PUBLIC ADMINISTRATION
DEBATED

PUBLIC ADMINISTRATION DEBATED

Herbert M. Levine

PRENTICE HALL, Englewood Cliffs, New Jersey 07632

Library of Congress Cataloging-in-Publication Data

Levine, Herbert M.
  Public administration debated.

  Bibliography: p.
  Includes index.
  1. Public administration. 2. Public administration—
United States. I. Title.
JF1351.L48 1987   350   86-25162
ISBN 0-13-737313-9

Editorial/production supervision: Ann L. Mohan
Cover design: George Cornell
Manufacturing buyer: Margaret Rizzi

This book can be made available to businesses, industry,
organizations, associations, and mail order catalogers at substantial
discou.ts when ordered in quantity.
For more information, contact:

Prentice Hall
Special Sales Department
College Division
Englewood Cliffs, NJ 07632
(201) 592-2863

© 1988 by Prentice Hall
A Division of Simon & Schuster
Englewood Cliffs, New Jersey 07632

Printed in the United States of America

10 9 8 7 6 5 4 3 2 1

ISBN 0-13-737313-9 01

Prentice-Hall International (UK) Limited, *London*
Prentice-Hall of Australia Pty. Limited, *Sydney*
Prentice-Hall Canada Inc., *Toronto*
Prentice-Hall Hispanoamericana, S.A., *Mexico*
Prentice-Hall of India Private Limited, *New Delhi*
Prentice-Hall of Japan, Inc., *Tokyo*
Simon & Schuster Asia Pte. Ltd., *Singapore*
Editora Prentice-Hall do Brasil, Ltda., *Rio de Janeiro*

To Jack and Susan Korsower

Contents

CHAPTER 2.   **The Political Setting of Public Administration   *41***

CHAPTER 4. **Organization Theory** *162*

15. *Is contracting out an effective means of
      providing government services?*

    YES. Stephen Moore, "How to Privatize
          Federal Services by 'Contracting
          Out' "   **223**

    NO. American Federation of State, County,
         and Municipal Employees, "Look Before
         You Leap: How Contracting Out Can Be
         Dangerous to Your Budget—and the
         Integrity of Government"   **230**

    QUESTIONS FOR DISCUSSION   **237**

    SUGGESTED READINGS   **237**

16. *Has airline deregulation done more harm than
      good to the airline industry and the public it
      serves?*

    YES. Wesley G. Kaldahl, "Let the Process of
          Deregulation Continue"   **238**

    NO. Herbert D. Kelleher, "Deregulation and
         the Troglodytes—How the Airlines Met
         Adam Smith"   **243**

    QUESTIONS FOR DISCUSSION   **252**

    SUGGESTED READINGS   **252**

17. *Should electronic broadcasting be deregulated?*

    YES. Bill Monroe, "Statement Before
          Congress"   **253**

    NO. Elaine Donnelly, "Statement Before
         Congress"   **260**

    QUESTIONS FOR DISCUSSION   **263**

    SUGGESTED READINGS   **263**

Preface

Because government is so big and takes such a vast share of American national income, much controversy has centered on not only the policies that government pursues but also the way that government agencies carry out their tasks. What government does and how it acts affect the lives of people in many ways, such as economic well-being, health, personal security, housing, and transportation. It is no wonder, then, that the public arena is filled with conflicting opinions about the work of government.

This book is an effort to introduce students to controversies over some of the important issues of public administration. Although there is no single universally accepted definition of public administration, we will define it as the study of the organization, processes, and work of government. The book is divided into five chapters dealing with broad aspects of the discipline. Chapter 1 presents an introduction highlighting some overriding issues of public administration. Other chapters examine the political setting of public administration, the tools of administration, organizational theory, and implementation and public policy.

Although public administration is a subject of importance in all political systems, this book is, for the most part, limited to American public administration. Some of the issues chosen for debate are subjects of long-standing controversy, such as the role of the bureaucracy in the American political process and the merits of decentralization. Other issues deal with more contemporary disputes, such as the fairness of affirmative action and the impact of airline deregulation.

The issues have been selected in an effort to supplement comprehensive public administration textbooks. Used in this manner, the book can show the conflicting arguments underlying some important public administration issues. A debate format is a teaching device which is designed to stimulate critical thinking and class discussion. A debate format, however, is not without its limitations. It implies that there are only two sides to every issue, when in fact there are many. In reading these debates, students may find that one or another side is convincing, but they may also want to find the most impressive points in either side in order to reach their own conclusions.

Although the book is not a comprehensive text, the headnotes in each chapter provide some context for understanding the debates. Each debate is followed by Questions for Discussion. A list of Suggested Readings is supplied so that students may pursue further research on the debate topic.

The articles in this book are drawn from a variety of sources, including academic journals, congressional hearings, books, and magazines. The authors include government officials, scholars, and interest group representatives.

In studying each debate, students may want to first understand the viewpoint of each author. They may then ask whether the conflict between the authors arises from differences over facts, over political ideology, over the institutional background of the authors, or over the perceived future consequences of this or that policy.

ACKNOWLEDGMENTS

In preparing this book, I had the professional help of people in both the academic and publishing worlds. Marvin Maurer at Monmouth College in New Jersey and Joseph Zentner at the University of Southwestern Louisiana read the manuscript and made suggestions for change. The editorial consultants were Professor Larry Elowitz, Georgia College; Professor Elinor Hartshorn, Western New England College; and Professor Steven W. Hays, University of South Carolina. Elizabeth O'Brien and Karen Horton were my editors at Prentice Hall. Ann L. Mohan, of WordCrafters Editorial Services, was the production editor. I am grateful to all of them for their efforts on my behalf.

Contributors

HERBERT M. LEVINE is a political scientist who taught at the University of Southwestern Louisiana for twenty years. He has written and edited several textbooks in political science, including *Political Issues Debated: An Introduction to Politics* (Prentice Hall) and *Challenge of Controversy: American Political Issues in Our Times* (Prentice Hall). He is currently a writer and lives in Chevy Chase, Maryland.

* * *

AMERICAN FEDERATION OF STATE, COUNTY AND MUNICIPAL EMPLOYEES is a labor union that was founded in 1936.

PHILLIP J. COOPER is Chair of the Department of Political Science at the Rockefeller College of Public Affairs and Policy, State University of New York at Albany. He is the author of *Public Law and Public Administration* and a forthcoming volume entitled *Hard Judicial Choices*.

DENNIS DECONCINI has been a United States Senator from Arizona since 1977. A Democrat, he has been a member of committees on judiciary, appropriations, and rules and administration.

LINDA S. DILLON is Associate Professor of Occupational Education at North Carolina State University, Raleigh. She was a fellow of the North Carolina Japan Center.

ELAINE DONNELLY is Special Projects Director of Eagle Forum, a conservative public interest group. She is the author of the handbook, *One Side vs. the Other Side—A Primer on Access to the Media.*

FRANK D. DRAPER is a staff associate in budget and planning with the National Science Foundation. He is a former Federal Executive Fellow in Economic Policy from the Brookings Institution. He is a lecturer at the University of Maryland.

RICHARD EDWARDS is Professor of Economics at the University of Massachusetts at Amherst. He is the author of *Contested Terrain* and *The Capitalist System.*

DANIEL J. EVANS is a United States Senator from the State of Washington. A Republican, he served as his state's governor from 1965 to 1977.

BRUCE E. FEIN is Senior Vice President, Telecommunications and Information Group, for Gray and Company. He served with the Federal Communications Commission and the Department of Justice.

HEIDI HARTMANN is the Study Director of the Committee on Women's Employment and Related Social Issues of the National Council of the National Academy of Sciences.

MARK O. HATFIELD is a United States Senator from Oregon. A Republican, he is a member of the Senate Appropriations Committee and served as its chairman when the Republicans controlled the Senate during the Reagan administration.

SIDNEY HOOK is Senior Research Fellow at the Hoover Institution of War, Revolution and Peace, Stanford, California. He is Emeritus Professor of Philosophy at New York University and is the author of numerous books.

DOUGLAS B. HURON is an attorney with Kator, Scott, and Heller in Washington, D.C. He is a former senior trial attorney in the Civil Rights Division of the Justice Department. He was Senior Associate Counsel to President Jimmy Carter.

DWIGHT A. INK has held several administrative positions in the federal government. He served as Executive Director of the President's Reorganization Personnel Management Project.

WESLEY G. KALDAHL is Senior Vice President of Airline Planning, American Airlines. He previously held other posts in the airline industry.

HERBERT D. KELLEHER is President and Chief Executive Officer, Southwest Airlines Co. He is an attorney who has been active in Democratic political campaigns in Texas.

TOYOHIRO KONO is Professor of Business Administration in the Department of Management at Gakushuin University in Tokyo. He is the author of Strategy and Structure of Japanese Enterprise.

RICHARD E. KOPELMAN is Professor of Management at Baruch College in New York. He is the author of Managing Productivity in Organizations: A Practical, People-Oriented Perspective.

LANCE T. LELOUP is Professor of Political Science at the University of Missouri, St. Louis. After receiving his Ph.D. from Ohio State University, he served on the staff of the Ohio Senate. He is the author of Budgetary Politics: Dollars, Deficits, Decisions and Politics in America: The Ability to Govern.

EDWIN A. LOCKE is joint Professor of Business and Management and of Psychology at the University of Maryland, College Park.

STEPHEN R. MCSPADDEN is counsel to the Subcommittee on Commerce, Consumer, and Monetary Affairs of the House Committee on Government Operations. He served as a trial attorney in the Antitrust Division of the Department of Justice.

R. SHEP MELNICK is Associate Professor of Politics at Brandeis University. He is the author of Regulation and the Courts: The Case of the Clean Air Act. He has been an associate staff member of the Brookings Institution since 1981.

H. BRINTON MILWARD is Associate Professor of Management and Public Administration at the University of Kentucky, where he is also Director of the Center for Business and Economic Research. He has published numerous articles on interorganizational networks, resource dependence and compliance, and policy implementation.

BILL MONROE served with NBC News for many years. He has been Moderator and Executive Producer of Meet the Press. He is a past president of the Radio-TV Correspondents Association.

STEPHEN MOORE is Policy Analyst with the Heritage Foundation. He is the editor of Slashing the Deficit, Fiscal Year 1987.

MICHAEL A. MURRAY is a professor at De Paul University in Chicago. He was formerly Associate Director of the Illinois Board of Higher Education. He has taught at the University of Illinois and Northwestern University.

THE NATIONAL ASSOCIATION OF NEIGHBORHOODS is a community action organization that was founded in 1975. It has 2,000 members from neighborhood organizations and city-wide coalitions in 120 cities.

K. NEWTON is Professor of Political Science

and Social Policy at the University of Dundee in Scotland.

JUNE O'NEILL is Assistant Staff Director, Program and Policy, of the U.S. Commission on Civil Rights. She served as Director of the Program of Policy Research on Women and Families of the Urban Institute.

CHIMEZIE A.B. OSIGWEH is Assistant Professor of Business Administration and a member of the graduate faculty at Northeast Missouri State University. His published articles have dealt with organization theory and behavior, economic issues, international management communication, and personnel relations.

JONE PEARCE is Assistant Professor of Administration in the Graduate School of Management at the University of California, Irvine. Her publications include articles on behavioral and interpersonal effects of various modes of compensation and related personnel practices.

JAMES L. PERRY is Professor in the School of Public and Environmental Affairs at Indiana University, Bloomington. His research on public organizations and management has focused on innovation, organizational effectiveness, and personnel and labor relations. He is coauthor of *Public Management: Public and Private Perspective*.

BERNARD T. PITSVADA is Program Director for the Department of the Army in the Pentagon. He received his Ph.D. in political science from the American University, Washington, D.C., and is a lecturer at George Washington University.

THE PUBLIC SERVICE RESEARCH COUNCIL is an organization engaged in research and education about public-sector unionism.

HAL G. RAINEY is Associate Professor in the Department of Administration and Policy Sciences Program at Florida State University. His most recent articles on bureaucratic performance, organizational incentive systems, and theories of public organizations have appeared in *Policy Studies Journal, Journal of Public Policy, Public Administration Review*, and *Administration and Society*.

GEORGE ROCHE is President of Hillsdale College in Michigan. He is the author of several books, including *The Bewildered Society*.

PETER W. RODINO is Chairman of the House Committee on the Judiciary. A Democrat from New Jersey, he is the dean of the New Jersey congressional delegation.

PUBLIC ADMINISTRATION
DEBATED

CHAPTER *1*

Introduction

When Jimmy Carter campaigned for the presidency in 1976, he complained about the growth of government and promised that he would reduce the size of the bureaucracy. He failed. When Ronald Reagan campaigned for the presidency in 1980, he, too, promised that he would reduce the size of the bureaucracy. He failed, too. Carter finished his term as president with a government bureaucracy bigger in numbers and in expenditures than when he entered. Reagan completed his first term as president with the same results. He campaigned for re-election in 1984 repeating the same idea that government had become too big, moreover.

Both presidents made efforts not only to reduce government expenditures but also to make government run more efficiently. Observers are not in agreement about whether either president accomplished anything of substance in achieving either of these goals, although they generally concur that both made vigorous efforts in that direction.

Reagan, particularly, became associated with a condemnation of big government. His rise to power as governor of California and later as a presidential candidate was partly based on political rhetoric critical of bureaucracy and government spending. While President Reagan was successful in slowing the rate of growth of the welfare sector, he adamantly increased government expenditures in the defense sec-

tor. Even in the domestic sector he discovered that there was much about federal government expenditures that was "uncontrollable."

We can better understand the reasons for Reagan's failure to achieve his objectives of reducing the size and cost of government if we evaluate the sources of government growth. In the United States as in other countries around the world—whether they be socialist or capitalist, dictatorships or democracies, or rich or poor—the size of government has grown, and the scope of government activities has broadened. Students of public administration attribute the major impetus behind the growth of government to many factors, but primarily to war and the threat of war, demands for the regulation of the economy, welfare, and the bureaucracy itself.

Some students of public administration contend that war is the chief reason for government growth. In the United States, for example, American involvement in the two world wars made America a world power. In the post-World War II period, the United States became a major participant in world politics—a development which meant that the use of American military power in distant areas was now to be a continuing possibility for policymakers. The technological changes which have been marked most notably by unprecedented means of rapid destruction through the devel-

1

opment, production, and deployment of nu- clear weapons and delivery systems have necessitated a military organization ready to take the most devastating military actions within a matter of minutes. Foreign-policy commit- ments of a big power status, moreover, have meant that America's military forces are de- ployed in many countries throughout the world ready to pursue the commands of central au- thorities in Washington, D.C. Since the 1960s, for example, American military power has been used most notably in Vietnam, the Dominican Republic, Cambodia, Iran, Lebanon, and Grenada. Even when not used in military com- bat, American military forces have been dis- played as a symbol of national will in other places, such as off the coast of Libya and in the Persian Gulf.

War, then, has made its contribution to American bureaucratic growth. Had the United States not become involved in wars in this cen- tury, however, its government would have grown in part because of the clamor for regu- lation of the economy. And so, government sought to regulate the railroads to prevent what was regarded as unfair business practices. An- titrust legislation established government agencies committed to keeping business com- petitive in areas which were increasingly dom- inated by a single corporation. Government regulatory agencies were established to deal with such matters as assuring that food prod- ucts were safe for human consumption, drug products were tested scientifically before being put on the market, construction of buildings was complying with fire and safety needs, an- tipollution devices were installed in factories so as not to contaminate air and water, and qualifying requirements were instituted to make certain that professionals in the fields of med- icine and law had proper credentials to serve the public.

Although often appeals for regulation were resisted by the groups who were to be regu- lated, this was not always the case. Sometimes, as the experience of airline regulation attests, some carriers sought to establish government regulation in order to prevent competition and, consequently, to assure profits—a topic which we shall consider in Chapter 5.

Military expenditures and economic reg- ulation, then, contributed to bigger govern- ment. So, too, did the welfare state, which was for the most part a creation of the twentieth century. In the America of the nineteenth cen- tury, a prevailing creed asserted the view that government is best which governs least. A so- ciety based on the principle of *laissez-faire* (lit- erally, to leave alone) would, it was argued, lead to greater prosperity in which the standard of living for the masses of people would im- prove. Although *laissez-faire* (or a market economy, as it is sometimes called) is still highly regarded in the United States, so, too, is the notion that every American citizen—regard- less of his or her economic condition—should be entitled to at least basic minimums in ed- ucation, health, housing, and income. And so, government—not only at the national level, but at state and local levels, as well—has in- creasingly provided funds for such purposes as building public schools and universities, sub- sidizing medical care for the indigent, con- structing public housing for the economically disadvantaged, and extending unemployment benefits for people out of work and financial assistance to the elderly. So much have welfare benefits been accepted by Americans that many welfare programs are regarded as "entitle- ments," benefits accorded to people because of their status as young or poor or sick or el- derly. It is these entitlements which are gen- erally regarded as contributing to spiraling government expenditures. This is not to say that entitlements cannot be diminished in any way. Political leaders have determined, how- ever, that when they try to deal with reducing the level of expenditures on entitlements, they run into sharp criticism by the groups who would be adversely affected by the cuts. They fear punishment at the ballot box.

Although national security concerns, reg- ulation of the economy, and the welfare state are principal factors in the growth of govern- ment, some people attribute a crucial reason for government growth to the government it- self. Specifically, they target the bureaucracy —that is, government employees—for bring- ing on government growth not because of some legitimate social need but rather for their own purposes—a theme which is discussed in a debate below.

Government, then, is big. It plays a role in most aspects of our lives—from cradle to grave. A government agency issues a birth certificate. Most people are educated in government-supported public schools—or sometimes even in private schools that receive direct or indirect government assistance. People are often hired by government agencies or engage in commercial ventures which are financed by government. The food we eat, the medicine we take, the health care we receive, the air we breathe, the cars we drive, the buildings we occupy, the money we earn, the television programs we view, the financial institutions in which we place our money, and the products we sell are all in some way regulated by government.

Because government is big and intrusive in our lives, it has become a source of considerable concern and dispute. Two fundamental areas of concern involve the activity of the bureaucracy and the relationship between government management and business management. It is these two subjects which will begin our debates in this public administration book.

IS BUREAUCRACY THE ENEMY OF THE PEOPLE?

For most people in American society, government is not regarded as an abstraction like truth and justice. Government behaves in specific ways which annoy some people and please others. Many modern liberals, for example, generally favor big government when that big government is used to provide greater support for education, health care, programs for minorities, environmental protection, and worker safety. They condemn government spending when that spending is applied to foreign aid to dictatorships, government assistance to parochial schools, or the purchase of computer equipment allowing police authorities to gather information about the private lives of citizens. For their part, many modern conservatives oppose government spending on welfare programs but favor it in national security, police

protection, and some social concerns, such as, say, antipornography campaigns. Often, then, many liberals and conservatives focus on the particular programs which the government is undertaking rather than the principle of government involvement in society itself.

Some critics of government attack the principle of government involvement itself and regard government in general and the bureaucracy in particular as a central political evil of our times. In this regard, the debate below considers whether government is the enemy of the people. George Roche provides a severe criticism of bureaucracy. He portrays American bureaucracy as "power hungry, inflexible, indifferent to human needs, servile, and draped in red tape." Roche denounces bureaucratic rules, the "bureaucratic mind," and bureaucratic waste. He contends that bureaucrats have a vested interest in making social problems worse and are, consequently, indifferent to human needs. He sees the bureaucracy as graft-riddled. Bureaucracy, according to Roche, is inefficient and destructive of freedom. Readers may note that for all the criticism that Roche heaps upon the bureaucracy, he attributes the growth of government to the desires of the American people to solve their problems.

A view which regards the bureaucracy in a more benevolent manner is asserted by H. Brinton Milward and Hal G. Rainey. They argue that the bureaucracy in the United States has been unfairly criticized. Agreeing that problems of excesses, waste, and other shortcomings of bureaucracy exist, they contend that these problems are exaggerated. The authors view excessive criticism of bureaucrats as leading to a faulty diagnosis of social problems. Such criticism, moreover, may make improvements in the bureaucracy even more difficult by lowering morale in many agencies and by a consequent departure from public service of many of the best people in the bureaucracy. The authors point to a number of factors that must be understood in order to evaluate government performance. They challenge the usual criticisms often leveled at government that it should be run like a business (a subject which will be debated more fully below by Michael A. Murray and Dwight Ink). They also contend that evaluation of government is difficult because of complex values that government must satisfy, higher performance standards than exist in the private sector, the requirements of special interests, imperialistic demands by Congress, a problem that the state is trying to do too many things, and budgetary constraints.

In judging the debate, consider the activities of different government institutions to see which of the contending viewpoints has more validity. Evaluate whether poor bureaucratic performance arises because of the self-serving character of the bureaucracy, bad construction of a government program, or some other reason. And ask whether better people in government service would lead to better public services or whether "better bureaucrats" is a contradiction in terms.

PRIVATE MANAGEMENT AND PUBLIC MANAGEMENT

The relationship between business and government has always been close in the American political system. Marxists say that the relationship has been too close, with government being controlled by business, working often behind the scenes to manipulate government for its own purposes. Critics other than Marxists have condemned business–government relationships, arguing that government is too supportive of business interests and sacrifices the public interest because of pressures from the commercial sector. Some conservatives rather than criticize government–business associations call for an even closer connection in practices and personnel.

Although there have been ebbs and flows in the influence of business on government, business and government are linked in a number of ways—through personnel, government programs, and management techniques, for example. In the twentieth century many business executives have served in government posts. In the post-World War II period, as a case in point, Charles E. Wilson, president of General Motors, became Secretary of Defense, a position later held by Robert McNamara, president of the Ford Motor Company. George Shultz, president of Bechtel Corporation, became Secretary of State, replacing Alexander Haig, who had come to that post as president of United Technologies. Many business people served as under secretaries and assistant secretaries of major departments and directors of government agencies and bureaus. Many, too, were appointed to advisory boards and presidential commissions.

Business representatives have traditionally sought to influence both the content of legislation and the way that government agencies actually function. In this regard, automobile companies tried to delay government regulations for mandatory installation of air bags. Shipping companies urged legislation requiring the overseas transport of foreign-aid items on American ships. Military contractors went after lucrative awards for research, development, and production of sophisticated weapons systems.

Much of the concern of public administration scholars, however, has been in the applicability of management techniques from the private sector to the public sector. American business has often boasted of its efficiency—an efficiency brought on by the demands of a free enterprise system. Proponents of the market economy argue that inefficient producers of goods will be driven from the market place since consumers will purchase similar products at a cheaper price resulting from competition. The free enterprise system, consequently, enforces efficiency.

For most of American history, Americans marveled at the achievements of the American economy. American industry created new products. Its goods were sold all over the world. It applied great efficiency to the Industrial Revolution, and by the twentieth century it became an economic giant. As we shall see in Chapter 4, American industry became dominated early in this century by Frederick W. Taylor's ideas of Scientific Management, which sought to rationalize industrial production in a manner to lead to the greatest efficiency and ultimately to universal prosperity. Some of the early writers in public administration hoped to apply the principles of Scientific Management to the public sector.

Even after the image of business was tarnished by the Great Depression of the 1930s and the seeming inability of industry to recover from that economic catastrophe, government sought the advice of business leaders to help government become more efficiently run. Herbert Hoover, a former president who had an early successful career as an engineer, was called upon by President Harry Truman to head a commission whose responsibility was to recommend ways in which waste and mismanagement could be reduced or eliminated in government. In more recent years President Ronald Reagan asked J. Peter Grace, president and chief executive officer of W. R. Grace & Company, to head the President's Private Sector Survey on Cost Control, a group of top executives whose job it was to look at every agency of government to see how wasteful government spending could be identified and reduced. The Grace Commission recommended that hundreds of billions of dollars could be eliminated from federal government spending if the federal government terminated some bad programs and instituted managerial reforms. Grace and many of his associates thought that government should be run more like a business.

To do that, however, similarities in the private sector and the public sector would be necessary. But is management in the private sector essentially similar to management in the public sector? That is the question considered by Michael A. Murray and Dwight Ink. While neither author talks in terms of absolutes, they come down on different sides of the question. Michael A. Murray makes the following points: (1) There has been a blurring of the distinction between public- and private-sector management. (2) Procedural matters, such as ethical behavior, are of concern to both public- and private-sector managers. (3) Comparisons of public- and private-sector management are often

unfair because unlike objects are being classified. (4) The perception of differences between public- and private-sector management is often based on myth. (5) Both public- and private-sector management rely on modern technical solutions to solve problems.

Dwight Ink notes, in contrast, the many differences between federal management and private-sector management. These are: (1) There is greater public scrutiny of the public-sector manager. (2) The sheer size of government weakens the ability of the president to have a meaningful dialogue with each agency head. (3) Federal managers are pulled in different directions by legislators with differing objectives. (4) Accountability is greater for public-sector managers. (5) The personal and professional risks are greater for public-sector than for private-sector managers. (6) Government bureaucrats deal frequently with inexperienced political appointees who have no background to run multibillion dollar programs. (6) The federal government has failed to provide sufficient funds to make a merit system of civil service work.

As you read this debate, think about the skills that are required of a manager in the private sector and how many of these skills may be applicable to the public sector. Consider, too, whether the changing nature of American business—from its nineteenth-century form in which business had great discretion as to how it would act until its twentieth-century form in which it is more involved with government—has any bearing on the issue being debated. Also, consider for purposes of discussion whether managerial skills in running, say, a private college are similar to or different from the skills required in managing a state college; or whether the skills in running Federal Express are similar to or different from the skills required in running the United States Postal Service.

ISSUES

1   YES   IS BUREAUCRACY THE ENEMY OF THE PEOPLE?

Bureaucracy: Enemy of the People
George Roche

He hath erected a multitude of New Offices and sent hither swarms of officers to harass our people, and eat out their substance.
—America's complaint about King George III and British rule, in the Declaration of Independence, 1776

Thomas Jefferson never heard of "bureaucracy," but nobody has described it more movingly than he did in the Declaration of Independence. It was to be free of bureaucracy and taxes that the colonists dared fight the mighty British empire. In that great revolution, subjects of the King became free Americans. They thought they would be free forever.

In pitifully few years, Jefferson was again obligated to warn us about bureaucracy, only this time the threat was from our own government rather than the British. ". . . [w]hen we must wait for Washington to tell us when to sow and when to reap," Jefferson wrote, "we shall soon want for bread."

Alas, the warning went unheeded. In the course of time the federal government built the biggest bureaucratic machine the world has ever seen. On a scale the kings of England never dreamed of, it has erected multitudes of new offices and sent forth swarms of officers to harass our people and eat out our substance. We call them bureaucrats.

No American today is safe from federal bureaucrats. If you eat, drink, breathe air, dress, work, play, go to school, drive, read, watch TV, listen to radio, travel, own a house, rent an apartment, operate a farm, run a business, buy, sell, advertise, publish, spend money, save money, borrow money, invest, ship goods, import and export, use the mails, have children, get sick, or grow old, you are au-

tomatically in the grasp of at least one major federal bureau, and within reach of scores or hundreds more. If you think you can escape by dying, you haven't reckoned on the ultimate bureau, the Internal Revenue Service.

To the private citizen, the activities of the federal bureaucracy may be bewildering, frustrating, wasteful, costly, or at times, hilarious. But too often its effects are tragic. The bureaucracy has wrapped the hurt and the needy in a web of rules, leaving them helpless and without hope. It has destroyed families. It has used free Americans in bizarre experiments that have drugged, crippled, blinded, and killed people. It has deformed, paralyzed, and killed people with dangerous drugs, and left countless thousands to suffer or die by denying them needed medicines. Its cost to each of us, in liberty and opportunity lost, as well as dollars, is brutal. Under feudalism, the serfs only had to work three months a year for the masters. *You* have to work four to support federal bureaucrats, and another month for state and local bureaucrats.

Not a day passes but that bureaucratic actions are blasted in editorials, or held up as examples of waste, futility, and sheer dizziness. Bureaucrats are the butt of endless jokes and cartoons. No one will even admit to being one. Ask a convention of bureaucrats what they do, and not one will stand and announce with pride, "I'm a bureaucrat." Yet there are millions of them around, and they seem to proliferate like mosquitoes in a fever swamp—with about the same contribution to human happiness.

Bureaucrats' vexatious methods have actually made it into the dictionary. According to Webster's Third New International Dictionary, unabridged, bureaucracy is "a system in administration marked by constant striving for increased functions and power, by lack of initiative and flexibility, by indifference to human needs or public opinion, and by a tendency to defer decisions to superiors and to impede action with red tape." Not exactly Jeffersonian in eloquence, but there you have it: the Bureaucrat is power-hungry, inflexible, indifferent to human needs, servile, and draped in red tape. Disgruntled citizens could no doubt expand on this description at length.

Bureaus rule you with rules. There are often dozens and sometimes hundreds of bureaus regulating a given activity. Every one of those bureaus has thousands of rules, and some have millions. If you look closely, you'll find rules in any bureau that contradict other rules, which in turn contradict rules in other bureaus. They can get you coming and going. An activity may be officially encouraged and discouraged, legal and illegal, required and prohibited, all at the same time. And every bureaucratic rule is binding. A bureaucrat need only dream up a regulation, publish it in the *Federal Register*, and it's the law. Nobody has ever read all the rules and regulations on the books. Nobody can count them. Yet if you run afoul of a single bureaucratic rule, out of all the uncounted millions of them, you may find yourself pinned under a bureaucrat's thumb.

This is madness. People do not live their lives the bureaucratic way, "by the book," nor do they want to. It is not normal, it is not natural. Force and force alone can impose such arbitrary and unnatural rules on our lives. If the rules were *good* for us, why would force ever be needed?

The rules we follow in private life are few, simple, and moral in nature. We do not obey the Ten Commandments because somebody forces us to, at gunpoint. We obey them because doing so enriches our lives and puts us in harmony with those around us.

Indeed, much or most of what we do in life has nothing at all to do with rules. What guides us is self-interest or motivation. That is, we do things because we enjoy them, or because they improve our condition and enhance our satisfactions in life. We deal with one another freely and voluntarily, meeting our differing needs, and resolving our differences, without force, in the marketplace. We cannot, after all, force others to do our bidding; that is slavery, and it is repugnant to those of us who would be free. Yet our own normal, free-willed, self-supporting actions as responsible people are just as repugnant to the bureaucrat.

The dedicated bureaucrat believes that all of life must be brought under the control of his rules. He may acknowledge that no one rule can possibly fit millions of individuals in millions of situations. But to him, it just means that he should have millions of rules to cover everything, all of them imposed by force. Millions of rules are exactly what he has today. And force is a government monopoly.

In a word, the bureaucratic mind and methods are *fundamentally* different from, and irreconcilable with, private life, the things we do in a free and normal way. The logic of bureaucratic coercion is that we, the people, cannot do things right on our own, cannot be trusted, and must be reduced to serfdom in the bureaucratic order. This, from so-called "civil servants" who supposedly work at our pleasure and are supported by our money and labor. The Servant has become Master.

* * *

What we call "bureaucracy," then, is the imposition of arbitrary rules, by force—literally, "rule by bureau." If we may judge it by its fruits, as we judge everything else, the wonder is that it could possibly exist. The bureaucracy is every bit as insane in practice as it is in theory.

"Dizziness" is not one of the bureaucratic qualities that made it into Webster's, but it should have been. People are forever using words like bonkers and wacko to describe it. Almost everybody I talk to has a pet horror story about bureaucracy, and the craziness of it is among the most persistent themes. I have a large collection of these stories, a few of which I'll share with you. First let me note that bureaucrats themselves are not crazy—at least no more so than anybody else. Most are known to lead quite normal lives, after they get off work at night. It's what they do on the job, "by the rules," that's wacky. Anyone else would see instantly that a given action is ridiculous; not the servant of the rulebook. He sees only the rules.

This is what we call the "bureaucratic mind" and here is some of its routine handiwork:[1]

- Federal bureaucrats drew up specifications for a mousetrap. The specs ran 700 pages long and weighed 3.3 pounds.

---

[1]Many of these items are thanks to *National Review* magazine, which for years has had an impish delight in chronicling bureaucratic boneheadedness. Its pages are by now probably the best single source of such material.

- The famous Abominable Snowman, also known as Bigfoot, Yeti, or Sasquatch, is on the federal endangered species list, in case somebody ever discovers one.
- The National Endowment for the Arts financed a film that repeatedly showed a dog being shot to death.
- The National Institute for Mental Health granted a professor $97,000 to study what he called the "social and behavioral relationships" in a Peruvian brothel. (Which worked out to $177 a night for the tireless researcher. Crazy Gringos!)
- The Federal Voting Rights Act specifies that areas that have a significant minority who speak a language other than English must be given ballots in the other language. Which is why federal bureaucrats, on behalf of the Lumbee Indians, ordered three counties of North Carolina to print ballots in Lumbee. The only trouble is, there is no Lumbee language. There was once, but the Lumbees abandoned it when white settlers moved into the area. The beleaguered North Carolina officials considered applying for a federal grant to invent a new Lumbee language and teach it to the Lumbees.
- Every year the Defense Department buys 48,000 heavy duty leather holsters for .45 caliber pistols. It has not gotten any new .45 pistols since 1945.
- In a surprise economy move, the Department of Health, Education, and Welfare decided after six years and half a million dollars, that it might not continue providing $81,000 a year to teach 28 Navajo medicine men the arts of ceremonies and taboos.
- Federal bureaucrats poured 76 million barrels of oil into a cave to create a "Strategic Petroleum Reserve," only to learn that they had forgotten to install pumps to get it out again.
- After a long delay, the White House finally took decisive action on streamlining federal aid programs. It issued an 11-volume study on the subject.
- David Berkowitz, the famed "Son of Sam" killer, has been receiving Social Security payments of some $300 a month in prison because he was ruled "mentally ill" and "unable to work."
- The Food and Drug Administration issued an urgent warning to the public not to eat those heart-shaped boxes your Valentine candies come in.

"Wonderland" is Washington, D.C's middle name, thanks to bureaucracy. But bureaucracy infects every level of government and every type of government. At times it seems that the state and local bureaucrats strive to do things even zanier and weirder than their big brothers in Wonderland, D.C.

- The government of Calumet Township, Indiana, nabbed one of its employees using witchcraft to get a welfare client to take part in a food stamp fraud. To avoid a recurrence, the city banned "voodoo, witchcraft, spiritualism and spells."

- California officials ruled that Mr. Ted Giannoulas can be a chicken anywhere but in San Diego. Whereupon Mr. Giannoulas became a parrot, and considered an offer to be a chicken in Atlanta, Georgia, where it's legal. Eventually he was permitted to be a chicken even in San Diego, so long as he was a different chicken.
- Seattle emergency vehicles helped deliver six babies one year, five of them to women.
- When George Willig climbed the World Trade Center in New York, he was arrested for "scaling a building without a permit," fined $1.10, and forced to eat lunch with Mayor Beame. Which New York bureau sells building scaling permits was not disclosed.
- Mr. Arnold Weber of Carmel, New York, was fined $320 for keeping an unlicensed cougar. To find the cougar license bureau, go three doors past the building scaling office and turn left.
- A man in Morganton, North Carolina, was fined $52 and given a suspended jail sentence for biting the tail off a snake.
- Police on a training mission in St. Louis planted several pounds of dynamite under the bumper of a civilian car in an airport parking lot. Before the trainees, using dogs, could find it, the owners retrieved their car and drove away.
- Unable to convict its rider, Idaho authorities filed suit against a 1970 Honda 750 motorcycle, for allegedly transporting marijuana.
- A Colorado woman who wants to be cremated on a funeral pyre when she dies made the dreadful mistake of asking whether it was legal. With faultless bureaucratic logic, her request was routed to the Colorado Air Pollution Control Board. Groping for just the right rule, and with the utmost in bureaucratic delicacy, the board ruled that the lady would need a permit—under the statute that prohibits the unauthorized burning of rubbish and trash.

Needless to say, wacky doings by bureaucrats are not limited to American government. Bureaucracy exists in every country, without regard to race, creed, sex, political system, or previous condition of servitude. It may have its own national or local flavor, but you know at once it's the bureaucratic mind at work when, for instance, Belgium made it a crime to show mercy to a caterpillar. The FDA-types in Denmark banned the coloring in Coca Cola, but do permit Danes to drink gray Coke. The Soviet bureaucracy is in such desperate condition that it brought mail handling equipment from us, to improve its postal service. But we'll let other countries worry about their own bureaucrats. Ours are quite enough to fret about, and besides, as a patriotic American, I happen to think that American bureaucrats can outwacko, outwaste, and outboondoggle any foreign competitors.

Behind dizziness, the quality about bureaucrats that most impresses people is their enormous capacity to waste money. *Our* money. Nobody wastes money more efficiently than Washington's corps of bureaucrats. Its appetite for waste is legendary, its skill at squandering is internationally renowned, and its budget will soon be measured in light-years. Federal bureaucrats not only waste money here but all over the world. They've even managed to waste some on the moon, on Venus, on Mars, Jupiter, Saturn and points west. In one case they even managed to blast a bureaucratic boondoggle clean out of our solar system,[2] a first in history.

Now, I don't think bureaucrats *try* to waste money. They don't get up in the morning and say, "I'm going to go down to the office and squander a bundle today." Some, a few, even try not to. However, for reasons we'll discuss later on, it's impossible for bureaucracy *not* to waste money. The wastage is inherent, built right into the bureaucratic method. The term "bureaucratic waste" is almost redundant. Combine this inherent tendency to waste money with the astronomical sums in the hands of federal bureaucrats, and you get stories like these. As the saying goes, easy come, easy go:

- The Federal Aviation Administration spent $57,800 studying stewardesses and determined that their noses average 2.18 inches long.
- The Pentagon spends $13.53 to make a grilled cheese sandwich.
- In 1978, U.S. Public Health hospitals were spending $6 million a year for plastic surgery—mainly facelifts for the wives of top military brass.
- The new Department of Energy, trying desperately to justify its existence, announced the discovery of a vast new source of energy, with reserves equal to 250 billion barrels of oil: peat. Ten billion dollars a

year for these boneheads, and they tell us to burn swamps.

- According to a National Science Foundation study costing $918,000, people who go camping do not like bugs or mosquitoes.
- In 1977, to save money, the Department of Energy decided to move to more austere quarters. Secretary Schlesinger had to give up his private dining room and Deputy Secretary O'Leary lost his shower. The move cost $17 million.
- Federal bureaucrats spend some $8 billion a year on travel, an average of $3,000 apiece.
- The Environmental Protection Agency has a lengthy application form with a $10 fee for farmers to discharge waste water on their own property. It costs the EPA $15.09 to process a farmer's check, and $376.10 to process an application.
- When a leak developed in the roof of the Kennedy Center in Washington, the bureaucrats spent $4,700,000 to fix it.
- As long as we're going through the roof, we may as well note that a $65,000 emergency repair to the ceiling of the National War College was finally completed for only $1,900,000.
- "No less an authority than *The New York Times* confirms the frightening fact that: 'Washington Unable to Spend Funds as Rapidly as It Planned This Year.' It also confirms that the experts are in pothers and dithers at this unexplained federal lethargy that leaves some eight billion dollars unslushed. Holy Keynes! That's a whole week's worth of slops untroughed, influence unpeddled, voters unbought and doggles unbooned. If the professionals can't waste it fast enough, what will become of us all?"

—*National Review* item, 1976

There is another, subtler sort of waste that results when bureaucrats, as they love to do, undertake projects of monumental triviality. This reflects a fact that people outside of government can scarcely grasp: true bureaucrats have no specific, definable job. For all their endless rules, there are no true guidelines as to what they are supposed to do or how well they are doing it. It is precisely this lack of guidelines, this institutional aimlessness, that sets bureaucracy apart from productive human activity. It is, in fact, what forces bureaucrats to operate "by the rules" instead of by their productivity or profit. We will encounter this factor over and over. Its effect is to make bureaucrats search constantly for actions on the job that *look* good, look important, look normal. Yet the same lack of guidelines blinds them to what really is good, normal, important, productive. Thus we often find bureaucrats pouring their energy—not to mention our money—into en-

---

[2] I refer to the Voyager spacecraft. I'm not criticizing its main, scientific mission, which included sending back those breathtaking photos of Saturn. The bureaucrats got into the act by putting a phonograph aboard, with a recorded message of greetings from Earth, in numerous languages. Just in case some Higher Intelligence out there finds the thing some day, see. And figures out how to work the phonograph. And happens to speak English, or Mandarin Chinese, or Tagalog, or Quechug. Fittingly enough, the record is made of solid gold. If there is any Higher Intelligence out there, it won't have any trouble figuring out that this was the bureaucratic mind at work.

terprises that are simply ludicrous. And, indeed, examples of these exercises in triviality can sound awfully funny. Inwardly, though, I am more inclined to sorrow at things so wasteful of human endeavor.

In any case, here are a few examples of how farfetched bureaucratic projects can become:

- "The Consumer Products Safety Commission, established October 27, 1972 for the purpose of reducing unreasonable risk of injury associated with consumer products—estimated 1976 fiscal year budget for policy development and support, $1,780,000; hazard identification, $3,950,000; hazard analysis and remedy, $10,233,000; information and education, $3,883,000; compliance and enforcement, $11,264,000; administration, $5,388,000; administrative law judges, $97,000; 890 full-time and 45 equivalent full-time positions, average paid employment 910, average salary, $17,916, total personnel compensation $18,427,000 plus $1,658,000 in benefits, total budget $36,595,000—has ordered the manufacturer to recall an unspecified quantity of Blobo Plastic Bubb-A-Loons."

  —National Review, 1976

- In its never-ending effort to protect American health, the FDA sued the manufacturers to force the recall of the Relco Bark Trainer and Wuf-E-Nuf electric dog collars.

- In June, 1973 the FDA, which thrives on triviality, ruled that all cherry pies sold in interstate commerce had to contain at least 24% cherries by weight, and no more than 15% blemished cherries, opening any number of jobs for cherry inspectors to snatch away the sixteenth blemished cherry out of every hundred that passed down the line. In the same month it announced that its next public health concern would be feminine hygiene sprays. A month later, after blasting breakfast cereals for lack of nutritional value, it blasted cereal makers for putting *more* vitamins and minerals into cereals. In December, 1975, it averted a tragedy of staggering proportions by forcing the recall of 17,000 cases of possibly dangerous pimentoes, forestalling a recall of untold millions of martinis. In November, 1976, it took decisive action to recall 500 cases of strawberry jam and 80,000 orange suckers, while assuring the public that the items were perfectly harmless.

This cascade of triviality from a single agency should give you a sharp picture of bureaucracy in general. Now consider that the FDA has perhaps the single most important assignment of any bureau, protecting our health—a life-or-death question to over 200 million Americans—and it worries about electric dog collars. Surely that will give you the idea. Yet I haven't even mentioned my very favorite story about the FDA, which goes back to October

1973. At that time, on an emergency basis, the FDA forced makers to recall glue in aerosol cans, a product almost indispensable to graphic artists for layout work. Why? Because it said it had discovered, God knows how, that spray glue would cause birth defects if *eaten* by pregnant women. Well, you know how it is with pregnant women. And bureaucrats.

"Studying" things sounds productive and important, so it has become perhaps the most popular of all bureaucratic ventures in triviality.

- Study of cultural, economic, and social impact of rural road construction in Poland—$85,000. Chasing wild boars in Pakistan—$35,000. Environmental testing of a zero gravity toilet (and I'd rather not think about what such tests entail)—$230,000. Analysis of violin varnish—$5,000. Study to find out why people say "ain't"—$121,000. Study to find out why kiddies fall off tricycles—$19,300. Study of frisbees—$375,000.

All of these, you ought to know, are from a single year, 1974, and don't even scratch the surface.

If the bureaucrats have any favorite thing to study, it's sex. Frankly, I didn't expect this at all. I would have thought bureaucracy would be as sexless as white bread. But it turns out that they are obsessed with sex, and lavish tax dollars without number on studies of the subject. Some of this—at least, if you dwell on it as much as the bureaucrats do—may seem pretty kinky, so parental discretion is advised.

- Study of Polish bisexual frogs—$6,000. National Science Foundation grant for studying polygamy among birds—$22,000. Study of the sexual strategies of milkweed—$24,000. Investigating the sociosexual behavior of the dabbing African black duck—$81,300. Study of whether marijuana stimulates men sexually—$121,000. (That one caused quite an uproar, because it involved giving male volunteers an illegal drug to start with, followed by showing them provocative movies, and measuring the results, and you can just imagine. And remember, you and I helped finance it.) My favorite tale of the bunch concerns the Department of Agriculture's efforts, in 1976, to peep at the screwing of sexworms, or perhaps it was the sex life of screwworms, and anyway the plan was to go out and catch a bunch of screwworm flies and tie little bitty electronic diode dinguses around their necks or something, and then watch what they do with lady screwworm flies on a sort of microwave radar, and all this for only $58,480.

No mention of the monumental trivialities of the federal bureaucracy would be quite complete without equal time for the monumental stupidities. But I'm afraid that even to touch the subject would be to open the floodgates. Besides, by citing stupidities, I would hardly be teaching you anything new about bureaucracy. Let me, then, tell you just one story as a gorgeous examplar of bureaucratic stupidity. It doesn't even involve the feds. It happened in Alabama, in 1977, to a 12-year-old boy.

- Jamie Ray, 12, of Florence, Alabama, got into big trouble with the law because his treehouse was too comfortable. Jamie's treehouse, measuring 8 × 12 feet, has a shingled roof, glass windows, and carpeting. Who shows up but the city's building inspection department (treehouse division?), to rule that the treehouse was "fit for human habitation." It then determined that Jamie's treehouse was less than 20 feet away from a city street, in violation of the zoning laws. Saying he was "admittedly sympathetic," but that "my responsibility is enforcement," the building inspector gave Jamie ten days either to destroy the treehouse or to move the tree.

We have to look at all this stupidity and waste with a smile. Taken seriously, it is just too upsetting, too sad to think about. It is human resources that are being wasted, our sustenance today, our dreams for tomorrow, and ultimately some part of our lives—wasted in astronomical numbers. The saddest part of all is that *none* of it is necessary. Almost every task given the bureaucracy to do, and do at such horrendous cost, can be handled in other, better ways. Indeed, throughout most of our history, we have handled these matters with nonbureaucratic methods, not only at far less cost, but with much greater success and justice. Surely we can do this again, once we understand the enormity of the bureaucratic failure.

We have seen the bureaucratic mind at work, and chronicled its prodigious waste. But there are many other qualities about bureaucracy that compound the distress it causes, and that we must be aware of. It is, for instance, notoriously slow in getting anything done—if it succeeds at all. It is famous for bumbling and bungling. In fact, when bureaus are created to solve social problems, they have an immediate vested interest in making those problems *worse*, to expand their own functions and power. Moreover, bureaus are rewarded not by the success of their efforts, but by their *size*. The bigger one gets, the more prestige and money it commands. The more you expand your empire, the more warm bodies you command, the higher your rank in the bureaucracy.

Its "by the rules" methods make bureaucracy notoriously unresponsive and indifferent to human need. Nobody suffers more at the hands of bureaucracy than its most needy "clients." This bureaucratic attitude leads, at times, to projects with a horrifying disregard for people's rights and even their lives.

What bureaus do care about is themselves. It is common for relief agencies to spend the large majority of their funds on themselves, and allow only a trickle of payments to those in need.

Bureaucracy is perpetually plagued with graft and fraud. This, like waste, seems inherent and ineradicable. Internal auditing and controls are so weak in bureaus that swindles are easy. Multiplying this problem enormously are the vast sums of money that pass through bureaucratic hands (sticking to many). Ultimately, of course, you and I pay for all this.

Everyone hates the endless paperwork, forms, and red tape associated with bureaucracy. The cost, in dollars and hours, is staggering, yet the bureaucrats demand more. The burden grows every year.

Other unpleasant qualities bureaucracy is known for include its inflexibility, its mindless meddling, and its authoritarianism.

As an educator, I have one other major grump about bureaucrats, namely, their capacity to expeditiously formulate, study, identify, develop, coordinate, recommend, administer, and finalize the dysfunctionization of intrasocietal linguistic modalities—which is to say, butcher the English language.

Examples of all of these bureaucratic failings find their way into the news every day. It would be profitable to ponder a few of them, if only in self defense. Know thine enemy!

The mills of bureaucracy grind slowly, but exceedingly coarse.

- The FDA banned sodium cyclamate in 1969—19 years after its researchers found evidence that the artificial sweetener causes tumors.[3]
- After more than three years of effort by its staff of 800, the Consumer Products Safety Commission issued its first hazardous product safety standard. The hazardous product: swimming pool slides.

_____

[3]The preponderant evidence today is that cyclamates are perfectly safe used in moderation. Yet the FDA is just as steadfast in refusing to allow its sale today as it was in refusing to ban it earlier. This is of no small concern, since obesity is the nation's number one health problem, and the only other artificial sweetener, saccharin, is suspected of being harmful.

In bureaucracy, "slow" can mean "never."

- Since its establishment in 1938, the Civil Aeronautics Board had not "certified"—its own word for approval—a single new trunk airline, until the deregulation of the 1980s.

The dictionary says "bungling" is doing things badly, clumsily, or in an awkward manner; mishandling or botching things. Washington's talent for it is such that the term "bureaucratic bungling" has become a cliche.

- In an effort to help the rare and endangered Kirtland Warbler by clearing away some brush, the U.S. Forest Service set fire to the bird's nesting area and burned out 25,000 acres.
- A hospital annex in San Francisco was built for the sole purpose of being torn down and rebuilt a year later, all at federal expense, into the new hospital that was needed in the first place, but for which no federal funds were available.
- The Army Corps of Engineers built two outhouses near Hastings, Minnesota. They were four-holers, with no heat or water, engineered "to meet federal environmental guidelines," and cost $25,000 each.
- A Securities and Exchange Commission reply to a congressional questionnaire took 13,000 pages and stood fifteen feet high.
- The IRS granted tax-exemption status to a "church" and two "charitable" organizations running homosexual boys' camps and peddling pedophilic pornography.

If that one surprises you, you don't know anything about the IRS. Or its friends.

We turn to a much more serious matter. A lot of people seem to have an endless and almost childlike faith that government agencies actually do what they are supposed to do. This is sadly mistaken, and it is the kind of public support that keeps the bureaucrats in power. If we *really* judged the bureaucracy by its results, it would be out of office tomorrow. Instead, we judge it by appearances, or take it for granted. If the government creates an "Environmental Protection Agency," it's protecting the environment—right? Wrong. Terribly wrong.

There are two rock-solid reasons that bureaus do not perform as advertised. First, they are not supposed to. Their real purpose is to serve themselves and enhance government power. Their ostensible assignment is merely a tool to this end. Second, it is not in the bureau's self-interest to do its job. If it solved the problem at hand, it would be out of work—a prospect contrary to every bureaucratic instinct. Its real interest is to make the problem worse, so that it can increase its own power and authority. The EPA, for example, only occasionally prohibits practices that rape the environment; usually, it *licenses* them. Fees payable to itself, of course.

In case you have any doubts at all about these points, let me give you three examples of how government really operates when it says it is protecting the environment. The first is a classic case of an agency creating the problem it is supposed to solve.

- On January 1, 1975, the U.S. Steel Company shut down its pollution-belching open hearth furnaces in Gary, Indiana. What federal agency frantically urged U.S. Steel to fire up the furnaces and start polluting again? The Environmental Protection Agency, of course. It seems the EPA had taken U.S. Steel to court and got a ruling that fined the company $2,300 a day—$2,000 payable to itself, the other $300 to the city of Gary—for each day the company continued polluting. So the company shut down, saying its operation either "is environmentally acceptable, or it is not—and doesn't become acceptable with the payment of a daily fine." With $2,000 a day at stake, the EPA practically begged U.S. Steel to pollute. Russell Train, head of the EPA, actually prepared figures showing it would only cost U.S. Steel 94¢ per worker per day, or 75¢ per ton of steel, to resume polluting. He even offered to negotiate a lower fine. To no avail. U.S. Steel went right on obeying the law.

So much for the EPA. Next, two other agencies crush the theory that the federal government is the greatest protector of our natural resources.

- Around June 1976 it was revealed that the Bureau of Land Management and the National Park Service had both approved uranium mining leases for the Exxon Corporation *in the Grand Canyon.* The Interior Department was very embarrassed about it. Why? Because *neither agency had required Exxon to file environmental impact statements.* Bureaucratic procedures had been violated. *First*, file an environmental impact statement, *then* tear up the Grand Canyon.

Indifference to human needs is one of those qualities of bureaucracy that made it into the dictionary, so we hardly need supply examples here. We see it all too often as it is. The indifference results from those ever-present rules, rules, rules. To the bureaucrat, the rules are more important than the people they are meant to serve.

There are, however, times when indifference grows into something far more sinister, a callous disregard for all human values. The following is a case of this. I was shocked when I first heard of it, and I still find it shocking. One would not believe things like this go on, but they do.

- In the summer of 1977, the Environmental Protection Agency issued a new policy order to the effect that it would no longer fund or approve tests, *on humans*, of substances known to cause cancer. The new policy grew out of a disclosure that two years earlier, senior EPA officials had nearly succeeded in funding a test to feed Mexicans massive doses of a fungicide known to be carcinogenic. The policy order specifically reserved the right for the EPA to continue to conduct tests on humans of substances merely *suspected* of causing cancer.

How could senior government officials undertake such a horrifying scheme? What was on their minds? What sort of insane atmosphere is there deep inside the bureaucracy that tolerates experiments like this, much less carries them out? I have struggled to understand it, and cannot. If there is a bureaucratic logic to it, it's the logic of Auschwitz.

Bureaucrats call themselves "civil servants," but it should be increasingly clear that they are in business to help themselves—"and pretty freely, too," as the Fairy Queen says in Gilbert and Sullivan's *Iolanthe*. This helps explain why noble-sounding endeavors like the "war on poverty" never work. Here are two examples among many.

- The Office of Economic Opportunity announced that it spends 81% of its budget on overhead—that is, on itself instead of on the poor.
- "(AP) A federal job placement program for welfare recipients cut public assistance payments by $400 million last year, but all but $22 million of the savings was gobbled up by the cost of running the program, the Labor Department says." Score: Bureaucrats, plus $378 million. Welfare recipients, minus $400 million.

When the bureaucrats aren't helping themselves, their relatives, friends, associates, and contractors may be. Sometimes it's legal . . .

- The Department of Health, Education, and Welfare ruled that the practice of officials of the National Institute of Drug Abuse awarding millions of dollars in contracts to their relatives and friends is not illegal, but does give a "substantial appearance of impropriety."

More often it's just plain graft, the camp follower of every bureaucratic scheme. Kickbacks, payoffs, account padding, ghost employees, undelivered goods, phony contracts, welfare frauds—

the opportunities are endless. Every week of two, it seems, we read about another case of corruption or scandal. The food stamp program is bilked out of $600 million a year, according to a GAO report. HEW admitted misplacing $6 or $7 billion one year—it wasn't sure quite how much—much of it due to fraud and abuse. The General Services Administration was found to be ridden with graft from top to bottom, and its top administrators were fired. This sort of thing is well known, and we needn't dwell on it.

Not as well understood, unfortunately, is the other side of this coin—the corrupting influence bureaucracy has on American life. And it seems the more "idealistic" a program starts out, the more corruption it spreads. Consider the Summer Foods Service Program, which provided $160 million for lunches for needy children. The lunches were purchased from food management companies, and distributed through some 2,000 churches and charitable organizations. Now, who would steal food from poor kids? Read on.

- *"U.S. PROBING CHILDREN'S FOOD PLAN.* Millions Believed Diverted From Lunches For Needy . . .

   "Justice and Agriculture Department investigators have found evidence that the government may have been defrauded of millions of dollars by food management companies that provide the free lunches . . .

   "[The] alleged fraud in the summer feeding program . . . included theft of food, substandard food, kickbacks, price-fixing, adult use of food intended for children and the dumping of extra food for which the government had paid.

   ". . . the FBI is investigating allegations that in some cases food suppliers agreed to kick back a portion of the over-charges to the sponsoring (religious or charitable) group . . .

   "In one Atlanta case, according to FBI documents, children were regularly served only a quarter glass of milk but were given a full glass on the day federal inspectors were expected.

   "In another case in Dublin, Ga., a preacher used his church as a day-care center, charged the government $16,384 for feeding children in June, 1970, but spent only $3,662 for their meals. He fabricated invoices to get reimbursed.

   "In South Carolina, a pastor collected $6,986 to cover costs of $1,767, with most of the money spent on ineligible children . . ."
   —From a *Washington Post* story

Programs that spread corruption among religious and charitable groups, that even tempt clergymen to steal, cannot be healthy. Yet this sort of result is all but unavoidable. Unless the program becomes an embarrassment, as this one did, the bureaucrats don't much care. It isn't their money being stolen, or their children being cheated. Their auditing procedures are too ineffectual to stop it anyway, even when rigorously applied, which is seldom the case.

- A GAO study of 34 federal agencies found that only two, the Smithsonian Institution and the Interior Department, were in compliance with government audit rules.

Paperwork, forms, red tape—is the bureaucracy bent on annoying us to death?

- In 1975, filling out federal forms was estimated to cost citizens and businesses $40 billion and 130 million man-hours a year. In a bold effort to reduce this burden, the government created a Commission on Federal Paperwork, which will undertake a two-year study of the problem.

Right. And file its report in sextuplicate. Here is what they came up with.

- "(AP) Americans most needing the help of government may be the least able to complete the forms required to get that help, the Federal Commission of Paperwork says.
  "Needy Americans complete more than 500 million federal forms each year, the commission found. Millions more forms are completed at the state and local level.
  "It may take the execution of as many as 60 separate forms to obtain . . . assistance, and a not atypical 10-year-old case was found to contain over 700 documents.
  "The commission quoted an April 1977 report of the Office of Management and Budget, which said individuals submit 231,211,159 responses annually requiring 65,643,952 hours to complete."

Very impressive. But one may be properly suspicious of such exact figures. One thing I've found is that nothing about the federal government ever comes up, believably, in exact figures, at least in recent years. Nobody even knows for sure how many bureaus, agencies, departments, subdepartments, subagencies, commissions, etc. it really has, or how much they spend, or how many different forms they use, much less how much time Americans spend filling them out. Ask "how much" or "how many" about anything in the government, and there is only one answer: "more than the human mind can comprehend."

Occasionally, agencies do try to make a dent in the paperwork problem.

- By a herculean effort, the Environmental Protection Agency managed to reduce one of its forms to a single page. But it had to provide a 90-page instruction book for filling out the form.

Just remember this: without all the information it gets from the forms and paperwork, how could the bureaucracy maintain its reputation for meddling?

Bureaus have to live with their own red tape and rules. Nothing is more amusing than one bureau meddling with another.

- HEW higher-ups sent this message down to the rank and file: "Please do not water the plants in your office. They are under the maintenance contract and will be taken care of properly."
- Citing Federal Property Management regulations, the GSA changed the locks on bureaucrats' bathrooms, to keep out bureaucrats with unsufficient rank.
- "Rules-minded investigators found some lower level transportation officials had more office windows than regulations allow. They went in to cover up two windows but were driven off by gales of laughter."
  —*The Wall Street Journal*

Sometimes innocent victims get caught in the crossfire when a couple of bureaus meddle with each other.

- OSHA ordered a Massachusetts supermarket to put a nonskid floor in its workspace. The Agriculture Department made the market take it out again, and put in a tile floor for sanitation.

Bureaucrats habitually conduct their business in a strange and somewhat threatening foreign language, sometimes called Bureaucratese. This complicates every problem in dealing with the bureaucracy, especially the forms and paperwork, into a bilingual nightmare.

Granted, every trade and every profession has its own jargon, mine not least. But Bureaucratese is in a class by itself. I suspect that bureaucrats use it deliberately, to separate the "ins" from the "outs," and to keep the "outs" from understanding what really goes on in the bureaucracy. I also suspect that fluency in Bureaucratese is the key to the Treasury. Here are a few of my favorite specimens.

- Jimmy Carter described his plan for cities as one "to strengthen linkages among macro-economic sectoral place-oriented economies."
- Trying to get reports written in plain English, the Interstate Commerce Commission formed a "Zero-Base Gobbledygook Committee." You can judge its

success by trying to figure out what a zero-base gob-bledygook committee is, in plain English.

- Examples of U.S. government publications for sale: "78S, Horse Bots, How to Combat Them, Rev. 1973. 7 P. il. A. 1.35:450/4 S/NO100-02787." Another hot number, "59S, Supplement to Digest and Index of Published Decisions of the Assistant Secretary of Labor for Labor-Management Relations Pursuant to Executive Order 11491, as amended July 1, 1972 through December 31, 1972. 1973. 189 pp. L. 1.151/3:972/supp.S/N 2900-00177." And my favorite, "82S, Rats, Let's Get Rid of Them. . . . Most people probably prefer to avoid a long-term relationship with a rat. . . . Rev. 1968. 8 p. il. 1 49.4:22/2. S/N 2410-00022." (And only 10¢).

Government language can be and is used to deceive. No outsider would have guessed that "A Bill to amend Part III of Subchapter O of the Internal Revenue Code of 1954" was in fact a measure to give tax relief to the Hilton Hotel chain.

One last quality about bureaucracy that is not well recognized, and ought to be, is that every federal agency and bureau is a police agency. The bureau's rules are meaningless unless it can enforce them, so every one has its own "compliance" or "enforcement" section—its own police force. Most have their own judges as well. Bureaus thus represent all three branches of government. They can make law, enforce it, and try and punish offenders, all in their own bailiwick.

Crime is seldom a laughing matter, but some of the "crimes" that result from bureaucratic rules get simply ludicrous.

- Three Texans bringing corn shucks from Mexico to make tamales were arrested for smuggling. The corn shucks didn't meet federal corn shuck sanitation standards.
- A 26-year-old woman caught swimming nude in Baker Hot Springs National Park refused to dress and was immediately arrested because she "had no identification at that time."
- Bruce's Restaurant in Tyler, Texas, was raided by seven uniformed and armed officers who suspected that Bruce was selling crappies rather than catfish. Scooping fish bones and remains off plates as evidence, the officers arrested Bruce and his patrons, and hauled them off to a justice of the peace, where all were fined. "They came in here with those big guns and made the waitresses cry," said Bruce.
- High drama at sea one dark night. A U.S. customs helicopter swoops down on suspected criminal activity. Two suspects flee in a speedboat. The customs agents radio for help. Local officials send another chopper and a speedboat. A wild three-hour chase

follows, during which the suspects ram a U.S. Coast Guard cutter that has joined the pursuit. Drug smugglers, of course? Not at all. The two were suspected of raking clams in waters that, according to federal regulations, were too polluted for clamming.

This concludes my review of federal bureaucracy in all its finery. You may have read a thousand stories like these, and yet when the next one comes along, you never cease to wonder: how could anyone be so boneheaded, slow, meddlesome, inconsiderate, weird?

It seems clear enough that the authors of the bureaucratic state, back in the New Deal days, never wondered about it. They had no serious experience with bureaucratic ways, and so didn't really know what sort of monster they created. There is no excuse, however, for the more recent architects of bureaucracy. The "yea" votes in Congress know full well that every time they create a new bureau, they are creating more bureaucratic headaches for America. But they say we, the people, demand it, and deny all responsibility. The fact is, they are fully and directly responsible; but they have a point.

The problem will persist as long as you and I, a majority of Americans, shirk our responsibilities and turn our problems over to the government for solution.

We should know by now that the government cannot solve our problems. It has no resources whatsoever that it did not take from us in the first place. And much of what it takes, it keeps. We think, or at least some people think, that we can unload our problems on somebody else. Then we end up with far more problems than we had to begin with. The "solutions" are forced on us, and we see them as boneheaded, slow, inflexible, inconsiderate, and weird.

And they are. You will have seen by now that bureaucrats work in a wholly different way from the rest of us. The difference is fundamental, going down to bedrock principles. Either we handle our affairs through free and voluntary association, or we turn them over to the bureaucrats, and have them handled with coercive rules and regulations. Those are really our only two choices. They are opposites and yield opposite results. Through free association, we produce what we need to survive and prosper. Under bureaucracy, we get rules upon rules telling what we can and cannot do. Bureaucracy produces nothing. Under bureaucracy we will, finally, starve.

Are there any common threads running through our experience with bureaucracy? I find three. First, all bureaucratic influence is based on its rules and regulations, rather than on what is sensible or economic. Second, all bureaucratic actions are imposed by force or threat of force, rather than being freely chosen. You and I are in the best position to decide how to manage our affairs, yet we are not permitted to. The bureaucracy, knowing little or nothing about it, does it for us. The point was explicit in Fascist Italy, which was plastered with posters of Mussolini with the caption, "He Will Decide." That is precisely what bureaucracy is all about.

The last common thread is taxes. Bureaucrats do not produce; they take. Everything they take comes off your table and mine. And what they take costs us more than food, clothing, and shelter—all the necessities of life—put together. Not counting any military spending, the current cost of federal bu-reaucracy is around $3,000 for every person in America. Little babies, people in nursing homes, everyone. Many of us would have trouble believing this, because it's far more than is deducted from our paychecks for income taxes and social security. But it's true. Rich people aren't paying your taxes for you, despite all the well-advertised "soak the rich" plans. You pay them, for the most part indirectly. Everything you buy or rent is marked up scores and hundreds of times to pay taxes. The money you bring home is marked down scores or hundreds of times to pay taxes. Inflation, which is nothing more than creating money, is a federal monopoly and another federal tax. You pay it in the higher price of goods and services. The bureaucrats spend it. Does your family budget allow $60 per person per week for feeding federal bureaucrats? Can you afford it? Let's hope so, because that's what bureaucracy costs you.

1 NO   IS BUREAUCRACY THE ENEMY OF THE PEOPLE?

Don't Blame the Bureaucracy!
H. Brinton Milward
Hal G. Rainey

1. THE DENIGRATION OF BUREAUCRACY

For over a decade, there has been increasing scepticism about the performance of the public bureaucracy in the United States. The problem has been a major theme in the last several presidential administrations, and has reached a high point in the Reagan administration. President Reagan's contempt for the bureaucracy is no secret. Ed Meese, one of the President's major counselors, came to a cabinet meeting with a rotund, faceless, large-bottomed doll. He announced that it was a bureaucrat doll; you put it on a stack of papers and it just sits there! (Raines, 1981).

If Presidents and their aides are acting this way, you can predict that they feel that most of the voters approve. Public opinion polls have in fact been detecting a widespread conviction that government is wasteful, meddlesome, and ineffective, and much of this concern focuses on public agencies and their employees as a major part of the problem. A Roper poll asked respondents to estimate how much of each $100 spent by the Social Security Administration goes for administrative costs. The median estimate was about $52.10. The actual cost is $1.30 (Germond and Witcover, 1981). In May of 1981 a Lou Harris poll found that 88 per cent of the 1,207 respondents felt that too much tax money is wasted by an inefficient bureaucracy.[1]

·From H. Brinton Milward and Hal G. Rainey, "Don't Blame the Bureaucracy!," *Journal of Public Policy* 3 (May 1983), pp. 149–68. Copyright © by Cambridge University Press. Reprinted with permission.

[1] Why the middle class supports Reagan, *Business Week*, 18 May 1981. The Institute for Social Research at the University of Michigan has been finding that very high percentages of the respondents to their polls feel that the government wastes a lot of money. See Smith, Taylor and Mathiowetz (1980).

Academics and journalists, including many who actually supported the growth of government agencies and programs in the past, show more and more concern over the intransigency and inefficacy of those agencies. Among many examples are Allen Barton and Carol Weiss, two prominent social scientists not necessarily inclined to hostility toward government, who recently published a book of readings entitled *Making Bureaucracies Work* (1980). The implications, of course, are that they are *not* working.

These doubts about public bureaucracy are part of a more general atmosphere of disenchantment with government in the United States, with what is seen as its poor performance, its excessive influence, and its huge cost. These concerns are echoed in other countries, including Britain under the Thatcher government. They have helped to fuel efforts by the Reagan administration and previous administrations to reduce and reform government. Well before President Reagan was elected, there was a downtrend in public employment (Serrin, 1981). At all levels of government, there were efforts to reduce taxes, cap or cut spending, curtail regulatory authority, return functions to the private sector, and otherwise cut down on government. The Reagan administration simply represents a high tide for such efforts. As the polls show, such actions are based in part on the perception that the bureaucrats and the bureaucracy are lazy and inept.

The central theme of this paper is that there are genuine dangers in this impulse to denigrate government in general and bureaucracy in particular. The danger is that oversimplifications, myths, stereotypes, and facile assumptions will distort decisions about the proper role of the public bureaucracy in the United States and other countries. There are major problems in managing the public bureaucracy, and we share concerns about excesses, waste, and other shortcomings which critics cite. Bad diagnoses lead to bad solutions, however, or to no solution. Using the public bureaucracy as a scapegoat for a variety of social and economic ills can effectively *prevent* the proper analysis of those problems. Verbal bludgeoning of bureaucrats can actually create a vicious cycle in which improvements can become even more difficult. Early on in the Reagan administration, for example, there were many newspaper reports of severely low morale in many agencies, and of the rapid departure from public service of many of the best people.

Too many people, including high-level policy makers and opinion leaders, are moving too quickly to propose cuts in public agencies and public programs without grappling with important points about the difficulty of evaluating those cuts and the true value of those programs. More people should be forced to confront those questions. Our public debate should show more sophistication in considering the role of the public bureaucracy in a modern, complex, technologically and socially advanced society. Virtually every other industrialized nation has a larger public sector than the United States, and issues continually come up which will require the involvement of government at all levels. Shortly after receiving the Nobel Prize in Economics, James Tobin observed that the rapid growth of the public sector in the United States had actually accompanied the greatest economic advances of any country in history, and that he knows of no evidence that government spending and growth are responsible for current economic difficulties.[2] We will continue to have a large, active, and expensive public sector, and it is time for this point to be incorporated into our public discussion. It is not a partisan matter. The conservative columnist George Will (1982), after noting that 40 per cent of our bridges are rated as deficient, and about 50 per cent of the Interstate Highway System will need major repairs by 1995, but that gas taxes had not increased since 1959, pointed out that private enterprise depends on a publicly provided infrastructure. It is neither optional, he said, nor inexpensive: 'A substantial portion—perhaps 80 per cent—of public spending is not really a subject of serious debate.'

The real challenge that the country faces is not simply the search for ways to slash the public sector and return functions to the private sector, as suggested in a number of recent treatises by ideological conservatives such as George Gilder (1981) and William Simon (1980). The challenge for modern societies is effectively posed in the book *Politics and Markets* by the political scientist Charles Lindblom (1976). He points out that modern societies have two major alternatives for administering the production of goods and services. They can allow independent decisions by individuals and firms responding to the signals of economic markets, or they can have a politically based, hierarchical system— a political body and a bureaucracy—direct what is

---

[2]*New York Times,* 3 January 1982, p. E5.

to be done and produced, by issuing laws and rules. We know that this political-bureaucratic alternative is, in Lindblom's words, 'all thumbs'. It is clumsy and inefficient in a number of ways, as President Reagan and many others have been telling us recently. The dilemma is that we also know that economic markets can fail, and fail badly, to provide all of the goods, services, and outcomes which we want and need. Of course, there are no countries which are run purely by one or the other of these methods, and as Lindblom describes in his book, the two are always mixed, modified, or balanced in a variety of ways. There lies the challenge. What is the best mix and balance for our complex society as we finish out this century and enter a new one?

A great many people assume we have gone too far in the political and bureaucratic direction, and need to move back towards heavier reliance on private markets. We do not claim to be certain that they are wrong, but we feel strongly that such decisions should not be made without considering some points about the performance and value of the public bureaucracy which we want to raise in this paper. Some of these points stress that the public bureaucracy may be more effective and valuable than often supposed. Other points emphasize that, if the bureaucracy performs badly in certain ways, the source of the problem may not be in the organizations and employees themselves. Blaming the bureaucracy, then, may be a very bad way of trying to improve things.

2. THE CRY FOR EFFICIENCY: 'RUN GOVERNMENT LIKE A BUSINESS'

The most popular current charge against the government bureaucracy is that government at all levels is inefficient and ineffective because of bad management. The solution proposed in Washington and in many state capitals and city halls is to 'run government more like a business'. Government's ship must be made tighter and more efficient, through centralization of power in the executive's hands, and elimination of waste, duplication, and overlap. This theme is nothing new in American public administration, but has been heavily emphasized recently. For example, President Reagan once said

that many of his budget cuts could be accomplished simply through the elimination of waste and mismanagement. Certain governors have made the call for more businesslike procedures into a theme for their administrations.

No one opposes efficiency in government, and many business practices should be used more frequently in government, but the call for 'running government more like a business' is often badly misconceived. It overlooks several serious points. One of these points is that heavy emphasis on operating efficiency may distort the role, purpose, and value of government in our society. The United States government, with its sharing of executive power between Congress and the President, was originally designed with less emphasis on simple efficiency than on avoiding concentrated power and centralized administration of the type European monarchies possessed. Indeed the same emphasis exists today. Samuel P. Huntington in *American Politics: The Promise of Disharmony* (1981) writes that the American people will not permit government to be what it must be for efficient operation, i.e., to possess some measure of hierarchy, inequality, arbitrary power, secrecy, deception and established patterns of superordination and subordination. These are the attributes which are necessary for efficiency but antithetic to the American ideal. Ironically, the Reagan administration represents that fear and distrust of government at the same time they advocate managerial solutions which will make it more fearsome. This unwieldly character of our government complicates the internal operation of agencies and programs and makes them appear inefficient or actually be that way.

A second misconception in the calls for more businesslike efficiency in government is their underestimation of the actual value that can be attached to government, if it really were viewed in businesslike fashion. Former Governor Dan Evans of Washington provided an excellent example of this when he grew tired of the constant calls for 'running government more like a business'. He had a document prepared titled *Report to the Shareholders of the State of Washington* (1976). In it he applied the corporate model to the state to show the inappropriate nature of the comparison. Imagine, he said, trying to run a company whose 'stockholders', the electorate, only gave you a razor thin vote of confidence; where the 'board of directors', the legislature, was often controlled by a rival group; and where your 'management team', the cabinet, was in part separately elected and partly picked by you. How would you like to manage this 'company' knowing you were limited by law to either one or two four-year terms? Evans went on to apply the accounting system used by Boeing, the largest company in Washington, to the assets and liabilities of the state. In spite of these constraints on management of the state, the analysis showed it to be far from a precarious financial position. Accepted accounting standards showed that the net worth of the state worked out to eighteen hundred dollars per citizen. The reason was that capital investments like buildings and highways previously had been treated as expenditures and were assumed to have no worth after construction.

Some observers even argue that the immense value of government assets and services are part of the problem in managing our economy. Lindblom (1976), points out that a great deal of government activity in the USA, now and in the past, has actually been devoted to the support and promotion of private business. James O'Connor, in *The Fiscal Crisis of the State* (1973), similarly argues that a major problem for our public finances is that private corporations, especially in certain noncompetitive industries, force major costs of their operations onto government. The taxpayers pick up the tab for roads, schools, cultural and entertainment facilities, police, public transportation, and numerous other assets and services which benefit business enterprises far more than they cost those enterprises. Yet public agencies usually receive the blame for the high costs. As one example, much has been made of the regulatory costs imposed on the automobile industry. Those costs may well be excessive, but the critics seldom note that the automobile industry's development has been directly linked to the hundreds of billions spent by taxpayers and government for roadbuilding. The huge costs of maintaining those roads and highways is emerging as a major issue, and government will have to take the heat and solve the problem. Is government a burden on the auto industry, or is it really the other way around?

Another shortsighted aspect of the cries for businesslike efficiency in government is that they often overestimate business efficiency and actually underestimate the efficiency with which government operates. It is commonly assumed that business is more efficient, but this is more easily assumed than proven. There is plenty of evidence of immense waste and inefficiency in business organizations, which makes it hard to say whether they are any better or worse than government organizations on that score.

Among many examples of this evidence of poor performance by some American business organizations is the current attack on them in two recent books (Ouchi, 1981; Pascale and Althos, 1981) and numerous articles which compare American management practices very unfavorably with those of the Germans and Japanese. These criticisms make one wonder whether American business organizations are really an ideal model for government to copy, and they point up an irony in some of the calls for more businesslike efficiency in government. The observers of Japanese industrial success say it results in large part from willingness to forego the short-term profit which comes at the expense of maintenance, capital investment in the plant, and humane management practices. Ironically, the changes urged on the public sector often involve financial techniques and control systems which focus on short-term efficiency and tightened control with little attention to long-term investment in the organization and commitment to it. One clear instance of this is the effort to remove civil service protections at many levels of government. While many successful business organizations here and abroad make long-term commitments to employees and emphasize their personal development, critics of government assume that government will become more productive if we make employees more afraid they will be fired.

The last point brings us to the ultimate jibe at the 'run the government like a business' argument. It is usually unclear, if not simply meaningless. It is a simple minded proposal that merits a simple response; should we run it like W. T. Grant, Penn Central and the fifty thousand businesses that go bankrupt every year; or should we run it like successful companies like IBM or Delta Airlines both of whom practice 'inefficient' practices like not laying off employees during cyclical downturns in business conditions? The simple proposal contains no clear advice as to what we should do.

The cries for more efficiency and for running government like a business are the easiest of the arguments to overturn. There are actually a number of related points which are more difficult to resolve, but which must be addressed.

3. VALUE COMPLEXITY: MULTIPLE, CONFLICTING, HARD-TO-MEASURE GOALS

We have made the point that government serves values more complex than operating efficiency. It is important to recognize the true variety and complexity of those additional values, the ways in which they complicate evaluation of the public bureaucracy, and most of all, to recognize that attention to them is simply inescapable. If the functions of government could be easily packaged for exchange on markets, then the private sector would normally get the jobs. Government gets the messy jobs, and government agencies have many goals imposed upon them. This naturally makes it harder to achieve all of them.

One reason for this is that the goals are often contradictory. Pursuit of one detracts from achievement of others. Wilson and Rachel (1977) provide a vivid illustration of this problem. Imagine, they say, a state highway department. It is largely composed of engineers who have been told by the legislature and governor to build a highway between two cities at the lowest cost given accepted engineering standards. Here we have a public agency with a goal which is actually clear and unambiguous compared to the goals of many public programs. Construction begins, however, and immediately efficient achievement of the goal is frustrated. The engineers are forced to pay the prevailing union wage, whether the workforce is union or not, because of the Davis-Bacon Act. Next, minority groups complain that the contractors have not given enough of the subcontract work to minority owned firms. The contractors claim that the minority subcontractors had higher bids and/or were less experienced than competing subcontractors. Nevertheless the law is clear and they must be given a piece of the action. Construction finally begins, and costs have already risen substantially, but the end appears to be in sight. Then the Sierra Club threatens to sue the contractors and the state if an alternate route is not chosen which avoids a swamp which is also a wildlife refuge. Again the law is clear and the state reroutes the highway at a cost of millions of dollars.

The road is finally completed several years late and millions over budget. Those groups who along the way pressed additional goals are happy but the public at large views the late completion and excessive cost as just another example of bureaucratic bungling.

The clear lesson from this example is that efficiency is a very important value but there are other values such as equity and protection of the environment which by law must be observed, and which compete with simple operating efficiency. If the road had been built efficiently the state would have been pilloried for spoiling the environment, supporting the vestiges of discrimination and being anti-union. Public agencies are often put in a no-win situation where the achievement of one goal insures poor performance on another.

The government agency may be seen as inefficient, but is actually incorporating into its own operations the value conflicts which must somehow be worked out in a complex society. Equity (defined as equal treatment of citizens) and governmental responsiveness and accountability are also very important values in our political life.

These values mean that there are multiple criteria for judging success or failure. A program can be run very efficiently and still be accused of being unresponsive, because to be efficient means that you cannot continually respond to this or that request or you will no longer be judged efficient. It is the ability of business to deflect many intrusions into how they operate that often makes them better able to perform on the efficiency criterion than government. Thus GM does not have to hold 'citizen participation' hearings before every major decision they make. Having to manage in a fishbowl and to have your files constantly open for public inspection—as the Freedom of Information Act allows—may be wonderful if judged from the criterion of accountability but it makes it very difficult to be efficient.

Equity is another value that is difficult to reconcile with efficiency. From an efficient standpoint it was economic madness to spend millions upon millions of dollars making public transportation accessible to the handicapped. Not only did it direct large amounts of money to a small proportion of the population but there were less costly ways to achieve the same goal of making public transportation available to the handicapped. Rather than retrofitting old buses, buying new ones with wider aisles and wheelchair lifts or putting elevators in subway stations (which then break down because of lack of use) cities could have more cheaply provided a system of wheelchair accessible minibuses that could be available on demand to take the handicapped person where he wanted to go. This alternative was rejected by organized groups representing the handicapped because handicapped people would not have the same access to the same facilities as non-handicapped people. Thus a great amount of money was spent complying with this interpretation of the law which said that federal funds must not be spent on facilities that are not accessible to the handicapped. The courts decreed that the money was to be spent to insure equity with no thought given to economic efficiency.

There is no better example of these difficulties of considering multiple values and avoiding stereotypes than that most frequent choice as the quintessential government giveaway program, 'welfare'. Public opinion polls and other sources consistently show that high percentages of Americans see 'welfare' as one of the major forms of government waste and major reason for higher taxes. Yet in the 1982 budget proposed by the Reagan administration, these programs normally considered welfare programs (AFDC, Medicaid, and several others) accounted for about $50 billion of the total of approximately $650 billion (Pechman, 1981, 55). Fifty billion dollars is a huge amount, and the programs may have huge problems, but it is clear that even if we eliminated them completely and passed all the money directly back to taxpayers, tax bills would not go down as much as 10 per cent. There is really not nearly that much which can be cut, of course, because we cannot let the poor starve in the streets, and most welfare recipients are not chiselers, but persons who work when they can or who simply are unable to work. It is clear that 'welfare' as a source of high taxes and bureaucratic waste is exaggerated in the minds of a great many Americans.

Still, some critics argue that we would do better to return the money to the private sector, and let business expand to absorb the welfare recipients. The private sector is assumed to be more efficient, so the money would be better used. But is this argument not a good example of the oversimplification about complex systems which plagues our public debate? One of the ways in which industry has made

its impressive gains in productivity is by displacing workers with machines. Industry has required higher and higher levels of skill from workers, and has less and less demand for the unskilled labor which most welfare recipients can provide. Government is given the task of providing for the persons least useful to industry, and is also saddled with the blame for the problem.

Complaints about the wasteful welfare system usually overlook the more general societal issues which are so complicated to resolve. Do we really know the social costs we are saving through the welfare system, even if it is riddled with waste, mismanagement, and disincentives? One could observe that the society is getting a perverse bargain, by buying off the impoverished lower end of the income scale with small payments, while the rest of us, including the much-pitied middle class, live in a state of comfort never dreamed of even by the aristocrats of a century or two ago. Another perspective is to view the system of welfare programs with a certain degree of pride, as a system which is flawed, but which has largely eradicated acute malnutrition and other aspects of abject poverty in a country not particularly inclined to address those problems. These arguments are oversimplifications themselves, but show how complicated the evaluation of even a widely-pilloried program can be.

This welfare example brings us to a final point about complex and intangible goals of public agencies. They make it harder for citizens, including experts, to see what government agencies are doing and how well. Functions are usually assigned to government because of their broad, diffuse impacts on society and the public interest. Public-sector goods and services usually cannot be exchanged on economic markets, and must be evaluated through the political process. Yet how can citizens make clear judgments of the value and contribution of national defense, public education, social welfare programs, and an elaborate interstate highway system? Since benefits are hard to see, it is easy to jump to the conclusion that there are not many benefits. It seems that people make such judgements largely through stereotypes, ideology, or concentration on a few issues of particular self-interest. The problem is that advancing technology and social complexity create more and demands for such government services, and we really have no alternative to finding more effective ways of evaluating their delivery.

4. PUBLIC SECTOR STANDARDS ARE HIGHER

The value complexity involved in evaluating public bureaucracy is also due to the higher performance standards which are applied to government. We feel a sense of ownership of government, and a caution about its powers. We demand that, in addition to being efficient, government must be fair, open, honest, accountable, consistent, and responsive.

A good example of these particularly high standards for government, ironically, is the matter of efficiency, where business is often assumed to be superior. What organization, public or private, doesn't waste five or ten per cent of its revenue? This 'waste' takes many forms—theft, breakage, spoilage, unnecessary perks for managers, poor decisions about projected demand, and slack resources to meet peak demand. All of these factors exist in both sectors, but they cause much more concern in the public sector. The federal government at the request of Congress is now requiring that Prime Sponsors under the CETA program account for and be responsible for every dollar spent by the autonomous training programs that they fund. No waste at all is allowed in a program which is supposed to be flexible and responsive to the needs of those who need job training. Most of the training programs which are storefront community organizations cannot afford accountants or trained financial managers, but the Prime Sponsor is held completely responsible for every dollar they spend (Barnes, 1980).

The same pattern holds in the matter of ethics. If Labor Secretary Raymond Donovan had still been a New Jersey contractor instead of Secretary of Labor, no one would bat an eye over his being accused of giving a union official with ties to the Mafia several thousand dollars to ensure labor peace at a construction site. In many northeastern states, this is part of the cost of doing business. Against a Secretary of Labor, however, this becomes a serious charge and, if proven, grounds for dismissal. Thus in ethics as in performance we seem to have created a double standard.

To this point, we have suggested that public bureaucracy has more value than is commonly recognized. As we have said, however, there are plenty of indications that government agencies often do perform poorly. Here again, it can be harmful simply to berate the bureaucracy, because the real source of the problem often lies outside it.

5. THE SPECIAL INTEREST STATE

This view of the bureaucracy problem has a number of different facets. Theodore Lowi originated this line of analysis in *The End of Liberalism* (1969) where he argued that the paralysis of liberal democracy resulted from its inability to judge the claims of special interest groups so the unjustified claims on society could be rejected and the just ones supported. Examples from the equal rights area abound. While Blacks and Indians have strong claims for affirmative action and special help, an argument can be made that each successive group clamoring for protection has a less strong claim on society's conscience. The logical result is no equal rights but preference extended to all groups with the result that we equate the claims of Blacks with the claims of Gays. Lowi argues that to fail to judge claims on society trivializes public policy. He calls this 'universalized ticket fixing' which breeds disrespect for government.

The result of 'universalized ticket fixing' is that the policy process (and government) are often immobilized. John Gardner, the founder of Common Cause, describes the special interest state this way:

> Imagine a checkers player confronted by a bystander who puts a thumb on one checker and says, 'Go ahead and play just don't touch this one,' and then another bystander puts a thumb on another checker with the same warning, and then another and another. Pretty soon all thumbs and no moves. The irony is that owners of the thumbs—the special interests—don't want to make the game unwinnable; they just don't want you to touch their checker. The result is they paralyze the policy-making process (Gardner, 1979, 32).

In addition to the immobility that comes from the checker game another aspect of the special interest state is that the pervasiveness of bureaucratic rules and regulations (the proverbial 'red tape') is caused by special interests and Congress, not rule-bound bureaucrats. What Samuel Halperin says of education can be applied to any policy arena:

> Much of the prescriptive language that occurs in federal statutes does not come from congressmen who are trying to oppress educators. Much of it comes from one group in society that doesn't trust or agree with another group in society (Halperin, 1978, 14–15).

The last special interest state argument concerns the fragmentation of policy and the lack of policy consistency one finds in federal programs. Joe Califano conducted an anti-smoking crusade at HEW while the Department of Agriculture was supporting price supports and acreage allotments for tobacco farmers and the Department of Commerce was not requiring manufacturers of tobacco to put the Surgeon General's health warning on cigarettes to be exported. The reason this occurs is not bureaucratic stupidity. Fragmentation arises precisely from a key function of democratic government—to respond to diverse demands from interests which are mutually incompatible. This leads directly to policies which tend to be directly contradictory.

All of the previous examples undergird the basic argument that the idiocies of bureaucracy (rule bound paralysis, inefficiency, fragmentation, waste, duplication and overlap) result not so much from the internal culture of bureaucracy as from the demands of powerful interest groups and congressional committees to which the agencies must respond.

> John Gardner . . . says it is a mistake to think of the Federal Government as a separate entity. 'It is a collection of fragments under the virtual control of highly organized special interests,' he said. 'In the special interest state that we have forged, every well organized interest owns a piece of the rock.' (Herbers, 1978).

6. CONGRESS ASKS BUREAUCRACIES TO DO THINGS WHICH NO ONE KNOWS HOW TO DO

This approach to the 'bureaucracy problem' locates the problem squarely in the Congress. Congress, due to the pressure of interest groups (some of them organizations of professionals who work for government), will pass laws calling for government agencies to do things that they or anyone else simply do not know how to do. Or if the technology is known, the Congress may be very reluctant to provide the necessary funds to perform the task adequately. Problems of this nature usually occur in organizations that are charged with changing the behavior of individual clients. Whether it is the prisons which are supposed to rehabilitate criminals or social workers who are supposed to change pathological behavior of some welfare clients involving spouse abuse, civil servants are being asked to do things that our society does not know how to do. If we do know how to do these things it is usually possible only in an individualistic setting where massive amounts of human and monetary resources are brought to bear on the client. This can hardly be the case in a resource-tight public sector that runs programs that must of necessity be geared to large numbers of clients and diffused over fifty states and ten thousand cities.

Congress and the American people have been unwilling to accept some harsh realities. As Peter H. Schuck (1980) points out, law as a tool of social change has limits. Politicization of some issues only makes them worse. There are few if any comprehensive solutions to problems like moral decay, declining cities, or welfare. Such matters are either unknowable or, for a variety of reasons, not achievable. While Congress can pass laws on any topic and spend money for any public purpose, implementing policies depends on bureaucracies being able to translate legislative intent into an implementable program. If there is no known cause and effect relationship between the theory underlying the program and what an agency is asked to do then the bureaucracy will once again become a scapegoat.

The most ridiculous current example comes not from the Democrats or social work do-gooders but from ultra-conservative Senator Jeremiah Denton (R-Ala). He introduced a bill in Congress to create a program to 'study the causes of teenage pregnancy' and develop ways of promoting chastity among teenagers. While the *causes* of teenage pregnancy are obvious the solutions are not and even if they were, the imposition of chastity belts in a democratic society would not be looked upon with great favor.

The politicization of social issues does not guarantee their solution. Public agencies have been expected to do things beyond their capacity—to halt moral decay, end wars and racial discrimination, prevent population growth, ensure equality, and eradicate crime.

7. GOVERNMENTAL OVERLOAD

This view of the problem is similar to the above argument concerning doing things we do not know how to do. It holds that because all issues become political and the special interest state has no criteria for refusing any request, the state will try to do everything (see King, 1975). Some things will be within its capacity, some will not, but all will be attempted. The result is that the carrying capacity of the government will become overloaded and because resources will be spread too thin the system will overload and falter.

A corollary to this is something called 'Moynihan's Law,' named for the senator from New York. It states that any program which depends for its success on there being large numbers of highly trained, intelligent, committed individuals will of necessity fail. This somewhat tongue-in-cheek maxim points out one problem that seems unique to government. Since there are no a priori grounds for refusing to intervene in areas that have been politicized, human or other resource constraints are not accepted as excuses for nonintervention. In contrast, no business would enter an area if capital or human resources were lacking. In the public sector one finds laws like the Safe Streets Act of 1968 which by a stroke of the pen created a profession that had previously not existed—Criminal Justice Planning—and because it was in the law programs had to be established to certify these people, even though no one knew what they did.

8. MACROECONOMIC MANAGEMENT HINDERS PROGRAM PERFORMANCE

The President and Congress live and die not on whether CETA is perceived as being an efficiently run program but rather on the rates of inflation and unemployment. These two summary statistics are far more important to political survival than any government program; because of this the management of the economy has become the single most important single task of government.

In Maryland an aide to Governor Harry R. Hughes points out that:

> The energy assistance program is designed to keep people warm in winter. But they (OMB) want to give you the money in equal amounts every quarter. We don't need the money in July, we need it now, and these guys in Washington are sitting on the money. You know why? They want to keep it in the bank and draw interest on it, and we've got people freezing (Herbers, 1982).

Steps designed to better manage or 'fine tune' the economy (across the board budget cuts, personnel reductions in force which lay off good workers and bad and personnel ceilings unrelated to the magnitude of the job to be done) can cripple the effectiveness of government programs. The US Office of Surface Mining issued 800 fewer mine violations in 1980 than in 1979. They attributed the decrease, rightly or wrongly, not to a change in policy from Carter to Reagan, rather they attributed it to not being able to replace mine inspectors who resigned during the federal hiring freeze.

9. STEREOTYPES OF BUREAUCRACY: TWO COGNITIVE LEVELS

The preceding points show how hard it is to say whether we are simply underestimating public bureaucracy or whether bureaucracy actually is doing badly because of burdens imposed on it. A problem in resolving the issue is that there are widely-held unfavorable stereotypes of public bureaucracy. It is hard to separate accurate evaluation from invidious myth. The views of public bureaucracy are also paradoxical, making it hard to say what people really want to do about bureaucracy.

In one of the most careful and interesting studies of such views ever done Daniel Katz and associates (1975) reported that the public's general evaluation of government agencies is not particularly favorable. They asked respondents to rate how well government agencies meet a number of performance criteria, such as solving clients' problems, prompt service, fair treatment, and others. About 25 to 35 per cent of the respondents gave generally unfavorable ratings of public agencies, and only small percentages gave highly favorable ratings. When asked to say whether business or government meets the standards better, about half of the respondents saw no difference, but of those who did, more than twice as many felt that business does better.

Strikingly, however, respondents' ratings of their own specific encounters with public agencies were much more favorable than their impressons of public agencies in general. Katz et al. concluded that their respondents' attitudes tended to be organized along two levels. The attitudes on specific matters —the way particular agencies have actually treated you—tended to be favorable. When the referent is less specific—public agencies in general—negative stereotypes have a greater influence and ratings become less favorable. There are also similar survey findings of unfavorable ratings of Congress as an institution by respondents who at the same time are pleased with their own Congressman. Only 20 per cent of the respondents in a University of Michigan poll taken in 1978 said Congress was doing a good job. In contrast, 65 per cent of those responding gave their Congressman a high rating on job performance. Polls consistently report similarly paradoxical views. People will say that they want less government and lower taxes, but more public services.

The problem of destructive stereotyping brings us back to the Ed Meese joke with which we started. The public employee is probably the easiest target for cheap shots in our political and economic system, and the criticisms have a very tangible impact. As we said earlier, there are many reports of demoralization, and of departure of good people from the public service in the first year of the Reagan presidency. An official working in Washington commented to one of us, only partly in jest, that the rhetoric there made him feel that as a public employee he had never earned an honest dollar.

The stereotype that 'bureaucrats' are lazy bunglers is so deeply embedded in our culture that it is hard to see how some people could live without it. It is very convenient for some people to be able to feel that many problems are due to the bungling bureaucrats, but the scapegoating makes a hard job

even harder. The complex values, pressures, and performance problems can be even more frustrating to the people who have to face them daily. Stephen Michelson (1980) has written about 'the working bureaucrat and the nonworking bureaucracy.' He points out that many public employees work hard in programs that appear not to work, because of the complexities we have discussed. Surveys of public employees have found that they report that they work very hard. Several researchers have concluded that frustrations over bureaucratic complexity are a significant morale and motivation problem for many public employees (Buchanan, 1975; Cherniss, 1980). Business executives in government-business executive exchange programs have commented that they were struck by the complex trade-offs and value considerations in public management, and the experience made them better understand the challenges public managers confront (Weiss, 1974).

10. CONCLUSION

We have argued two main points which it is dangerous to overlook. First, the public bureaucracy in the United States is more valuable, and is performing more effectively, than many people assume. We noted that its performance and value cannot be evaluated only in terms of simple operating efficiency, because of the need for complex controls of the public bureaucracy and the need to assess its impact on complex societal objectives. We pointed out the immense and often underestimated value of the functions and services provided by public agencies, and argued that those agencies are not as wasteful and inept as is often casually assumed. Among the reasons that they may seem to be performing badly are that we assign them particularly complex, multiple, hard-to-measure goals, which often conflict with each other, and at the same time we hold their performance up to particularly high standards.

The second main point is that when public bureaucracies do perform badly, the problem is often due to external factors rather than internal laziness, incompetence, or mismanagement. Public agencies must respond to demands of multiple special interests within the society. They are asked to do things which are immensely difficult or sometimes impossible, and are often overloaded with responsibilities relative to the resources they have for carrying out those responsibilities. Chief executives and legislatures emphasize macroeconomic management in a way that hinders internal program management and efficiency. We also pointed out that public agencies and officials must operate in an environment of crude, contradictory stereotypes, where berating bureaucrats and the bureaucracy are favorite pastimes. These stereotypes can be self-fulfilling, and in themselves create performance problems.

Failure to consider these points can be harmful because it is obvious that the United States is going to continue to have a large, influential public sector. There is no alternative but to try to learn ways to improve our management of it, but that process will be hindered by oversimplifications about its value and performance and about the reasons for poor performance when it occurs.

The huge scope and size of the public sector are obvious. After careful analysis, Eli Ginzburg and George Vojta (1981) concluded that about one out of every three jobs is attributable to the public sector, rather than one out of six, as often reported. The apparent excesses involved in some of this extensive size, together with the points we ourselves made about governmental overload and impossible tasks, can be taken as suggestions that the public sector should be cut back. Certainly there are numerous ways in which the public sector, like all major institutions, can be usefully reduced and streamlined.

Yet devising such cuts and improvements is more complicated than many critics of the bureaucracy would like to believe, because it is also true that the public sector grew not simply because of greedy special interests, self-serving bureaucrats, porkbarrel politicians, or bleeding-heart liberals. All advanced modern societies have large public sectors, and in fact the United States ranks about eighth among the major industrialized democracies in percentage of gross domestic product accounted for by the public sector, even though the other countries devote smaller proportions of their GNP to defense (Pechman, 1981). It is clear that governmental sectors grow because of technological, social, and economic imperatives in all advanced societies, which cause government to be called on to provide a range of essential functions and services. Ginzburg and Vojta themselves argue that it is wrong to regard public investment and employment as necessarily

unproductive. They note that government provides essential infrastructure for industry, such as highways and airports, and contributes to private sector productivity through education, which adds value to human capital. There may be important marginal adjustments to the size of government which should be made, but large public bureaucracies and programs are here to stay. What absolutely must be done is to keep trying to improve the management of them.

It is ironic, then, that some of the most virulent attacks on government and bureaucracy, and the most determined efforts to cut them back, are coming just at a time of rapid development in thought and training about public management and public policy. At certain major universities there have been programs in higher education for the public service for a long time, but only within the last decade has there been a marked proliferation of such programs across the United States. Similarly, there has been a substantial increase in the literature and research on public management and public policy, covering a number of related topics and issues such as evaluation of public programs, public policy analysis, public finance and public sector economics, the social responsibility of business and the relationship between business and the public sector, and the application of a variety of management concepts and techniques to the public sector. Some of this activity is criticized as faddish busywork by self-serving bureaucrats and academics. One can also argue, however, that these are essential steps in developing our ability to handle the immensely complex, intangible, value-laden administrative issues faced by advanced modern societies, which simply cannot be handled through exchanges on decentralized economic markets.

As part of this trend, there has been progress in development of the concept of public management.[3] To discharge the complex, essential functions of the public sector, there is a need for individuals trained in this growing body of knowledge we have mentioned, and for continued de-

---

[3]For examples, see Allison (1979); Bower (1977); Lynn (1981). There is also a voluminous relevant literature in public administration, which has developed over a longer period but which has been developing more rapidly in recent years.

velopment of the body of research and thought itself. Management in any setting faces complicated problems, but the role of public management involves some particularly complex challenges and constraints.

Public management must operate within a complex institutional and political setting, which imposes extensive external direction and control, assigns abstract, value-laden goals, and constrains managerial authority in various ways. Civil Service constraints on personnel decisions are one much-discussed example of these constraints, but there are other examples which receive less attention. One arises from the elaborate structure of government in the United States, in which a public manager's problems and programs are rarely coterminous with the agency in which he or she is located. Joseph Bower (1977) provides an illustration of this when he notes that the Health Commissioner of New York City controls only a few of the hospitals and health care organizations in the city but has responsibility for the health policy of the city.

Similarly, government programs which pay for particular goods and services often play little or no direct role in providing them. Public managers are often agents who turn over money to private non-profit agencies which provide social services or to corporations such as defense contractors, who provide goods for government. While presidential administrations have tried various ways of simplifying some of them, these complex relations between agencies, sectors, and levels of government are simply not going to be easily eliminated. They will be more likely to increase with increasing defense expenditures and involvement of the private sector in public services.

These elaborate relations and structures call for highly effective management procedures and control systems. Public management, however, has also been faced with constraints which have hindered development of such systems. For all the talk about excessive public spending, constraints on the amount and form of spending for such things has caused many management systems—accounting systems, financial controls, and management information systems—to be either antiquated or poorly developed in the public sector. Their further development is an absolute necessity. We actually rejected simple-minded 'run government like a business' proposals to defend more responsible versions of such proposals. Some of this development may take the form of careful adaptation of successful business practices.

Another major constraint has been the limitations on rewards for public managers. Pay ceilings at the highest levels affect not only those levels but career choices of talented people at lower levels. As we noted, the complex bureaucratic systems and political controls can be discouraging and frustrating. Ironically, however, we need very special individuals to fill these roles. Not only must they be energetic, talented managers, they must also be altruistic enough to pursue the public interest with limited financial rewards relative to private-sector counterparts. They must have the flexibility and tolerance for ambiguity to deal with difficult value questions in a complex institutional and political setting. Yet in addition to the constraints on incentives, we make it even harder to attract and keep such people by subjecting them to insults and stereotypes.

Given the opprobrium attached to being a 'bureaucrat' why would anyone want to become involved in public management? The reason is that the very challenges we have discussed make the job interesting and essential. The work is imbued with social purpose. The public sector deals with some of the most difficult and important problems faced by the society.

We may be able, then, to continue to attract good people to the public service. There is also reason to hope that we will make progress in confronting the management problems of the public sector. The outcomes of the current emphasis on cutback and fiscal constraint are uncertain at this writing, but it is clear that no one is going to dismantle government. The United States—and other industrialized countries—will continue to need effective large-scale public management. The public service which discharges those functions must be subject to public criticism, so a certain degree of blaming the bureaucracy is inevitable. More of our citizens and leaders, however, need to begin to think like managers themselves. We must respond to problems with clear thinking and an intelligent search for solutions, and deny ourselves the luxury of easy excuses, oversimplifications, scapegoating, myths, and damaging stereotypes. Only if we do so can we successfully address the challenges of governing a complex, advanced society.

REFERENCES

ALLISON, G. T. (1979) Public and private management: are they fundamentally alike in all unimportant respects? In *Setting Public Management Agendas*, Proceedings of the Public Management Research Conference, 19–20 November 1979, Washington DC: The Brookings Institution.

BARNES, P. W. (1980) CETA audits of local funds spark protest, *Wall Street Journal*, 26 August 1980.

BARTON, A. and C. WEISS (eds) (1980) *Making Bureaucracies Work*. Beverly Hills, California: Sage.

BOWER, J. L. (1977) Effective public management, *Harvard Business Review*, March–April, 131–40.

BUCHANAN, B. (1975) Government managers, business executives, and organizational commitment, *Public Administration Review*, 35, 339–47.

CHERNISS, G. (1980) *Professional Burnout in Human Service Organizations*. New York: Praeger.

EVANS, D. J. (1976) *Report to the Stockholders of the State of Washington*. Olympia, Washington.

GARDNER, J. (1979) The special interest state, *Encounter*, 52(1).

GERMOND, J. and J. WITCOVER (1981) GOP playing numbers, *The Tallahassee Democrat*, 19 July 1981.

GILDER, G. (1981) *Wealth and Poverty*. New York: Basic Books.

GINZBERG, E. and VOJTA, G. (1981) The service sector of the US economy, *Scientific American*, 244 (March), 48–55.

HALPERIN, S. (1978) Emerging education policy issues in the federal city. Occasional Paper No. 42, The National Center for Research in Vocational Education, The Ohio State University.

HERBERS, J. (1978) Special report on governing America, *New York Times*, 14 November 1978.

HERBERS, J. (1982) Budget cuts, tax hikes confront many states, *Lexington Herald Leader*, 3 January 1982.

HUNTINGTON, S. P. (1981) *American Politics: The Promise of Disharmony*.

ISR Newsletter (1979) Deepening distrust of political leaders is jarring public faith in institutions, *ISR Newsletter*, Autumn 1979, p. 4. Institute for Social Research, University of Michigan.

KATZ, D., B. A. GUTEK, R. L. KAHN and E. BARTON (1975) *Bureaucratic Encounters: A Pilot Study in the Evaluation of Government Services*. Ann Arbor, Michigan: Survey Research Center, Institute for Social Research, University of Michigan.

KING, A. (1975) Overload: problems of governing in the 1970s, *Political Studies*, 23, 162–74.

LINDBLOM, C. (1976) *Politics and Markets*. New York: Basic Books.

LOWI, T. (1969) *The End of Liberalism*.

LYNN, L. E. (1981) *Managing the Public's Business*. New York: Basic Books.

MICHELSON, S. (1980) The working bureaucrat and non-working bureaucracy. In A. Barton and C. Weiss (eds), *Making Bureaucracies Work*, Beverly Hills, California: Sage.

O'CONNOR, J. (1973) *The Fiscal Crisis of the State*. New York: St. Martin's Press.

OUCHI, W. (1981) *Theory Z, How America Can Meet the Japanese Challenge*. Reading, Mass.: Addison-Wesley.

PASCALE, R. T. and A. G. ALTHOS (1981) *The Art of Japanese Management*. New York: Simon and Schuster.

PECHMAN, J. A. (ed.) (1981) *Setting National Priorities: The 1982 Budget*. Washington DC: The Brookings Institution.

RAINES, H. (1981) Bureaucrats: The scapegoats again for Reagan and staff, *The Louisville Courier Journal*, 23 October 1981.

SCHUCK, P. H. (1980) A Carter mirror of our political innocence (a review of *In the Absence of Power*, by Haynes Johnson), *Wall Street Journal*, 11 April 1980.

SERRIN, W. (1981) Government employment down, *The Louisville Courier Journal*, 17 December 1981.

SIMON, W. (1980) *A Time for Truth*. New York: Berkeley.

SMITH, T. W., D. G. TAYLOR and N. A. MATHIOWETZ (1980) Public opinion and public regard for the Federal government. In A. Barton and C. Weiss (eds), *Making Bureaucracies Work*, Beverly Hills, California: Sage:

WEISS, H. L. (1974) Why business and government exchange executives, *Harvard Business Review*, July/August, 129–40.

WILL, G. (1982) Tax dollars needed to fill potholes, *The Tallahassee Democrat*, 18 April 1982.

WILSON, J. Q. and P. RACHEL (1977) Can government regulate itself? *The Public Interest*, 46 (Winter, 1977), 3–14.

QUESTIONS FOR DISCUSSION

1. Do bureaucrats have a vested interest in making social problems worse? Why?

2. Would the environment be in better shape if environmental protection agencies did not exist? Why?

3. Is graft more likely to occur in the public or private sector? Why?

4. What effect does intense criticism of the bureaucracy have on the bureaucracy?

5. Are some government agencies run more efficiently than others? Why?

SUGGESTED READINGS

ELLING, RICHARD C., "Bureaucratic Accountability: Problems and Paradoxes; Panaceas and (Occasionally) Palliatives," *Public Administration Review*, 43 (Jan./Feb. 1983), 82–89.

GAPPERT, GARY, "The Enduring Nightmare: The 1984 Bureaucracy," *The Futurist*, 17 (Dec. 1983), 49–51.

GOODSELL, CHARLES T., *The Case for Bureaucracy: A Public Administration Polemic*, 2nd ed. Chatham, NJ: Chatham House, 1985.

GRACE, J. PETER, *Burning Money: The Waste of Your Tax Dollars*. New York: Macmillan, 1984.

KAUFMAN, HERBERT, "Fear of Bureaucracy: A Raging Pandemic," *Public Administration Review*, 41 (Jan./Feb. 1981), 1–9.

KELMAN, STEVEN, "The Grace Commission: How Much Waste in Government?," *Public Interest*, No. 76 (Winter 1985), 62–82.

PETERS, B. GUY, "The Problem of Bureaucratic Government," *Journal of Politics*, 43 (Feb. 1981), 56–82.

ROSEN, BERNARD, *Holding Government Bureaucracies Accountable*. New York: Praeger, 1982.

VON MISES, LUDWIG, "A Note on Bureaucracy," *Regulation* (Sept./Oct. 1985), pp. 44–45.

WEISS, CAROL H., AND ALLEN H. BARTON, eds. *Making Bureaucracies Work*. Beverly Hills, CA: Sage, 1980.

WRISTON, MICHAEL J., "In Defense of Bureaucracy," *Public Administration Review*, 40 (Mar./Apr. 1980), 179–83.

2 YES IS MANAGEMENT IN THE PRIVATE SECTOR ESSENTIALLY SIMILAR TO MANAGEMENT IN THE PUBLIC SECTOR?

Comparing Public and Private Management: An Exploratory Essay
Michael A. Murray

Historically in America two different institutional approaches to management science have developed: one in the private sector and one in the public sector. This dual development, however, has not gone unchallenged. For perhaps two generations scholars and practitioners have realized that management can be viewed as a generic process, with universal implications and with application in any institutional setting—whether a private firm or a public agency. More recently, on the assumption that public and private management have much to share, a new body of literature has developed around the idea of general management. Especially significant, entire new management schools are being founded on the generic model. The historic "separate but equal" doctrine is being challenged by a nascent integrationist movement.

Like the movement in the race area, however, the integrationist policy is not progressing with "due speed." There are many reasons for this. One is the traditional mistrust or misunderstanding between the public and private practitioner. Another is the perceived threat which the merger poses to free-standing schools of business and to schools of public administration. A more significant reason perhaps, is the lack of development of the concept that public and private management have points in common. If one examines the literature, or pages through the brochures of the new schools of management, there is little specific comparative analysis that is discussion of points where public and private management converge or diverge.

The important question then is what are the areas of comparison; and what specifically are the similarities and differences? In short, are public and private management comparable?

The central purpose of this article is to explore this relationship. A related purpose is to fill the gap

From Michael A. Murray, "Comparing Public and Private Management: An Exploratory Essay," reprinted with permission from *Public Administration Review*, 35, pp. 364–71. ©1975 by the American Society for Public Administration, 1120G Street, N.W., Suite 500, Washington, D.C. All rights reserved.

in the literature and hopefully to provide the student or practitioner with a ready checklist of comparisons. The method used is uncomplicated: the article lists the traditional management activity and then presents the arguments which explain or illustrate similarities and differences.

To categorize the issues the article is divided into two parts. Part I discusses substantive areas of comparison. Part II focuses on procedural activities in management.

I. SUBSTANTIVE ISSUES: INHERENT CONFLICT OR NATURAL CONGRUENCE?

The key substantive issue is whether there is an inherent conflict between the rational, private management model with its criteria of economic efficiency, and the political public management model with its criteria of consensus and compromise. Obviously these are idealized types and this perhaps is the first and most important point to be made.

Fact vs. Value: The Context of Decision Making

Although conventional taxonomy divides society into two sectors, public and private, the actual similarities between a business firm and a government organization are increasingly apparent. In any complex organization, "defining purposes and objectives, planning, organizing, selecting managers, managing and motivating people, controlling and measuring results, and using a variety of analytical, problem solving and managerial techniques . . . are essential."[1] The point is that these elements are relevant in any complex organization and are common aspects of a universal or generic management process, whether in the private or the public sector.

But are they the same? That is, are similar activities comparable even though the institutional setting differs? In his famous discussion of fact and value, Herbert Simon argued no. Simon argued that the means of administration (the facts) are quite different from the ends (the values). To ignore this

central difference, he said, is to ignore the importance of the end or value as the major independent variable. The inference is that the values of the public sector, aimed at consensus, are different than the values of the private sector, aimed at profits. Hence, it is a misrepresentation to say that the value, or the context of the decision, is not important. What is important in the managerial relationship is not the tool, the means, but the context of the decision, the ends. If the context is different, then the values are different, and thus the application and function of the tool is different. In brief, Simon argued that the *process* of management has a value component itself and that fact cannot be separated from value.[2]

Many public administrators cite this argument as evidence of the chasm separating public administration and business administration. But as Norton Long has pointed out, Simon's distinction between fact and value has one fatal flaw. "It does not accord with the facts of administrative life."[3] Though the quest for scientific distinctions has a psychological appeal, it runs the risk of becoming ivory tower escapism.[4] The same can be said of Simon's implication that business and government administration are different. Built on the sandy base of logical positivism, Simon's argument derives from formal distinctions and ignores the *informal* mix between public and private activities. There is another problem with Simon's argument. Even if we accept his distinction between fact and value, the question remains: are the ends of government and business different?

Profits vs. Politics

To ask whether the values of the private sector differ from the objectives of the public sector is to ask a large question and a normative question; a question surrounded by a great deal of controversy. The issues will not be resolved in this paper, but the question remains: are the differences real or superficial?

To begin, the notion that profits are the sole or main reason for the existence of private business is

---

[1]Fredric H. Genck, "Public Management in America," *AACSB Bulletin*, Vol. 9, No. 3 (April 1973), p. 6.

[2]Herbert A. Simon, *Administrative Behavior* (New York: Macmillan, 1949).

[3]Norton Long, "Public Policy and Administration: The Goals of Rationality and Responsibility," *Public Administration Review*, Vol. 14, No. 1 (Winter 1954), p. 22.

[4]*Ibid.*

itself misleading. First of all, profits are an essential requirement for existence; but the focus on profits as the single objective distorts or minimizes other advantageous business activities such as products, services, employment, and all of the "hidden hand" effects of community and social contribution. A second point is that while profits are a handy measure, benefits and costs do not always lend themselves to a monetary judgment of effectiveness.[5]

On the other hand, to say that profits are never the objective of public sector activities is equally misleading. Government projects are notoriously subject to cost-benefit analysis, and efficiency in government is a by-word of bureaucrats. Once stereotypes are discarded, similarities emerge.

To carry the argument further, however, a distinction made is that the criteria of political decisions are based on objectives of compromise, consensus, and democratic participation, and that these are quite different from the private sector objectives of efficiency, rationality, and profit or product maximization. But this also is an idealized type. As Theodore Levitt argues, "The culture of private bureaucracies is . . . basically the same as that of public bureaucracies. . . ."[6] That is, the desire for personal power and security is the same; responsiveness to outside pressures is the same. In short, once general priorities are established, private and public bureaucracies operate about the same.

Are the Objectives Measurable?

Beyond the abstract question of whether rational man differs from political man, the issue is whether objectives in the public and private areas are capable of comparison. The problem arises because objectives in the private sector often can be reduced to clear, concise, and quantifiable statements. Many public organizations must deal in social intangibles such as the right to privacy, increased political participation, or improving quality of life. Those are difficult to articulate in any clear specific way.

One example of this is the notion of divisible and indivisible services. In the private area goods and services can be purchased on an individual basis. Hence they can be defined and delivered in specific tangible ways. In the public sector many services such as clean air, decent housing, and adequate education are indivisible in the sense that these are communal services which increasingly have to be "purchased" jointly. Hence the problem of individual values has to be stated in the general terms of social choice. Such a conceptualization can only be stated in generalizations.[7]

Which One Is Better: The Normative Issue

Another normative argument is that the modern technologies of business administration are somehow superior to the less systematic and structured tools of the public sector. Indeed the popular disdain toward the public sector is reflected in choice of terms. For example, we often use the term management when referring to private business, but substitute the term administration when talking of public organizations. In part this reflects the acceptance of the private enterprise ethic in our social labels. In part it reflects the less attractive position of the public service in a country where for the past century industrialization was the most exciting thing happening. Recently some of this has changed.

Perhaps because of the Depression, but certainly dating from that point, the myth of the well-managed firm has been challenged. The legend of private efficiency lives in company brochures but is seldom realized in the lives of millions of Americans who fight the daily battle with insurance agencies or auto mechanics or TV repairmen. As early as 1945 the dean of public administration, Paul Appleby, argued that the alleged superiority of business represented a gross over-generalization which did not withstand close analysis.[8] Today we can ask the same kinds of comparative questions as 30 years ago. Is business less corrupt than government? Are public administrators less moral than business executives? Is fiscal management better in the aerospace industry than it is in Health, Education, and

[5]Fredric Genck, op. cit., p. 7.

[6]Theodore Levitt, The Third Sector (New York: Amcom, 1973), pp. 28–29.

[7]See The Future of the American Government, Daniel Pearlman (ed.) (Boston: Houghton-Mifflin, 1968), especially Foreword by Daniel Bell.

[8]Paul H. Appleby, Big Democracy (New York: Knopf, 1945), pp. 50–51.

Welfare? The point is that what we find overall are more similarities than differences; a blending and mix between public and private. Neither sector has a corner on the morals market.

Government Attitudes vs. Business Attitudes

In the end many of these normative issues are related to questions of attitude. This is a central point in the comparative literature: "that the dissimilarity between government and all other forms of social action is greater than any similarity among those other forms themselves," and that the major difference is one of attitude.[9]

Today we are beginning to question even this attitudinal difference. For example, is it true that former businessmen cannot adjust to the chaotic world of government? The fact is that some can and some cannot, but generalizations do not hold. Likewise, it is inaccurate to say that all public officials are non-materialistic do-gooders who disdain the profit motive. These are obviously stereotypes which do not fit the facts. In short, in a democracy there is a great deal of consensus on values and norms; and attitudes between businessmen and career bureaucrats are not necessarily contradictory. More and more old stereotypes are being challenged. Nonetheless, these attitudinal, normative issues are difficult to resolve. Hence, we turn to more specific criteria for comparison.

II. PROCEDURAL ISSUES: IS MANAGEMENT A UNIVERSAL PROCESS?

In a procedural context, management might be defined as any activity or behavior concerned mainly with the means for carrying out prescribed ends. Although the ends of the business sector and government agencies might be different, often the means of achieving these ends are quite similar. These common procedural elements or aspects permit academics and practitioners to view management as a universal process.

But is it? We know from Part I that there are

important distinctions between public and private values and objectives. Do these substantive differences affect procedural matters as well? Or are we so conditioned to examining the boundaries of things that we miss the thing itself?

The Accountability Factor: The Goldfish Bowl vs. The Closed Board Room

Almost 50 years ago John Dewey said that the line between public and private "is to be drawn on the basis of the extent and scope of the consequences of acts which are so important as to need control. . . ."[10] Consequences which affect only those directly involved in the transaction are private. Consequences which affect others beyond those immediately concerned are public, and need to be regulated.

In this concept of consequence and regulation we find the germ of the procedural difference between public and private management. What Dewey is saying, and what others have said before and after, is that the key distinction between the public and private sectors is the accountability factor, the degree to which the institution is responsible to others for its actions.

The argument is that the business sector operates in relative, although not complete, autonomy and perhaps secrecy; free of the checks and balances of the public arena. The public sector, on the other hand, is subject to the pressure of the press and to public scrutiny, it operates in a "goldfish bowl."

For example, government's susceptibility to public criticism is sometimes carried to extremes, and at the very least complicates public management and brings into play organizational forms and methods of accountability which explain many of the differences between public and private administration. An example of this is the public corporation. In creating such corporations, government intended to establish businesslike agencies that would permit government institutions to provide services in a modern businesslike manner. But because of the political environment in which public agencies

---

[9]*Ibid.*, p. 1.

[10]John Dewey, *The Public and Its Problems* (New York, 1927), p. 15.

function, guidelines and measures were introduced, aimed mainly at establishing fiscal accountability, which undercut the principal advantages of the corporation device.

This is the point repeated in the literature, that government administration differs from all other administrative work because it is subject to public scrutiny and outcry. Every change in government has to be thought about in terms of the possible public agitation resulting from it.[11]

But in the past quarter century conditions have changed. As Daniel Bell argues, in the post-industrial society every organization is politicized, including the private firm. A specific change is increase in public regulation of the so-called "private firm." The regulation of air and water pollution is only one example; automobile safety and airline schedules are others. In an age of communal pressure and political mobilization even private firms are not dispensed from public scrutiny. The line between public and private has blurred, and today the businessman faces as much public as the public official. Consider the fact that bureaucrats often operate in relative privacy while businessmen squirm under the glare of the public eye.

Evaluation Techniques: Social Good and Fiscal Control

A second comparison concerns the application of evaluation techniques. Simplified, the argument is as follows. In the private sector it is quite easy to go to the bottom line and determine whether the firm or organization is measuring up to its organizational goal. This can be translated very easily in terms of profits and losses.

In the public sector, even though modern, businesslike fiscal control techniques are utilized, they are less easily transferable to public "social good" questions. A good example of this might be the popular pressure to apply cost-benefit analysis to War on Poverty programs. As proponents of the community action program argued, some of the objectives of the War on Poverty were to reverse apathy and powerlessness, the chief characteristics of

the poor. This meant designing political mobilization activities to counter-condition long-range and inbred psychological attitudes of shiftlessness and withdrawal; to generate feelings of pride and involvement. Such psychological or intrapsychic reflections of economic disparity are often difficult, if not impossible, to measure in terms of traditional or even modern businesslike techniques. Recall the debate of a few years ago when OEO officials complained that *economic* cost-accounting tools were irrelevant to measuring the long-range *political* goals of the poverty program.

This "bottom line" distinction has other implications. It also means, for example, that government and public agencies do not have that measure of achievement which the business sector enjoys. Without clear standards of government performance often public administration results in sloppy or irrational activities. Things slide along often to the detriment of accountability. The point is that it is very difficult in the public sector to clarify objectives and then to apply the sophisticated, precise tools of profit and loss to measure performance.

A final point, however, it that it is difficult to measure quality in both sectors and that the attempt to apply fiscal control simply represents a first step in developing science in either sector.

Criteria of Decision Making: Rational Man vs. Political Man

Although decision making is the basic operation of management, it has been argued that this operation varies in the public and private sectors. For example, even though the *formal steps* in decision making are technically the same (definition of problem, outlining options, crystallizing preferred response, allocating resources, etc.), the *criteria* of decision making is different. That is, the logic, or mode of thinking, the movement from point to point, is different. In a word, it is often argued that the technology of decision making varies from private to public areas.

An understanding of the term technology is important here. As used in this paper, the term technology means . . . "not simply a 'machine', but a systematic, disciplined approach to objectives, using a calculus of precision and measurement and a concept of system that are quite at variance with

[11]Paul H. Appleby, *Big Democracy, op. cit.*

traditional and . . . intuitive modes.''[12] The difference may be one of degree but the reality is that the systems approach has triumphed in the private sector while it is viewed with some distrust in the public sector.

There are several reasons for this. One is the fact that a technological conception of a problem limits the focus to those factors that can be expressed quantitatively and which fit certain models.[13] This encroachment of economics into intrinsically political processes is inherently contradictory. The emphasis, automatically, is on neatness and order versus social disorder; technical precision versus confusion and conflict; gestalt theories instead of ad hoc piecemeal fragmentation; efficient management versus "bumbling bureaucracy.''[14] In short, the distinction is between a process of management based on criteria of economy, efficiency, and rational results, versus a process of decision making based on ideas of consensus, the broadest social good, and "muddling through."

Another reason why "technology" has been resisted in the public sector is the assumption that governmental problems are basically social in nature. Although many of society's pressing problems have been generated or aggravated by technological change and development (e.g., transportation problems, housing design), the technical solution is not automatically transferable. Referring to a range of social ills, Ida Hoos analogized that "calling upon an engineer to cure them is much like asking an economist to treat a heart ailment because the patient became ill over money matters.''[15]

The counterpart is that whether or not technology, and particularly systems analysis, is appropriate to public decisions, it is in fact being applied. Some would say that Bertram Gross' fears about a new breed of technipols have been realized. In this sense, government has accepted business as its model and economics as its decision-making means. Hence,

the theoretical differences in modes of public and private criteria may well be moot as this point.

Personnel Systems

In reflecting on comparisons between business and government, Paul H. Appleby argued:

> It is exceedingly difficult clearly to identify the factors which make government different from other activity in society. Yet this difference is a fact and I believe it to be so big a difference that the dissimilarity between government and all other forms of social action is greater than any dissimilarity among those other forms themselves. Without a willingness to recognize this fact, no one can even begin to discuss public affairs to any good profit or serious purpose.[16]

The single most determinative factor that Appleby identified was personnel. One aspect of this difference has to do with recruiting patterns; a second element has to do with socializing processes.

In the private sector candidates theoretically are recruited through formal credentialing systems. In the public sector, recruitment, especially for top-level positions, is often informal, ad hoc, and on a personal (who do you know) basis. At least this is the accepted notion. Realistically, it is difficult to say whether there is more or less nepotism in business than in government. Are appointments in government more or less a function of pull and privilege than in the business world? Obviously, it would be hard to prove the argument one way or the other.

With regard to differences in socialization, a number of points can be made. On the one hand, some observers view background as the critical variable. For example, some businessmen do poorly in government. They come into government service with strong personalities and are unable to adjust to situations which they cannot control. There is a contradiction between the businessman's attitude and government needs. The businessman sees his role as executive, as decision maker. Yet the reasons for bringing him into government may have been simply to coopt his support, to win legitimacy for

---

[12]Daniel Bell, "Trajectory of an Idea," in *Toward the Year 2000*, Daniel Bell (ed.) (Boston: Houghton-Mifflin, 1968), p. 5.

[13]Ida R. Hoos, *Systems Analysis in Public Policy: A Critique* (Berkeley: University of California Press, 1972), p. 26.

[14]*Ibid.*, p. 89.

[15]*Ibid.*, p. 24.

[16]Appleby, *op. cit.*, p. 1.

policies made, or to seek his prestige in order to maintain national unity. These are political as opposed to business reasons.

On the other hand, businessmen have traditionally succeeded in government executive positions indicating that their skills are transferable. This is likely to continue especially given the current disaffection with the politician image. In fact, businessmen may, because of their supposed neutrality, be in even greater demand. The operational question is the reverse of this: whether ex-government people can shift into the private sector. On this score, there is some evidence that former administration officials are prime candidates for top corporate positions and that public experience is not an undesirable reference.

Planning

Planning is an activity common to both the public and private sectors. Although the term refers generally to the process of uniting ideas with action, it needs to be analyzed in its specific institutional setting.

There are two ways to view planning: as a process of decision making or as a means of control. In terms of process, planning means lateral consultation, sharing of information, discussion of short- and long-range objectives. It implies a participatory process in order to come up with mutually satisfactory goals.

Planning as a means of control refers to a system of gathering information and marshalling available resources in a sequential priority framework in order to maximize agreed-upon objectives.

The advantages and disadvantages of each approach have been discussed elsewhere.[17] The question for this article is whether one mode is used more in business or in public. As in many of the areas discussed, distinctions blur when applied to actual situations. Consider the fact that the vital circumstances surrounding any planning effort are intangible, ad hoc, and uncertain. In both the public sector and the private sector, this is evidenced by the first impulse of planners, to "get more, or better,

data." Planning is an eclectic science with no distinct theoretical base. As such it is hardly a precise science. It is true that planners seem more common in government circles than in private firms. But this may be simply a matter of labels, i.e., calling the corporate finance officer financial analyst instead of resident planner, or calling the city planner by that title instead of research associate. In either area planning is at best a secondary function, and the point is that in actual situations the process of planning appears to be the same.

The Efficiency Question

Too much has been written on the subject of government waste and business efficiency for this article to dispel any widespread notions. But a few comments are in order.

If one accepts the notion that the business of government is politics (the allocation of authority for a society) and that the goal is not efficiency by resolution of conflict, then it is impossible to say that government is less efficient than business.

There are three important points to be made. First, in terms of efficiency it is difficult to compare the two areas. It is the old apples and oranges problem. Is the Supreme Court less efficient in protecting the first amendment than General Motors is in producing cars? Is Boeing Aircraft more efficient in what it does than TVA is in producing electricity? To go even further, it is difficult to make comparisons within a particular area, public or private. For example, in the so-called private sector, is *The New York Times* more or less efficient in producing news than the Chicago Bears organization is in producing entertainment? The point is obvious: if this quantity efficiency cannot easily be measured within one supposedly similar area, then how are comparisons to be made between different areas?

There is a second point. In government what appears to be inefficiency is sometimes essential to the public purpose of the agency. For example, millions of dollars spent every year on public scrutiny of government activities operates in the public interest, and the net effect is to make the agency more efficient in terms of its central purpose which is political responsiveness.

The third point is that in terms of efficiency the private sector is not without criticism; business has its share of horror stories. The facts emerging from

---

[17]Aaron Wildavesky, *The Politics of the Budgetary Process* (Boston: Little Brown, 1964), especially ch. 5.

the aerospace industry belie the notion of rational, efficient operations in private industry. Efficiency and waste it seems are more a matter of case by case analysis than across the board generalizations.

Theoretically similar principles of hierarchic control, comprehensive coordination, the rule of merit, and line of authority apply in both the public and private sectors. A word on each of these is in order.

With regard to the principle of hierarchic control, the theory of the scalar process, or the application of superior-subordinate relationship is honored in every formal organizational chart but seldom in fact. This applies to the private sector myth of "chairman of the board" and to the ceremonial role of the "agency director" in public affairs. In either case the head is often a ceremonial figure with political as opposed to operational duties.

Coordination, a second principle, means the rational allocation of resources to meet needs and depends on two factors: (1) definition of need, and (2) availability of resources. Coordination is, however, a similar process in any operation since it relates to maximization of agency goals.

The rule of merit is protected by informal systems, as well as by formal codes and contracts in both public and private sectors, but it is violated with equal impunity in either area. The temporary assignment in the civil service has as its counterpart the position of management consultant in private industry.

Another principle is that authority should be commensurate with responsibility. This is the cardinal rule of management and a central objective of public and private practitioners. The fact that it remains a central objective underscores its absence in either area.

CONCLUSION

1. Substantive Issues: More Blurring Than Bifurcation

The large issue, the central question, is whether public and private management are inherently different. Based on this exploratory survey of the issues, the answer is a cautious no, not at this time. In Daniel Bell's post-industrial society, characterized by a diffusion of goods, there may be a growth

of public decision making which so overwhelms the free market as to radically alter the society. As yet this has not happened. The situation that seems to be evolving is a mixture of public-private, government-market decision making with a blurring of the lines rather than a distinct bifurcation of responsibilities. This is reflected in the analysis of the substantive areas like objective setting and evaluation techniques. Few lasting differences were found. For example, the central issue of different value systems seems to be more a difference of degree and emphasis than of substance. Politics conditions judgment in both areas; private decisions transcend immediate application in either sector. Boundaries between public and private activity seem to be blurring. At any rate, in areas such as attitudes and values it will require a good deal more behavioral research to establish the fact of difference as opposed to the sentiment of difference.

2. Procedural Issues: Distinctions Not Differences

As Justice Holmes once remarked to a lawyer making a fine legal point: that's a distinction, but not a difference. The same dictum applies to the survey of procedural areas. For example, in the area of ethics it is true that the public sector conduct is characterized by clear, formal, even legal guidelines (the Constitution, conflict of interest laws, etc.). It is also true that these laws are honored as much in the breach as in the fact. In the private sector, although pressures and constraints may be informal, studies have shown that private executives are extremely sensitive to the appearance of ethical behavior. Some argue that this has led to a conformist type mentality in the private sector. At any rate, ethical questions seem to be reemerging as legitimate issues in either sector and where differences exist they are formal and superficial, i.e., legalistic in nature. In actual practice this difference dissipates.

3. Apples and Oranges

A third conclusion has to do with the "apples and oranges" syndrome of comparing unlike objects. On the question of efficiency, for example, it is impossible to match political efficiency with economic efficiency. One must judge one agency's political efficiency with another agency's political efficiency, and so on. It is unfair and illogical to use the efficiency criteria alone and apply it to the public and private sector.

4. Myths and Sentiments

A fourth conclusion is that some of our most cherished and popular myths do not hold up under cold analysis. For example, is private management superior to public administration in terms of waste management? Not by aerospace industry standards. Is the public sector run more openly and democratically? Not if public sentiment and recent criminal cases against officials is any measure. The view of "big bureaucracy" as a mismanaged monolith is as unrealistic as the view of business as a social rip off. The law of variations tells us that the situation differs as management practice varies—from case to case.

5. The Primacy of Method

The essential issue it seems is not what procedural or substantive distinctions or differences exist, but what *management tools* are applied to problem solving, whether in the public or the private sector. The choice of tools and models is the critical intervening variable between the definition of the problem and the crystallization of a policy. With regard to public-private activities it is clear that what may be acceptable in the private sector in the technical sense may be completely unsatisfactory in the public area where social questions cannot be subordinated to technical approaches.

The issue, of course, is only part of a larger question facing a society enamored of systems approaches, and empirical models and quick technological solutions. As suggested above, it may be too late to raise the issue; the public sector already relies on modern technical solutions to a great degree. Ida Hoos has noted:

The main myths in the business world that most needed exploration and explosion have become doxology in government circles, with

critical inquiry tantamount to heresy. Indeed, he who has the temerity to raise questions runs the risk of being considered not only anachronistically and iconoclastically unscientific but probably a bit subversive and unAmerican as well.[18]

At the risk of being unpatriotic, it is this reckless application of cheap, visible, quantitative solutions to social problems which poses the greatest threat to problem solving and ultimately to harmonious interface between the public and private sectors. As Robert Merton has said:

The technician sees the nation quite differently from the political man: to the technician, the nation is nothing more than another sphere in which to apply the instruments he has developed. To him, the state is not the expression of the will of the people nor a divine creation nor a creature of class conflict. It is an enterprise providing services that must be made to function *efficiently*.[19]

Or as others have said: data does not automatically solve problems; human beings, with the help of data, are capable of problem solving.

Rather than conceptualizing management in the public sector as an extension of private sector practices and values, this article points toward an increasing convergence in management processes in the public and private sectors. Traditional barriers and distinctive patterns in decision making and goal definition are breaking down. While prevailing ideal-type models stress the uniqueness of public organizations as opposed to private organizations, this article argues that in the post-industrial society, which is emerging in the U.S., the old distinctions are no longer operational. Both in the handling of substantive issues and procedural matters, actual management practices point to a blurring of public and private sectors rather than to a bifurcation. Public and private management procedures, operations, and goals cannot be viewed as separate processes.

---

[18]Hoos, *op. cit.*, p. 196.

[19]Frank Trippet, "The Shape of Things as They Really Are," *Intellectual Digest* (December 1972), p. 28.

2   NO
IS MANAGEMENT IN THE PRIVATE SECTOR ESSENTIALLY SIMILAR TO MANAGEMENT IN THE PUBLIC SECTOR?

Public Management and Private Management
Dwight Ink

. . . There is a persistent myth that if federal managers could be replaced with those who would run agencies like a business all would be well. This view fails to recognize that there are some very important differences between operating a business and operating an agency.

As an agency head, for example, I had many millions of stockholders; every voter and every taxpayer in the country, each one of whom had a right to publicly question and criticize whatever I and my managers did or said from day to day.

My boss I rarely saw. The organization of the federal government has become so fragmented it is physically impossible for the President to have a meaningful dialogue with each agency head.

My board of directors had over 500 members. They were Senators and Congressmen, each strong figures with diverse philosophy and generally sharply conflicting views as to what I should do, and where my priorities should be.

Public accountability is also very different from corporate accountability. Unlike a private business, every action a government official takes, and every action one does not take, may appear within days, hours, or minutes on television, perhaps nationwide. And as any member of Congress knows full well, the news story generally has to be told in a negative way in order to create readership, becoming a story replete with innuendo and motivations which never occurred to the official involved.

One of 25 to 50 documents a public manager may sign during a typical day and to which one can squeeze only an average of five minutes of attention may greatly upset some citizen in Iowa or Texas—the constituent of some diligent member of Congress and a friend of the local editor—after which

the official and his or her staff may spend hundreds of hours dealing with that 5 minute action. The auditors, investigators and reporters may then spend days reviewing in detail the circumstances of the 5 minute action. If the resulting attention level is reasonably high, the likely end result will be the birth of a brand new regulation, further limiting the ability of a public manager to act, and adding to the hidden cost of government.

There are personal and professional risks in government of a type which one rarely encounters in business. Businesses expect their managers to take risks and to make some mistakes in the process. If the correct decisions outweigh the incorrect by a substantial margin, the private manager is advanced. If not, the problems are discussed by a small group of the firm's executives, and if the mistakes are too numerous or serious, the manager is eased out or reassigned with little or no press attention. When mistakes occur in the public sector, they tend to become public events, and one is likely to be subjected to public criticism over an extended period and a series of well-advertised investigations. The ensuing news stories can be very traumatic for one's wife and children, as well as devastating to one's career even if no wrongdoing is involved. At times the problem may really be no more than a mistaken press report or a policy disagreement, yet the family strain may be intense and prolonged. Risk taking and innovation do not thrive under these circumstances.

A serious shortcoming in the federal government is the frequent failure of political leadership to use much common sense skill in dealing with the career service.

Among other things, we frequently impose on careerists and on the taxpayers, political appointees who have had no background to prepare them for the business of running multibillion dollar programs and managing tens of thousands of employees. We would never dream of looking to a nonengineer to design an airplane or a nonpilot to fly an airliner.

Statement of Dwight Ink, U. S. Cong., Senate, *Management Theories in the Private and Public Sectors*, Hearings before the Subcommittee on Civil Service, Post Office, and General Services of the Committee on Governmental Affairs, 98th Cong., 2nd Sess., 1984, pp. 351–55.

How many private companies have chosen chief operating officers who have had no business experience? Experience is taken for granted as essential for responsible assignments in other important fields; why should we impose on the American people managerial amateurs in the appointing of many men and women in key government posts? Presidential loyalty is essential for political appointees, but it is a grave mistake to believe that loyalty alone is sufficient. Too often, the appointee stays about long enough to begin to learn the job and how to work with the careerists when he or she finds it impossible to make the financial sacrifice required to stay in office. The appointee leaves, eventually another managerial neophyte is appointed, and the cycle is repeated.

A number of these appointees have publicly campaigned vigorously against the bureaucrats, the very people on whom they and the President will have to depend to carry out their programs. Again, this is in contrast to most modern business executives who strive hard to motivate company employees. Here is one of those instances in which we do have much to learn from industry.

Another problem. We established a merit pay system for federal employees—a move I regard as sound—and then failed to provide the funds to make it work. By definition, without meaningful dollar incentives, merit pay is not really merit pay.

The Civil Service Reform contemplated a greatly increased emphasis on the positive aspects of personnel management by the new OPM [Office of Personnel Management] and the various departments, as well as a determined attack on existing disincentives to federal employee morale and productivity. Employee development opportunities, for example, were to be given a strong boost. Training is given a very important role in most corporations in contrast to the extremely limited and rather haphazard training efforts found in most nondefense agencies of government. The Civil Service Reform sought a reversal of this sad state of affairs. Great emphasis also was to be placed on personnel research and pilot projects such as one finds in the more progressive corporations.

The fact is that very little of this has occurred, and in some respect we have lost ground. We have moved forward with the legal skeleton of Civil Service Reform, but we have failed to give it flesh and blood, except in a few agencies with progressive political and career leadership. We have not really breathed life into the opportunity this reform gave us for enlightened personnel management. In my view we have not kept faith with our public service men and women, and they deserve better.

These are some of the reasons I believe government does not work as well as we believe it should. Reasons why it is ridiculous to fantasize about straightening out the bureaucracy by simply replacing the "foot dragging career bureaucrat" with innovative risk taking business executives who can run an agency the way they run a business. . . .

QUESTIONS FOR DISCUSSION

1. Are there some government agencies that are better suited than other government agencies to be run by business people? Explain.
2. What should be the criteria for determining efficiency in a government agency?
3. Should efficiency be the sole criterion for evaluating the performance of a government agency? Why?
4. Which is run more efficiently: government or industry? Why?
5. What skills do business managers bring to government?
6. Are business managers less accountable to the public than government managers? Explain.
7. The late Wallace Sayre once remarked that public and private management are fundamentally alike in all unimportant matters. Do you agree or disagree with that assessment? Why?
8. On the basis of what you know about American business leaders throughout American history, can it be correctly said that they have come more to resemble public managers today than was the case 50 or 100 years ago? Explain.

SUGGESTED READINGS

ALLISON, GRAHAM T., JR., "Public and Private Management: Are They Fundamentally Alike in All Unimportant Matters?," in *Current Issues in Public Administration* (2nd ed.), ed. Frederick S. Lane. New York: St Martin's Press, 1982, pp. 13–33.

GOLD, KENNETH A., "Managing for Success: A Comparison of the Private and Public Sectors," *Public Administration Review*, 42 (Nov./Dec. 1982), 568–75.

GRACE, J. PETER, "A Businessman's View of Washington," *The Bureaucrat*, 13 (Summer 1984), 14–17.

HANSEN, MICHAEL G., "Management Improvement Initiatives in the Reagan Administration: Round Two," *Public Administration Review* (Mar./Apr. 1985), 441–46.

HARTLE, TERRY W., "Sisyphus Revisited: Running the Government Like a Business," *Public Administration Review*, 45 (Mar./Apr. 1985), 341–51.

LEVINE, CHARLES H., ed., *The Unfinished Agenda of Civil Service Reform: The President's Private Sector Survey on Cost Control.* Washington, DC: Brookings Institution, May 1985.

LOVERD, RICHARD A., "Taming Techniques for Public Purposes: Some Business Views and an Overview," *Public Administration Review*, 42 (Sept./Oct. 1982), 484–87.

RAINEY, HAL G., ROBERT W. BACKOFF, AND CHARLES H. LEVINE, "Comparing Public and Private Organizations," *Public Administration Review*, 36 (Mar./Apr. 1976), 233–44.

REGAN, EDWARD V., "Why Can't Government Be Run Like a Business?," *Vital Speeches of the Day*, 45 (Sept. 15, 1982), 714–17.

SAVAS, E. S., *Privatizing the Public Sector.* Chatham, NJ: Chatham House, 1982.

U. S. CONGRESS, SENATE, *Management Theories in the Private and Public Sectors*, Hearings before the Subcommittee on Civil Service, Post Office, and General Services of the Committee on Governmental Affairs, 98th Cong., 2nd Sess., 1984.

CHAPTER 2
The Political Setting of Public Administration

Government administrative organizations operate within a political environment. The goals they pursue and the power they possess are dependent largely upon how they relate to external actors in the American political process both in and outside of government. The Constitution establishes the framework in which government agencies function in American government. The behavior of government administrative organizations, however, is also influenced by political developments, customs, laws, interest groups, the media, and political parties. This chapter focuses on how administration and policies may be affected by some of the principal actors in the American political arena.

The Constitution established a system which divides power among various institutions at the national level—president, Congress, and the Supreme Court—and between the federal government and the states. At the national level, the separation of powers in which each of the principal actors is granted some exclusive powers and shares others with one or both of the other branches is a dominant factor influencing administration. So, too, is the division of powers between the national government and the states.

Although the Constitution established the framework for political activity, political developments and customs also contributed to

shaping that behavior to a significant degree. The Constitution says nothing about political parties because political parties did not exist in eighteenth-century America; however, political parties have played an important role in influencing government. The Constitution, moreover, says nothing about judicial review —the power of the Supreme Court to declare any act of Congress or the executive to be unconstitutional—and yet the Court clearly has acquired that power. To be sure, there are some scholars who contend that the founding fathers intended for the Supreme Court to have the power of judicial review both at the national and state levels, but it was a power scarcely used by the Court prior to the American Civil War—although, when used, it clearly established important constitutional precedents. Many of the kinds of cooperative arrangements between the national government and the state governments brought on by the proliferation of government programs are also not mentioned in the Constitution, and yet these have come to characterize much of federalism today.

In addition to the Constitution, laws have shaped administrative behavior in many ways. Congress has established departments and reorganized agencies. It has, through its power of appropriations, strengthened some government units and weakened others. In some cases, it has written legislation to force government agencies to do some things or not to do others. Through the constitutional power to confirm presidential appointments, the Senate has been able to play a role in not only selecting executive personnel but in influencing policy, as well.

In a democratic system, the public influences government decisions. Interest groups seek to achieve their goals through lobbying in both the executive and legislative branches. The media help set the national agenda by putting the spotlight on the actions of government. Political parties play a role in staffing government executive agencies at political appointee levels.

The debates that follow present some issues involving the political context in which administrative agencies function. Specifically, they examine the line-item veto for the president, the legislative veto, the relationship between independent agencies and Congress, the role of the Supreme Court in affecting public administration, and decentralization.

LINE-ITEM VETO

As indicated above, the president and Congress each has powers derived from the Constitution, laws, political practices, and custom to influence policy and administration. Of central concern to both policy and administration is money. The Constitution gives Congress the power to raise revenues and appropriate funds. Spending bills, like other bills, are subject to a veto by the president, which would prevent a bill from becoming a law. The Constitution provides that a veto may be overridden by a two-thirds vote in both the House of Representatives and the Senate.

The written Constitution, however, does not tell the entire story about power relationships in the budgetary process. In the first century of American history, Congress was the dominant institution in spending matters. But the level of government spending was relatively small as a percentage of the gross national product. In the twentieth century, the level of government spending has increased for reasons discussed in Chapter 1. The presi-

dent's power over the budget was strengthened with the enactment of the Budget and Accounting Act of 1921, which established a Bureau of the Budget. The president now presented a budget to Congress, and the power to recommend appropriations made government agencies more subject to presidential control.

The budgetary process will be discussed further in Chapter 4. Here we will note that Congress has taken steps to restore some of its authority through the enactment of the Budget and Impoundment Act of 1974, which limited the power of the President to impound funds appropriated by Congress and also established a Congressional Budget Office to present its own assessment of the economy. Conflict and cooperation mark the relations between Congress and the president on budgetary matters. As federal government deficits soared in the past decade, proposals were made to reduce government expenditures or, if that could not be accomplished, at least to lower deficits. One proposal which has been offered by several presidents to achieve this objective is granting the president the power of a line-item veto.

Under the Constitution, the president must either veto an entire bill or sign it. Often, Congress includes items in a bill that the president does not like. These items would, in many cases, be rejected by the president if they were presented as separate bills. And so, when presented with a bill containing both favorable and unfavorable provisions, the president is in a dilemma: to veto an entire bill in the hope that Congress will then repass the bill without provisions that he finds offensive or to make the best of a somewhat bad situation by signing the bill into law.

In his State of the Union message of 1986, Ronald Reagan asked Congress to give him a line-item veto, a power which exists already for governors in 43 states. Proposals for a presidential line-item veto have been offered for more than a century now.

Would a line-item veto for the president strengthen the president in controlling federal spending? The subject of the line-item veto is here debated by two United States senators—Daniel J. Evans of Washington and Mark O.

Hatfield of Oregon. The debate is drawn from a congressional hearing considering one version of such a proposal that would contain a two-year expiration clause. Technically, the proposed bill (S. 43) would not actually provide for a line-item veto authority for the president. In effect, however, it does. Under S. 43 the appropriate officers of each congressional chamber would instruct the enrolling clerks to enroll for presentation to the president each item (defined as all unnumbered paragraphs and numbered sections) in appropriations bills as separate pieces of legislation. The president would then be allowed to approve or disapprove each piece of legislation. If the president vetoed a measure, Congress would be able to override the veto by a two-thirds vote of each chamber.

In his defense of the line-item veto Evans argues: (1) The line-item veto would not create an imbalance in the constitutional system of checks and balances favoring the president; rather, it would restore power to the president which has experienced encroachment by Congress. (2) The budgetary savings from a line-item veto would be significant. (3) Congress, rather than the Clerk of the House and the Secretary of the Senate, will have the power to determine the structure of a bill. (4) The question of constitutionality of the proposal appears to be resolved.

Hatfield takes a Negative view of the proposal. He contends: (1) The line-item veto would have a minor role in limiting federal government expenditures since less than 15 percent of the budget, the nondefense domestic discretionary appropriation items, would in reality be subject to presidential use of the veto. (2) The use of the line-item veto by governors in 43 states is not an argument in defense of the proposal because (a) the federal government is bigger than state governments and (b) per capita government spending in states where governors have line-item veto authority is somewhat higher than in states where the governor does not have this authority. (3) The proposal would constitute an unnecessary decline in the power of Congress with respect to the president. Hatfield develops his third point by arguing that Congress has acted responsibly on

appropriations; that the president would, if the bill were adopted, still not be able to veto particular items he finds objectionable and might, consequently, veto worthy items, as well; that the president already possesses impoundment powers; and that, in effect, the president now really possesses "de facto" line-item veto authority.

As you read the debate, consider the reasons why presidents veto bills and evaluate the consequences of the veto to legislation and executive–legislative relationships. On the basis of your assessment, speculate about whether a line-item veto for the president would result in similar or different consequences.

LEGISLATIVE VETO

The Constitution provides that the president alone has the power to veto bills. In 1932, however, Congress introduced a *legislative* veto in a bill which gave President Herbert Hoover power to reorganize executive agencies. Over the years, Congress increased its use of this device in other matters, including arms transfer sales, the ability of the president to commit American troops to combat areas, and actions of regulatory agencies.

Under the legislative veto (or congressional veto, as it is sometimes called), Congress allows the president, a government agency, or an independent regulatory commission to take certain kinds of actions subject to a veto by (depending upon the specific legislation) both the House and the Senate, by one chamber of Congress, or even by a committee of one chamber of Congress within a specified period of time—often 30 or 60 days. If the appropriate congressional authority did not exercise a veto, then the president or the agency could do what was proposed. The purpose of the procedure is to allow Congress authority to reject executive acts.

The legislative veto grew rapidly in the 1970s, particularly with the enactment of regulatory laws that dealt with complicated matters requiring enormous time and technical competence to comprehend. Presidents continuously argued that the legislative veto was unconstitutional but complied with all of the laws that included that provision.

In 1983 the Supreme Court decided in *Immigration and Naturalization Service* v. *Chadha* that the legislative veto used in the case under consideration was unconstitutional. The decision implied that the legislative veto in all laws was unconstitutional. It was the most important decision on the separation of powers since the White House tapes case of the Watergate investigations in the Nixon presidency. In an instant, 200 laws containing legislative vetoes would either have to be rewritten to exclude the veto provisions or face the prospects of being invalidated as unconstitutional.

Is the legislative veto an important instrument of congressional control of administration? Dennis DeConcini, a United States Senator from Arizona, thinks that it is. He introduced a proposed constitutional amendment (S. J. Res. 135) to reinstitute the legislative veto. DeConcini made the following major points in defense of this power: (1) The congressional veto is necessary to make the bureaucracy accountable to Congress. (2) The congressional veto allows Congress to fulfill its designated role as the nation's lawmaker. (3) Congress is now faced with the choice of either refraining from delegating its authority to the bureaucracy to make rules or to transfer wholesale its lawmaking functions to the executive. (4) The absence of the legislative veto will result in more conflict between the president and Congress.

Peter W. Rodino, Jr., chairman of the House Committee on the Judiciary, believes that the importance of the legislative veto has been overstated. After describing why Congress has adopted the legislative veto, he indicates why he has long opposed this and related devices. He notes: (1) Such devices encourage Congress to avoid setting clear national policy when it delegates statutory authority in the first place. (2) The more Congress adopts such procedures, the larger becomes the congressional staff necessary to oversee the bureaucracy. (3) The legislative veto and its alternatives will strengthen special interest pleading and political pressures. (4) The devices would take too much congressional time. (5) They would delay administrative action. (6) They would make it difficult to implement laws advancing the common good.

As you read this debate consider whether the absence of the legislative veto has led to greater friction between the president and Congress. Consider, too, whether presidential power over administration has increased since the *Chadha* decision.

CONGRESS AND INDEPENDENT AGENCIES

Congress has a variety of powers to influence administration, including legislative, budgetary, appointment, and oversight. Some of these powers have already been described. Through its legislative powers, Congress can create departments and agencies and write in specific instructions governing what agencies must and must not do. Its budgetary power allows it to strengthen some agencies and weaken others. Without the funds for hiring investigators, for example, the Environmental Protection Agency would be unable to administer laws against air and water pollution.

One chamber of Congress—the Senate—has the power to confirm presidential appointments. It uses that power on occasion to reject a nominee when it considers that particular person to be lacking qualifications for that position or when it believes that the nominee would pursue policies of which many in the Senate would disapprove.

Congress supervises the activities of government agencies through its legislative oversight responsibilities. It exercises this role largely through congressional committee investigations of the agencies.

While there is general agreement that Congress has legitimate authority to exercise its oversight powers over administration, a controversy exists about how that power should be exercised over independent agencies. Agencies are called "independent" when they exist outside of executive departments. Independent regulatory commissions and independent executive agencies constitute independent agencies. Independent regulatory commissions are technically arms of the Congress. They are freer from executive controls than are federal departments. The president cannot dismiss commission members for political reasons. These commissions deal with making rules and establishing standards in various sectors of the economy, such as communications and finance. Independent regulatory commissions include Interstate Commerce Commission, Federal Reserve System, Federal Trade Commission, Federal Communications Commission, Securities and Exchange Commission, National Labor Relations Board, Equal Employment Opportunities Commission, Nuclear Regulatory Commission, and Consumer Product Safety Commission.

Independent executive agencies, although independent of executive departments, report directly to the president. They perform a variety of functions, including "housekeeping" and serving particular clients. Among these agencies are the Veterans Administration, General Services Administration, Environmental Protection Agency, Small Business Administration, National Aeronautics and Space Administration, and the Office of Personnel Management.

The debate below considers whether independent agencies should, under certain conditions, resist congressional investigations in order to protect confidentiality. Bruce Fein, who served as the general counsel of the Federal Communications Commission, argues that it should. He notes that Congress uses its investigatory power of independent agencies beyond legally permissible bounds to breach confidentiality which should be accorded independent agencies. He points out, in this regard, that congressional committees insist on the disclosure of confidential agency information or seek to investigate the mental processes of commissioners to influence the outcome of pending adjudication, investigation, or rulemaking proceedings. Committees, moreover, have sought confidential records to embarrass agencies. Fein calls upon agencies to resist congressional "intrusion" into an agency's past confidential deliberations or investigations if no legitimate legislative purpose is served. In this way, the principle of separation of powers will be vindicated.

Stephen R. McSpadden, counsel to the Subcommittee on Commerce, Consumer, and Monetary Affairs of the House Committee on Government Operations, argues against Fein's proposal. He contends that the proposal would terminate effective and meaningful oversight of independent agencies. He denounces Fein's solution as being unnecessarily overbroad and restrictive, unsupported by law, and running counter to legitimate public interest, which requires accountability of government agencies.

As you read this debate, consider the practicality of Fein's argument in terms of the benefits to an independent agency resisting congressional oversight. In this regard, evaluate the power of such an agency to make its resistance worth the effort.

COURTS AND THE BUREAUCRACY

Like the president and Congress, the federal courts play a role in shaping administration. Although the courts are not as involved in administrative acts as the other branches of government, their influence can be strongly felt.

Court decisions influence bureaucratic behavior in many ways. They may, for example, determine that government employees were improperly fired or that a regulatory commission acted illegally in applying particular rules or that proper procedures were not followed by a government agency in reaching its decisions or that specific agency rulings were in conflict with the law or the Constitution and were, consequently, illegal.

In the 1960s and 1970s, Supreme Court decisions were particularly influential in changing procedures police followed in the criminal justice system and in overseeing antidiscrimination practices. Court decisions in these policy areas subjected the court to considerable criticism.

At times, federal judges have become involved in the most detailed aspects of administrative decisions, as when they evaluated and approved racial integration policies of local school officials or when they determined precise living conditions for criminals held in prison. Have federal judges usurped the authority of administrative agencies? Political scientist R. Shep Melnick takes the Affirmative side of this argument. He contends: (1) The courts have used new procedural requirements and techniques of statutory interpretation to strengthen subcommittees and special interests at the expense of the president. (2) Judicial review has been used by the courts to expand government expenditures in ways not sought by legislators approving the law. Melnick cites examples from laws on the environment and the handicapped to make his case.

Political scientist Phillip J. Cooper takes the Negative view. He asserts that some tension must exist between the judges and administrators as courts must reconcile administrative discretion with the rule of law, but this tension should not lead to a misunderstanding of what federal courts have been doing. Specifically, he draws the following conclusions from his study of recent court rulings: (1) Courts care about the fiscal implications of their decisions for public administration. (2) Courts are willing to defer to the expertise of administrators. (3) The Supreme Court is not continually expanding the authority of federal district courts to issue complex remedial orders obstructing administrative operations. (4) The Supreme Court is not expanding legal protections available to employees at the expense of managers' discretion. (5) The Supreme Court has not consistently issued rulings that make it easier to bring suit in federal court. (6) Federal courts are not constantly expanding the threat to administrators from tort liability judgments.

As you read this debate, consider the expertise available to judges in deciding cases dealing with complex administrative matters. Consider, too, whether Professors Melnick and Cooper share any agreement in describing the behavior of federal courts in their dealings with government agencies.

DECENTRALIZATION

One problem of government administration is: What should be the relationship between the central and regional units? Even in unitary political systems in which authority is concentrated at the center, efforts are sometimes made to allow for some measure of autonomy by regional and local units. The American political system, however, is a federal system in which authority is legally divided between central and regional units—the states—so that some decentralization is constitutionally required.

Even in states, however, demands are heard for further decentralization—calling upon power for the counties, the cities, or the neighborhoods. In federal laws, state laws, and municipal ordinances, a certain measure of autonomy at a decentralized level is often recognized. In the 1960s, antipoverty legislation required that "maximum feasible participation" by community members themselves was required in decisions dealing with the expenditure of federal government antipoverty funds. Local school boards in some municipalities, moreover, have been given some say in educational policy, hiring of school employees, and disbursement of funds.

As far as the relationship between government and people is concerned, is small beautiful? In the debate below, the National Association of Neighborhoods, representing a number of neighborhood organizations in the United States, argues that it is. The National Neighborhood Platform, which reflects the association's values, asserts a case for decentralization. Among its main points are: (1) Existing government institutions have grown too large and too remote. (2) Large institutions force many Americans to become apathetic about political matters. (3) Neighborhood associations will enhance civic participation. (4) Those people who are affected by the decisions of government must be consulted. The platform calls for specific steps that should be taken by government to serve the needs of people who live in neighborhoods.

K. Newton challenges the view that small is beautiful. Specifically, he argues: (1) Large units are no less efficient and can be more effective than small ones. (2) Large units of government are no less democratic than small ones and, in some respects, are more so.

As you read the debate, consider the kinds

of government services that are offered to communities and whether all, some, or none of them can be more effectively administered at a decentralized level, such as a neighborhood. Consider, too, how much participation in government decision making can be asked of people in terms of the time they have available after they meet their work and family obligations. At various times in the past few decades, decentralization in the form of calls for "power to the people" or "local control" has been advocated by radical, liberal, and conservative groups. What conclusions can be drawn from this fact?

ISSUES

3 YES   WOULD A LINE-ITEM VETO FOR THE PRESIDENT STRENGTHEN THE PRESIDENT IN CONTROLLING FEDERAL SPENDING?

[The Case for the Line-Item Veto]
Daniel J. Evans

Mr. Chairman, ranking minority member and other distinguished members of the Committee on Rules and Administration, I wish to express my thanks to the committee for holding this hearing and providing me with the opportunity to express my views on this important issue of line-item veto.

Last week, this committee reported a resolution to establish a temporary select committee to study the congressional budget process. To a major extent, this action was in response to a growing dissatisfaction with how we deal with this Nation's budget.

The line-item veto should be considered in the same light—one budgetary tool that can assist us in crafting a lean, responsible Federal budget.

This line-item veto proposal can be characterized as a low-risk/high reward proposition. As a low-risk proposition, the legislation includes a 2-year expiration clause. If it does not work it will die on its own. If we try it and it does work, the potential reward is great by allowing a President the privilege and the opportunity of using this one tool, in conjunction with others, to bring our budget def-

icits under control. If it has the effect even as a small spending control tool, then I suspect Congress might well continue such a proposal, perhaps on a 2-year basis, so Congress would always retain control to continue it or let it die.

Even with such a low-risk/high-reward proposition, there continues to be opposition. Perhaps it would be of greatest benefit to review and discuss the major arguments raised by those opposed to the line-item veto.

1. *Granting the President too much authority and ating an imbalance of the constitutional checks   balances.*—Some suggest that by granting the Pr   ident line-item veto authority, the balance between Executive and legislative power over the allocation of Federal resources will be upset. Let us look, however, at recent practice.

Since the beginning of the Truman administration, 14,081 public bills have passed, with only 355 vetoed—a veto rate of 2.5 percent. 10.1 percent of these vetoes were overridden. Twenty-three appropriation bills were vetoed during this same period, but the rate of success for the Congress in overriding appropriations vetoes is 30.4 percent—triple that of the normal rate for all public bills. I suggest this can be interpreted to indicate that Congress has maintained and perhaps increased its influence over the ultimate passage of appropriation bills, while restraining the Presidential use of veto authority.

Mr. Chairman, allow me to digress into the not so recent past to examine what has happened to Pres-

From U. S. Cong. Senate, *Line-Item Veto*, Hearings before the Committee on Rules and Administration, 99th Cong., 1st Sess., 1985, pp. 69–71.

idential veto authority. In the Federalist Papers, both James Madison and Alexander Hamilton argued against an absolute veto and for a qualified veto on the grounds that a qualified veto will be used more frequently. Let me emphasize that. A qualified veto will be used more frequently. Hamilton stated the general opinion that the absolute veto is, "A power odious in appearance, useless in practice." Hamilton concluded that, "There would be greater danger of the President not using his power when necessary, than of his using it too often or too much."

In recent years, Congress has developed practices that often convert the qualified veto into something closely akin to the absolute veto, a device too rigorous to be used as a security against bad laws. Congress has adopted the practice of adding riders to bills and in particular legislative riders and pork-barrel appropriations to vital bills that cannot stand on their own merit. This practice has impaired and diminished that qualified veto significantly. Current legislative practice presents the President with the choice of take all of what is offered or nothing. Such proposals have no other purpose than to intimidate the President, to emasculate the veto power, to foreclose the opportunity for reconsideration.

The veto was designed not only to provide the benefits of reconsideration but also those of anticipation—the foresight that brings self-control. As Hamilton pointed out, it is not just an actual veto but the anticipation of a veto that will provide check and balance. Congress has invented techniques that give it less reason to anticipate a veto, thus less reason to be restrained and responsible.

Current legislative practice subverts the veto power provided in the Constitution by providing Congress with an alternative to self-discipline. The alternative is a form of blackmail, extortion of the Executive's approval through threat, and a process to add trainloads of unworthy projects that could not stand on their own merit. Congress has turned the tables on the President making the veto work for legislature license instead of against it.

The qualified veto is a part of the internal balance of the Constitution. It is a counterforce that offsets potential abuse of power by the Legislature. Since the founding, Congress has encroached on this veto power. This proposal that we are discussing today will address this concern—not that we're granting the President with greater authority, but returning balance to the relationship between the President and Congress.

2. *Affecting only a small portion of the Federal budget.*—Some suggest that only a small portion of the Federal budget will be subject to the provisions of this proposal. They say that the President wouldn't exercise his veto authority on defense items. Entitlement and interest spending and revenue measures could not be reached. All that is left is about 15 percent of Government spending categorized under nondefense discretionary spending.

Admittedly, to curb Government spending we must look at mandatory spending—control and reform. But as to the remainder of the budget, nothing should or can be sacred. I personally would suggest that at some future point in time we should look seriously at including tax expenditures and authorization measures. For the present, however, we should start with appropriations and stop second-guessing the President as to where he, or future presidents may use this authority—we must provide the opportunity.

Mr. Chairman, a more appropriate question to look at is not the portion of the budget subject to a line-item veto, but how does the President find access to these spending items.

Perhaps one of the finest examples of recent years has been the fiscal 1985 continuing resolution. This resolution contained almost $400 billion of spending and 8 of 13 appropriations acts. It delayed us to the extent that 500,000 Government workers were furloughed. This year, will we further intimidate a President by putting all 13 appropriations bills into a single continuing resolution? Will we add to it, as we attempted to last year—Superfund, Grove City, busing, tutition tax credits, gun control, comparable worth, and whatever else we might think valuable? Then wrap it into one package and present it to the President, saying "take it or leave it," or may-be even more appropriately "find it, it's in there."

I suggest that while some may ridicule the line-item veto authority as being insignificant, even these small reductions amount to something that cannot be concluded to be insignificant.

3. *Investing new powers in the enrolling clerks.*—This line-item veto proposal directs the Senate enrolling clerks to divide appropriations bills into items which stand as separate bills. A few suggest that this is granting these clerks new powers at the expense of Members of Congress. Nothing is more ludicrous.

The Clerk of the House and the Secretary of the Senate currently share the responsibility to review bills and ensure accuracy with what was passed by Congress; direction is then provided to the enrolling clerks.

Members of Congress retain the authority to determine the structure of a bill; an "item" will be determined by the structure of appropriations bills considered and passed by Congress.

The United States Code gives direction as to a numbered section; "each section (of a bill) shall be numbered, and shall contain, as nearly as may be, a single proposition."

These three points ensure that no increased authority and discretion will be delegated to the enrolling clerks.

4. *Questioning its constitutionality.*—The question of constitutionality appears to be resolved through the use of the precedents established by the Gephardt rule. Also with the review and endorsement of the President and the Office of Management and Budget and with a growing number of supportive members

in this body, we can leave behind the question of constitutionality and get on with discussions that examine the merits of a line-item veto.

Mr. Chairman, as a three-term Governor of the State of Washington, I valued the line-item veto more than any other budget tool. Benefits were not only derived from the ability to remove waste from the budget, but also served as a check for germaneness. I seldom was presented a bill that was not clear and consistent within the framework of the title under which it passed. Admittedly, there is a difference between this Congress and State legislatures and between a President and a Governor. But what I find most disturbing is the fact that we, here in this present-day Congress, lay on the President's desk huge trainloads of pork attached to vital pieces of legislation. We make it almost impossible for the President to veto what is absolutely necessary to carry on the operations of Government. When he signs such legislation, he also must accept a whole series of expenditures which could not stand on their own merits.

A recent Gallup poll suggests that 67 percent of those asked thought the President should have line-item veto authority. It is time we join these citizens and seek the benefits of this line-item veto proposal—benefits in the areas of (1) budget control, (2) germaneness, (3) reconsideration, (4) anticipation and (5) balance between the executive and legislative branches.

It is time for us to test the value of the line-item veto—not just for the present, not just for this administration, not just for this Congress, not as a miracle cure to our continuing deficit concern—but as an important first toward fiscal responsibility.

3   NO   WOULD A LINE-ITEM VETO FOR THE PRESIDENT STRENGTHEN THE PRESIDENT IN CONTROLLING FEDERAL SPENDING?

[The Case Against the Line-Item Veto]
Mark O. Hatfield

Mr. Chairman, I appreciate the opportunity to testify before the Committee today. My position on the line-item veto is no secret. I am unalterably opposed to it in any form.

Legislation to grant the President authority to veto items in appropriation bills is proffered as a tool to eliminate extravagant and wasteful government spending. It is a simple solution on its face, but wrong. I hope this Committee, in considering this legislation, will look beyond the immediate public appeal of this proposition. If enacted, it will have serious institutional and political impacts.

At the outset, it should be made clear in any discussion of the line-item veto that it is not a mechanism to achieve meaningful reductions in the Federal deficit. A look at the composition of Federal spending indicates otherwise. As proposed, line-item veto authority would apply only to individual items in appropriation bills. It would not be used on revenue measures. It also would not be applied

against the largest and fastest growing portions of the budget, such as permanently-funded entitlement spending and other mandatory costs such as interest on the Federal debt. These items account for half the budget and are not funded in appropriation bills.

Of the remaining half of the budget subject to appropriation, more than half goes for defense. I doubt very much that the current administration, even though committed to spending restraint, would exercise this grant of power much on defense or foreign aid items. Nor could this veto be used to reduce entitlements funded in annual appropriation acts—items which cannot be reduced or eliminated without changes in substantive law.

What it boils down to is less than 15 percent of the budget, the non-defense domestic discretionary appropriation items. These activities include education assistance, community and regional development, law enforcement, environmental protection, health research, energy development, agriculture aid, and a host of other vital Federal responsibilities.

This small fraction of the Federal budget—the target of the line-item veto—has actually been the

From U. S. Cong., Senate, *Line-Item Veto*, Hearings before the Committee on Rules and Administration, 99th Cong., 1st Sess., 1985, pp. 51–52.

only declining portion of the Federal budget in recent years, falling from $97.3 billion in fiscal year 1980 to $65.0 billion in fiscal year 1985 in 1972 constant dollars, a 33 percent reduction.

It baffles me that we are considering a proposal that seeks to control the only portion of the budget we have been able to control—not only control, but reduce—in recent years. This is not the path to meaningful deficit reduction. Indeed, we could eliminate all non-defense domestic discretionary appropriation items and the deficit would still exceed $100 billion in fiscal year 1986.

Much has been made of the fact that 43 states currently grant their governors some form of line-item veto authority. The argument here is that what works for states ought to work for the Federal government.

We should be careful to consider the differences between State governments and the Federal government. Notable differences include the structure of State budgets, the fact that State legislatures meet only for a limited portion of the year, and that most states operate under a balanced budget requirement. The most obvious difference, however, is simply the size and power of the Federal government. The greater the scope and reach of the power, the more critical it is that such power be held in check, balanced between the three, co-equal, branches of government.

Philosophical considerations aside, the practical matter is that the line-item veto may not work in the states either. The February 1985 Annual Report of the President's Council of Economic Advisors states: "Approval of line-item veto may not have a substantial effect on total Federal expenditure. The experience of the States indicates that per capita spending is somewhat higher in States where the Governor has the authority for line-item veto, even when corrected for the major conditions that affect the distribution of spending among States."

To be blunt, Mr. Chairman, this proposal has little to do with spending reduction. It has everything to do with the balance of power in our government. This proposal represents a significant grant of power and passing of responsibility to the Chief Executive at the expense of the Legislative Branch, and there are no sound reasons why this shift in power should occur.

First, the Congress has acted responsibly on appropriations. Total funds appropriated by the Congress have remained very close to the Administration's requested levels. Enacted appropriations over the past six years have been under the President's request by slightly less than one percent. This is not evidence of the Congress wielding a "free-wheeling" hand in spending federal resources. It is evidence of responsible appropriations action by the Congress.

Second, there is a misconception that this grant of power will allow the President to veto spending for a certain project or activity in one area of the country or another; that it will allow the President to remove funding for so-called "pork-barrel" projects. This could occur only on a very limited basis. If, for example, the President opposed funding for an Army construction project located in a particular state, he could line-item veto the total appropriation for the "Military Construction, Army" account. That would deny funding for all Army construction projects, but it would not simply delete the objectionable project. The same is true for a single water construction project, a particular Park Service land acquisition, and a host of other individual projects and activities. It would be necessary to veto the entire appropriation for the account to turn down one minute detail of it. And, that is only if the account fits the definition of an "item."

What would result is regular appropriation bills being enrolled as perhaps as many as a hundred or so separate bills. General appropriation measures might be converted into literally hundreds of separate bills. The President would be swamped with paper and we would have difficulty keeping track of things. In addition, it remains unclear to me what the application of this proposal would be if a bill or conference report is incorporated by reference into a general appropriation measure. We should equally be concerned that legislative intent may be completely overridden when items intentionally linked and sequenced together are separately enrolled.

Third, the President can use his current impoundment powers to delete funding for subaccount details considered to be wasteful or unnecessary. Proposals to defer or rescind funding for these items can be made by the President, getting to a level of detail the line-item veto cannot.

Fourth, the President already possesses "de facto" line-item veto authority. The President, through his aides, is in close touch with each bill as it progresses through the legislative process, making his opposition known and exercising a great deal of influence over the bill's particulars before it is ever sent to him for signature. The jobs bill supplemental of fiscal year 1983 is a case in point. A provision to accelerate the fourth-quarter payment of general revenue sharing funds was dropped from the bill because of a threatened Presidential veto, despite the fact that there was strong sentiment for the proposal in both the House and Senate. The argument is no longer valid that the President must approve appropriation bills and swallow the good with the bad or permit the government to shut down. Short funding extensions are traditionally granted to allow time to negotiate out an acceptable measure.

The veto authority the President now possesses under the Constitution is a powerful tool. To enhance a President's veto authority further with the grant of an item veto could be to hand a President a powerful political weapon. It could be used to dictate Presidential priorities and thwart the will of the Congress.

Mr. Chairman, I am not appearing before you today as the Chairman of the Senate Appropriations Committee—out to protect the Committee's turf. The objections I raise to the line-item veto proposal are ones I believe should be of grave concern to this Committee and to all members of the Congress.

The item veto will not lead to significant deficit reduction. It may not result in any budget savings. What it will do is unnecessarily and inadvisably change the relationship of the President and the Congress. The separation of powers and the balance of power are coveted principles embodied in our Constitution. I see no need to change them.

It is tempting to support a mechanism to shift the blame and responsibility from our shoulders and go back home and tell our constituents that we have just given the President a tool to eliminate wasteful spending. That will not make it happen. It is the responsibility of the Congress to spend funds and to raise revenue. We may need to do a better job, but relinquishing this responsibility is the wrong answer and the line-item veto is the wrong solution.

QUESTIONS FOR DISCUSSION

1. Who is more responsible for high government spending: the president or Congress? Explain.
2. How would a line-item veto affect the bargaining process between president and Congress in determining the size of the budget?
3. Had the president been granted a line-item veto in appropriations when the Constitution was first adopted, what difference would it have made to federal spending practices?
4. Would the president be strengthened or weakened by the line-item veto? Why?
5. Would social programs in education, health, and housing be helped or hurt by a line-item veto authority for the president?

SUGGESTED READINGS

ABNEY, GLENN, AND THOMAS P. LAUTH, "The Line Item Veto in the States: An Instrument for Fiscal Restraint or an Instrument for Partnership?," *Public Administration Review*, 45 (May/June 1985), 372–77.

AMERICAN ENTERPRISE INSTITUTE FOR PUBLIC POLICY RESEARCH, *Proposals for Line-Item Veto Authority: 1984*. 98th Cong., 2nd Sess., 1984. Washington, DC: American Enterprise Institute for Public Policy Research, 1984.

BEST, JUDITH A., "The Item Veto: Would the Founders Approve?,"*Presidential Studies Quarterly*, 14 (Spring 1984), 183–88.

COHEN, RICHARD, "Congress Plays Election-Year Politics with Line-Item Veto Proposal . . . ," *National Journal*, 16 (Feb. 11, 1984), 274–76.

CRONIN, THOMAS E., AND JEFFREY J. WEILL, "An Item Veto for the President?," *Congress and the Presidency*, 12 (Autumn 1985), 127–49.

PALFFY, JOHN, "Line-Item Veto: Trimming the Pork," Heritage Foundation *Backgrounder*, No. 343 (Apr. 3, 1984).

RINGELSTEIN, ALBERT C., "Presidential Vetoes: Motivations and Classifications," *Congress and the Presidency*, 12 (Spring 1985), 43–55.

ROSS, RUSSELL M., AND FRED SCHWENGEL, "An Item Veto for the President?," *Presidential Studies Quarterly*, 12 (Winter 1982), 66–79.

SPITZER, ROBERT J., "The Item Veto Reconsi-dered," *Presidential Studies Quarterly*, 15 (Summer 1985), 611–17.

U. S. CONGRESS, SENATE, *Line-Item Veto*, Hearing before the Subcommittee on the Constitution of the Committee on the Judiciary, 98th Cong., 2nd Sess., 1984.

4   YES   IS THE LEGISLATIVE VETO AN IMPORTANT INSTRUMENT OF CONGRESSIONAL CONTROL OF ADMINISTRATION?

[The Case for the Legislative Veto]
Dennis DeConcini

Mr. President, at the conclusion of my remarks, I intend to introduce a Senate joint resolution that will amend the Constitution to permit legislation to provide for a legislative veto process. This constitutional amendment will reverse the recent Supreme Court decision in Immigration and Naturalization Service against Chadha which ruled that legislative veto provisions violated the traditional scheme of the separation of powers and was unconstitutional. I disagree with the decision, but I also recognize that arguments concerning the basis for the decision are certainly not clearcut. As a legislator who believes that the legislative veto has a valid place in the lawmaking process, I hope through my proposed amendment, not only to restore the ability of Congress to exercise legislative veto powers, but also to clearly set out the constitutional basis for this power.

I will direct the majority of my comments to the disturbing effects that the Chadha case imposes upon the balance of powers within our Government.

As a legislator, I am troubled by Chadha. I am troubled because Chadha erodes the fundamental position of the legislative branch as the lawmaker of our Government. We, the Members of Congress, must act to retain our power to make the laws in this Nation.

My proposed amendment will restore congressional power over the lawmaking functions of Government by enabling Congress to oversee the manner in which the executive branch uses any legislative power which Congress had delegated to it. My proposed amendment will allow Congress to exercise a one House or two House legislative veto.

Mr. President, the text of this proposed amendment is very clear and concise. It states:

> Executive action under legislatively delegated authority may be subject to the approval of one or both Houses of Congress, without presentment to the President, if the legislation that authorizes the executive action so provides.

The amendment permits Congress to select a one or two House legislative veto. Congress merely has to specify in the enabling legislation which sort of veto it believes is appropriate.

Under this amendment, Congress would sanction independent and departmental agency actions taken by the executive branch of our Government. Congress would express these sanctions by a vote of approval or disapproval.

This amendment would not permit Congress to veto actions constitutionally assigned as executive functions. For example, a legislative veto on an inherently executive function, such as that of initiating prosecutions, would not be permissible under the provisions of this amendment. Only executive ac-

From *Congressional Record*, July 27 1983, pp. S11015–17.

tion taken under power which was delegated from Congress to the executive branch would be subject to a legislative veto.

The amendment essentially restores the status quo which existed before the Chadha decision. In Immigration and Naturalization Service against Chadha, the Supreme Court on June 23, 1983, ruled by 7-to-2 vote, that the one House legislative veto is unconstitutional. While the substantive ruling was not unexpected, the reach of the Court's rationale came as a surprise to many. The encompassing nature of the ruling is reflected in Justice Powell's observation that "the Court's decision apparently will invalidate every use of the legislative veto."

The Court's opinion rests upon the view that the Constitution mandates a bicameral consideration, and a presentment to the President for his signature or veto, of all exercises of legislative power by Congress. The Court broadly defined legislative power as actions which "alter the legal rights, duties, and relations of persons outside the legislative branch."

In Chadha, the Supreme Court limited the doctrine of separation of powers, as embodied in the Constitution, to the interaction of the bicameral and presentment clauses. That is the fundamental basis of my disagreement with the Court's decision. I do not agree with the Supreme Court's interpretation that these clauses of the Constitution incorporate the doctrine of separation of powers as the framers of the constitution intended that doctrine to be interpreted and employed.

I consider the spirit of the doctrine of separation of powers to flow throughout the Constitution as a whole. To understand the constitutionality of any law, we must look not only to the written words of the Constitution, but also to the spirit which that document embodies.

The requirement of presentment of legislative action to the President and the process of bicameral action was founded upon the framers' fear of a concentration of power in one branch of the Government at the expense of another branch.

The framers perceived that the accumulation of all powers, be they legislative, executive, or judiciary, in the same hands, whether of one, a few or many, and whether hereditary, self-appointed, or elective, may justly be pronounced the very definition of tyranny. When the framers formed the Constitution, they put into effect measures which

they believed would curb abuses of power by our Government.

The framers created a three-branch Government to oversee our Nation's business. The judicial branch was created with the power to interpret our laws. The executive branch was empowered to enforce our laws. And the congressional branch was deemed to be the lawmaking body within our Government.

The purpose of separating the authority of government is to prevent unnecessary and dangerous concentration of power in one branch. For that reason, the framers saw fit to divide and balance the powers of government, so that each branch would be checked by the others. Virtually every part of our constitutional system bears the mark of this judgment. It is the checks and balances aspect of the doctrine of separation of powers which the Chadha decision so grievously violates. To understand this violation, we must review the development of our Government during this century.

This Nation has entered a modern industrial and technological age. Problems and needs of a national scope have required a congressional response. From the end of the last century, with the establishment of the first independent agencies, through the period of the Great Depression, with the creation of agencies under Franklin Roosevelt's New Deal, to the post-Vietnam era, with the formation of consumer and environmental agencies, Congress has met the challenges of the modern epoch.

Especially since the time of the New Deal, the modern bureaucracy has mushroomed. Congress wisely recognized that many modern problems which required a response were in fact so complex in scope that only the creation of a special administrative body could adequately address the situation. Consequently, Congress delegated more and more of its legislative authority to Federal agencies.

The escalating growth of Federal agencies reveals itself in the statistics concerning our Government. Between 1930 and 1939, a total of 154 Federal agencies were created. This contrasts with 552 agencies created between 1970 and 1979. In 1939, agency regulations filled 5,007 pages of the Federal Register. In 1979, this number had increased to 77,468 pages. In 1982, Federal agencies drafted approximately 105,000 pages of regulations.

For some time, the sheer amount of law made

by agencies, has surpassed in quantity the lawmaking engaged in by Congress through the traditional legislative process. For every statute Congress passes, the bureaucracies have put out 18 regulations.

There is no question but that agency rulemaking is lawmaking in any functional or realistic sense of the term. When agencies are authorized to prescribe law through substantive rulemaking, the administrator's regulation is not only due deference, but is accorded "legislative effect." These regulations bind courts and officers of the Federal Government. They may preempt State law. They can grant rights to and impose obligations upon the public. In sum, they have the force of law.

Our Nation's development into a complex social structure has made it necessary for Congress to delegate some of its legislative authority to those agencies which, with their national scope and technical expertise, are well suited to attend to the day-to-day problems under their jurisdictions. From pollution to production, executive agency action impacts the fundamental fabric of our lives.

As each regulation becomes law, Congress' constitutional responsibility to make the laws of the land is placed into the hands of the unelected administrators of our Government. The rise of these bodies which are not restrained by the electoral process, has been the most significant legal trend of the last century. They have become a veritable fourth branch of the Government, which has fundamentally disturbed our three-branch legal theories.

Congress is responsible for having created this administrative age. But in doing so, it has not acted irresponsibly. Instead, we have created mechanisms to secure the accountability of this fourth branch of government. The legislative veto was the central means which Congress employed.

The modern legislative veto was established in 1932 during the Hoover administration's reorganization plan. The President and the Congress adopted the veto as a means by which Congress could delegate to the executive branch the authority to carry out its expanding duties, while maintaining Congress' constitutional role as the Nation's lawmaker.

Since that time, this body has acted with the President to expand the use of the veto. Justice White, in his dissent of the Chadha case, noted that the "Legislative veto balanced delegation of statutory authority in new areas of governmental involve-

ment." Congressional utilization of the legislative veto in the Congressional Budget Impoundment Control Act of 1974 and the War Powers Act of 1973, for example, earmarked the veto as a tool for resolving problems of policy between Congress and the President.

There have been approximately 300 veto provisions placed in legislation over the past 50 years. The majority were enacted since 1970. It is not surprising that the number of veto provisions has grown proportionally with the growth of the agencies.

The history of the legislative veto makes it clear that it has not been a sword which Congress has used to aggrandize itself at the expense of the other branches. Rather, the veto has been a means of defense. The veto reserves the ultimate authority necessary if Congress is to fulfill its designated role as the Nation's lawmaker. The legislative veto is commonly seen to be a check upon rulemaking by administrative agencies and upon broad-based policy decisions by the executive branch.

The legislative veto is more than efficient, convenient, and useful. It is an important, if not indispensable, political invention that allows the President and Congress to resolve major constitutional and policy differences. It preserves Congress' control over lawmaking.

With the Chadha decision, this accepted constitutional practice, the legislative veto, was destroyed. The Chadha case has far reaching ramifications. As Justice White states in his dissent, the Chadha decision "strikes down in one fell swoop provisions in more laws enacted by Congress than the Court has cumulatively struck down in its history." Chadha forces us into a tumultuous period of readjustment.

Congress is now faced with the choice of either refraining from delegating its authority to legislate, which would impose upon Congress the impossible task of writing laws with the specificity necessary to cover the endless number of special circumstances which may arise over the entire policy spectrum, or transferring wholesale its lawmaking function to the executive branch. Neither of these choices is acceptable.

The loss of the legislative veto means the reconsideration of hundreds of existing statutes. I foresee a trend toward more specific laws, granting very detailed authority. Committee scrutiny will increase. The progress of needed legislation will be slowed.

The absence of the legislative veto opens a battleground between Congress and the President. We will nip-and-tuck over the appropriation of Federal funds. We will do battle with an extensive use of riders to appropriate bills. Confrontation will erupt over the deferral of appropriated funds.

Such extensive ramifications demonstrate that this body needs to approve an amendment to overturn the decision in Chadha. We must reinstate the legislative veto as an effective congressional tool. We need the power to attach a legislative veto to the broad delegation of powers which modern-day government requires. I believe that the doctrine of the separation of powers is violated by a scheme of government which allows the delegation of legislative power to the President and the departments under his control, but forbids a check on the exercise of that power by Congress. I believe that the legislative veto is a mechanism by which our elected representatives preserve their voice in the governance of the Nation. It is consistent with the purposes of article 1 and the principles of the separation of powers, which are reflected in that article and throughout the Constitution.

The history of the separation of powers doctrine is a history of accommodation and practicality. The Constitution does not contemplate total separation of the three branches of government. Madison emphasized that the principle of the separation of powers is primarily violated where the whole power of one department is exercised by the same hands which possess the whole power of another department. However, this should not preclude partial involvement or oversight of one department over another.

According to Montesquieu, the legislature is uniquely fit to exercise an additional function: To examine in what manner the laws that it has have been executed. The legislative veto merely provides Congress with that opportunity. It allows us to approve or disapprove what an agency has done with the power which we have delegated to it.

A legislative veto over agency actions is a necessary check on the expanding power of the agencies, both executive and independent, as they engage in exercising authority delegated by Congress. As President Reagan suggested when he was a candidate, it is the legislative veto which presents a way to check the excesses in the Federal bureaucracy.

The Court's decision in Chadha, that all "law-making" must be shared by Congress and the President, ignores the fact that legislative authority is routinely delegated to the executive branch and to the independent agencies. If congressional action under the legislative veto technique is "legislative" action that must be shared, why is the same true of executive or administrative promulgation of orders, rules, and regulations, which the legislative veto attempts to control?

This amendment allows Congress to reserve a check on legislative power for itself. Absent the veto, the agencies receiving delegations of legislative power may issue regulations having the force of law without bicameral approval and without the President's signature.

The fact that the Supreme Court has handed down its opinion that the veto is unconstitutional does not alter or dilute the original rationale which persuaded Congress to adopt and utilize the legislative veto in the first place. The crux of the issue is this: Who shall be responsible for the laws of the land?

In a democracy, it is the elected legislators which the electorate holds accountable. I fear that without a legislative veto, fundamental policy decisions in our society will be made not by the body elected by the people to make the laws, but by appointed officials, not answerable to the public.

The legislative veto offers the means by which Congress could confer additional authority, while preserving its own constitutional role. Under my amendment, the President would retain his power to initially approve or disapprove the delegation of the power which has a legislative veto attachment. Congress could make a wholesale delegation of power to the executive branch, or it could attach a veto provision to any delegation. Such policies would have to be worked out between the President and the Congress.

This amendment would restore the ability of Congress and the President to determine the best method to control the actions of the Executive and independent agencies. Only within the last half century has the complexity and size of the Federal Government's responsibilities grown so greatly that the Congress must rely on the legislative veto as the most effective, if not the only means, to insure their role as the Nation's lawmakers.

The legislative veto which would be created

by this amendment would provide a "check" upon agency action. That "check" is desperately called for under the principle of separation of powers. I simply believe that unacceptable agency actions must be checked and that Congress is the appropriate body to do so.

Thomas Jefferson once predicted that the people will see and amend any error in our Constitution which makes any branch independent of the Nation. The recent Chadha decision effectively creates a fourth branch of our Government, an administrative branch, which is not elected, nor answerable to any officials of our Government. Let us follow Mr. Jefferson's advice. Let us amend our Constitution so that no branch of our Government will remain unchecked and independent of the Nation.

Mr. President, as ranking minority member of the Constitution Subcommittee of the Judiciary Committee, I intend to push for immediate hearings on this proposal. I urge my colleagues to support efforts to restore the legislative veto and I ask unan-

imous consent that the text of this amendment appear in the RECORD.

There being no objection, the bill was ordered to be printed in the RECORD, as follows:

S. J. RES. 135

Resolved by the Senate and House of Representatives of the United States of America in Congress assembled, (two-thirds of each House concurring therein), That the following article is proposed as an amendment to the Constitution of the United States, which shall be valid to all intents and purposes as part of the Constitution when ratified by the legislatures of three-fourths of the several States within seven years after the date of its submission by the Congress:

"ARTICLE _____

"SECTION 1. Executive action under legislatively delegated authority may be subject to the approval of one or both Houses of Congress, without presentment to the President, if the legislation that authorizes the executive action so provides."

4 NO IS THE LEGISLATIVE VETO AN IMPORTANT INSTRUMENT OF CONGRESSIONAL CONTROL OF ADMINISTRATION?

[The Case Against the Legislative Veto]
Peter W. Rodino

WHY CONGRESS HAS ADOPTED LEGISLATIVE VETO

During the 20th century, the role of the Federal Government, particularly in domestic affairs, has changed dramatically. It is now involved in many matters, such as health, welfare, and safety, that were once the sole province of State and local governments. As a result of this expanded role, Congress has faced a tremendously growing workload. Yet under the Constitution it could deal with these new responsibilities only through the legislative process—as you well know, an often cumbersome, time-consuming, and frustrating task.

_____
From U.S. Cong., House, *Legislative Veto after Chadha,* Hearings before the Committee on Rules, 98th Cong., 2nd Sess., 1984, pp. 400–406.

Because of the sheer size and complexity of this Federal role, Congress increasingly found it necessary to delegate authority to the executive branch, which, with its greater manpower and resources, seemed best adapted to handling the detailed implementation of laws.

Often these statutory delegations included only the most generalized standards for implementation of the delegated authority. The executive branch became more powerful as its delegated authority grew.

The executive branch, of course, exercised the power Congress gave it—at times in ways some, or even most of us, did not like. Congress often felt frustrated by this exercise of power by the executive branch. Some Members felt we were incapable of assuring that the laws we pass were "faithfully executed." In addition, we were expected by our constituents to do something or prevent something about whatever problem concerned them. At times we were powerless to produce what our constituents wanted. Congress began to feel it was sitting on the sidelines while the executive branch ran the Government.

The original legislative vetoes, such as the first one in 1932 which applied to a statute authorizing executive reorganization by the President, consisted of accommodations of the overlapping constitutional responsibilities of the legislative and executive branches. The Congress agreed that the President would have the authority to make certain decisions in these areas of shared authority. At the same time, however, the President's decision would be subject to a veto by one or both Houses of Congress.

By the 1970's, however, legislative veto began to be extended to areas quite distinct from its original arena of overlapping powers. Two circumstances propelled this development.

First, during Watergate, the period which covered the last years of the Nixon administration, there was tremendous tension and distrust between then President Richard Nixon and the Congress. As a result, numerous veto provisions were enacted in order to assure that the laws would be properly executed. These vetoes were not limited to areas of overlapping responsibility under the Constitution.

The second circumstance that led to the extension of legislative veto was the enactment in the 1960's and early 1970's of many new environmental and safety laws. These laws frequently contained broad delegations of authority, with only vague standards for agency action. They often dealt with complex issues that required technical and scientific findings as a basis for implementation. Agencies were directed to implement these laws through the issuance of detailed regulations. Businesses, State and local governments, and others that had to comply with the regulations complained that they were faulty, excessive, and unnecessarily burdensome. Congress, which had delegated regulatory authority to the agencies, began to be held politically accountable for these regulations. Many in Congress felt a need to demonstrate that Congress was the preeminent lawmaking branch of Government, and

they saw legislative veto as the convenient response to this problem of political accountability.

Legislative veto did create the appearance of congressional control. Therefore, more and more frequently such provisions were added to all types of statutory delegations. Congress increasingly used legislative veto to control the executive branch in its most "executive" activity: The daily management of government.

Congressional efforts to expand legislative veto provisions reached their peak in nearly successful efforts in 1975 and again in 1982 to enact legislation that would apply legislative veto to all agency regulations. These efforts failed, but by 1983, more than 200 laws containing more than 350 separate legislative veto provisions had been enacted, and 126 veto provisions applying to 207 types of Executive action were in effect. . . .

SHOULD ANY ALTERNATIVES TO LEGISLATIVE VETO BE ADOPTED?

In my view, the importance of legislative veto as a device for controlling the implementation of law has been vastly overstated. While legislative veto provisions reflect an understandable frustration with the legislative process, they are not a very effective response to the changing nature of the Federal Government.

Despite the large number of statutes which contain a legislative veto provision, the mechanism itself has not been frequently used. Since 1932, legislative vetoes overturning Presidential or regulatory actions have been adopted approximately 125 times. Sixty-six of these vetoes have been requests for deferrals of spending authority under the Congressional Budget and Impoundment Control Act of 1974; 24 were disapprovals of Executive reorganization plans; and only 25 involved agency regulations. The remainder addressed policy or other matters not regulatory in nature.[9]

[Editor's note: text and citations for notes 1 through 8 were omitted here.]

[9]"Data on and examples of Congressional Disapproval of Rules and Regulations," Clark F. Norton, Congressional Research Service, Library of Congress, July 8, 1983.

Before addressing whether we should seek alternatives to legislative veto, I must first state that I have long opposed the adoption and use of this device. My opposition is based on several factors and would apply to most other "quick-fix" mechanisms that would somehow seek to short circuit the regular constitutional legislative process.

First, such alternatives encourage Congress to avoid setting clear national policy when it delegates statutory authority in the first place. The tough political choices are simply avoided and pushed to the end of what is often a long and complex decision-making process. I believe Congress should make these choices, and make them clearly, at the time the statutory authority is originally delegated.

Second, the proliferation of alternatives to legislative veto will necessarily result in an increase in congressional staff. If the Congress seeks to perform the functions of the Executive, it will find it necessary to duplicate the staff of the Executive. Rather than creating greater political accountability, one of the stated goals of legislative veto, such duplication actually reduces political accountability. With both the executive branch and Congress involved in a particular decision, neither branch will be truly responsible for that decision. Moreover, a congressional bureaucracy will not necessarily be more expert or enlightened than the executive bureaucracy that already exists.

Third, the original purposes of most delegations of statutory authority, particularly in the area of regulations, were to assure that a decision would be made only after expert evaluation of the facts, and to assure that due process would be afforded to affected groups and individuals. Legislative veto and its alternatives threaten the integrity of this process by opening it to special interest pleading and political pressure. They invite closed-door dealings with Members of Congress or their staffs, with decision being made on the basis of power, not facts.

Fourth, legislative veto and its alternatives necessarily plunge an already overburdened Congress into a morass of Executive and administrative decisions, ranging from such matters as the amount of pulp required for lemon juice to the safety procedures for nuclear powerplants. While each of these issues is important in its own context, one of the main reasons for delegations of authority in the first place was that Congress lacked the time to deal with the complex and necessarily detailed matters involved in implementing the law. Congressional involvement in all such decisions will deny Congress the time it needs to concentrate on the broad domestic and foreign policy issues which only it can address.

Fifth, legislative veto type devices add another time-consuming step to the decisionmaking process. Such delay can itself impose significant burdens. For example, the failure to promptly issue regulations can prevent businesses from making vital decisions on such matters as redesignating products or making capital investments to modernize facilities. Delay can also make it difficult for State and local governments to administer federally mandated programs effectively.

Finally, legislative veto type devices make it difficult to implement laws advancing the common good. While the beneficiaries of a law are generally dispersed through the population, those who must directly comply with the law are often a clearly identifiable group with a specific interest in how a law is implemented. Such groups frequently have a strong incentive to prevent aggressive implementation. For example, under a statute which mandates a decrease in air pollution, an agency might issue regulations that require costly capital investment to install smokestack scrubbers. Manufacturers would like to avoid these expenditures. They might bring pressure on Congress to veto the regulation—raising every objection from increased unemployment to balance-of-payment problems. Each of these is a legitimate concern for Congress to consider in setting national environmental policy. However, if Congress responds serially to each such concern, the law that was enacted for the common good can be gutted by congressional rejection of any specific implementation.

Legislative veto was aimed at the end point of the decisionmaking process. It short circuited the regular legislative process. It did not require a careful balancing of facts, interest, and equities—it simply said "no" to whatever the Executive had decided. It did not require any clear assessment of the situation or any choice of contending policies, but it did give Congress the appearance of decisiveness and control.

In view of my position on legislative veto, it comes as no surprise that I generally oppose adopting new devices or mechanisms to replace the original forms of legislative veto. However, I do believe that Congress must address the situation resulting from the *Chadha* decision.

Congress must first concern itself with statutory delegations that are subject to unconstitutional legislative veto provisions. The major problem involved here is that of severability. Each statutory provision subject to legislative veto must be examined to determine whether the Congress wishes to continue the delegation without the limitation of a legislative veto.

This process should be undertaken as expeditiously as possible, because there now is doubt as to the validity of the legal obligations imposed by these statutes. Congress must determine whether to continue these delegations, perhaps with specific limitations and guidelines, or whether to entirely rescind the authority.

Only when this immediate and rather urgent task is accomplished should Congress consider alternatives to legislative veto.

It is my view that before searching alternatives, Congress should carefully examine the modern relationship between the executive and legislative branches in the light of separation of powers and effective Government process. I believe this examination will demonstrate that it is unnecessary to adopt new mechanisms of congressional control. The political clout and legislative authority of Congress have not been measurably diminished by the loss of a mechanism that, perhaps with the exception of the areas of overlapping constitutional responsibilities, was very poor policy in the first place. Congress already has effective, constitutional means to insure that the laws are fully implemented.

What is needed is for Congress to exercise more effectively the power it currently possesses.

First, Congress should be more careful with the laws it enacts. In new statutes, Congress can legislate with greater specificity and clearer standards, making in the beginning the hard political choices that it has often avoided through broad delegations with vague standards. Congress can also reexamine existing statutes from a more exacting perspective. If the purposes of these statutes are not being met, or if delegated authority is being improperly used, Congress can legislate to clarify, limit, or, if necessary, withdraw the delegation.

Second, Congress can delegate authority to the executive branch for limited periods of time. This will require the executive branch to justify the renewal of statutes or programs otherwise scheduled for termination. It will also give Congress an opportunity to require a change in executive implementation of the delegated authority, if experience shows that change is necessary.

Third, Congress can direct that certain Executive decisions may not go into effect until it has had a set time to review the decision. This would allow Congress to pass legislation to override Executive decisions before they take effect. These "report and wait" provisions have been used effectively in the past, and in the Rules Enabling Act to which I referred earlier. However, in my view, this approach should be limited to major decisions that need not go into effect immediately and that occur only occasionally, such as executive branch reorganizations.

Fourth, Congress has final say over the Government's pocketbook. Congress can use the appropriations process to direct or prohibit the expenditure of funds for a particular purpose. This is a powerful tool because the President and agencies are unlikely to risk consistently incurring wrath by the controller of the pocketbook. Experience has shown that accommodations with the executive branch are often possible before direct action through the appropriations process is necessary.

Fifth, the Senate must confirm the appointment of high-level Presidential appointees (article II, section 2, clause 2). Under the Constitution, this is a final, unreviewable power. In a confrontation with the President over the execution of the law, the Senate can disapprove an appointment until a certain condition is satisfied or it can withhold its approval until it extracts a commitment that the law will be executed in a specified manner.

Sixth, Congress can impeach executive branch officials. The House of Representatives and the Senate together hold the power to remove from office executive branch officers who fail to carry out the duties of office in a proper manner. This is a drastic remedy, but it can be used if necessary.

Finally, Congress must face the defects in its own organization, where numerous committees and subcommittees have overlapping jurisdiction that makes effective legislative oversight weak, fragmented, and, at times, contradictory. Reform of the committee system could lead to enhanced congressional power and more efficient government.

Ultimately, if the Executive is acting in an unauthorized or excessive manner, Congress can restrain and redirect it. The question is not one of power, but one of will. Congress has the power to shape national government and policy; the question is whether it has the will to do so.

QUESTIONS FOR DISCUSSION

1. Does the absence of a legislative veto necessarily mean greater conflict between the president and Congress? Why?

2. To what extent was the legislative veto a device that allowed Congress to be less accountable for its actions?

3. What alternatives does Congress have to the legislative veto as a check upon the bureaucracy?

4. Did the *Chadha* decision weaken Congress' ability to oversee administration? Why?

5. Why did the enactment of legislative veto provisions in different laws increase so rapidly in the 1970s?

SUGGESTED READINGS

"Controversy over the Legislative Veto: Pro & Con," *Congressional Digest* (Dec. 1983), whole issue.

DECONCINI, DENNIS, AND ROBERT FAUCHER, "The Legislative Veto: A Constitutional Amendment," *Harvard Journal on Legislation*, 21 (Winter 1984), 29–59.

FISHER, LOUIS, "Judicial Misjudgments About the Legislative Veto Case," *Public Administration Review*, 45 (Nov. 1985), 705–11.

GILMOUR, ROBERT S., AND BARBARA HINKSON CRAIG, "After the Congressional Veto: Assessing the Alternatives," *Journal of Policy Analysis and Management*, 3 (Spring 1984), 373–92.

LEVITAS, ELLIOTT H., AND STANLEY M. BRAND, "The Post Legislative Veto Response: A Call to Legislative Arms," *Hofstra Law Journal*, 12 (Spring 1984), 593–616.

OLSON, THEODORE B., "Restoring the Separation of Powers, "*Regulation* (July/Aug. 1983), 19–22, 27–30.

SUNDQUIST, JAMES L., "The Legislative Veto: A

Bounced Check," *Brookings Review*, 2 (Fall 1983), 13–16.

U. S. CONGRESS, HOUSE, *Legislative Veto After Chadha*, Hearings before the Committee on Rules, 98th Cong., 2nd Sess., 1984.

U. S. CONGRESS, SENATE, *Congressional Review of Agency Rules*, Hearing before the Subcommittee on Administrative Practice and Procedure of the Committee on the Judiciary, 98th Cong., 2nd Sess., 1984.

U. S. CONGRESS, SENATE, *Constitutional Amendment to Restore Legislative Veto*, Hearing before the Subcommittee on the Constitution of the Committee on the Judiciary, 98th Cong., 2nd Sess., 1984.

U. S. CONGRESS, SENATE, *Rulemaking Procedures Reform Act of 1985*, Hearing before the Subcommittee on Administrative Practice and Procedure of the Committee on the Judiciary, 99th Cong., 1st Sess., 1985.

5   YES
SHOULD INDEPENDENT AGENCIES RESIST CONGRESSIONAL INVESTIGATIONS IN ORDER TO PROTECT CONFIDENTIALITY?

Fighting Off Congress: A Bill of Rights for the Independent Agency
Bruce E. Fein

I.

Independent government agencies are frequently confronted with demands from congressional committees for agency records or testimony that would reveal confidential adjudicatory, investigatory, or rulemaking deliberations or information. These demands are ordinarily constitutionally irreproachable if actuated by a reasonable suspicion of government corruption or maladministration. As the Supreme Court explained in upholding a congressional inquiry into alleged wrongdoing in the Department of Justice:

> . . . the subject to be investigated was the administration of the Department of Justice —whether its functions were being properly discharged or were being neglected or misdirected, and whether the Attorney General and his assistants were performing or neglecting their duties in respect of the institutions and the prosecution of proceedings to punish crimes and enforce appropriate remedies against the wrongdoers; specific instances of alleged neglect being recited. Plainly the subject was one on which legislation could be had and would be materially aided by the information which the investigation was calculated to elicit.[1]

Congressional power to investigate allegations of crime or misconduct, however, is bounded. That power cannot defeat the need for confidentiality in the performance of executive functions by other branches of government unless a compelling demonstration is made that a breach of confidentiality

"is critical to the performance of [Congresses'] legislative functions."[2]

In addition to investigating allegations of criminal conduct or improprieties, congressional committees, occasionally imperiously insist on disclosure of confidential agency information or seek to examine the mental processes of a commissioner in order to influence the outcome of a pending adjudication, investigation, or rulemaking proceeding. Political annals have also recorded occasions where committees have sought confidential records to embarrass an agency, thereby fostering an atmosphere of agency docility toward committee importunings.

Our constitutional architects anticipated such aggrandizing demarches of Congress against other branches of government. As James Madison remonstrated in the *Federalist Papers*:

> The legislative department is everywhere extending the sphere of its activity and drawing all power into its impetuous vortex . . . its constitutional power being at once more extensive, and less susceptible of precise limits, it can, with greater facility, mask, under complicated and indirect measures, the encroachments it makes on the coordinate departments.[3]

Accordingly, the Framers embraced principles of separation of powers in delimiting the powers of the federal government as a constitutional mainstay primarily against abuses of legislative authority.[4] Un-

---

From Bruce E. Fein, "Fighting Off Congress: A Bill of Rights for the Independent Agency," *District Lawyer*, 8 (Nov./Dec. 1983), pp. 37–42. Reprinted with permission.
[1]*McGrain* v. *Daugherty*, 273 U.S. 135, 177 (1927).

[2]*Senate Select Committee* v. *Nixon*, 498 F.2d 725, 732 (D.C. Cir. 1974).
[3]*The Federalist* No. 48 (J. Madison) at 157 (J.S. Mills ed. 1952).
[4]*See* 2 Farrand 1937, *The Records of the Federal Convention of 1787*, at 74, where James Madison, at the Constitutional Convention, declared:

der these principles, the court explained in *Nixon v. Administrator of General Services*,[5] Congress is foreclosed from obstructing the accomplishment of functions constitutionally assigned to other branches of government.

Fearful of Congress' formidable oversight and appropriations powers, independent agencies have historically complied with alacrity to any congressional committee request for information, confidential or otherwise. Comprehensive research unearthed only five occasions where an independent agency successfully resisted congressional information demands. All involved the Securities and Exchange Commission and the withholding of investigatory files. A recent survey of the independent agencies[6] confirms that unquestioning obedience to congressional demands for agency records is a practice as constant as the north star in contemporary times. An agency typically justifies such supine behavior on the theory that it is an "arm of Congress," and thus is legally defenseless against any congressional probing. Since Congress by statute created independent agencies, it is said, Congress is legitimately entitled to exercise unbounded supervision and

control over their functions. That reasoning cannot withstand scrutiny.

Congress, by the exercise of legislative power, is also the parent of all executive branch departments or agencies, such as the Department of Defense or the Environmental Protection Agency. All lower federal courts are likewise the offspring of congressional legislative action, and can be abolished by repeal of pertinent statutes.[7] Notwithstanding their statutory dependence on Congress, executive departments and the federal judiciary are constitutionally protected from congressional obstruction in discharging their respective legal responsibilities.[8] It seems beyond constitutional cavil, for example, that Congress could not compel disclosure of internal deliberative materials of federal courts regarding adjudications, at least when no wrongdoing or maladministration is reasonably suspected.[9]

It might be argued, however, that unfettered congressional access to confidential, deliberative or investigatory records of agencies is permissible if continued secrecy of the information is pledged. Congressional maintenance of confidentality, it might be said, would prevent any obstruction of an agency's adjudicatory, investigatory, or rulemaking proceedings. The answer to this argument has several components.

All branches of the federal government are crowned with only limited powers. Congress lacks constitutional authority to investigate matters over which it cannot legislate. As Justice Harlan elaborated in *Barenblatt* v. *United States*:

> The scope of the power of inquiry in short, is as penetrating and far-reaching as the potential

---

Experience in all the States had evinced a powerful tendency in the Legislature to absorb all power into its vortex. This was the real source of danger to the American Constitution; and suggested the necessity of giving every defensive authority to the other departments that was consistent with republican principles.

See also Id. at 299, 300, 407, 428, 551. *The Federalist* No. 48 (J. Madison) at 157 (J.S. Mills ed. 1952), further states: "[I]t is against the enterprising ambition of this department that the people ought to indulge all their jealousy and exhaust all their precautions. . . ." Moreover, *The Federalist* No. 49 elaborates that: "[T]he tendency of a republican government is to aggrandisement of the legislative at the expense of the other departments." *Id.* at 160.

[5]433 U.S. 425, 442–443 (1977).

[6]This informal survey encompassed the following independent agencies: Civil Aeronautics Board, Commission on Civil Rights, Commodity Futures Trading Commission, Consumer Product Safety Commission, Equal Employment Opportunity Commission, Federal Communications Commission, Federal Election Commission, Federal Energy Regulatory Commission, Federal Maritime Commission, Federal Reserve System, Federal Trade Commission, International Trade Commission, Interstate Commerce Commission, Merit Systems Protection Board, National Labor Relations Board and Occupational Safety and Health Review Commission.

[7]*See Stuart* v. *Laird*, 5 U.S.. (1 Cranch) 299 (1803).

[8]*Nixon* v. *Administrator of General Services*, 433 U.S. 425 (1977); *United States* v. *Nixon*, 418 U.S. 683 (1974); *Senate Select Committee* v. *Nixon*, 498 F.2d 725 (D.C. Cir. 1974).

[9]*Senate Select Committee* v. *Nixon*, 498 F.2d 725, 729 (D.C. Cir. 1974). *See also United States* v. *Morgan*, 313 U.S. 409, 422–423 (1941), where the Supreme Court elaborated:

> It will bear repeating that although the administrative process has had a different development and pursues somewhat different ways from those of the courts, they are to be deemed collaborative instrumentalities of justice and the appropriate independence of each should be respected by the other.

power to enact and appropriate under the constitution. Broad as it is, the power is not, however, without limitations. Since Congress may only investigate into those areas which it may potentially legislate or appropriate, it cannot inquire into matters that are exclusively the concern of the judiciary. Neither can it supplant the executive in what exclusively belongs to the executive. And Congress, in common with all branches of the government, must exercise its powers subject to the limitations placed by the constitution on governmental action, more particularly in the context of this case the relevant limitations of the Bill of Rights.[10]

When an agency adjudicates, investigates, or issues a rule pursuant to a statute, it is involved in the execution or administration of a law. Separation of powers principles would denounce any endeavor by Congress by statute to direct an agency as to how particular statutes should be administered.[11] It would be unconstitutional, for instance, for Congress to enact a statute directing an agency to institute enforcement proceeding against designated parties.[12]

Of course, Congress possesses legislative power to repeal, codify, or alter any rule promulgated by an agency.[13] But this power does not undermine the

---

[10]360 U.S. 109, 111 (1959).

[11]See Buckley v. Valeo, 424 U.S. 1, 121–122 (1976) (per curiam).

[12]Such a statute would unconstitutionally arrogate the executive function of how laws should be enforced (See United States v. Nixon, 418 U.S. 683 (1974); United States v. Cox, 342 F.2d 167 (5th Cir. 1965)), and might also constitute a prohibited bill of attainder (See United States v. Lovett, 328 U.S. 303 (1946); United States v. Brown, 381 U.S. 437 (1965); Ex parte Garland, 71 U.S. (4 Wall.) 333 (1867); Cummings v. Missouri, 71 U.S. (4 Wall.) 277 (1867)).

[13]For example, Congress directed the Consumer Product Safety Commission to amend its standards for walk-behind power lawn mowers. See Omnibus Budget Reconciliation Act of 1981 (Pub. L. 97–35, 95 Stat. 357, signed by the President on August 13, 1981). The Commission standard originally required that a mower blade stop within 3 seconds of the release of the handle and that mowers with only manual starting controls must stop the blade without stopping the engine. The statute provides that a lawn mower with only manual starting controls which meet the requirement of the present standard except that the blade control system stops the blade by stopping the engine, shall be allowed if 1) the engine starting controls for the lawn mower are located within 24 inches of the top of the mower's handle, or 2) the mower has a protective foot shield which extends 360 degrees around the mower housing. The Commission amended its standard accordingly. See 46 Fed. Reg. 54932 (Nov. 5, 1981); 16 C.F.R. § 1205.5(9)(1)(iv).

Moreover, in 1974 Congress enacted the Motor Vehicle and Schoolbus Safety Amendments of 1974, Pub. L. No. 93–492, §109, 88 Stat. 1482 (codified at 15 U.S.C. § 1410b) in response to public disapproval of the ignition interlock system ordained by the Department of Transportation. The statute: 1) banned any federal motor vehicle safety standard requiring ignition interlocks or continuous buzzers to warn that seatbelts were not in use (15 U.S.C. § 1410b (b)(1)) and 2) sharply reduced DOT's discretion to modify Standard 2098, 37 Fed. Reg. 3911 (Feb. 24, 1972), in the future. If a modified standard could be sat-

isfied by any system other than seatbelts only, the amended safety standard would have to be submitted to Congress where it might be vetoed by concurrent resolution of both houses. 15 U.S.C. § 1410b (b)(2). A new mandatory passive restraint regulation was issued by DOT in 1977. See 42 Fed. Reg. 34, 289 (July 5, 1977). This regulation, ordered a "phasing-in" of passive restraints based on vehicle size, beginning with large cars manufactured for the 1982 model year and extending to all cars being manufactured for the 1984 model year. See 42 C.F.R. §571.208. Although Congress did not exercise the legislative veto provision of the 1974 amendments, it attached riders to appropriations bills for 1979 and 1980 that prohibited DOT from implementing the passive restraint standards in those years. Pub. L. No. 95–335, § 317, 92 Stat. 435, 450 (1978); Pub. L. No. 96–131, § 317, Stat. 1023, 1039 (1979).

Congress also overruled anticipated agency rulemaking in the Saccharin Study Labeling Act. Pub. L. No. 95–203, 91 Stat. 1451 (1977). On March 9, 1977, the Food and Drug Administration (FDA) announced its intention to propose a ban on the use of saccharin, the only artificial, non-nutritive sweetener then available in the United States, on the basis of a study sponsored by the Canadian government which showed that saccharin, when fed in high doses to rats, causes bladder cancer. Under the provisions of the Delaney Amendment, 72 Stat. 1784, 21 U.S.C. § 321 (1958), of the Federal Food, Drug and Cosmetic Act of 1938, as amended, Pub. L. No. 87–781, 76 Stat. 781 (1962), any food additive which is shown to cause cancer in man or animals must be banned. The FDA proposal to ban saccharin evoked a storm of public interest, and in 1977 Congress enacted the Saccharin Study Labeling Act which, inter alia, prohibited the Secretary of Health, Education, and Welfare from taking action with regard to saccharin for eighteen months.

Congress enacted the Clear Air Act Amendments of 1977, Pub. L. No. 95–95, 91 Stat. 685 (signed by the President on August 7, 1977), which: 1) delayed an auto emission standards for 1980 and 1981 model year automobiles; 2) set new standards to protect areas with clean air from experiencing a deterioration of air quality; and 3) extended previously set deadlines for air quality standards for most cities and industries. As a result, the Environ-

principle that there is no constitutionally legitimate reason for Congress to inquire into confidential, deliberative or investigatory materials of an agency, absent reasons to suspect misconduct or corruption the disclosure of which is critical to vindicating a legislative function.[14]

Furthermore, inadvertent, contrived, or ingenuous public disclosures of confidential information submitted to Congress is a commonplace of American political life. Pledges of congressional confidentiality, therefore, are oceans apart from ironclad guarantees of secrecy. Moreover, such pledges are constitutionally unenforceable. The Supreme Court has established that a member of Congress is beyond the judicial power under the Speech and Debate Clause if he reads materials into the public record during a congressional hearing. In *Gravel* v. *U.S.*, the court declared that Senator Gravel was shielded from executive or judicial scrutiny for placing 47 volumes of the Pentagon Papers into the public record during a subcommittee meeting.[15]

---

mental Protection Agency amended its regulations which limit the lead content of gasoline, in order to exempt small refiners in conformance with the instructions in the Clean Air Act Amendments of 1977. *See* 42 U.S.C. §§ 7413(d), 7601 (August 1, 1979).

Under the Federal Mine Safety and Health Act of 1977, Pub. L. No. 95–164, 91 Stat. 1211 and 1299 (1977), Congress transferred the responsibilities of the Secretary of the Interior under Section 101 of the Federal Coal Mine Health and Safety Act of 1969, Pub. L. No. 91–173, to the Secretary of Labor on March 9, 1978. In order to be consistent with Section 202(e) of the Federal Mine Safety and Health Act of 1977, the Department of Labor amended its mandatory health standards, Title 30, Code of Federal Regulations, Part 70, as to the definition of respirable dust and the procedures for sampling respirable dust in underground coal mines. Included in these amendments are revised requirements for certification of persons conducting sampling of respirable dust and calibrating sampling equipment. This rule also amended the definition of respirable dust in Parts 11, 71, 75, and 90.

Also, in response to congressional edict, the Environmental Protection Agency amended Title 40, Code of Federal Regulations, by adding a new Part 25, which sets forth minimum requirements and suggested program elements for public participation and activities under the Clean Water Act, Pub. L. No. 95–217 (1977), the Resource Conservation and Recovery Act, Pub. L. No. 94–580 (1976), and the Safe Drinking Water Act, Pub. L. No. 93–523 (1974). *See* 44 Fed. Reg. 10292 (February 16, 1979).

[14]*Senate Select Committee* v. *Nixon,* 498 F.2d 725, 731 (D.C. Cir. 1974).

[15]408 U.S. 606, 615–626 (1971).

To summarize, despite the lack of any customary practice or unequivocal judicial precedent, sound constitutional theories can be expounded to resist illegitimate congressional intrusion into an independent agency's adjudicatory, investigatory, or rulemaking processes. When an illegitimate request is made by a committee, the agency must shoulder the burden of articulating the basis of a constitutional privilege in order to justify withholding documents or to resist answering certain categories of questions. Analogous to the executive privilege, the agency constitutional privilege is qualified and can be surmounted in special circumstances. As the claim of executive privilege to confidentiality of communications must yield to reasonable judicial needs to try allegations of criminal activity,[16] Congress can override the assertion of the independent agency privilege by articulating a reasonable foundation for suspecting agency maladministration or misconduct and a critical legislative need for disclosure.[17]

The need for independent agency privilege is at its zenith when Congress seeks to unbosom confidential materials pertinent to a pending adjudication, investigation, or rulemaking. Many harms to agency functions ascribable to disclosure of confidential or deliberative information would be substantially ameliorated if Congress desists from invoking its oversight powers regarding particular proceedings until they are definitively concluded. Nevertheless, if no legitimate legislative purpose for congressional intrusion into an agency's past confidential deliberations or investigations exists, an agency is entitled to deny disclosure in order to vindicate venerable separation of powers principles.

II.

When Congress obstructs an agency's discharge of its adjudicatory functions by employing its investigatory or oversight powers to influence the outcome of a particular proceeding, twin constitutional in-

---

[16]*United States* v. *Nixon,* 418 U.S. 683, 708, 712–713 (1974); *Nixon* v. *Sirica,* 487 F.2d 700, 717 (D.C. Cir. 1973).

[17]*See* *McGrain* v. *Daugherty,* 273 U.S. 135, 177 (1927); *Senate Select Committee* v. *Nixon,* 498 F.2d 725, 731 (D.C. Cir. 1974).

fractions are perpetrated. A litigant before an in-dependent agency is endowed with constitutional due process right to have his case adjudicated without the stain of congressional hectoring or interference. This constitutional right may be invoked by an agency to fend off improper congressional probing.[18]

In *Pillsbury* v. *FTC*,[19] the Federal Trade Commission issued a complaint against Pillsbury charging that two acquisitions violated Section 7 of the Clayton Act. During the pendency of the case, the Senate and House Judiciary Committees held hearings to explore pertinent legal theories that the Commission might invoke in its decisionmaking process. The Chairman of the Commission, several members of his staff, and the General Counsel appeared before the committees and were exhorted by committee members to apply a disputed legal doctrine that would condemn *per se* the Pillsbury acquisitions if they substantially increased Pillsbury's relevant market share. Protracted congressional questioning specifically focused on the Pillsbury case, sought to explore the mental processes of the FTC Chairman regarding the relevant law and evidence, and demonstrated animosity toward any Commission ruling that might exonerate the acquisition.

Several years after the congressional grilling, the FTC held Pillsbury's acquisitions unlawful under the Clayton Act. The Court of Appeals reversed, holding that the congressional committee hearings constitutionally tainted the FTC adjudicatory process. Writing for a unanimous panel, Chief Judge Tuttle maintained:

[C]ommon justice to a litigant requires that we invalidate the order entered by a quasi-judicial tribunal that was importuned by members of the United States Senate, however innocent they intended their conduct to be, to arrive at a conclusion which they did reach.[20]

Congress, Judge Tuttle insisted, lacked authority to intervene in an agency's judicial function:

[W]hen [a congressional] investigation focuses directly and substantially upon the mental decisional processes of a commission in a case which is pending before it, Congress is no longer intervening in the agency's legislative function, but rather, in its judicial function. At this latter point, we become concerned with the right of private litigants to a fair trial, and, equally important, with their right to the appearance of impartiality which cannot be maintained unless those who exercise the judicial function are free from powerful external influence.[21]

The *Pillsbury* decision is in accord with the longstanding doctrine of *United States* v. *Morgan* which frowns on any attempt by either the Judiciary or Congress to force disclosure of the deliberative process by which an agency adjudicatory or rule-making body or individual reached a decision.[22] Such intimate probing, the Supreme Court acknowledged in *Morgan*, would be destructive of adjudicatory or executive responsibilities.[23]

It might be argued that congressional violation

---

[18]In *Singleton* v. *Wulff*, 428 U.S. 106, 114–118 (1976), the Court concluded that a litigant may advance the constitutional rights of a third party where there are genuine obstacles to the direct assertion of the rights, the litigant is the best available spokesman, and the rights are inextricably bound to the activities the litigant wishes to pursue or resist. It would be difficult, if not impossible, for the subject of an adjudicatory hearing to seek an injunction against an agency's disclosure of confidential adjudicatory information to Congress that could taint the proceeding. The subject might be unaware of such a request, and Speech and Debate Clause problems would bedevil any claim to an injunction against Congress. *See Eastland* v. *United States Servicemen's Fund*, 421 U.S. 491, 507 (1975). Moreover, an agency would have the same interest as the subject of the adjudication to issue a constitutionally justified ruling in the first instance.

[19]354 F.2d 952 (5th Cir. 1966).

[20]*Id.* at 963.

[21]*Id.* at 964.

[22]313 U.S. 409, 422 (1941).

[23]*Id.* at 422–23. The Supreme Court held that:

[T]he Secretary should never have been subjected to this examination. The proceeding before the Secretary 'has a quality resembling that of a judicial proceeding'. *Morgan* v. *United States*, 298 U.S. 468, 480, 56 S.Ct. 906, 911, 80 L.Ed. 1288. Such an examination of a judge would be destructive of judicial responsibility. We have explicitly held in this very ligitation that 'it was not the function of the court to probe the mental processes of the Secretary'. 304 U.S. 1, 18, 58 S.Ct. 773, 776, 82 L.Ed. 1129. Just as a judge cannot be subjected to such a scrutiny, compare *Fayerweather* v. *Ritch*, 195 U.S. 276, 306, 307, 25 S.Ct. 58, 67, 49 L.Ed. 193, so the integrity of the administrative process must be equally respected.

of the due process rights of litigants before agencies can be corrected on appeal,[24] and thus the agency is unprivileged to resist such unconstitutional gambits. But the Supreme Court unequivocally held in *Ward* v. *Village of Monroeville*,[25] that litigants are entitled in the first instance to a trial before a disinterested and impartial judicial officer under the Due Process Clause of the Fourteenth Amendment.[26] The guarantee of an untainted *de novo* trial in a second proceeding, the Court asserted, cannot rectify any unconstitutional bias in the first proceeding. Accordingly, neither an agency nor litigants before it are required to capitulate to a congressional assault on due process rights before launching defensive action under the banner of the Constitution.

A second constitutional theory for protecting the confidentiality of an agency's adjudicatory processes emerges from the celebrated *Chadha*[27] decision. Congress created in the Administrative Procedure Act[28] a statutory right to impartial agency adjudications unsullied by external interference. The Act stands as a fortress against any attempt by Congress to undermine the policy of adjudicatory impartiality and independence, absent the exercise of legislative power that would repeal or modify this standard. As the Supreme Court explained in *Chadha*, to exercise such legislative power requires affirmative action on a bill by both houses of Congress and its presentation to the President for his approval or veto. A vote by a congressional committee or a single house of Congress to invade the Administrative Procedure Act standard of adjudicatory neutrality through subpoenas, interrogation of agency adjudicators, or otherwise would flout the *Chadha* doctrine that such policy departures from an existing

statute must surmount the procedural requirements for enacting legislation.

The conclusion that independent agencies may assert a constitutional shield to assure the confidentiality of its adjudicatory proceedings is strengthened by analogy to Article I Courts. Article III of the Constitution entrusts the judicial power of the United States to Article III Judges with life tenure and protection against reduced compensation. Congress, however, may also create so-called Article I or "Legislative" Courts to adjudicate in specialized areas that also fall within the constitutional jurisdiction of Article III Courts. The United States Tax Court and Territorial Courts are illustrative of Article I Courts. Article I Judges lack any constitutional guarantee of life tenure and safeguard against reduced salary.[29] When independent agencies exercise their quasi-judicial powers, they function as veritable Article I Courts. The agencies thus should be armed with a constitutional privilege as formidable as that wielded by Article I Courts to insure against compromising independence and impartiality in the adjudicatory process through congressional investigations or oversight.

III.

Independent agencies, as the Supreme Court recognized in *FTC* v. *Ruberoid Co.*,[30] possess an ill-defined constitutional status. In that case, the court observed:

> The use of administrative bodies probably has been the most significant legal trend of the last century and perhaps more values today are affected by their decisions than by those of all the courts, review of administration decisions apart. They also have begun to have important consequences on personal rights. Cf. *United States* v. *Spector*, 343 U.S. 169. 72 S. CT. 591. They have become a veritable fourth branch of government which has deranged our three-branch legal theories . . . administrative agencies have been called quasi-legislative, quasi-executive or quasi-judicial, as the occasion required, in order

[24]Gelford, *Judicial Limitation of Congressional Influence on Administrative Agencies*, 73 Nw.U.L. Rev. 931, 936–937 (1979).

[25]409 U.S. 57 (1972).

[26]*Id.* at 61–62.

[27]*Immigration and Naturalization Service* v. *Chadha*, 51 U.S.L.W. 4907 (June 23, 1983). The Supreme Court clearly concluded that the *Chadha* decision was applicable to independent agencies by its summary affirmances in *Consumers Union, Inc.* v. *Federal Trade Commission*, 51 U.S.L.W. 3935 (June 28, 1983) and *Consumers Energy Council of America* v. *Federal Energy Regulatory Commission*, 51 U.S.L.W. 3935 (June 28, 1983).

[28]5 U.S.C. § 551 *et seq.*

[29]*Northern Pipeline Construction Co.* v. *Marathon Pipe Line Co.*, 458 U.S. 50,—S. Ct.—, 73 L.Ed. 2d 598, 625 at n.39, 637 (1982).

[30]343 U.S. 470 (1952).

to validate their functions within the separation-of-powers scheme of the constitution.[31]

Whether exercising quasi-legislative, quasi-executive, or quasi-judicial power, independent agencies invariably act to administer their charter and related statutes. Illustrative of this conceptual taxonomy would be divergent enforcement tools that the Securities and Exchange Commission might unfurl to enforce the statutory prohibition against securities fraud etched in Section 10(b)(5) of the Securities Exchange Act. The Commission could issue a rule delineating with specificity the scope of the statutory proscriptions. Such an endeavor would fall within the *Ruberoid* concept of quasi-legislative action. The Commission could also investigate and determine to prosecute alleged violations of the statute or implementing rules. This exercise of authority would be characterized as quasi-executive. The Commission could further adjudicate a complaint charging a statutory or rule violation. In so doing, the Commission would be performing a quasi-judicial function. The conceptual unity of the three courses of action open to the SEC pursuant to Section 10(b)(5) is that all represent methods of administering or enforcing the statute.

As James Madison observed in *Federalist 47*, an essential function of the Constitution's separation of powers was to foreclose the possibility that Congress would combine law making with law enforcement or administration. Lionizing the ageless wisdom of Montesquieu, Madison lauded one of the former's political maxims:

> When the legislative and executive powers are united in the same person or body, there can be no liberty, because apprehensions may arise lest *the same* Monarch or Senate should *enact* tyrannical laws to *execute* them in a tyrannical manner.

The Supreme Court, in *Buckley* v. *Valeo*,[32] expounded on the government task that separation of powers principles intended to deny to Congress in order to prevent the dangerous marriage of law making with law administration or execution. *Buckley* involved a challenge to the constitutionality of a congressionally dominated Federal Election Commission entrusted with various powers relating to the enforcement of the Federal Election Campaign Act.

The Commission was made the principal repository of numerous reports and statements required to be filed by those engaging in regulated political activities. Commission duties regarding this information included filing and indexing, making it available for public inspection, preservation and auditing and field investigations.

Beyond these recordkeeping, disclosure, and investigative functions, the Commission was endowed with extensive rulemaking and adjudicatory powers, including the issuance of substantive policy rules, advisory opinions regarding possible campaign law violations, and the adjudication of alleged violations. The Commission was further authorized to institute lawsuits in federal courts to enforce the Campaign Act and to administer provisions for presidential campaign financing.

The Court held that the congressionally controlled FEC could not constitutionally exercise functions with respect to the Commission's task of fleshing out the statute, namely, promulgating rules or issuing advisory opinions. Likewise, functions necessary to ensure compliance with the statute and rules—informal procedures, administrative determinations and hearings, and civil suits,—could not constitutionally be entrusted to a Commission dominated by Congress. The cornerstone of the Court's reasoning was that such an amalgamation of power by the legislature would mock the separation of powers prophylactic against the combination of law making with law administration.[33]

The *Buckley* decision seemingly establishes that Congress lacks any legitimate constitutional interest in seeking to control or dominate an agency rulemaking proceeding by forcing disclosure of confidential agency deliberations or records. Rulemaking, the court in *Buckley* suggested, constitutes administration of a statute that cannot constitutionally be held subservient to congressional power. Thus, Congress has no rightful interest in obtaining access to the confidential rulemaking deliberations of an independent agency, unless credible charges of corruption or improprieties have been alleged. Otherwise, Congress could hobble an agency's

---

[31]*Id.* at 487.
[32]424 U.S. 1 (1976) (per curiam).

[33]*Id.* at 139–143.

rulemaking functions by chilling candor and a robust exchange of views among Commission members and staff.[34]

The decision in *Texas Medical Association* v. *Mathews*[35] rebuking efforts by members of Congress to influence an HEW policy pronouncement in administering a statute reinforces the view that any attempt by the legislature to inject itself into agency rulemaking is legally suspect. At issue in *Texas Medical* was a regulation promulgated by the Secretary of Health, Education and Welfare under the Professional Standards Review Organization (PSRO) Stat-

ute of 1972. The regulation divided the State of Texas into nine PSRO areas, despite an overwhelming expert consensus that a single statewide PSRO would be preferable. Evidence adduced at trial showed that the Secretary's questioned regulation represented a volte-face from a preliminary policy statement made by a subordinate official of HEW. The Secretary's preference for multiple PSRO units in Texas emerged in the aftermath of extensive discussions between HEW employees, Senator Bennett, and a senior staff member of the Senate Finance Committee, which exercised jurisdiction over HEW's budget. The Senator and Committee staff member unflaggingly insisted that both the law and enlightened policy precluded any statewide PSRO unit in Texas.

The District Court held the PSRO regulation invalid under the Administrative Procedure Act as not in accordance with law. Applying an administrative law doctrine that agency action is invalid if based, even in part, on succumbing to congressional pressure,[36] the Court concluded that the steely exhortations from Senator Bennett and the Senate Finance Committee staff had tainted the Secretary's decisionmaking process regarding the PSRO regulation. The *Texas Medical* decision and kindred cases[37] support the principle that Congress is legally foreclosed from interference with confidential agency rulemaking or policy deliberations undertaken in the course of administering statutes.

Independent agency investigations of alleged

---

[34]The Government in the Sunshine Act, 5 U.S.C. § 552b, does not undermine this conclusion. The statute generally requires agencies, subject to enumerated exceptions, to conduct open meetings when deliberations involve a quorum or "at least the number of individual agency members required to take action on behalf of the agency," and where "such deliberations determine or result in the joint conduct or disposition of agency business." 5 U.S.C. § 552b(a). Commission or Board members are ordinarily able to engage in confidential rulemaking deliberations, notwithstanding the Sunshine Act, by communicating with their staffs or with other members on a bilateral basis because in such circumstances a quorum does not obtain. Rulemaking deliberations involving three member agencies, such as the Federal Home Loan Bank Board, Federal Deposit Insurance Corporation, Federal Labor Relations Authority, or National Credit Union Administration, cannot employ these arrangements to protect confidentiality in rulemaking proceedings because two members constitute a quorum, unless such deliberations are merely informational or exploratory. See Berg & Klitzman, *An Interpretive Guide to the Government in the Sunshine Act* at 9 (1978). Moreover, members of such agencies may exchange confidential communications by memoranda to avoid application of the Sunshine Act because the exchanges would not constitute a "meeting." *See Communications Systems, Inc.* v. *FCC*, 595 F.2d 797, 800 (D.C. Cir. 1979). In addition, formal agency rulemaking deliberations fall within Exemption 10 of the Act, 5 U.S.C. 552(b)(10), and thus can be closed to the public. *See* 1976 U.S. Code Cong. & Ad News 2219; 42 Fed Reg. 13288. Finally, all predecisional deliberations of agencies that culminate in formal opinions are privileged from discovery or use in adjudicatory proceedings attacking agency action, even if the original agency action takes place at an open meeting in accordance with the Sunshine Act. The refusal of the judiciary to examine agency deliberations opened to the public under the Sunshine Act for the purpose of defeating agency action substantially ameliorates any inhibiting effect that Act might otherwise have on agency candor essential to enlightened execution of the law. *See Kansas State Network, Inc.* v. *FCC*, No. 82–1319, slip op. at 12 (D.C. Cir., Oct. 25, 1983).

[35]408 F. Supp. 303 (W.D. Tex. 1976)

[36]*Id.* at 306, where the Court states:

> The controlling principle of law thus enunciated in *D.C. Federation* v. *Volpe* is that agency action is invalid if based, even in part, on pressures emanating from congressional sources. Through an array of administrative law precepts reviewing courts are properly constrained from substituting their own judgment for that of the administrative agency. But those precepts presuppose that the judgment being thus protected is the agency's own legitimate judgment. Where pressures emanating from congressional sources have, in the words of *D.C. Federation* v. *Volpe*, 'intruded into the calculus of considerations on which the Secretary's decision was based,' then the resulting judgment is unlawful *ab initio* and not entitled to the sanctuary accorded untainted agency judgments.

[37]*See also Koniag, Inc.* v. *Andrus*, 580 F.2d 601 (D.C. Cir. 1978); *Koniag* v. *Kleppe*, 405 F.Supp. 1360 (D.D.C. 1975); *Peter Kiewit Sons' Co.* v. *U.S. Army Corps of Engineers*, 534 F. Supp. 1139 (D.D.C. 1982).

law violations or prosecutorial decisions constitute law enforcement functions under the *Buckley* constitutional taxonomy.[38] Congress, thus, cannot obstruct accomplishment of these functions by forcing disclosure of confidential agency investigatory or prosecutorial decisional materials. If an agency privilege of confidentiality were not recognized for such materials, Congress would be empowered to exert pivotal influence over law enforcement decisions, a result that would defeat a major purpose of the Constitution's separation of powers.[39]

IV.

The independent agency privilege that protects the confidentiality of agency communications is not born of a formalistic application of Separation of Powers Doctrines. To the contrary, the privilege is a centerpiece of wise and enlightened government. It is underwritten by the same policy reasons that the Supreme Court expounded in recognizing a presidential privilege of confidentiality of communications in *United States* v. *Nixon*.[40] There the court explained:

> The expectation of a president to the confidentiality of his conversations and correspondence, like the claim of confidentiality of judicial deliberations, for example, has all the values to which we accord deference for the privacy of all citizens and, added to those values, is the necessity for protection of the public interest in candid, objective, and even blunt or harsh opinions in presidential decisionmaking. A president and those who assist him must be free to explore alternatives in the process of shaping policies and making decisions and to do so in a way many would be unwilling to express except privately. These are the considerations justifying a presumptive privilege for presidential communications. The privilege is fundamental to the operation of government and inextricably rooted in the separation of powers under the Constitution.[41]

Independent agencies have a greater need to a constitutional privilege than the President. The latter can threaten vetoes, promise judgeships or other high office, award handsome grants and draw on other powers to defend against congressional overreaching. Independent agencies possess none of these formidable weapons of self-defense, and frequently appear as mere supplicants before congressional committees asking for adequate funds. Without a judicially recognized constitutional privilege to protect confidentiality, independent agencies are unlikely candidates to police congressional trespasses on Separation of Powers Doctrines.

V.

Independent agencies should reexamine practices of bent obedience to every congressional request for confidential agency records or information. Rather than embracing the fiction that as an "arm of Congress" they must suffer legislative intrusion into their confidential adjudicatory, investigative, and rulemaking processes, agencies should stand erect and resolute in furtherance of our constitutional scheme of separation of powers. Flinty responses to congressional attempts to arrogate agency functions may be necessary in certain circumstances. In the area of executive privilege, the Supreme Court has invoked historical practice as persuasive evidence of its constitutional foundation.[42] A similar historical record of independent agency fortitude against congressional encroachments will bolster the assertion of agency privilege before the judiciary. The

---

[38]The cases of *United States* v. *Nixon*, 418 U.S. 712 (1974) and *United States* v. *Cox*, 342 F.2d 167 (5th Cir. 1965) support the proposition that prosecutorial discretion is an inherent executive function.

[39]On January 31, 1983, the Securities and Exchange Commission (SEC) entered into a Memorandum of Understanding (MOU) with the General Accounting Office for the purpose of expediting an inquiry into the Commission's enforcement program requested by Congressman John D. Dingell, Chairman of the Subcommittee on Oversight and Investigations of the House Committee on Energy and Commerce. The MOU sets forth mutually acceptable procedures for limited disclosure, maintenance, and retention of the SEC documents at issue, including material from open law enforcement files and pending litigation files. The MOU demonstrates a congressional proclivity to seek law enforcement files despite an absence of any articulated suspicion of agency maladministration or wrongdoing.

[40]418 U.S. 683 (1974).

[41]*Id.* at 708.

[42]*Id.* at 711.

Constitution, the integrity of independent agency functions, and the due process rights of agency litigants will be vindicated by judicial recognition of such a privilege.

5 NO
SHOULD INDEPENDENT AGENCIES RESIST CONGRESSIONAL INVESTIGATIONS IN ORDER TO PROTECT CONFIDENTIALITY?

Don't Cripple Congress
Stephen R. McSpadden

Bruce Fein's article, "Fighting Off Congress: A Bill of Rights for the Independent Agency," masterfully portrays these agencies as the victims of an overbearing and unscrupulous Congress seeking access to confidential agency information. In keeping with the Reagan Administration's attempts to choke off information to the Congress, as well as to the public, the FCC general counsel's proposed solution would effectively terminate effective and meaningful congressional oversight of these agencies. Fein claims that independent agencies already provide too much information to Congress and strongly argues that Congress has no right to inquire into confidential, deliberative, or investigative agency material, including law enforcement and adjudicative records, unless certain stringent conditions are met, and then only for narrow oversight purposes. His solution is unnecessarily overbroad and restrictive, is not supported in law, and runs counter to legitimate public interests in effective congressional oversight of independent agencies, which are accountable to no other entity.

Based on my own experience, I question the accuracy of (1) Fein's statement about the overwhelming agency compliance with congressional requests for information and (2) the responses to Fein's survey of 16 independent agencies, confirming unquestioning obedience to congressional demands for agency records. Having worked almost six years for a House of Representatives' oversight subcommittee (which has jurisdiction over several of the agencies cited, but not the FCC), I can attest that this is not so. Agency officials far too easily and readily assert a general interest in confidentiality to prevent both congressional and public scrutiny of their activities. Some agencies routinely comply fully with congressional requests for confidential information; others do not. A survey of congressional oversight subcommittees would have disclosed that most Federal agencies—both independent and executive branch—routinely overclassify agency material (particularly anything potentially embarrassing), often invoke an unspecified privilege against the disclosure of "confidential intra-agency deliberations and processes," or otherwise attempt to impede congressional access to their material. Government agencies can be as intransigent in turning over material as attorneys in major private litigation.[1]

Fein is on stronger ground when he indicates that it may be improper under many circumstances for the Congress to attempt to influence the outcome in favor of or against a particular person or business during an agency's adjudicatory proceeding. (In The Pillsbury Co. v. the F.T.C., the Fifth Circuit Court of Appeals held that significant congressional interference in an adjudication pending before an in-

From Stephen R. McSpadden, "Don't Cripple Congress," District Lawyer, 8 (Jan./Feb. 1984), pp. 16, 18–21. Reprinted with permission.

[1]To obtain agency material under these conditions becomes a test of wills and an exhaustion of resources. In a typical scenario, a congressional subcommittee will enter into weeks of letter-writing and negotiating to obtain material in some usable form. As often happens, the subcommittee will have to convene to vote on a subpoena and, if subsequently necessary, to vote on a contempt citation; or, alternatively, the subcommittee will have to accept a generally worded response in lieu of actual documents, because of pressing congressional workloads, the difficulty in assembling subcommittee members to vote on a subpoena, and the tremendous time and subcommittee resources required to carry this matter to an ultimate conclusion, in face of vastly larger agency staffs arrayed against the subcommittee.

dependent regulatory agency tainted and invalidated the agency's final decision.[2] Nevertheless, even here, Congress does have an oversight role. Major policy changes are often made through adjudications—for example, the FTC's consideration of the General Motors–Toyota Joint Venture—and therefore drawing that line is difficult. If an agency is straying beyond its mandate, significantly altering preexisting law, or failing to implement or enforce the law in a particular adjudication (or rulemaking), Congress has the authority to examine this occurrence, even if there is no final conclusion, and the legislators have the right to voice their views. It is the agency's responsibility to take steps to prevent undue influence or the premature release of official views or prejudgments, both of which occurred in the *Pillsbury* case.

However, Fein calls for restraints far beyond pending adjudications. He would limit Congress' authority to obtain agency material in past matters.

Congress possesses a unique and ultimate responsibility to examine the policies and operations of the agencies it has created. Congressional subcommittees, including the one I work for, on a number of occasions have needed to examine law enforcement material, interagency and intra-agency memoranda, and internal documents to determine if the agency involved was effectively administering and enforcing the law. These examinations often will reveal significant problems and will result in subcommittee (and committee) hearings and the issuance of valuable critical reports or letters. Often, disclosure to Congress of confidential, deliberative, or investigatory material is the *only* way to uncover reasons for and sources of the problems. Agency officials and the press are quick to dismiss congressional criticism of agencies, unless they are supported by tangible evidence.

For example, there was some question whether the Commodity Futures Trading Commission (CFTC) adequately and timely responded in 1979 to the Hunt Brothers' attempt to corner the silver markets. The subcommittee I work for examined CFTC records and material. Only by obtaining tapes of CFTC meetings and other "sensitive" agency information was the subcommittee able to show that the CFTC knew about price manipulations in the silver market

at an early stage and could have taken specific preventative and emergency actions then, but failed to do so.

Fein correctly asserts that there must exist a legitimate legislative purpose for congressional intrusion into an agency's past confidential deliberations or investigations. However, the existence of a legitimate purpose does not depend on supportable congressional allegations of credible charges of corruption or improprieties, sufficient to satisfy an agency, as suggested by Fein.

To the contrary, in *Watkins* v. *United States* the Supreme Court articulated a much broader, less restrictive, and more suitable standard:

> The power of the Congress to conduct investigations is inherent in the legislative process. That power is broad. It encompasses inquiries concerning the administration of existing laws as well as proposed or possibly needed statutes. It includes surveys or defects in our social, economic, or political systems for the purpose of enabling the Congress to remedy them. It comprehends probes into departments of the Federal Government to expose corruption, inefficiency, or waste.[3]

In *Wilkinson* v. *United States*, the Supreme Court delineated the boundaries of congressional oversight and enumerated criteria for the courts to consider in confronting constitutional challenges to such oversight: Congressional investigatory authority is properly asserted in a particular case if (1) the committee's investigation of the broad subject matter has been authorized by Congress (in practice, either by rule or resolution); (2) the investigation is pursuant to a valid legislative purpose (as set forth below); and (3) the specific inquiry involved is pertinent to the broad subject areas which have been authorized by the Congress.[4] The Supreme Court has sanctioned congressional investigations for the following legislative purposes: the determination of whether or not legislation is appropriate, oversight of the administration of laws by the executive branch, the essential function of Congress informing itself in matters of national concern, and the primary

[2]354 F.2d 952, 963 (5th Cir. 1966).

[3]354 U.S. 178, 187 (1957).
[4]365 U.S. 399, 408–09 (1961).

functions of legislating and appropriating.[5] A court's purview is therefore limited. It should only inquire as to whether the investigation being undertaken is within Congress' constitutional authority and powers and whether the information requested is relevant to that investigation.[6] The grounds for an agency's denial of information should be thusly limited.

Justifiably, the courts have never limited Congress' right to review material relating to independent agency rulemaking or adjudicative, investigative, or policy deliberations in the manner which Fein suggests. They have not recognized the applicability to Congress of the privilege against the disclosure of "confidential intra-agency deliberations and processes,"[7] neither have they limited congressional examinations only to possible corruption, misconduct, or improprieties, but have included possible waste or inefficiences. Also, the courts have not required Congress to specifically allege the problems it expected to find if the material were produced.

If the law were modified as Fein suggests, the subcommittee I work for could not have recently examined and obtained material on one independent agency's extremely long delays in ten rulemaking proceedings, dating back to 1976 and 1977. Without obtaining information necessary to uncover the reasons for these delays, it would have been impossible for the subcommittee to detail and allege the causes of the delay, whether the delays were warranted, and whether the agency had functioned inefficiently or improperly.

Fein's article emphasizes the separation of powers among the branches of government. However, pursuant to our constitutional tradition, the judicial and legislative branches do possess the authority to examine the activities and policies of the executive branch and the independent agencies created by the Congress. It is not accidental that in most crucial exercises of power, such as the power to appropriate funds and control expenditures and the power to override presential vetoes and enact laws, the greatest authority is reposited in Congress, subject only to narrow constitutional challenges before the judiciary.

The Congress is the only branch of government responsible for the accountability of commissioners and other appointed independent agency officials, who are rarely accountable to the President. It is inconsistent and somewhat surprising that officials appointed by an Administration which emphasizes the need to make bureaucrats and agencies accountable to the public take positions which will cause less public accountability.

While independent agencies do complain about spending precious time and resources to respond to congressional requests for information, particularly on subjects of lesser importance to them, agencies cannot circumscribe Congress' role or deny it information on those grounds, in view of the larger public goals and interests which should be served. The Congress, not the agency, must set the priority and determine the subjects, scope, and depth of its oversight activities.

Fein's article ends as a "call to arms" for independent agencies to stand resolute to congressional attempts to obtain "sensitive" agency material and urges recognition of a privilege for that purpose. If heeded, this call will increase agency secrecy, block public scrutiny, and diminish agency accountability. If Congress is confronted with and must continually battle against these repeated denials of information, Congress' constitutional authority to inquire will severely deteriorate. And the public's interest in effective and accountable government will greatly suffer. Let us hope that Fein's arguments do not win agency, congressional and judicial acceptance.

---

[5]*Quinn v. United States*, 349 U.S. 155, 161 (1955); *McGrain v. Daugherty*, 273 U.S. 135 (1927), *Sinclair v. United States*, 279 U.S. 263, 295 (1929); *United States v. Rumely*, 345 U.S. 41 (1953); and *Barenblatt v. United States*, 360 U.S. 109 (1959).

[6]Rosenthal & Grossman, in *Congressional Access to Confidential Information Collected by Federal Agencies, Harvard Journal on Legislation*, Vol. 15:1, 1977, p. 100, have also suggested the same standard for executive branch challenges, in lieu of a "balancing of interests" test. In this article the authors deal primarily with (1) the conflicting interests of keeping private third party information relating to trade secrets which has been submitted to an agency, (2) Congress' right to that information, and (3) ways to balance those rights and interests. Appropriately, this issue was not addressed in Fein's article.

[7]Fein has correctly not linked such a privilege to the claim of executive privilege, since it is clear that independent agencies cannot validly assert such a claim. *Ibid*, p. 99, note 99.

QUESTIONS FOR DISCUSSION

1. What should be the proper role of Congress in overseeing independent agencies?
2. What checks does Congress have in overseeing independent agencies?
3. Who should determine whether congressional involvement in an independent agency's adjudicatory, investigatory, or rulemaking processes is illegitimate? Why?
4. What is a "legitimate legislative purpose" for congressional intrusion into an agency's past confidential deliberations or investigations?
5. From a practical point of view, would an independent agency be likely to adopt Fein's recommendation? Why?
6. What effect would Fein's proposal have on the kinds of information that independent agencies make available to the public?

SUGGESTED READINGS

BRIGMAN, WILLIAM E., "The Executive Branch and the Independent Regulatory Agencies," *Presidential Studies Quarterly*, 2 (Spring 1981), 244–61.

COHEN, JEFFREY E., "Presidential Control of Independent Regulatory Commissions Through Appointment: The Case of the ICC," *Administration and Society*, 17 (May 1985), 61–70.

COOPER, ANN, "Fowler's FCC Learns Some Hard Lessons About What It Means to Be 'Independent'," *National Journal*, 17 (Apr. 6, 1985), 732–36.

DAVIS, JEFFRY L., "Regulatory Reform and Congressional Control of Regulation," *New England Law Review*, 17, No. 4 (1981/82), 1199–1235.

HIBBING, JOHN R., "The Independent Regulatory Commissions Fifty Years After *Humphrey's Executor* v. *U. S.*," *Congress and the Presidency*, 12, (Spring 1985), 57–68.

PERTSHUK, MICHAEL, *Revolt Against Regulation: The Rise and Pause of the Consumer Movement*. Berkeley: Univ. of California Press, 1982.

TOLCHIN, SUSAN J., AND MARTIN TOLCHIN, *Dismantling America: The Road to Deregulate*. Boston: Houghton Mifflin, 1983.

U. S. CONGRESS, HOUSE, *Congressional Review of Agency Rulemaking*, Hearings before the Subcommittee on Rules of the House of the Committee on Rules, 97th Cong., 1st Sess., 1981.

U. S. CONGRESS, SENATE, *Regulatory Reform Act —S. 1080*, Hearing before the Subcommittee on Regulatory Reform of the Committee on the Judiciary, 97th Cong., 1st Sess., 1981.

VISCUSI, W. KIP, "Presidential Oversight: Controlling the Regulators," *Journal of Policy Analysis and Management*, 2 (Winter 1983), 157–73.

WEST, WILLIAM F., *Administrative Rulemaking: Politics and Process*. Westport, CT: Greenwood Press, 1985.

6   YES   HAVE FEDERAL JUDGES USURPED THE AUTHORITY OF ADMINISTRATIVE AGENCIES?

The Politics of Partnership
R. Shep Melnick

In 1971 Chief Judge David Bazelon of the Circuit Court of Appeals for the District of Columbia marked the arrival of "a new era in the long and fruitful collaboration of administrative agencies and reviewing courts" by ordering recalcitrant administrators to initiate proceedings to ban the pesticide DDT.[1] A dissenting judge grumbled that the court was "undertaking to manage the Department of Agriculture."[2] The D.C. Circuit soon had many bureaucrats grumbling as well. All the court's talk about "partnership" and "collaboration" could not hide the fact that this court and many others were overruling agency decisions at an accelerating rate, were criticizing administrators for acting arbitrarily, parochially, and sloppily, and were demanding compliance with complex new rule-making procedures. With partners like this, who needs enemies?

Yet over a decade later it is clear that judicial rhetoric about a court-agency partnership is more than just a clever disguise for judicial usurpation of administrative authority. While a few agencies—most notably the Federal Communications Commission and the Nuclear Regulatory Commission—continued to fight with the courts for years, most adapted to the courts' requirements and have even applauded their efforts. "The effect of such detailed factual review by the courts on the portion of the agency subject to it," wrote one Environmental Protection Agency attorney after careful investigation, "is entirely beneficial."[3] Similar sentiments are frequently expressed by lawyers in other agencies as well.[4]

THE PARTNERS' OBJECTIVES

What are the objectives of this new partnership? The answer most frequently provided in judicial opinions is "open, fair, and rational decision making." This means most immediately that agencies must present rationales supporting their major decisions and that these rationales must be technically sound. To this end, the courts have read a number of new requirements into the notice and comment rule-making provisions of the Administrative Procedures Act.[5] When agencies propose new regulations, they must make public the data, methodology, and arguments on which they have relied. Not only must they invite comment on this material, but they must also respond to all "significant" criticism. Then they must provide a detailed explanation of how they arrived at their final rule. All this information must be compiled in a record which can be reviewed by the appropriate court. The reviewing court will give

[1]*Environmental Defense Fund* v. *Ruckelshaus*, 439 F.2d 589,597 (D.C. Cir. 1971).

[2]*Ibid.*, p. 598 (Judge Robb, dissenting).

[3]William F. Pederson, "Formal Records and Informal Rulemaking," *Yale Law Journal*, vol. 84 (1975), pp. 59–60.

[4]William H. Rodgers Jr. discusses the broad acceptance of heightened judicial scrutiny in "A Hard Look at *Vermont Yankee*: Environmental Law Under Close Scrutiny," *Georgetown Law Journal*, vol. 67 (1979), p. 699. On cooperation between EPA and the courts, see R. Shep Melnick, *Regulation and the Courts: The Case of the Clean Air Act* (Washington, D.C.: Brookings Institution, 1983), especially pp. 379–383.

[5]"Notice and comment" or "informal" rule making is governed by Section 553 of the Administrative Procedures Act. For years the courts applied the lenient "arbitrary and capricious" standard in reviewing informal rule making. Important examples of the more demanding judicial review of informal rule making include *Kennecott Copper Corp.* v. *EPA*, 462 F.2d 846 (D.C. Cir. 1972); *Portland Cement Assoc.* v. *Ruckelshaus*, 486 F.2d 375 (D.C. Cir. 1973); and *South Terminal Corp.* v. *EPA*, 504 F.2d 646 (1st Cir. 1974). The evolution of judicial review is described in Pederson, *op.cit.*, and Richard B. Stewart, "The Reformation of American Administrative Law," *Harvard Law Review*, vol. 88 (1975), p. 1667.

a hard look at the record, insisting that the agency "articulate with reasonable clarity its reason for decision and identify the significance of the crucial facts, a course that tends to assure that the agency's policies effectuate general standards, applied without unreasonable discrimination."[6] Courts have insisted upon undertaking such searching and careful review even when it requires immersing themselves in highly technical material.

Going hand-in-hand with the goal of assuring adequate analysis is the objective of assuring participation by all affected interests. In part the latter serves the former: when all can speak, more information and alternatives are presented for consideration. But the concerted efforts of the courts to open the door to participation by such non-traditional groups as environmentalists, civil rights organizations, and consumer groups also reflect their concern about the political biases of administrative agencies. In the late 1960s the courts began to complain that administrators were focusing too narrowly on the accepted missions of their agencies, losing sight of the public interest in the process. At best, agencies were unimaginative; at worse, they had been captured by the powerful industrial interests they were created to control. Led by the D.C. Circuit, the courts sought to open up these "iron triangles" by giving a variety of interests the chance to be heard.[7] The "reformation" of administrative law, as Richard Stewart explained, "changed the focus of judicial review . . . so that its dominant purpose is no longer the prevention of unauthorized intrusion on private autonomy, but the assurance of fair representation for all affected interests in the exercise of the legislative power delegated to agencies."[8] Just as the technical components of agency decision making would be scrutinized for accuracy, the more political components would be scrutinized for fairness and breadth of view.

Who could object to this? Certainly not the agencies, which would hardly claim the right to be irrational or unfair. Certainly not Congress, which constantly criticizes bureaucratic myopia. Before long, Congress had written these judicially created procedures into many regulatory statutes.[9] Certainly not the press, for which openness is next to godliness. And certainly not legal scholars, who want nothing more than for government to be as fair and reasonable as the most distinguished members of their profession. To be sure, a few judges complained of the enormous burden this put on the courts; but this was a cross most judges would gladly bear.

ADDING BITE TO ITS BARK

For all this to work, however, judges must be able to spot fair and reasonable policies when they see them—or, more accurately, be able to recognize unfair and unreasonable policies. One factor contributing to the difficulty of this task is the amount of scientific and technical uncertainty which inevitably accompanies public policy making. Another is that on most important public issues even when the facts are undisputed people still disagree strenuously about what is fair and reasonable, with neither side clearly wrong. As agencies dutifully gathered more information, uncertainty seemed to grow rather than diminish. As they listened to more people, they found their options widening rather than converging. Given the fuzziness of the reasonableness and fairness standards, resourceful administrators, it would seem, can easily learn how to jump through all the hoops—and then do whatever they want. What agencies would lose in delay they would gain in improved public relations.

This possibility led one leading commentator, Joseph Sax, to claim in the early 1970s that these judicial efforts would prove futile.[10] He was wrong. The "new era" in administrative law did not fade into procedural irrelevancy because judges were

---

[6]*Greater Boston Television Corp.* v. *FCC*, 444 F.2d 841, 851 (D.C. Cir. 1970).

[7]*Moss* v. *CAB*, 430 F.2d 891 (D.C. Cir. 1970); *Office of Communications of the United Church of Christ* v. *FCC*, 425 F.2d 543 (D.C. Cir. 1969); *Calvert Cliffs Coordinating Committee* v. *AEC*, 449 F.2d 1109 (D.C. Cir. 1971); *Scenic Hudson Preservation Conf.* v. *FPC*, 354 F.2d 608 (2nd Cir. 1965).

[8]Stewart, *op. cit.,* p. 1712.

[9]Examples include the Clean Air Act Amendments of 1977 and the Magnuson-Moss Warranty—Federal Trade Commission Improvement Act.

[10]Joseph Sax, "The (Unhappy) Truth about NEPA," *Oklahoma Law Review*, vol. 26 (1973), p. 239.

able to devise more specific standards to give bite to their intensified scrutiny. The source of these standards was an agency's enabling statute, or, more precisely, the courts' often creative interpretation of such statutes. It is the statute as interpreted by the court that determines which factors are relevant, and thus what lines of analysis can be considered reasonable.[11]

Statutory interpretation adds a third partner to the policy-making firm: Congress. In Judge Harold Leventhal's words, "the courts are a kind of partnership for the purpose of effectuating the *legislative* mandate." Added Judge Skelly Wright, "Our duty, in short, is to see that the legislative purposes heralded in the halls of Congress, are not lost in the vast halls of the federal bureaucracy."[12] Judges, of course, have always insisted that administrators comply with explicit statutory requirements that bar them from exceeding their legal authority. In recent years, however, courts have been increasingly willing to second-guess administrators when the meaning of the statute is far from evident. Many a statute, as Justice John Harlan so colorfully put it, "reveals little except that we have before us a child born of the silent union of legislative compromise." Congress frequently "voice[s] its wishes in muted strains and [leaves] it to the courts to discern the theme in the cacophony of political understanding."[13] In the 1970s judges gained confidence in their ability to discern the harmonies of the Muses amid the static emanating from Capitol Hill. As the courts were giving increasing scrutiny to legislative enactments, Congress itself was going through dramatic changes both internally and in its relations with the president. This transformation gave new significance— and additional allies—to judicial activism.

---

[11]The "relevant factors" language comes from the landmark case, *Citizens to Preserve Overton Park* v. *Volpe*, 401 U.S. 402, 416 (1971). The importance of aggressive statutory interpretation was obvious not just in this case (especially at pp. 415–416), but also in the equally important case of *EDF* v. *Ruckelshaus*, 439 F.2d at 593–596. Legal commentators have generally focused on the procedural aspects of these decisions, ignoring their use of "creative" statutory interpretation.

[12]*Calvert Cliffs Coordinating Committee* v. *AEC*, 449 F.2d at 1111. The Leventhal quotation comes from *Portland Cement Assoc.* v. *Ruckelshaus*, 486 F.2d at 394.

[13]*Rosado* v. *Wyman*, 397 U.S. 397, 412 (1970).

CONGRESSIONAL RESURGENCE

In the late 1960s when the new administrative law was beginning to take shape, it would not have been inaccurate to make three generalizations about Congress. First, when Congress takes action on major issues, it generally follows the president's lead —"the president proposes and Congress disposes." Second, Congress usually speaks in vague language, using such phrases as "the public interest," "convenience," and "necessity." And third, except in extraordinary circumstances (such as after the 1932 and 1964 Democratic landslides), the conservative coalition of Republicans and Southern Democrats can block passage of important liberal legislation.

By 1975 when the new administrative law hit full stride, these generalizations had become demonstrably false. For more than five years the Democratic Congress engaged in battle with President Richard Nixon on both regulatory and spending matters. Increasingly numerous Northern liberal Democrats broke the hold of the conservative coalition and instituted major structural reform in Congress. The most important reforms were those that increased the number, power, autonomy, and staff of congressional subcommittees. Already a decentralized institution, Congress became even more so. Only this time it was the younger, more activist, and entrepreneurial members, not their more stolid and conservative adversaries, who controlled the subcommittees. Using subcommittee resources, members initiated new programs and revised old ones, challenging the president for the title of "chief legislator." No longer would Congress respond to calls for action by passing vague legislation telling the executive to do something. Now Congress was writing detailed statutes which not infrequently deviated from the president's program. Subcommittees were also using oversight hearings to make sure that administrators paid heed not just to the letter of their legislation, but to its spirit as well.[14]

---

[14]There is a huge literature describing these changes in Congress. Most helpful are the following: Lawrence C. Dodd and Bruce I. Oppenheimer (eds.), *Congress Reconsidered*, 3d ed. (Washington, D.C.: Congressional Quarterly Press, 1985; Thomas E. Mann and Norman J. Ornstein (eds.), *The New Congress* (Washington, D.C.: American

Efforts to make these powerful subcommittees representative of Congress as a whole were abandoned as each member sought a piece of the action and was allowed to choose the type of action he or she favored.[15] Environmental advocates flocked to subcommittees on environmental protection; those advocating expansion of social welfare programs chose their favorite subcommittees on the Labor and Public Welfare and the Education and Labor committees. The influence of the more cautious "insider" committees—Rules, Ways and Means, and Appropriations—plummeted. As more and more legislation reached the floor, non-committee members had less and less time to scrutinize each enactment. Sensing an imbalance, members attempted to increase party control over legislation and to create a new budget process capable of setting rational budget priorities. But party and budget reform wilted in the face of subcommittee government.[16]

Presidents Nixon, Ford, Carter, and Reagan could hardly ignore these developments. Since 1970 all presidents, Democratic as well as Republican, have tried to reduce federal spending and to limit regulatory demands placed on private enterprise. In doing so they have increased the power of the organization best equipped to translate these presidential directives into legislative and administrative action—the Office of Management and Budget (OMB). The role of the president as budget-cutter and the power of OMB were most apparent in 1981 when Congress adopted the Reagan administration's proposal to reduce annual spending by $35 billion. But Nixon's impoundments, Ford's numerous vetos of spending bills, Carter's use of the budget act to cut $10 billion from the budget in 1980, and executive-congressional conflicts since 1981 remind us of the *institutional* causes of continuing differences over the scope of government activity.

A major consequence of this struggle between Congress and the president is that federal administrators frequently find themselves caught between the competing demands of congressional subcommittees on the one hand, and the White House and OMB on the other. OMB cuts agency budget requests; subcommittees condemn administrators for failing to carry out their missions. Subcommittees urge regulators to read statutes broadly; OMB insists that they regulate only when they are sure that benefits will outweigh costs.

Courts hearing administrative law cases are often forced to resolve these conflicts between subcommittee advocates and lieutenants of the president. The spate of recent cases involving the Reagan administration's efforts to relax regulatory requirements is only the most graphic illustration of this pattern.[17] While few judges or law professors will admit it, administrative law is increasingly becoming a forum for resolving interbranch competition for control of the bureaucracy.

THE REAL PARTNERS

When put in this political context, the courts' new procedural requirements and techniques of statutory interpretation take on new significance. The courts have strengthened congressional subcommittees at the expense of the presidency. One must say subcommittee rather than Congress because major administrative law cases seldom, if ever, involve instances in which Congress as a whole has spoken clearly. When courts look to congressional intent to resolve ambiguity, they usually find the intent of the program advocates who dominate subcommittees. The real partners in the new administrative law, to put it bluntly, are the courts, subcommittees, and those administrators who wish to be freed from the influence of OMB and the president.

The most obvious way in which courts increase the influence of subcommittees is by relying heavily on legislative history. Most of the elements of legislative history—reports, floor statements, and hear-

---

Enterprise Institute, 1981); James Sundquist, *The Decline and Resurgence of Congress* (Washington, D.C.: Brookings Institution, 1981); and Arthur Maass, *Congress and the Common Good* (New York: Basic Books, 1983).

[15]Maass, *op. cit.*, pp. 99–103.

[16]Allen Schick, *Congress and Money: Budgeting, Spending, and Taxing* (Washington, D.C.: Urban Institute, 1980) (budget); Maass, *op. cit.*, pp. 54–63; and Lawrence C. Dodd and Bruce I. Oppenheimer, "The House in Transition: Change and Consolidation," in *Congress Reconsidered, op. cit.* (party).

[17]Examples include *Chevron* v. *Natural Resources Defense Council*, 52 U.S.L.W 4845 (1984); *Motor Vehicle Manufacturers Assoc.* v. *State Farm Mutual*, 103 S. Ct. 2869 (1983); *ASH* v. *CAB*, 699 F.2d 1209 (D.C. Cir. 1983); and *Building and Construction Trade Dept.* v. *Donovan*, 553 F. Supp. 352 (D.D.C. 1982).

ings—are produced by subcommittee leaders and staff. Subcommittee staff has become adept at creating enormous legislative histories, portions of which are carefully designed for later judicial consumption.[18] As legislative histories grow longer (the legislative history of the Clean Air Act compiled by the Congressional Research Service runs on for 7,500 pages), it becomes less likely that ordinary members of Congress will be familiar with them. Indeed, major components of legislative histories are often manufactured by staff members without any participation by elected members of Congress.[19]

More subtle is reliance on statutory purpose to tilt statutory interpretation to the advantage of program advocates. All statutes combine purposes with constraints. We want to protect the environment, but not put people out of work. We want to aid families with dependent children, but not spend too much money. We want to provide the handicapped with an appropriate education, but not impinge upon the states' prerogative to control their schools. To the extent that courts increase their emphasis on statutory purpose, they strengthen the hands of those who advocate achieving these objectives at the expense of those who seek to impose constraints.[20]

These are, of course, tendencies rather than iron laws. There is far too much play in the joints of statutory interpretation to permit definitive generalization. Statutes differ in their structure; judges in their emphasis; subcommittees in their unity, skillfulness, and single-mindedness; agencies in their loyalty to the president. Indeed it is the difficulty of generalization on statutory construction that has led students of the judiciary to downplay its significance. For this reason it is all the more important to consider how the courts affect relations among members of Congress, administrators, and presidential aides in a variety of policy arenas.

How the courts, led by the D.C. Circuit, cemented an alliance between the Environmental Protection Agency (EPA) and environmental protection advocates in Congress and substantially reduced White House influence over air pollution policy has been explained in detail elsewhere.[21] Here are a few examples. Relying on the Clean Air Act's purpose to "protect and enhance the quality of the Nation's air resources," the courts ordered EPA to devise the huge prevention of significant deterioration (PSD) program. The Senate Subcommittee on Environmental Pollution chaired by Edmund Muskie cheered from the sidelines, even though two years before it had not bothered to mention this program either in the detailed Clean Air Act of 1970 or in a lengthy Senate report on the act. Although the Nixon and Ford administrations opposed the entire program, EPA dutifully complied with the court order. The Muskie subcommittee blocked the administration's efforts at legislative repeal and eventually succeeded in writing PSD into the statute.[22] Similarly, while the Muskie subcommittee and the Nixon administration were fighting over the use of tall stacks by coal-burning power plants, the Fifth Circuit ruled that despite the statute's silence on the matter, Congress could not have intended to allow polluters to substitute pollution dispersion for pollution reduction. EPA agreed and refused to appeal the decision to the Supreme Court. Again the Muskie subcommittee refused to consider the administration's proposal to overturn the court decision.[23] On another major issue, the setting of air quality standards, the D.C. Circuit relied heavily on language in the 1970 Senate report and 1977 House report to prohibit EPA from considering the cost of alternative standards. The agency clutched tightly to these decisions to insulate itself from White House pressure to set standards on the basis of cost-effectiveness.[24]

---

[18]For an example, see Bruce A. Ackerman and William T. Hassler, Clean Coal/Dirty Air (New Haven: Yale University Press, 1981), pp. 48–58.

[19]Michael Malbin, Unelected Representatives (New York: Basic Books, 1980), p. 30.

[20]This is particularly clear in aid to families with dependent children (AFDC) cases such as Lewis v. Martin, 397 U.S. 552 (1970). For an example of its application to a regulatory statute, see NRDC v. Gorsuch, 685 F.2d 718 (1982).

[21]Melnick, op. cit., n. 4.

[22]The case is Sierra Club v. Ruckelshaus, 344 F. Supp. 253 (D.D.C. 1972), discussed in Melnick, op. cit., ch. 4.

[23]NRDC v. EPA, 489 F.2d 390 (5th Cir. 1974), discussed in Melnick, op. cit., ch. 5.

[24]The key cases are Ethyl Corp. v. EPA, 541 F.2d 1 (D.C. Cir. 1976); Lead Industries Assoc. v. EPA, 647 F.2d 1130 (D.C. Cir. 1980); and American Petroleum Institute v. Costle, 665 F.2d 1175 (D.C. Cir. 1981), all discussed in Melnick, op. cit., ch. 8. The Supreme Court's recent decision in Chevron v. NRDC, 52 U.S.L.W. 4845 (1984), could alter this general pattern. It is too early to know if the lower courts will follow the Supreme Court, or ignore it, as they often do on administrative law issues.

ENTITLEMENTS

For many years federal courts intervened far less frequently in spending programs than in regulatory ones. Not only did judges view spending as an activity most appropriately controlled by the other branches of government, but few federal statutes spelled out in detail who should receive how much money (the old age insurance section of the Social Security Act being the glaring exception). Within Congress the purse strings were controlled not by the authorizing committees that wrote legislation establishing spending programs but by the appropriations committees that put together the annual budget. In deciding how much to include in the budget, the appropriations committees paid much more attention to the recommendations of OMB (then known as the Bureau of the Budget) than to the far higher recommendations of the authorizing committees.

This changed dramatically in the late 1960s and early 1970s. Increasingly aggressive authorizing committees convinced Congress to enact "backdoor" spending measures not subject to annual review by the appropriations committees and OMB. The most important form of backdoor spending is the entitlement, which guarantees the payment of a certain sum (often including a cost-of-living adjustment) to all eligible individuals, regardless of the total cost of such payments. In 1972, 66 percent of the budget was "uncontrollable"; by 1982 this figure was nearly 80 percent.[25] Thus, shortly after the courts altered legal doctrines to open the courthouse doors to recipients of government largess,[26] changes within Congress produced a multitude of detailed spending statutes for judges to interpret. As with regulatory statutes, the members of Congress most involved in writing entitlement laws were those most interested in expanding government programs.

There was, however, an additional complication. Many federal programs do not provide money directly to private individuals but rather funnel the money through the states. Such statutes establish general program guidelines, but they delegate administrative responsibility to the states and offer the states considerable discretion in setting eligibility standards and funding levels. Federal administrators are expected to enforce federal rules by cutting off funds to states that fail to comply "substantially." In practice this means that federal statutory requirements can easily be flaunted, since the penalty can have a devastating effect on program recipients and, consequently, will seldom be employed. Liberalizing reforms approved at the national level can easily be blocked by state legislatures and governors tenaciously guarding the public fisc.[27]

To deal with this problem, the federal courts deployed an arcane but potent judicial weapon, the private right of action. When a court discovers that a federal statute contains or implies a private right of action, it offers alleged beneficiaries the opportunity to bring suit against states or private parties to vindicate their statutory rights—even if a federal agency has been given primary responsibility for assuring compliance with the statute.[28] This means not only that private parties gain control over enforcement mechanisms but also that federal courts gain additional opportunities to determine what benefits statutes promise to private citizens. The private right of action has special significance in joint federal-state spending programs. If an alleged beneficiary could only bring suit against a federal administrator for failing to enforce federal standards, the only relief the court could offer successful plaintiffs would be an injunction cutting off federal funds to the state. In most cases, this would mean that victorious litigants would lose money. But when potential recipients can bring suit against the state for failure to comply with federal requirements, the

---

[25]Schick, op. cit., p. 27; and Congressional Quarterly, Budgeting for America (Washington, D.C.: Congressional Quarterly Press, 1982), p. 49.

[26]In the legal literature this change goes under the rubric of "the demise of the rights-privilege distinction." Goldberg v. Kelly, 397 U.S. 254 (1970) is usually considered the key case, and Charles Reich's article, "The New Property," Yale Law Journal, vol. 73 (1964), p. 733, is the classic argument for the change.

[27]The best description of the behavior of federal administrators before the transformation of legal doctrines is Martha Derthick, The Influence of Federal Grants: Public Assistance in Massachusetts (Cambridge, Mass.: Harvard University Press, 1970).

[28]The leading cases on private rights of action are Cort v. Ash, 422 U.S. 66 (1975), and Maine v. Thiboutot, 448 U.S. 1 (1980). While court decisions have been changing and inconsistent, it appears that the Supreme Court is becoming less inclined to find implied rights of action in federal statutes, but increasingly is willing to find authority for such lawsuits in 42 U.S.C. §1983, originally passed as part of the Civil Rights Act of 1871.

court can compel the state to pay the plaintiff the money owed. The private right of action, thus, significantly alters the balance of power between the federal government and the states.

I did not take program advocates at the national level long to recognize the advantages of the new regime. Officials of the Department of Health, Education, and Welfare (HEW) began to issue more detailed regulations and joined with private plaintiffs in attacking state practices in federal court. Few judges asked why these administrators were challenging the very programs they had formally approved just months before. Congress responded to this opportunity to expand federal control over joint programs by adding more elaborate eligibility requirements, writing lengthy legislative histories, and passing broad cross-cutting mandates which apply to all state programs receiving federal funds.[29]

AIDING THE HANDICAPPED

Nowhere are the political consequences of these institutional and doctrinal developments more evident than in programs for the handicapped. In the 1960s and 1970s, a number of public interest groups and professional associations brought to public attention a multitude of problems facing the handicapped, ranging from lack of adequate transportation to exclusion from public schools to inhumane conditions in state institutions. These groups began to achieve success in Congress just as the potential for using private rights of action was becoming evident. A cohesive subcommittee-agency-court-interest group alliance managed to build strong programs and to pass most of the costs along to the states.

As the problems of the handicapped were brought to the attention of Congress, subcommittees investigating the issue multiplied. Few members of Congress were unsympathetic to the plight of the handicapped. The problem was that relief would cost a great deal of money, and the Nixon and Ford administrations were seeking to avoid large deficits.

One congressional response was to add new mandates without adding more money. Such was the strategy of Section 504 of the Rehabilitation Act

of 1973. This section, little noticed at the time of passage, prohibits discrimination on the basis of handicap in any program receiving federal funds, however, it fails to define "discrimination." When the Republican administrations did little to implement this provision, the handicapped went to court. Relying on language inserted in a conference committee report issued one year after passage of Section 504, the federal district court for the District of Columbia ordered HEW to issue and enforce regulations implementing the new federal mandate. After still another suit, a change of administrations, and a sit-in at his office, Secretary Joseph Califano reluctantly published new rules. Many other courts subsequently found an implied private right of action in Section 504. They could not, after all, leave enforcement of the law to administrators who seemed so reluctant to put it into effect. Judicial interpretation of Section 504 helped push the cost of the program into the billions of dollars.[30]

On the issue of education for handicapped children, subcommittees on education and the handicapped in the House and the Senate took a more direct approach. Insisting (erroneously) that federal courts had ruled that all children have a constitutional right to an education, they championed an authorizations bill that would provide billions of dollars to help states meet the judicial mandate. The Nixon and Ford administrations threatened a veto. The subcommittees reduced the authorization levels, and President Ford signed the Education for All Handicapped Children Act into law in 1975. Subsequently the appropriations committees, following the advice of OMB, kept actual funding at only a fraction of authorization levels.

The Education for All Handicapped Children Act is far more than just a funding act. It contains elaborate procedures and guidelines to ensure that all handicapped children receive an "appropriate" education. Local schools must construct an individualized education program (IEP) for each handicapped child. Parents have the right to participate in the formulation of the IEP, and they can appeal any provision in the IEP first to an independent hear-

---

[29]Advisory Commission on Intergovernmental Relations, *Regulatory Federalism: Policy, Process, Impact, and Reform* (Washington, D.C.: ACIR, 1984), ch.1.

[30]The key decision was *Cherry v. Mathews*, 419 F. Supp. 922 (D.D.C. 1976). The importance of this case was pointed out to me by Robert Katzmann of the Brookings Institution, who is completing a major study of the politics of Section 504 and transportation policy.

ing officer and then to the state board of education. While the procedural aspects of the act are elaborate, nowhere does it specify what constitutes a "free appropriate public education." There is logic to this: the major decisions on appropriateness are made by state and local educators who can study each case in detail and who bear responsibility for footing most of the bill.

The Senate bill said little about judicial review of IEPs, and the House bill subjected state and local decisions to a lenient standard of judicial review. However, the conference committee, which reconciled the bills of the two houses quietly but drastically, altered the role of the courts. In the final version of the legislation there appeared a new judicial review provision that enabled parents to challenge IEP's in federal court and required judges to "make an *independent* decision based on a preponderance of the evidence" and to "grant all appropriate relief." Final authority to decide what constitutes an appropriate education thus was transferred from state and local officials to federal judges. Program advocates on the conference committee had used a seemingly technical change to alter the balance of power between the states and the federal government.[31]

The Education for All Handicapped Children Act has generated scores of federal court cases. While judges have expressed concern about the huge cost of providing an appropriate education for the handicapped, they have nonetheless ordered schools to provide residential care for severely retarded and emotionally disturbed children, prohibited states from limiting the academic year for the handicapped to the normal 180 days, required schools to perform such quasi-medical procedures as catheterization, and even ordered schools to pay compensatory damages for past student misplacements.[32] Before

being overruled by the Supreme Court, several circuit courts held that an appropriate education means the best possible education a school can provide.[33] Partly as a result of these decisions, the cost of the act has become enormous. One estimate puts it at $10 billion per year. Federal appropriations have leveled off at about $1.2 billion, far less than was promised to the states in the authorization passed in 1975.[34]

The fact that the federal courts are available to put bite into a vague statutory mandate provides program advocates with two strategic advantages. Most obviously, judicial review creates a mechanism for maintaining the flow of benefits even when federal budgets grow tight. If congressional appropriations committees reduce federal funding, state and local budgets must absorb the differences.[35] A more subtle consequence is that state and local officials then become lobbyists in the appropriations process, protecting the appropriations base and demanding federal spending increases. This strategy has worked: federal spending for education of the handicapped has remained constant while other education programs have sustained major cuts.

THE PRICE OF SUCCESS

Some writers have characterized policy making for the handicapped as dominated by a new "iron triangle" of subcommittee, agency, and interest group.[36] Given the pivotal role of the lower courts, it is tempt-

---

[31]Senate Report No. 168, 94th Cong; House Report No. 332, 94th Cong.; and Senate Conference Report No. 455, 94th Cong. Erwin L. Levine and Elizabeth Wexler, *PL 94–142: An Act of Congress* (New York: Macmillan, 1981) provides a detailed review of congressional activity on education of the handicapped.

[32]*Doe* v. *Anrig*, 692 F.2d 800 (1st Cir. 1982); *Kruelle* v. *Biggs*, 489 F. Supp. 169 (D. Del. 1980); *Battle* v. *Commonwealth of Pennsylvania*, 629 F.2d 269 (3rd Cir. 1980); *Crawford* v. *Pittman*, 708 F.2d 1028 (5th Cir. 1983); *Tatro* v. *Texas*, 468 U.S. _____ (1984); *Boxall* v. *Sequoia Union High School Dist.*, 464 F. Supp. 1104 (N.D. Cal. 1979).

[33]*Hendrick Hudson Dist. Bd.* v. *Rowley*, 458 U.S. 176 (1982).

[34]John C. Pittenger and Peter Kuriloff, "Educating the Handicapped: Reforming a Radical Law," *The Public Interest* (Winter 1982), p. 72; *Congressional Quarterly Weekly Report*, November 5, 1983, p. 2317.

[35]This holds true even for states that refuse federal funds under the act. The Department of Education has ruled that Section 504 incorporates all regulations issued under the act.

[36]Levine and Wexler, *op. cit.*; Pittenger and Kuriloff, *op. cit.*; Diane Ravitch, *The Troubled Crusade: American Education 1945–1980* (New York: Basic Books, 1983), pp. 305–312. Martin Shapiro uses the act as an example of a "new iron triangle" of agency, court, and interest group, leaving out subcommittees, in "The Presidency and the Federal Courts," in Arnold J. Meltsner (ed.), *Politics and the Oval Office* (Institute for Contemporary Studies, 1981).

ing to speak of an "iron rectangle" instead. But the metaphor is probably not worth saving. As Hugh Heclo has pointed out, contemporary "issue networks" of policy advocates inside and outside government tend to be larger and less coherent than classic iron triangles.[37] Subcommittees are too numerous and fickle, public interest groups too varied and transitory, and federal courts too decentralized and unpredictable to move in lock step. Most importantly, the costs of many of these programs have grown too large for outsiders to ignore. The iron triangles of old maintained their autonomy by keeping their programs out of the limelight, either by passing costs along to taxpayers at a time when taxes were relatively low and competition for federal money less intense or by passing them along to consumers in the form of higher prices. Inflation put the political spotlight on rising prices. Huge deficits are doing the same for rising agency budgets.

The very success of the court-agency-subcommittee-interest group partnership can reduce its autonomy by exposing program costs. Exposure can be especially dangerous for those who have ingeniously built extensive programs on narrow political bases—to be more direct, those who have constructed legislative histories in lieu of legislative coalitions.

For the partnership the challenge becomes finding ways to reduce the visibility of program costs without curtailing program operations. In regulatory programs the best way to do this is to ease up on enforcement against existing employers. EPA, Congress, and the courts have all cooperated in giving polluters with established work forces much more time to comply with pollution requirements. At the same time they have increased the burdens on new facilities that have not yet established constituencies.[38] For programs requiring extensive government spending, advocates have increasingly relied on two strategies: spreading costs over federal, state, and local governments and making total spending a function of thousands of individualized decisions that are hard to control from above. Unfortunately, these cost-disguising strategies can have undesirable consequences. Placing heavier burdens on new facilities than on old ones is inefficient and discourages innovation. Relying on individualized decision making, including litigation, for the education of the handicapped, directs disproportionate resources to children of upper-middle class parents and to those requiring expensive residential care.[39]

In sum, behind the judicial rhetoric about a court-agency partnership lies a new political reality. The old administrative law evolved during the New Deal when liberal reformers such as Felix Frankfurter could aid their cause from the bench merely by deferring to administrators chosen by Roosevelt to carry out New Deal legislation.[40] By 1970 the presidency had become a threat to liberal reforms now championed by congressional entrepreneurs, often in cooperation with bureaucratic careerists. At this point the courts switched institutional partners, protecting program advocates in the bureaucracy from presidential interference, reading statutes to reflect the intention of subcommittee activists, and substantially increasing federal administrative control over the states. New Deal politics was high visibility, breakthrough politics. Dramatic legislative victories were followed by well-publicized action by self-confident whiz kids. Recent activism is far less at home in the limelight. It is complex, low visibility, administrative politics. As the courts voluntarily became "in a real sense part of the total administrative process,"[41] they simultaneously became part of an as yet poorly understood political coalition. While one cannot tell how long this coalition will survive, it has unquestionably left its mark on the American polity.

[37]"Issue Networks and the Executive Establishment," in Anthony King (ed.), *The New American Political System* (Washington, D.C.: American Enterprise Institute, 1978).

[38]Lester Lave and Gilbert Omenn, *Cleaning the Air: Reforming the Clean Air Act* (Washington, D.C.: Brookings Institution, 1981), p. 41; and Melnick, *op. cit.,* ch. 7.

[39]Richard A. Weatherly, *Reforming Special Education: Policy Implementation from State Level to Street Level* (Boston: MIT Press, 1972), especially pp. 124–127 and 137–140.

[40]See Martin Shapiro, *op. cit.,* and "The Constitution and Economic Rights," in M. Judd Harmon (ed.) *Essays on the Constitution of the United States* (Port Washington, N.Y.: Kennikat Press, 1978).

[41]*Greater Boston Television Corp.* v. *FCC,* 444 F.2d at 852.

6   NO   HAVE FEDERAL JUDGES USURPED THE AUTHORITY OF ADMINISTRATIVE AGENCIES?

Conflict or Constructive Tension: The Changing Relationship of Judges and Administrators
Phillip J. Cooper

Administrators these days often express frustration, resentment, and anxiety over judicial intervention into administrative operations. The indictment is familiar. Beginning in the late 1960s and early 1970s, the story goes, federal courts began a movement toward greater interference in administrative matters that has become progressively more intrusive. The trend, the argument runs, continues to this day.

It should not be at all surprising that administrators resent judicial rulings limiting their discretion and mandating procedural or substantive policy changes in agency operations. After all, one of the administrator's primary tasks is to anticipate and eliminate contingencies in the organizational environment.[1] Judicial rulings would seem to be just one more troublesome factor constraining administrative flexibility.

However, the courts perform a variety of essential functions required of them by the Constitution and statutes. They must ensure that administrators do not exceed their statutory authority, ignore basic procedural requisites, conduct themselves in a manner that is arbitrary and capricious or an abuse of discretion, make important policy determinations without some kind of reasoned decision based upon a record, or violate the provisions of the Constitution.[2] Neither these functions nor the courts designated to perform them are going to be eliminated.

The problem then is to develop an effective working relationship between judges and administrators. But before such an accommodation can be reached it will be necessary to assess the current relationship between these legal and administrative institutions. The starting point for such a reassessment must be a realization that the federal courts, led by the Supreme Court, have changed the law governing administrative agencies in ways more charitable to administrators. It is not true that there is a continuing trend toward greater interference in administration. Recent cases indicate an increasing judicial sensitivity to management problems and priorities.

This article examines the premises underlying current tensions between judges and administrators. It then turns to a consideration of the various counts in the indictment brought by administrators against the courts indicating the importance of recent federal court rulings. There is one new era of tension developing between courts and agencies, cases in which administrators refuse to act at all or engage in administrative deregulation. Judicial reactions to this problem are also assessed. Finally, the article suggests that law is a discretion-reinforcing agent, a fact that argues for improved judicial-administrative relations and against continued hostility.

LAW AND ADMINISTRATION: NATURAL ANIMOSITY OR CONSTRUCTIVE TENSION?

Two premises are essential to any discussion about law and administration. First, discretion is an essential commodity in modern public administration. Problems are simply too diverse and specialized and the environment too dynamic for legislators to provide more than a moderate amount of guidance to those who must administer public programs. Beyond that, managers must have sufficient flexibility to adapt their organizations and practices to changing conditions in order to perform effectively and efficiently. A lack of discretion would stifle creativity and confine administrators to rigid behavior patterns producing a panoply of bureaucratic

From Phillip J. Cooper, "Conflict or Constructive Tension: The Changing Relationship of Judges and Administrators." Reprinted with permission from *Public Administration Review*, 45 (Nov./Dec. 1985), 643–52. © 1985 by the American Society for Public Administration, 1120 G. Street, N.W., Suite 500, Washington, D.C. All rights reserved.

[1]Victor Thompson, *Bureaucracy and the Modern World* (Morristown, N.J.: General Learning Press, 1976), p. 10.

[2]5 U.S.C. §706.

dysfunctions long feared by scholars of organizational theory.[3]

The second premise is that law is intended to, and does in fact, limit discretion. Internal checks acquired by careful recruitment and training of promising public servants and the external checks provided by executive supervision and legislative oversight have never been thought adequate substitutes for the opportunity to call an official into court to demonstrate the validity of his or her actions. "No man in this country," the Supreme Court has admonished us, "is so high that he is above the law. No officer of the law may set that law at defiance with impunity. All of the officers of government, from the highest to the lowest, are creatures of the law, and are bound to obey it."[4]

From these two premises it follows that there will inevitably be tension between judges and administrators. Adding to that conflict are the differing perspectives of legally trained professionals and management educated professional administrators.[5] The former tend to treat as core values the utility of law as a defense against government intervention in personal and business affairs, the commitment to due process of law, an insistence upon equal protection of the law, and a concern for substantial justice. The latter, on the other hand, are by degrees more concerned with the latitude necessary to apply expertise to complex problems, the need for flexibility in meeting new challenges, and the goal of efficiency—what Gulick referred to as "the basic good."[6]

However, the fact that some tension exists between judges and administrators is not necessarily destructive nor should it transform natural tension into animosity. Such a polarized view of the judicial-administrative relationship would be understandable only if managers could successfully argue that absolute discretion is absolutely good and necessary or if legalists could contend that all discretion is bad. Neither argument has merit. Discretion does not necessarily have a straight-line correlation with efficiency.[7] The relationship is more curvilinear. No discretion would paralyze management. On the other hand, complete discretion may undermine efficiency. Sofaer, for example, found in his study of an agency with extremely wide discretion that broad flexibility can lead to "inconsistency, arbitrariness, and inefficiency."[8] He concluded that "the evidence seemed to refute the hypothesis that discretion results in less costly, speedier administration. . . . The presence of discretionary power seemed throughout the administrative process, disproportionately to attract political intervention."[9] Legalists have the same problem. The relationship between just decisions and discretion is again nothing so simple as a straight-line negative correlation. Absolute discretion would mean a high probability of arbitrary and inconsistent administrative judgments. On the other hand, no discretion would mean rule-bound administration without accommodation for equity or any other consideration of individualized justice.

The challenge, then, is to find useful mixes of discretion and checks on abuses of discretion not only to achieve just decisions and bolster accountability but also to protect necessary administrative flexibility so that managers can administer their organizations efficiently. The most useful approach to thinking about law and administration is not a juxtaposition of law against administration, but development of an understanding of the interaction of courts and agencies as a necessarily ongoing relationship.

Before progress can be made in improving the judicial-administrative relationship, administrators must be made aware of some of the important changes in the law. There are indications in a variety of recent rulings of increased judicial sensitivity to administrative concerns.

---

[3]See Robert K. Merton, "Bureaucratic Structure and Personality," in Merton et al. (eds.), *Reader in Bureaucracy* (New York: Free Press, 1952).

[4]*United States* v. *Lee*, 106 U.S. 196, 220 (1882).

[5]It is, of course, understood that many are administrators as a second profession and that a substantial proportion of those managers have not received advanced training in public administration. See Frederick Mosher, *Democracy and the Public Service* (New York: Oxford University Press, 1984).

[6]Luther Gulick and L. Urwick (eds.), *Papers on the Science of Administration* (Fairfield, N.J.: A.M. Kelley, 1977), p. 192.

[7]Phillip J. Cooper, *Public Law and Public Administration* (Palo Alto, Calif.: Mayfield, 1983), pp. 217–219.

[8]Abraham Sofaer, "Judicial Control of Informal Discretionary Adjudication and Enforcement," *Columbia Law Review*, vol. 72 (December 1972), p. 1374.

[9]*Ibid.*, pp. 1301–1302.

JUDGES NEITHER UNDERSTAND NOR CARE ABOUT ADMINISTRATIVE PROBLEMS: MYTHOLOGY AND REALITY IN RECENT LEGAL DEVELOPMENTS

A common misconception is that a straight-line progression of judicial assumption of authority has occurred, substituting legal judgment for administrative discretion. Examination of administrative law cases over the past decade, however, indicates that part of this management perception is based upon a number of myths or misunderstandings, which are not generally supported by the case law. True, there are important controversies, but the relationship is not as adversarial as it may seem.

The last decade or so has witnessed significant changes in direction within the Supreme Court and some lower courts in issues of importance to administrators. In several areas, judges have openly recognized the importance of administrative discretion and have moved to protect it. One way to understand the importance of these rulings is to consider the charges issued by administrators against the judiciary and the manner in which a federal judge might respond to them.

1. Courts Do Not Care About Costs. There is substantial evidence to the contrary. Consider the development of standards for administrative due process, judicial acknowledgment of the need to avoid supplanting legislative budgeting, and the recognition of fiscal problems faced by administrators in institutional reform litigation.

Even before the important recent changes in the requirements of administrative due process, the Supreme Court acknowledged the need to permit a flexible approach to due process to accommodate administrative circumstances. In a 1976 ruling, *Mathews* v. *Eldridge*, the court went even further.[10] In *Eldridge*, the court found that Social Security disability recipients were not entitled to a hearing before the termination of their benefits, though they would have an opportunity to be heard at some point later in the process. The significance of this decision lies not in permitting administrators to deny claimants any due process, but in granting flexibility in assessing what process is due under varying ad-

ministrative conditions. In *Eldridge*, the Supreme Court developed a balancing test for determining how much process is due someone before an administrative agency which specifically recognizes fiscal and administrative burden as a major element of the balance. In order to decide what process is due, the court said, one must consider:

> first, the private interest that will be affected by the official action; second, the risk of an erroneous deprivation of such interest through the procedure used, and the probable value, if any, of additional or substitute safeguards; and finally, *the Government's interest, including the function involved and the fiscal and administrative burdens that the additional or substitute procedural requirements would entail.*[11] (Emphasis added.)

The *Eldridge* balancing test has been the controlling due process standard since 1976.[12] The court has consistently rejected calls for expanded administrative due process since that time and has, in fact, relaxed some of the requirements imposed in earlier cases.[13]

This approach to due process overtly considers the problems of financial and administrative burden so important to administrators. There are other indications that judges at both the Supreme Court and lower court levels are increasingly aware that their rulings have substantial fiscal implications for public administration.[14]

---

[10]*Mathews* v. *Eldridge*, 424 U.S. 319 (1976).

[11]*Ibid.*, p. 335.

[12]Evidence for this is provided in my study on administrative due process since *Goldberg* v. *Kelly* which was reported in "Due Process, the Burger Court, and Public Administration," *Southern Review of Public Administration*, vol. 6 (Spring 1982), pp. 65–98.

[13]See, e.g., *Parham* v. *J.R.*, 422 U.S. 584 (1979); *Bishop* v. *Wood*, 426 U.S. 341 (1976); *Paul* v. *Davis*, 424 U.S. 693 (1976); *Board of Curators* v. *Horowitz*, 435 U.S. 78 (1978); and *Ingraham* v. *Wright*, 430 U.S. 651 (1977). The court has spoken of the *Eldridge* balancing formula as "the familiar test prescribed in Mathews v. Eldridge." *Schweiker* v. *McClure*, 72 L. Ed 2d 1, 9–10 (1982).

[14]One federal district judge put it this way: "Subject to constitutional limitations, Arkansas is a sovereign State. It has a right to make and enforce criminal laws, to imprison persons convicted of serious crimes, and to maintain order and discipline in its prisons. This Court has no intention of entering a decree herein that will disrupt the Penitentiary or leave Respondent and his subordinates helpless to deal with dangerous and unruly convicts.

The Sixth Circuit Court of Appeals recently made the point rather forcefully that courts should not supplant the budgetary process. The case resulted from a challenge by parents to the closing of an innovative day treatment facility, known as Jewel Manor, by the Kentucky Department of Human Resources. The reason for the elimination of the facility was budgetary pressure. Disappointed parents argued that the closing of Jewel Manor meant a change of placement for their children within the meaning of the Education for All Handicapped Children Act (EHCA). As such, they insisted, the state was precluded from closing the facility unless it could justify the change of placement or establish some other equally acceptable program. The court of appeals admonished the district judge to grant wide deference to state and local governments in matters of program modification.

> These [state] authorities do not, by electing to receive funds under the EHCA, abdicate their control of the fiscal decisions of their school systems. . . . Congress did not compel, as the price for federal participation in education for the handicapped, a wholesale transfer of authority over the allocation of educational resources [away] from the duly elected or appointed state and local boards. . . .[15]

The Supreme Court has extended that expression of concern about compulsion of state expenditures. The Third Circuit Court of Appeals affirmed a district court ruling ordering reform of Pennsylvania mental health programs in part on grounds that the Disabled Assistance and Bill of Rights Act of 1975 mandated minimum requirements for appropriate treatment in the least restrictive setting. The state received funds under that act and was therefore obligated to comply with the statute's standards. The Supreme Court reversed finding that the legislation "intended to encourage, rather than

mandate, the provision of services to the developmentally disabled."[16] In reaching this conclusion, the court observed:

> The fact that Congress granted to Pennsylvania only $1.6 million in 1976, a sum woefully inadequate to meet the enormous financial burden of providing "appropriate" treatment in the "least restrictive" setting, confirms that Congress must have had a limited purpose in enacting [this section of the law]. . . .

> Our conclusion is also buttressed by the rule of statutory construction established above, that Congress must establish clearly its intent to impose conditions on the grant of federal funds so that the State can knowingly decide whether or not to accept those funds.[17]

As the dissenters pointed out, the court's reading of the statute was extremely generous to the states involved.

Thus, evidence shows that judges are aware of some of the fiscal implications of their judgments and are concerned about the need to minimize these burdens. That does not mean they are willing to accept a budgetary justification for violating constitutional rights, but neither are they oblivious to administrative problems.

Some question exists, however, as to whether administrators have tried in complex litigation to assist judges to understand relevant fiscal dimensions and to work out accommodations where necessary to minimize judicial-administrative tension. For example, in one northern school desegregation case, the state, when called upon by the judge to produce a proposed remedy, sent six plans, recommended none of them, and provided only one witness for the remedy hearing whose only role was to explain what was in the plans.[18] The state provided the judge no help whatsoever in understanding the administrative and fiscal problems involved in implementing any of the proposed remedies. In an Alabama case, state mental health officials were given six months to take action to remedy unconstitutional conditions at state mental health facili-

---

"The Court has recognized heretofore the financial handicaps under which the Penitentiary system is laboring, and the Court knows that Respondent cannot make bricks without straw." Holt v. Sarver, 300 F. Supp. 825, 833 (E.D. Ark. 1969). See also Ralph Cavanagh and Austin Sarat, "Thinking About Courts: Toward and Beyond a Jurisprudence of Judicial Competence," Law & Society Review, vol. 14 (Winter 1980), p. 408.
[15]Tilton v. Jefferson County Bd. of Ed., 705 F.2d 800, 804–805 (6th Cir. 1983).

[16]Pennhurst State School v. Halderman, 451 U.S. 1, 20 (1981).
[17]Ibid., p. 24.
[18]See, generally, Bradley v. Milliken, 345 F. Supp. 914 (E.D. Mich. 1972).

ties, but they took no action at all. Moreover, the state refused offers of assistance from federal agencies. After indicating his understanding that state administrators may have lacked funds to implement reforms, the judge asked just how that prevented the administrators from producing a plan that could be implemented when funds did become available.[19]

Administrators can improve their relationship with judges in such cases by making careful decisions about when to fight and when to negotiate. They can present detailed and understandable explanations of their concerns about financial and administrative feasibility. They can resist the temptation simply to ignore likely judicial action until it is forced upon them.

2. Courts Are Increasingly Unwilling to Defer to the Expertise of Administrators.

Again, there have been a number of opinions, particularly Supreme Court rulings, demanding deference to administrative expertise. The court has issued these admonitions in two types of cases, rulemaking review and institutional reform litigation.

The court's leading ruling on judicial review of administrative rulemaking was the unanimous opinion issued in *Vermont Yankee Nuclear Power Corp. v. United States Nuclear Regulatory Commission.*[20] *Vermont Yankee* warned lower courts against fashioning procedural requirements beyond those contained in the statutes administered by the agency involved. Lower courts are to examine the record prepared by the agency during rulemaking, and, if it is adequately supported and within the statutory authority of the agency, the action is to be affirmed.[21] While there has been disagreement among members of the court as to precisely how much deference is due,[22] the prime forces expanding rulemaking procedural requirements in recent years have been legislation and executive orders, not judicial mandates.

The court subsequently issued a number of rulings demanding lower court respect for and deference to administrative expertise at the state as well as the federal level. Two of the more forceful decisions concerned administration of programs for handicapped children and mental health treatment.

Amy Rowley's parents objected to the individual education plan (IEP) developed for their daughter by the Hendrick Hudson School District under the requirements of the Education for All Handicapped Children Act. While school officials had provided an FM microphone, training for teachers, tutorial assistance, and speech therapy for the hearing-impaired child, they refused the Rowley's request for a sign language interpreter in the classroom. Amy was acknowledged by all to be a bright child who read lips well enough to earn passing marks at least in her elementary grades in a regular classroom. But she did this in spite of the fact that she could only understand about half of the information conveyed. In sum, she was not able to perform up to anything like her potential without the additional assistance of a sign language interpreter. For that reason, they argued, Amy was denied the "free appropriate public education" required by the EHCA. The lower courts agreed, but the Supreme Court reversed.

The court concluded that the act did not require the state to do more than ensure that "personalized instruction is being provided with sufficient support services to permit the child to benefit from instruction" plus meet the procedural requirements for parental participation in development of plans. If that was done, the child was by definition receiving a "free appropriate public education."[23] Perhaps of equal importance, however, was the court's discussion of how judges are to decide whether the child is in fact receiving benefit from the plan. The court insisted upon increased deference to administrative expertise.

> In assuring that the requirements of the Act have been met, courts must be careful to avoid imposing their view of preferable educational

[19]*Wyatt* v. *Stickney*, 334 F. Supp. 1341, 1344 (M.D. Ala. 1971).

[20]*Vermont Yankee Nuclear Power Corp.* v. *U.S. Nuclear Regulatory Commission*, 435 U.S. 519 (1978).

[21]See, e.g., *Federal Communications Commission* v. *WNCN Listeners Guild*, 450 U.S. 582 (1981) and *Office of Communications of the United Church of Christ* v. *FCC*, 707 F.2d 1413 (D.C. Cir. 1983).

[22]See, e.g., *Industrial Union Dept, AFL-CIO* v. *American Petroleum Institute*, 448 U.S. 607 (1980) and *American Textile Manufacturers Institute* v. *Donovan*, 452 U.S. 490 (1981).

[23]*Hendrick Hudson Bd. of Ed.* v. *Rowley*, 458 U.S. 176, 189 (1982).

methods upon the States. The primary responsibility for formulating the education to be accorded a handicapped child, and for choosing the educational method most suitable to the child's needs was left by the Act to state and local educational agencies in cooperation with the parents or guardian of the child. . . .

We previously have cautioned that courts lack the "specialized knowledge and experience" necessary to resolve "persistent and difficult questions of educational policy."[24]

But the court's admonition to judges on the need for deference was not limited to this particular program. In the same term, the court issued a decision in *Youngberg* v. *Romeo* which, though it recognized a constitutional claim for protection against abuse and a requirement for some mental health care for institutionalized retarded persons, carried a strong warning against judicial second-guesses of expert administrative judgement.[25] Justice Powell insisted that "courts must show deference to the judgment exercised by a qualified professional." He concluded:

> By so limiting judicial review of challenges to conditions in state institutions, interferences by the federal judiciary with the internal operations of these institutions should be minimized. Moreover, there certainly is no reason to think judges or juries are better qualified than appropriate professionals in making such decisions [about the kind of care and treatment needed by a patient]. . . . (Courts should not "second-guess the expert administrator on matters on which they are better informed.")[26]

This was a suit which asked, among other things, for damages against hospital and state officials for the lack of treatment. Pressing the need to protect administrative discretion and recognize fiscal difficulties, the court wrote:

> [L]iability may be imposed only when the decision by the professional is such a substantial departure from accepted professional judg-

ment, practice, or standards as to demonstrate that the person responsible actually did not base the decision on such a judgment. In an action for damages against a professional in his individual capacity, however, *the professional will not be liable if he was unable to satisfy his normal professional standards because of budgetary constraints. . . .*[27] (Emphasis added.)

In other cases, the court has held that judges must "design procedures that protect the rights of the individual without unduly burdening the legitimate efforts of the states to deal with social problems"[28] and insisted that "courts cannot assume that state legislatures and prison officials are insensitive to the requirements of the Constitution or to perplexing sociological problems of how best to achieve the goals of the penal function in the criminal justice system. . . ."[29]

3. The Supreme Court Is Continually Expanding the Authority of Federal District Courts to Issue Complex Remedial Orders Obstructing Administrative Operations.

There are two important factors to be considered in assessing the remedial decree cases. First, administrators have often welcomed suits against prisons and mental hospitals as means to pressure legislators for increased appropriations.[30] Thus, it is not always clear that the relationship of court to agency in these cases is primarily adversarial.

In fact, for a decade now the Supreme Court has been moving to make it harder for trial judges to justify issuance of a remedial order,[31] narrowing

---

[24]*Ibid.*, p. 208.

[25]*Youngberg* v. *Romeo*, 457 U.S. 307 (1982).

[26]*Ibid.*, pp. 322–323.

[27]*Ibid.*

[28]*Parham*, 422 U.S. at 608, n. 16. This case involved commitment of juveniles to state mental hospitals.

[29]*Rhodes* v. *Chapman*, 452 U.S. 337, 352 (1981), a case challenging conditions at Ohio's principal maximum security prison. See also, *Bell* v. *Wolfish*, 441 U.S. 520, 539 (1979).

[30]Stephen L. Wasby, "Arrogation of Power or Accountability: 'Judicial Imperialism Revisited,' " *Judicature*, vol. 65 (October 1981), p. 213. See also, Stonewall B. Stickney, "Problems in Implementing the Right to Treatment in Alabama: The Wyatt v. Stickney Case," *Hospital & Community Psychiatry*, vol. 25 (July 1974), pp. 454–455.

[31]See, e.g., *San Antonio Independent School District* v. *Rodriquez*, 411 U.S. 1 (1973); *Washington* v. *Davis*, 426 U.S. 229 (1976); *Personnel Administrator* v. *Feeney*, 442 U.S. 256 (1979); *Rizzo* v. *Goode*, 423 U.S. 362 (1976); and *Rhodes* v. *Chapman*, op. cit.

the scope of such orders[32] and limiting the duration for which district judges may retain supervisory jurisdiction over administrative institutions.[33] In cases involving school desegregation, mental health, and prison conditions, the court has admonished lower courts to avoid unnecessary orders, to carefully tailor those which are necessary to remedy constitutional violations without undue interference in agency operations, and to terminate control over those institutions as soon as possible.

4. The Supreme Court Keeps Expanding Legal Protections Available to Employees at the Expense of Managers' Discretion.

An expansion of employee rights did occur in the late 1960s and early 1970s. Once again, however, care must be exercised in judgments about judicial interference with administration. In the first place, many employee rights were created by statute or executive order and not judicial rulings.[34] It is, of course, true that federal courts added protections, particularly in the area of First Amendment free speech and association as well as due process requirements in adverse personnel actions. However, important changes have been made in recent Supreme Court decisions that define employee rights, particularly in the First Amendment and due process fields.

Using the *Eldridge* balancing formula, the court has drawn back from what were some years ago expanding administrative due process requirements in employee terminations concerning which employees are entitled to a hearing[35] and the type and timing of any hearing that is required.[36] These cases have indicated that the court will be reticent to require more elements of due process than are specified in statutes and regulations. Moreover, they have rejected claims by employees that civil servants are entitled to a hearing before they are removed from their jobs rather than some time later in the administrative process.

In the First Amendment field, the court has shifted the burden and increased the level of proof required for the employee to prevail on complaints of unlawful termination in violation of First Amendment free speech protections.[37] The most direct statement of the court's intention to leave managers free of unnecessary judicial involvement in personnel decisions came recently in *Connick* v. *Myers*.[38]

The *Connick* case arose when Myers, a deputy district attorney in Orleans Parish, Louisiana, got into a disagreement with her supervisor regarding a job transfer. She had been offered a transfer and promotion based upon her performance, but she resisted the step up because it would have required her to prosecute cases in the court of a judge with whom she had been working for some time on an offender diversion program. She saw the move as a conflict of interest. When her supervisor disagreed and insisted upon the move she charged that this was another example of his poor administration of the office. Her criticism alleged a range of administrative problems including attempts to coerce employees into participating in partisan political activities. The supervisor indicated her views were not widely shared within the office. At that, Myers went home and prepared a questionnaire which she circulated to other employees. Her supervisor summoned Myers who was summarily dismissed. The district court awarded damages on grounds that there was no question that she had been fired because of her First Amendment protected speech and there was no showing of significant impairment of organizational operations as defined by previous case law that justified the termination.[39]

The Supreme Court reversed, finding that Myers had not adequately demonstrated the public signif-

[32]See, e.g., *Milliken* v. *Bradley*, 418 U.S. 717 (1974); *Dayton Bd. of Ed.* v. *Brinkman*, 433 U.S. 406 (1977); *Columbus Bd. of Ed.* v. *Penick*, 443 U.S. 449 (1979); *Dayton Bd. of Ed.* v. *Brinkman*, 443 U.S. 526 (1979); and *Firefighters Local Union No. 1784* v. *Stotts*, 81 L. Ed 2d 483 (1984).

[33]*Pasadena Bd. of Education* v. *Spangler*, 427 U.S. 424 (1976).

[34]Indeed one purpose of the Civil Service Reform Act of 1978 was to assemble and clarify the various statutory protections for civil servants provided by, among others, the Civil Rights Act of 1964 as amended, the Age Discrimination in Employment Act of 1967, the Fair Labor Standards Act, and the Rehabilitation Act of 1973. 5 U.S.C. §2302(b) (1978).

[35]*Bishop*, 426 U.S. 341, and *Paul*, 424 U.S. 693.

[36]*Arnett* v. *Kennedy*, 416 U.S. 134 (1974).

[37]Consider the shift from *Pickering* v. *Bd. of Education*, 391 U.S. 563 (1968), to *Mt. Healthy Bd. of Ed.* v. *Doyle*, 429 U.S. 274 (1977), to *Givhan* v. *Western Line Consolidated School Dist.*, 439 U.S. 410 (1979).

[38]*Connick* v. *Myers*, 75 L. Ed 2d 708 (1983).

[39]*Myers* v. *Connick*, 507 F. Supp. 752 (ED La. 1981), *aff'd* 654 F.2d 719 (5th Cir. 1981).

icance of her speech. In so doing, the court added a new requirement to the existing burden an employee must carry in defending his or her speech against reprisal. It was not, however, merely the court's change of this test regarding when an employee can be disciplined that made the case so important, but it was also Justice White's insistence upon deference to management discretion in such matters.

> When employee expression cannot fairly be considered as relating to any matter of political, social, or other concern of the community, government officials should enjoy wide latitude in managing their officers, without intrusive oversight by the judiciary in the name of the First Amendment. Perhaps the government employer's dismissal of the worker may not be fair, but ordinary dismissals from government service which violate no fixed tenure or applicable statute or regulation are not subject to judicial review even if the reasons for the dismissal are alleged to be mistaken or unreasonable.[40]

> We hold that where a public employee speaks not as a citizen upon matters of public concern, but instead as an employee upon matters only of personal interest, absent the most unusual circumstances, a federal court is not the appropriate forum in which to review the wisdom of a personnel decision taken by a public agency allegedly in reaction to the employee's behavior. . . .

> When close working relationships are essential to fulfilling public responsibilities, a wide degree of deference to employers' judgment is appropriate. Furthermore, we do not see the necessity for an employer to allow events to unfold to the extent that the disruption of the office and the destruction of working relationships is manifest before taking action.[41]

The court's language in Connick coupled with its cautions against extensive judicially imposed due process requirements indicates a significant shift toward deference to administrative interests.

5. The Supreme Court Has Consistently Issued Rulings That Make It Easier to Bring Suit in Federal Court. It is true that in the late 1960s and early 1970s the Warren court relaxed the rules governing who could bring a suit in federal court permitting a wider range of litigation. However, the Burger court has issued a string of decisions placing significant limits on standing to sue and other procedural standards governing access to federal courts.[42] In fact, it is in the area of court access rules that the Burger court has made some of the most dramatic changes from the Warren court precedents.

The Burger court has sent other signals indicating that groups interested in changing policy should look to arenas other than the federal courts. For example, it rejected the claim that public interest groups acting as private attorneys general could collect attorneys' fees when they sued successfully.[43] (Congress later reversed that ruling by statute.) The court has also restricted the ability of private groups to claim a right to sue under statutes that do not specifically authorize private litigation, the so-called implied right of action.[44] Just because there may be a violation of law that government is unable or unwilling to prosecute, does not mean that a group of private individuals may step into the breach and demand court action. For several reasons, then, it simply is not true that the trend of the Warren court years to open the doors of the federal courthouse to more lawsuits has been continued by the current court.

6. Federal Courts Are Constantly Expanding the Threat to Administrators from Tort Liability Judgments. The controversy surrounding the vulnerability of officials and units of

---

[40]Connick, 75 L. Ed 2d at 719–720.
[41]Ibid.

[42]See Allen v. Wright, 82 L. Ed 2d 556 (1984); Valley Forge Christian College v. Americans United for Separation of Church and State, 454 U.S. 464 (1982); Duke Power Co. v. Carolina Environmental Study Group, 438 U.S. 59 (1978); Simon v. Eastern Kentucky Welfare Rights Organization, 426 U.S. 26 (1976); and Warth v. Seldin, 422 U.S. 490 (1975).
[43]Alyeska Pipeline v. Wilderness Society, 421 U.S. 240 (1975).
[44]Middlesex County Sewerage Authority v. National Sea Clammers Assn., 453 U.S. 1 (1981); California v. Sierra Club, 451 U.S. 287 (1981); Touche Ross & Co. v. Redington, 442 U.S. 560 (1979); and Cannon v. University of Chicago, 441 U.S. 677 (1979).

government to damage claims is considered elsewhere in this symposium. But since administrators' frustration and anxiety about tort lawsuits is an important part of the conflict between judges and managers, some caveats are worthy of brief mention here.

First, while the Supreme Court has permitted more types of suits for damages over the past decade, it has brought about a kind of trade-off for administrators. At the same time that it has been allowing a wider range of damage suits, it has been limiting broad remedial orders that interfere with ongoing administration.[45] The message to lower courts is to limit interference with current administrative operations, but to let claimants come into court after the fact and collect damages if they can make their case.

Second, recent liability rulings are not unrestricted invitations to sue public officials. Even in the decisions expanding the range of possible damage claims, the Supreme Court has created a series of immunities making it relatively difficult for a plaintiff to win a case.[46] More recently, the court has recognized that its official liability decisions have placed added burdens upon public administrators discouraging initiative and producing time-consuming and costly litigation.[47] In *Harlow* v. *Fitzgerald*, the court expanded the standard immunity afforded public officials in federal tort suits and instructed judges to guard against unnecessary pretrial discovery and other burdensome procedures.[48]

In sum, the rules and judicial trends affecting the judicial-administrative relationship are not part of a continuing judicial assault on public administration. In a variety of areas the federal courts have demonstrated a sensitivity to the problems administrators must face. That does not mean that they have been willing to serve as rubber stamps for administrative action, but it does give lie to some of the more extreme charges that the courts are about the business of undermining administrators.

ADMINISTRATIVE DEREGULATION AND REFUSAL TO ACT: A DEVELOPING JUDICIAL-ADMINISTRATIVE TENSION

In one area an increase has recently occurred in judicial-administrative tension. Historically, legal challenges to administrators have primarily concerned efforts to limit overzealous use of administrative discretion. In the administrative environment of the late 1970s and the 1980s, however, attention has shifted to situations in which administrators either refuse to act at all or withdraw from previously developed policies. Although the need to compel administrative action as well as guard against excessive administrative zeal is rarely discussed these days, it is an important issue that was stated by Carl Friedrich more than 40 years ago.

> Too often it is taken for granted that as long as we can keep government from doing wrong we have made it responsible. What is more important is to insure effective action of any sort. . . . An official should be as responsible for inaction as for wrong action; certainly the average voter will criticize the government as severely for one as for the other.[49]

The efforts of the Carter and Reagan administrations to deregulate and generally move administrative agencies to less proactive approaches to their work have been the focal point of controversy. It is important in any discussion of administration and law to consider not only limits on the discretion to act but also the legal forces compelling the exercise of discretion. The cases calling for mandatory use of administrative authority have been basically of four types: (1) those objecting to an administrative refusal to launch a fact-finding or policy-making process; (2) agency refusal to issue rules; (3) intentional delay in agency action; and (4) rescission of existing or proposed policies.

---

[45]See, *Rizzo*, 423 U.S. 362. See also, David Rosenbloom, "Public Administrators' Official Immunity: Developments During the Seventies," *Public Administration Review*, vol. 40 (March–April 1980), pp. 166–173.

[46]See, e.g., *Butz* v. *Economou*, 438 U.S. 478 (1978).

[47]457 U.S. 800 (1982).

[48]*Ibid.*, pp. 817–818.

[49]Carl Friedrich, "Public Policy and the Nature of Administrative Responsibility," in Friedrich and E. S. Mason (eds.), *Public Policy* (Cambridge, Mass.: Harvard University Press, 1940), p. 4.

Controlling the agency agenda is an important element of administrative discretion. Deciding what problems to address and assigning priorities is often more than a question of efficient management. It may involve a strategic decision. Administrators would frankly prefer to avoid some problems. Take the case in which the involvement of the Food and Drug Administration (FDA) was demanded in the capital punishment controversy. Death row inmates petitioned the FDA to launch an investigation to determine whether the pharmaceuticals used for execution by lethal injection were safe and effective for the specific application to which they were put. Drugs could only meet that criteria if they brought about quick and painless death, but the inmates alleged there was substantial evidence that in improper dosage and administration the drugs currently used could "leave a prisoner conscious but paralyzed while dying, a sentient witness of his or her own slow lingering asphyxiation." FDA refused to investigate on grounds that it lacked jurisdiction to review state-sanctioned uses of drugs for these purposes. The agency did not argue that it lacked the capacity to inquire into the matter, but that it was without jurisdiction in the case. Moreover, the agency claimed that even if it had jurisdiction, it also had complete and unreviewable enforcement discretion concerning whether and when to take administrative action. The FDA refused to act on the basis of that discretion.

The D.C. Circuit Court of Appeals, however, found that the agency did have jurisdiction which it had previously asserted, for example, in drug experiments involving state prison inmates. The court rejected the claim to unreviewable enforcement discretion and found the FDA refusal to launch an investigation arbitrary and capricious. The court wrote:

In this case FDA is clearly refusing to exercise enforcement discretion because it does not wish to become embroiled in an issue so morally and emotionally troubling as the death penalty. Yet this action amounts to an abnegation of statutory responsibility by the very agency that Congress charged with the task of ensuring that our people do not suffer harm from misbranded drugs. . . . As a result of the FDA's inaction, appellants face the risk of cruel execution and are deprived of FDA's expert judgement as to the effectiveness of the drugs used for lethal injection. . . .[50]

While the court will not dictate the outcome or the particular administrative process to be employed, the simple assertion of absolute discretion will be challenged.

Another problem area is the refusal to make rules. The Eighth Circuit Court of Appeals recently found that the secretary of agriculture had abused his discretion by refusing to issue rules under a statute governing farm loan foreclosure. A family charged that the Department of Agriculture had an obligation under the statute to promulgate rules and provide adequate notice to those affected concerning possible deferments of foreclosures. The government argued that the statute "merely created an additional power to be wielded at the discretion of the agency, or placed in the Secretary's back pocket for safekeeping."[51] The court found the refusal to make rules or institute any kind of process of reasoned decision making a "complete abdication" of responsibility.[52]

In some ways related to the refusal to make rules is the tactic of delaying for as long as possible the issuance of rules required by statute. Here again, courts seem willing to draw a line. Efforts by the Environmental Protection Agency (EPA) to delay implementation of rules required by the Resource Conservation and Recovery Act covering toxic wastes were successfully challenged in a number of lawsuits. Among the remedies sought by the plaintiffs in one of the cases was an award of attorney's fees under the Equal Access to Justice Act. The court awarded the fee finding that the intentional delaying tactics employed by the agency were "exactly the type of arbitrary governmental behavior that the EAJA was designed to deter."[53]

Finally, a number of challenges have been brought against efforts of administrators to deregulate by rescinding existing agency regulations or

[50]*Chaney* v. *Heckler*, 718 F.2d 1174 (D.C. Cir. 1983).
[51]*Allison* v. *Block*, 723 F.2d 631, 633 (8th Cir. 1983).
[52]*Ibid.*, p. 638.
[53]*Environmental Defense Fund* v. *EPA*, 716 F.2d 915, 921 (D.C. Cir. 1983). The other key case compelling production of rules was *Illinois* v. *Gorsuch*, 530 F. Supp. 340 (D.D.C. 1981).

withdrawing pending rules. The Federal Communications Commission (FCC) efforts to reduce its regulatory control over broadcasting have prompted several such lawsuits. Another recent example is the withdrawal of mandatory automobile passive restraint rules by the Department of Transportation. In both cases, administrators claimed that the decision to reduce regulation administratively was not really policy making and was a purely discretionary matter not subject to judicial examination. The courts rejected that claim in both cases and insisted that a change in policy is a policy decision whether it results in promulgation of a new rule or abandonment of an old one. In fact, a panel of the D.C. Circuit Court of Appeals said, "such abrupt shifts in policy do constitute 'danger signals' that the Commission may be acting inconsistently with its statutory mandate. . . . We will require therefore that the Commission provide a reasoned analysis indicating that prior policies and standards are being deliberately changed, not casually ignored."[54] Having said that, however, the court upheld the FCC deregulation. It cautioned the commission that it was perilously close to violating its statutory responsibility but found enough evidence to say the FCC had met its requirements of reasoned analysis.

The Supreme Court did not find the necessary foundation for the rescission of the passive restraint rule and remanded the matter to the agency. It concluded that an "agency changing its course by rescinding a rule is obligated to supply a reasoned analysis for the change beyond that which may be required when the agency does not act in the first instance."[55] Since a rule was presumably adopted in the first instance on the basis of a careful reasoning process using the agency's expertise and available evidence, there is a presumption in favor of the rule. The court concluded:

> In so holding, we fully recognize that "regulatory agencies do not establish rules of conduct to last forever, . . . and that an agency must be given latitude to adapt their rules and policies to the demands of changing circumstances. . . ." But the forces of change do not

always or necessarily point in the direction of deregulation. In the abstract, there is no more reason to presume that changing circumstances require the rescission of prior action, instead of a revision in or even the extension of current regulation. If Congress established a presumption from which judicial review should start, that presumption—contrary to petitioner's view—is not *against* safety regulation, but *against* changes in current policy that are not justified by the rulemaking record.[56] (Emphasis in original.)

There is one final problem of what might be termed negative discretion. Administrators often argue that judges should defer to their administrative expertise regardless of the type of policy under consideration. However, judges sometimes doubt that administrators are entitled to such deference when there does not appear to be a policy at all but rather a failure to make any policy or to enforce existing standards. Justice Brennan, for instance, observed that while judges ought to defer to the expertise of correctional administrators, the prison conditions frequently in dispute often arise not from a policy decision based upon administrative expertise but from sheer neglect. "There is no reason of comity, judicial restraint, or recognition of expertise for courts to defer to negligent omissions of officials who lack the resources or motivation to operate prisons within the limits of decency."[57]

Federal District Judge Bruce Jenkins of Utah came to a similar conclusion recently in a case involving claims made against the government by the families of alleged victims of nuclear testing. The court awarded damages to those who demonstrated that their illnesses stemmed from the testing. Jenkins rejected the notion that there should be a deference to administrative discretion in this sort of case. There was, he said, "no official policy of indifference to safety."[58] The "actions taken were negligently insufficient—not as a matter of discretion at all—as a matter of deliberate choice making—but as a matter of negligently failing to warn, to measure and to inform, at a level sufficient to meet the stated

---

[54]*Office of Communications of the United Church of Christ*, 707 F.2d at 1425.

[55]*Motor Vehicle Manufacturers' Assn.* v. *State Farm Mutual*, 77 L. Ed 2d 443, 457 (1983).

[56]*Ibid.*

[57]*Rhodes*, 452 U.S. at 362 (Brennan, J., concurring in part, dissenting in part).

[58]*Irene Allen* v. *United States*, 588 F. Supp. 247, 337 (D. Utah 1984).

goals of the Congress, the executive branch and the Atomic Energy Commission."[59]

In sum, administrators may not assume absolute administrative discretion when they refuse to act as compared to cases where they are alleged to have acted too vigorously. The problem of relating administrative discretion and judicial obligations to ensure accountability is all the more difficult when there is no policy for a given action but an actual departure from stated policy or simple neglect. This concept of negative discretion is an aspect of the judicial-administrative relationship that is very much a developing matter and worthy of attention.

LAW AS A DISCRETION-REINFORCING AGENT

There are and always will be natural tensions between administrators and judges over the nature and boundaries of administrative authority. Yet there is a simultaneous positive aspect to this law-administration relationship. It is worthwhile to assess the reasons administrators ought to attempt to foster better working relations with judges, notwithstanding the difficulties such a prescription entails.

Knowledge of the legal elements of administration is an enabling force. Formal authority of administrators is derived from a statute or executive order. Care in using such authority supports effective administration. There is an admittedly rough but useful analogy to the budget process. An agency without adequate fiscal resources is in serious trouble. The amount of funds available is a significant factor in the agency's ability to perform. It is both an enabling force and, in a sense, a constraint. The fact that budgetary politics are complex and often disappointing does not indicate that a good manager ought to abandon concern for the subject or cease efforts to improve relationships with appropriations committees. The same is true of law and administration.

An understanding of legal developments is also important as a defensive matter. It can help to avoid liability judgments, prevent the loss of invested time and effort when agency decisions are reversed, avoid loss of control over one's agency to a complex re-

medial court order, and lead to savings of money as well as time from having to replicate and improve work rejected in judicial review.

Two other key functions are served by enhancing the relationship between administrators and judges. Understanding the relationship provides increased predictability which is critical to any manager. The first task is to understand judicial trends sufficiently to anticipate likely judicial responses to agency actions. An awareness of legal limits on administration provides an ability to predict not only what courts will do with respect to one's own but also to other agencies. Administrators thus informed can manage their operations with some expectation of how other agencies will be able to respond. Administration without attention to law would not mean more efficiency, it would mean chaos.

Finally, administrators need legal support for their claim to legitimacy within government and, perhaps more importantly, within the larger society. There is a certain irony in the fact that administrators busy challenging the legitimacy of judicial involvement in policy making are in danger of being convicted by their own arguments. Many of the charges made against judges can be made in only slightly modified form against administrators. They are not elected. Many cannot be removed from office except for cause. It is extremely difficult to keep them responsive and responsible. They frequently do precisely what the majority of the people do not wish them to do. The list goes on. Beyond that particular threat to legitimacy, however, is the need for assistance in establishing a legitimate place for administrators in the constitutional framework. Our constitutional authority is derivative. We obtain our authority by inference and indirectly.[60] We must always be able to trace our authority back through the chain of statutes and judicial rulings that support us.

CONCLUSION

This article has assessed common assumptions about the evolving relationship between federal courts and administrators. It has provided evidence that despite the natural tensions between administrators and

---

[59]*Ibid.*, p. 338.

[60]I am indebted for this idea, if not these precise words, to John Rohr.

judges, it is an overstatement to charge that federal judges neither understand nor care about the harm their rulings may cause to management. In fact, legal authorities and opinions, if properly understood, are enabling and protecting forces providing sources of administrative discretion and protecting its use.

Moreover, the federal judiciary, led by the Supreme Court, has in several respects drawn back from intervention in administration in open recognition of the need for managerial flexibility. That good reasons exist for not applauding some of those deferential rulings does not change the fact that they do support more discretion. One rapidly developing area of judicial-administrative challenge is likely to remain of importance in the near term at least: the refusal of administrators to use the discretion that they possess.

Good reasons exist for administrators to develop their relationship with courts, reasons of an extremely practical nature and others of wider import, including the need to have law as a support for the legitimacy of public administration. In the final analysis, administrative discretion does not exist for its own sake. Administrators are vested with particular authority to serve public purposes in a society predicated on a rule of law. Natural tension, yes, but necessary as well.

QUESTIONS FOR DISCUSSION

1. What should be the legitimate function of federal courts in reviewing administrative decisions?

2. What have been the factors leading to judicial intervention in administrative matters?

3. What is the significance of "legislative intent" in judicial decisions dealing with administrative practices?

4. What should the courts do when agencies refuse to act according to the requirements of law?

5. What have been the fiscal consequences of judicial involvement in administrative decisions?

SUGGESTED READINGS

DASCHLE, TOM, "Making the Veterans Administration Work for Veterans," *Journal of Legislation*, 11 (Winter 1984), 1–14.

EDWARDS, HARRY T., "Judicial Review of Deregulation," *Northern Kentucky Law Review*, 11, No. 2 (1984), 229–83.

GARLAND, MERRICK B., "Deregulation and Judicial Review," *Harvard Law Review*, 98 (Jan. 1985), 507–91.

HARRIMAN, LINDA, AND JEFFREY D. STRAUSSMAN, "Do Judges Determine Budget Decisions?: Federal Court Decisions in Prison Reforms and State Spending for Corrections," *Public Administration Review*, 43 (July/Aug. 1983), 343–51.

HARTLE, TERRY W., "The Law, the Courts, Education and Public Administration," *Public Administration Review*, 41 (Sept./Oct. 1981), 595–601.

HOROWITZ, DONALD L., *The Courts and Social Policy*. Washington, DC: Brookings Institution, 1977.

KOCH, CHARLES H., JR., "Confining Judicial Authority over Administrative Action," *Missouri Law Review*, 49 (Spring 1984), 183–250.

LEHNER, PETER H., "Judicial Review of Administrative Inaction," *Columbia Law Review*, 83 (Apr. 1983), 627–89.

MELNICK, R. SHEP, *Regulation and the Courts: The Clean Air Act*. Washington, DC: Brookings Institution, 1983.

MILSTONE, JAMES, "Automatic Occupant Restraints and Judicial Review: How a Federal Agency Can Violate Congressional Will and Get Away with It," *Valparaiso University Law Review*, 19 (Spring 1985), 693–727.

ORFIELD, GARY, *Must We Bus?: Segregated Schools and National Policy*. Washington, DC: Brookings Institution, 1978.

ROSENBLOOM, DAVID H., *Public Administration and Law: Bench v. Bureau in the United States*. New York: Marcel Dekker, 1983.

7 YES
IS DECENTRALIZED GOVERNMENT MORE RESPONSIVE AND DEMOCRATIC THAN CENTRALIZED GOVERNMENT?

The National Neighborhood Platform[1]
The National Association of Neighborhoods

DEVELOPMENT OF THE NATIONAL NEIGHBORHOOD PLATFORM

In November 1978, at the National Association of Neighborhoods' Eighth National Meeting in Hartford, Connecticut, member neighborhood organizations from around the country recognized the need for a public policy agenda for and by neighborhoods. At this meeting the groundwork was laid for a nation-wide series of local Neighborhood Platform Conventions culminating in a National Neighborhood Platform Convention to be held in November 1979. This was the beginning of the National Neighborhood Platform Campaign.

A Director of the Platform Campaign was hired early in 1979 to coordinate and support the efforts of N.A.N. leaders and members in the Campaign process. Regional organizers were assigned to various sections of the country to provide encouragement and assistance to sponsors of local Conventions.

During 1979, nearly 50 local Neighborhood Platform Conventions were held around the country. These local Conventions served two valuable purposes. The production of each local Platform Convention allowed a variety of neighborhood groups to come together to share ideas, to exchange information, and to devise common solutions for their problems. In many cities, this effort established or strengthened an effective city-wide coalition of neighborhood organizations. Local Platforms will serve as action agendas for these coalitions in the coming years. Each is a comprehensive statement of neighborhood beliefs, designed for policy input at neighborhood, ward, city, county and state levels of government.

_____
Submitted for the record in U. S. Cong., *Neighborhood Conditions*, Hearing before the Joint Economic Committee, 97th Cong., 1st Sess., 1981, pp. 48–52.

[1]Written and adopted by the National Association of Neighborhoods National Neighborhood Platform Convention, Nov. 11, 1979.

Equally as important, these local Platform Conventions served as the basis of the National Platform Convention. Participants in the local Conventions elected delegates to represent them at the National Neighborhood Platform Convention. The resolutions of the local Conventions were compiled to produce an impressive document of resolutions regarding neighborhood government, public safety, housing, employment, economic development, our environment, transportation, education, rural development and human rights. The National Neighborhood Platform was based upon these resolutions.

Seven hundred N.A.N. members, local Convention delegates, and other neighborhood advocates convened in Louisville, Kentucky from November 9–11, 1979 to develop the National Neighborhood Platform. They met in twenty issue committees to draft resolutions. Additional resolutions were added by petition, and then all resolutions were voted upon by the delegates as a whole. The result of this monumental, year-long effort is the National Neighborhood Platform—the neighborhoods' agenda for the 1980's.

THE NATIONAL NEIGHBORHOOD PLATFORM

Preamble

Two centuries ago, our nation was founded on the proposition that all people are created equal and are endowed with the inalienable rights to life, liberty, and the pursuit of happiness. Governments are properly instituted among people to secure these rights. While the world has changed, our faith in this proposition remains unchanged.

As our ancestors fashioned institutions to secure and enhance their rights, so do we. As our ancestors sought to form a more perfect union, establish justice and secure the blessings of liberty, so do we. As successive generations have sacrificed much in order to give new birth to freedom and to guarantee that government of the people, by the people, and for the people shall not perish, so shall we.

In the two centuries since our founding, our institutions have grown too large and too remote to allow us to meet face-to-face to seek the common good. Thus, many Americans have withdrawn into apathy or have been overwhelmed by forces too powerful for any individual to withstand.

In response, we now turn to our neighborhoods and communities to fulfill our human capacities as citizens by participating in making those decisions which directly affect our lives. Rediscovering citizenship in our neighborhoods, we reaffirm the principles of freedom, justice, and equality upon which our nation was founded. We believe that those who are affected by the decisions of government must be consulted by those who govern; that it is the right of citizens to have access to the instruments of power; and that it is their duty to learn to use them effectively and wisely.

We reaffirm our belief in the N.A.N. Neighborhood Bill of Responsibilities and Rights which we adopted in 1976 when we declared that governments and private institutions must recognize:

The right of neighborhoods to determine their own goals, consistent with the broad civic ideals of justice and human equality;

The right of neighborhoods to define their own governing structures, operating procedures, names and boundaries;

The right of democratically organized neighborhoods to receive a just share of private and public resources necessary for the implementation and support of neighborhood decisions;

The right of democratically organized neighborhoods to review in advance and decisively influence all stages of planning and implementation of all actions of government and private institutions affecting the neighborhood; and

The right of neighborhoods to information necessary to carry out these rights.

Rediscovering democracy, we join with neighbors in communities across our land to create a neighborhood movement built upon the belief that people can and should govern themselves democratically and justly. The neighborhood is a political unit which makes this possible; since the smallness of the neighborhood enables all residents to deliberate, decide, and act together for the common good.

We share our neighborhoods with individuals and families of diverse needs, interests, backgrounds, and beliefs. We cooperate and work with the labor movement, church groups, and all other groups with whom we share common goals. The full humanity of every person must be affirmed in our neighborhoods. Therefore, we continue our determined opposition to every form of racism, classism, or sexism. Justice is only possible when neighbors, in their collective decisions, respect their diversity and their interdependence with other neighborhoods.

People organized in neighborhoods, responding to their fellow residents as human beings and families, rather than as clients, are best able to provide needed services. People organized in neighborhoods are best able to pronounce and amplify in firm tones the voice of citizens so as to command the respect of government and private institutions. People organized in neighborhood assemblies are best able to create government under their control.

The key problem addressed by our National Neighborhood Platform is the problem of displacement. By displacement we mean the calculated efforts of large corporations, banks, real estate and utility contracts with the cooperation of the federal government, to bring about the wholesale racial and economic resegregation of the cities of this country, both large and small. This displacement of our people from the neighborhoods includes the processes of gentrification as well as disinvestment and destruction of basic community institutions, public facilities and educational facilities. Our national program calls for ways and means to stabilize communities, provide and maintain low and moderate income housing, provide community control of the economic and community development processes and provide accountability of corporations which are investing and disinvesting in our cities. Our Platform is a program that addresses the most crucial issue in our nation: Will this country be developed for the majority of the people, or the few?

This Platform which we have set for ourselves shall not be soon accomplished. But we, the people of America's neighborhoods and communities, seek by its declaration to turn our country in a new direction. We seek to restore a sense of trust and mutuality in public life, to open up our government to citizen participation, to unleash the power of people deciding together their own future. Many institutions will have to change, many policies will have to be revised, many actions are yet to be taken, but nothing is so powerful as the ideal of freedom, justice, and equality when its time has come, and when the people are prepared to sacrifice to make it prevail.

We do declare that it is the will of the people residing in America's neighborhoods that these actions be taken. We do declare that they are just, and represent the counsel of reason, as well as the support of numbers. We mutually pledge to each other unremitting effort to enact this Platform and to bring, once again, a rebirth of freedom and democracy to our land. Recognizing that many past decisions by government and private institutions have not been in the common interest of all Americans, and secure in our faith that citizens will participate in governing their neighborhoods if given the power and authority to do so, we declare that it seems best to the people residing in America's neighborhoods that the following actions be taken to empower neighborhood organizations, promote neighborhood government and ensure citizen participation, secure public safety, provide physical improvements to our neighborhoods, ensure employment and economic development, maintain a pure environment, provide adequate transportation and education, develop rural areas, and protect the human rights of all who live in our neighborhoods.

Empowering Neighborhoods

We believe that by meeting together in our own communities and by empowering neighborhood organizations, we can take our destiny into our own hands. The following are necessary if neighborhood organizations and governments are to achieve increased citizen responsibility, justice, and equality in our neighborhoods and in our nation.

Neighborhood organizations and governments must have adequate and direct funding from both public and private sources.

Neighborhood organizations and governments must have adequate technical assistance.

Neighborhood organizations and governments must have access to all information necessary to carry out their programs and activities, obtained through state and local "freedom of information" acts, if necessary.

Neighborhood Government

Our government jurisdictions have become so large, distant and unresponsive to peoples' lives and concerns that our communities are now, to a serious degree, ungoverned. Administrative neglect and private actions have endangered the safety and justice of our communities. We believe it is the responsibility of citizens in our democratic republic to govern the affairs of their own neighborhood communities in common deliberation, with binding jurisdictional power, and in constitutional relationship to other communities.

We propose that neighborhood residents be empowered to define their own geographic boundaries and establish directly elected or representative neighborhood government which must then be recognized by city and state governments, endowed with legal status and public powers, and supported by tax revenues.

We propose that the federal government not distribute any revenue-sharing or block grant funds to states which do not provide enabling legislation for establishing neighborhood governments or to local authorities which refuse to recognize duly established neighborhood governments.

We propose that duly established neighborhood governments have at least the following powers:

A. The ability to raise tax revenues.
B. The ability to incur bond indebtedness.
C. The ability to enter into interjurisdictional agreements.
D. The ability to settle neighborhood disputes.
E. The ability to contract with City or with private providers of services.
F. The ability to conduct elections.
G. The ability to sue or be sued.
H. The ability to determine planning, zoning and land use.
I. The ability to exercise limited eminent domain.
J. The ability to undertake public investment.
K. The ability to provide public and social services.
L. The ability to operate enterprises.

Citizen Participation Through Neighborhood Organization

We believe that government should provide for citizens' maximum authority over decisions that affect them, through the vehicle of neighborhood organizations, and toward the particular goal of ending racial inequality.

We propose that local governments should be restructured to empower neighborhoods to exercise maximum authority over decisions affecting them, consistent with the goal of ending racial segregation. Since federal programs designed to assist neighborhoods have frequently been administered without the involvement of neighborhood residents and without regard to their needs, to secure rights of maximum authority the following steps must be taken:

A. Elected neighborhood representatives must be given a policy voice in all decisions regarding federal funds in the neighborhood.
B. Neighborhood organizations must have the ability to prepare and present a neighborhood development plan to guide all federal, revenue-sharing and economic development expenditures in the neighborhood.
C. Neighborhood organizations must have the ability to obtain legal counsel to contest federal expenditures.
D. Independently funded and staffed neighborhood organizations must have the ability to monitor program operation and government financial expenditures in their neighborhoods.
E. Neighborhood organizations must have franking privileges.

We propose that neighborhood organizations actively encourage non-partisan voter registration, voter education and voter turn-out.

We propose that all policy-making boards and forums of local and state government be made up of representatives from the neighborhoods, elected by the people in non-partisan elections. Terms must be staggered and equitably represent affirmative action concerns, the elderly and disabled.

We propose that full Congressional voting rights be granted to the District of Columbia.

Volunteerism

The quality and freedom of community life require deep and widely shared voluntary citizen action and commitment by neighborhood residents. The activities of volunteers in neighborhood organizations should be increased and strongly supported by the public and private sectors.

We believe that the efforts of individual volunteers should be supported by providing them with leadership, skill and policy development training at the neighborhood level.

We believe that youth should be involved in decision-making at the neighborhood level, and propose that such methods as school credit, leadership development, vocational internships and stipends be developed for their participation in neighborhood organizations.

We propose that volunteers serving with non-profit neighborhood organizations be allowed to declare allowable, non-reimbursed out-of-pocket costs for income tax purposes, or to receive a direct stipend.

We propose that HR 4209 be passed, giving now ineligible neighborhood and community organizations the ability to use bulk mailing rates.

We propose that the federal government increase its financial support of the ACTION Agency for the VISTA (Volunteers in Service to America) and RSVP (Retired Senior Volunteer Program) programs.

Social Service Delivery

Certain social services must be provided to the residents of our neighborhoods, and the provision of these social services must promote self-sufficiency, not dependency. Neighborhood organizations are best equipped to identify and provide the social service needs of residents in a way that enhances their human dignity.

We propose that, in order to promote self-sufficiency, public funding must be made directly available to neighborhood organizations to plan, deliver, monitor and evaluate social service programs in the neighborhood and that such programs must be based in the neighborhood.

We believe that child care is a right, not a privilege. To promote this right, neighborhood organizations must run community child care programs, including day and night care (up to 17 years), recreation, job training, supplementary education and family support services. To implement and administer funding to such programs, state-wide boards (with equal representation from neighborhood residents, child care workers and parents) should be elected from the neighborhood. They should be empowered to develop, review, change and enforce regulations for all child care programs.

We believe that comprehensive physical and mental health care are basic rights.

We believe that health care as a profit-oriented business will never meet the needs of the people and oppose the destruction of public health care in the inner city as a part of a corporate and government policy of deliberate dislocation and genocide.

We propose that neighborhood-based and community-controlled comprehensive health-care facilities be established and emphasize preventive health care and health education. All neighborhood residents should have access to such facilities in their neighborhoods.

We believe that the development of community-based and controlled support systems for de-institutionalized persons must be encouraged, and that education programs must be established to promote community acceptance of such persons.

Displacement

Human beings are injured by forced removal from their communities. Housing and residential stability are essential to human dignity and well-being. Neighborhood organizations must defend their residents against displacement.

We believe that people have a right to housing and residential stability and that neighborhood residents must maintain control of the neighborhood to ensure this right.

We believe that neighborhood organizations must form active partnerships with federal, state and local governments and the private sector to preserve and restore existing, structurally sound, housing stock.

We propose that, for those individually and collectively agreeing to be displaced, the public or private sources of displacement must provide resident-approved relocation schemes. These must include equal or improved replacement housing, an equal or improved social and economic environment, and relocation funds.

We propose that developers in a neighborhood be required to reserve adequate new development units for original residents, including tenants.

We propose that public funds avoid displacement and support the maintenance and development of economically, racially and ethnically diverse neighborhoods through the following means:

A. Conversion of tenants to homeowners.
B. Strengthening of the Uniform Relocation Act.
C. Making 80 percent of homesteading, mortgage subsidies and low interest improvement loans available to low income and poor people.
D. Making the allocation of federal funds to local governments dependent upon the existence of local antidisplacement plans which independent neighborhood organizations must help develop, implement and monitor.
E. Expansion of state and federal programs for minor home repairs for elderly homeowners.

We believe that the government and private sectors should aggressively support neighborhood organization antidisplacement strategies such as community development corporations, community credit unions, land-banking, neighborhood planning, and neighborhood housing counseling.

We propose that the following steps be taken by local and federal government (as appropriate) in order to avoid displacement due to condominium conversion:

A. Consent of 75 percent of tenants be required to convert multifamily rental units to condominiums, cooperatives or hotels.
B. Lifetime tenancy to be guaranteed to senior citizens and families with incomes of $20,000/year or less.
C. Establishment or enforcement of the tenants' "first right of refusal."
D. Promotion of cooperative housing.
E. Strengthening of disclosure requirements on ownership, financing and third party contractual agreements.

We propose that tenants be guaranteed the first option to purchase their homes from their landlords, and that they receive sufficient technical assistance and private funds to exercise this right.

We propose that anti-speculation taxes be adopted to tax windfall profits on all residential and commercial property sales by non-resident owners (in cases where resale takes place in under five years and without significant rehabilitation). Funds so generated should be used to provide property tax relief to low and moderate income people (where legislation mandates such relief) or put into community-based cooperative funds.

We propose a moratorium on the use of "eminent domain" by public and non-public bodies un-less 75 percent of the residents of the affected area agree to the proposed activity.

7 NO IS DECENTRALIZED GOVERNMENT MORE RESPONSIVE AND DEMOCRATIC THAN CENTRALIZED GOVERNMENT?

Is Small Really So Beautiful? Is Big Really So Ugly? Size, Effectiveness, and Democracy in Local Government*

K. Newton

Discussing the appropriate size for units of government, Robert Dahl observes that 'The smaller the unit the greater the opportunity for citizens to participate in the decisions of their government, yet the less of the environment they can control. Thus for most citizens, participation in very large units becomes minimal and in very small units it becomes trivial.'[1] This is the heart of a problem which plagues attempts to reform modern government: on the one hand, large units of government are necessary for the efficient and effective provision of public services; on the other, small units are more conducive to grass roots democracy, a sense of belonging, a high rate of individual participation, and close contact between political elites, leaders, and ordinary citizens. For the sake of brevity these competing claims will be referred to as functional effectiveness and democracy.[2]

The incompatibility of functional effectiveness and democracy has presented political scientists and politicians with a conundrum ever since the early days of the Greek *polis*, but the problem is specially acute for local government, where it is not only possible to re-draw political boundaries, but advisable to do so as the shape of urban-industrial society changes to form ever larger continuously built-up areas. Thus the Redcliffe-Maud Commission, for example, saw an adjustment between democracy and efficiency as one of its fundamental considerations. By this it meant, 'the best practical balance between the needs of efficiency (in terms of population, geography and resources of money, manpower and technical equipment) and the requirements of effective representation'.[3] Local government reform in the United Kingdom, as well as in Sweden, Belgium, and Denmark, has had to seek ways of striking this balance, and, since, in most cases, the result has been larger units of government, the claims of effectiveness appear to have been stronger than those of democracy. The issue is also a live one in the United States where the merits of metropolitan consolidation and community control have been contested in terms very similar to those of Dahl and the Redcliffe-Maud Commission.[4]

This paper will argue that the classical conundrum is a false one, and that large units of local

From K. Newton, "Is Small Really So Beautiful? Is Big Really So Ugly? Size, Effectiveness, and Democracy in Local Government," *Political Studies* (Oxford), 30 (June 1982), 190–206. Reprinted with permission.

*This paper started life as a contribution to a seminar at Nuffield College, Oxford, was rewritten for the Political Studies Association meeting at Warwick in 1978, and then appeared in the Studies in Public Policy series of the Centre for the Study of Public Policy, the University of Strathclyde. I am most grateful to Frank Bealey, John Bochel, Patrick Dunleavy, Ed Page, Paul Peterson, Jim Sharpe, and Jeff Stanyer for their constructive criticism.

[1] R. A. Dahl, 'The City in the Future of Democracy', *American Political Science Review*, 61 (1967), p. 960.

[2] Various writers use different terms to express essentially the same things—see R. A. Dahl and E. R. Tufte, *Size and Democracy* (London, Oxford University Press, 1974), pp. 110–17; L. J. Sharpe, 'American Democracy Reconsidered: Part II and Conclusions', *British Journal of Political Science*, 3 (1973), pp. 130–44; R. Honey, 'Conflicting Problems in the Political Organisation of Space', *Annals of Regional Science*, 10 (1976), 45–60.

[3] *Report of the Royal Commission on Local Government in England* (London, HMSO, 1969, Cmnd. 4040), p. 6.

[4] See, for example, N. I. Feinstein and S. S. Feinstein, 'The Future of Community Control', *American Political Science Review*, 70 (1976), p. 905.

government are no less effective and efficient than small ones, and no less democratic. The paper will reach this conclusion by showing that:

1. the democratic merits of small units of government have often been exaggerated and romanticized, while their democratic deficiencies have been overlooked;
2. large units are as economically efficient as small ones, and have a greater functional capacity;
3. large units do not seem to be deficient in democratic qualities and may even be more democratic in some respects;
4. hence there is no necessary incompatibility between the size necessary for functional effectiveness and that required for democracy.

It is not a matter of saying how big is 'big', and then labelling units of local government 'good' and 'bad' according to their size. Nor is it a matter of searching for an optimum size. Rather, the aim must be to trace the relative effects (if any) of size on the structures and processes of local government, allowing for the possibility that increasing size may well improve some aspects of functional effectiveness and democratic performance, while detracting from others, and also for the possibility that these effects may well change, creating U and ~ shaped curves as size increases. In other words, rather than drawing an arbitrary line between big and small, the (changing) relationship between size, on the one hand, and the various dimensions of functional effectiveness and democracy, on the other, should be examined. It may then be possible to say how and why the question of size should be considered in debates about local government reform.

For present purposes size refers primarily to population size, and to those social characteristics which are generally (but not invariably) associated with it, such as geographical size, population density, a local economy that is mainly industrial and commercial, and all the multifarious characteristics of life in urban-industrial areas. Such a broad and loose definition would be inadequate for many purposes, but it suffices here for two reasons. First, few empirical studies try to unravel the effects of different aspects and correlates of size, so to do so here would be a largely empty exercise.[5] Some studies

carefully isolate the effects of population size as such, some systematically examine the effects of population density and overcrowding, and others trace urban and rural differences, but for the most part the variables that are usually closely associated with population size are not clearly separated from size as such. However, the fact that the clear distinctions are not always drawn is not a crucial matter, which leads to the second reason. The problem of size is most acute in the large metropolitan centres of urban-industrial society, and these invariably have large populations covering wide areas, high population densities, and a tendency towards overcrowding, and all the social and psychological merits and deficiencies of life in the modern city. This simplifies the definitional problem since, from the policy-making point of view, the practical issue is how to organize local government in large urban agglomerations with populations of about (for the sake of argument) a quarter of a million or more. Consequently, it is not of overwhelming importance to distinguish between the effects of size and its correlates, for in the real world, the most important problem is how to organize local government in large, urban areas. Big city government is the main concern.

This paper will be organized around the assumption, explicit in some studies, but implicit in most, that the two main functions of local government are to maximize functional effectiveness and local democracy.[6] It will start with functional effectiveness and will bring as broad a range of secondary data as possible to bear on the two issues.

I. SIZE AND FUNCTIONAL EFFECTIVENESS

Three main arguments are used against large units of local government so far as their functional effectiveness is concerned. The first, a remarkably poor one, is used by Dahl who writes that 'the mouse and the sparrow have outlasted the brontosaurus and the sabre-toothed tiger'.[7] The reply to this is that the elephant and giraffe have survived as long as

---

[5]For criticism of studies which confuse the effects of size and density see J. J. Palen, 'Density, Crowding and Pathology: Research and Reappraisal', paper presented to the Ninth Congress of the International Sociological Association, Uppsala, Sweden, 1978, p. 7.

[6]J. Stanyer refers to these as the service provision and community principles in 'Are Two Tiers the Best Buy for the Big Cities?', *Municipal Review*, 596 (1979), p. 128.
[7]Dahl, 'The City in the Future of Democracy', p. 969.

the mouse and the sparrow, and that all four have outlived the dodo. The enormous size of dinosaurs certainly catches the imagination, but there are probably just as many extinct creepy-crawlies, and, in any case, dinosaurs survived for many millions of years. Size is irrelevant.

The second argument, which concerns diseconomies of scale, is not on much firmer ground. The subject has been researched at length in many countries because changing boundaries and population sizes is one of the few things local government reformers can do with any certainty, but the research results are far from unambiguous. For example, of seventy-three attempts to ascertain the relationship between population size and service costs in British local government, thirty-eight found statistically significant relationships, eighteen found significant but substantively trivial relationships, and the remaining seventeen uncovered significant and quite substantive figures. This would not be so bad were it not for the fact that the last group of figures has both positive and negative signs attached to them, suggesting economies of scale for some services, but diseconomies for others. The results for counties and county boroughs also varied making the general pattern even more complex. The search for optimum size, therefore, has proved to be as successful as the search for the philosophers' stone, since optimality varies according to service and type of authority.[8] We can conclude with confidence that, under certain not well understood circumstances, it may, or may not, be more, or less, economical to have larger, or smaller, local authorities. In short, it is not possible to make out a case against large authorities on grounds of diseconomies of scale.

It is easy to show that the largest cities have high per capita expenditure on some services, but this is not proof of the diseconomies of scale. Big cities may spend more because they have better services, because they have a better tax base or greater service needs (or both), or because they have a wider range of specialized services.[9] Cities such as Birmingham, Manchester, and Liverpool pay for a whole range of specialized services which are less frequently found in smaller authorities—special schools, sports and recreational centres, museums, art galleries, parks, concert halls, theatres, and libraries, for example.[10] In addition, big cities usually attract commuters and visitors, who use them for business and pleasure, and consequently expenditure on highways, transport, police, public health, and refuse collection tends to be high.[11] In short, the fact that large cities spend heavily on public services may have something to do with diseconomies of scale, but there again, it may have much to do with other things, and the point has never been proved either way.

The third main argument against large units of government points to a special type of diseconomy and inefficiency, namely the general public's favourite *bête noire*, bureaucratic expense and wastefulness. In spite of the popular belief that large government creates bureaucrats and red tape at an alarming rate, this theory, too, fails the empirical test. A recent and thorough study of Scotland, which has some of the largest local authorities in Western Europe, finds a *negative* correlation between district size and proportion of the local budget spent on

[8]The research is summarized in K. Newton, 'Comparative Community Performance', *Current Sociology*, 26 (1976), pp. 50–5. For an even longer and more inconclusive set of American studies see W. F. Fox, J. M. Stam, W. M. Godsey, and S. D. Brown, *Economies of Size in Local Government: An Annotated Bibliography* (Washington D.C., United States Department of Agriculture, Rural Development Research Report No. 9). For the philosophers' stone analogy see H. W. Richardson, 'Optimality in City Size, Systems of Cities and Urban Policy', in G. C. Cameron and L. Wingo (eds). *Cities, Regions, and Public Policy* (Edinburgh, Oliver and Boyd, 1973), pp. 29–48. The same conclusion for Germany is reached by G. F. Schaefer, 'Size, Efficiency, and Democratic Control of Local Governments', paper presented to the Council for European Studies Conference of Europeanists, Washington D.C., 1979.

[9]The assumption that high expenditures are due to diseconomies of scale is still common although it was questioned by O. D. Duncan many years ago—'Optimum Size of Cities', in P. K. Hatt and A. J. Reiss (eds). *Readings in Urban Sociology* (Glencoe, The Free Press, 1951), p. 766.

[10]The argument and some evidence is presented in K. Newton, 'Central Place Theory and Local Public Expenditure in Britain', paper presented to the annual meeting of the Political Studies Association of the United Kingdom, 1980.

[11]One important American study concludes that it is not the size of the central city, but that of the suburban population which mainly determines level of service expenditure, see J. D. Kasarda, 'The Impact of Suburban Population Growth on Central Service Functions', *American Journal of Sociology*, 77 (1972), p. 1121. Kasarda's conclusions are supported by a recent research report of R. P. Appelbaum and R. Follett, 'Size, Growth, and Urban Life', *Urban Affairs Quarterly*, 14 (1978), pp. 158–62.

administration, and no relationship between size of regional and administrative costs.[12] These results confirm earlier research which suggests that administrative costs do not rise, and may well fall proportionately as size of government increases.[13]

Even these counter-intuitive findings are only half the story, the other half involving central government's administrative costs in dealing either with a small or a large number of local authorities. The former is likely to be relatively cumbersome and expensive, the latter more streamlined and efficient. A comparison of the United Kingdom and the United States is interesting in this respect, for the United Kingdom has a small number of relatively large authorities, while the United States has a large number of relatively small ones. Total full-time employment in all civilian departments in British central government increased 6.7 per cent between 1968 and 1975, but the Department of the Environment, which is mainly responsible for local government, reduced its proportion of the total from 19.6 per cent in 1968 to 17.3 per cent in 1975, an absolute drop of 4,800 employees.[14] In the United States paid civilian employment in all Federal agencies decreased by 2.4 per cent, 1970–5, but the agencies most directly concerned with local government, Health, Education, and Welfare (HEW) and Housing and Urban Development (HUD), increased their proportion of the total from 2.6 per cent to 5.0 per cent, and from 0.46 per cent to 0.59 per cent respectively. Between 1970 and 1975, HEW and HUD increased their employment by 32.8 per cent and 10.5 per cent respectively.[15] While it would be unwise to draw

firm conclusions from these figures, they are, nevertheless, consistent with the proposition that a large number of small local units are likely to impose high administration costs on central government.[16]

The economic case against large units of local administration is, therefore, unconvincing; but arguments in favour of them have a good deal of power. In the first place, as urban-industrial society becomes larger and more complex so must local government. We may deplore this, but have to recognize it as a fact of life. It is impossible to run a large urban area as if it were nothing so much as a collection of small, pre-industrial communities. This is not to say that community-based governments cannot be nested in a large city-wide structure, but it does mean that many services such as planning, housing, water, sewage, and transportation must be organized on a large scale. Besides it has been found that quite a large population is necessary for some rather specialized services such as residential children's homes, special educational institutions, temporary accommodation for the aged, and facilities for the physically and mentally handicapped.[17] Financial planning also seems to be better in large authorities.[18]

The case for small and autonomous local units is further undermined by the requirements of equality and territorial justice which require a degree of centralization of the whole system, at least as far as the collection of taxes and the distribution of grants is concerned. A system which obliges local authorities to rely upon their own resources will be inegalitarian in so far as wealth is rarely distributed equally throughout regions, or different areas within cities. While it is possible that local authorities will

---

[12]E. C. Page and A. F. Midwinter, 'Remote Bureaucracy or Administrative Efficiency. Scotland's New Local Government System', *Studies in Public Policy*, No. 38 (Glasgow, Centre for the Study of Public Policy, 1979), p. 45.

[13]K. S. Lomax, 'A Criterion of Efficiency in Local Administration', *Journal of the Royal Statistical Society*, Series A, 115 (1952), pp. 521–3; and C. S. Page, 'The Administrative Costs of Local Authorities', Royal Commission on Local Government in Scotland, *Research Studies*, No. 1 (Edinburgh, HMSO, 1969). Another study produces mixed and generally inconclusive results, see S. P. Gupta and J. P. Hutton, Royal Commission on Local Government in England, Research Study No. 4, *Economies of Scale in Local Government Services* (London, HMSO, 1968).

[14]Central Statistical Office, *Annual Abstracts of Statistics, 1975* (London, HMSO, 1976), p. 152.

[15]U.S. Bureau of the Census, *Statistical Abstract of the United States*, 96th edn (Washington D.C., 1975), pp. 242–3.

[16]For a powerful critique of the USA's local government system with respect to Federal government grant programmes see R. D. Reischauer, 'Governmental Diversity: Bane of the Grants Strategy in the United States', in W. E. Oates (ed.), *The Political Economy of Fiscal Federalism* (Lexington, Mass., Heath, 1977), pp. 115–27.

[17]B. P. Davies, A. J. Barton, and I. McMillan, *Variations in Children's Services Among British Urban Authorities* (London, Bell, 1972), p. 112; B. P. Davies and A. J. Barton, 'Child Care Services', Royal Commission on Local Government in England, Research Study No. 1, *Local Government in South East England* (London, HMSO, 1968); J. N. Danziger, *Making Budgets* (London, Sage, 1979), p. 95.

[18]Page and Midwinter, 'Remote Bureaucracy', p. 50.

II. SIZE AND DEMOCRACY

agree among themselves to redistribute, as the old London boroughs did, a large measure of redistribution is likely to require centralization at the level of national government. Second, if local authorities have to rely largely upon their own resources, they will inevitably compete with one another to maximize their tax base and minimize their expenditure needs. Anything which tends to decrease the tax base or increase spending needs, such as the building of low-income housing or of hostels for the poor, will be avoided, while anything which has the reverse effect, such as building high-income housing, will be encouraged. Such a system of small, competing units of local government is unlikely to produce a wide range of public goods, and is likely to reinforce territorial inequalities.[19] By combining rich and poor neighbourhoods in the same municipality, large units of government can (not necessarily will) help to reduce territorial inequalities, and by redistributing at the national level, the problem can be further reduced.

So far as the service-providing functions of local government are concerned, therefore, it seems that large units are no less efficient and can be a good deal more effective than small ones. But as it was argued in the introduction to the paper, this does not cover all, or even the best part of the debate. It might be said that local government should not be judged by its efficiency or rationality, since its prime purpose is to sustain a genuine grass-roots democracy, and to counter-balance the increasingly remote and impersonal politics of national and international government. This point of view should be taken seriously, and so the second part of the paper will turn to the relationship between size and democracy.

The larger the political unit, so it is argued, the more difficult it is to sustain democracy: as the unit grows beyond manageable and human proportions, citizens lose their sense of community, they start to develop feelings of alienation and inefficacy, they start to know less and care less about public affairs, their attitudes towards government become unfavourable, the social and political distance between leaders and citizens starts to grow, and the costs of individual political participation increase to a point where sustained activity is the preserve of the few. In short, the transition to mass society is completed. Government takes on a monolithic structure and an inhuman face. The curious thing is that although these arguments are often used in bar room and seminar room discussions, there is little evidence to support them. On the contrary, research seems to show that city size is largely irrelevant to democratic culture and behaviour.

We all know of the experiments with overcrowded rats, and their implications for the high rate of violent crime in Manhattan are clear—until it is pointed out that central Paris, most of Tokyo, and the whole of Hong Kong have considerably higher densities than Manhattan but only a fraction of its crime. More to the point, studies of human beings outside laboratory conditions show that city size and density have remarkably little impact upon psychological states, or upon rates and types of social and political participation. It is possible to reel off lists of references, from the Bethnal Green community studies onwards, which find that urban life does not destroy the social fabric of primary relations, does not induce feelings of uprootedness, alienation, hostility, and anomie, and that it may well have some positive effects on political psychology, in so far as it has any effects at all.[20]

[19] The point has been made by many writers on metropolitan fragmentation in the United States. See, for example, R. Vernon, 'The Myth and Reality of Our Urban Problems', in B. Chinitz (ed.), *City and Suburbs: The Economics of Metropolitan Growth* (Englewood Cliffs, N.J., Prentice-Hall, 1964), 97–109; James Heilbrun, 'Poverty and Public Finance of the Older Central Cities', reprinted in M. Edel and J. Rothenberg (eds), *Readings in Urban Economics* (New York, Macmillan, 1972), 523–45; and R. Wood, *Suburbia* (Boston, Houghton Miffin, 1961), pp. 212–21. On the centralizing tendencies of egalitarian politics see L. J. Sharpe, 'Decentralist Trends in Western Democracies: A First Appraisal', in L. J. Sharpe (ed.), *Decentralist Trends in Western Democracies* (London, Sage Publications, 1979), p. 14.

[20] See, *inter alia*, J. D. Kasarda and M. Janowitz, 'Community Attachment in Mass Society', *American Sociological Review*, 39 (1974), 328–39; A. Hunter, 'The Loss of Community: An Empirical Test Through Replication', *American Sociological Review*, 40 (1975), 537–52; C. S. Fischer, 'On Urban Alienations and Anomie: Powerless and Social Isolation', *American Sociological Review*, 38 (1973), 311–26; C. S. Fischer, *The Urban Experience* (New York, Harcourt, Brace, Jovanovich, 1976), pp. 125–77; B. J. L. Berry and J. D. Kasarda, *Contemporary Urban Ecology* (New York, Macmillan, 1977), Ch. 3; R. W. Marans and W. Rodgers, 'Toward an Understanding of Com-

These studies of the general psychological and social wellbeing of large city dwellers are wholly consistent with the picture which emerges clearly from the Redcliffe-Maud Commission's Research Study No. 9, which deals with community attitudes and local government. As the summary figures in Table 1 show, the study found no systematic variation between authorities of different type and size and a whole range of social and political indicators, including rates of participation, knowledge of the local government system, attitudes to local services, readership of local papers, knowledge of the location of town hall and council offices, or opinions about the right size of local authorities. To double-check these results, the study factor analysed the responses to produce two dimensions of community involvement which were labelled 'social attachment' and 'interest in local affairs'. With only minor exceptions, local authority size was not related to these two factors.[21]

The Maud Committee's research on the local government elector also showed that size is largely irrelevant to attitudes towards local government. The study used three scales, measuring alienation (criticism of councillors reflecting a sense of distance between councillors and citizens), democracy (criticism of the party system and system of representation), and the selection of representatives (based upon criticism of personalities and the demographic composition of councils). The study found that unfavourable attitudes were no stronger in large than in small local authorities. On the contrary, they bore little relationship to size or type of authority.[22]

Surveys of British electors also show that there is little variation between residents of different sizes and types of local authority according to their knowledge of local authority responsibilities for different services, or their knowledge about the time and place of the next council meeting.[23] If anything, residents in the largest urban units of the old system (the county boroughs) were better informed about local affairs than those in other and smaller authorities. They were more likely to know the location of their council offices, more likely to know that town clerks and housing officers were appointed not elected, better able to name their Mayor, more likely to have heard of council activities in the previous month, and more likely to have read a recent news item about council matters in a local paper.[24]

The same general picture emerges when we examine figures for actual or claimed participation. There is a tendency for smaller authorities to have higher rates, but the differences by size of authority are slight by comparison with variations according to age, sex, education, and length of residence in the area. The pattern is repeated for participation in local public services,[25] and in the extent to which electors initiate contact with their local authority.[26] Voting turnout is, of course, the hardest measure of participation, although not necessarily the best, but here the pattern is complex, in the United Kingdom, at least. On the one hand, turnout generally decreases as one goes down the system of government from national government, to local government, to community councils. On the other, turnout decreases as size increases within the same level of government. General election turnout is usually above 70 per cent, local election turnout is closer to 40 per cent, and community council turnout is around 19 per cent, but the larger the local authority or community council, the lower the turnout.[27] And

munity Satisfaction', in A. Hawley and V. Rock (eds), *Metropolitan America in Contemporary Perspective* (New York, Halstead Press, 1975), pp. 299–354; A. W. Finifter, 'Dimensions of Political Alienation', *American Political Science Review*, 64 (1970), pp. 403–4; S. Verba and N. H. Nie, *Participation in American Life: Political Democracy and Social Equality* (New York, Harper and Row, 1972), Ch. 13; C. S. Fischer, 'The City and Political Psychology', *American Political Science Review*, 69 (1975), 568–9; B. N. Boots, 'Population Density, Crowding, and Human Behavior', *Progress in Human Geography*, 3 (1979), 13–63; T. R. Dye, 'Population Density and Social Pathology', *Urban Affairs Quarterly*, 11 (1975), 265–75.

[21] Royal Commission on Local Government in England, Research Studies, No. 9, *Community Attitudes Survey: England* (London, HMSO, 1969), pp. 148–9.

[22] Committee on the Management of Local Government, Volume 3, *The Local Government Elector* (London, HMSO, 1967), p. 71.

[23] *Community Attitudes Survey*, p. 86; *The Local Government Elector*, p. 59.

[24] *The Local Government Elector*, pp. 6–42.

[25] *Community Attitudes Survey*, p. 75.

[26] *The Local Government Elector*, pp. 47–55.

[27] For turnout figures and correlations between population size and turnout see Danziger, *Making Budgets*, p. 90; N. Boaden, *Urban Policy-Making* (Cambridge, Cambridge University Press, 1971), p. 126; M. Masterson, 'Forming Community Councils—East Kilbride', *Local Government Studies*, 4 (1978), p. 72.

TABLE 1   Local Authority Size and Political Attitudes and Behaviour

	County Boroughs			Municipal Boroughs/Urban Districts				
	Conur-bation	*250,000+*	*60,000 to 250,000*	*Conur-bation*	*60,000 to 100,000*	*30,000 to 60,000*	*Up to 30,000*	*Rural Districts*
% Regular readers of 1 local paper	85	82	86	88	81	90	88	86
% Participation in Council politics	2.7	2.9	4.8	4.4	3.8	5.2	5.8	9.9
Correct answers to questions about local authority services	6.3	6.3	6.6	5.6	4.9	5.2	5.1	4.3
% mentioning at least 1 well-run service	71	76	76	68	68	77	71	71
% mentioning at least 1 service not well run	50	47	42	73	55	51	52	53
% with correct knowledge of location of town hall or council offices	87	88	92	95	89	88	94	—
Optimum size of local authority area:								
% wanting bigger ones	17	19	30	18	24	17	19	14
% wanting smaller ones	8	4	1	5	3	6	2	6
% wanting same size	57	54	49	58	57	62	59	59
Social attachment								
% low	42	45	40	41	46	42	31	—
% high	9	7	9	10	7	8	17	—
Interest in local affairs								
% low	38	48	39	41	34	39	37	—
% high	4	5	7	10	6	7	10	—

Source: Royal Commission on Local Government in England, Research Studies No. 9, *Community Attitudes Survey* (London, HMSO, 1969), *passim*.

yet, paradoxically, the low turnout in local elections in large cities may reflect relatively high levels of political activity, for even hopeless seats are often contested by the parties, and it is these seats which typically register a low poll. In smaller and more rural authorities, a much higher proportion of seats are uncontested, a fact which is not revealed by the polling statistics, and which may well conceal relatively low levels of political activity.[28] In countries outside the United Kingdom there is no general tendency for large units to have a low voting turnout, so we can draw no hard and fast conclusions about the relationship between size and turnout, or any other form of individual participation for that matter.[29]

The *Community Attitudes Survey* also presents some interesting information about how citizens judge local authority performance. The first question asked 'Are there any of these services, or any others, which are quite well run in this local authority area?' Responses did not differ by local authority size, feelings of satisfaction and dissatisfaction being randomly distributed in this respect. The second question asked whether the size of local authorities should be changed. Not surprisingly, there was a strong preference for the status quo, but slightly more people wanted larger rather than smaller authorities. Yet again, responses varied very little by local authority size, and yet again there is no evidence to support the idea that the residents of large authorities are particularly hostile or dissatisfied with their local government.[30]

The second part of the paper has concentrated, so far, on evidence about mass attitudes and be-

[28]The argument is spelled out in L. J. Sharpe, *A Metropolis Votes* (London, London School of Economics, Greater London Papers, No. 8, 1962), p. 21.

[29]Dahl and Tufte, *Size and Democracy*, p. 61 conclude that 'there is no general relationship between turnout and unit size'.

[30]*Community Attitudes Survey*, p. 89, p. 129.

haviour, but what about local political leaders? Do they not become more remote and elitist as the size of the administrative unit grows? Being on a parish or community council, playing darts in the village pub, and meeting constituents at Sunday church is one thing, but sitting on a metropolitan council and representing a large and ever-changing big city ward is quite another. But once again, the British evidence is counter-intuitive. In the old system of local government it was the county boroughs which had more representative councils, in the sense of a better cross-section of the population. They had a larger proportion of younger people, more women, more working-class and low-income members, a greater proportion with an average education, and a more typical range of housing tenures. The existence of developed party systems in the county boroughs probably accounts for their more broadly based councils.[31]

Even more important, perhaps, is the fact that in the largest urban authorities councillors showed an unusually strong attachment to their areas. Compared with other councillors, they were more likely to have been born and to have worked in the area they represented, more likely to have lived in it for over twenty-five years, and to claim that all or most of their friends lived there.[32] Part of the explanation for this lies in the fact that the very size of county boroughs makes it possible to move large distances within the local boundaries, and yet the strong attachment of big city councillors to their areas is not consistent with the popular image of urban life as being amorphous, rootless, faceless, and impersonal. This seems to be true of neither big city residents nor their representatives.

If the argument so far has been cast entirely in terms of individual attitudes and behaviour this is because the overwhelming majority of social scientists treat it this way. And yet cities are more than the sum of their individual residents. That is, large authorities are not just bigger versions of small ones.

They develop their own distinctive characteristics, which create qualitative variations between units of different sizes. Four of these seem to be of special importance to the present discussion, and they are community organizations, political parties, the mass media, and the relationship between size, system capacity, and participation. They also should be considered before drawing any conclusions about size and democracy.

Hard evidence is in short supply, but there does seem to be a tendency for large urban areas to have proportionately more voluntary organizations, citizens associations, and community groups than smaller ones.[33] Certainly American and Swedish evidence indicates that large cities have a higher rate of organizational participation, and on this basis Dahl and Tufte conclude that there is 'a persistent tendency for organizational and partisan activity to increase with size of community'.[34] British data is consistent with this. Although mass membership of voluntary organizations is no higher in large authorities, county and county borough councillors seem to belong to more organizations, and spend more time with organizations than councillors in smaller authorities. In fact, unlike most of the figures reported so far, the hours spent with voluntary organizations varies far more by type and size of authority than with individual variables such as age, sex, and social class.[35]

These findings suggest that while rates of individual participation do not differ in authorities of different size, organizational participation is rather more important in larger authorities. The possibility—no more than this, given the state of knowledge—that some types of political participation may be relatively higher in larger units of government is overlooked in most of the size and democracy literature because it concentrates on individual participation. And yet organizational in-

[31]L. J. Sharpe, 'Elected Representatives in Local Government', *British Journal of Sociology*, 13 (1962), 169–209; *The Local Government Councillor*, pp. 15–43; J. Gyford, *Local Politics in Britain* (London, Croom Helm, 1976), pp. 25–7; K. Newton, 'Local Elites in Britain', in J. Lagroye and V. Wright (eds), *Local Government in Britain and France* (London, Allen and Unwin, 1979), 105–13.

[32]*The Local Government Councillor*, p. 39.

[33]D. H. Smith (ed.), *Voluntary Action Research* 1973 (Lexington, Mass., Lexington Books, 1973).

[34]Dahl and Tufte, *Size and Democracy*, p. 98.

[35]*Community Attitudes Research*, p. 56; *The Local Government Elector*, p. 114; *The Local Government Councillor*, p. 93, pp. 188–94. American research also shows that councilmen in the larger, industrial cities had the most favourable attitudes towards groups and group activity, see B. H. Zisk, *Local Interest Politics: A One-Way Street* (Indianapolis, N.Y., Bobbs-Merrill, 1973), p. 67.

volvement can be particularly important because organizations provide collective resources for those who have relatively few individual resources to rely upon. In other words, those with relatively little time, money, or education can pool their resources in an attempt to overcome their individual disadvantages. Hence the slogan: united we stand, divided we fall.

The same general line of argument applies to the presence of political parties in local government, in that the larger and more urban the authority the more likely it is to have not just a party system, but also a developed and competitive party system[36] Parties are, of course, just as crucial to local as to national democracy partly because they can (but not necessarily do) represent the interests of those who have inadequate individual resources to protect themselves, and partly because they are able to recruit to positions of political power a range of people who would not otherwise rise through the political system. This helps to explain the fact, noted earlier, that large urban authorities have councils which are more representative of the general population than smaller and more rural ones.

Swedish data also suggest that party competition in the larger local government communes may well help to keep councillors in line with constituent opinion, and hence the discovery of a fairly high agreement between leaders and citizens in both large and small communes.[37] There are no British data on the particular point, although there is evidence to suggest that parties can act as channels of communication which keep local leaders in touch with public opinion.[38] And lastly, the fact that parties at least contest elections means that voters are offered some sort of choice on election day, and the larger and more densely populated the authority the lower the likelihood of uncontested elections.[39]

The third characteristic of large urban local authorities is their somewhat greater chance of having a serious, daily coverage of local affairs in their own papers, radio and television stations. As Berry and Kasarda observe 'we would expect larger social systems to divert relatively greater proportions of their human resources to communicative functions'.[40] To put the matter a different way, only large cities can support local dailies such as the *Birmingham Post*, the *Glasgow Herald*, or the *Liverpool Daily Post/Echo*, which try to cover local council affairs reasonably fully. This probably helps to explain the fact (noted earlier) that county borough residents knew considerably more about local affairs than residents of smaller and more rural authorities. Demographic differences did not, in this instance, explain the variation.[41] Besides, the local press is still by far and away the most important single source of information of public affairs in the community, it being mentioned more than twice as much as all the other sources put together.[42] Moreover, although there is little variation in the proportion of local residents reading a local paper regularly (outside London which is dominated by the national media), considerably more (25 per cent) in the county boroughs had read an item about council news in the past month, than in the rural districts, where the figure was only 13 per cent.[43]

The fourth and last property of large units of government involves their greater system capacity, and the effects this may have on level of public participation. Dahl and Tufte convincingly argue that larger systems are in a better position (though they do not always take advantage of it) to do more

---

[36]J. E. Alt, 'Some Social and Political Correlates of County Borough Expenditures', *British Journal of Political Science*, 1 (1971), p. 53; D. E. Ashford, 'Parties and Participation in British Local Government, and Some American Parallels', *Urban Affairs Quarterly*, 11 (1975), 58–81; R. A. W. Rhodes, 'The Changing Political-management System of Local Government', paper given to the workshop on European Urbanism: 'Policy and Planning', ECPR Joint Sessions, London, 1975. For Dutch, Swiss, and American evidence supporting the generalization see Dahl and Tufte, *Size and Democracy*, pp. 98–107.

[37]Dahl and Tufte, *Size and Democracy*, p. 86.

[38]K. Newton, *Second City Politics* (Oxford, Oxford University Press, 1976), pp. 106–13.

[39]Danziger, *Making Budgets*, p. 90; Sharpe, *A Metropolis Votes*, p. 21; Ashford, 'Parties and Participation', p. 72; General Register Office, *The Registrar General's Statistical Review of England and Wales*, 1967, Part II (London, HMSO, 1986), p. 99.

[40]Berry and Kasarda, *Contemporary Urban Ecology*, p. 339

[41]*The Local Government Elector*, pp. 7–42.

[42]*The Local Government Elector*, p. 28.

[43]*The Local Government Elector*, p. 28.

[44]Dahl and Tufte, *Size and Democracy*, Ch. 7. See also T. R. Dye and J. A. Garcia, 'Structure, Function, and Policy in America Cities', *Urban Affairs Quarterly*, 14 (1978), p. 109.

than smaller ones,[44] and there is hard evidence to confirm this so far as British local authorities are concerned.[45] This may have consequences for local democracy in so far as the more a unit of government can and does do, the more citizens are likely to involve themselves in its affairs. Conversely, the less a government is able to do, the less its citizens will bother themselves about its petty affairs. Political scientists have argued that system capacity and democracy are quite separate, while others assume that level of citizen input determines level of government output; in contrast to both these views, it is also possible that level of government output may influence the level and intensity of public input, so affecting the participatory and democratic nature of the system.[46]

The evidence for this proposition is highly inconclusive, but at the national level, election turnout in sixteen Western industrial societies correlates at 0.56 (significant at 0.01) with the percentage of GNP spent by the central government.[47] At the subnational level, American research shows that the broader the functional scope of city government the higher its election turnout, although it must be said that the relationship, though statistically significant, is not strong.[48] To the very limited extent that one can generalize from such flimsy evidence, it seems not altogether impossible that large scale units of local government may encourage relatively high levels of political participation, partly because their greater capacity to provide public goods and services may attract public involvement, and partly

because large cities do seem to stimulate activity on the part of pressure groups and political parties, as well as support media coverage of events. In short, large units of local government may be more democratic in some respects than small ones.

All this raises one last problem; if size is largely irrelevant to efficiency and democracy in local government, and if large units actually seem to have many economic advantages and some democratic ones, why is so much ink spilled and breath wasted celebrating the virtues of the small? There seem to be three main answers to this question. First, small communities and small units of government are often seen in an unrealistic and romantic way by many writers who share little, other than their anti-urban sentiments.[49] Apart from the intimacy and 'togetherness' of their social life, which is contrasted (incorrectly, as we have already seen) with the anonymity and alienation of the big city, small communities are often supposed to have highly developed forms of direct democracy. This seems to be largely wishful thinking. After all the Greek *polis* excluded women, slaves, and young males from democratic participation, and chronic warfare between the cities could be tolerated only as long as their soldiers wielded nothing more dangerous than swords and spears.[50] New England townships are another model for the "small is beautiful" school, although they seem to have been hierarchical, socially exclusive, intensely conservative, and run by a small elite of businessmen and land owners.[51] The English village is another model, although it, too,

[45]*Report of the Royal Commission on Local Government in England*, pp. 33–44. See also the references cited in footnote 17 above.

[46]In his review of Dahl and Tufte's *Size and Democracy*, Barry takes the authors to task for confusing system capacity and democracy, see B. J. L. Barry, 'Review of *Size and Democracy*', *Government and Opposition*, 9 (1974), p. 495.

[47]Turnout is defined as the number of valid votes expressed as a percentage of the voting age population. The data comes from B. M. Russett, H. R. Alker, K. W. Deutsch, H. D. Lasswell, *World Handbook of Social and Political Indicators* (New Haven, Yale University Press, 1964). The data file was assembled and analysed by the author and Mike Aiken, Department of Sociology, the University of Wisconsin, Madison.

[48]R. J. Liebert, *Disintegration and Political Action* (New York, Academic Press, 1976), pp. 120–1.

[49]See Ruth Glass 'Urban Sociology in Great Britain', in R. E. Pahl (ed), *Readings in Urban Sociology* (Oxford, Pergamon Press, 1968), pp. 63–73.

[50]Dahl, 'The City in the Future of Democracy', p. 955 and Dahl and Tufte, *Size and Democracy*, p. 9. On the Kafkaesque and repressive nature of a medieval French village see Emmanuel Le Roy Ladurie, *Montaillou* (Harmondsworth, Middx., Penguin Books, 1980), pp. 10–23.

[51]I have defended this view in 'Conflict Avoidance and Conflict Suppression: The Case of Urban Politics in the United States', in K. R. Cox (ed.), *Urbanization and Conflict in Market Societies* (Chicago, Maaroufa Press, 1978), pp. 78–9. The analysis is based largely on A. J. Vidich and J. Bensman, *Small Town in Mass Society* (Garden City, N.Y., Anchor Books, 1960)

[52]See, for example, R. Frankenberg, *Communities in Britain* (Harmondsworth, Middx., Penguin Books, 1965), pp. 255–75; H. Newby, *The Deferential Worker* (London, Allen Lane, 1977).

tends to be socially and politically closed and easily dominated by the local squirearchy.[52] Open, democratic society and government does not appear to figure very largely among the qualities of small and rural communities. On the contrary, it may be that the smaller the community the greater the pressures for social conformity, and the greater the tendency to suppress political dissent and conflict.

Complementing the rather rosy view of small communities, there is a widespread pessimism about urban places. In particular, there is a dislike of the relatively high levels of conflict which sometimes mark urban politics. As Dahl and Tufte write: 'Until comparatively recent times, dissent, diversity, and conflict were usually regarded as unequivocal dangers to republics.'[53] In fact, conflict is still widely regarded as a 'bad thing', which may help to explain some of the attraction of small communities that are popularly supposed to 'provide a haven from which the weary can escape the conflicts of larger communities'.[54] All other things being equal, of course, lack of conflict is preferable to its presence, but all other things are not equal when it comes to comparing large and small communities, a fact which makes small communities less harmonious than they sometimes appear.

First, there is widespread and rather good evidence that small groups and communities often suppress their disagreements because they find it rather difficult to handle.[55] Absence of conflict, therefore, it not necessarily a sign that all is well, and it may indicate the opposite. Second, if and when conflict does break out in small places, it may well take a particularly acrimonious and rancorous form. As Dahl puts it: 'Anyway, I suspect that the village probably never was all that it is cracked up to be. The village, including the pre-industrial village, is less likely to be filled with harmony and solidarity than with the oppressive weight of repressed deviation and dissent which, when they appear, erupt

explosively and leave a lasting burden of antagonism and hatred.'[56] Third, it may not be size, *per se*, so much as social homogeneity which matters. Although it can be argued on purely formal and mathematical grounds that the larger the group, the greater the chance of conflict between individuals,[57] in the real world it seems to be the composition of the community rather than its size which precipitates conflict. Thus Black concludes 'the virtues of "smallness" may be greatly overstated, particularly because the proponents of "smallness" usually assume that "smallness" implies homogeneity.'[58] It is obviously true that the larger the population, particularly in urban areas, the more mixed it is likely to be, but, nevertheless, it may not be size so much as social heterogeneity which encourages conflict. And fourth, what is wrong with conflict? It is not to be valued in its own right any more than peace and quiet, but if it stops short of physical violence to people, if it is fruitful, and if it is the result of striving for liberty, equality, and fraternity, then there may be more to be said for it than for its absence.

The third and last source of antagonism towards large units of government derives from a strong preference for the kind of direct, individual participation which is possible (in theory, even if strong social pressures make it difficult in practice) in small, face-to-face communities. Indirect, collective participation, via pressure groups and political parties, is thought to be an extremely poor substitute for prolonged, first-hand political commitment. This biased, not to say intolerant, view of the world is not shared by most people, who want to be left alone to get on with the important things in life, whether this is succeeding in their job, bringing up their children, growing roses, or playing football. For most people, politics does not warrant more than the odd attendance at a meeting, and allowing pressure groups and parties to defend their interests in between. Political scientists do not like this sort of spasmodic and indirect participation, but then politics is both profession and pastime for them, and they should not expect everyone to be like this.

---

[53]Dahl and Tufte, *Size and Democracy*, p. 89.

[54]G. S. Black, 'Conflict in the Community: A Theory of the Effects of Community Size', *American Political Science Review*, 68 (1974), p. 1261.

[55]See, for example, L. Coser, *The Functions of Social Conflict* (London, Routledge and Kegan Paul, 1965), pp. 67–85; J. S. Coleman, *Community Conflict* (New York, The Free Press, 1967), pp. 21–3; P. M. Blau, *Exchange and Power in Social Life* (New York, Wiley, 1964), p. 6.

[56]Dahl, 'The City in the Future of Democracy', p. 961.

[57]J. J. Mansbridge does so in 'Size and Common Interest', paper presented to the Eleventh World Congress of the International Sociological Association, Moscow, 1979.

[58]Black, 'Conflict in the Community', p. 1261.

CONCLUSIONS

The first conclusion must be that any conclusion about the relationship between size, effectiveness, and democracy must be tentative because in spite of an ample supply of common knowledge about the subject, there is relatively little hard information. Nevertheless, the evidence to hand points to two general tendencies. First, local authorities of different sizes, whether urban or rural, do not differ by more than a small amount, if they differ at all, on many measures of functional effectiveness and democracy. Large units do not suffer from the diseconomies of scale, or from the cumbersome and expensive administration which is often claimed for them, and nor do they have many of the democratic ailments which are commonly diagnosed. Second, so far as size does make a difference, large units seem to have something of an advantage in some respects: they are better able to provide a range of specialized facilities which are beyond the capacity of most smaller units; they are better able to organize some services such as planning, transport, police, and fire which must be provided on a city wide basis, and which cannot sensibly be broken down and organized on a sub-city or neighbourhood basis; and they may have something of an advantage when it comes to organized (as opposed to individual) participation in politics, namely that of community groups, political parties, and the media. Moreover, an equalization of resources and services between areas demands authorities which are large enough to include both the rich and poor neighbourhoods within their boundaries as well as a redistribution of resources at the national level.

It might be said, in criticism of these conclusions, that the various measures of functional effectiveness and democracy used here are deficient, and although there is truth in this, it is also true that they cover a wide range of measures and indicators for a broad range of countries. The onus is upon those who are dissatisfied to produce better measures and show their association with size. Others might argue that the simple bi-variate analysis of many studies is unlikely to show up the true effects of size. This criticism fails to account for the null findings of those who have used multivariate techniques, and it also overlooks the fact that many studies, whatever their methods, do underline the importance of variables such as age, sex, education, and occupation, whose importance is beyond doubt in other fields of research. Besides, size does not differentiate between British cities when it comes to comparing their social, economic, and political characteristics.[59]

We are driven back to the conclusion that size is largely irrelevant to many aspects of functional effectiveness and democracy, although its effects seem to be beneficial rather than the opposite in some regards. Whereas most of the discussion is based upon the assumption that size is fundamentally incompatible with local democracy, this appears to be not the case. It does not follow that local government should be as big as possible, for it is as silly to make a fetish of the big as the small, and, besides, the population should have the form of government it is most comfortable with, even if its views on the matter are inconsistent with empirical evidence. Nevertheless, small is not as beautiful as commonly supposed, and big is not nearly so ugly.

---

[59]C. A. Moser and W. Scott, *British Towns* (Edinburgh, Oliver and Boyd, 1961), p. 61.

QUESTIONS FOR DISCUSSION

1. Who benefits and who is hurt by decentralization? Explain.
2. Is greater popular participation in government desirable? Why?
3. Are decentralized political institutions more responsive to the people than centralized political institutions? Explain.
4. How do you recognize a neighborhood when you see one?
5. Are decentralized political institutions more efficient than centralized political institutions? Why?
6. Are people who participate in decision making at a decentralized level more representative of citizens at that level than elected representatives in more centralized governing units? Why?

SUGGESTED READINGS

BARBER, BENJAMIN, *Strong Democracy: Participatory Politics for a New Age*. Berkeley: Univ. of California Press, 1984.

BOYTE, HARRY C., *Community Is Possible: Regaining America's Roots*. New York: Harper & Row, 1984.

COMMAGER, HENRY STEELE, "Tocqueville's Mistake: A Defense of Strong Central Government," *Harper's Magazine* (Aug. 1984) 70–74.

CRENSON, MATTHEW A., *Neighborhood Politics*. Cambridge, MA: Harvard Univ. Press, 1983.

FUERST, J. S., "Decentralization: An Elusive Idea," *American City and County*, 99 (Nov. 1984), 58–60.

KOTLER, MILTON, *Neighborhood Government: The Local Foundations of Political Life*. Lanham, MD: University Press of America, 1983.

PATEMAN, CAROLE, *Participation and Democratic Theory*. Cambridge, England: Cambridge Univ. Press, 1970.

STEVER, JAMES A., "Contemporary Neighborhood Theories: Interpretative Versus Romance and Reaction," *Urban Affairs Quarterly*, 13 (Mar. 1978), 263–84.

VENTRISS, CURTIS, "Emerging Perspectives on Citizen Participation," *Public Administration Review*, 45 (June 1985), 433–40.

YIN, ROBERT K., "Decentralization of Government Agencies: What Does It Accomplish?," *American Behavorial Scientist*, 22 (May/June 1979), 525–36.

CHAPTER *3*
Tools of Administration

In conducting its work, a government organization is not as free as its private-sector counterpart to exercise its responsibilities. It is constrained by laws, executive policies, and judicial decisions, not only in the policies it pursues but in the way it pursues them. And so, a government bureaucracy generally must conform to more stringent rules governing employment and administration than private companies. This is not to say that private companies are completely free to do what they wish since they, too, are restricted by law in such matters as employment and administration. But clearly, the private company has greater discretion than the public organization.

This chapter deals with issues governing some of the tools of administration. Like a business organization, a government organization seeks to recruit the best people to perform particular tasks. If it is going to have effective workers, it must reward the most qualified and most productive employees. However, a government organization not only seeks efficiency but also pursues other goals, such as fairness in hiring practices. Debates in this chapter treat four issues concerning how government organizations relate to their employees. Specifically, merit pay, affirmative action, comparable worth, and collective bargaining are examined.

MERIT PAY

A task of management, whether in the public or private sector, is to recruit qualified personnel and to encourage excellence in performance. In the private sector, excellence may sometimes be readily recognized. An automobile sales representative may be regarded as "excellent" if he or she sells more cars than other sales representatives. A typist may be excellent if he or she produces more accurately typed pages within a specified period of time than other typists. Even in the private sector, however, it is not always easy to distinguish the performance of workers in those cases in which there is no precise mechanism to measure performance as there is in, say, sales. In this regard, it is difficult to measure performance of Customer Assistance representatives in terms of pleasantness to customers.

The public sector offers even fewer measurable ways to evaluate performance. Managers have had to devise some way to reward people who perform better than others in work for the organization. One method which has been used by government has been a merit pay system in which higher pay is ostensibly linked to better performance. Such a system has received the greatest attention in teaching but has been applied to other occupations, as

114

well. Partially because in government it is extraordinarily difficult to fire someone on the basis of general incompetence, political leaders and government managers have sought to acquire management tools that will spur great effort in government employment. To be sure, government employees can be fired and have been when they engage in some impropriety or do not show up. But often, bureaucrats are protected in a variety of ways, including complex appeals machinery, union intercession, tenure, and judicial constraints.

Merit pay has received the most notoriety in teaching at both the el-hi and university levels. It has also been applied in other fields. As president, Jimmy Carter made merit pay an important part of his program for administrative reform. The Civil Service Reform Act of 1978 provided for merit pay for government employees.

Is merit pay a good way to encourage excellent performance from government and private-sector employees? Richard E. Kopelman, Professor of Management at Baruch College, argues that linking pay to performance is a proven management tool. He bases his case on expectancy theory, which shows that the greater a person's expectancy (i.e., subjective probability) that effort expenditure will lead to various rewards, the greater the person's motivation to work hard. He draws three conclusions from the theory: (1) The stronger the performance–reward relationship, the higher the average organization-wide level of work motivation. (2) The stronger the performance–reward relationship, the more likely it is that high-performing employees will be retained and the most productive employees will tend to be the most satisfied and the least likely to quit. (3) In such a system, the happy worker will be the productive worker only if productivity is a precondition for happiness. Kopelman cites research support for his view. He also shows how a merit system should be applied.

James Perry and Jone Pearce, who conducted research on merit pay while faculty members in the Graduate School of Management at the University of California, Irvine, disagree with this view of the merit pay system.

On the basis of extensive research of employee attitude surveys and analysis of the effects of merit pay on objective criteria of office productivity within the Southern California area of the Social Security Administration, they conclude that merit pay, in its first two years of operation at the federal level, had no discernible positive impact on motivation or performance. As reasons for this conclusion, they put forth these points: (1) Merit pay failed in accurately and completely measuring performance. (2) Federal merit pay requires a ranking of employees; such a ranking system resulted in a significant drop in employee commitment to the organization. (3) A fixed merit pay budget heightens the demoralizing effect of comparative ratings. (4) The federal merit pay system allows for "managed" ratings to prevent payout inequities, and this detracts from the very idea of objective performance standards to evaluate merit. Perry and Pearce conclude by arguing that the merit system has inherent flaws that make it unsuitable for both the public and the private sectors.

As you read notice whether the authors of the articles qualify their views. Would you expect that Kopelman would object to certain aspects of the federal merit pay system as it has operated in practice? Would Perry and Pearce consider any improvements in the existing federal merit system to meet their criticisms?

AFFIRMATIVE ACTION

For most of American history discrimination in employment—both public and private—was practiced against many groups. In the past few decades, strong efforts have been made to remove barriers against discrimination based on race, gender, age, or condition of physical handicap. Although many groups have benefited from civil rights laws making discriminatory practices illegal, minority members and women have had the most direct gain from the new laws.

Although the campaign for equal rights was sharply contested, by the late 1970s few people would openly argue that black people should not be allowed to be admitted into professional schools or that women should not be appointed to top government posts. In practice, however, discrimination persisted although its new form was more subtle than was the case before civil rights laws were adopted.

One means which began to be used in the 1960s and continued thereafter to end discrimination was affirmative action. Although there was no universally accepted definition as to what affirmative action actually meant, it was based upon the notion that legislating against racial or gender discrimination was not enough to end discrimination; there had to be, in addition, concrete results in the form of jobs or admission programs so that real equality would be achieved. Government agencies at the national, state, and local levels were asked to establish goals and timetables in those instances where women and minority members were underrepresented. Critics of affirmative action argued that, in effect, goals and timetables became quotas, and this was in conflict with the law, Supreme Court decisions, and the Constitution. In fact, the Supreme Court endorsed, in a July 1986 decision, the use of affirmative action in the workplace to cure past discrimination against minority groups when other approaches would not suffice. The issue of affirmative action affects employment in both the public and private sectors. The principle is based on similar premises in either sector.

Is affirmative action a proper remedy to end discrimination? Douglas B. Huron, a former senior trial attorney in the Civil Rights Division of the Justice Department, writes that it is. He argues: (1) In many circumstances, minority members have been discriminated against thoughtlessly because it has been the fashion not to hire them. (2) In such instances, affirmative action may be valid tools to respond. (3) Huron cites a specific state, Alabama, which applied affirmative action in hiring government employees so that 13 years after judicial actions requiring affirmative action were taken, that state's agencies are more integrated today than ever before. (4) Affirmative action is not a panacea but should be used as a last resort to end discrimination based on race and gender considerations.

Philosopher Sidney Hook objects to affirmative action. He argues: (1) Discrimination is an evil, and those guilty of discriminating in violation of the law should be punished. (2) Affirmative action is based on the principle of collective—rather than individual—guilt, a principle at odds with American tradition. (3) Today affirmative action works to discriminate against a generation of white males who had nothing to do with discrimination of the past. (4) It is unfair to penalize a group of people today for injustices that were done to groups in earlier generations. (5) Affirmative action represents a condescending and disparaging attitude toward an entire race, an attitude which many blacks quite properly resent.

As you read the debate, consider what criteria should be used to determine whether a government agency has engaged in employment discrimination against blacks and women. If discrimination did exist, determine the best means that should be used to end it.

COMPARABLE WORTH

Affirmative action programs have been one device to remedy discrimination against both minorities and women. Another antidiscrimination program, but one designed exclusively to deal with equality for women, is comparable worth.

Comparable worth may be defined as a system in which women are paid on the basis of their worth in terms of education, experience, and training for a particular category of jobs. Whereas the Equal Pay Act of 1963 makes it illegal for a firm to pay different wages to men and women who perform the same job and have the same experience, comparable worth involves equal pay for work of comparable value. And so, for example, jobs which traditionally have been occupied by women, such as nursing and teaching, should, according to the notion of comparable worth, be paid more than is currently the case—particularly since jobs requiring much less education and training, but which are occupied predominantly by men, are paid more.

By the spring of 1985, five states had already adopted comparable worth legislation and others were debating or considering it. As a result of litigation, the State of Washington agreed to restructure its pay scales to raise in pay those government jobs largely held by women.

Should comparable worth be adopted as one remedy for discrimination against women? In a discussion sponsored by the magazine *New Perspectives*, Heidi Hartmann, study director of the Committee on Women's Employment and Related Social Issues of the National Council of the National Academy of Sciences, takes the Affirmative side; and June O'Neill, director of the Program of Policy Research on Women and Families of the Urban Institute, takes the Negative case. Hartmann deals with the fact that in the aggregate, a working woman in the United States averages 59 cents in pay for every dollar earned by a man. She attributes much of the disparity in income to gender discrimination. This can be seen from an examination of the scholarly studies. When a study was made of some specific groups of people, such as holders of Masters' degrees in business administration, for example, it showed that women's salaries over time declined with respect to men even before women married and had children.

Hartmann says that women do not receive the same opportunities as men because managers assume that training women will not be economically advantageous for firms. In her view, jobs that are predominantly held by women are paid less than equally rated men's jobs because of gender discrimination. Hartmann, consequently, sees comparable worth as benefiting women since it will lead to women getting more pay for the work that they are doing and for women securing better jobs.

June O'Neill disagrees. She contends that there are many factors that produce the pay gap between men and women and they cannot always be explained in terms of discrimination. For example, the education of women in the labor force declined relative to that of men since the late 1950s—a view shared by Hartmann. Since the late 1970s, moreover, the average working woman over the age of 35 worked about 60 percent of the time since completing school while her male counterpart worked more or less continuously. O'Neill also argues that most working women have two careers—one at home and one at work—so that the types of jobs they take and the size of their paycheck reflect this fact. In her view, women make specific choices to emphasize their home rather than business life and, consequently, reject more lucrative jobs because of the demands on their time.

O'Neill opposes comparable worth. For her, market forces are sufficient to remedy discrimination. Companies that discriminate against qualified women will be forced to hire men at higher wages, resulting in inefficient economic organizations which will not be able to compete in the market. She argues that comparable worth would interfere with market forces and would discourage women from moving into nontraditional jobs.

As you read this debate, ask yourself whether the contending authors differ about the basic facts or about evaluating the facts. Consider, too, the role of government if comparable worth is adopted.

COLLECTIVE BARGAINING

The history of trade unionism in America is mostly a story of labor–management relations in the private sector. The role of government in such relationships centered on the use of its authority and power to support or oppose management or labor (or to mediate between the two) in such matters as strikes, picketing, and union representation. Collective bargaining, which involves the right of unions to form and to strike for the purpose of achieving higher wages and greater benefits, became an established principle by the time of the administration of Franklin Roosevelt after a long period of conflict in different industrial sectors.

With the expansion of the size and services of government at the national, state, and local levels in the post-World War II years, efforts were made to allow collective bargaining in the public sector. In 1954, New York City became the first city to accept the principle that public employees could organize and bargain collectively. In 1959, Wisconsin became the first state to allow such practices for state employees. The right of federal government employees to organize into unions was established by executive order of President John F. Kennedy in 1962 (although the unions were not given the power to strike).

Government employees have organized into many unions. The largest public-sector union is the American Federation of State, County, and Municipal Employees (AFSCME). AFSCME and other public-sector unions have sought many of the same goals as their private-sector counterparts: job security, basic economic improvements, and fringe benefits. One particular unique area of public-sector union concern is the extent of patronage appointments. In general, public-sector unions have sought to expand the size of the civil service at the expense of political appointments.

As in the private sector, the strike is the ultimate weapon of many public-sector unions. And so, in cities and states, teachers, firefighters, transit employees, sanitation workers, and other government employees have, on occasions, gone out on strike. In most cities and states, the right of public employees to strike is illegal—particularly in what is regarded as essential services, such as public safety and health. Court injunctions to halt strikes have been issued, and sometimes union officials have been jailed because they refused to stop a strike.

One of the more notable recent strikes was that of the Professional Air Traffic Controllers (PATCO) in 1981. When PATCO went out on strike—an action that was in conflict with federal law—the Reagan administration fired the strikers and hired new air controllers. It successfully destroyed the union. As is true of the private sector, the power of unions to strike has been influenced by the amount of money available. The strike weapon is feasible in private industries experiencing boom times and weak during periods of economic distress. The income of public employees has also been subject to the level of funds available even when the source of those funds is the public treasury.

Does collective bargaining in the public sector give unions in that sector extraordinary power that is harmful to the public? The Public Service Research Council, an organization formed for research and education about public-sector unionism, argues Yes. It makes the following points: (1) Governments should not engage in collective bargaining because the collective bargaining process undermines democratic processes. (2) There is a correlation between compulsory public-sector collective bargaining legislation and heightened strike activity. (3) Public-sector unions should not be permitted to strike since such action harms the health, welfare, and safety of citizens and taxpayers.

Chimezie A. B. Osigweh, Assistant Professor of Business Administration at Northeast Missouri State University, argues No to the question of extraordinary union power in the public sector. He contends: (1) Public-Sector unions do not have a disproportionately favorable economic base from which to bargain. (2) The amount of benefits given to public employees is subject to financial constraints, such as the tax base of the government's area of jurisdiction, the legal or legislative restraints placed on the government's ability to raise its revenue, and the unwillingness of elected public officials to vote for increased taxes. (3) The existence and activity of public-sector unions are subject to political constraints, such as the emergence of groups challenging their goals.

As you read the debate, consider the strengths and weaknesses that the principal actors in the public-sector union bargaining process possess. Evaluate whether labor–management relations in the public sector should be governed by the same laws reflecting negotiation and the right to strike regardless of the activity performed by a particular government agency.

ISSUES

8   YES

IS MERIT PAY A GOOD WAY TO ENCOURAGE EXCELLENT PERFORMANCE FROM GOVERNMENT AND PRIVATE-SECTOR EMPLOYEES?

Linking Pay to Performance Is a Proven Management Tool
Richard E. Kopelman

As John W. Gardner, former Secretary of Health, Education and Welfare, has observed, there are three bases a society can use for distributing its resources: birthright, egalitarianism and competition.[1] Similarly, organizations can distribute their resources based on such approaches as nepotism (or more broadly, "who you know, not what you know"), across-the-board payments ("everyone gets the same"), and merit allocations ("let the best person win").

While philosophers and politicians continue to debate the merits of these three approaches from a societal perspective, an extensive body of the theoretical and empirical research has developed at the organizational level.

Recently, Charlie Brown, while walking past Woodstock's feeding bowl, commented as follows: "The research they're doing these days on finding old sunken ships is amazing. . . . Some people think there might even be sunken ships from the War of 1812 right here. . . . I suppose one theory is as good as another."[2] Of course, it is a dubious proposition that all theories are equally valid.

One theory of motivation that has received considerable attention during the past 15 years is expectancy theory. Because expectancy theory has typically demonstrated superior predictive validities in comparison to other theories, it is generally viewed as a dominant, if not predominant, theory of work motivation.[3]

Expectancy theory is based on the principle of expected value. People are seen as making choices (e.g., about effort expenditure) based on the expected payoffs associated with different behavioral alternatives. Simply put, the greater a person's expectancy (i.e., subjective probability) that effort expenditure will lead to various rewards, the greater the person's motivation to work hard.

Similarly, the more highly a person values the various rewards that may be obtained (and the more undesirable the penalties that may be avoided) the greater the person's work motivation. Because a multiplicative relationship is posited, highly valued rewards will not prompt high motivation if the person sees no chance of obtaining them; nor will a high expectancy of obtaining rewards (or avoiding punishers) produce high motivation if the outcomes of effort are viewed as trivial.

It follows, therefore, that the stronger the relationship between job performance and rewards, the higher the expectancy that effort expenditure will lead to rewards. (It might be noted that this idea, essentially, is a restatement of the Law of Effect: behaviors that are reinforced are more likely to be repeated; behaviors that are punished are less likely to be repeated.) Also, the stronger the performance-reward tie, the more highly valued rewards will be. The rationale for this notion is that

Reprinted with permission from Richard E. Kopelman, "Linking Pay to Performance Is a Proven Management Tool," *Personnel Administrator*, 28 (Oct. 1983), pp. 60, 62–63, 65, and 67–68, Copyright 1983, The American Society for Personnel Administration, 606 North Washington Street, Alexandria, VA 22314, $40 per year.

[1]Gardner, J. W. *Excellence: Can We Be Equal and Excellent Too?* New York: Harper and Row, 1961.

[2]Schulz, "Peanuts." United Feature Syndicate. May 11, 1983.

[3]Mitchell, T. R. "Organizational Behavior," chapter in M. K. Rosenzweig and L.W. Porter (Eds.) *Annual Review of Psychology*, 1979, Vol. 30, pp. 243–281.

rewards which are obtained as a result of one's performance will have more psychological value than rewards obtained for nonperformance reasons.

Thus, the seven percent salary increase obtained in an organization where the average is five percent will likely be more highly valued than an across-the-board seven percent increase. Certainly, a person can take little credit for achieving an across-the-board increase; it merely signifies that the person has survived for another year. (Perhaps this explains why the youngster who delivers newspapers all year long to buy a bicycle takes better care of it than the youngster who receives a bicycle as a gift.)

Although many implications for practice can be derived from expectancy theory, three in particular warrant discussion. First, the stronger the performance-reward relationship, the higher the average organization-wide level of work motivation. Consequently, in organizations where rewards are largely unrelated to job performance, many employees can be expected to exhibit little work motivation. Some individuals, those with a high need to achieve, might be expected to work hard despite the absence of reward and recognition. However, it has been estimated that only a small minority of people, roughly 10 percent, have a high need to achieve.[4]

Second, the stronger the performance-reward relationship, the more likely it is that high-performing employees will be retained. But in organizations where rewards are largely unrelated to job performance, the most productive employees will tend to be the least satisfied and the most likely to quit; indeed, many will conclude that "there has to be a better way."

Further, in such settings the least productive employees will tend to be the most satisfied and the least likely to quit. Unfortunately, no matter what type of reward system an organization adopts, it is virtually impossible to satisfy all employees. However, is it rational to invest in the satisfaction and the retention of those employees who contribute the least?

Third, it might be noted that whereas rewards importantly influence satisfaction, it is the reward *system* that importantly influences work motivation and job performance. While increased rewards will generally raise job satisfaction, satisfaction is not an antecedent of motivation and performance. Rather, highly satisfied workers will hang around and smile

a lot. The happy worker will be the productive worker only if productivity is a precondition for happiness —i.e., if rewards are based on performance.

THE EVIDENCE

Research on reward systems has focused primarily on the effects of output-based merit reward systems (where performance is measured objectively in terms of quantifiable outputs). Nash and Carroll, in their book *The Management of Compensation*, cite the results of five early surveys encompassing more than 4,700 interventions. Average increases in productivity after switching from time-based to output-based pay plans ranged from 29 to 63 percent, the median increase being 34.5 percent.[5] More recently, an extensive literature review found that, on average, individual incentive plans increased output by 30 percent; group incentive plans typically increased output by 18 percent.[6] Additionally, a comprehensive review of productivity experiments reported the results of seven studies which examined the effects of financial incentives. Results were positive in all cases, with performance increases ranging from 18 to 46 percent.[7]

Clair Vough, in his book *Productivity: A Practical Program for Improving Efficiency*, describes how IBM increased labor productivity in the manufacturing of typewriters by nearly 200 percent over a 10-year period. According to Vough, one-half of the increase in productivity was due primarily to two practices: pay for productivity, only for productivity; and promote for productivity, only for productivity. In his words, increased efficiency arose from "giving every person a tangible, visible, *personal* stake in the division's productivity."[8]

While Vough does not claim that pay and pro-

[4]Luthans, F., *Organizational Behavior* (Third Ed.), New York: McGraw-Hill, 1981, p. 160.

[5]Nash, A. N., and Carroll, S. J., Jr., *The Management of Compensation*, Monterrey, CA: Brooks, Cole, 1975, pp. 199–202.

[6]Locke, E. A., Feren, D. B.: McCaleb, V. M., Shaw, K. N., and Denny, A. T., "The relative effectiveness of four methods of motivating employee performance," in K. D. Duncan, M. M. Gruneberg, and D. Wallis (Eds.), *Changes in Working Life*, New York: Wiley, 1980, pp. 363–388.

[7]Katzell, R. A., Bienstock, P., and Faerstein, P. H., *A Guide to Worker Productivity Experiments in the United States 1971–75*, New York: New York University Press, 1977.

[8]Vough, C. F., *Productivity: A Practical Program for Improving Efficiency*, New York: Amacom, 1979, p. 2.

motion are the only useful incentives, he does argue that they are the most important. He recommends that managers perform the following mental experiment: "Go down the list of status-and-satisfaction factors at your company, and ask yourself what would happen if it were removed."[9] Clearly, if pay were removed, most people would not continue to work: only a few would choose to be volunteers, working just for laughs. But the same cannot be said of other incentives and motivational techniques (e.g., job enrichment, alternative work schedules, goal setting, and so forth).

Notes Mitchell Fein, a consultant to more than 500 companies, "By any measure, pay tied to performance is the most powerful motivator of improved work performance . . . it is undeniable that from floor sweepers to presidents all (employees) raise their productivity when their pay is tied to productivity."[10]

Similarly, John Miner has concluded that whatever the literature one reads, "the evidence of the motivating effects of . . . contingent incentives is quite overwhelming."[11] Perhaps this explains why psychologists speak about the Law of Effect, rather than the Theory or Hypothesis of Effect.

Relatedly, two field studies have examined the effects of going from a performance-based reward system to a time-based one. In one case involving a large manufacturer of paper and paper products, the result was a dramatic and significant reduction in productivity.[12] In the other case, a piece-rate system was discontinued in favor of an hourly wage plan, and the result was failure—performance went down and turnover went up. However, two years later, a plant-wide incentive system was installed. Suddenly, productivity went up 45 percent, and turnover dropped to a lower level than before the piece rate plan was dropped.[13]

---

[9]Ibid., p. 14.

[10]Fein, M., "An alternative to traditional managing," unpublished paper, 1977, pp. 12–13.

[11]Miner, J., in "Performance appraisal: the barrier to pay for performance," Proceedings, 1978 National Meeting of the American Compensation Association. p. 46.

[12]Greene, C. N., and Podsakoff, P. M., "Effects of removal of a pay incentive: a field experiment," Proceedings of the 1978 National Meeting of the Academy of Management, pp. 206–210.

[13]Lawler, E. E., III, "Reward systems," chapter in J. R. Hackman and J. L. Suttle (Eds.), Improving Life at Work, Santa Monica, CA: Goodyear, 1977, pp. 163–228.

Certainly, the results to date are consistent with the predictions of expectancy theory. Moreover, it is not surprising to find numerous case studies and reports of lethargy and inefficiency in public sector organizations—organizations that typically have opted for the across-the-board approach to reward distribution. Consider, for example, the following (unsolicited) testimonial provided by a supervisor working for an agency of a large municipal government:

> Over the course of 15 years with the city. . . .
> I have observed that policies, attitudes and perverse techniques of administration and management have tended to drive out the most able employees in the work force. With good people leaving on a continuing basis, the agency finds itself saddled with an inordinate number of low performers, "crazies," and nonfunctioning people.
>
> To such an extent is this true, that the agency faced with reduced staff and more work, cracks down even harder. . . . In my own unit I find it ever more difficult to retain the best worker, who tells me he wants to leave . . . he feels "burned out" because he has come to realize that his co-workers cannot perform well. Therefore, he feels that he has to put out more.

Ironically, although most of the empirical research to date on reward systems has focused on output-based pay plans (in comparison to time-based plans), the majority of workers today do not produce countable outputs. Indeed, the knowledge sector of the U.S. economy—the jobs that produce and distribute information and ideas—accounts for roughly 50 percent of GNP.

Clearly, for these information-related jobs it is difficult, if not impossible, to measure performance in terms of units produced. There are numerous important differences across types of legal cases, engineering problems, computer programs and college courses. Although objective measures are sometimes available, they represent at best only partial indicators of work behavior or job performance. Hence, the use of judgment is inescapable in measuring the performance of most of today's workers.

Although organizations frequently claim to employ judgmental merit reward systems, espoused policies are often very different from actual practices. This discrepancy in part arises because the consequences (reinforcers) associated with saying something are different from the consequences associated with doing the same thing; in brief, because talk is cheap. Yet there exists a relatively objective way of assessing the robustness of a judgmental merit reward system—namely, by computing correlations (across individuals) between rated performance scores and various organizationally provided rewards (e.g., pay, job title).

To date, only two studies have computed performance-reward correlations for different organizational units and compared these correlations with differences in average levels of work motivation or judgmental job performance scores. In both studies, results were consistent with the predictions of expectancy theory: the stronger the performance-reward relationship, the higher the average level of work motivation or job performance.[14]

PRACTICAL APPLICATION

How can these findings be put to use in the world of work? Here are a few suggestions:

- *A responsive system:* Managers should ensure that a strong connection exists between rated job performance and various organizationally mediated rewards. Importantly, a relatively objective procedure exists for assessing the robustness of a judgmental merit reward system —namely, the computation of correlations (across individuals) between rated performance and rewards. This procedure permits comparisons to be made over time and across subunits. It should be noted, though, that a strong correlation cannot be obtained if all individuals receive the same performance score, or the same level of rewards.

- *Substantial differences in rewards:* To use pay, or any other incentive, to motivate improved performance, it is essential that substantial differences exist in the range of benefits actually

provided (as distinct from the range of benefits theoretically attainable). If, for example, the top performers receive a seven percent salary increase, average performers a six percent increase, and low performers a five percent increase, the correlation between performance and pay increase will be high—but the range of rewards will likely prove too small to affect motivation. As Lawler has pointed out, using pay to motivate improved job performance is not a "piker's game."[15]

To be sure, employees are rather adept at sizing up the tradeoffs associated with performance alternatives, and they are quick to spot a bad deal.[16] Not surprisingly, therefore, *Business Week* surveys report that companies are expanding the range of pay raises they offer, and increasing the variability in the timing of these increases.[17]

Illustrative of these trends are the following pay increase ranges in use at prominent companies: Digital Equipment, 0 to 30 percent; Xerox Corp., 0 to 13 percent; Westinghouse Electric, 0 to 19 percent. Relatedly, many companies are turning to the use of annual performance bonuses in place of the customary annual salary increase (which over time resembles an annuity). Increasingly, the emphasis is on current performance (i.e., "What have you done for me lately?"), rather than on the faded "press clippings" of achievements dating back over many years, or decades.

Clearly, with the use of performance bonuses, differences in payment can be substantial; in contrast, with the conventional step-grade approach, salary increase differences tend over time to become minimal, as people reach the top steps of salary grades.

- *A mixed-consequence system:* Evidence indicates that the most powerful motivational systems are those that provide rewards for good performance, and that take rewards away for

---

[14]Kopelman, R.E., "Organizational control system responsiveness, expectancy theory constructs, and work motivation: some interrelations and causal connections," *Personnel Psychology*, 1976, Vol. 29, pp. 205–220; also Kopelman, R. E., and Reinharth, L., "Research results: the effect of merit-pay practices on white collar performance," *Compensation Review*, 1982, Vol. 14, No. 4, pp. 30–40.

[15]Lawler, E. E., III, *Pay and Organizational Effectiveness: A Psychological View*, New York: McGraw-Hill, 1971.

[16]Smith, H. R., "Brother to the ox," *Management Review*, November 1975, Vol. 64, pp. 4–12.

[17]"A change pattern in allocating pay hikes," *Business Week*, June 23, 1975, pp. 67, 70, also "The tightening squeeze on white-collar pay," *Business Week*, September 12, 1977, pp. 82–94.

poor performance.[18] If good performance merely leads to token increase in rewards while poor performance is ignored, many people will conclude that it pays to do as little as possible and performance will fall to the lowest acceptable level. Managers, therefore, should see to it that the reward system is a two-edged sword. The consequences of performance should be leveraged across all levels of performance, not just the higher levels.

More specifically, poor performers should be notified about performance deficiencies, and provided coaching or additional job training if needed; poor performers should also be denied pay increases until performance is satisfactory. In the event of continuing poor performance, management should offer counseling, and consideration should be given to job reassignment or termination.

Unfortunately, many managers find it difficult to uphold performance standards due to three disabling emotions: guilt, pity and fear (i.e., intimidation). Certainly, it is not realistic to expect lower level managers to uphold standards if higher level managers are unwilling to lend their support, if not their active encouragement, to such efforts.

• *Demanding performance standards:* Good performance should be defined in terms of reasonably high levels of accomplishment. A considerable body of research (more than 100 studies) attests to the positive effects of setting difficult, as compared to easy, performance goals.[19] If managers expect very little from subordinates, subordinates are not likely to sparkle; rather, low expectations will tend to be self-fulfilling. Certainly, in the world of sports, the most successful managers (e.g., Lombardi, Wooden) have demanded excellence. Excellence rarely results from expectations of mediocrity. As Carol Kopelman has observed, one must suffer to be beautiful.

• *Valid measurement of performance:* An effective judgmental merit reward system requires a valid method of measuring job performance. Deficient or excessive performance measures can cause dysfunctional consequences.[20] If, for example, managerial performance is defined in terms of having a tidy desk, and managers are rewarded on the basis of "performance," desk-cleaning behavior will accelerate while other, more relevant work behaviors will tend to occur less often.

It is essential, therefore, that job analyses be conducted, and that performance measures reflect all the important job responsibilities and behaviors. Moreover, the existence of relevant measures does not ensure accuracy. Rater errors (e.g., leniency, halo) and rater biases are important threats that have to be minimized. A number of steps can be taken in this regard, including: the use of multiple ratings (i.e., ratings provided by multiple raters); the use of behaviorally-based rating forms (which focus on specific, observable, overt behaviors rather than on vague performance dimensions such as "attitude," or "leadership skill"); and the provision of extensive rater training.[21]

To summarize, an extensive theoretical and empirical literature attests to the utility of financial incentives for improving performance. A recent review of 10 prominent techniques used to improve organizational functioning, indicates that there is no more effective way to improve productivity than by financial incentives.[22] The major problem in implementation is that judgment is necessarily involved in assessing job performance. While steps can be taken to improve the validity and accuracy of performance ratings, rater errors and rater biases cannot be eliminated altogether. However, the major alternative approach to reward distribution—the across-the-board method—has been found to be an efficient recipe for organizational decline and degradation.

[18]Kazdin, A. E., *The Token Economy*, New York: Plenum Press, 1977; also Kopelman, R. E., and Schneller, G. O., IV. "A mixed-consequence system for reducing overtime and unscheduled absences," *Journal of Organizational Behavior Management*, 1981, Vol. 3, pp. 17–28.

[19]Locke, E. A., Shaw, K. N., Saari, L. M., and Latham, G. P., "Goal setting and task performance: 1969–1980," *Psychological Bulletin*, 1981, Vol. 90, pp. 125–152.

[20]Ridgway, V. F., "Dysfunctional consequences of performance measurements," *Administrative Science Quarterly*, 1956, Vol. 1, pp. 240–247.

[21]Latham, G. P., and Wexley, K. N., *Increasing Productivity Through Performance Appraisal*, Reading, MA: Addison-Wesley, 1981.

[22]Kopelman, R. E., *The Management of Productivity: An Organizational Behavior Perspective*, New York: McGraw-Hill, forthcoming.

IS MERIT PAY A GOOD WAY TO ENCOURAGE EXCELLENT PERFORMANCE FROM GOVERNMENT AND PRIVATE-SECTOR EMPLOYEES?

Statement . . . on Merit Pay
James Perry and Jone Pearce

Thank you, Madam Chairwoman:

My name is James Perry and I am a Professor in the Graduate School of Management and a Research Associate of the Public Policy Research Organization at the University of California, Irvine. With me this morning is Jone Pearce who is also a faculty member of the Graduate School of Management and a Research Associate of the Public Policy Research Organization. We want to thank the Subcommittee for this opportunity to share the results of our research on federal merit pay and performance appraisal.

Jone and I, together with faculty colleagues Lyman Porter, William Stevenson and Alana Northrop, have been studying the Civil Service Reform Act of 1978 for the past five years. Our research was initially supported by a research contract with the U. S. Office of Personnel Management [OPM] Although the research was originally intended to cover a five-year period, from October 1979 until September 1984, it was terminated after 20 months. Despite the loss of OPM funding, we were able to continue the research at a reduced level with support from other sources, including the National Aeronautics and Space Administration and the University of California, Irvine.

We conducted an intensive study of a small, diverse set of federal headquarters and field offices: The Transportation and Public Utilities Service (TPUS) of the General Services Administration (Washington, D.C.); the Naval Ship Weapon Systems Engineering Station (NSWSES) in Port Hueneme, CA; NASA [National Aeronautics and Space Administration]-Ames Research Center (Moffett Field, CA); 21 Social Security Administration (SSA) field offices in the Southern California area; and both the National (Washington, D.C.) and California State (Davis,

CA) offices of the Department of Agriculture's Farmers Home Administration (FmHA) and Soil Conservation Service (SCS). We were able to study only a small portion of all federal organizations, but our research findings are generally consistent with those reported by other investigators.

We believe our research has shed light on two general questions that concern this committee. These questions are: Has merit pay met its intended objective of fostering increased efficiency through performance-based raises for federal managers?; and, Is merit pay both practically and theoretically defensible as a means for motivating managerial performance in the federal sector?

HAS MERIT PAY INCREASED PERFORMANCE?

In answering the first of these two questions, let me briefly summarize the results of our evaluations. They indicate that federal managers do not appear to be more highly motivated nor are they performing at a higher level under merit pay than under the previous time-in-grade compensation policies. This conclusion is based on our analysis of employee attitude surveys and analysis of the effects of merit pay on objective indicators of office productivity (e.g., processing time for claims, accuracy of documentation) within the Southern California area of the Social Security Administration. *Based on our analyses, we have concluded that merit pay, in its first two years, had no discernible positive impact on motivation or peformance.*

Given these disappointing results, we tried to explore why merit pay did not meet its objectives.

1. We have identified a major weakness in the current assumptions behind merit pay. It is not that federal managers do not value pay as a reward, since they report that it is among the handful of important rea-

From U.S. Cong., House, *Civil Service Amendments of 1984 and Merit Pay Improvement Act*, Hearing before the Subcommittee on Compensation and Employee Benefits of the Committee on Post Office and Civil Service, 98th Cong, 2nd Sess., 1984, pp. 71–81.

sons for remaining in their current positions. Where merit pay fails as a motivational program is in the ability to accurately and completely measure performance. Since performance appraisal was initiated these managers report a decline in the contribution of appraisals to their job or agency effectiveness.

Managers apparently do not believe that "good performance" will result in a "good rating" under existing appraisal systems. Consistent with all the available theory and research, merit pay cannot be expected to motivate unless it is tied to an accurate measure of performance.

Qualitative evidence from our visits to SSA offices illustrates the disruptions that can occur when an attractive reward such as merit pay is tied to a performance appraisal system that cannot reflect actual contributions. Setting specific standards of performance for merit pay managers in local claims offices had a large impact on managers' behaviors. There was clear evidence that the setting of these specific standards focused managerial actions on their attainment; managers worked hard to obtain good ratings on those measured standards. Yet not all of those actions could be considered "good management." Each manager and supervisor we interviewed related stories of "gaming" the statistical measures of performance, since most of SSA's performance statistics could be manipulated with no direct harm (or benefit) to the claimant. We had no way of knowing whether or not gaming was truly pervasive, but suspicions were widespread and these suspicions—irrespective of their accuracy—were detrimental to morale.

2. Federal merit pay requires that appraisal ratings be converted into an implicitly comparative rank-ordering for pay purposes. Previous research has indicated that overly precise, implicitly comparative appraisal systems are dysfunctional (e.g., lowered self confidence, alienation and increased turnover among high performers) in private sector organizations. We found similar effects: the receipt of a satisfactory but not outstanding rating was associated with a distinct and significant drop in employee commitment to the organization. Furthermore, the commitment of these satisfactory performers stayed at this reduced level for the remainder of our study, more than 12 months after its initial decline. Thus, *it may be counterproductive in the long term to develop a system that separates the "stars" from the "also rans."*

3. A fixed merit pay budget heightens the demoralizing effect of these comparative ratings. As in all rank-ordering systems, simply improving one's own performance is not enough, one must increase one's relative ranking by displacing another. *Because one employee's gain is another employee's loss, it becomes more difficult to create expectations that rewards will be contingent on performance; thus, we found that managers did not see any greater link between their efforts and a salary increase under merit pay.*

4. There is an inherent contradiction in the policy that calls for accurate, objective appraisals along with "managed" ratings to prevent payout inequities. Performance appraisal ratings must be accurate representations of a manager's performance, and they must also be managed by pay pool managers and personnel specialists to maintain equity across pay pools, with a sufficient dispersion of ratings within a pool to ensure that the size of the increase received by the "best" managers is large enough to motivate their effort. If the ratings are accurate, why should they be manipulated? Will this not make them less accurate? In fact, this contradiction seems to be based on several assumptions: that all pay pools contain the same proportion of high/average/low performers; that managerial performance is naturally distributed in a manner that allows high performers to receive increases two to four times greater than low performers; and, finally, that the only reason actual ratings do not reflect this is that raters either willfully, or through ignorance, distort their ratings. These assumptions are tenuous at best.

To summarize our results, merit pay has had a negative impact on the morale of federal managers, without any compensating increase in managerial or governmental performance. The only evidence of improvement since merit pay is the significant increase in reports of clearer performance expectations. There is no evidence that it has produced any benefits in terms of economies, improved efficiency, or increased fairness in compensation. In response to the first question we posed at the beginning of our statement, we conclude that performance-based pay has not achieved its intended objectives.

CAN MERIT PAY INCREASE PERFORMANCE?

Returning now to the second question we posed at the outset: Is merit pay both practically and theoretically defensible as a means for motivating performance in the federal sector? The research findings we summarized above do not necessarily preclude subsequent improvement of the system so that it could at some time in the future measure up to initial expectations. However, we believe the concept of merit pay itself has inherent flaws that militate against its continuing use as a compensation program for all managers, private or public. These flaws are suggested by recent observations in the popular press, among them:

> Ford Motor Company's decision to consider eliminating performance appraisals because they may be detrimental to continued improvements in quality and, in the words of Donald Peterson, Ford's president, "There is untold waste of human resources with traditional evaluation systems." (San Francisco Examiner, March 2, 1984)

> Reports that companies which rely on a simple set of qualitative values to motivate performance do much better than those which depend on elaborate "objective" measures of job performance with pay raises directly dependent on them. (Peters and Waterman, In Search of Excellence)

> An American company abandons a piece-rate incentive at a high-technology manufacturing plant because management found this kind of compensation to be incompatible with the firm's new Theory Z philosophy of cooperation and employee commitment. (Ouci, Theory Z)

We believe that underlying these shifting practices in the private sector is the realization that merit pay based on carefully metered objectives-based appraisal is counterproductive. As evidence for this argument we offer the following:

1. *While many scholars advocate performance based pay systems, they recognize that under certain conditions such pay systems may be more dysfunctional than functional.* Among the conditions cited as reasons for not using merit pay are low trust levels, performance that cannot be accurately and completely measured, and lack of significant pay increases for the best performers. All of these conditions characterize the federal context and, therefore, serve as a practical basis for eliminating the federal merit pay program. Any federal merit pay system has to overcome an inherently ambiguous performance environment, tight budgetary restraints, freedom of information about individuals' salaries, diffuse authority for implementation, major managerial successions, and significant changes in organizational goals. These factors are continuing features of the federal context for merit pay and, therefore, it is difficult to imagine how any merit pay system could succeed.

2. *Managerial jobs are inherently complex and ever-changing.* These characteristics of managerial jobs suggest that objective measures of managerial performance may not be specifiable in advance. One expert suggests that the complexity of the managerial job may account for the lack of consistent success for managerial goal setting (e.g., MBO programs). In the absence of the ability to measure managerial jobs, merit pay systems are unlikely to be effective.

3. *There is no systematic research that supports the widely held belief that merit pay enhances organizational performance.* Although there have been empirical studies of the effect of merit pay for assemblers and sales personnel, there have been only two systematic studies (including ours) of the actual performance improvements associated with managerial merit pay and neither has found a relationship between merit pay for managers and organizational performance.

4. *Managerial control over organizational performance is complex and often problematic.* The role of management is not simply supervision of employee productivity, even in organizations employing a simple technology, such as the distribution of Social Security benefits.

The arguments above suggest that merit pay—while appealing in theory—has serious, probably fatal, flaws. The federal context is not conducive to the stability and predictability that a merit pay system requires. Furthermore, managerial jobs may be too complex and permit too little control for them to be suitable for merit pay. From our viewpoint, these factors provide conclusive evidence that merit pay is neither practically nor theoretically defensible as a means for motivating performance in the federal sector.

ARE THERE BETTER WAYS TO ENCOURAGE PERFORMANCE?

What should replace merit pay? We cannot provide a detailed design of a substitute, but we can offer some guidelines for performance management and compensation systems that we believe are more promising. These guidelines are based upon both our research and our professional experiences in a variety of organizations.

1. *Eliminate competition for a fixed amount of money.* The zero-sum ("I win, you lose") quality of the existing systems does not encourage better performance. Satisfactory performers should be assured comparability increases, with merit awards coming from a separate pool of funds large enough to encourage employees.

2. *Avoid fine distinctions among satisfactory performers.* Implicitly comparative, overly precise appraisal systems serve no constructive organizational purpose. Federal administrative and management objectives would be adequately served by a two- or three-level system.

3. *Avoid tying rewards rigidly to last period's performance.* The allocation of rewards needs to account for factors other than recent measured performance, including prior years' performance, job tasks and difficulty, and responsiveness to changing demands.

4. *Develop organization-level performance management systems.* More attention should be given to how well each federal agency does as a whole, its objectives, and its overall efficiency and effectiveness. This is a more direct route toward CSRA's primary objective—to improve agency performance. Performance targeting, Scanlon-type plans and similar programs that focus on group performance and group rewards are potentially promising devices for reorienting federal performance management.

5. *Decentralize responsibility for performance management and reward systems.* We believe the variety of jobs and organizations in the federal government demands a diversity of reward systems. We also believe that the responsibility for the design of these systems should be located with departments and their subunits. This realignment of functions might have sev-

eral benefits. Since the design of reward systems would be in the hands of line agencies, it should lead to motivational programs that better suit their needs and those of their employees. It might also lead to a refocusing of OPM and Congressional oversight activity from matters such as the mechanics of merit pay to the performance of agencies and their employees.

CONCLUSION

Based upon our research, we believe, as do many of our academic colleagues, that federal merit pay has failed. Futhermore, we do not expect that it will contribute to better federal performance. Given this prospect, it is advisable that the search begin for new performance management and reward systems that can achieve the promises originally associated with merit pay.

QUESTIONS FOR DISCUSSION

1. What criteria should be used in measuring performance in the public sector?

2. What effect does a low merit rating have on the productivity of a government employee?

3. To what extent can it be credibly argued that a merit pay system strengthens the power of managers but not the productivity of their employees?

4. What alternatives are there to a merit pay system in public employment? Are these alternatives better or worse than the merit pay system?

5. Should there be a merit pay system for university teachers? If so, what should be the criteria for evaluating university teachers? What do you think would be (is?) the effect of a merit pay system at colleges and universities on (a) student grades, (b) cooperation among faculty members in the same department, (c) relationships between a department head (or ranking committee) and other department members, and (d) relationships between university administrators and the faculty members?

SUGGESTED READINGS

COHEN, DAVID K., AND RICHARD J. MURNANE, "The Merits of Merit Pay," *Public Interest*, No. 80 (Summer 1985), 3–30.

FINN, R. H., AND P. A. FONTAINE, "Performance Appraisal: Some Dynamics and Dilemmas," *Public Personnel Management*, 13 (Fall 1984), 335–43.

GABRIS, GERALD T., AND WILLIAM A. GILES, "Improving Productivity and Performance Appraisal Through the Use of Non-Economic Incentives," *Public Productivity Review*, 7 (June 1983), 173–89.

GAERTNER, KAREN N., AND GREGORY H. GAERTNER, "Performance-Contingent Pay for Federal Managers," *Administration and Society*, 17 (May 1985), 7–20.

LAWLER, EDWARD E., "Merit Pay: Fact or Fiction?," *Management Review*, 70 (Apr. 1981), 50–53.

MEDOFF, JAMES L., AND KATHARINE G. ABRAHAM, "Are Those Paid More Really More Productive? The Case of Experience," *Journal of Human Resources*, 16 (Spring 1981), 186–216.

MIHAL, WILLIAM L., "Merit Pay: More Research

Is Needed; Goals May Motivate Better," *Personnel Administrator*, 28 (Oct. 1983), 61–63, 65, and 67.

NALBANDIAN, JOHN, "Performance Appraisal: If Only People Were Not Involved," *Public Administration Review*, 41 (May/June 1981), 392–96.

THAYER, FRED C., "Civil Service Reform and Performance Appraisal: A Policy Disaster," *Public Personnel Management*, 10, No. 1 (1981), 20–28.

U. S. CONGRESS, SENATE, *Merit Pay and Proposed Pay-for-Performance Regulations*, Hearing before the Subcommittee on Civil Service, Post Office, and General Services of the Committee on Govermental Affairs, 98th Cong., 1st Sess., 1983, Parts 1 and 2.

ZEMKE, RON, "Is Performance Appraisal a Paper Tiger?," *Training*, 22 (Dec. 1985), 24–26 and 29–32.

9   YES   IS AFFIRMATIVE ACTION A PROPER REMEDY TO END DISCRIMINATION?

Equality of Opportunity or Equality of Results? Results
Douglas B. Huron

It may be fashionable to insist that affirmative action, and especially quotas for minorities, don't work. But not for the first time, the fashion is wrong. In many kinds of situations these remedies do work, providing job opportunities for qualified (or easily qualifiable) people who otherwise would not have them.

This does not mean we should turn to affirmative action to solve all the problems of America's unemployed and underemployed minorities. Affirmative action provides useful tools, not panaceas. Affirmative action cannot make an illiterate person literate, or teach good work habits, or turn someone with janitor's skills into an engineer. There is no substitute for education, training and apprenticeship. . . .

In many circumstances, members of minority groups have been discriminated against casually, thoughtlessly—because it has been the fashion not to hire them. Thus, many big city police and fire departments traditionally hired no blacks; many craft unions accepted no blacks as members; many big companies put no blacks in positions higher than kitchen help and janitors. When patterns of discrimination are apparent, affirmative action and

quotas may be valid tools to respond. And they may also be useful for an employer who recognizes the problem and wants to change it voluntarily.

The utility of affirmative action and quotas was demonstrated in 1983 in hearings held by Reps. Don Edwards (D-Cal.) and Patricia Schroeder (D-Colo.). In those hearings I talked about public sector employment in Alabama, something I learned about as an attorney in the Justice Department's civil rights division in the Nixon-Ford administration. Another witness at the same hearings was Fred Cook, vice president for human resources at Mountain Bell in Denver.

Alabama has seen dramatic changes in the level and type of black employment in public agencies over the past decade. Most of that change is directly attributable to litigation and specifically to affirmative action and quota decrees entered by Judge Frank Johnson of Montgomery. And it is tough to imagine how blacks would have gotten those state jobs in Alabama without them.

In the late 1960s, the 70-odd Alabama state agencies employed only a handful of blacks above the menial level. At that time the Justice Department sued seven of the larger agencies which together employed over half the state government's work force. Following trial, Judge Johnson found that of the 1,000 clerical employees in these agencies, only one was black. Of over 2,000 workers in semi-professional and supervisory positions, just 26 were black.

From Douglas B. Huron, "Equality of Opportunity or Equality of Results? Results," *Human Rights*, 13 (Fall 1985), pp. 19–20, 22, and 42. Published by the Section of Individual Rights and Responsibilities, American Bar Association.

This paucity of black employees was no accident, since the state refused to recruit at black schools and in black media and also maintained segregated cafeteria facilities.

Even more telling, on those occasions when black applicants appeared at the top of employment registers, agencies simply passed over them in favor of low-ranked whites.

To try to remedy these entrenched discriminatory patterns, Judge Johnson enjoined the passing-over of qualified blacks and required the state to attempt to recruit black applicants. He also ordered the hiring of some 62 blacks who had been passed over and who could be identified following a laborious process of records analysis. In short, Frank Johnson in 1970 ordered everything W. Bradford Reynolds, the current assistant attorney general for civil rights, would require of an employer guilty of discrimination.

But nothing substantive changed, despite Alabama's compliance with the specific elements of Judge Johnson's decree. Perhaps the state's attitude was still too grudging, or blacks were still too skeptical, or perhaps other factors were at work. Whatever the explanation, black employment in Alabama agencies remained low.

The one exception to this otherwise gloomy picture lay in the area of temporary employment. There Johnson had simply imposed a ratio—a quota—on temporary hires. The ratio was fixed at 25 percent—approximately the black population percentage in Alabama—and the goal was met. But there was still no improvement in permanent positions.

Then in January 1972, the Alabama NAACP filed suit against the Department of Public Safety—the state troopers. At that time everyone in Public Safety was white—the troopers, the officers and the support personnel. No blacks had ever been employed there. Throughout the '50s and '60s—from the schoolhouse door to the Selma bridge—the troopers had been the most visible instrument defending segregation.

Judge Johnson set an early trial date, then ruled from the bench, finding that Public Safety had engaged in a "blatant and continuous pattern and practice of discrimination." Having learned from his experience with the other Alabama agencies, Johnson immediately imposed a quota: he required the state to hire one black trooper for each new white hired, until blacks reached 25 percent of the trooper force. He also applied the same formula to support personnel.

The state complied, and the results have been little short of astounding. Within weeks, Alabama had hired its first black troopers. Within two years, there were a substantial number of blacks on the force, and the director of Public Safety later testified that they were competent professionals.

Today, 13 years after the entry of Judge Johnson's decree, Alabama has the most thoroughly integrated state police force in the country. Over 20 percent of the troopers and officers—and nearly 25 percent of the support personnel—are black. The day is fast approaching when Public Safety will be freed of hiring constraints. And although 13 years may seem a long time for a court order to remain in effect, the problem was years longer in the making.

When Justice contrasted the initial results on the trooper force with the lack of progress in other Alabama agencies, the department went back into court, asking that hiring ratios be applied to entry-level jobs in the other Alabama agencies. Judge Johnson gave the agencies plenty of time—over two years—to mend their ways.

When little changed, he issued a decision finding statewide discrimination, but he demurred to Justice's plea for quotas. He said that "mandatory hiring quotas must be a last resort," and he declined to order them. But he noted that the denial would be "without prejudice" to Justice's seeking the same relief one year later: "In the event substantial progress has not been made by the 70 state agencies, hiring goals will then be the only alternative."

The message—the threat—could not have been clearer, and the agencies immediately began to come around. In the eight largest departments, which together account for close to 75 percent of all state workers, black employment increased by over half between 1975 and 1983 and now stands at over 20 percent. And black workers, who used to be concentrated in menial jobs, now appear in substantial numbers in nearly all the larger job categories.

No doubt problems remain in Alabama, but the only fair conclusion is that dramatic progress has been achieved in public employment for blacks over the past decade. And in view of the history of the Alabama litigation, it is clear that this would not have occurred if Judge Johnson had not first imposed a hiring quota on the state troopers—and then threatened to extend it statewide if the other agencies did not alter their discriminatory practices.

At Mountain Bell—an affiliate of AT&T before divestiture—affirmative action was also needed. In 1972, AT&T entered into a six-year consent decree with the EEOC and the Justice Department to substantially increase the number of minority and female workers, as well as the number of women in non-traditional jobs such as installers, cable repairers and frame attendants.

It was not easy at first. Fred Cook said Mountain Bell did not meet its goals for the first year of the decree, but the company then intensified its recruiting efforts and was on target for the next five. As a result, minority managers at the company have increased from under 200 to over 1,400, and there are now nearly 1,200 women in non-traditional jobs, compared to 81 in the year before the decree.

Cook defends Mountain Bell's employment practices in the '50s and '60s, saying that his company was more responsive than most to the aspirations of minorities and female workers. But, he frankly admits that the consent decree focused the company's efforts in a particularly acute and compelling way. As he put it, "It became as important as the bottom line." If it weren't for the decree, with its affirmative action goals, the progress Cook recounted would not have been made.

It is also significant that affirmative action has helped Mountain Bell in a very practical way. Fred Cook said recently that, before the consent decree, "we were reflecting society. We were not using all the talent available." Under the decree, though, the company discovered that its minority and female work force was a "gold mine" for high-quality managers.

And in the wake of Mountain Bell's own efforts, blacks, Hispanics, and women formed organizations aimed at helping one another and at assisting the company in identifying still more talent. Cook praised the work of these groups, and he said that the net result is that Mountain Bell has done a "very good job, especially since the consent decree has ended." The company has no interest in turning back. According to Cook, "it is good business sense to take this kind of affirmative action." It is ironic that it took government action to sharpen Bell's business judgment.

Affirmative action can be a potent weapon, so it should be used only with great care. An effective affirmative action program should have a limited duration, should be aimed only at genuine problems caused by past discrimination, and should not lower standards. Otherwise the problem of selection based on race or sex may be perpetuated indefinitely.

In deciding whether affirmative action is desirable or required, the key question is, what caused a company to exclude blacks from its work force, or keep them in menial jobs? When the answer is that blacks did not have the requisite skills or training, then affirmative action is unlikely to be an effective remedy.

But when the cause is discrimination, whether it is overt or casual discrimination, affirmative action may then be required.

9 NO IS AFFIRMATIVE ACTION A PROPER REMEDY TO END DISCRIMINATION?

Rationalizations for Reverse Discrimination
Sidney Hook

The progress of civilization is marked, among other things, by the abolition of the blood feud. This is the practice of continued hostility over generations often marked by murder based on the views of col-

From Sidney Hook, "Rationalizations for Reverse Discrimination," *New Perspectives*, 17 (Winter 1985), pp. 9–11.

lective, inherited guilt for a crime committed in the past. Although the blood feud often involves murder, those who engage in it deny that their killing is murder if murder is defined as the killing of the innocent. But since it is not difficult to establish the innocence of most victims of blood feuds, when that is established, other rationalizations are sought for the practice. Sometimes religious justifications are introduced. There is the biblical pronouncement "I shall visit the sins of the fathers upon the heads of the children unto the third and fourth generation." Yet no one can morally justify such a view of collective guilt over time. The law in all enlightened jurisdictions recognizes that guilt is individual.

There is, to be sure, a distinction between collective guilt and collective responsibility; one can accept the validity of the latter concept in some situations without accepting the former. In the West, however, the responsibility for the commission of immoral or illegal acts is generally recognized as individual, not collective. Since invidious discrimination against persons on the basis of race, color, sex or national origin is rightfully regarded as immoral today, no one can reasonably object to the punishment of individual persons guilty of such discrimination. The punishment may take many forms in order to redress the sufferings of those victimized. But it is clear that current applications of affirmative action, by going beyond the outlawing of present day discrimination and requiring preferential hiring practices on the basis of race and sex, constitute a form of punishment based on the concept of collective rather than individual guilt and responsibility. This is evidenced by the manifest injustices committed against white males who by no stretch of the imagination can be regarded as responsible for present or past practices of invidious discrimination. I myself am acquainted with half a dozen young white males who, after long years of intense preparation, have been prevented from achieving an academic career in the humanities, and are compelled to look elsewhere for work by the refusal of administrative officers in the institutions where they applied even to grant them interviews. This was an injustice not only to these highly qualified candidates but to all students—black and white—in the institutions which accepted less academically qualified applicants in place of those summarily rejected for reasons of race or sex.

There are some situations in which the claims of justice may be overridden on behalf of other values—e.g., safety and social stability. And there are some advocates of affirmative action based on reverse discrimination who do in fact acknowledge its injustice with respect to young white males and to student bodies but insist that these are the necessary and unavoidable costs of beneficent social

policy. Such judgments are based on empirical estimates of consequences. I doubt, however, whether anyone can establish that the results of quota systems, lax or discriminatory open admissions policies or reverse discrimination in hiring practices have contributed to the quality and discipline of the educational experience or that strict application of the merit principle would pose a threat to basic peace and social order. On the contrary, were the Supreme Court to reverse itself and mandate that the claims of the seniority system were subordinate to those of the affirmative action quota programs, the result would be chaos and conflict in many institutions and industries. Indeed, on the basis of *their* empirical experience, a majority of whites and blacks in some opinion surveys have time and again declared themselves opposed to reverse discrimination and quotas.

Militant advocates of discriminatory affirmative action programs insist that despite the objections raised, these programs are based on justice. They assert that even if minorities and women are given equal opportunities in the present, even if they are not subjected to any invidious discrimination, they still suffer collectively under the weight of past discrimination. They claim that despite enlightened treatment of minorities and women in the recent past, despite all encouragement and remedial programs, these victimized groups suffer from the cumulative effects of the previous discrimination against their forbearers, and that among these effects from the distant past are loss of confidence, self-contempt and lower expectations resulting from the absence of role models in many areas of life.

It is further argued that even if some women and members of minority groups have not themselves suffered directly from the environment in which they grew up, they have suffered debilitating consequences *indirectly* from the discrimination against their brothers and sisters of earlier times and that present day society should therefore make amends to them even if by so doing it does less than justice to some white males. The latter, it is asserted, even if not guilty themselves of having wronged minorities and women, have profited from the wrongs imposed and the opportunities denied to minorities and women by the past policies of the community.

This line of argument seems to me to be very far fetched and invalid. For one thing, the present descendants of *any* group that suffered severe discrimination in the past, could, by the same mode of argument, make similar claims for preferential treatment and hiring. Faced by such claims in any particular situation, we would have to determine the relative degree, intensity and duration of the injustices of the past with respect to each candidate. Anyone who knows the history of the United States knows of the persecutions to which the Jews, the Irish, the Mormons, the Chinese and Japanese were subjected, to mention only major groups. Yet none of these groups has asked for preferential treatment. All they have ever demanded is that one equitable standard be applied to all. Of course, our knowledge of American history also tells us that none of the aforementioned groups, even when periodically subjected to mayhem, suffered the evils and consequences of slavery. But surely there are *some* individuals from discriminated groups not recognized today as protected minorities for purposes of preferential treatment who have suffered as much as or more than *some* present day individual blacks who may be competing for the same position. It would be absurd to attempt to undertake an inquiry in each individual case to make comparative evaluations.

Secondly, if it is the community which is responsible for the injustice of the past to minorities and women, why should the burden of compensating such injustices now fall upon young white males alone? To allege that the white male who may himself be from a poor and underprivileged family has necessarily profited from the deprivations and psychic damage of present day descendents of the enslaved is a claim that borders on fantasy. Wisdom suggests that instead of correcting the injustices of yesterday by creating the new injustices of today, it is better to recognize a statute of limitations on present day accountability for man's inhumanity to man in the distant past.

In many areas, society has already long acknowledged the need for a statute of limitations on the obligations incurred by injustices of the past when the effect of attempting to counteract or undo long past wrongs is to create new and possibly greater wrongs. There is no doubt that property was unjustifiably seized or fraudulently acquired by early American settlers from the native population. But even if it were possible to establish the truth about these spoliations centuries ago, to contest or deny legitimate title to the current possessions of those who purchased them in good faith would generate

social chaos. Similar considerations apply to the current recognition of squatters rights. Even in the area of criminal law, except for treason and capital crimes, statutes of limitation of varying durations are the rule. In various state jurisdictions, contractual obligations lapse after a certain period of time.

There is one particular response that is often made to the proposal that we recognize a statute of limitations on accountability for injustices of the distant past and conscientiously and honestly abide in the present and future by the merit principle. This response invokes a deceptive analogy: "If you handicap a runner at the outset of the race," say the advocates of preferential hiring, "by burdening him with heavy chains, you cannot make it a fair race by removing the chains from his limbs when the race has been half run. He will still suffer unfairly from the effects of that handicap."

Of course, this is perfectly true for the individual runner in this particular race and possibly in subsequent races in which he engages. He is certainly entitled to special consideration and treatment to overcome his handicap. This is nothing but a simple application of the principle of justice on which there is universal agreement, viz., that any person who has been unfairly discriminated against in the past is entitled to the compensatory treatment. But surely this does not entitle the descendants of the originally handicapped person who are running against others in subsequent races to a privilege of handicap over them. Who knows but that the ancestors of the others in the race were also handicapped unjustly in past races.

There is also something very nebulous about postulating the harm done to individuals by social practices that undermine their self-confidence. The same conditions that depress and discourage one person may inspire another to revolt against these conditions, or to rise to a challenge. Further, when we have to make a choice between specific candidates, how do we balance the possible lack of confidence of a minority because of past discrimination against members of his group and the danger of a crisis of self-confidence that often arises when one profits from discrimination and subsequently encounters the judgment of one's professional peers that the post or award was not earned by merit but by special favor?

To give weight to possible injustices from the past, and their alleged continuing debilitating effect on individuals in the present, without tracing the specific proximate causes of discriminatory actions, encourages fantastic speculations of a conflicting kind. Because some blacks have said that they prefer their present status in the United States to that of the present African descendants of blacks whose ancestors were not sold by their chiefs or kidnapped by Arab raiders into slavery, should the relatively superior status of American blacks, as compared to what would have been their lot if their ancestors had remained in Africa, be entered into the equation when calculating what society owes them? This would be absurd. Here we are dealing with hypothetical possibilities that defy not only quantification but significant comparison.

Another questionable assumption by those who speculate about the might-have-beens of the past is that we can retroactively determine what would have been the vocational interests of members of discriminated-against minorities if they had not experienced any prejudice against them. We therefore can reasonably assess—so it is argued—the advantages thereby gained by contemporary white males in particular fields from the cumulative frustrations of the lives of the minorities in the past and make it clear what the former owe the latter. This presupposes, among other things, that in the absence of persecution and discrimination, all groups will manifest interest in various vocational fields roughly in the same proportions. It overlooks the variety of cultural, religious and historical factors that may operate in determining the vocational orientations of different groups. (It is, moreover, an elementary fallacy to infer merely from the statistical inequalities of representation, without evidence of individual discrimination, an overall practice of past or present discrimination. No informed person or one with a sense of humor would infer from the fact that 92 percent of the captains of tug boats in New York harbor and adjoining waters are Swedish, and from the fact that not a single Jew is among them, that the industry is anti-Semitic or, for that matter, anti-black.)

One must acknowledge that the experiences of the blacks who endured slavery and the Jim Crow laws of the post-Reconstruction era were worse than the humiliations and handicaps of any other minority group in this country except the American Indians. But one cannot convert this acknowledgement into a sufficient criterion for public policy in making positions available to the descendants of blacks regardless of their qualifications. After all, there are black immigrants to the United States who were never slaves or were slaves for a short time before being liberated. And how shall we assess the effects of oppression on persons of mixed blood? Implicit in the very essence of a social policy of preferential treatment based on race is the assumption that members of victimized minorities in the past were a compact, passive mass, incapable of differentiated responses and lacking all initiative and responsibility for making choices, however limited, that would in some way have altered their lot. Stripped of its moralistic rhetoric, the reverse discrimination approach represents a condescending and disparaging attitude towards an entire race, an attitude which many blacks quite properly resent.

We should also question the assumption that minorities were seriously handicapped because they were deprived of role models, especially in the educational system at the level of college and university life. The fact that there were once no role models for aspiring black athletes in some professional sports, particularly major league baseball, a field from which American blacks were unfairly and shamelessly excluded, did not prevent blacks from acquiring the skills of star players and—once Jackie Robinson broke the color bar—from achieving outstanding careers in all major sports. The best players were recruited for baseball, football and basketball teams, regardless of the percentage of black and white players represented on the team in relation to the distribution of blacks and whites in the general population. In this field we do not hear of setting up numerical goals and definite time periods within which these goals are to be achieved.

There is no reason to doubt the potential ability of blacks, other minorities and women when given the opportunities in an atmosphere free of invidious discrimination to reach achievement comparable to those of the general population. It requires, of course, the sacrifice or postponement of immediate gratifications in order to achieve success. Preferential treatment, quota systems, reverse discrimination of any variety, are likely in actual effect to harm the prospects of achievement for blacks by wrongly suggesting to them that there is a shortcut to success.

The black experience in professional sports may in fact be taken as a paradigm case of how to combat invidious discrimination without a demand for reverse discrimination. If the bars of racial discrimination are removed in *all* fields and remedial programs are introduced to supplement the educational activities of those interested in learning, who is to predict what the outcome will be? One thing, however, is certain. Just as skill and success in athletics are not simply gifts bestowed at birth but are the result of harnessing native talents to a hard and sustained discipline, so too will meaningful achievement in any field of endeavor depend upon that same sort of effort and commitment.

QUESTIONS FOR DISCUSSION

1. Are numerical goals the same thing as quotas? Explain.
2. How should it be determined which groups should have hiring preference according to affirmative action principles?
3. Is affirmative action reverse discrimination? Explain.
4. Why do some groups excel professionally more than others?
5. What alternatives are there to affirmative action? Are they better or worse than affirmative action?

SUGGESTED READINGS

ALLEN, WILLIAM B., DREW S. DAYS III, BENJAMIN L. HOOKS, AND WILLIAM BRADFORD REYNOLDS, "Is Affirmative Action Constitutional?," *Regulation*, 9 (July/Aug. 1985), 12–18 and 39–45.

DOMETRIUS, NELSON C., AND LEE SIGELMAN, "Assessing Progress Toward Affirmative Action Goals in State and Local Government: A New Benchmark," *Public Administration Review*, 44 (May/June 1984), 241–56.

DRINAN, ROBERT F., "Another Look at Affirmative Action," *America*, 152 (Feb. 9, 1985), 104–106.

EPSTEIN, JEROME L., "Walking a Tightrope Without a Net: Voluntary Affirmative Action Plans After Weber," *Univ. of Pennsylvania Law Review*, 134 (Jan. 1986), 457–75.

GALLAS, NESTA M., "Representativeness: A New Merit Principle," *Public Personnel Management*, 14 (Spring 1985), 25–31.

HOFFMANN, CARL, "Affirmative Action Programs That Work," *New Perspectives*, 17 (Summer 1985), 16–23.

KINSLEY, MICHAEL, "Equal Lack of Opportunity," *Harper's* (June 1983), 8–10.

LOURY, GLENN C., "Goals Are Quotas," *Washington Post*, March 11, 1986, p. A19.

MANSFIELD, HARVEY C., Jr., "The Underhandedness of Affirmative Action," *National Review* (May 4, 1984), 26, 28–30, 32, and 61.

NAGEL, THOMAS, "Caste Struggle?," *New Republic* (Jan. 23, 1984), 13–15.

ROMZEK, BARBARA S., AND J. STEPHEN HENDRICKS, "Organizational Involvement and Representative Bureaucracy: Can We Have It Both Ways?," *American Political Science Review*, 76 (Mar. 1982), 75–82.

SCHWARTZ, HERMAN, "In Defense of Affirmative Action," *Dissent*, 31 (Fall 1984), 406–14.

SIGELMAN, LEE, H. BRINTON MILWARD, JON M. SHEPARD, AND MICHAEL DUMLER, "Organizational Responses to Affirmative Action: 'Elephant Burial Grounds' Revisited," *Administration and Society*, 16 (May 1984), 27–40.

TEMPLE, ANDREW J., AND JAMES M. TOLLIVAR, "Affirmative Action—Making It Effective in the Public Sector," *Public Personnel Management*, 12 (Summer 1983), 211–73.

THOMPSON, WALTER G., "Affirmative Action," *Journal of Social, Political and Economic Studies*, 7 (Winter 1982), 377–86.

10   YES / NO   SHOULD COMPARABLE WORTH BE ADOPTED AS ONE REMEDY AGAINST DISCRIMINATION AGAINST WOMEN?

The Comparable Worth Controversy
Heidi Hartman
June O'Neill

NEW PERSPECTIVES: Let's start off with the so-called 59 percent wage gap. What is it?

HEIDI HARTMANN: Basically that's the ratio of the earnings of women who work full-time, year 'round to the earnings of men who work full-time, year 'round.

NP: Has the wage gap narrowed over time?

HARTMANN: I don't see any pattern of narrowing. The recent Rand report argues that it has been narrowing recently and will continue to do so, but very, very slowly, so that by the year 2000 it will still be 74 percent.

JUNE O'NEILL: One problem with comparing full-time annual earnings is that full-time for men tends to be close to ten percent more hours than for women. Another problem is that annual earnings are more difficult to remember and report. And the restriction to only those who work 50 to 52 weeks eliminates many of the more highly paid women, like teachers. If you look instead at the hourly earnings of workers in their current job, the wage gap is considerably less—about 72 percent.

NP: Whatever the size, why is there any gap?

O'NEILL: There are some factors that help explain the pay gap and changes in it over time—work experiences and education for instance. In the early 1950s, women actually had about one and a half more years of education than working men. During the late 1950s and early 1960s there was a large increase in the labor force participation of older, less-educated married women, while at the same time, the educational level of working men rose. As a result, the education of women in the labor force declined relative to that of men—and the wage gap at that time widened.

NP: Is the return on investment in education greater for men than women?

O'NEILL: That's hard to say. Women appear to have a greater return on schooling than men. But I

think this captures both returns on education and returns on career commitment. More highly educated women are more attached to the labor force. As of the late 1970s, the average working woman over the age of 35 had worked about 60 percent of the time since completing school, while her male counterpart worked more or less continuously. That points to the real source of the wage gap.

NP: Is it true that the salaries of college-educated working women are comparable to their male counterparts?

HARTMANN: It might be true for women in selected fields who are between 20 and 25.

NP: What about the older working women? Have the salaries of those who have remained in the labor force for their entire adult lives kept up with men?

O'NEILL: The differentials are larger for the mothers of the baby boom generation who dropped out of the labor market while their husbands built up valuable work experience.

NP: Where do the women who stayed in the labor force stand?

HARTMANN: I suspect the differential for women and men with comparable education and experience there is about 20 percent.

NP: Are you saying that the differential was halved for those women who stuck it out in the labor market?

O'NEILL: We both seem to agree that about half of the differential is explained by a few basic factors, such as years of schooling and years of work experience.

We may disagree more about the unexplained half. I would argue that important variables are omitted; variables which may not be measurable. For example: the importance of a career in one's life. Most working women have two careers—one at home and one at work. Many women are in the same situation as a student who works to put himself through school. That student is not going to earn what he could if he gave up school and found a job that demands his full attention and energy. Women are in a very similar situation. Time budget studies

From "The Comparable Worth Controversy: An Interview with Heidi Hartmann and June O'Neill," *New Perspectives,* 17 (Spring 1985), pp. 28–33.

show that women work many more hours at home than men. And as I have said, they don't spend as much time at work. You have to expect that this difference will be reflected in the type of jobs women can feasibly take and in the size of their paychecks.

HARTMANN: June might argue that, if you add up the effects of all of the intangibles, like willingness to move (that we don't quite know how to measure yet), you might be able to explain away the remaining gap. I say the evidence doesn't show that. If we look at some very specific groups of people—take people with master's degrees in business administration coming right out of graduate school—the wage differentials between men and women are pretty small. Five years later—before they've married, before they've had babies, before they have done anything differently than men—the women's salaries are substantially lower. That is probably due in whole or in part to discrimination.

NP: Well, what is going on here? Why would an employer not discriminate when someone gets out of college and then start discriminating as a person picks up skills and becomes more valuable to his business?

HARTMANN: I think employers tend to believe, "Well, they haven't gotten married yet, but they will. They will have babies, then I don't know what will happen to them." There is just an awful lot of evidence, in workplace-oriented studies, suggesting that women don't get the same opportunities on the job for advancement or promotion because it is assumed that training women won't pay off for the firm.

O'NEILL: I see a tremendous amount of circumstantial evidence suggesting that most of what you're referring to has to do with choices that women are making. Many of the women who went to graduate school with me gave up job offers that were very lucrative because they preferred to spend more time with their families.

HARTMANN: On the other hand, maybe women are being placed in slightly different kinds of jobs, positions with fewer promotional opportunities attached to them. The perception of these limited opportunities perhaps then leads women to "choose" family life.

O'NEILL: But maybe they do choose them freely. We don't know. A recent article in *The Wall Street Journal* reported on a survey of successful women in management. A substantial percentage of them were not married, and if married, were childless. They felt there would be a conflict between the responsibilites of a marriage and a demanding job. Some of them did say that they felt they were treated

differently or that they could have advanced further than they had. When you get down to concrete cases it is really very hard to tell whether discrimination is a factor.

HARTMANN: You're right. We do not have absolute proof. We don't know how much is choice and how much is discrimination. But we do have evidence and we have judgment. Knowing as we do that women have historically been discriminated against in the market, I think it is reasonable to conclude that discrimination is still a major factor.

O'NEILL: Well, what percentage of women were paid differently than men on the same job in the past? There is evidence that with piece work, women were paid less per hour than men because they turned out fewer pieces. But men and women were paid identical piece rates for each piece they produced.

NP: One thing that troubles me is that we do not have massive evidence that there was wage discrimination against women over the past 100 years. So why should we now pass legislation or have a court make a ruling that assumes that the difference between men's and women's wages is due to discrimination? Does it make sense to base policy on a phenomenon for which we have no clear explanation?

HARTMANN: Well, I think there is lots of evidence of discrimination. Job evaluators have studied men and women at work in Washington State (and in the past at Westinghouse and General Electric) and have consistently found that women's jobs are paid about 20 percent less than equally rated men's jobs.

NP: Because of discrimination? Would an employer, for example, say "I have women who work for me and I will pay them less than I would pay a man because they are women"?

HARTMANN: Some of it certainly is intentional discrimination. Some companies have generalized policies placing women in different jobs and paying them less than similarly qualified males.

There is also a lot of institutional discrimination. For example, you could have a company policy that rewards heads of households in various ways, most of whom might very well be men.

O'NEILL: I define discrimination as unequal treatment for workers who have identical productivity. Competition in the market makes discrimination expensive. If an employer shuns a particular group of workers simply because of their sex, then that employer will have to pay more to get workers of the "preferred" sex. In a free market—and I know of no evidence of collusion in this regard—another employer will hire on a sex-blind basis. As a result, he will be more competitive and tend to drive the discriminating employer out of business.

Also, prejudicial male workers may refuse to work with women. In that case, some employers would hire only men and others would hire only women. Still, there wouldn't be any reason for wages to differ between the groups. If an employer hiring men paid higher wages for the same work, his profits would be lower. There are penalties imposed on employers for discriminating.

NP: Dr. Hartmann, what do you think about this?

HARTMANN: I think June's definition of discrimination is fine. But I think she seriously underestimates the amount of fat in the market. You know, Saks Fifth Avenue can lose a million dollars worth of fur coats in a warehouse and the loss just gets absorbed. The point is that employers can afford to indulge in lots of discrimination.

O'NEILL: I think that there's much more competition out there than Heidi suggests. Even the largest companies—e.g., automobile companies—eventually face competition from others, here or abroad. They can't continue to pay any wage, pass it on in the form of higher prices for cars, and get away with it. They have to face the consumers. And large department stores do close if they are not managed properly.

HARTMANN: I do not believe competition in the U.S. economy is sufficient to eliminate discrimination. It hasn't done so yet. And you're forgetting that discrimination can take many forms. It might not be overt. You might not even bother to *apply* because a company discriminates.

NP: How is comparable worth going to deal with barriers to jobs? How will raising the wages for jobs that seem to be of comparable value make it easier for women to move into traditionally male jobs?

HARTMANN: I don't think comparable worth is so different from a lot of other things. Take the Equal Pay Act. Once an employer is forced to pay women as much as men he comes to view their labor power differently. He could say, "Hey, since I've got to pay them the same as men, I'll just make sure I get the same productivity out of them that I get out of men." And one way of doing that is by assigning them to tasks traditionally performed by men.

O'NEILL: I think the reverse is more likely. Comparable worth would discourage women from moving into non-traditional fields. Right now younger women have higher career expectations than their older sisters or certainly their mothers did, and they

are qualifying themselves for different occupations, mainly through formal schooling. They realize that they are going to be spending a lot of their adult lives working and they want to have higher pay. If you artificially raise the pay for women's jobs, the desire to do so will be blunted. They'll figure they can stay in the jobs that are easier to fit into a married life and still get higher pay. The real down side to this is that as the pay goes up, employers will begin to phase out the traditional jobs, with the result that fewer women will be hired. Lucky women, those with more education, and more valuable characteristics will be retained. Others—the relatively disadvantaged and those with fewer work skills— will lose out.

HARTMANN: I think June is right in principle. There might be some layoffs. But none of us knows how many there would be. And I don't think higher pay in "female" jobs will blunt women's desire to enter other jobs. That has independent dynamics of its own that will not be altered by comparable worth. I want to go back and say what I think comparable worth is and what it isn't and what it would and wouldn't do. We were talking about the wage gap and discrimination. Maybe we could start there. I find it useful to distinguish two types of discrimination that contribute to the wage gap. Barbara Bergmann argues that women have been kept out of certain occupations and are thereby crowded into others, consequently earning lower wages than they would otherwise. So job discrimination indirectly affects wages. There is also direct wage discrimination. If men were nurses or secretaries, those occupations would probably pay more. Because the culture undervalues women for what they do, those occupations tend to be paid less. Comparable worth is an attempt to eliminate the effects of both types of discrimination. It asks what would those occupations pay if there were no discrimination in the labor market, if women could get any job they were qualified for, and if women's work were not culturally undervalued.

It addresses the single employer and it asks the employer not to discriminate in setting the wages of female-dominated jobs. If comparable worth proceeds on an employer-by-employer basis, much like other EEO policies, wages would be gradually realigned and massive unemployment would be extremely unlikely. The most significant effect would be that women would earn more money. We might even reduce female poverty as the salaries of low wage "female" jobs were increased.

O'NEILL: I cannot agree with Heidi's claim that comparable worth corrects, or even addresses, discrimination. The fact that a firm does not base wages for different occupations on a comparable worth job evaluation does not mean that the firm discriminates, any more than it would if it charged different prices for fruits and vegetables with the same nutritional value, weight, and esthetic appeal.

Moreover, comparable worth is not like existing equal pay and employment policies which do not require that firms abandon market forces and pay wages that exceed the worker's productivity. Under EEO policies a firm that treats workers with the same skills in the same fashion should not have any difficulty with the law. Under comparable worth, a firm will never know how it will be judged since the standard of comparability has no single, objective meaning.

It is possible that women are kept out of certain occupations by discriminatory and artificial barriers. If so, the obvious remedy is to remove the barriers. But choice may also account for gender differences in occupation. In fact, the work that I and others have done is more consistent with the interpretation that women are in certain occupations because of their own uncoerced choices. And younger women are moving into what were once male occupations because their career outlooks are different from those of their mothers and so are their choices.

Furthermore, I don't believe that predominately female occupations would pay more if men held them. There are certainly male occupations that pay low wages—for example, farm work or the clergy.

HARTMANN: Women do want to get into men's occupations, even physically demanding ones, that pay relatively well, such as coal mining or the military. There is definitely a pattern of women's jobs being systematically devalued as well as barriers to entry to other jobs.

O'NEILL: I can tell you exactly what I found after looking at approximately 300 occupations. For every ten percentage point increase in the percent female in an occupation, pay went down by one and a one-half percent, which is not very much. That's after holding constant easily measured variables like education and age, but not taking account of equally important, but less easily measured factors, such as the intensity of effort required or the flexibility of working conditions.

NP: Dr. Hartmann, you have argued that overcrowding is due not just to discrimination, but to a whole range of cultural factors affecting women while they're growing up. Subtle things that eventually influence their career choices. For example, a guidance counselor might steer them away from courses that would prepare them for a "male" job. Of course,

you could go further back than that and say that many women are discouraged by their parents from preparing themselves for various kinds of jobs.

HARTMANN: I'm in favor of trying to educate the parents, telling them that their daughter is not likely to be supported by a man for her entire life given the divorce rate. They ought to be paying some attention to how she's going to support herself, if and when she gets divorced.

O'NEILL: I think you have just cited the reasons why women have changed, why they are gaining more work experience and changing their occupations.

HARTMANN: I also think that the problem is sufficiently serious that schools should get involved. They should actively encourage girls to take courses that will qualify them for "male jobs" when they leave school.

NP: Dr. Hartmann you wrote in a paper presented at an Eagle Forum conference that "many women have come to believe that their work is undervalued because it is simply women's work. They believe that such factors of jobs as caring and nurturing, being polite and friendly are undervalued, reflecting the monetary value society places on them." Likewise, nurses argue that their responsibility for life and death goes unrecognized. Do you contend, or are you just reporting a fact, that some women believe that certain characteristics of jobs are not presently given as much value as they should?

HARTMANN: The kinds of job evaluation systems that have been used tend to stick pretty much with the established variables. Variables like responsibility and skill. What comparable worth advocates say, and I agree, is that the job evaluation plan should look at all the different kinds of responsibility found in jobs. Women may have different kinds of responsibilities than men on average. Nurses have responsibility for life and death, secretaries have responsibility for coordinating and scheduling and so on. Men have financial and supervisory responsibilities. So if we are going to factor in the variable responsibility, let's make sure we measure it in all of its different manifestations.

NP: Let's return to the question about caring and nurturing. I think part of a nurse's job entails being friendly and having a nurturing attitude toward patients. Does it make any sense then to do a job evaluation of a nurse's job and not include these factors? Isn't that an argument against the kind of job evaluations that don't include them as factors?

HARTMANN: Well, job evaluation is an extremely flexible tool. You can include anything you believe should be valued. Some job evaluations have

15 job factors—there is even a type of job evaluation that's called task analysis which inventories 200 different features of each job on the average.

NP: Yes. But you are saying that job evaluations that have been used are fine, while many comparable worth advocates are saying there is something fundamentally wrong with them: they don't take into consideration some of the most important aspects of their jobs. You can't have it both ways it seems to me.

HARTMANN: Well, not exactly. Present job evaluation systems do need to be improved, but even the unimproved ones tend to suggest women's jobs are undervalued.

O'NEILL: I do a lot of statistical analysis of the factors relating to pay. I can tell you that I would never want anyone to use them to set my pay. Their purpose is to gain insight into the way different factors affect earnings. Most studies can explain only about 35 percent of the difference in pay among individuals. By using such a crude tool, you are obviously not measuring a lot of things that affect pay. Moreover, some of the things you measure are only proxies for other variables. It may not really be factor "X" that's producing the effect. It is for reasons like this that planned economies are so inefficient. They attempt to substitute planning for the market. The Soviets have sophisticated computers and computer scientists, and they try to measure demand and the likely supply of inputs, but these factors are too complex and change too fast for any planner to keep up with. Since they don't allow functioning markets to tell them how to set wages for different jobs and how to set prices for consumer goods, they never get the right mix. A job evaluation doesn't tell you the appropriate—i.e., the market clearing—wage to pay; it only tells you how a given group of job evaluators measure certain job characteristics. Most companies do not even use job evaluations. Those that do are usually large, bureaucratic enterprises that need to establish some hierarchy within clusters of jobs. For example, they look at the cluster of clerical jobs and they try to assign points to each, the purpose often being to establish a ladder for promotions so that workers within the group will know where they stand and why. As to the cluster itself, the firms know that they are competing in a market for the skills that the cluster calls for. Thus, in the final analysis, it is to the market that the firm must turn to find out the wages it must pay. I don't think that any job content evaluator can tell a firm the wage it should pay for any job because the job evaluation doesn't address the market situation, which is always changing.

HARTMANN: In fact, job evaluators market their systems to companies based on their ability to "capture the market." They say "Look, we have a system that identifies the factors that are compensated in the marketplace and if you use this to adjust the internal hierarchy of jobs in your firm you won't be totally out of wack with the marketplace." The same kind of job evaluation plans are being used in comparable worth cases and they have at least two problems. One you identified: they may not identify the factors that are important in women's jobs, such as nurturing and caring. That is one problem. Second, evaluators may just perpetuate discrimination in the marketplace in the way they identify and weight factors. That is less true in places where workers are organized enough to demand a comparable worth study, in which case they work with the job evaluators. Typically, there is a committee of workers and managers set up to advise the job evaluation consultants.

O'NEILL: Then it immediately loses its objectivity, because it becomes a political decision. You can imagine what goes on in the room when the head of the nurses' association sits on a panel that assigns points. You can be pretty sure that nurturing will be weighted very heavily indeed.

NP: Is it like a bargaining situation?

O'NEILL: Yes, it's negotiating over what's to be considered valuable. What do you do with two occupations both of which require a college degree, but one essentially uses math skills and the other one uses verbal skills. Are they equal? It all depends on how many people have the math skills—how hard it is to get someone with these skills as against someone with verbal skills. Job evaluations can't tell the two jobs apart, but the market sure can.

I think this points to the reason why job evaluations tend to show that women are paid less than men for "equally valuable" jobs. The only objective factor the evaluators have to grab onto is years of schooling. I think if you look at years of schooling that would probably explain most of the variation in the job points.

And women and men are not that far apart in years of schooling. They are far apart in other characteristics, such as years of on-the-job training, or field of study in school, but not in years of schooling.

HARTMANN: It is generally the skill variables that explain most of the differential. Skill can be measured in a variety of different ways. Schooling is just one way. But other factors do enter in.

NP: How about the politicization of the process that June is talking about. Does it take away from the objectivity of a comparable worth study?

HARTMANN: You can call it political infighting if you want. You can also call it consensus building. Comparable worth, through job evaluation, says this: whatever you want to value in a job, let's make sure you value it equally for all different kinds of jobs. If we are going to value nurturing let's make sure we look at the different kinds of nurturing. Men's jobs can involve nurturing. The senior mechanic who shows the ropes to the junior mechanics—he nurtures. And you can still use the marketplace but try to eliminate the part that is discriminatory.

O'NEILL: Say what you will, the job evaluation is going to be subject to biases of all sorts. Once a group gains control of the process, it can make the points come out to meet its own objectives. Any job evaluator will tell you that. What happened in Washington State is a good example of what I'm talking about.

NP: What happened there?

O'NEILL: Basically, women's jobs, like nursing and secretarial occupations, got a lot of points. Nurses were the highest ranked occupation in the state, higher than the highest level computer systems analyst, higher than the highest level actuary, or the highest level chemist or physicist.

NP: Dr. Hartmann, how would you account for the fact that nurses scored so high in comparison to Ph.D. scientists?

HARTMANN: I do not recall the specific factors they looked at or the weights assigned to them. One result I am aware of seemed perfectly reasonable to me. Licensed practical nurses came out with about the same points as correctional officers. And yet the nurse made about $4,000 a year less.

O'NEILL: A practical nurse is not very much different from a housekeeping job. It is a low scale job.

HARTMANN: So is being a guard.

O'NEILL: But a guard can be shot.

HARTMANN: And a practical nurse can be exposed to life threatening diseases. There is a lot of risk.

O'NEILL: Of course your assessment and mine are not what counts—which is the main point. There is no real way of measuring the possibility of contracting a disease against the possibility of being shot. They're like apples and oranges. You can only tell what's an attractive job and what's an unattractive job by looking at the behavior of people. And you can only tell what's valuable and what's not valuable to firms by looking at their behavior. And the only way to balance a worker's tastes and a firm's needs is by letting supply and demand operate.

HARTMANN: But if there is discrimination we must do something to correct the market. Not only because it's the right thing to do; eliminating discrimination also makes the market more efficient. Resources aren't reasonably allocated when some people are underpaid and others are overpaid, relative to their contribution to the employer. Slavery wasn't efficient. When minorities were paid a lot less for doing the same work and they weren't hired for jobs because of their race, we lost GNP. Congress has an estimate of how much GNP we lose because of the inefficiencies in allocation due to discrimination. Comparable worth seeks to readjust wages to remove the discriminatory element in the market and to improve efficiency. If we pay secretaries too little, for example, we use too many secretaries.

O'NEILL: If you pay too low—you usually get too few workers. But you are saying that there are too many. Are all of these women being compelled to do this underpaid work?

HARTMANN: The personnel office of GAO [General Accounting Office] has a sign that says they are always short of secretaries. That suggests they want more than they can get at the wages they offer.

O'NEILL: If you looked at the queue of who is waiting to get into government employment, I suspect you would find that there is a long line of people who wish to be secretaries. If there is no queue and no applicants can be found, that would suggest the federal government is not offering enough in pay or other compensations at this particular time. But this is not an argument for comparable worth. The situation could arise with any occupation. It is an argument for making government more sensitive to market forces.

HARTMANN: It is also an argument that the market may not operate the same way for women's jobs as it does for men's.

NP: What about the implementation of a comparable worth plan?

O'NEILL: Bureaucracies would eventually be required to regulate all firms. Government bureaucrats would look over employers' shoulders to see if they were evaluating jobs in a nondiscriminatory way.

HARTMANN: Nobody is going to be looking over their shoulders unless somebody files a complaint. I do not believe it would be any different from what we do right now with equal pay and affirmative action enforcement. All the enforcement agencies combined don't have a fraction of the Defense Department's budget. What's being advocated is an employer-by-employer approach where if you use a job evaluation system you are going to have to use it in an unbiased manner.

O'NEILL: It's a vastly easier task to decide whether two key punch operators are being paid the same, if they have the same seniority and so on. It is a vastly more difficult task to require that firms compare totally different kinds of occupations to see whether they are being paid the same for jobs of comparable worth when there really is no definition of comparable worth. In other words, there is no agreed upon measuring rod.

HARTMANN: I think comparable worth advocates are simply saying that if employers use job evaluation, they should use it fairly. The EEOC could issue guidelines on the fair use of job evaluation just as they issued guidelines on the fair use of testing.

NP: What if a firm doesn't have a job evaluation plan and the women workers complain about their pay and demand a job evaluation analysis?

HARTMANN: Well, probably the government won't require a firm to carry out a job evaluation for comparable worth purposes. The cases so far have arisen after the employer has agreed to do the job evaluation and then has not abided by its results.

NP: Well, wait a second—if an employer discriminates against women wouldn't you want the government to put a stop to that? No one has yet gone and told the employer you have to do the job evaluation. But if job evaluation systems are a way of measuring discrimination, eventually someone is going to get the bright idea that she ought to go to court and demand that her employer do a job evaluation.

HARTMANN: That could happen eventually. But I'm willing to let the field develop in a case-by-case approach and see what happens. That's how social change comes about. I would argue that on the whole comparable worth is going to improve the market because it is going to create wage rates that do not reflect discrimination and will therefore improve the allocation of resources. And women will earn more money and be better off.

O'NEILL: It will do what administered pricing systems often do. It will create havoc in the market and lots of women are going to be hurt in the process.

NP: Thank you very much.

QUESTIONS FOR DISCUSSION

1. Does the fact that working women on average earn 59 cents for every dollar earned by a man mean that the American economic system discriminates against women? Explain.

2. If there is discrimination against women in employment, would you argue that there is a difference in the degree of discrimination between public and private employers? Explain.

3. If large numbers of men were nurses and secretaries, would these occupations pay more? Explain.

4. What criteria should be used in establishing a wage scale for different government positions so as to be free of gender discrimination?

5. Who should decide pay for government positions? Why?

6. Could comparable worth be supervised by a government agency in a fair manner? Explain.

SUGGESTED READINGS

BELLACE, JANICE R., "Comparable Worth: Proving Sex-Based Wage Discrimination," *Iowa Law Review*, 69 (Mar. 1984), 655–704.

BERGMANN, BARBARA R., "Women's Plight: Bad and Getting Worse," *Challenge*, 26 (Mar./Apr. 1983), 22–26.

CHI, KEON S., "Comparable Worth Progresses Slowly in the States," *State Government News*, 28 (Sept. 1985), 12–14 and 16.

Comparable Worth: Issue for the 80's: A Consultation of the U. S. Commission on Civil Rights. Washington, DC: Commission on Civil Rights, 1984, 2 vols.

"Comparable Worth: Special Issue," *Public Personnel Management*, 12 (Winter 1983), whole issue.

COWLEY, GEOFFREY, "Comparable Worth: Another Terrible Ideal," *Across the Board*, 21 (May 1984), 44–48.

GRUNE, JOY ANN, AND NANCY REDER, "Addendum—Pay Equity: An Innovative Public Policy Approach to Eliminating Sex-based Wage Discrimination," *Public Personnel Management*, 13 (Spring 1984), 70–80.

JOHANSEN, ELAINE, "Comparable Worth: The Character of a Controversy," *Public Administration Review*, 45 (Sept./Oct. 1985), 631–35.

LEVIN, MICHAEL, "Comparable Worth: The Feminist Road to Socialism," *Commentary* (Sept. 1984), 13–19.

SCHLAFLY, PHYLLIS, "Shall I Compare Thee to a Plumber's Pay?," *Policy Review*, No. 31 (Winter 1985), 76–78.

U. S. CONGRESS, HOUSE, *Federal Pay Equity Act of 1984*, Hearings before the Subcommittee on Compensation and Employee Benefits of the Committee on Post Office and Civil Service, 98th Cong., 2nd Sess., 1984.

11   YES   DOES COLLECTIVE BARGAINING IN THE PUBLIC SECTOR GIVE UNIONS IN THAT SECTOR EXTRAORDINARY POWER THAT IS HARMFUL TO THE PUBLIC?

Public Sector Bargaining and Strikes
The Public Service Research Council

During a May 1973 legislative hearing on the initial experience with Act 195, Pennsylvania's primary collective bargaining statute, Mr. Harry Boyer, president of the Pennsylvania AFL-CIO, "declared that the Pennsylvania AFL-CIO played 'no small part' in the enactment of Act 195. He stated that there were 'many' strikes before the enactment of the law, but that 'Now, with the limited, restricted right-to-strike included in the law, such strikes were minimal.' "[1] Either Mr. Boyer computed differently than his colleagues or he was guilty of purposeful misrepresentation. For in fact, from 1958 through 1968, Pennsylvania's public employees engaged in 72 work stoppages. In the first three years of experience under Act 195, there were 215 work stoppages.

The question that arises from this evidence concerns the nature of the relationship between the enactment of collective bargaining legislation and the frequency of strikes. An examination of the facts relating to this question through the use of statistical data and its interpretation is the primary focus of this study.

THE RISE OF UNIONISM

The emergence of collective bargaining as a labor-management tool of state and local governments and the parallel growth of public sector unions has been referred to as "among the half dozen most far-reaching legal developments of this century."[2]

In 1959, only one state, Wisconsin, had enacted public sector collective bargaining legislation. In all others, the collective bargaining process was a special arrangement tolerated by a small number of local governments. Strikes were rare with the vast majority of public sector unions accepting their illegality and officially rejecting their use.

From The Public Service Research Council, *Public Sector Bargaining and Strikes*, 6th ed. Vienna, VA: The Public Service Research Council, 1982. Reprinted with permission.

[1]Alderefer, Harold F., "Follow-up on the Pennsylvania Public School Strikes," *Labor Law Journal*, March 1974, p. 167

[2]Summers, Robert S., *Collective Bargaining and Public Benefit Conferral: A Jurisprudential Critique*; Institute of Public Employment Monograph 7 (Ithaca, NY: New York State School of Industrial and Labor Relations, Cornell University), (1976) p. vii

By 1980 matters were very different. By then thirty-seven states had enacted some type of bargaining or meet-and-confer legislation. Membership in public sector unions had virtually quadrupled, and whereas there were only 15 strikes by public employees in 1958, there were 536 in 1980. Strikes also tended to last longer and involve more employees than strikes prior to the 1960's.

In 1958, public sector union membership was 1,035,000. By 1978 membership in public sector unions and associations had grown to 6,019,000. Private sector unions, in 1956, represented 24 percent of the total work force with 16,575,000 members. At the same time, public sector union membership represented only 1.3 percent of the total work force. By 1978, the difference between the two segments of the union movement had narrowed noticeably. Private sector union and association membership stood at 16,779,000 or 16.4 percent of the total work force. In the public sector, the 6,019,000 members of unions and associations represented almost 6.0 percent of the total work force.

In 1956, 27 percent of the private sector work force belonged to unions. By 1978 that figure had fallen to 19.3 percent. In contrast, public sector union membership, as a percentage of the government work force, had increased from 12 percent in 1956 to 39 percent in 1978.

The growing importance of the public sector union movement is indicated in other statistics. From 1968 through 1978, the two fastest growing unions in the country operated in the public sector. During this period, the American Federation of State, County and Municipal Employees (AFSCME) increased its membership by 180.2 percent. The American Federation of Teachers (AFT) posted a gain of 203 percent.

In addition, the National Education Association (NEA) which has, over the last decade and a half, evolved from a professional association into a labor organization, now ranked among the largest unions. Its 1,700,000 members place it second only to the Teamsters in size.

These developments were accompanied by a radical change in the attitudes of the leadership of the union movement toward public sector collective bargaining. "In 1955, AFL-CIO President George Meany wrote: 'It is impossible to bargain collec-

tively with the government.' "[3] But it was not possible to ignore the growing union membership in the public sector.

In 1974, the AFL-CIO created a Public Employee Department (PED). In his speech at the PED founding convention, George Meany evidenced a different perspective on public sector labor relations. Not only did he now feel it was possible to bargain collectively with government, Meany now endorsed the use of militant tactics. "You just quit working for the guy who's kicking you around. And if that guy happens to be the mayor of the city or the governor of a state, it doesn't make a damn bit of difference." By this time, many public sector unions had already amended their constitutions and by-laws to remove strike prohibitions.

INCREASE IN STRIKE ACTIVITY

The growth of unionization and collective bargaining in the public sector has been accompanied by an increase in strike activity. This increase has occurred despite the fact that all but eight states prohibit strikes in the public sector. The states legalizing strikes in a limited form are: Alaska, Hawaii, Minnesota, Montana, Oregon, Pennsylvania, Vermont and Wisconsin.

In 1958 there were 15 public sector strikes, involving 1,730 workers and resulting in the loss of 7,520 man-days. By 1980 the number of public sector strikes had increased to 536, involving 223,600 workers and resulting in the loss of 2,347,800 man-days. The decade of the seventies averaged 423 public sector strikes per year.

During this period, public attitudes toward strikes against government underwent change. While opinion on the issue was almost evenly divided in the mid-1970's, support for strikes had eroded by the end of the decade. A 1975 Gallup Poll provided the following results on public support for strikes by various types of public employees: sanitation workers—45% YES, 48% NO; teachers—45% YES, 48% NO; firefighters—39% YES, 55% NO; police—41% YES, 52% NO.

---

[3]Steiber, Jack, *Public Employee Unionism: Structure, Policy, Growth*, Brookings Institution, Washington, D.C., 1973, p. 116

TABLE A

	States with Bargaining Legislation	Public Sector Union Membership*	Public Sector Union and Association Membership*	Number of Strikes
1958	0	1,035,000	—	15
1959	1	—	—	25
1960	1	1,070,000	—	36
1961	2	—	—	28
1962	2	1,225,000	—	28
1963	2	—	—	29
1964	2	1,453,000	—	41
1965	9	—	—	42
1966	10	1,717,000	—	142
1967	13	—	—	181
1968**	15	2,115,000	3,857,000	254
1969	23	—	—	411
1970	28	2,318,000	4,080,000	412
1971	30	—	—	329
1972	31	2,460,000	4,520,000	375
1973	34	—	—	387
1974	36	2,920,000	5,345,000	384
1975	36	—	—	478
1976	36	3,012,000	5,852,000	378
1977	36	—	—	413
1978	37	3,625,000	6,019,000	481
1979	37	—	—	593
1980	37	***	***	536

*data on public sector union and association membership compiled by the Bureau of Labor Statistics biannually.

**data on public sector association membership only available since 1968.

***data unavailable for 1980.

Over the next few years attitudes toward strikes by sanitation workers and teachers remained relatively unchanged. There was a gradual decline in support for strikes by police and firefighters.

Polls taken in 1981, however, showed a dramatic change. The Gallup Poll of that year reported public support for strikes by sanitation workers had fallen to 40% and support for police and firefighter strikes had dropped to 27%. An NBC News/Associated Press Poll taken in August, 1981, provided similar results. When asked whether certain types of public employees should be permitted to strike, the public responded as follows: teachers—39% YES, 57% NO; police and firefighters—26% YES, 70% NO; postal workers—27% YES, 67% NO.

These poll results suggest a growing public dissatisfaction with strikes by public employees and their unions. Yet, the public may not be aware of the relationship between strikes and the advent of collective bargaining and collective bargaining laws in the public sector.

Table A illustrates that the increase in states with bargaining legislation was accompanied by an increase in union membership and strikes in the public sector. Dr. Sylvester Petro examined this trend in the public sector and compared it with events in the private sector following passage of the Wagner Act. He came to the following conclusion:

Proceeding as cautiously as possible because statistical analysis is an inconclusive business, one emerges with this fact: the introduction of compulsory collective bargaining legislation in the public sector coincided with both a sharp increase in unionization and a sharper increase in the number of strikes, despite their illegality, than occurred in the private sector with the introduction of compulsory collective bargaining legislation there.[4]

RATIONALE FOR BARGAINING

According to Myron Lieberman and Michael Moskow, authors of *Collective Negotiations for Teachers*, there were five important factors that contributed to the development of collective bargaining in public education: (1) the need of teachers for more effective representation at the local level; (2) consolidation of school districts; (3) developments outside of education (more militant activities of other public employees); (4) the changing attitudes of teachers themselves (from docile to assertive—especially in their willingness to strike); and (5) organizational rivalry.[5] While Dr. Lieberman now feels that there may be a need for some reevaluation of these factors, they nonetheless remain relevant, not only in the area of public education, but for the public sector in general.

One of the most important factors has been organizational rivalry. The inherent difficulty of unseating a certified exclusive representative has led to intense competition between unions.

The rapid spread of bargaining after enactment of a state bargaining law is not due to widespread rank-and-file demands for immediate bargaining. Instead, it is the result of union leadership efforts to achieve incumbency before being frozen out by a rival union.[6]

State legislators were no less helpful in providing a suitable environment for the growth of bargaining. They justified adoption of such statutes partly on the grounds that legislative remedies were too slow and ineffective to resolve labor-management problems in the public sector.

. . . There was some thought that once the legislatures had provided bargaining rights at the local level, they would get out of the business of legislating statewide terms and conditions of employment. They could legitimately say that they had established a mechanism for dealing with these problems at the local level and that they did not intend to usurp the function of local public employers. In fact, no such legislative reaction seems to have occurred, at least on a national basis.[7]

The model for public sector labor relations has been the private sector experience. In many states, the language drafted for use in public employee collective bargaining statutes, was not significantly different from that of the National Labor Relations Act (NLRA). There are, however, legitimate distinctions between the responsibilities of public and private sector employees that we ignore at our peril. These distinctions are central not only to questions of whether public sector unions should be permitted to strike, but also, to the root issue of whether governments should engage in collective bargaining.

The relationship between government and its employees has undergone a radical metamorphosis within the last twenty years. The emergence of collective bargaining, coupled with traditional civil service systems, have placed many public employees in the position of enjoying protections and privileges not shared by workers in the private sector.

Perhaps first among these special privileges is a developing body of case law which holds that public sector employees have a constitutionally protected and supported "property interest" in their continued employment. There is no such benefit conferred on private sector workers.

The U.S. Supreme Court's decision in *Perry* v. *Sindermann*, 408 U.S. 593, (U.S. 1972) was an integral link in establishing the concept of property right to employment. Mr. Justice Stewart, delivering the opinion of the Court stated

We have made clear in *Roth* . . . that "property" interests subject to procedural due process protection are not limited by a few rigid, technical forms. Rather, "property" denotes a broad range of interests that are secured by

---

[4]Petro, Sylvester, *Sovereignty and Compulsory Public-Sector Bargaining*, Wake Forest Law Review, Vol. 10, No. 1, March 1974, p. 35–36

[5]Lieberman, Myron and Moskow, Michael H., "Collective Negotiations for Teachers" (Chicago: Rand McNally, 1966) p. 55–61

[6]Lieberman, Myron, *Public-Sector Bargaining* (Lexington, Mass., Lexington Books, 1980) p. 15

---

[7]Ibid., p. 16–17

'existing rules or understandings' . . . A person's interest in a benefit is a "property" interest for due process purposes if there are such rules or mutually explicit understandings that support his claim of entitlement to the benefit and that he may invoke at a hearing. . . .

A teacher, like the respondent, who has held his position for a number of years, might be able to show from the circumstances of this service—and from other relevant facts—that he has a legitimate claim of entitlement to job tenure.[8]

The consequences of this constitutionally supported right, as it relates to the issue of collective bargaining, are just now beginning to be understood.

The Supreme Court has frequently ruled that unions cannot negotiate away the basic statutory rights of employees set forth in Section 7 of the NLRA. Thus, it would be most unlikely to permit unions to negotiate away constitutional rights. As the Court stated in a leading First Amendment case, "one's right to life, liberty and property . . . and other fundamental rights may not be submitted to a vote; they depend on the outcome of no election."[9]

These strictures have important implications. Perhaps the most important of these concerns the rationale for the extension of collective bargaining to the public sector, because if, in fact, the constitutional guarantees are upheld, "public employers and public employee unions cannot make and enforce agreements that would be completely viable in the private sector."[10]

CONSTITUTIONAL FALLACY

Among many policymakers there has been a mistaken interpretation of the constitutional rights of public employees to organize and press for collective negotiations. For instance, when Representative Edward Roybal of California introduced legislation in Congress in 1977 to federally mandate collective bargaining for all state and local government employees, he stated:

The denial by some public employers of the right of employees to organize and the refusal by some employers to accept the procedure of collective bargaining deprives public employees of the effective exercise of rights guaranteed under the Constitution of the United States. Such refusal also leads to strikes and other forms of unrest. . . .[11]

The glaring fallacy in Roybal's statement is that *collective bargaining even in the private sector, is a creation of national legislation and not a constitutionally guaranteed right.*

The U.S. District Court for the Western District of North Carolina stated in *Atkins* v. *City of Charlotte,*

There is nothing in the United States Constitution which entitles one to have a contract with another who does not want it. . . . The right to a collective bargaining agreement, so firmly entrenched in American labor-management relations, rests upon national legislation and not upon the federal constitution.[12]

THE QUESTION OF SOVEREIGNTY

The prohibitions and arguments against extending collective bargaining rights to public employee unions can be traced as far back as 1937 when President Franklin D. Roosevelt declared:

All government employees should realize that the process of collective bargaining, as usually understood, cannot be transplanted into the public service. It has its distinct and insurmountable limitations when applied to public personnel management. The very nature and purposes of government make it impossible for administrative officials to represent fully or to bind the employer in mutual discussion with government employee organizations. The em-

---

[8]*Perry v. Sindermann*, 408 U.S. 593, (U.S. 1972)

[9]Lieberman, Myron, op. cit., p. 109

[10]Ibid., p. 107

[11]From the preamble to H.R. 1987, introduced in the 95th Congress by Rep. Edward Roybal (D-CA).

[12]*Atkins v. City of Charlotte*, 296 F. Supp. 1068 (W.D,N.C. 1969)

ployer is the whole people who speak by means of laws enacted by their representatves in Congress. Accordingly, administrative officials and employees alike are governed and guided, and in many cases restricted, by laws which establish policies, procedures or rules in personnel matters.[13]

Herein is reiterated the principle of sovereignty; governments operate on the principle that their decisions, when all appeals are exhausted, are final and universally applied. Only duly elected representatives of the people may share in the delegated powers of government. Dr. Sylvester Petro provides a succinct statement about the inherent conflict between collective bargaining and governmental sovereignty. He says:

. . . the unchallenged, undivided, and supreme power to govern is vital to ordered society and is in fact recognized as such even by those who consider the sovereignty doctrine somehow "outmoded" and not a fit subject for sustained scholarly discussion of the issues raised by compulsory public sector bargaining.

. . . there is an absolute and ineradicable incompatibility between government sovereignty and compulsory public sector bargaining, an incompatibility which must necessarily weaken if not ultimately destroy effective governing power and the integrity of government vis-à-vis the general citizenry, since the necessary consequence of according public employee unions exclusive bargaining status is to encourage among government employees a tendency to repose their loyalties primarily in the unions which they have been induced to believe are their protagonists.[14]

Government and unions do bargain, however, and the result has been that the process has become an appendage to the political process that changes the dynamics of government's most vital operations, i.e., budget development and the determination of state and local policy. Petro comments:

The most ominous threat that compulsory public-sector bargaining poses is to the basic political institution of the United States. Call it representative government, or popular government, or popular sovereignty, or the "normal" American political process; the name does not matter; it is the reality that counts. The system whatever called, presupposes that government programs will represent a consensus, somehow derived, on all the varied, intersecting, sometimes conflicting interests of the American people as a whole. Here as elsewhere, as Whitehead might have said, it is the process that counts. The process with which we are concerned is one in which a free people acting singly or in voluntary groupings, none of them possessed of monopolistic powers rivalling those of government itself, seeks to secure from government the kind of services upon which a majority can agree without doing too much harm to minority interests.[15]

Currently, collective bargaining excludes major sections of the electorate from decisions affecting budget allocations and policy development. One private interest group, unaccountable to the public, the union, realizes enhanced power over these decisions to the detriment of other legitimate interest groups.

The U.S. District Court for the Middle District of North Carolina, in a decision upholding that state's ban on public sector bargaining, stated:

[To the] extent that public employees gain power through recognition and collective bargaining, other interest groups with a right to a voice in the running of the government may be left out of vital political decisions. Thus, the granting of collective bargaining rights to public employees involves important matters fundamental to our democratic form of government. The setting of goals and making policy decision are rights inuring to each citizen. All citizens have the right to associate in groups to advocate their special interest to the government. It is something entirely different to grant any one interest group special status and access to the decision-making process.[16]

[13]Rosenman, "The Public Papers and Addresses of Franklin D. Roosevelt", 1937 Vol. 1 p. 325 (1941)
[14]Petro, Sylvester, op. cit., p. 110–111

[15]Ibid., p. 112
[16]Winston-Salem/Forsyth County Unit of the North Carolina Association of Educators v. Phillips (DCNC 1974) 381 F. Supp 644

PUBLIC SECTOR STRIKES DISRUPTIVE

The fact that public sector bargaining is not consistent with elements of the democratic process is most visable and easily understood in strike situations.

Strikes, as impasse resolution procedures, designed to force changes or improvements in "wages and terms and conditions of employment," constitute pressure to modify public policy. Justice Lewis Powell observed that "the ultimate objective of a union in the public sector, like that of a political party, is to influence public decision-making in accordance with the views and perceived interests of its membership. . . ."[17] If that is so, then in a sense, a public sector strike represents a unique and ultimately damaging political act.

One of the basic rationales for government provision of police, firefighter, teacher and other essential services is that it could better provide an uninterrupted flow of service. A strike against government disrupts the normal flow of a public benefit for which there is no alternative source of supply and, in the case of essential services, the absence of which jeopardizes the public good. Strikes in the private sector generally do not affect the public to the same degree. The usual reaction to the strike is pressure on elected officials to restore the disrupted service. Thus, the victim becomes the unwitting ally of the union. If the cost of restoring the disrupted service is capitulation to union demands, elected officials caught between angry strikers and an angry public, usually must do so. Thus, public sector strikes enjoy a heightened degree of effectiveness not shared by private sector work stoppages.

Professors Harry H. Wellington and Ralph D. Winter, in their Brookings Institution Study, "The Unions and the Cities," focus on this problem concerning the strike weapon:

> The trouble is that if unions are able to withhold labor—to strike—as well as to employ the usual methods of political pressure, they may possess a disproportionate share of effective power in the process of decision. Collective bargaining would then be so effective a pressure as to skew the results of the "normal" American political process.

. . . Since interest groups other than public employees, with conflicting claims on municipal government, do not, as a general proposition, have anything approaching the effectiveness of the strike—or at least cannot maintain that relative degree of power over the long run—they may be put at a significant competitive disadvantage in the political process.[18]

OTHER CONSIDERATIONS

The strike, or restrictions against it, presents problems in the area of public policy that have deeper reverberations. For instance, if members of a local policemen's union are prohibited by law from striking, what can be done by the governing bodies of that jurisdiction if the police do strike? After injunctive relief is sought and found to be of no avail, should the next step be the arrest of the entire participating body of striking policemen? What type of barriers are being erected against future amicable relations between the citizens and their protectors if such action is taken? What type of protection can citizens expect if the majority of the security force is behind bars? Should those responsible for making public policy fire all the strikers or should they accept tardy responses to judicial decrees and grant amnesty which includes no reprisals?

Strike prohibitions and penalties are seldom consistently applied. This inconsistency in enforcement results in an erosion of respect for the rule of law. Leon Jaworski, special Watergate prosecutor, said in an address before a group of law school graduates:

> . . . despite the existence of laws that forbid policemen, firemen, teachers and other public employees to strike and the issuance of court orders restraining them from continuing their conduct and ordering their return to work, both laws and court decrees have been ignored and wantonly flouted. . . . To my dismay, here were large groups of teachers . . . jeering, shouting epithets, and engaging in various disorders and generally acting like ruffians and rogues. Some of them were arrested, sentenced for contempt of court and confined where, as jailbirds, they were exemplifying citizenship behavior for their students to emulate. . . .

---

[17]*Abood v. Detroit Board of Education* (1977) 431 U.S. 209, 228

[18]Wellington, H.H. and Winter, R.K., *The Unions and the Cities* (Brookings Institution, Washington, D.C., 1971) p. 25

The question naturally arises: What is to be expected of the young as they grow older? Is it to be expected that they will become citizens respectful of the law, or is it likely that they will recall the precepts and examples of their teachers . . .?[19]

The 1968 National Commission of the Causes and Prevention of Violence stated in its majority report:

. . . every time a court order is disobeyed, each time an injunction is violated, each occasion on which a court decision is flouted, the effectiveness of our judicial system is eroded. How much erosion can it tolerate? It takes no prophet to know that our judicial system cannot face wholesale violation of its orders and still retain its efficacy. Violators must ponder the fact that once they have weakened the judicial system, the very ends they sought to attain—and may have attained—cannot then be preserved.[20]

Given the growth of compulsory public sector collective bargaining and the adverse impact of public sector strikes, one obvious question should concern us. Is there a relationship between public sector collective bargaining and strikes?

BARGAINING AND STRIKES RELATED

Proponents of compulsory public sector collective bargaining have argued that such laws would serve to reduce public sector strike activity. They claim that forcing government to recognize and bargain with unions would remove the cause of strikes by providing formal channels for the resolution of differences.

It is claimed that bargaining legislation, by reducing the number of recognition strikes, would result in a net reduction in public sector strike activity. Jack Stieber, author of a Brookings Institution study entitled *Public Employee Unionism*, is often cited to support this contention.

In fact, Stieber fails to recognize the relationship between such laws and strikes. His full quote indicates this:

Clearly, there is little relationship between the incidence of government strikes and state laws regulating labor relations in public employment. Michigan, one of the three states with the largest number of strikes, has had a comprehensive law since 1965, while Ohio and Illinois, the other two, have no state statute providing collective bargaining for public employees. Other state patterns are similarly inconclusive. The one effect of laws that can be documented is that they reduce greatly the number of strikes over the issue of union recognition. But other issues, particularly wages, have apparently *increased the number of strikes sufficiently to more than compensate for the elimination of union recognition as an important issue in states with public employment laws.* [Emphasis added][21]

Fortunately, the Bureau of Labor Statistics of the U.S. Department of Labor began to keep detailed statistics on public sector strike activity in 1958. This data base allows us to examine strike activity before and after enactment of bargaining legislation.

In order to provide a more thorough examination of the data, this study employs two differing statistical analyses. The first is the state-by-state comparison used in previous editions, expanded to include 1980 figures.

The average number of strikes per state per year was calculated for the periods before and after the enactment of bargaining legislation, omitting the year of legislation. In the overwhelming majority of cases, the passage of a bargaining law did not result in a reduction of strike activity.

In many cases, strike activity was notably higher in the period following legislation. As a national compilation, states without or prior to legislation averaged 1.34 strikes per year while states after legislation averaged 5.00 strikes per year—over three and a half times more. (See Table B)

However, public sector strike activity in general has increased dramatically since the mid-1960's. It would be reasonable then to question whether the results displayed in Table B reflect this general trend rather than changes in legislative status. Table

[19]Commencement address of Leon Jaworski at George Mason University School of Law: Saturday, August 23, 1980
[20]From the majority report of National Commission on Causes and Prevention of Violence: as quoted from a speech by Leon Jaworski at George Mason University School of Law; Saturday, August 23, 1980

[21]Stieber, Jack, op. cit., p. 163

TABLE B Public Sector Strikes Before and After Enactment of Bargaining Legislation 1958–1980
   (Compiled by Public Service Research Council)

State	Strikes/ yr. before Legislation	Year of Legislation	Strikes/ yr. after Legislation
ALABAMA	3.78	—	—
ALASKA			
teachers	0.00	1970	.60
all others	.50	1972	2.00
ARIZONA	.70	—	—
ARKANSAS	.65	—	—
CALIFORNIA			
higher education	.81	1979	3.00
state employees	.38	1971	1.66
teachers	.14	1965	11.07
all others	.33	1961	13.05
COLORADO	1.57	—	—
CONNECTICUT			
state employees	0.00	1975	.60
all others	.86	1965	6.73
DELAWARE			
teachers	0.00	1969	1.45
state and some local	0.00	1965	1.33
all others	.09	—	—
FLORIDA	3.19	1974	3.33
GEORGIA	2.74	—	—
HAWAII	.08	1970	1.00
IDAHO			
firefighters	0.00	1970	.10
teachers	.08	1971	1.22
all others	.43	—	—
ILLINOIS			
state employees	1.20	1973	4.57
all others	20.78	—	—
INDIANA			
teachers	1.93	1973	6.00
all others	3.61	—	—
IOWA	1.38	—	—
KANSAS			
teachers	0.00	1970	.10
state	.15	1971	.44
all others	.78	—	—
KENTUCKY	2.74	—	—
LOUISIANA	1.78	—	—
MAINE			
state employees	.06	1974	0.00
univ. employees	.06	1975	.20
all others	0.00	1969	.82
MARYLAND			
teachers	.27	1969	.64
all others	1.22	—	—
MASSACHUSETTS	.57	1965	7.13
MICHIGAN			
state employees	.22	—	—
state police	0.00	1978	0.00
all others	.14	1965	50.60
MINNESOTA	.38	1971	5.33
MISSISSIPPI	.65	—	—
MISSOURI			
teachers and police	1.83	—	—
all others	2.00	1967	4.23
MONTANA			
nurses	0.00	1969	.64

State	Strikes/ yr. before Legislation	Year of Legislation	Strikes/ yr. after Legislation
teachers	.15	1971	1.33
all others	.40	1973	3.57
NEBRASKA			
teachers	0.00	1967	0.00
all others	0.00	1969	.55
NEVADA			
state employees	0.00	—	—
all others	0.00	1969	.18
NEW HAMPSHIRE			
state employees	0.00	1969	0.00
police	0.00	1972	.13
all others	.75	1970	1.10
NEW JERSEY	3.10	1968	25.08
NEW MEXICO	.74	—	—
NEW YORK	4.22	1967	20.62
NORTH CAROLINA	2.48	—	—
NORTH DAKOTA			
teachers	0.00	1969	0.00
all others	.09	—	—
OHIO	30.26	—	—
OKLAHOMA			
teachers, police and firefighters	.23	1971	.44
all others	.52	—	—
OREGON			
teachers	0.00	1965	.60
all others	.20	1973	2.14
PENNSYLVANIA			
police and firefighters	.10	1968	2.17
all others	6.00	1970	76.70
RHODE ISLAND			
teachers	.25	1966	3.64
local employees	.11	1967	1.46
state employees			
police and firefighters	.25	1970	1.70
SOUTH CAROLINA	.30	—	—
SOUTH DAKOTA	.09	1969	.09
TENNESSEE			
teachers	.90	1978	5.00
all others	1.88	—	—
TEXAS	2.09	—	—
UTAH	.48	—	—
VERMONT			
state employees	0.00	1969	0.00
teachers	0.00	1969	.45
all others	0.00	1973	.14
VIRGINIA	.74	—	—
WASHINGTON			
teachers	0.00	1965	3.13
state, community college and univ. employees	.15	1971	1.89
all others	.22	1967	2.69
WEST VIRGINIA	2.91	—	—
WISCONSIN			
state employees	0.00	1966	.64
all others	0.00	1959	6.38
WYOMING			
firefighters	0.00	1965	0.00
all others	.09	—	—
NATIONAL AVERAGE STRIKES/YR.	1.34		5.00

TABLE C Average Number of Strikes per State

	Employees Not Covered by Legislation	Employees Covered by Legislation
1958	.30	—
1959	.52	—
1960	.66	2.00
1961	.52	0.00
1962	.42	1.00
1963	.54	1.00
1964	.74	2.00
1965	.76	2.00
1966	1.96	5.22
1967	2.28	5.30
1968	2.83	8.23
1969	5.42	11.47
1970	4.64	9.29
1971	3.17	7.70
1972	4.26	8.00
1973	3.81	8.90
1974	4.21	8.35
1975	4.74	10.58
1976	4.38	7.52
1977	4.45	8.52
1978	5.97	8.97
1979	6.17	12.12
1980	5.52	10.94

C presents on a year-to-year basis, the average number of strikes per state by employees covered and not covered by bargaining legislation.

The chart does reveal a general increase in the level of strike activity in the public sector. However, the level of strike activity by employees covered by bargaining legislation has been consistently higher than that of employees not covered by legislation.

PRA ANALYSIS

The second statistical analysis was prepared by Policy Research Associates (PRA), of Fairfax, Virginia for use in this study. The cumulative strike rates and strike acceleration rates were calculated for each employee group affected by collective bargaining legislation. In order to make comparisons with groups not covered by legislation, similar calculations were made for the periods before and after 1969, which is both the mean and modal year for the passage of public sector collective bargaining legislation.

Through the use of the strike acceleration rate for the pre-collective bargaining legislation (Pre-CBL)

period, it is possible to predict strike levels for the post-collective bargaining legislation (Post-CBL) period. Strike activity above the predicted levels is regarded as "excess strike activity." The question is whether this "excess strike activity" can be attributed to the presence of collective bargaining legislation? The PRA analysis contends there is a linkage.

Causation in science is (or can be) an intensely philosophic morass which becomes even trickier when translated to social phenomena not subject to experimentation in the laboratory sense. Nevertheless, it is reasonable to attribute (with the qualification noted below) changes in the post-CBL acceleration pattern to the CBL itself because it is the single most stable change in the underlying circumstances of the group. Other phenomena might certainly play a role, but their various effects are at least partially cancelled out by the undeniable fact that, over all CB groups, the point in time at which the CBL entered the cumulative pattern varied from 1959 to 1979.[22]

An examination of the data for those employee groups covered by collective bargaining legislation reveals a significant amount of "excess strike activity" for the post-legislation period. A comparison of the strike acceleration rate predictions for the post-legislation period with the actual levels of strike activity show an excess of 2,498 strikes involving 376,141 workers and resulting in the loss of 9,953,785 man-days that theoretically would not have occurred in the absence of collective bargaining legislation.

It is possible, however, that there occurred over this period of time general changes in the patterns of public sector strike activity. Factors such as greater union militancy, declining managerial effectiveness, growth in public employment, etc., may have contributed to a climate more conducive to public sector strikes. While some of the factors may be related to the enactment of public sector collective bargaining legislation, we will assume that such a relationship does not exist.

In order to ascertain the presence of this general change in the strike climate and to correct for it, those employee groups not covered by legislation

---

[22]Policy Research Associates, Fairfax, VA., *Public Employee Strike Behavior Statistical Analysis* (Unpublished Report)

were used as a control. When the comparisons described above were applied to the non-bargaining legislation sub-set, excess strike activity for this group was revealed. Specifically, there were 325 strikes involving 116,770 workers resulting in the loss of 2,636,067 man-days above the levels predicted by the strike acceleration rate.

The final problem stems from the fact that the collective bargaining legislation sub-set is larger than the non-legislation group. By making a simple proportional adjustment it was possible to arrive at a correction factor of 628 strikes, 225,199 workers and 5,083,844 man-days.

By subtracting this correcting factor from the previously derived excess activity levels for the bargaining legislation group it is possible to determine a level of "excess strike activity" that can be laid at the doorstep of the collective bargaining legislation: 1,870 strikes; 150,942 workers; 4,869,941 man-days.

CONCLUSIONS

Briefly stated, the questions examined in this study concern (1) whether governments should engage in collective bargaining, (2) whether the collective bargaining process leads to an increase in strike activity, and (3) whether public sector unions should be permitted to strike.

In the case of the first, evidence would lead us to answer in the negative. As Robert S. Summers, professor of law at Cornell University, explains, "Collective bargaining and the process of democratic public benefit conferral are not felicitous bedfellows."[23] Specifically, the process gives a special interest group the ability to set policy and determine municipal fiscal matters uninhibited by the wishes or interests of other citizens; it provides the unions with a disproportionate amount of influence which is used to the detriment of other interest groups with legitimate claims on the resources of the community; and it removes responsible decision-making from duly elected officials and vests it in a special group with a limited membership.

As to our second concern, the data would indicate the development of certain trends. Namely,

public sector unions representing bargaining units covered by collective bargaining legislation have exhibited a greater tendency to strike after enactment of legislation than before and a greater tendency than units not covered by legislation. While the levels of public sector strike activity have risen across the country, they have risen higher and faster in areas covered by compulsory collective bargaining legislation.

It is admittedly impossible to empirically prove a causal relationship. However, the data have exhibited a pattern of such consistency that we can acknowledge the existence of a correlation between compulsory public sector collective bargaining legislation and heightened strike activity.

The connection between collective bargaining and strikes has been noted and there is abundant evidence as to the detrimental effects of strikes on the health, welfare and safety of citizens and taxpayers. Public sector strikes distort normal democratic processes by virtue of their ability to hold vital management decisions "captive" until the issues in question are settled. The hesitancy with which governments invoke strike penalties and the flagrant violations of injunctions against the strike gives silent assent to those who subvert the rule of law.

What may be achieved to correct the imbalances and damaging effects of extending collective bargaining to public sector unions is at present a matter of speculation. However, Lieberman suggests that the solution does not lie in new or futuristic methodology, he says:

> . . . At the risk of oversimplification, the public sector union is a hybrid union-political party, with most of the advantages of both and none of the disadvantages of either. It would be desirable to have a new organizational structure to replace public sector unionism, but such a structure is not required to justify deunionizing public employment. All things considered, the conventional ways of resolving public-sector labor disputes prior to public-sector bargaining were better for our society. Some were much better than others, and some were hardly defensible, but overall, they were not as harmful. In any event, there is no justification for waiting until something better than public-sector bargaining comes along. It was here and left. The more a new structure is consistent with democratic political processes, the more it will be

———
[23]Summers, Robert S., op. cit., p. 65

unacceptable to public-sector unions anyway. The choice is not between public-sector bargaining and something better. Without in any way idealizing what preceded public-sector bargaining, it was better.[24]

[24]Lieberman, Myron, op. cit., p. 162

11   NO   DOES COLLECTIVE BARGAINING IN THE PUBLIC SECTOR GIVE UNIONS IN THAT SECTOR EXTRAORDINARY POWER THAT IS HARMFUL TO THE PUBLIC?

Collective Bargaining and Public Sector Union Power
Chimezie A. B. Osigweh

INTRODUCTION

Keen observers have for decades debated the status of union-management relations in the public setting as compared to the private sector (Hart, 1961; Loewenberg and Moskow, 1972; Lewin, Feuille and Kochan, 1977). A review of the arguments indicates that several claims have been made in favor of private sector collective bargaining. A great deal of uneasiness, however, seems to persist about the potential power of unions in the public sector (Wellington and Winter, 1969, 1970, 1971; Summers, 1976). When Stieber (1973:213) predicted that "by the end of the 1970s all state and local government employees probably will be protected in their right to organize and bargain collectively," he could not have anticipated the persistence, ten years later, of the uneasiness that still surrounds any mention of union power and bargaining in the public sector. The analysis that follows revisits the "power-nonpower" aspects of this debate by exploring the economic, financial, and political contexts of public sector collective bargaining.

From Chimezie A. B. Osigweh, "Collective Bargaining and Public Sector Union Power," *Public Personnel Management Journal*, 14 (Spring 1985),pp. 75–84. Also published as "Public Sector Union Power and the Economic, Financial, and Political Contexts of Collective Bargaining," *Akron Business and Economic Review*, vol. 16, no. 1, (Spring 1985), pp.24–30. Reprinted with permission.

THE ECONOMIC CONTEXT

As Rees (1962:70–73) summarizes, many of our theoretical explanations for the private sector labor unions' economic sources of power can be traced to Alfred Marshall's four principles of the derived demand for labor. According to these principles, we are to expect the most powerful unions when: 1) there is inelastic demand* for the product; 2) labor is an essential factor in the production process; 3) labor costs are a very small percentage of total production costs; and 4) supply for alternative factors of production, such as non-union labor or capital, is inelastic.

Let us use these conditions as our dimensions for a descriptive evaluation of union power in public sector collective bargaining. The central question focuses on whether the above conditions bestow great advantages of economic power on public sector unions.

Demand Inelasticity

Some scholars would contend that these conditions enable public sector unions to begin negotiations from a disproportionately favorable economic base.

*Demand "inelasticity" refers to a situation when there is continuing high demand for the product despite possible price increases.

According to a major proposition, the demand for public sector labor is highly inelastic—at least, more inelastic than in the private sector. One argument is that public employers have no right to withhold services such as sanitation, police service, street maintainance, fire protection, etc. (Ray, 1967). Underlying this is the premise that these employers are specifically chartered by the people for the continuous provision of some services not available from private industry. This translates into a lack of impetus for the public employer to engage in lockouts, or to minimize costs. Since there is no need to minimize costs in order to remain competitive and make reasonable profits, public employers will simply not bargain hard.

This position has been developed further by Wellington and Winter (1971:12–32). They suggest an absence of a competitive market in the public sector, which warrants chronic inelasticity of demand for public services. Because citizens rely on the public employer as their single source of services such as police and fire protection, the demand for the public services are insensitive to price changes. Public demand for the services remain constantly high, even with increases in price.

Ashenfelter and Ehrenberg (1975) are often cited to lend empirical support to the inelasticity argument. But their results also indicate that the degree to which employment levels fall when wages are increased (i.e., elasticity) varies greatly among public services. It is greater in states where the population density, in persons per square mile, is high (e.g., Rhode Island, New Jersey, Massachusetts, Connecticut, New York, Maryland, Pennsylvania, Ohio, etc.), than in low density states (e.g., Alaska, Wyoming, Nevada, Montana, New Mexico, Idaho, North Dakota, South Dakota, etc.) Moreover, it should be noted that data for the study were collected for the 1958–1969 period. The study was thus based on data collected for a period when demand for the public sector was rapidly expanding.

That the Ashenfelter-Ehrenberg study is frequently cited by proponents of the inelasticity argument reveals the tendency to unfairly judge public sector labor unions by using data from the formative period of a new industrial relations system. However, the early expansion in the public sector has topped off. Indeed, public employment is declining

in some areas, suggesting that the inelasticity argument may not be very valid. New York City, after the boom of the 1960s, became one of the most publicized examples. The number of workers on the city payroll declined steadily between 1974 and 1979 due to layoffs and attrition (Weitzman, 1979). Schlossstein (1975) finds that in fiscal 1975, there were layoffs of 140,000 government employees at the state and local levels.

Moreover, public employers appear to be increasingly willing to subcontract work rather than give in to union demands. For example, Burton and Krider (1972:277) record that Warren, Michigan ended an impasse by actually executing its threat to subcontract; while the striking city employees of Santa Monica, California returned to work when the city threatened to subcontract.

These examples of general reduction in growth and the threat or use of subcontracting offer evidence that the public sector is not altogether immune to competition or elasticity in the labor market. One suggestion is that the demand for labor in the public sector is perhaps more elastic now than during the period studied by Ashenfelter and Ehrenberg. Indeed, some recent studies show this more explicitly. For example, Thornton (1979) concludes that the elasticity of demand for employees in the public sector is comparable to that for private-sector workers, based on a comparative empirical analysis of the demand for teachers in the public and private sectors.

The Essentiality Argument

It has also been argued that public services are of high strategic importance: that public services are essential and indispensable. Carmen D. Saso (1970) is a major proponent of this thesis. The argument is that collective bargaining empowers public sector employees with an awesome force—the freedom to commit "a siege" or to engage in "a mass abduction"—with which society's indispensable services are made hostage and consequently held for ransom.

It is very difficult to generalize that all services in the public sector are essential, because public sector employees carry out very diverse functions. Yet the "essentiality" thesis suggests that all public services are essential. This, indeed, is an attempt at proving the unprovable. For example, the duties performed by corrections personnel, the police, the firefighters and perhaps the sanitation workers may provide an indisputable source of power to their unions. On the other hand, we cannot see the services performed by park maintenance employees, teaching assistants (where unionized), clerical personnel, or library workers as essential. Moreover, several other occupations can be seen as falling somewhere in the middle range along the essential-nonessential continuum. Examples are teachers, college professors, street or highway maintenance personnel, etc., who may be seen as essential, but whose services can be interrupted without great loss to society.

That public services are not all essential has been documented by bureaucratic practice in the public sector. Governments at all levels (e.g., local, state, federal) usually group their public services under the rubrics of "essential" and "nonessential." It is no surprise that courts are likely to issue injunctions when public sector collective bargaining impasses result in strikes in the essential services—while the likelihood of injunctions against those in the nonessential services is less (Aboud and Aboud, 1974). Another example is Burton and Krider's (1972) finding that striker replacements are sought more often in the essential services, and less often when the strike occurs in the nonessential services.

These observations imply that the collective bargaining units found in the public sector are likely to vary greatly when considered by the services they perform. As a result, great variations also exist in the power enjoyed by public sector unions (or bargaining units). Furthermore, the wide variation in the sources of power for public sector unions implies that some private sector unions may even enjoy more power than some of those in the public sector. For, as *Anderson Federation of Teachers v. School City Anderson* (252 Ind. 558, 251 N.E. 2d 15, Cert. Denied, 399 U.S. 928, 1970) suggests, some private sector services may be "more 'essential' " than some services rendered by the public sector.

Cost of Labor

The third economic dimension deals with labor costs as a percentage of total costs. This dimension is

often overlooked by those who propose that the power of public sector unions is excessive. This tendency is not surprising. First, the high percentage of total governmental expenditures devoted to labor cost is perhaps the most important single economic constraint on the power of public sector unions. Bahl, Greytak, Campbell and Wasylenko (1972) show that payroll costs represent 60% of local and 40% of total state government expenditures. Besides, most public sector occupations (e.g., fire service, sanitation, police, teaching, etc.) are labor intensive. The result is that pay increases for any of the groups will translate to high costs of total production. Since the costs of producing public goods are usually passed on to the public in the form of higher taxes, the public may be enraged by being asked to pay more. It is to be expected that this will create very strong incentives for the public employer to resist pressures from the unions for negotiated wage increases, weakening the public sector union's power position.

Thus, the labor intensive nature of public sector occupations results in high labor-product costs which, in view of public resistance to higher taxes, strengthens the public management's incentive to resist union coercion. This detracts from, rather than adds to, the public sector union's source of power.

Alternative Factor Considerations

The fourth dimension focuses on the use of alternative factors in the public sector. More specifically, it deals with the prospects for replacing union labor with other factors of production (e.g., capital, nonunion labor, etc.). The argument is that the labor intensive nature of the public sector makes it difficult to replace union labor with innovations in technology. There is, however, a trade-off that is frequently overlooked. The difficulty in adopting technological innovations in the public sector may also account for the low productivity growth in that sector, since improved technology is associated with increased productivity. Experience in manufacturing suggests that increased average productivity results in increased average wages. Indeed, it has been found that firms rank productivity trends as the fourth most important set of criteria considered when establishing wages and benefits (Kochan, 1980:217; Freedman, 1979). This means that the low productivity due to the difficulty of adopting technological innovations in the public sector may also translate to lower wages (than the private employees) for the public sector employees, regardless of public sector union activities. Besides, being labor intensive suggests that the public sector enjoys a high labor-to-total cost ratio. Evidence indicates that the higher the labor-to-total cost ratio, the lower the wage level and the lower the rate of wage increase (Kochan, 1980; Freedman, 1979).

THE FINANCIAL CONTEXT

The financial arguments are mainly traced to the various problems associated with public taxes. In private sector contract negotiations, the cost of a settlement package can be covered if the employer enjoys good productive efficiency, profits, or favorable product prices. Company representatives are likely to make fewer concessions and bargain harder when faced with little profits, limited efficiency, or low prices. Product prices may be raised, and costs easily passed on to consumers, if the firm encounters an unexpected or very costly contract settlement. The public sector employer, on the other hand, deals mainly in public services. Additional revenues can be obtained mainly by raising the price of public services through tax increases. This means that the different levels of government primarily obtain their revenues from different forms of taxes or user charges such as sales taxes, income taxes, and property taxes.

Of course, there are some other minor sources of government revenue. For example, governments may also borrow. State and local governments may obtain additional revenue from federal aid. And local governments may receive state aid. Bureau of the Census (1972) data show that property taxes alone account for as much as 40 percent of local government revenue. While federal aid increased at an annual rate of 20–25 percent from 1970 to 1975, it accounted for only between 4–10 percent of local government budgets (Lewin, et al., 1977:19).

Even where governments borrow to finance their budgets, the debts are usually repaid by tax monies. Consequently, the major financial constraints on public employers derive from: the tax base of the government's area of jurisdiction; the legal or leg-islative restraint placed on the government's ability to raise its revenue; and the unwillingness of elected public officials to vote for increased taxes.

Bahl et al. (1974) find, for example, that the number of public and private sector jobs has been steadily declining in many large cities. This indicates that many cities, especially those of the Northeast, are confronted with shrinking tax bases. Unfortunately, the flight of jobs away from large cities does not correspond to any decrease in population for them. The result is that there remains a very high need for public services in those cities for the people who remain behind.

One would therefore expect that most of the cities are already being pushed against their legal or constitutional tax limits. Besides, a government may not be able to raise funds through borrowing if its debt is already high. The limit on tax increases becomes a pressure on the budget. But legislatures are severely limited in their abilities to control budgetary matters, especially at the city and state levels. It may be unrealistic to expect that a local councilman, or state legislator, will totally understand, within the short time available, the intricate nuances of a budget that took three or four bureaucrats two to three months to complete. The tremendous number of fiscal items and the overwhelming complexity that shrouds the budgetary process forces legislators toward a constant inclination to press for an "across-the-board" budget slash. The mere threat of across-the-board cuts is a constant reminder to government administrators that big budget proposals are likely to be slashed. It reveals how legislative approval serves as a constraint that effectively sets upper limits to budget requests. It also suggests that public negotiators will assume tougher bargaining postures in the light of the administration's foreseeable budget allowances.

There is also the existence of the taxpayer-voter, and the vote-conscious public official. Most public officials are vote conscious not without reason. Opposition parties are always quick to seize upon tax increases as campaign battlegrounds, often used to arouse voter ill-will toward the current administration. The underlying slogan seems to be: "let's throw out the tax-hiking rascals." Moreover, the American taxpayer is also becoming more unwilling to accept tax increases. This was illustrated in 1979 by the well-publicized passage of California's "Proposition 13," which limits property tax increases to only two percent per year. Being in constant fear of taxpayer reprimands at the polls, public officials seem to have become even more reluctant to vote for higher taxes.

As a result, public administrators are often caught between employee compensation demands, public willingness to vote for increased operating levies, shrinking tax bases, opposition interests, and the legislatures' reluctance to allow governments the freedom to impose any kind of tax(es) at will. Under these conditions, it is to be expected that public sector unions will encounter more rigorous public employer bargaining, with public negotiators presenting tougher positions on the bargaining fronts. This will undermine, rather than boost, the public sector unions' source of bargaining power.

THE POLITICAL CONTEXT

Several other arguments by the opponents of public sector bargaining are revealed as we turn to the political context of collective bargaining. First is one borrowed from the Hobbesian notion of sovereignty. As Blackstone once put it, the "king can do no wrong." This suggests the sacred, ecclesiastical reverence accorded kings during the Hobbesian era. And, since "kingdom" interprets as "government" in an American sense, several implications can be drawn therefrom. To start with, the government can do no wrong. As such, it should be revered and respected. This vein of thought has been documented in the *Government Employee Relations Reporter* (51:101) by the Advisory Commission on Intergovernmental Relations as it writes that allowing government employees to strike would arouse a climate of disrespect for the government and its laws. The government is supreme, and therefore possesses the final power—the "divine prerogative" to cater responsively to the interests of its subjects and constituencies. It knows the interests of all, and must retain, on behalf of all, the fundamental power to establish what shall be policy.

In brief, the "sovereignty theory" holds that it is the sole responsibility of the government, through its legislators and executives, to make budgets, set rates, create jobs, determine working conditions, and fill jobs with citizens who are satisfied with its rates, conditions, or general terms. To concede to the union the right to bargain for rates and conditions, or to strike against terms set and judged fair by the government is to relinquish the government's sovereign responsibility. It contravenes the public interest by allowing public sector unions to manipulate the government's divine predispositions. The suggestion is that public employees should not be allowed to collectively bargain, because such an act will exemplify the waiving of "sovereign immunity," and will be tantamount to granting the employees enough power to subvert the political process.

This argument is not very persuasive, however. First, a word of caution. It is not that the government does no wrong. Rather, the government should not be allowed to do any wrong. Present-day experience vindicates this way of thinking. It is common practice that policy makers and legislatures often waive the government's "sovereign immunity" in other areas of law, governance, or the political process. That any public units or agencies can be sued on counts of negligence serves as an illustration. Yet this has never been viewed as disrespect for our government and its sets of laws. Second, simple observation reveals that suppliers of hardware, materials and equipment to the government (e.g., Xerox, Rockwell International, McDonnell Douglas, etc.) are permitted to negotiate construction, delivery and price terms. This is not usually viewed as an abdication of governmental responsibility. Neither has it been popularly viewed as an arrangement that gives the groups unusual powers to manipulate the government's sole function. One wonders if allowing suppliers of services (e.g., firefighters, teachers, the police and sanitation workers) to do the same does, indeed, signify any greater denial of governmental sovereignty.

Third, it is quite possible to isolate government's administrative responsibilities from those that are policy-making or legislative. Perhaps the notion of "sovereignty" should not be automatically extended to the operating function, even if it is an attribute of the legislative prerogative. Fourth, "government sovereignty" in the traditional American sense suggests that the people's will is supreme. It indicates that the people are sovereign, and that the people's wishes as manifested in legislative action must always be given precedence. Thus, it does not rule out the possibility of legislating any worker-management relationships, be it the right to bargain collectively on all possible subjects, or the right to do any other thing(s) that our imaginations may conjure up. For certainly, it may be the will of the people that their public employees be allowed (more power), to collectively bargain.

Beyond this, however, experience shows that the traditional notion of sovereignty pervades our system so much that its mere existence effectively checks the expanded power of public sector unions. For example, what one finds as the American political process is a congregation of heterogeneous groups or political actors—each possessing an independent and sovereign power base, but none dominating the other(s). New interest groups form as reactions against the successes and activities of existing actors (Truman, 1971). Heartless bargaining and outlandish gains by the unions would thus give rise to reactive counter groups. Appropriate checks and balances would be imposed by the new counter interests. Because the checks and balances may be too severe, public sector unions are likely to exercise restraint and soften their demands: first, to prevent the formation of vociferous taxpayer or business groups poised against them; and second, to moderate the extent of efforts to be directed against them by the counter groups. That the American Federation of State, County, and Municipal Employees (AFSCME) has been known to endorse the maxim, "Better to ask for half a loaf, upset no one and get it, than to ask for two loaves, arouse significant opposition and get nothing" (Belasco, 1972:243-244) suggests that public sector unions are not unaware of the described imperatives of our notion of sovereignty.

This is the nature of the pluralistic political process that has, without question, established America as the world's number one democracy. The survival of such a democracy requires the maintenance of the fundamentals of its political process. The foundations of such a political process cannot be properly maintained if any of the groups enjoy continued domination of the others. No group (such as the public management group) may be allowed to keep dominating any other (such as the public employee group) through the purposive denial or limitation of the fundamental right to bargain collectively. In this sense, Truman (1971) reminds us that the American political process is a constellation of groups and individuals all sharing power.

Yet it has been put forward that collective bargaining gives public employees more political power than other political actors, especially at the local and municipal levels. The result is that public employees may influence most public policies that relate to their interest while excluding several other public issues from the consideration of policy makers (Wellington and Winter 1970; 1971).

The core question reverts to whether collective bargaining in the public sector distorts the "normal" American political process. This analysis answers in the negative. For one thing, it is inconceivable that only one group of political actors, which perhaps marginally possess more power than the average group, will indeed "distort" the normal American political process. But even if public employees are found likely to distort the political process by virtue of possessing some power leverage in collective bargaining, we are also to find that they are not the first offenders. Neither are they the only ones with such powers in the political system.

CONCLUSION

It is often argued that collective bargaining for public sector employees will bestow a disproportionately high bargaining power (and advantage) on public sector unions. An examination of the economic, financial and political contexts of collective bargaining reveals a mixed assessment. Collective bargaining does not provide public sector unions with unusual sources of bargaining power. Indeed, the power of public sector unions is occasionally constrained more severely than that of private sector unions. Besides, public sector collective bargaining is not incongruent with the notions of group politics and representative democracy which, indeed, defines the American pluralist political process.

REFERENCES

ABOUD, ANTONE and ABOUD, GRACE S. *The Right To Strike in Public Employment.* New York: Cornell University Press, 1974.

ADVISORY COMMISSION ON INTERGOVERNMENTAL RELATIONS. "Labor Management Policies for State and Local Government," Bureau of National Affairs, *Government Employee Relations Reporter.* Reference File 51:101.

ASHENFELTER, ORLEY C. and EHRENBERG, RONALD G. "The Demand for Labor in the Public Sector," in Daniel S. Hamermesh (ed.), *Labor in the Public and Nonprofit Sectors.* Princeton, New Jersey: Princeton University Press, 1975.

BAHL, ROY W., D. GRAYTAK, A. K. CAMPBELL, and M. S. WASYLENKO. "Intergovernmental and Functional Aspects of Trends in Public Employment in the United States." *Public Administration Review,* Vol. 32, November-December, 1972.

BAHL, ROY W., et al. *Taxes, Expenditures and the Economic Base.* New York: Praeger, 1974.

BELASCO, JAMES A. "Municipal Bargaining and Political Power," in Loewenberg and Moskow (eds.) *Collective Bargaining in Government.* New Jersey: Prentice-Hall, 1972.

BUREAU OF THE CENSUS. *Guide to Recurrent and Special Government Statistics.* State and Local Government Special Studies (Social and Economic Statistic Division). No. 62, May, 1972.

BURTON, JOHN F. Jr., "The Extent of Collective Bargaining in the Public Sector." In Benjamin Aaron, Joseph R. Grodin, and James L. Stern (eds.), *Public Sector Bargaining.* Madison, Wisconsin: Industrial Relations Research Association, 1979.

BURTON, JOHN F. and C. KRIDER. "The Roles and Consequences of Strikes by Public Employees," in Loewenberg and Moskow (eds.), *Collective Bargaining in Government.* Englewood Cliffs, New Jersey: Prentice-Hall, Inc., 1972.

COHEN, SANFORD. "Does Public Employee Unionism Diminish Democracy?" *Industrial and Labor Relations Review,* Vol. 32, No. 2, January 1979.

FREEDMAN, AUDREY. *Managing Labor Relations.* New York: The Conference Board, 1979.

HART, WILSON R. *Collective Bargaining in the Federal Civil Service.* New York: Harper and Brothers, 1961.

KOCHAN, THOMAS A. *Collective Bargaining and Industrial Relations.* Homewood, Illinois: Richard D. Irwin, 1980.

LEWIN, DAVID, PETER FEUILLE and THOMAS A. KOCHAN (eds.). *Public Sector Labor Relations.* Glen Ridge, New Jersey: Thomas Horton and Daughters, 1977.

LOEWENBERG, JOSEPH J. and MOSKOW, MICHAEL H. (eds.) *Collective Bargaining in Government.* Englewood Cliffs, New Jersey: Prentice-Hall, Inc., 1972.

RAY, JACK N. "The Compatibility of Public Employment Collective Bargaining with Public Interests." *Labor Law Journal,* Vol. 18, 1967.

REES, ALBERT. *The Economics of Trade Unions.* Chicago, Illinois: University of Chicago Press, 1962.

SASO, CARMEN D. *Coping with Public Employee Strikes.* Washington, DC.: Public Personnel Association, 1970.

SCHLOSSTEIN, RALPH. "State and Local Government Finances During Recession." *Challenge,* Vol. 18, July-August, 1975.

STIEBER, JACK. *Public Employee Unionism: Structure, Growth, Policy.* Washington, D.C.: The Brookings Institution, 1973.

SUMMERS, ROBERT S. *Collective Bargaining and Public Benefit Conferral: A Jurisprudential Critique.* Ithaca: Institute of Public Employment, New York State School of Industrial and Labor Relations, 1976.

THORNTON, ROBERT J. "The Elasticity of Demand for Public School Teachers." *Industrial Relations,* Vol. 18, Winter, 1979.

TRUMAN, DAVID B. *The Governmental Process,* 2nd ed., New York: Alfred Knopf, 1971.

WEITZMAN, JOAN P. "The Effects of Economic Restraints on Public Sector Collective Bargaining: The Lessons from New York City," in Hugh D. Jascourt (ed.), *Government Labor Relations: Trends and Information for the Future.* Oak Park, Illinois: Moore, 1979.

WELLINGTON, HARRY H. and RALPH K. WINTER. "The Limits of Collective Bargaining in Public Employment." *The Yale Law Journal,* Vol. 78, No. 7, June, 1969.

WELLINGTON, H. H. and R. K. WINTER. "Structuring Collective Bargaining in Public Employment." *Yale Law Journal,* Vol 79, April, 1970.

WELLINGTON, H. H. and R. K. WINTER. *The Unions and the Cities.* Washington, D.C.: The Brookings Institution, 1971.

QUESTIONS FOR DISCUSSION

1. Is there a difference between the right of unions to be formed in the public and private sectors? Explain.

2. Should all employees in the public sector be forbidden by law to strike? Why?

3. Does collective bargaining in the public sector undermine democratic processes? Explain.

4. Is the demand for public-sector labor elastic or inelastic? Why?

5. What alternatives to collective bargaining exist that would be acceptable to public-sector employees?

6. In an age of scarce government funds, is public-sector unionism outmoded? Explain.

SUGGESTED READINGS

COHEN, SANFORD, "Does Public Employee Unionism Diminish Democracy?," *Industrial and Labor Relations Review*, 32 (Jan. 1979), 189–95.

FINKIN, MATTHEW W., "The Limits of Majority Rule in Collective Bargaining," *Minnesota Law Review*, 64 (Jan. 1980), 183–274.

HENKEL, JAN W., AND NORMAN J. WOOD, "Collective Bargaining by State Workers: Legislatures Have the Final Voice in the Appropriation of Funds," *Journal of Collective Negotiations in the Public Sector*, 11, No. 3 (1982), 215–23.

KERSHEN, HARRY, ed., *Collective Bargaining by Government Workers*. Farmingdale, NY: Baywood, 1983.

LEVINE, MARVIN J. AND EUGENE C. HAGBURG, eds., *Labor Relations in the Public Sector: Readings, Cases, and Experimental Exercises*. Salt Lake City, UT: Brighton Pub. Co., 1979.

LEVITAN, SAR A., AND ALEXANDRA B. NODEN, *Working for the Sovereign: Employee Relations in the Federal Government*. Baltimore, MD: Johns Hopkins Univ. Press, 1983.

PERRY, JAMES L., "Collective Bargaining—The Search for Solutions, *Public Administration Review*, 39 (May/June 1979), 290–94.

PHELPS, ANN T., "The Right to Strike in the Public Sector: A View of Eight States," in *Centenary Issues of the Pendleton Act of 1883: The Legacy of Civil Service Reform*, ed. David H. Rosenbloom. New York: Marcel Dekker, 1982, pp. 63–84.

SHILS, EDWARD B., "The State Government Dilemma: Civil Service vs. Collective Bargaining Laws," *International Social Science Review*, 57 (Autumn 1982), 210–25.

TROY, LEO, AND NEIL SHEFLIN, "The Flow and Ebb of U. S. Public Sector Unionism," *Government Union Review*, 5 (Spring 1984), whole issue.

VEGLAHN, PETER A., "Public Sector Strike Penalties and Their Appeal," *Public Personnel Management*, 12 (Summer 1983), 196–205.

CHAPTER 4

Organization Theory

Organization theory deals with how organizations work or ought to work. It describes their internal structure and processes and their external environment. This chapter examines three issues of organization theory that have generated controversy: incrementalism, Scientific Management, and Japanese management techniques.

INCREMENTALISM

One theory that has received much attention in public administration is incrementalism, a theory which asserts that political decisions tend to be made in gradual, limited steps. One of the leading proponents of this notion is Charles E. Lindblom, who made a classic argument in its defense in an article published in 1959 (cited in the Suggested Readings for this debate). Other social scientists have supported the concept, including Aaron Wildavsky, Richard Fenno, and Ira Sharkansky.

In contrast to the rational model of decision making in which comprehensive evaluations of problems are made, incrementalism argues that most decisions are made which slightly modify previous decisions. Much effort of incrementalists has been directed to applying incrementalism to budgetary theory. Does incrementalism explain the budgetary process

in the federal government? Bernard T. Pitsvada and Frank D. Draper argue that it does. They see five basic factors of growing importance that have added to the utility of the incremental approach. These are: (1) There are eight major federal programs that are indexed to the rate of inflation. (2) Government agencies are required to prepare budget requests through appropriations for three-year periods. (3) Congress has for several years used continuing resolutions, that is, the mechanism by which Congress grants authority to agencies to continue obligating funds in the absence of an annual appropriations act. (4) Through the Budget and Impoundment Act of 1974, the president is required to submit a current services budget, and the Congressional Budget Office is required to submit reports reflecting budgetary options. (5) Agencies prepare their budgets from a basically incrementalist perspective. The authors conclude that common sense supports the incremental analysis since Congress reflects popular will and popular votes do not change dramatically from year to year.

Lance T. LeLoup, Chairman of the Department of Political Science at the University of Missouri, St. Louis, argues that incrementalism does not describe the budgetary process in government in the United States. He notes: (1) There is a surprising amount of change in budgetary outcomes for specific agencies. (2)

The analytical choices of the supporters of incrementalist theory limit the applicability of the theory in such areas as level of aggregation, time and object of analysis, and dependent and independent variables. (3) The theory of incrementalism contains many problems, including definitional difficulties, a failure to take into account in any given year the externally determined parameters to the amount of change that can occur, and a tendency to characterize budgetary studies in either/or terms. LeLoup asserts that incrementalism is not totally wrong, but needs to be modified. He concludes by providing a tentative framework for an analysis of national budgeting in the United States.

In reading this debate on budgeting consider the criteria that the contending authors use in evaluating the validity of incremental theory. Consider, too, the areas of agreement between the two viewpoints.

SCIENTIFIC MANAGEMENT

The study of public administration has been shaped by contributions from different disciplines, including management, psychology, sociology, and political science. One theory of the early twentieth century which greatly influenced the discipline was Scientific Management, a theory so associated with one man, Frederick W. Taylor, that it is sometimes called Taylorism, although other writers have conducted major studies in this field. Scientific Management had its origins in business management, which sought to make the workplace more efficient and productive. Taylorism, which is described below in the article by Edwin A. Locke, analyzed the workplace and worker behavior in order to maximize productivity. Although most applicable to business, it has been used in government to rationalize the structure and responsibilities of different levels of government and to organize day-to-day operations for some kinds of government agencies. It has been an impetus to the movement for promoting economy and efficiency in government. It influenced public administration theorists who argued that management in the public sector could be studied and applied scientifically.

Among the theorists influenced by this thought were Leonard White, Henri Fayol, F. W. Willoughby, Luther Gulick, and Lyndall Urwick.

Are the principles of Taylorism valid? Edwin A. Locke argues that the ideas of Frederick W. Taylor on management have been proven valid and that most of the criticisms that have been made of him have been unjustified. Specifically, Locke notes the major ideas of Taylor that have been accepted as true: (1) A scientific management approach (that is, one based on proven fact rather than on tradition, rule of thumb, guesswork, precedent, personal opinion, or hearsay) should be taken. (2) Management and labor would both benefit from greater productivity. (3) Techniques of work could be developed in a scientific manner, such as through preparing a time and motion study, standardizing tools and procedures, assigning workers specific tasks, using money as an incentive, relying on individual rather than group rewards, training of workers by management experts, selecting "first-class" workers, and granting shorter working hours.

Locke notes that criticisms of Taylor are not warranted, including: (1) that Taylor had an oversimplified view of human motivation; (2) that he was unaware of the importance of social factors in worker productivity; (3) that he believed in blind obedience to authority; (4) that he overemphasized specialization; (5) that he treated men as machines; (6) that Scientific Management exploited workers; (7) that Taylor was antiunion; and (8) that he was dishonest. Locke concludes with tables evaluating the status of Taylor's ideas and techniques in contemporary management and the validity of criticisms of Taylor's ideas.

While recognizing the contributions that Taylorism has made to management, Richard Edwards points out the limitations of Taylorism: (1) Taylorism did not create all the management elements that have been attributed to it. (2) The actual impact of Taylorism in business practices was limited. (3) Many changes in management practices had little to do with Taylorism.

In reading the debate, note the areas of agreement between the authors about the contributions of Scientific Management. Consider, however, the areas of contention in the evaluation of Taylorism.

JAPANESE MANAGEMENT

Because of the increased interdependence of nations, the world has been characterized as a global village. More and more, the economies of nations are interconnected. Travel and communication across national boundaries have become more frequent. Many corporations use more resources from different countries to create their products and services than ever before. Where a particular country or organization excelled in production and management skills, it began to be copied by those who sought to benefit from its success. In the nineteenth century, British industry served as the model of excellence as entrepreneurs copied its production, organization, and management techniques. In the aftermath of World War II, American industry became the model for the world.

In the 1970s and 1980s, the economic accomplishments of Japan have led managers and scholars from other countries to examine the ingredients of Japanese success. That success was attributed in part to Japanese management techniques which emphasized human relationships in a business setting. A number of studies showed that job security, worker participation in decision making, and worker loyalty to an organization were factors contributing to the Japanese economic miracle.

Often overlooked in the praises of Japanese management is the fact that the Japanese did not invent such ideas. A number of American corporations had applied human relations concerns to the work place for many decades. American literature in management and public administration, moreover, had recognized the importance of the human side of management.

One Japanese technique that has received considerable attention is the Quality Circle (QC). The QC consists of a group of employees who share similar work responsibilities and meet at regularly scheduled times to improve their own work and performance. It is based upon the notion of worker cooperation through team ef-

fort and has begun to be applied in some American corporations which have seen Japanese industry thrive from its usage. Some efforts have been made in the United States to apply QCs not only in the private sector but in government, as well.

Can Japanese management techniques be applied in the United States? Toyohiro Kono, Professor of Business Administration at Gakushuin University, argues the Affirmative side. He notes that there are three key features of the Japanese style of management: (1) It is innovative. (2) It is a "soft" organization in which jobs are ambiguous and employees are willing to do many related tasks. (3) It is a community organization in which employees are considered to be partners in the organization. While some of these features are rooted in the uniqueness of Japanese culture, many of them have been adopted from the practices of other countries and are universally effective and transferrable.

Linda S. Dillon, Assistant Professor of Occupational Education at North Carolina State University, Raleigh, takes the Negative position. She contends that much of the success for Japanese management is rooted in Japanese culture. In Japan, 30 percent of the employees of major corporations are given lifetime employment. This can be done in part because women are hired as temporary or part-time employees who are let go when the corporation experiences a decline in demand. Japan has a practice of slow evaluation and promotion which is based upon selection of the most talented individuals. The Japanese, consequently, have a rigorous educational tradition based upon intense competition. The Japanese have a tradition of collective decision making and responsibility. They also have a tradition of a holistic approach to business matters in which workers feel a sense of trust and commitment to their work places. In Dillon's view, Japan learned much from American business practices in the period following World War II. It was the ability of Japan to apply these practices to Japanese culture, however, that allowed it to make such massive economic gains. According to Professor Dillon, it would be a mistake to assume that the United States could borrow and use Japanese management techniques as easily as the Japanese adopted American management techniques.

As you read this debate, consider the similarities between business and public management in the United States. Ask yourself whether some of the economic and social factors of Japanese society are more readily adopted in the public sector than in the private sector of the United States.

ISSUES

12   YES   DOES INCREMENTALISM EXPLAIN THE BUDGETARY PROCESS IN THE FEDERAL GOVERNMENT?

Making Sense of the Federal Budget the Old Fashioned Way—Incrementally*
Bernard T. Pitsvada and Frank D. Draper

Since Wildavsky and Fenno applied Lindblom's concept of pluralistically-based incrementalism to the budgetary process during the 1960s, incrementalism has become the dominant analytical model for describing how budgeting in the federal government really works.[1] The caricature of incrementalism that has arisen is that of a decision-making process taken up for the most part with negotiations over increases and decreases to an existing "base," and not with a review of the budget in its entirety. Over the years others have successfully elaborated and

built upon what remains the dominant paradigm in the field of budgetary research.[2]

The theory has not been without its many critics, however. One challenge that was voiced almost immediately by Natchez and Bupp focused more on specific programs within agencies rather than the "totals."[3] Thus, just because budgets appear to be incremental (or decremental) in absolute dollar amounts, does not always mean that base programs are being ignored, or that great changes in the programs are not taking place. Others have accurately pointed out that when annual changes in certain budget requests approach 20 to 30 percent, this strains the traditional definition of incrementalism.[4] Then again, some critics have noted that the "base"

From Bernard T. Pitsvada and Frank D. Draper, "Making Sense of the Federal Budget the Old Fashioned Way—Incrementally." Reprinted with permission from *Public Administration Review*, 44 (Sept./Oct. 1984), pp. 401–07. © 1984 by The American Society for Public Administration, 1120 G Street, N.W., Suite 500, Washington, D.C. All rights reserved.

*The views expressed here are those of the authors and do not necessarily represent those of the Department of the Army or the National Science Foundation.

[1]Charles Lindblom, "The Science of Muddling Through," *Public Administration Review* 29 (Spring 1959), 79–88, and Lindblom and Robert Dahl, *Politics, Economics and Welfare* (New York: Harper & Row, 1953); Aaron Wildavsky, *The Politics of the Budgetary Process* (Boston: Little, Brown and Company, 1964); and Richard Fenno, *The Power of the Purse* (Boston: Little, Brown and Company, 1966).

[2]For example, O. A. Davis, M. A. H. Dempster, and Aaron Wildavsky, "A Theory of the Budgetary Process," *American Political Science Review* 60 (September 1966); Peter B. Natchez and Irwin C. Bupp, "Policy and Priority in the Budgeting Process," *American Political Science Review* 67 (September 1973); and Ira Sharkansky, "Agency Requests Gubernatorial Support and Budget Success in State Legislatures," *American Political Science Review* 62 (December 1968).

[3]Natchez and Bupp, *op. cit.*

[4]See, for example, Charles Schultze, *The Politics and Economics of Public Spending* (Washington, D.C.: The Brookings Institution, 1968), p. 77ff.

has different meanings.[5] For example, where the "base" is primarily a sum of transfer payments to individuals and organizations, agencies are probably less protective than when the "base" supports ongoing discretionary programs or operating costs of agencies. There were, also, other voices of concern.[6]

Recent changes in the scope and nature of federal budgeting have brought the status of incrementalism as an explanatory tool of how resources are allocated into even more serious question. One recent article in the *Public Administration Review*, for example, noted that changes in the budget process brought about by the Budget and Impoundment Control Act of 1974, as well as Reagan administration attempts to dictate changes from the "top-down," diminish "the explanatory power of incrementalism" in periods of "budget shrinkage."[7]

We do not necessarily disagree with all the observations of the critics of incrementalism. We do believe though that, on balance, incrementalism still remains the best method of explaining and understanding budgets. We see five basic factors of growing importance in federal budgeting that have added to, rather than reduced the tendency toward incrementalism in budget analysis, and thus have increased the utility of this approach. An examination of these factors can bring into clearer focus the realities, as distinct from the rhetoric, surrounding budget decisions facing the federal establishment in mid-decade.

INDEXING AND INFLATION

There are eight major federal programs that are indexed to the rate of inflation, usually the Consumer

---

[5]John R. Gest, " 'Increment' and 'Base' in the Congressional Appropriations Process," *American Journal of Political Science* 21, No. 2 (May 1977), 242; and Mark S. Kamlet and David C. Mowery, "The Budgeting Base in Federal Resource Allocation," *American Journal of Political Science* 24, No. 4 (November 1980), 808–810.

[6]See, for example, Lance T. LeLoup, "The Myth of Incrementalism: Analytical Choices in Budgetary Theory," *Polity* (Summer 1978), 488–509; and John J. Bailey and Robert J. O'Connor, "Operationalizing Incrementalism: Measuring the Muddles," *Public Administration Review* 35 (January/February 1975), 60–66.

[7]Barry Bozeman and Jeffrey D. Straussman, "Shrinking Budgets and the Shrinkage of Budget Theory," *Public Administration Review* 42 (November/December 1982), 509–515.

Price Index (CPI). The programs range from the Social Security System (by far the largest), to civil service and military retirement, to food stamps and child nutrition. These programs accounted for more than $195 billion of outlays in Fiscal Year 1982 (with Social Security payments accounting for about 70 percent of this amount), or more than one-quarter of all federal outlays that year. The Congressional Budget Office (CBO) Baseline Projections for Fiscal Year 1984–89 estimate that almost one-third of federal spending for that period is directly indexed. It is difficult to make a case that anything other than incrementalism directs these programs upward, since the rates of outlays are primarily increased by the incremental adjustment made for indices such as the CPI. While all these indexed programs are "entitlements," i.e., any person who meets the criteria stated in the enabling statutes is entitled to payments, it is hardly the number of new claimants that caused these programs to increase so greatly in the past few years. Without indexing or congressional action to increase payments there would probably not have been the Social Security "problem." We recognize that it is possible that Congress may have enacted legislation to increase these programs even more than the CPI (as it did in 1972 when Social Security benefits were increased by 20 percent), but Congress did not have to take such action because of indexing. Nevertheless, even if Congress had been required to pass periodic increases, Congress would probably have used some measure of the price level as a basis for protecting these programs from inflation.

The observation that may be made from this is that the more a budget contains indexed programs, the more it is likely to become incremental in nature. It will be incremental because indexing is an annual adjustment along a steady glide path related primarily to the CPI, and not a sporadic or periodic adjustment made by Congress every few years to "catch up" with past inflation. Such a situation holds true if the increase is, say, two percent or 12 percent because of the nature of how the added budgetary costs are calculated and applied. They simply are a net change, to an existing amount, that is established impersonally by rules based on previous legislation. The same situation theoretically would hold true if the CPI went down for a full year and the entitlements were reduced to each eligible beneficiary.

When Wildavsky and Fenno wrote, they paid

little attention to indexed programs or transfer payments such as Social Security. The combination of the two as we now know them did not even exist until the 1970s. Nevertheless, as transfer payments, indexed or not, become such a large part of the federal budget—the FY 1984 budget claims that 42 percent of outlays are transfer payments—the budget will likely become more incremental. Indexing merely ensures that a major part of it will.

Indexing represents just one method for coping with inflation. Another method, which is widely used for non-entitlement programs by the Department of Defense (DOD), is actually to budget for anticipated "cost growth," i.e., inflation. Since FY 1978, the DOD has been authorized by legislation (Public Law 94–361) to request additional obligational authority in the budget to cover the projected increased cost of purchasing defense-related goods. The budget justification material submitted to Congress by the DOD clearly differentiates increases from year to year for "program growth" and "cost growth." In fact, the DOD FY 1984 budget "reductions" proposed by Secretary Weinberger were, in part, the result of changing budgetary assumptions that projected a lower rate of inflation for that year than was originally expected. As a result the inflationary impact of these items purchased represents an incremental change to the budget.

Another long-standing method of budgeting for inflation is used by all federal agencies. The annual October pay raise for government employees is simply an inflation-based adjustment to existing federal pay levels. While the next October pay raise does not get included in the annual January budget submission, the impact of the previous year's pay raise is included in the budget as part of the existing agency base. The net result of this procedure is to cause a slow but steady creep upward in the budget as a mandatory cost of doing business.

MULTIYEAR BUDGETING

In his budget message that accompanied the FY 1980 budget, Jimmy Carter announced a relatively little-noticed budget reform that has also contributed to increasing the influence of incremental analysis in the federal budget. According to Carter, "For the first time, the budget reflects the 3-year budget planning system I have initiated to gain better control of the longer-range effects and direction of government policies."[8] By way of further explanation it was noted that while budgets since 1970 had displayed five-year projections of total outlays and receipts, agencies were now required to prepare budget requests by appropriation that extended two years beyond the budget year. This change was designed, among other things, to expand the government's planning horizon and identify long-term consequences of programmatic changes to the budget.[9] By displaying three-year costs it became necessary for agencies to project the future changes that current year programs would entail. Since such an approach does not call for analyzing prospective changes in resource levels resulting from additional *program changes* in future years, the basic approach must be limited to consider incremental adjustments to the *status quo* policy from the budget year. This change also has the effect of giving the first succeeding year a budgetary base accepted by all parties, including OMB and Congress, from which to begin the next budget cycle. The focus of the next year's effort becomes the incremental change above the prior year base. This is almost a perfect description of Wildavsky's "aids to calculation."[10]

To confirm that this is in fact how budgeting proceeds we need only to examine the longest continuing multiyear budgeting effort in the federal government. When Robert McNamara, as secretary of Defense, introduced his much-heralded Planning, Programming and Budgeting System (PPBS) into the DOD in 1961, a component part of that system was the Five Year Defense Plan (FYDP). This so-called FYDP, which in reality is a seven-year display of resources (current year, budget year, and five program or "outyears"), is used as a basis of planning multiyear budgetary decisions and integrating various different appropriations into a single programmatic effort, such as building and fielding a Minuteman missile or Polaris submarine. Projecting budgetary outlays in a single year, such as the budget year, is a relatively imprecise science; projecting four years farther out is even more speculative. Nevertheless, the DOD usefully applied and still continues using the FYDP because outyears tend to

[8]*The Budget of the U.S. Government, Fiscal Year 1980,* Budget Message (Washington, D.C.: Government Printing Office, 1979), p. 7.

[9]*Ibid.,* p. 31.

[10]Wildavsky, *The Politics of the Budgetary Process, op. cit.,* p. 15.

be viewed as relatively minor extensions of the pre-ceding year or years. The FYDP totals serve as a base from which the next annual cycle begins. Changes brought about by congressional action, cost growth, or strategic decisions are then implemented as incremental adjustments to the five-year program totals already in place. Thus, while some decisions made by the DOD hierarchy may be major and result in sizeable changes in future budgets, the *process* of making such changes within the DOD is viewed as incremental in that changes are applied to a given and accepted base that all participants use in program development. The use of this aid to calculation was never more apparent than when the Carter administration introduced Zero-Base Budgeting (ZBB) to the federal government in 1977. The Defense Department merely grafted ZBB onto its existing resource allocation mechanism, the PPB System. The DOD did not examine all resources from a zero base as the name implies but limited its analysis to 9 percent of the resources at the margin of its existing FY 1979-83 FYDP.[11]

While Wildavsky and Fenno both excluded DOD budgets from their studies, there is little reason to believe that other federal agencies do not follow a course similar to the DOD. It is simply easier and more realistic for agencies to operate this way. Once Congress sees outyear projections for a given program, adjustments to that program are likely to draw questions in terms of why projections changed incrementally as they come closer to reality. Multiyear budgets provide all actors in the process with a better basis for performing comparative analysis. If this were not the case budgets would not be structured to display prior-year, current year, and budget-year totals side by side. Projecting two years beyond the budget-year merely provides more data upon which to focus in order to identify marginal changes from year to year. This is the stuff of which incrementalism is made.

CONTINUING RESOLUTIONS

Continuing resolutions are the authority Congress grants to agencies to continue obligating funds in the absence of an annual appropriations act. Such resolutions also act to further budgetary decision making by incremental steps.

Initially, the federal fiscal year was the same as the calendar year. But ever since the second appropriations act, in March 1790, Congress has had difficulty in passing appropriations before the beginning of the fiscal year.[12] It was this difficulty that caused Congress, in 1842, to change the date of the beginning of the fiscal year from January 1 to July 1, and in the Budget and Impoundment and Control Act of 1974 from July 1 to October 1. Since the president is still required to submit the budget to Congress 15 days after Congress convenes in January of each year, moving the fiscal year to October 1 was designed to give Congress three more months to review the budget and pass the appropriate legislation. It has not worked out that way despite the best of intentions.

Table 1 reflects that over the last seven years late enactment of appropriations, and thus reliance on continuing resolutions, has become a fact of life for much of the federal government. (Of course, many federal programs operating on the basis of trust funds and/or permanent appropriations are not affected by the absence of annual appropriations acts. Such programs have standing legislative authority.) Even the House which during Fiscal Years 1977 and 1978 had a reasonably good record in passing appropriations on time, has slipped in the last five years and especially the last two. One reason for the most recent difficulty in the House rests with the budget reductions proposed by the Reagan administration budget requests. As a means of resolving the heightened budgetary conflict brought about by these requests, Congress has employed a decision-making technique that attempts to cushion most of the areas of disagreement; that is, to resort to continuing resolutions. In this sense, a continuing resolution is the most incremental approach possible since it permits funding levels for agencies to be set based upon either or both houses' adjustment to the prior year totals or budget request.

The traditional approach in continuing resolutions places obligational authority at the lower figure of either house if both have passed separate bills but have not reconciled the differences; or if only one house has passed the appropriation, ob-

[11]Frank D. Draper and Bernard T. Pitsvada, *A First Year Assessment of Zero-Base Budgeting in the Federal Government—Another View* (Arlington, Va.: Association of Government Accountants, 1978), p. 3.

[12]See Stanley Katz, "The Federal Fiscal Year; Its Origin and Prospects," *National Tax Journal* 13, No. 4 (December 1959), 346–366.

Making Sense of the Federal Budget

TABLE 1 Enactment of Appropriation Acts, FY 1977–83

Fiscal Year	Passed House by Oct. 1	Enacted by Oct. 1	Enacted after Oct. 1	Not Enacted Separately
1977	13	10	3	0
1978	13	9	4	0
1979	13	5	7	1
1980	12	3	7	3
1981	12	0	8	5
1982	9	0	10	3
1983	5	1	5	7

ligations may continue at the lesser amount appropriated or the current rate, which generally means the rate of the previous year.[13] The FY 1983 continuing resolution was somewhat different in that it set different rates of spending for various agencies by including much of the original appropriations act language in the resolution, thereby making it a sizeable piece of legislation. Nevertheless, Congress seemed intent on using the continuing resolutions as a means of putting its stamp on an incremental control of the budget. The one thing the Congress wanted to avoid throughout the entire review of the FY 1983 budget was the use of the reconciliation process as had been done the year before. The reconciliation process of the FY 1982 budget simply did too much violence to the legislative process. To allow budgetary decisions to be made on a once-and-for-all, "thumbs up" or "thumbs down" vote on a reconciliation bill flies in the face of Congress' conception of decentralized power. It would appear that as budgetary conflict increases, Congress uses continuing resolutions to restore order to the budget process by restoring the traditional grounds of negotiation, bargaining and incrementalism. "Partisan mutual adjustment," "satisficing," "muddling through"—all part of the lexicon of the incrementalist approach to decision making—are what continuing resolutions seem to be all about.

BASELINE REVIEWS

Section 605 (a) of the Budget and Impoundment Control Act of 1974 requires the president to submit a "current services" budget to the Congress each

year. The law requires the submission "on or before November 10" but it has become customary to submit it along with the president's budget the following January. This current services estimate displays budget authority and outlays for the fiscal year ". . . if all programs and activities were carried on during such ensuing fiscal year at the same level as the fiscal year in progress and without policy changes in such programs and activities." Schick correctly points out that while the current services budget could be viewed as a neutral document, Congress has used it as a vehicle for achieving "incremental stability." According to Schick, "Congress institutionalized incrementalism in the form of the current services budget."[14] Congress has relied on the current services totals to represent the *status quo* and as a protection vehicle for agency "bases" and ongoing programs. The vehicle has also enabled certain non-indexed programs a degree of protection from inflation because what are displayed are totals designed to maintain a level of "services" rather than the current level of funding. Higher costs of doing the same work can be accommodated in a current services budget.

In addition, the same legislation (Section 202 (f)) also requires the Congressional Budget Office to submit by April 1 of each year a report to the Budget Committees which reflects budgetary options, which means alternative levels of revenues, outlays and budget authority. For the FY 1984 budget this report took the form of three separate reports. The key report was called *Baseline Budget Projections for Fiscal Years 1984–1988*. This document provided the CBO alternative to the executive branch estimates and projections. Considerable confusion resulted in the review of the budgets for Fiscal Years 1982 and 1983 because both branches insisted upon using their own baselines, which were different because of differing economic assumptions. Regardless of the differences, the key point is that established baselines were used by both the Congress and the administration. In some ways these baselines have substituted for the president's budget request as the point of departure for decision making.

Budgetary baselines, even though they represent multiyear projections which are not forecasts of future outcomes, tend to have the same incremental effect as the Defense Department's Five Year

---

[13]Robert W. Hartman, "Congress and Budget-Making," *Political Science Quarterly* 97, No. 3 (Fall 1982), 392.

[14]Allen Schick, *Congress and Money* (Washington, D.C.: The Urban Institute, 1980), p. 217.

Defense Plan or multiyear budgets. They provide what the CBO calls "a useful starting point," which is given a great deal of credibility in the budgetary process. It is possible to view these multiyear projections as extending the concept of the single year budget base into a multiyear budget base. This has been how agencies that did not operate off a multiyear planning process, such as the Five Year Defense Plan, have tended to interpret the figures. Certainly these multiyear estimates were designed for other reasons: they were primarily intended to give Congress a multiyear view of its past actions and to preclude seeing just the "nose of the camel." Nevertheless, since the practice started in the mid-1970s (at about the same time that it became widely recognized that we were entering a period of fiscal constraint), Congress was quick to recognize that such documents had a strategic as well as informational use. A strong point in favor of budgetary baselines is that they can be used in the alliance between the participants in the "Iron Triangle" (i.e., congressional committees, agencies, and constituency groups) against an administration that attempts major budgetary changes. Baselines are sacred for these participants and incrementalism preserves baselines.

INCREMENTAL (DECREMENTAL) BUDGET DISPLAYS

There remains one other major force supporting incrementalism. Agencies prepare their respective budgets from a basically incrementalist perspective. How else can we explain how budgets resisted change when faced with major reforms imposed by presidents in terms of the way budgets were to be prepared? Neither the PPB System nor ZBB caused major changes to agency budgets. These two, so-called "rational-comprehensive" models of budget preparation were supposed to change how agencies looked at, prepared and justified their budgets. If this had really happened why was this not reflected in budgetary outcomes? While "top-down" perspectives may have expected programs to be evaluated against one another in the PPB System, or alternative levels of funding among existing programs to be "ranked" in ZBB, neither really came to pass. Congress rejected the PPB system and Wildavsky recounts the tale of how the House Appro-

priations Committee even threatened to abolish funds for an agency's office that had prepared the PPB documents.[15] The assessment of congressional use of ZBB was generally along similar lines.[16] In the end, agencies eventually presented their budgets to Congress in much the same way they had always done: reflecting incremental changes.

Just a cursory look at any agency's budget request document to Congress (as well as to the OMB) reflects how incrementally-oriented the display of budget material is, and how the display is designed to draw out incremental decisions. This display is a part of all agencies' "justification books." These books are submitted to Congress in conjunction with the president's budget request. They provide a more detailed explanation of the budget, primarily in terms of where and why this budget makes changes to agency activities and programs. Format and size of these justification books differ from agency to agency. They do, however, have one common thread: just like the president's budget they tend to focus on a three-year period—past year, current year, and budget request year. "Trails" are provided showing increases and decreases over these years. Congressional review of these budgets proceeds along similar lines. Thus, while the books display an agency's total budget request, the book is really an incremental adjustment. Appropriately,

> . . . programs that continue at about the same level of funding from year to year are generally not highlighted for the simple reason that they show no change. . . . On the other hand, new programs or activities are displayed in greater detail for scrutiny because they represent changes from the preceding year. This structure, when coupled with the display of past year totals for comparison purposes, is at the heart of the Congressional incremental budget review."[17]

---
[15]Aaron Wildavsky, *Budgeting* (Boston: Little, Brown and Company, 1975), p. 313.

[16]Frank D. Draper and Bernard T. Pitsvada, "Congress and Executive Branch Budget Reform: The House Appropriations Committee and Zero-Base Budgeting," *International Journal of Public Administration* 2, No. 3 (1980), 331–374.

[17]Frank D. Draper and Bernard T. Pitsvada, "Limitations in Federal Budget Execution," *Government Accountants Journal* 30, No. 3 (Fall 1981), 22.

CONCLUSION

Probably the most compelling reason that supports an incremental view of the federal budget is the common sense one. We accept the fact that the budget is a reflection of societal needs as embodied in programs enacted by Congress as representatives of the majority will of "the people." If Congress is a reasonable reflection of popular will, then Congress simply enacts programs that people want. If it can be assumed that popular wants do not change drastically from year to year, neither should the budget, if one is a reasonably accurate reflection of the other. Thus, for example, permanent entitlement programs, protected from inflation, represent a baseline of stability that is reflected in how budgets are prepared and what they contain. Only drastic social upheaval (war), major depression, or revolution are likely to change this. (The first Castro budget was probably a lot different from the last Batista budget.) Changes in political philosophy do obviously change budgets; budget "systems" do not. As one official who actively participated in his state's implementation of ZBB said: "One's political philosophy [and the acceptance of such a philosophy] is far more important than one's budgeting technique in dertermining the size of government."[18] Political philosophies do not change all that often. Nor do budgets. To expect budgets to vary significantly from year-to-year, while at the same time expect social needs and wants to remain relatively stable from year-to-year defies logic in a democratic society.

Also, if one introduces a time perspective to the stability surrounding budgets, it is easy to understand why some participants in the budget process, such as those in the "Iron Triangle," still cling essentially to incremental analysis. At any given point in time a federal agency is executing one budget, probably defending another budget before Congress, preparing a third budget to submit to the OMB, and planning subsequent year budgets. These various budgets, by definition, must relate to one another since that is how agencies perceive them.

Further, in any process that results in increases or decreases to programs, compromises weigh heavily

on budgetary outcomes. But the great bulk of resource allocation decisions occur below the threshold of outside observation. What results is a relatively stable pattern of bureaucratic decision making that considers bureaucratic expectations, routines and arrangements—all factors that tend toward stability and incrementalism. Ironically, the "problem" with stability (i.e., increments or decrements to an existing base) is that it is not very visible. "Top down" budget making, which might be called the "big bang" approach, makes headlines; the "long whimper" mode (decremental budgeting) usually does not.[19] Any president can immediately attract attention by the threat of the "big bang," or a radical change in a program. Let the OMB issue annual guidance, however, to agencies to prepare their budget requests for the coming fiscal year at alternative levels of funding only slightly above or below last year's funding and the event goes unrecorded. Yet, the latter is often of more significance to an agency. Proposed severe reductions, for example, are easier for an agency to defend against; it is the drops of water over time that really cause the damage. As one observer of how the "big bang" approach is used in killing programs has noted,

> Because the conflict generated by big-bang termination efforts is more public and intense, examples of this process (both successful and unsuccessful) are easier to identify and more interesting to study. Indeed, how do you even distinguish a serious but unsuccessful attempt to achieve termination through decremental budgeting from the normal fluctuations in the policy budget? *There is no empirical evidence to suggest that termination occurs more frequently or more successfully as a result of sudden and vigorous efforts than as a result of a prolonged and subtle one. The big-bang mode is simply easier to identify and study.*[20] (Emphasis added)

---

[18]Quoted in Allen Schick and Harry Hatry, "Zero-Base Budgeting: The Manager's Budget," *Public Budgeting and Finance* 2, No. 1 (Spring 1982), 85.

[19]The terminology is that of Robert D. Behn, "How to Terminate a Public Policy: A Dozen Hints for the Would-Be Terminator," in Charles H. Levine, ed., *Managing Fiscal Stress* (Chatham, N.J.: Chatham House Publishers, 1980), 327–342.

[20]*Ibid.*, p. 338. Since Behn's article was written—it first appeared in *Policy Analysis* in 1977—there has been, however, one "big bang" event: the demise of the Community Services Administration (CSA). After attempting in the early 1970s to abolish the Office of Economic Opportunity (OEO) by the "big bang" approach (requesting

Others have noted similar typology in killing programs by decremental budgeting.[21]

no appropriations for it in the second year of its authorization), and after finding its path blocked by Congress and the courts, the Nixon administration chose the decremental route: Using his executive authority, Nixon scattered OEO's responsibilities and its organizational units throughout the federal government. OEO's successor, the Community Services Administration, picked up what budget pieces were left and was then subjected to a decremental budget attack over the next several years. The agency had a mild comeback in FY 1977, only to see its budget slip away from it once again in the Carter years. By that time, after nearly a decade of the "long whimper," President Reagan administered the "big bang" (though some might call it the coup de grace). No new obligational authority was requested for it in FY 1982 and the last of its outlays were due to be expended in FY 1983.

[21]See, for example, W. Henry Lambright and Harvey M. Sapolsky, "Terminating Federal Research and Development Programs," *Policy Sciences* 7 (June 1976), 199–213. Of particular relevance for today's decision makers is Lambright and Sapolsky's examination of the successful attempt during the 1970s to abolish NASA's Sustaining University Program (SUP), a program designed to aid students who were training in doctoral fields relevant to aerospace. A series of decremental budgets, ranging from $46 million to $9 million over four years, finally resulted in the program's abolishment in FY 1970. As the authors noted, "Rather than confronting the students and universities with a stark decision that would have affected their interests immediately, the decremental approach gave them time to adjust, to seek new support, or to learn to live with less" (p. 203).

In summary, the federal establishment uses incrementalism because over the years incrementalism and all its trappings—indexing, multiyear budgeting, continuing resolutions, baseline reviews, and budget displays—provide a useful tool in avoiding and sometimes solving budgetary conflict. Incrementalism is reflective of stability, something that lawmakers and administration officials like to project more often than not. At the same time incrementalism is a two-edge sword: with stability has also come a steady and inexorable growth in federal expenditures. But here again incrementalism has something to say for itself. For just as incrementalism provided the vehicle for growth in the 1970s, so decrementalism (or at least a slower incremental path) may be the only realistic way of curbing growth in the remaining years of the 1980s. The radical paring of programs that occurred beginning in 1981 would appear to be going nowhere in the environment of mid-1980s. Considering the vested interests that are entrenched behind current programs, i.e., the "Iron Triangle" participants, the use of decremental budgeting may well be the only viable alternative in reducing such growth. The fact that this may occur from the "top-down," by either the OMB, the president, or by congressional budget resolution, is immaterial. Whoever said that incrementalism (or decrementalism) had to be exclusively a "bottom-up" approach?

12   NO   DOES INCREMENTALISM EXPLAIN THE BUDGETARY PROCESS IN THE FEDERAL GOVERNMENT?

The Myth of Incrementalism: Analytical Choices in Budgetary Theory
Lance T. LeLoup

I. INTRODUCTION

Of all the subfields of political science budgeting is most dominated by one theory to the exclusion of competing theories. For over a decade *incremen-*

From Lance T. LeLoup, "The Myth of Incrementalism: Analytical Choices in Budgetary Theory," *Polity*, 10 (Summer 1978), pp. 488–509. Reprinted with permission.

talism has dominated conceptualization, analysis, and description of the budgetary process. The present essay attempts to show that this dominance has been detrimental to an overall understanding of the dynamics and processes of budgeting. Incrementalism was developed as a fully articulated theory on the basis of a number of implicit analytical choices appearing so obvious as to preclude the consideration of alternatives; however, they were costly in providing a misleading view of budgeting.[1]

A growing number of studies challenge the incremental theory of budgeting. The coherent integration of previously isolated challenges in terms of analytical and interpretive choices in the development of budgetary theory will be attempted here. This will not only help to clarify incrementalism but also suggest a number of alternative approaches and explanations. New directions refocusing budgetary theory on annual budgeting and multiyear budgetary decisions will be proposed as more promising for theoretical development. Finally, the conclusion will review the persistence of incrementalism and its relevance to budgeting.

II. INCREMENTALISM AS BUDGETARY THEORY

When V. O. Key lamented the lack of a budgetary theory, he was referring to the lack of normative theory to guide allocative decisions under conditions of scarcity.[2] Subsequently attempts were made, perhaps in response to Key, to specify a normative theory of budgeting,[3] and the literature supporting Planning Programming Budgeting (PPB) can be seen as a recent extension of such efforts.[4] While incrementalism has a normative foundation in pluralism,[5]

our analysis seeks to avoid the explicitly normative dimensions and instead concentrates on explanatory and descriptive aspects of budgetary theory.

The "incrementalists" are the authors of the most influential works on budgeting in the last two decades: Lindblom, Wildavsky, Fenno, Davis et al., and Sharkansky. In "The Science of Muddling Through," Lindblom suggests that in governmental decision-making, successive limited comparison of policies is more feasible and rational than comprehensive analysis.[6] Limited, noncomprehensive, incremental change, representing mutual adjustment of participant groups, is portrayed as the most common method of policy formulation.[7] Muddling through is not only what *is* done, it is what *should* be done.

Incorporating Lindblom's thesis, the fully developed and most influential statement of incremental budgeting is found in Wildavsky's, *The Politics of the Budgetary Process*, where he examines the interaction of agencies and Congress and the resulting appropriations decisions.[8]

> Budgeting is incremental, not comprehensive. The beginning of wisdom about an agency budget is that it is almost never actively reviewed as a whole every year in the sense of reconsidering the value of all existing programs as compared to all possible alternatives. Instead, it is based on last year's budget with special attention given to a narrow range of increases or decreases.[9]

Incrementalism explains the strategies and behavior of participants as well as the observed patterns of budgetary stability. The incremental process of mutual adjustment is built around the reinforcing roles and expectations of the participants; agencies attempt to establish a base and then gradually expand it. Their strategy is to ask for an increase, but a modest increase. While they expect to be cut back and take this into account in their calculations, too large a request might result in severe cutbacks. Con-

---

[1]This theme could logically be discussed in terms of paradigm dominance and change as suggested by Thomas Kuhn in *The Structure of Scientific Revolutions* (Chicago: University of Chicago Press, 1970). However, because of the controversy among philosophers of science and some highly problematic applications of Kuhn's ideas by political scientists, this approach is avoided. Also see Imre Lakatos and Alan Musgrave, *Criticism and the Growth of Knowledge* (Cambridge: Cambridge University Press, 1970).

[2]V. O. Key, "The Lack of a Budgetary Theory," *American Political Science Review* 34 (December 1940): 1137–1144.

[3]Verne B. Lewis, "Toward a Theory of Budgeting," *Public Administration Review* 12 (Winter 1952): 42–54. Arthur Smithies, *The Budgetary Process in the United States* (New York: McGraw Hill, 1955).

[4]Fremont J. Lyden and Ernest G. Miller, eds., *Planning Programming Budgeting* (Chicago: Markham, 1972). Charles Schultz, *The Politics and Economics of Public Spending* (Washington, D.C.: Brookings, 1968). David Novick, ed., *Program Budgeting* (Cambridge, Massachusetts: Harvard University Press, 1965).

[5]Allen Schick, "Systems Politics and Systems Budgeting," *Public Administration Review* 29 (March/April 1969): 137–151.

[6]Charles Lindblom, "The Science of Muddling Through," *Public Administration Review* 19 (Spring 1959): 79–88.

[7]Lindblom, "The Science of Muddling Through," p. 88.

[8]Aaron Wildavsky, *The Politics of the Budgetary Process* (Boston: Little, Brown and Company, 1964, 1974).

[9]Wildavsky, *The Politics of the Budgetary Process*, p. 15.

gress, through the Appropriations Committee and subcommittees, makes incremental cuts in agency requests, since it expects the agencies to request more than they need.

Focusing on the appropriations process in Congress, Richard Fenno detailed the roles assumed by the Appropriations Committees.[10] As "guardians of the public purse," subcommittees normalize their decision-making by routinely making cuts in request.[11] As political sub-systems, they develop stable relationships over time with the agencies. Looking at annual changes in agency appropriations Fenno concludes:

> Committee decisions are primarily incremental ones. These kinds of decisions represent the logical outcome of incrementalism which appears in the agency's expectations about committee action and in the committee's perception of agency budgets.[12]

It is apparent that incrementalism is used in at least two different senses: (1) to characterize the decision-making process of mutual adjustment and bargaining, and (2) to describe the budgetary outcomes that result from that process.[13] Using Fenno's data, Wildavsky interprets budgetary outcomes as incremental because in a majority of cases the final appropriation varies within a range of ±10 percent of the previous year's appropriation. This is the closest one gets to a firm definition of an incremental income. Fenno's conclusion that committee decisions reveal a basic incrementalism is similarly made without establishing the necessary criteria.

The work of Lindblom, Wildavsky, and Fenno was essentially descriptive of the process of calculation, decision, and the budgetary outcomes. The most important explanatory variable is the budget base, specifically, last year's appropriation.

From descriptive incrementalism, the theory was elevated to what Moreland has called "analytical

incrementalism," that is, mathematical representation of the process using regression equations.[14] The empirical models of agency appropriations by Davis, Dempster, and Wildavsky are the most influential tests of the theory.[15] In the initial model (1966), eight equations were hypothesized to explain the decision rules used by the participants. The dependent variable was the final appropriation voted by Congress. Using data from 56 domestic agencies from 1946 to 1963, Davis et al. found they could account for 86 percent of the appropriation decisions. One model each for Congress and the agencies best represented the decisions. The dominant agency decision rule in calculating requests was to take a fixed percentage increase over last year's appropriation. The dominant congressional decision rule in voting appropriations was to make a fixed percentage cut in the agency's request. These two simple calculations summarize the process and the results of incrementalism: the "striking regularities of the budgetary process" that are indicative of the stable decision rules employed by the participants.[16] Change in appropriation patterns are defined as "random shocks in an otherwise deterministic system," the result of "disturbances" and "special circumstances."[17] The causes of disturbances, special circumstances, shift points, or changes in decision rules are left largely unexplained.

The final elevation of incrementalism was to a predictive theory using econometric modeling tech-

---

[10]Richard Fenno, *The Power of the Purse* (Boston: Little, Brown and Company, 1966), p. 15.

[11]Richard Fenno, *Congressmen in Committee* (Boston: Little, Brown and Company, 1973), pp. 47–51.

[12]Fenno, *The Power of the Purse*, p. 354.

[13]John Bailey and Robert O'Connor, "Operationalizing Incrementalism: Measuring the Muddles," *Public Administration Review* 35 (January/February 1975): 60–66.

[14]William Moreland, "A Nonincremental Perspective on Budgetary Policy Actions," in R. Ripley and G. Franklin, eds., *Policy Making in the Federal Executive Branch* (New York: Free Press, 1975), chap. 3.

[15]Michael Davis, Michael Dempster, and Aaron Wildavsky, "A Theory of the Budgetary Process," *American Political Science Review* 60 (September 1966): 529; idem., "On the Process of Budgeting II: An Empirical Study of Congressional Appropriations," in Byrne et al., eds., *Studies In Budgeting* (Amsterdam and London: North Holland Publishers, 1971); idem., "Toward a Predictive Theory of the Federal Budgetary Process" (Paper delivered at the Annual Meeting of the American Political Science Association, New Orleans, La., Sept. 1973); idem., "Towards a Predictive Theory of Government Expenditure: U.S. Domestic Appropriations," *British Journal of Political Science* 4 (October 1974): 419–452.

[16]Davis et al., "A Theory of the Budgetary Process," p. 529.

[17]Ibid., p. 531.

niques.[18] This represented an effort to explain what were previously assumed to be random shift points. These shifts had been detected in years of partisan political change; added to this factor were a number of social, economic, administrative, and political explanatory variables. The inclusion of these environmental variables increased the explanatory power of the models, but since the R^2 were so high under the initial model, the improvement was only marginal.[19] Environmental factors were included as binary variables, "to model the abrupt changes in behavior in response to exogenous forces."[20] Agencies performing services to the administration and population and in the natural resources areas were found to be most susceptible to environmental influences. The impact of the political, social, economic, and administrative variables was found to be evenly distributed among the categories.[21] The latest refinement, although recognizing for the first time the potential impact of external factors, is based on the same theoretical assumptions and reinforced the conclusions of earlier work.

The theory of budgetary incrementalism is not limited in application to the United States federal budget; subsequent studies have applied it to virtually every level of United States government as well as to other nations and international organizations. Separate studies by Sharkansky and Anton concluded that incrementalism explained budgeting in the American states.[22] John Crecine extended the focus to municipal budgeting with the important caveat that incremental calculations are constrained by revenue projections.[23] Gerwin found incrementalism in school district budgeting.[24] Cowart et al. extended the theory to Norway,[25] and Hoole et al. found incremental decision rules in the United Nations, the World Health Organization, and the International Labor Organization.[26] Wildavsky's latest work, developing a comparative theory of budgeting, makes some important distinctions between governments on the basis of wealth and predictability.[27] The common basis of budgeting in his comparative theory, however, revolves around the concepts of incrementalism. Because of the tremendous scope of these studies, they cannot be examined here, and we shall therefore limit ourselves to United States federal budgeting. A final testament to the pervasive dominance of incrementalism, however, is found in secondary works. Incrementalism has filtered down and is heavily relied on in a range of basic texts on American government, state and local, Congress, the bureaucracy, public policy, etc.[28] The range of different meanings applied to the term and to the theory has further confused the issue.

In spite of its widespread acceptance, some scholars have been critical of the theory. Some of the criticism is on the normative level; as an outgrowth of pluralism it is said to dignify an irrational, biased process with rational status.[29] More general criticism has objected to the view of budgeting it

[18]Davis et al., "Towards a Predictive Theory of Government Expenditure."

[19]Aaron Wildavsky, *Budgeting: A Comparative Theory of Budgetary Processes* (Boston: Little, Brown and Company, 1975), table 3–2, p. 52.

[20]Ibid., p. 51.

[21]Ibid., p. 65–68.

[22]Ira Sharkansky, "Four Agencies and an Appropriations Subcommittee: A Comparative Study of Budget Strategies," *Midwest Journal of Political Science* (August 1965), pp. 254–281; idem., "Agency Requests, Gubernatorial Support and Budget Success in State Legislatures," *American Political Science Review* 62 (December 1968): 1222; Thomas Anton, *The Politics of State Expenditure in Illinois* (Urbana: University of Illinois Press, 1966).

[23]John Crecine, "A Computer Simulation Model of Municipal Budgeting," *Management Science* (July 1967), pp. 786–815. Idem., *Government Problem Solving, A Computer Simulation of Municipal Budgeting* (Chicago: Rand McNally, 1969).

[24]Donald A. Gerwin, *Budgeting Public Funds: The Decision Process in an Urban School District* (Madison: University of Wisconsin Press, 1969).

[25]Andrew Cowart, Tore Hansen, and Karl-Erik Brofoss, "Budgetary Strategies and Success at Multiple Decision Levels in the Norwegian Urban Setting," *American Political Science Review* 69 (June 1975): 543–558.

[26]Francis Hoole, Brian Job, and Harvey Tucker, "Incremental Budgeting and International Organizations," *American Journal of Political Science* 20 (May 1976): 273–301.

[27]Wildavsky, *Budgeting*.

[28]Without undertaking a thorough survey of texts, readers are referred to familiar books used in classes.

[29]Schick, "Systems Politics and Systems Budgeting," p. 95.

provided, producing as it does a uniform set of re-sults in the face of political bargaining. The upshot is an almost apolitical, deterministic, mechanistic explanation of budgeting. Some have attacked the failure to account for the most important points: the bases from which incrementalism proceeds.[30] The present critique of incrementalism will focus on in-terpretative questions and the analytical framework itself.

III. INTERPRETATIVE QUESTIONS

Are budgetary outcomes clearly incremental as Wil-davsky, Fenno, and others have stated? Some sug-gest that the incrementalists did not interpret their descriptive data correctly. Bailey and O'Connor claim that this misinterpretation is a result of the confusion between incrementalism in the process and incre-mentalism in outcomes.[31]

> When incremental is thus defined as bargain-ing, we are aware of no empirical case of a budgetary process which is nonincremental. Further, the working assumption has been that the products of bargaining are incremental out-puts. If this is accepted as true by definition, then incrementalism as a descriptive concept is simply not useful. Indeed, the interesting question concerns the range of outputs from bargaining processes and the linkages between nonincremental outputs and the processes which generate them.[32]

Re-examination of Fenno's data reveals a surprising amount of change, greater than 10 percent. Addi-tional budgetary data reveal a similar diversity in budgetary outcomes. Looking at state, federal, and comparative foreign budgetary data, Bailey and O'-Connor conclude that all reveal a broad range of results.[33] From 1960 to 1971 the Army Corps of Engineers had nine of eleven annual changes (82%) in the ±10 percent range; during the same period the United States Office of Education had only one of eleven changes (9%) in that range.[34] While there may be some question as to the exact definition of an incremental outcome, it seems clear that there exists a broader range of budgetary outcomes than the incrementalists have described.

A second major question concerns the inter-pretation of the regression equations. Both More-land and Gist suggest that the high correlations found by Davis et al. are the direct result of not controlling for secular trends in the data.[35] Controlling for col-linearity, Gist found that at least 50 percent of the variance in requests and appropriations is explained by the secular trend alone.[36] Examining the impact of administrative maturity on budget outcomes while controlling for collinearity, Moreland concluded that agencies in the Department of Agriculture could only count on receiving 44 cents of each dollar appropriated in the previous year.[37] Both found that when serial correlation is accounted for, the impact or existence of incrementalism is dramatically re-duced.

A related criticism was made by John Wanat.[38] Using sensitivity analysis he concluded that strategic interpretations of budgetary incrementalism are not warranted on the basis of the correlation analysis of Davis et al. He found that the magnitude of cor-relations in randomly generated data approximates those found by Davis et al. Therefore, one cannot validly support the existence of budgetary decision rules on the basis of high correlation coefficients.

Based on their request/appropriation figures the incrementalists concluded that there is a basic sim-ilarity in agency strategies; that is, requesting a mod-erate (incremental) increase. One of the first critics of this interpretation was Ira Sharkansky (who none-theless remained supportive of the theory). He com-plained that this conclusion was reached without a

---

[30]B.L.R. Smith, "Letters to the Editor," *American Political Science Review* 61 (March 1967): 150–152.

[31]Bailey and O'Connor, "Operationalizing Incremental-ism," p. 60.

[32]Ibid., p. 65.

[33]Ibid., p. 65.

[34]Lance T. LeLoup, "Agency Policy Actions: Determinants of Non-Incremental Change," in Ripley and Franklin, eds., *Policy Making*, chap. 5, p. 76.

[35]John R. Gist, "Mandatory Expenditures and the Defense Sector: Theory of Budgetary Incrementalism," *Sage Profes-sional Papers in American Politics*, vol. 2, series 04–020 (Beverly Hills and London: Sage Publications): 13–14. Moreland, "A Nonincremental Perspective," p. 49.

[36]Gist, "Mandatory Expenditures," p. 31.

[37]Moreland, "A Nonincremental Perspective," p. 61.

[38]John Wanat, "The Bases of Budgetary Incrementalism," *American Political Science Review* 68 (September 1974): 1221–1228.

comparison of individual agency strategies.[39] He suggested that some agencies are more assertive than others in that they ask for larger increases and concluded that different strategies exist in the form of varying degrees of assertiveness affecting budgetary outcomes. To get more, agencies need to ask for more. Examining the same phenomena, Sharkansky's interpretation ran counter to Wildavsky, Fenno, and Davis et al., who had argued that agencies asking for large increases are cut back more severely.

Changing requests in the president's budget for eight agencies revealed that agencies requesting larger increases tended to have significantly greater budget growth.[40] A recent study found a great deal of variation in agency strategies and outcomes.[41] The incrementalists make the assumption that agency requests contained in the president's budget reflect the goals and desires of agencies. In the study of agencies in the Department of Agriculture (DOA), data on initial agency estimates, department requests, and Office of Management and Budget (OMB) recommendations were all included in the analysis. The results indicated a much greater variation in agency behavior and demonstrated the error of assuming that requests in the president's budget are indicative of agency strategies. In two out of three cases the agencies requested an increase of more than 10 percent, and in one quarter of the cases, the agencies requested increases of more than 50 percent.[42]

Additional findings in this study call in question the incremental dichotomy of "spenders" versus "savers." The budgetary roles assumed by the DOA and the OMB appeared to be significantly different. The DOA assumed what might be called a balancing role, tending to increase requests for agencies which requested a cut in funding while, concomitantly, severely cutting back agencies which requested the largest increases. The OMB, on the other hand, tended

to make across the board cuts in agency requests regardless of the size of the increase asked for. The findings confirmed the existence of alternative strategies to the single incremental strategy of moderation and showed that assertiveness has an important impact on budgetary results and that further differentiation among roles is necessary.

Much of the theory of incremental budgeting rests on Wildavsky's and Fenno's interpretation of their extensive descriptive data and on empirical tests. Their work contains a great deal of interesting information on the appropriations process. It appears, however, that incremental assumptions structured their analysis and conclusions. Re-analyzed and reinterpreted, their empirical data could support a more differentiated set of conclusions.

IV. ANALYTICAL CHOICES AND ALTERNATIVES

In addition to its questionable interpretation of results, incrementalism as a theory of budgeting is built on a number of analytical choices that affect its forms of empirical validation and applicability. No attempt is made to delimit the application of incrementalism to only certain budgetary decisions; the clear implication is that it applies to the full range of phenomena. Their choices were not necessarily the wrong choices but strictly limit the applicability of the theory.

This section attempts to specify a number of interrelated analytical choices, their implications, critical responses, and some alternatives. Three main areas of analytical choice are: (1) level of aggregation, (2) time and object of analysis, (3) dependent and independent variables.

Level of Aggregation

The incrementalists chose to focus on domestic budget items aggregated at the agency level. This was an obvious choice for analysis; totals are available, agency officials and members of Congress are certainly concerned with the final appropriation, and it is commonly a visible figure. A number of recent studies have shown, however, the negative consequences of using this level of aggregation.

Aggregating at the agency level treats all components of an agency's request and appropriation

[39]Sharkansky, "Four Agencies"; idem., "Agency Requests."

[40]Lance T. LeLoup, Explaining Agency Appropriations Change, Success and Legislative Support: A Comparative Study of Agency Budget Determination (Ph.D. diss., Ohio State University, 1973).

[41]Lance T. LeLoup and William Moreland, "Agency Strategies and Executive Review: The Hidden Politics of Budgeting," Public Administration Review (forthcoming).

[42]Ibid.

as equal; the highest common denominator is dollars. But agency budgets can be disaggregated into different components. Gist asserts that agency budgets must be divided into mandatory and controllable components.[43] He suggests that mandatory spending items preclude any strategic manipulation in incremental strategies. If these decisions are previously determined, incrementalism cannot explain budget stability in such categories.[44] Gist further refines this point in a subsequent study. Because of the increase in uncontrollable spending, the budget base is not only reviewed but has become a fairly regular target for reductions.[45]

> The contention of incrementalism that the budget base is not reviewed cannot be sustained. While attention to the annual increment may be the normal state of affairs . . . , it has not characterized congressional budget behavior over the past decade or so . . . , Congressional budgeting has become as often "basal" as "incremental."[46]

Wanat also differentiates between components of appropriations. Agency budgets consist of three parts: the base, mandatory needs, and programmatic desires.[47] Wanat's mandatory component has a different meaning from the conventional use of mandatory or uncontrollable spending.[48] It refers to the new costs required to keep the agency operating at the same level as last year: an inflation factor. The program component represents the desire for new programs or expansion of old ones. Examining the Department of Labor budget, he found that agencies differentiate between these components in their presentations to Congress. Results, according to Wanat, can be empirically explained on the basis of an agency's mandatory needs. His study makes the important point that agencies conceptualize

components differently and that budgetary decisions are subject to external constraints (this theme will be pursued later).

Another alternative level of budget aggregation is the intraagency program level. Several studies have concluded that the agency level of aggregation used by the incrementalists leads to erroneous conclusions about policy stability. Natchez and Bupp argue that a stable appropriation pattern may belie substantial program shifts occurring at lower levels.[49] Looking at the Atomic Energy Commission, the authors show patterns of growth, decay, and fluctuation among AEC programs in nuclear rockets, high energy physics, thermonuclear research, and nuclear weapons, all within the context of stable, apparently incremental budget totals.[50] They conclude that significant policy change is missed by the incremental perspective; the most interesting questions of social and political change require more extensive probing into the lower levels of the administrative process where key decisions are made:

> In this regard, Davis, Dempster and Wildavsky's stochastic models perpetuate a fundamental error about the way the government operates. . . . We have seen that real change does occur within this "massive stability," reflecting real conflicts over purpose and priority.[51]

Arnold Kanter makes a similar observation by uncovering significant program variation in the Department of Defense.[52] The risk of a higher level of aggregation is that variation is often masked, gains and losses by competing programs cancel each other out in the totals, and that it has a tendency to bias results towards incremental interpretations. Gist also breaks down the defense sector budgets into their major program components. Both Kanter and Gist find that after disaggregating totals, nonincremental patterns actually dominate. The rate of growth in procurement and research and development were

---

[43]Gist, "Mandatory Expenditures," p. 15.

[44]Ibid., p. 10.

[45]John Gist, " 'Increment' and 'Base' in the Congressional Appropriations Process," *American Journal of Political Science* 21 (May 1977): 341–352.

[46]Ibid., pp. 350–351.

[47]Wanat, "The Bases of Budgetary Incrementalism," p. 1225.

[48]Barry M. Blechman, Edward M. Gramlich, and Robert W. Hartman, *Setting National Priorities, the 1976 Budget* (Washington, D.C.: Brookings, 1975), pp. 191–192.

[49]P. B. Natchez and I. C. Bupp, "Policy and Priority in the Budgetary Process," *American Political Science Review* 67 (September 1973): 951–963.

[50]Ibid., p. 960.

[51]Ibid., p. 963.

[52]Arnold Kanter, "Congress and the Defense Budget: 1960–1970," *American Political Science Review* 66 (March 1972): 129–143.

significantly greater than growth in the overall defense budget.[53] Gist includes a similar dissaggregation of the budgets of the National Aeronautics and Space Administration (NASA), the AEC, and the State Department. While the incremental model still predicts accurately in some cases (more frequently for Congress than the agencies), nonincremental decisions are evident in every budget item analyzed.[54]

In choosing total agency budgets as the level of aggregation, the incrementalists made the assumption that all dollars in the budget were the same. Such a choice and concomitant assumptions helped to insure finding incremental results. The alternative analytic choices discussed above facilitate a fuller understanding of underlying processes and policy changes in the budgetary process.

Time and Object of Analysis

Related to the choice of level of aggregation is that of time and object of analysis. Incremental theorists focus on annual appropriation decisions. This, too, is an apparently obvious choice since the yearly submission and review of appropriation requests are perhaps the most salient feature of the budgetary process. But annual appropriations are not the only important budgetary decisions and may not even be the most important.

The annual budget consists of a revenue as well as an expenditure side. Of critical importance to appropriation decisions are revenue estimates, taxation decisions, and decisions on the approximate size of the deficit (or surplus) and most recently, expenditure ceilings. Based on these decisions, there is a certain maximum amount of change that can occur in a given year. While the tax structure in the United States is not reviewed in an orderly yearly fashion and has been relatively stable, some major changes have occurred in the past decade in the sources and nature of federal revenues.[55] Decisions on revenues, deficit, and outlays constrain the appropriations process. With the implementation of new budget procedures in Congress, decisions on these totals are made consciously, and they create

tighter parameters for subsequent decisions.[56] Using appropriations as the sole object of analysis eliminates the possibility of detecting relationships between decisions on the whole and decisions on parts.

Along with annual decisions are a host of multiyear spending decisions that affect the budget. These include a number of substantive legislative and administrative decisions on the so-called uncontrollable spending items that are not reviewed every year.[57] The previous consideration of level aggregation referred to the need to separate out mandatory spending items. Yet the resolution of this problem by excluding these categories, estimated to be approximately 75 percent of the budget for fiscal year (F/Y) 1978,[58] from analysis is unsatisfactory. This is a point that has been ignored by the critics of incrementalism as well as by the incrementalists themselves. The analytical choice of single years as the time frame precludes theoretical explanation of three quarters of the budget. The impact of long-term spending decisions has become so great that one cannot hope to understand budgeting without considering them. The next section discusses in more detail some suggestions for a nonannual perspective; it is important to recognize here that selection of annual appropriations represents an analytical choice that virtually excludes these other important budgetary decisions.

Dependent and Independent Variables

A third set of related analytical choices concerns specific dependent and independent variables. The selection of final appropriations as the variable to be explained has led the incrementalists to specify single important explanatory variables: last year's appropriation for agencies; this year's request for Congress. Certainly these are key variables in budgetary decision-making. Alternative measures of

[53]Gist, "Mandatory Expenditures," p. 18; Kanter, "Congress and the Defense Budget," p. 133.

[54]Gist, "Mandatory Expenditures," p. 36.

[55]Blechman et al., *Setting National Priorities*, chap. 6.

[56]Budget and Impoundment Control Act, 1974, Public Law 93–344.

[57]Murray Weidenbaum, "Institutional Obstacles to Relocating Government Expenditures," in R. Haveman and J. Margolis, eds., *Public Expenditures and Policy Analysis* (Chicago: Markham, 1970), pp. 232–245.

[58]U.S. Office of Management and Budget, *Budget of the United States Government, Fiscal Year 1978* (Washington, D.C.: U.S. Government Printing Office, 1977).

budgetary results are available, however, and suggest a broader range of relevant independent variables. Changing the dependent variable from final appropriations to the percentage change in appropriations may suggest a new set of theoretical variables.[59] In one study, the level of presidential support for an agency was shown to relate to changes in requests and appropriation growth.[60] Priorities expressed in the public statements of the president affect changes in the rate and amount of change in agency budgets. At the same time, change in appropriations in the previous year had virtually no impact on percentage changes in agency requests or appropriations. This dependent variable does not preclude finding stability; if rates of change were constant, this would be reflected in the results. Davis, Dempster, and Wildavsky's 1974 study including a variety of environmental variables represents a substantial improvement. Their inclusion as binary variables in the model, however, only begins to suggest the potential impact of political, social, and economic factors on budgetary change. Shull has found that coalitions in Congress and the executive branch affect appropriation outcomes.[61] The partisan makeup of Congress and the presidency, the degree of congressional support for the president, and the level of conflict in Congress all have an impact on agency budgets.[62]

As described earlier, Sharkansky, and LeLoup and Moreland found that variation in agency strategies affects budget results. Variations in the level of support from departments and the Budget Office also affect success and growth.[63] Moreland indicated that agency size and administrative experience of the agency staff correlate with greater appropriations. An additional analytical alternative is to use annual appropriation data with secular trends removed and examine the residuals.[64] As Gist has shown, analysis of residuals can confirm incremental conclusions, but it also reveals evidence of nonincremental decision rules.

V. THE VALIDITY AND APPLICABILITY OF INCREMENTALISM

It would be a simple task to debunk a theory if disconfirming evidence were obtained from a "straightforward" test. But with incrementalism, where empirical validation of the highest order continues to result, the nature of the tests themselves insures something close to incremental results. There are several critical problems in dealing with the theory. Beyond the confusion between incremental decision-making (mutual adjustment) and incremental results (small annual changes), there is a general confusion surrounding the term: it has taken on a host of nontheoretical meanings. In most secondary, casual treatments (introductory texts, for example) it simply refers to the truism that budgets (or governments) do not change radically from year to year. But why? Because most spending commitments are for periods of longer than a year, and in any given year there are externally determined parameters to the amount of change that can occur. Incrementalism takes no account of these critical factors, which must be included in budgetary theory. More serious than the general confusion associated with the term is the tautological nature of the theory itself and the self-confirming nature of the empirical tests. Wildavsky's barb at critics is suggestive:

> The huge increase in the size of the budget—should end the vacuous debate over the importance of making decisions in small increments as opposed to large proportions of the total. For one of the secrets of incrementalism is that the base is as important as the rate of increase.
>
> Another secret of incrementalism is that one can get a long way by rapid movements, if they continue long enough.[65]

[59]Ripley and Franklin, eds., *Policy Making in the Federal Executive Branch* (New York: Free Press, 1975). Selections in this volume suggest several different sets of relevant variables.

[60]LeLoup, "Agency Policy Actions," p. 83.

[61]Steven A. Shull, "Coalitions and Budgeting" (Paper presented at Annual Meeting of Midwest Political Science Association, Chicago, Illinois, May, 1975).

[62]LeLoup, "Agency Policy Actions"; and Shull, "Coalitions and Budgeting."

[63]LeLoup and Moreland, "Agency Strategies and Executive Review."

[64]Gist, "Mandatory Expenditures," pp. 30–36.

[65]Wildavsky, *The Politics of the Budgetary Process*, preface to the Second Edition (1974), pp. xix, xx.

When a theory applies to all situations at all times without the possibility of disconfirming evidence, it is no longer a theory and of little use for explanation or even description.

An additional problem related to the dominance of incrementalism is the tendency to characterize budgetary studies in either/or terms. A nonincremental approach does not necessarily have to assume that budgeting is unstable, that all components of the budget are reviewed from the ground up every year, or that budgeting conforms to the rational-comprehensive model.

In spite of this, it would not be accurate to say that incrementalism is totally wrong. It correctly describes some aspects of annual budgetary decision-making in some agencies and some congressional subcommittees. However, its applicability is limited to a subset of annual appropriations decisions; it provides a misleading view and explanation of the overall budgetary process. To be sure, some of the underlying concepts of incremental budgeting are relevant, but they are in need of modification:

1. *Complexity*: Budgeting is complex, and participants employ aids to calculation. Yet some participants deal with the budget as a whole (president, OMB, Budget Committees) and are generalists, using aids in calculation required by the complexity of the process which are not mentioned by the incrementalists. Other participants may use nonincremental aids in making calculations at the agency level.

2. *Budget Base*: Last year's appropriation may not be the only base for agency calculations, and the multiple components of the base itself are treated differently by the actors. Changes are made by reviewing bodies in the controllable base and the increment.[66] For those responsible for budget totals, last year's budget may be of less value than current policy estimates of a "standpat" budget.[67]

3. *Roles*: The roles adopted by participants are more complex than the simple advocate/guardian dichotomy. Within the executive branch, agencies, departments, and the OMB differ in their behavior and

may adopt multiple or mixed roles. In Congress, differing roles adopted by authorization, Appropriations, and Budget Committees are apparent. For example, the authorization committees behave like advocates to the Budget Committee, but as guardians to the agencies.

4. *Bargaining*: The incrementalists correctly claim that budgeting is political; allocations cannot be and are not made "rationally" on the basis of a total view of the public interest. Yet some actors do bargain over the totals. The scope, object, and intensity of bargaining differ across policies, decision-making levels, and time. Conflict and its resolution shifts dramatically depending on the actors involved, partisan control of the presidency, economic conditions, and other external factors.

5. *Outcomes*: Bargaining matters; it does not always result in a deterministic pattern of stability. Change cannot be assessed without defining the time frame. Over the longrun, significant reallocation can and has occurred. But even in the shortrun, budgeting produces a set of results that cannot simply be described as "incremental." Within the budget, at lower levels of aggregation, significant changes can occur within a pattern of overall stability.

The incremental theory of budgeting was formulated on the basis of a number of interrelated analytical choices. As has been shown, these choices played a critical role in determining what was found and what conclusions were drawn. Focusing on striking regularities, crucial changes were obscured; in a relatively simple explanation of budgetary decision making, complex alternatives were ignored. The history of incrementalism presents a dramatic example of the pitfalls of social science theory. What appeared to be an obvious and self-evident analytical approach actually involved numerous choices and excluded alternatives. The consequences of these choices are a set of findings highly skewed toward a single interpretation.

VI. DEVELOPING BUDGETARY THEORY

Significant changes have occurred in the composition of the federal budget in the past thirty years. Income security increased its share of the budget 700 percent, health 2000 percent, and social services 2100 percent between 1946 and 1976.[68] At

---

[66]John Crecine et al., "Controllability of 'uncontrollable' Expenditures: Manipulation of Ambiguity in Budgetary Decision Making" (Paper presented at Midwest Political Science Association, April 21, 1977, Chicago, Illinois). Preliminary findings suggest that uncontrollables are manipulated within the executive branch as well as controllables.

[67]Current Policy Estimates (Congressional Budget Office) and Current Services Estimates (OMB) are projections of outlays in the next fiscal years if no programs are changed and services maintained at a constant real level.

[68]*Budget of the U.S. F/Y 1976*, p. 66.

the same time the defense share of the budget fell from 64 percent to 27 percent of the total. The most dramatic changes in the budget have occurred within the last decade. The growth in uncontrollable spending has aroused concern over the amount of annual discretion for decision-makers. Changes have also taken place in the budgetary process. The Bureau of the Budget became the OMB in 1970, and more significantly, Congress overhauled its procedures in 1974. The relevance of budgetary theory depends on its ability to comprehend the changing composition of the budget within the context of a set of external and internal constraints on the actions of key actors in the budgetary process.

In attempting to suggest new directions in developing budgetary theory, several key factors must be included. The shortcomings of incrementalism can be as instructive to the scholar as the observations and alternatives suggested in the many studies cited. Five key considerations should be recognized in attempting to advance our theoretical understanding of budgeting:

1. Perhaps the most important step is to expand the definition of relevant decisions. Besides the agencies and Appropriations Committees, many actors make decisions that affect the levels of revenues and expenditures. The authorization committees have become particularly important but are often excluded since their main function is not budgeting.

2. Time is essential in the reformulation. Most decisions are nonannual, having a duration of more or less than one year.

3. Budgetary decisions are made at different levels from different perspectives. Some actors are responsible for the whole budget, most for just a part of the budget. Budgetary decision-making differs considerably depending on how general or specific the decisions themselves are.

4. Annual budgeting is not simply a one way process, aggregating from small parts to the whole. One of the weaknesses of incrementalism is that budgeting is portrayed only as building increments on a base. This ignores the existence of external parameters, decisions on totals, that constrain the process. Budgeting can be seen as both an upward and downward process, with relevant theoretical questions focusing on the existence of parameters, their determination, and their impact.

5. Finally, budgetary theory must analyze discretion. How much flexibility do decision-makers have in the shortrun? Even the distinction between controllable and uncontrollable spending does not provide an accurate determination of the actual range of discretion for decision-makers.

Based on these key points, we are suggesting below a tentative framework for the analysis of national budgeting in the United States. While incrementalism has had a much wider application, our critique has focused on its application at this level. With appropriate modifications, some of the proposals may suggest new directions in other applications of budgetary theory.

"Levels" of Decisions

Budgetary decisions range from the broad and the general to the narrow and the specific. Decisions can be classified in terms of three categories:

• *Priority decisions:* these are a set of choices on budget totals for expenditures, revenues, deficit, and spending subtotals in functions such as defense, health, agriculture, etc. Priority decisions are macrobudgeting actions representing priorities in economic and fiscal policy. Such decisions are made annually, and are the most general type of budgetary actions.

• *Program decisions:* these concern program authorizations, agency appropriations, entitlement programs, construction projects, and a variety of decisions concerning agencies and programs. Decisions made at the program level review the legal basis of programs, fund existing programs, and may initiate new programs. Decisions at this level may be annual, multiyear, or open ended.

• *Operations decisions:* these allocate and obligate funds to specific purposes. Included are decisions on the timing of spending, the amount of spending, carrying over balances, future funding, reprogramming, and transferring funds between accounts. Operations decisions are continual, occurring daily, weekly, monthly, quarterly, etc., and are the most specific type of budgetary actions.

Key Actors

Different sets of actors are most prominent in the decision-making processes on the three levels. Priority decision-makers include the president and his advisors, Congress (the Budget Committees), and the OMB. Implementation of the Budget Control and Impoundment Act has made the decisions on totals more explicit in Congress and the bargaining between the president and Congress more visible. Program decisions involve the largest group of actors, and participants may vary depending on whether decisions are annual or multiyear. Appropriation decisions center on the familiar relationship between agencies and appropriations subcommittees. Key actors making authorization decisions (annual, multiyear, permanent) include agencies, standing committees, interest groups, and occasionally the president, OMB, and Congress. Specific entitlement programs and long-term construction projects involve combinations of these actors. Operations decisions are dominated by agencies, and include periodic interactions with appropriations committees and subcommittees and the OMB.

Key Relationships

Decisions at different levels are highly interrelated and interdependent. The most important limiting factors are the spending commitments made in previous years. Within the parameters imposed by these continuing commitments, it is possible to identify interrelationships between the general (higher level) and the specific (lower level) decisions. Higher level decisions establish *constraints* for lower level decisions; that is, priority decisions set boundaries for program and operations decisions. At the same time, budgeting involves combining smaller items into larger ones; *aggregation* may be defined as the process of successive combinations of lower level into higher level decisions. For example, priority decisions on totals may represent the aggregation of various program level decisions. Budgeting, then, is an interactive process combining constraint and aggregation. At any given time, one set of relationships may be ascendant. For example, prior to 1975, congressional budgeting was closer to an aggregative process, although presidential totals were sometimes used as reference points. The implementation of budget reform has increased the constraints imposed on authorization and appropriation decisions by totals agreed to in the concurrent budget resolutions.

Environmental Factors

Finally, decisions at all levels are affected by external factors, such as economic, social, and political trends. Economic changes may have the most significant direct impact. Rising unemployment, under existing statutory requirements, decreases tax collections and increases expenditures for unem-

ployment, welfare, etc. Cost of living escalators translate general increases in price levels into larger expenditures for social security, federal retirement, etc. Other political and social trends have a less direct impact, but often affect changes in budgetary directions.

Figure 1 summarizes the concepts and relationships discussed above and suggests a variety of hypotheses. For example, one may speculate on the degree of constraint, the relative dominance of Congress or the executive at different levels, or the impact of external changes in the environment. Specific policies and actors may predominantly occupy a certain level; others cut across levels.

Discretion

It is not enough just to recognize that a large proportion of the budget is uncontrollable because controllability, as officially defined, does not translate into discretion.[69] Expenditures classified as "uncontrollable" are not equally uncontrollable. Fixed costs (such as interest on the national debt) constitute firmer commitments than long-term construction of weapons, dams, etc. These projects, in turn, offer less possibility for control than entitlement programs. Efforts made in 1975 and 1976 to tighten eligibility for foodstamps, to restrict cost of living escalators, and to hold back mandated federal pay increases demonstrate that some potential for control exists. While the percentage that may change in a given year is small, the fact that these expenditures constitute just under half of the total budget allows more discretion than many "controllable" expenditures that make up only a small portion of the total.

Similarly, all expenditures categorized as "controllable" are not equally controllable. Since most of the controllable portion of the budget consists of personnel costs, civil service rules concerning severance pay, sick leave accumulation, etc., making large scale changes is very difficult. It has been estimated that in 1976 only $5–7 billion could be cut from the controllable portion; this is approxi-

---

[69]Lance T. LeLoup, "Discretion in National Budgeting: Controlling the Controllables," *Policy Analysis* (Fall 1978), see this for a detailed attempt to estimate discretion.

FIGURE 1 A Framework for Budgetary Analysis

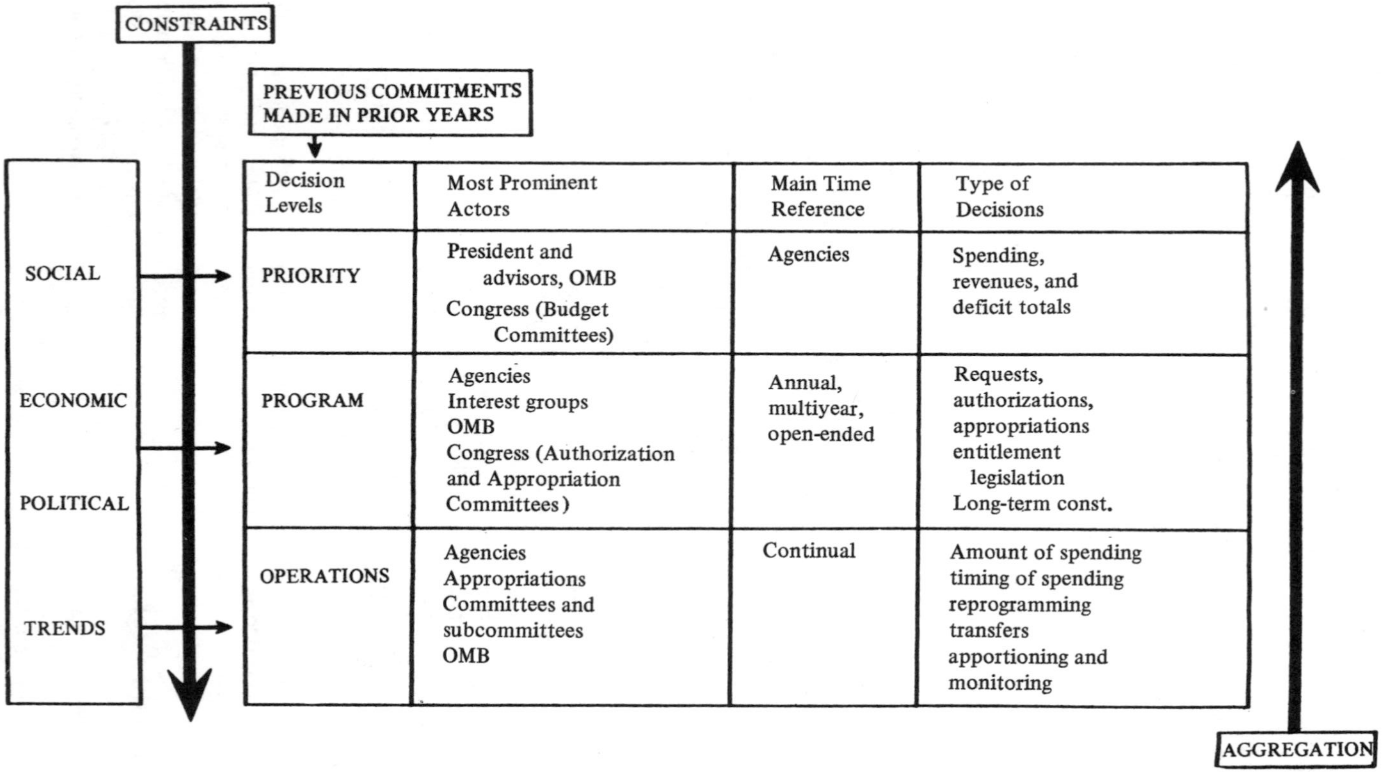

CONSTRAINTS

PREVIOUS COMMITMENTS MADE IN PRIOR YEARS

AGGREGATION

Decision Levels	Most Prominent Actors	Main Time Reference	Type of Decisions
PRIORITY	President and advisors, OMB Congress (Budget Committees)	Agencies	Spending, revenues, and deficit totals
PROGRAM	Agencies Interest groups OMB Congress (Authorization and Appropriation Committees)	Annual, multiyear, open-ended	Requests, authorizations, appropriations entitlement legislation Long-term const.
OPERATIONS	Agencies Appropriations Committees and subcommittees OMB	Continual	Amount of spending timing of spending reprogramming transfers apportioning and monitoring

SOCIAL

ECONOMIC

POLITICAL

TRENDS

mately the same amount that could be cut from the uncontrollable portion.[70]

The official controllable/uncontrollable dichotomy can be misleading; a continuum from most to least controllable expenditures would provide a more useful notion of discretion. The limits of annual discretion and the importance of multiyear decisions show that budgeting is a much more dynamic process than the correlation of consecutive appropriations patterns would indicate.

VII. SUMMARY AND CONCLUSIONS

In all probability incrementalism will remain in prevalent use regardless of findings to the contrary; it is a truism that government changes only marginally from year to year. Even though the precise descriptive validity of the term has been challenged,

many devotees of incrementalism will persist in the belief that government and budgeting will remain "incremental." Unfortunately, its self-fulfilling nature renders incrementalism nearly useless for social science theory. If it retains any validity after process is distinguished from outcomes, it is only in relation to a relatively narrow range of annual appropriations decisions.

This study has attempted to clarify the meaning of incrementalism as a theory of budgeting and integrate recent studies which challenge the theory. From the perspective of the social scientist, incrementalism appears predicated on a number of implicit analytical choices. Specification of these choices and alternatives clarifies the biases of incrementalism and suggests some of the difficulties encountered in the construction of theory.

The main bias of incrementalism is towards stability and against change. Analytical alternatives and the general suggestions for the development of budget theory presented here undoubtedly have their own biases. But in light of the experience of the previous decade, these alternatives may have greater promise for developing a balanced set of budget theories relevant to both the stability of budgeting and the mechanisms of change.

---

[70]Blechman et al., *Setting National Priorities*, pp. 192–194; see also Weidenbaum, "Institutional Obstacles," pp. 234–238; Joel Havemann, "Ford, Congress seek handle on 'uncontrollable' spending" *National Journal* 6, no. 48 (Nov. 29, 1975).

QUESTIONS FOR DISCUSSION

1. What criticisms have been made of incremental theory?

2. What percentage of increase or decrease in the level of spending by agencies would prove or disprove the validity of incremental theory? Explain.

3. To what extent can it correctly be said that incrementalism does not take into account

externally determined parameters to the amount of change that can occur?

4. To what extent have developments since the early 1970s strengthened the incrementalist argument?

5. What are the factors that contribute to rapid increases in spending for an agency over a short period of time?

SUGGESTED READINGS

ADAMS, BRUCE, "The Limitations of Muddling Through: Does Anyone in Washington Really Think Anymore?," *Public Administration Review*, 39 (Nov./Dec. 1979), 545–52.

BALZER, ANTHONY J., "Reflections on Muddling Through," *Public Administration Review*, 39 (Nov./Dec. 1979), 537–45.

CATES, CAMILLE, "Beyond Muddling: Creativity," *Public Administration Review*, 39 (Nov./Dec. 1979), 527–32.

DROR, YEHEZKEL, "Muddling Through—'Science' or Inertia?," *Public Administration Review*, 24 (Sept. 1964), 153–57.

ETZIONI, AMITAI, "Mixed Scanning: A 'Third' Approach to Decision-Making," *Public Administration Review*, 27 (Dec. 1967), 385–92.

GREENWOOD, ROYSTON, "Incremental Budgeting: Antecedents of Change," *Journal of Public Policy*, 4, (Nov. 1984), 277–306.

LINDBLOM, CHARLES E., "The Science of 'Muddling Through,' " *Public Administration Review*, 19 (Spring 1959), 79–88.

———, "Still Muddling, Not Yet Through," *Public Administration Review*, 39 (Nov./Dec. 1979), 517–26.

RUBIN, IRENE S., *Shrinking the Federal Government: The Effect of Cutbacks on Five Federal Agencies*. New York: Longman, 1985.

SCHICK, ALLEN, "Incremental Budgeting in a Decremental Age," *Policy Sciences*, 16 (Sept. 1983), 1–25.

TUCKER, HARVEY J., "Incremental Budgeting: Myth or Model?," *Western Political Quarterly*, 35 (Sept. 1982), 327–38.

WHITE, JOSEPH, "Much Ado About Everything: Making Sense of Federal Budgeting," *Public Administration Review*, 45 (Sept./Oct. 1985), 623–30.

WILDAVSKY, AARON, *The Politics of the Budgetary Process*, 4th ed. Boston, MA: Little, Brown & Co., 1984.

13   YES   ARE THE PRINCIPLES OF TAYLORISM VALID?

The Ideas of Frederick W. Taylor: An Evaluation[1]
Edwin A. Locke

Few management theorists have been more persistently criticized than has Frederick W. Taylor, the founder of scientific management, despite his being widely recognized as a key figure in the history of management thought (Wren, 1979). Taylor and scientific management frequently were attacked in his own lifetime, prompting, among other responses, Gilbreth's *Primer* (Gilbreth, 1914/1973), and the criticisms have continued to this day.

The present author agrees with Drucker (1976), although not with all of his specific points, that Taylor has never been fully understood or appreciated by his critics. Many criticisms either have been invalid or have involved peripheral issues, and his major ideas and contributions often have gone unacknowledged.

From Edwin A. Locke, "The Ideas of Frederick W. Taylor: An Evaluation," *Academy of Management* Review, 7 (June 1982), pp. 14–24. Reprinted with permission.

[1]This paper is based on the Annual Frederick J. Gaudet Memorial lecture given at the Stevens Institute of Technology, Hoboken, N. J., on April 17, 1980. The author is greatly indebted to J. Myron Johnson of the Stevens Institute and Daniel Wren of the University of Oklahoma for their helpful comments on an earlier draft of this paper, as well as to Marvin Levine for his helpful input on the issue of labor–management relations. The preparation of this paper was supported in part by Contract N00014-79-C-0680 between the University of Maryland and the Office of Naval Research.

Wren (1979) did a superb job of showing how Taylor's major ideas permeated the field of management both in the United States and abroad. However, Wren was not concerned primarily with evaluating all of Taylor's techniques or the criticisms of his ideas. Boddewyn (1961), Drucker (1976), and Fry (1976) have made spirited defenses of Taylor, but more by way of broad overviews than in systematic detail. The present paper summarizes Taylor's major ideas and techniques and considers both their validity and their degree of acceptance in contemporary management. In addition, the major criticisms made of Taylor are systematically evaluated.

TAYLOR'S PHILOSOPHY OF MANAGEMENT

An essential element of Taylor's philosophy of management, as the name of the movement implies, was a scientific approach to managerial decision making (Taylor, 1912/1970b; Sheldon, 1924/1976). The name was intended to contrast his approach with the unscientific approaches that characterized traditional management practices. By scientific, Taylor meant: based on proven fact (e.g., research and experimentation) rather than on tradition, rule of thumb, guesswork, precedent, personal opinion, or hearsay (Taylor, 1911/1967).

There can be no doubt that this element of Taylor's philosophy is accepted in modern management. This is not to say that all contemporary managers are fully rational decision makers. Clearly this is not the case. However, most would subscribe to the principle of scientific decision making and many actually practice it, at least with respect to some of their decisions. In most business schools there now is a specialized field called management science (which includes operations research), but the scientific approach is reflected in other areas of business as well (e.g., cost accounting). [See Kendall, (1924/1976) for a discussion of Taylor's early influence.] Taylor's goal was to forge a "mental revolution" in management, and in this aim he clearly succeeded. Drucker wrote that "Taylor was the first man in history who actually studied work seriously" (1976, p. 26).

A second element of Taylor's philosophy of management, and the other key aspect of the mental revolution that he advocated, concerned the relationship between management and labor. At the turn of the century, management-labor strife was widespread, violence was not uncommon, and a number of radical labor groups were advocating the violent overthrow of the capitalist system. Many believed that labor-management conflict was virtually inevitable.

Taylor argued that this view was false, that, at root, the interest of both parties were the same. Both would benefit, he argued, from higher production, lower costs, and higher wages, provided that management approached its job scientifically. Taylor believed that there would be no conflict over how to divide the pie as long as the pie were large enough (Taylor, 1912/1970b).

In logic, one cannot argue with Taylor's fundamental premise of a community of interest between management and labor. There were virtually no strikes in plants in which he applied scientific management (Taylor, 1911/1967; 1912/1970a). Wren (1979) argues that during the 1920s Taylor's hopes for union cooperation in introducing scientific management and in reducing waste were realized to a considerable extent in two industries. Unfortunately this attitude of cooperation ended in the 1930s when unions turned their attention to the passage of prolabor legislation.

In general, management-labor relations now are far more amicable than they were at the turn of the century, but all conflict has not been eliminated. One reason for this is that no matter how big the pie is, there still can be disagreements over how to divide it up. Taylor did not anticipate that as the pie got bigger, aspirations would rise accordingly.

TAYLOR'S TECHNIQUES

Time and Motion Study

Before Taylor, there was no objective method for determining how fast a job should be done. Most managers simply used past experience as a guide. Taylor's solution was to break down the work task into its constituent elements or motions; to eliminate wasted motions so the work would be done in the "one best way" (Taylor, 1912/1970a, p. 85)—a principle even more strongly emphasized by Frank Gilbreth (1923/1970); and to time the remaining motions in order to arrive at an expected rate of production (a proper day's work).

Time study now is used routinely in industrialized countries. However, there has been no final solution to the problem of (partially) subjective elements in time study (e.g., fatigue allowances); nor has worker resistance to time study disappeared, although it should be noted that resistance is most likely when there is a lack of trust in management (Bartlem & Locke, 1981). Such lack of trust often is earned by practices such as rate-cutting—something that Taylor explicitly warned against.

Standardized Tools and Procedures

Before scientific management, every workman had his own private tool box. This resulted in great inefficiencies because the proper tools were not always used or even owned. Taylor pushed strongly for standardization in the design and use of tools. The tools and procedures were standardized in accordance with what designs that experiments had shown to be most effective in a given context (e.g., the best size and shape for coal shovels).

Like time study, the principle of standardization is now well accepted. Combined with the principle of designing tools to fit people, the technique of standardization has evolved into the science of human engineering. Standardization also has been extended beyond the sphere of tool use to include other types of organizational procedures, especially in large firms.

The Task

Taylor advocated that each worker be assigned a specific amount of work, of a certain quality, each day based on the results of time study. This assigned quota he called a "task" (Taylor, 1911/1967, p.120). The term task (which was not original to Taylor) is roughly equivalent to the term goal. Thus, the use of tasks was a forerunner of modern day goal-setting. It is worth noting that Wren's (1979) discussion of scientific management at DuPont and General Motors implies that there is an historical connection between it and the technique of management by objectives (MBO). Pierre DuPont adapted Taylor's cost control ideas in order to develop measures of organizational performance (such as "return on investment") for the DuPont Powder Company. One of his employees, Donaldson Brown, further developed the return on investment concept so that it could be used to compare the efficiency of various departments *within* DuPont. When Pierre DuPont became head of General Motors, he hired Brown and Alfred P. Sloan, who institutionalized Brown's ideas at General Motors. Thus, although the technique of MBO may have been an outgrowth of scientific management, it developed more directly from the concepts of feedback, performance measurement, and cost accounting than from the task concept. Taylor had introduced an interlocking cost and accounting system as early as 1893 (Copley, 1923, Vol. 1).

Drucker acknowledges that Sloan was one of the earliest users of the MBO technique, but the term evidently was coined by Drucker (1954) himself, based not just on his studies at GM but on his work at General Electric with Harold Smiddy (Greenwood, 1980). At GE, the technique of MBO came to mean objectives set jointly by the manager and his superior rather than simply assigned objectives and/or work measurement.

Another term used widely today is organizational behavior modification (OB Mod); most OB Mod studies merely involve goal-setting with feedback, described in behavioristic terminology (Locke, 1977). Virtually every contemporary theory of or

approach to motivation now acknowledges the importance of goal setting either explicitly or implicitly (Locke, 1978).

The main effect of the post-Taylor research has been to support the validity of his practices. For example, it has been learned that specific challenging goals lead to better performance than do specific, easy goals or vague goals such as "do your best" or "no" goals (Locke, 1968; Locke, Shaw, Saari, & Latham, 1981). Taylor anticipated these results. The tasks his workers were assigned were, in fact, both specific (quantitative) and challenging; they were set by time study to be reachable only by a trained, "first class" workman (Taylor, 1903/1970). Remarkably, Alfred P. Sloan himself said: "The guiding principle was to make our standards difficult to achieve, but possible to attain, which I believe is the most effective way of capitalizing on the initiative, resourcefulness, and capabilities of operating personnel" (Odiorne, 1978, p. 15).

Further, it now seems clear that feedback (knowledge of one's progress in relation to the task or goal) is essential for goal setting to work (Locke et al., 1981), just as it is essential to have goals if feedback is to work (Locke et al., 1968). Again Taylor anticipated these findings. His workers were given feedback at least daily indicating whether or not they had attained their assigned task (Taylor, 1911/1967). A precursor of evaluative feedback for workers, developed a century before Taylor, was Robert Owen's "silent monitor" technique, described by Wren (1979, p. 72).

The Money Bonus

Taylor claimed that money was what the worker wanted most, and he argued that the worker should be paid from 30 percent to 100 percent higher wages in return for learning to do his job according to scientific management principles, that is, for "*carrying out orders*" (Boddewyn, 1961, p. 105), and for regularly attaining the assigned task.

Although money has been attacked frequently by social scientists from the time of the Hawthorne studies to the present, on the grounds that it is an inadequate motivator, Taylor's claim—that money is what the worker wants most—was not entirely misguided. A plethora of new incentive schemes have developed since Taylor's time, and new ones are still being tried (Latham & Dossett, 1978), not only for workers but for managers as well. Most labor-management conflicts still involve the issue of wages or issues related to wages, such as seniority, rate setting, layoffs, and fringe benefits. New analyses of the Hawthorne studies indicate that their disparagement of money as a motivator was wrong (Carey, 1967; Franke & Kaul, 1978; Sykes, 1965; Lawler, 1975), and recent books and articles again are advocating the use of money to motivate workers (Lawler, 1971; Locke, 1975; Vough, 1975).

Pay has become a major issue even in the famous Topeka experiment at General Foods, which was intended to stress job enrichment and participation (Walton, 1977), and it is a key element in the still popular Scanlon Plan (Frost, Wakeley & Ruh, 1974), long considered a human relations/organizational development technique. The pendulum now clearly seems to be swinging back toward Taylor's view (Locke, Feren, McCaleb, Shaw, & Denny, 1980). It is notable that one of the most outspoken contemporary advocates of money as a motivator is, like Taylor, an industrial engineer, Mitchell Fein. Fein has developed a new plant-wide incentive system called "Improshare" (Fein, 1977), which is coming into increasingly wide use.

Individualized Work

Taylor was a staunch advocate of individual as opposed to group tasks, as well as individual rewards, because he believed that group work and rewards undermined individual productivity, due to such phenomena as "systematic soldiering." Taylor wrote, "Personal ambition always has been and will remain a more powerful incentive to exertion than a desire for the general welfare" (1912/1976, p. 17). In this respect, Taylor's views are in clear opposition to the trend of the past four to five decades, which has been toward group tasks.

Nevertheless, Taylor's warnings about the dangers of group work have proven to have some validity. For example, Janis (1972) has demonstrated that groups that become too cohesive are susceptible to groupthink, a cognitive disorder in which rational thinking is sacrificed in the name of unanimity. Latané, Williams and Harkins (1979) have documented a phenomenon called "social loafing," in which people working in a group put out less effort than when working alone even when they claim to be trying their hardest in both cases.

Studies of group decision making indicate that there is no universal superiority of groups over individuals or vice versa. Although a group might outperform the average individual member, the best group member is often superior to the group as a whole (Hall, 1971).

The current view seems to hold that although people may work less hard in groups (as Taylor claimed), the benefits in terms of cooperation, knowledge, and flexibility generally outweigh the costs. Overall, the evidence is not conclusive one way or the other. Most likely the final answer will depend on the nature of the task and other factors.

Management Responsibility for Training

In line with his emphasis on a scientific approach to management, Taylor argued that employees should not learn their skills haphazardly from more experienced workers, who may not be using the "one best way," but from management experts who are thoroughly familiar with the job. There can be no doubt that most contemporary managers fully accept the notion that training new employees is their responsibility. Furthermore, the objective evaluation of training is becoming increasingly common.

Scientific Selection

Taylor advocated selecting only "first class" (i.e., high aptitude) men for a given job because their productivity would be several times greater than that of the average man. Colleague Sanford E. Thompson's use of a measure of reaction time to select bicycle ball bearing inspectors (Taylor, 1911/1967) was one of the earliest efforts at objective selection.

Thompson's selection testing antedated the pioneering work of Hugo Munsterberg (1913) as well as the more systematic attempts at validation of selection tests conducted by American psychologists for the Army during World War I. Since that time, personnel selection has mushroomed enormously and has become a science in its own right. Wren (1979) notes that Taylor's emphasis on scientific selection was an impetus to the development of the fields of industrial psychology and personnel management.

Shorter Working Hours and Rest Pauses

Taylor's experiments with pig iron handlers and ball bearing inspectors determined that fatigue would be reduced and more work would be accomplished if employees were given shorter working hours and/ or rest pauses during the day in proportion to the difficulty of the work. The findings with respect to shorter work week were corroborated by the British experiments during World War I (Vernon, 1921) and are now fully accepted. Similarly, the beneficial effects of periodic rest pauses have been documented in numerous experiments. Ryan (1947) summarizes the evidence on both issues.

CRITICISMS OF TAYLOR

View of Work Motivation

A number of criticisms have been made of Taylor and his ideas. Taylor is frequently criticized for having an oversimplified view of human motivation. Although he never claimed to have a complete view (Taylor, 1911/1967), he did claim that what the worker wanted most was money. Taylor believed that men would not work or follow directions unless they attained some permanent, personal benefit from it. This assumption is fully in accord with the tenets of expectancy theory (Vroom, 1964).

What is the evidence for the power of money as motivator? The present author and his students recently analyzed all available field studies that examined the effectiveness of four motivational techniques: money, goal setting, participation in decision making, and job enrichment (Locke et al., 1980). It was found that the median performance improvement resulting from individual incentive systems was 30 percent. This figure was far higher than that for any of the other incentives. The median figure for group or plantwide incentive schemes was 18 percent, still higher than for any nonmonetary technique. These findings (which were based mainly on studies of blue collar workers) coincide with the results of numerous recent studies which indicate that extrinsic incentives such as money are more important for blue collar than for white collar employees (Locke, 1976). This should not be taken to imply that money is unimportant to white collar and professional workers.

Taylor's other major motivational technique was goal setting, that is, assigning specific tasks. A critical incident study by White and Locke (in press) found that goal setting and its equivalents (e.g., deadlines, a heavy work load) were associated with high productivity (and absence of goal setting or goal blockage with low productivity) more frequently than were any other factors. In the Locke et al. (1980) analysis referred to above, goal setting was the second most effective motivational technique. The mean improvement in performance in studies in which workers were assigned specific, challenging goals was 16 percent.

If the effects of Taylor's two main motivators, money and goals—or the task and the bonus, as he called them—are combined, there is an expected or potential performance improvement of 46 percent. The figure is very close to the figure of a 40 percent mean performance improvement obtained in studies of individual task and bonus systems (Locke et al., 1980). A survey of 453 companies (Fein, 1973) found that task and bonus systems combined yielded productivity increases even greater than 40 percent. This figure far exceeds the combined effect of two more recently promulgated motivational techniques, job enrichment and participation (Locke, et al., 1980). Although Taylor offered nothing approaching a complete theory of human motivation, one must be impressed by the effectiveness of his techniques and by the little that has been added, at least by way of effective techniques, since his time.

Social Factors

The Hawthorne studies (Roethlisberger & Dickson, 1939/1956) were supposed to represent a great enlightenment. They allegedly "discovered" the influence of human relations or social factors on worker motivation. It has been noted that most of the conclusions that the Hawthorne researchers drew from their own data were probably wrong (Franke & Kaul, 1978). But, beyond this, much of what they said was not even original. Much has been made of the studies in the Bank Wiring Observation room, which found that workers developed informal norms that led to restriction of output. It has been claimed that this discovery refuted Taylor's alleged assumption that workers respond to incentives as isolated individuals. Actually Taylor made no such assumption. In fact, he had identified exactly the same phenomenon as the Hawthorne researchers several decades earlier. He called it "systematic soldiering." (See also comments by Boddewyn, 1961.) Not only did Taylor recognize restriction of output, but one of the chief goals of scientific management was to eliminate it! He viewed soldiering as wasteful and as contrary to the interests of both management and the worker. The main difference between Taylor and Mayo (director of the Hawthorne studies) was that Taylor viewed soldiering as a problem caused by a poor management and one that could and should be eliminated by scientific management; Mayo saw it as a reflection of an ineradicable human need.

Nor was Taylor unaware of the effort of social comparisons on worker morale. Discussing the need for the worker to perceive incentive systems as fair, relative to what other workers were getting, he said, "sentiment plays an important part in all our lives; and sentiment is particularly strong in the workman when he believes a direct injustice is being done him" (Copley, 1923, Vol. 2, p. 133). Taylor also was aware of social factors at a deeper level. Scientific management itself involved a social revolution in that it advocated replacing management-labor conflict with cooperation.

Authoritarianism

Authoritarianism means the belief in obedience to authority simply because it is authority—that is, obedience for the sake of obedience. Such a doctrine clearly was in total contradiction to everything Taylor stood for. First and foremost he stood for obedience to facts—to reason, to proof, to experimental findings. It was not the rule of authority that he advocated but the rule of knowledge. To quote Taylor biographer F. B. Copley, "there is only one master, one boss; namely, knowledge. This, at all events, was the state of things Taylor strove to bring about in industry. He there spent his strength trying to enthrone knowledge as king" (1923, Vol. 1, p. 291).

Taylor did not advocate participation in management matters by his uneducated, manual workers because they did not have the requisite knowledge to do their jobs in the one best way. For example, he shortened the working hours of ball bearing inspectors even when they opposed any such reduction (despite the promise of no loss in pay), because

the evidence indicated that their work day was too long (Taylor, 1911/1967). The positive results vindicated his judgement. Similarly, most workers, when they first heard about the task and bonus system, wanted no part of it. But when Taylor (1903/1947) showed them how such a system would actually benefit them (sometimes, to be sure, accompanied by pressures) most embraced it enthusiastically and performed far better as a result. Taylor was not averse to suggestions from the workers. He wrote, "Every encouragement . . . should be given to him to suggest improvements in methods and in implements" (1911/1967, p. 128). (See also Gilbreth, 1914/1973.) Fisher quotes Copley on this issue as follows: "If you could prove that yours was the best way, then he would adopt your way and feel very much obliged to you. Frequently he took humble doses of his own imperious medicine" (1925/1976, p. 172).

Specialization of Labor

There is little doubt that Taylor emphasized maximum specialization, not only for workers but for foremen (e.g., functional foremanship) and managers as well. His argument was the traditional one, that specialization decreases learning time and increases competence and skill. To evaluate the criticism that Taylor overemphasized specialization one must ask: How much emphasis is overemphasis?

Advocates of job enrichment have argued with some validity that extreme specialization leads to boredom and low morale and lack of work motivation due to underutilized mental capacity. However, it should be noted that Taylor always argued for a matching of men to jobs in accordance with their capacities. People who do jobs that require very little mental capacity should be people who have very little mental capacity (Taylor, 1903/1947). Those with more capacity should have more complex tasks to perform (e.g., by being promoted when they master the simple tasks). See Gilbreth (1914/1973) and Taylor (1912/1970a). In this respect Taylor might very well approve of individualized job enrichment, although, as noted earlier, its effects on performance may be limited. The present author does not agree, however, with Drucker's (1976) claim that Taylor anticipated Herzberg's theory.

There is a potential benefit of job enrichment (e.g., multicrafting and modular working arrangements), however, that Taylor did not foresee. There are fewer and fewer jobs in existence today that stay unchanged for long periods of time. If such jobs exist, they eventually are automated. People are more versatile than machines precisely because of their greater flexibility and adaptability. In times of rapid technological change, such as the present, spending months training a worker for one narrow specialty would not be very cost-efficient. It is more practical to have each worker master several different jobs and to work each day or hour where they are most needed.

With respect to supervision, Taylor's concept of functional foremanship clearly has not been accepted and probably is not very practical.

Men as Machines

The criticism that Taylor's system treated men as machines is related to the previous one. It usually refers to scientific management's requirement of complete uniformity for a given job with respect to the tools and motions used by the workmen (the one best way). As noted earlier, Taylor was not against the workers making suggestions for improvements, provided they first mastered the best known methods. Taylor's well-chosen example of this principle was that of training a surgeon: "he is quickly given the very best knowledge of his predecessors [then] . . . he is able to use his own originality and ingenuity to make *real additions to the world's knowledge, instead of reinventing things which are old*" (1911/1967, p. 126). The alternative to treating men as machines in the above sense was the prescientific method of management, which allowed men to choose tools and methods based on personal opinions and feelings rather than on knowledge.

It often is forgotten that standardization included the redesign of machines and equipment in order to enable men to become more skilled at the tasks they performed. Taylor applied this principle as much to himself as to others. His unique modifications of the tennis racket and the golf putter for his own use are cases in point. (Both items are on display at the Stevens Institute of Technology.) As noted earlier, he did not force people to fit existing equipment. He, and the Gilbreths, (re-)designed equipment to fit people. It might be more accurate to say that Taylor, rather than treating men as machines, helped to develop the science of integrating men with machines.

Exploitation of the Workers

During Taylor's lifetime, socialist Upton Sinclair and others claimed that Taylor's system was exploitative because, although under scientific management the worker might improve his productivity by around 100 percent, his pay was generally increased by a lesser amount. In fairness, they argued, the pay increase should match the productivity increase.

Taylor easily refuted this argument (Fisher, 1925/ 1976; Copley, 1923, Vol. 1). He pointed out, for example, that the increase in productivity was not caused by the worker only, but also by management; it was management who discovered the better techniques and designed the new tools, at some cost to themselves. Thus they deserved some of the benefits as well (Taylor, 1911/1967).

Ironically, Lenin, the self-proclaimed enemy of so-called "capitalist exploitation," himself strongly advocated the application of scientific management to Russian industry in order to help build socialism. However, socialist inefficiency, hostility to capitalist ideals, and resistance to change prevented the application of virtually all scientific management techniques in Russia except for the Gantt chart (Wren, 1980). The Soviets, however, may have been influenced by the Polish manager and theorist Karol Adamiecki, who developed his own scientific management theory independently of Taylor (Wesolowski, 1978).

Antiunionism

The criticism that Taylor was antiunion is true in only one sense. Taylor foresaw no need for unions once scientific management was properly established, especially because he saw the interests of management and labor as fundamentally the same (Copley, 1925/1976). It is worth noting in this respect that companies that are known for treating their employees well, such as IBM, do not have unions. The belief that unions were unnecessary under the proper type of management did not indicate lack of concern for employee welfare. The leaders of the scientific management movement, including Taylor, showed great concern about the effects of company policies on employee well-being (Sheldon, 1924/1976). For example, they were constantly preoccupied with eliminating or reducing fatigue. This benevolence, however, did not always characterize the followers of Taylor, who often tried to shortcut the introduction of his methods and engaged in rate-cutting and other deceptive practices.

Dishonesty

The strongest condemnations of Taylor, specifically of Taylor's character, have come in two recent articles (Wrege & Perroni, 1974; Wrege & Stotka, 1978). The first asserts that Taylor lied about the conduct of the famous pig iron handling experiments at Bethlehem Steel, and the second claims that Taylor plagiarized most of his *Principles of Scientific Management* from a colleague, Morris L. Cooke.

As for the pig iron experiments, it seems clear from Wrege and Perroni (1974) that Taylor did stress different things in the three reports that appeared in his writings. However, these descriptions were *not* contradictory to one another, they differed only in terms of emphasis and in the amount of detail presented. This in itself does not constitute dishonesty. Taylor apparently was in error as to certain details (e.g., the amount of tonnage of iron involved), but this could have involved errors of memory rather than deliberate deception. Nor do these details change the thread of his arguments.

Wrege and Perroni also claim that Schmidt (actual name: Henry Knolle) was not selected scientifically for the job of pig iron handling as claimed, but was simply the only worker who stuck with the task from the beginning to the end of the introductory period. This claim would appear to be true unless James Gillespie and Hartley Wolle, who conducted most of the research, omitted pertinent information in their report. However, if one accepts the idea that by a "first class" workman Taylor meant one who was not just capable but also highly motivated, then the choice of Schmidt was not inconsistent with Taylor's philosophy.

In addition, Wrege and Perroni could find no evidence that local papers had opposed Taylor's experiments as he had claimed. However, it is possible that Taylor was referring to some other paper or papers. Wrege and Perroni do not indicate whether the papers they looked at were the only ones published in the Bethlehem area or surrounding areas at that time.

Wrege and Perroni argue further that Taylor never acknowledged that his "laws of heavy laboring" were based on the work of "two extraordinary workers" (1974, p. 21). However in *Principles of Scientific Management*, Taylor clearly states that "*a first class laborer,* suited to such work as handling pig iron could be under load only 42 percent of the day and must be free from load 58 percent of the day" (1911/1967, p. 60, footnote 1; italics added). In short, these laws were specifically *for* extraordinary workers.

Wrege and Perroni claim that Taylor lied about giving the workers rest pauses, because all of the rest periods referred to involved only the return walk after loading the pig iron rather than an actual seated or motionless rest period. However, if one reads Taylor's *Principles* carefully, one notes that he specifically described his laws of heavy laboring in terms of how much of the time the worker can be "under load" (1911/1967, pp. 60–61, footnote 1). This implies that the return walk was the part not under load. Furthermore, near the end of footnote 1, Taylor states, "Practically the men were made to take a rest, generally by sitting down, after loading ten to twenty pigs. *This rest was in addition to the time which it took them to walk back from the car to the pile*" (1911/1967, p. 61, italics added). No evidence in Wrege and Perroni's (1974) paper contradicts this assertion; nor do they even mention it.

As to the Wrege and Stotka (1978) claim that Taylor plagiarized most of his *Principles* from a manuscript written by a colleague, Morris Cooke, several facts should be noted. First, Cooke's manuscript was based on a talk written and presented by Taylor himself. Apparently Cooke added to it, but the source of the additional material is not actually known; it could have been from other talks by or discussions with Taylor. Cooke himself gave Taylor credit for this allegedly plagiarized material (Wrege & Stotka, 1978). Fry argues, "It is ludicrous to accuse Taylor of plagiarizing Cooke if in fact Cooke's material was based on Taylor's own talks" (1976, p. 128). Second, Taylor published *Principles* with Cooke's full knowledge and apparent consent. Third, Taylor offered Cooke all the royalties lest his book reduce the sales of a similar book Cooke planned to author himself. All of this is hardly consistent with Wrege and Stotka's implication that Taylor was a dishonest exploiter. Actually, the reasons why Cooke agreed to let Taylor be sole author of the manuscript are not known. At most Taylor can be accused of lack of graciousness due to his failure to acknowledge Cooke's editorial work. It also is puzzling why, if Cooke actually wrote most of *Principles*, Wrege, Perroni, and Stotka did not accuse Cooke as well as Taylor of dishonesty in reporting the pig iron experiments.

Wrege and Perroni (1974) also accuse Taylor of not giving credit to Gillespie and Wolle for their work on the Bethlehem studies. Although Taylor did not acknowledge in print every assistant who ever worked with him, in *Principles* he did acknowledge his indebtedness to many colleagues, including, Barth, Gilbreth, Gantt, and Thompson. He also used the term "we" when describing the Bethlehem experiments. Thus he was clearly not in the habit of taking all credit for himself, as Wrege and Stotka (1978) charge. Again, however, a footnote acknowledging the work of Gillespie and Wolle would have been appropriate.

In the present author's opinion, not only is the evidence that Taylor was dishonest far from conclusive, it is virtually nonexistent. On the grounds of practicality alone, it seems doubtful that Taylor, who worked and performed experiments with so many different people, would deliberately attempt to distort what was done or who did it and thus leave himself open to exposure by any one of them.

CONCLUSION

With respect to the issues of a scientific approach to management and the techniques of time and motion study, standardization, goal setting plus work measurement and feedback, money as a motivator, management's responsibility for training, scientific selection, the shortened work week, and rest pauses, Taylor's views not only were essentially correct but they had been well accepted by management. With respect to the issues of management-labor relations and individualized work, Taylor probably was only partially correct, and he has been only partially accepted. These issues are summarized in Table 1.

With respect to criticisms, the accusations regarding the following points are predominantly or wholly false: Taylor's inadequate model of worker motivation, his ignorance of social factors, his authoritarianism, his treatment of men as machines, his exploitation of workers, his antiunionism, and

TABLE 1   Status of Taylor's Ideas and Techniques in Contemporary Management

	Valid?	Now Accepted?	Manifested in (outgrowths):
Philosophy			
Scientific decision making	Yes	Yes	Management science: operations research, cost accounting, etc.
Management-labor cooperation	Yes	Partly	Greater management-labor cooperation (but conflict not eliminated)
Techniques			
Time and motion study	Yes	Yes	Widespread use; standard times
Standardization	Yes	Yes	Standardized procedures in many spheres; human engineering
Task	Yes	Yes	Goal setting, MBO, feedback
Bonus	Yes	Increasingly	Proliferation of reward system, Scanlon Plan, Improshare, need to consider money in job enrichment/OD studies
Individualized work	Partly	Partly	Recognition of dangers of groups, groupthink, social loafing, contextual theories of group decision making (but group jobs sometimes more efficient)
Management training	Yes	Yes	Management responsibility for employee training
Scientific selection	Yes	Yes	Development of fields of industrial psychology and personnel management
Shorter hours; rest pauses	Yes	Yes	40 hour (or less) work week; common use of rest pauses

TABLE 2   Validity of Criticisms of Taylor's Ideas

Criticism	Valid?	Relevant facts
Inadequate theory of work motivation	Specious, because no complete theory offered	Money and goals are the most effective motivators
Ignored social factors	No	SM designed specifically to facilitate cooperation and to eliminate negative effects of social factors; awareness of sentiments
Authoritarianism	No	Stressed rule of knowledge (the essence of SM)
Overspecialization	Partly	Specialization maximized expertise; matched men to job requirements (but ignored possible benefits of multicrafting)
Treated men as machines	No	Methods based on knowledge, not feelings
Exploitaton of workers	No	Management deserves some of the benefits of increased efficiency based on its contribution
Antiunionism	No	Unions not needed under good management
Dishonesty	No	Accusations based on incomplete or false information

his personal dishonesty. Several of them verge on the preposterous. The accusation of overspecialization seems partly but not totally justified. See Table 2 for a summary of these points.

Considering that it has been over 65 years since Taylor's death and that a knowledge explosion has taken place during these years, Taylor's track record is remarkable. The point is not, as is often claimed, that he was "right in the context of his time" but is now outdated, but that *most of his insights are still valid today.* The present author agrees with those who consider Taylor a genius (Johnson, 1980). His achievements are all the more admirable because, although Taylor was highly intelligent, his discoveries were not made through sudden, brilliant insights but through sheer hard work. His metal-cutting experiments, for example, spanned a period of 26 years (Taylor, 1912/1970a)!

Drucker (1976) claims that Taylor had as much impact on the modern world as Karl Marx and Sigmund Freud. This may be true in that Taylor's influence was certainly worldwide and has endured long after his death (Wren, 1979). Of the three, however, the present author considers Taylor's ideas to be by far the most objectively valid. But the historical figure that Taylor most reminds one of is Thomas Edison (Runes, 1948)—in his systematic style of research, his dogged persistence, his emphasis on the useful, his thirst for knowledge, and in his dedication to truth.

REFERENCES

BARTLEM , C. S., & LOCKE, E. A. The Coch and French study: A critique and reinterpretation. *Human Relations,* 1981, 34, 555–566.

BODDEWYN, J. Frederick Winslow Taylor revisited. *Academy of Management Journal,* 1961, 4, 100–107.

CAREY, A. The Hawthorne studies: A radical criticism. *American Sociological Review,* 1967, 32, 403–416.

COPLEY, F. B. *Frederick W. Taylor: Father of scientific management* (2 Vols.). New York: Harper & Row, 1923.

COPLEY, F. B. Taylor and trade unions. In D. DelMar & R. D. Collins (Eds.), *Classics in scientific management.* University, Ala.: University of Alabama Press, 1976, 52–56. (Originally published, 1925.)

DRUCKER, P. F. *The practice of management.* New York: Harper, 1954.

DRUCKER, P. F. The coming rediscovery of scientific management. *Conference Board Record,* 1976, 13 (6), 23–27.

FEIN, M. Work measurement and wage incentives, *Industrial Engineering,* 1973, 5, 49–51.

FEIN, M. An alternative to traditional managing. Unpublished manuscript, 1977.

FISHER, I. Scientific management made clear. In D. DelMar & R. D. Collins (Eds.), *Classics in scientific management.* University, Ala.: University of Alabama Press, 1976, 154–193. (Originally published, 1925.)

FRANKE, R. H., & KAUL, J. D. The Hawthorne experiments: First statistical interpretation. *American Sociological Review,* 1978, 43, 623–643.

FROST, C. F., WAKELEY, J. H., & RUH, R. A. *The Scanlon*

plan for organization development: Identity, participation, and equity. East Lansing: Michigan State University Press, 1974.

FRY, L. W. The maligned F. W. Taylor: A reply to his many critics. *Academy of Management Review*, 1976, 1 (30), 124–139.

GILBRETH, F. B. Science in management for the one best way to do work. In H. F. Merrill (Ed.), *Classics in management.* New York: American Management Association, 1970, 217–263. (Originally published, 1923.)

GILBRETH, F. B. *Primer of scientific management.* Easton, Pa.: Hive Publishing Co., 1973. (Originally published, 1914.)

GREENWOOD, R. Management by objectives: As developed by Peter F. Drucker assisted by General Electric's management consultation services. Paper presented at the Academy of Management meetings, 1980, Detroit.

HALL, J. Decisions, decisions, decisions. *Psychology Today*, 1971, 5 (6), 51ff.

JANIS, I. *Victims of groupthink.* Boston: Houghton Mifflin, 1972.

JOHNSON, M. J. Fred Taylor '83: Giant of non-repute. *Stevens Indicator*, 1980, 97 (2), 4–8.

KENDALL, H. P. A decade's development in management trends and results of scientific management. In D. DelMar & R. D. Collins (Eds.), *Classics in scientific management.* University, Ala.: University of Alabama Press, 1976, 118–133. (Originally published, 1924.)

LATANÉ, B., WILLIAMS, K., & HARKINS, S. Social loafing. *Psychology Today*, 1979, 13 (4), 104ff.

LATHAM, G. P., & DOSSETT, D. L. Designing incentive plans for unionized employees: A comparison of continuous and variable ratio reinforcement schedules. *Personnel Psychology*, 1978, 31, 47–61.

LAWLER, E. E. *Pay and organizational effectiveness: A psychological view.* New York: McGraw-Hill, 1971.

LAWLER, E. E. Pay, participation and organization change. In E. L. Cass & F. G. Zimmer (Eds.), *Man and work in society.* New York: Van Nostrand Reinhold, 1975, 137–149.

LOCKE, E. A. Toward a theory of task motivation and incentives. *Organizational Behavior and Human Performance*, 1968, 3, 157–189.

LOCKE, E. A. Personnel attitudes and motivation. *Annual Review of Psychology*, 1975, 26, 457–480.

LOCKE, E. A. The nature and causes of job satisfaction. In M. D. Dunnette (Ed.), *Handbook of industrial and organizational psychology.* Chicago: Rand McNally, 1976, 1297–1349.

LOCKE, E. A. The myths of behavior mod in organizations. *Academy of Management Review*, 1977, 2, 543–553.

LOCKE, E. A. The ubiquity of the technique of goal setting in theories of and approaches to employee motivation. *Academy of Management Review*, 1978, 3, 594–601.

LOCKE, E. A., CARTLEDGE, N., & KOEPPEL, J. Motivational effects of knowledge of results: A goal-setting phenomenon? *Psychological Bulletin*, 1968, 70, 474–485.

LOCKE, E. A., SHAW, K. N., SAARI, L. M., & LATHAM, G. P. Goal setting and task performance: 1969–1980. *Psychological Bulletin*, 1981, 90, 125–152.

LOCKE, E. A., FEREN, D. B., MCCALEB, V. M., SHAW, K. M., & DENNY, A. T. The relative effectiveness of four methods of motivating employee performance. In K. Duncan, M. Gruneberg, & D. Wallis (Eds.), *Changes in working life.* Chichester, England: Wiley, 1980, 363–387.

MUNSTERBERG, H. *Psychology and industrial efficiency.* Boston: Houghton Mifflin, 1913.

ODIORNE, G. S. MBO: A backward glance. *Business Horizons*, October 1978, 14–24.

ROETHLISBERGER, F. J., & DICKSON, W. J. *Management and the worker.* Cambridge, Mass.: Harvard University Press, 1956. (Originally published, 1939.)

RUNES, D. D. (Ed.). *The diary and sundry observations of Thomas Alva Edison.* New York: Philosophical Library, 1948.

RYAN, T. A. *Work and effort.* New York: Ronald, 1947.

SHELDON, O. Taylor the creative leader. In D. DelMar & R. D. Collins (Eds.), *Classics in scientific management.* University, Ala.: University of Alabama Press, 1976, 35–51. (Originally published, 1924.)

SYKES, A. J. M. Economic interest and the Hawthorne researchers. *Human Relations*, 1965, 18, 253–263.

TAYLOR, F. W. *Shop management* (published as part of *Scientific management*). New York: Harper, 1947. (Originally published, 1903.)

TAYLOR, F. W. *The principles of scientific management.* New York: Norton, 1967. (Originally published, 1911.)

TAYLOR, F. W. Time study, piece work, and the first-class man. In H. F. Merrill (Ed.), *Classics in management.* New York: American Management Association, 1970, 57–66. (Originally published, 1903.)

TAYLOR, F. W. The principles of scientific management. In H. F. Merrill (Ed.), *Classics in management.* New York: American Management Association, 1970a. (Originally published 1912.)

TAYLOR, F. W. What is scientific management? In H. G. Merrill (Ed.), *Classics in management.* New York: American Management Association, 1970b, 67–71. (Original testimony given 1912.)

TAYLOR, F. W. Profit sharing. In D. DelMar & R. D. Collins (Eds.), *Classics in scientific management.* University, Ala.: University of Alabama Press, 1976, 17–20. (Originally written, 1912.)

VERNON, H. N. *Industrial fatigue and efficiency.* New York: Dutton, 1921.

VOUGH, C. F. *Tapping the human resource.* New York: Wiley, 1964.

VROOM, V. *Work and motivation.* New York: Wiley, 1969.

WALTON, R. E. Work innovations at Topeka: After six years. *Journal of Applied Behavioral Science*, 1977, 13 (3), 422–433.

WESOLOWSKI, Z. P. The Polish contribution to the development of scientific management. *Proceedings of the Academy of Management, 1978.*

WHITE, F., & LOCKE, E. A. Perceived determinants of high and low productivity in three occupational groups: A critical incident study. *Journal of Management Studies*, in press.

WREGE, C. D., & PERRONI, A. G. Taylor's pig-tale: A his-

torical analysis of Frederick W. Taylor's pig-iron experiments. *Academy of Management Journal*, 1974,
17, 6–27.
WREGE, C. D., & STOTKA, A. M. Cooke creates a classic:
The story behind F. W. Taylor's principles of scientific
management. *Academy of Management Review*, 1978,
3, 736–749.

WREN, D. A. *The evolution of management thought* (2nd
ed.). New York: Wiley, 1979.
WREN, D.A. Scientific management in the U.S.S.R., with
particular reference to the contribution of Walter N.
Polakov. *Academy of Management Review*, 1980, 5,
1–11.

13 NO ARE THE PRINCIPLES OF TAYLORISM VALID?

The Ambiguous Results of Scientific Management
Richard Edwards

. . . Frederick Winslow Taylor, founder and chief propagandist of the movement, diagnosed the problem [of strengthening management control of the speed of production] as essentially one of "soldiering"—that is, of workers habitually choosing to produce at less than their maximum possible rate. Taylor and the "efficiency experts" who followed him believed that, through a careful study of individual jobs and judicious selection of incentives or bonus pay, employers could structure the workplace so that soldiering (or soldiering workers) would be eliminated. Their efforts, variously known as "Taylorism" or "scientific management," promised to resolve the crisis of control through scientific study.[19]

It has become fashionable to interpret scientific management as an enormous breakthrough in the history of work relations. Thus it is said that "Taylorism dominates the world of production" and that "work itself is organized according to Taylorian principles."[20] But this view overestimates scientific

management's impact. For one thing, not all those elements of which Taylor wrote were new with the Taylor system. The thrust toward standardization of tools and tasks, the fragmentation of jobs, and the increased use of semiskilled or unskilled workers— all of which the Taylorites stressed—were tendencies that had long been evident in American development. A second error has been the tendency to confuse Taylorism as a management theory (and it did cause considerable stir among the professionals who advised businesses) with Taylorism in practice, where its impact was considerably more limited. Finally, the Taylor movement has been confused with the broader reorientation of management that occurred during the transition period; many parts of this reorientation, however, had little or nothing to do with scientific management per se.[21]

Closer analysis suggests that scientific management played a more circumscribed, though still important, role. Its significance was that it showed the possibilities of applying corporate resources to the control problem in a systematic way. Although widely debated among professional management theorists, it was not introduced into industry on any broad scale, and by the First World War its potential as a workplace panacea had been destroyed by the intense labor opposition that it generated. Like welfare capitalism, it failed to solve the crisis of control in

___

From *Contested Terrain: The Transformation of the Workplace in the Twentieth Century* by Richard Edwards (pp. 97–104). Copyright © 1979 by Basic Books, Inc., Publishers. Reprinted by permission of the publisher.

[19]Histories of the scientific management movement, with their almost mandatory recounting of Taylor's famous "Schmidt" experiment, are common and have recently undergone yet another revival. See for example Lyndall Urwick and E.F.L. Brech (1945, 1946, 1948), Milton Nadworny (1955), Hugh Aitken (1960), and Harry Braverman (1974).

[20]Harry Braverman (1974), p. 87. Peter Drucker (1954, p. 280) makes virtually the same statement, completing the left-to-right consensus.

[21]Harry Braverman (1974, p. 89), citing Lyndall Urwick and E.F.L. Brech (1945), acknowledges that "Taylor was the culmination of a pre-existing trend," though he still credits Taylor with the innovation. David Brody (1968, p. 152) attributes welfarism to Taylor's inspiration, though there is little evidence for this other than Taylor's own claims.

the firm. Yet, also like that other movement but perhaps more directly, scientific management contributed experience and ideas to corporate capitalists that eventually led them to modern forms of control.

Scientific management presented both an analysis of work relations and a new philosophy of the workplace—that is, it made both a material and an ideological assertion. In its analysis of work, Taylorism asserted that the managers' inability to control soldiering resulted from their inadequate knowledge of the actual techniques of production. Most of the specific expertise—for example, knowledge of how quickly production tasks could be done—resided in the workers and to some extent in the foremen, many of whom had come up through the ranks. But higher management had no access to it. Taylor wrote that he

> realized that the greatest obstacle to harmonious cooperation between the workmen and the management [Taylor's euphemism for greater management control] lay in the ignorance of the management as to what really constitutes a proper day's work for a workman.[22]

How could management bargain for a "fair day's work" if it didn't even know how much could be done during the workday? Thus, for management to control production, employers had to dispossess workers of their special knowledge and gain for themselves mastery of specific production expertise.

Taylor's analysis of work grew directly out of employers' experiences with piece-rates. Piece-rates always carried the allure of payment for actual labor done (rather than for labor power), thus promising an automatic solution to the problem of translating labor power into labor. Two difficulties invariably intervened to spoil this solution. First, when workers used their employer's machinery, capitalists had as much stake in seeing that the machinery worked hard as in inducing workers to speed up. Paying workers only according to their self-established pace (as piece-work attempted to do) became unattractive if it meant that the machinery ran at less than full speed; in this case the piece-rate would cut down on the labor cost, but it would not necessarily bring profits. Thus, capitalists could never be in-

different to the worker's pace, even if the piece-rate meant that the employer was only paying for work done.

The second, more serious difficulty was that piece-rates always contained an incentive for workers to deceive employers and restrict output. Since the pay structure was necessarily anchored on some expectation of how quickly a job could be done, the system clearly led workers to make jobs appear to take as long as possible. On the other hand, if all or most workers responded to the piece-rates with enough production to raise their wages substantially, then the expected job completion time would fall, and the piece-rate would be adjusted accordingly. To prevent this, workers tended to restrict output.

As long as management depended on its workers for information about how fast the job could be done—that is, as long as workers had a monopoly on that "special knowledge"—there was no way to make the piece-rate method deliver its promise. Scientific management directed its material assertion at exactly this issue and offered "scientific study of work" as a new independent source of special knowledge.

The Taylorites' ideological assertion was that both workers and employers would benefit from increased production. Thus both had a stake in seeing that "science" and "scientific methods" were used to determine the one best way that each task should be done. As Taylor himself put it, "What constitutes a fair day's work will be a question for scientific investigation, instead of a subject to be bargained and haggled over."[23] Since the real objective was to wrest from workers control over special knowledge, and since "scientific investigation" was likely to be employed (literally) by management, the results of such a procedure could hardly be in doubt. Yet the effect of this maneuver should not be minimized: the objectivity of science was being appropriated to bolster management prerogative.

Thus science was to produce a new body of special knowledge, and this new learning would be lodged in management's hands. The methods by which this change was to be effected involved all three elements of control systems, but by far the most revolutionary concerned the first, the direction of work tasks.

---

[22]F.W. Taylor (1911), p. 53.

[23]Ibid., pp. 142–143.

Taylor and his followers understood that unless management knew in detail how production occurred, precise direction of work tasks was impossible. To achieve an understanding of production, the Taylorites proposed time and (later) motion studies and, more generally, systematic study of the production flow. "Scientific analysis" produced a vast body of task standards, best or quickest techniques, and the like, and the stopwatch became the most important tool in the efficiency engineer's kit. The data were so vast, in fact, that individual managers could not be expected to master them, so Taylor recommended establishing a company planning department that could systematize and thereby effectively use such information. Finally, the newly defined tasks needed to be communicated to the workers who were to carry them out, and this involved specifying to workers exactly what they were expected to accomplish each day. Taylor recommended that each worker receive an instruction card at the beginning of each workday, giving explicit written form to this communication process. In other words, direction of work tasks was to emerge from orderly processes of information discovery, organization, and communication.

Scientific management also proposed revision of the second control system element, the evaluation of work done. In prior systems, of course, the foreman himself had monitored performance in a more or less capricious way. Under the new system, piece-rates constituted the chief form of pay, so at one level judging each worker's performance was to be merely a matter of measuring output. Yet Taylor realized that this was much too crude a measure of performance and proposed "functional foremanship" instead. The traditional foreman's job was to be fragmented into eight parts or functions and a separate individual assigned to undertake each part. Three of the new foremen were kept busy directing the work and one meted out punishment, but the remaining four were all put to the task of performance evaluation: checking to see that machines were driven at proper speeds, inspecting the quality of work, ensuring that workers took proper machine maintenance measures, and recording the times and costs of work. The point was to systematize the evaluation process.

Finally, the matter of reward and punishment —the third control element—was entrusted to what was termed the "differential rate piece-work" sys-

tem. As with all the piece-rate methods that had been so fervently promoted during these years, Taylor's system attempted to avoid the pitfalls of deliberate deception and output restriction. Taylor's idea was to split the rate structure, with a considerably higher piece-rate—30 to 100 percent higher, as Taylor so frequently repeated—applying to workers who met the established time standards for the task. (Since the higher piece-rate typically required a 200 or 300 percent increase in output, employers were pleased to make this offer.) Work study was intended to eliminate the possibilities for deception by providing a new source of special knowledge, so the piece-rate could be unambiguously aimed at inducing higher production.

Scientific management thus presented an ambitious agenda. It proposed a thorough-going change in all three elements of control, designed to eliminate soldiering. More broadly, it claimed to eliminate the conflict between workers and employers, rendering labor unions—with their "bargaining and haggling"—unnecessary. Taylor often boasted that "during the thirty years that we have been engaged in introducing scientific management there has not been a single strike."[24] Here, clearly, was a promising solution to the control crisis in the firm.

Yet if we look at Taylorism as a management practice rather than as an idea, the promise was never fulfilled. For one thing the system was complicated, and employers often grew impatient long before the final elements were ready to be installed. At the American Locomotive Company, for instance, one of Taylor's early converts, David Van Alstyne, began introducing elements of the efficiency system. But higher management, which saw the program as experimental, was not ready to undertake the scale of changes required for full implementation. Under pressure to obtain results, Van Alstyne began taking shortcuts, and the full system was never installed. This experience repeated the past—at Bethlelem, Taylor himself had been fired before he was able to complete the job—and foretold future difficulties.[25]

More significantly, Taylorism failed to solve the crisis of control because most big corporations failed

[24]Ibid., p. 135; see also Taylor (1912), p. 193.

[25]Milton Nadworny (1955), pp. 27–28 and p. 11. See also David Nelson and Stuart Campbell (1972, p. 13) on the impatience and eventual alienation of the Bancroft management.

even to give it a try. The extent and incidence of scientific management has always been something of a mystery, but the available evidence suggests that Taylorism was largely confined to smaller, usually nonunionized enterprises.[26] In any event, the new industrial giants—U.S. Steel, International Harvester, and the others—showed little interest in it. Of the twenty-five "representative" firms using scientific management that Robert Hoxie investigated in 1915, only two (Westinghouse and Jones & Laughlin) ranked among the largest industrial firms.[27] Other big firms experimented with bonus systems and time and motion studies, but none appeared willing to undertake large-scale reorganization along Taylorian lines.

One reason for the big firms' coolness may have been that Taylorism seemed to express a philosophy that ran counter to the image so carefully contrived in the other labor programs of the big firms. Despite Taylor's rhetoric of labor-management cooperation, workers and bosses alike understood that stopwatch methods constituted a real challenge to the workers. The Taylor system, when stripped of its "scientific" veil, attempted to remove the decisions over work pace and sequence from the bargaining between foremen and workers—bargaining in which workers participated and exercised some power. In order to impose the new Taylorized standards, management had to break the workers' power to resist. On the other hand, welfare capitalism (and later the "plans of representation") attempted to convince workers that harmony, not conflict, would bring rewards to workers.

One place where the tension between Taylorism and welfarism was clearly visible was the textile firm of Joseph Bancroft and Sons of Wilmington.[28] An entrepreneurial firm, Bancroft had grown slowly through the second half of the nineteenth century, but in the 1890s the firm's labor force nearly tripled, as merger and internal growth rapidly extended its scale. The old paternalistic relations of entrepreneurial control no longer held the expanded work-

force in sufficiently tight harness; a "crisis of control" loomed, and a new system was required.

The Bancroft management chose not one but two new approaches: Elizabeth Briscoe was hired in 1902 to introduce welfare work, and Taylor's disciple H. L. Gantt was retained in 1908 to begin reorganizing production along scientific lines. The first effort sought to rebuild a sense of personal bonds between employer and workers. The second effort attempted simply to introduce more efficient methods of production. Since welfare work did not directly affect the production flow—it focused on workers' housing, plant safety and sanitation, medical services, and so on—whereas Taylorism was aimed only at the work process itself, Bancroft managers saw no conflict between these two approaches.

Yet the company's experience demonstrated that Taylorism and welfarism coexisted uneasily if at all. As Gantt began reorganizing production, speeding up work, and dismissing recalcitrant (or "non-first-class") employees, the workers became resentful. Directly undercutting the intent of the welfare programs, the efficiency methods provoked conflict between management and workers. The road jointly taken seemed to diverge: the company was forced to choose between the strong-arm tactics needed to install Taylorism and the positive incentives embodied in welfarism. (In this case, welfarism won and Gantt was dismissed, although soon after, Briscoe was demoted as well.)

The main failure of Taylorism, however, was that it failed to solve the crisis of control in the firm because workers simply fought it to a standstill. Taylor's claim that scientifically managed shops had never suffered a strike was contradicted by the record. At American Locomotive, for example, Van Alstyne's attempt to introduce Taylorism had been met with serious union opposition. The unionized boilermakers secured an agreement that exempted them from the new system, and unorganized machinists were so provoked that they established an International Association of Machinists local and promptly went out on strike. Later, when the company went back on its agreement with the boilermakers, they struck and stayed out for three weeks. The strike was settled only by the removal of Van Alstyne and his system. Similarly, as we have seen, the new arrangements at Bancroft and Sons were

[26]No comprehensive list of applications of scientific management is available.

[27]Compare Robert Hoxie's (1915, pp. 3–4) list with the firms listed in Richard Edwards (1975a, Appendix Table V).

[28]See Daniel Nelson and Stuart Campbell (1972).

abandoned in the face of rising worker frustration and resistance, manifested in the higher turnover and growing in-plant conflict.[29]

The decisive battle came at the government's Watertown (Mass.) Arsenal. The War Department used the arsenal both to produce military materiel and to provide an independent check on the costs of similar equipment procured from private producers. But it was old, its machinery was obsolete, and its manufacturing costs were too high to be useful for either competition or comparison. So in 1909 the Army called in efficiency experts to improve the situation. The installation of scientific management proceeded smoothly for two years, during which time a planning department was established, engineering studies completed, inventory control improved, and so on.[30]

When the Taylorites moved into the shops to introduce the bonus-pay plan and to begin stopwatch timing of particular jobs, however, conflict immediately flared. The skilled molders, whose jobs were chosen as the first to be timed, walked out. Their strike immediately galvanized the International Association of Machinists into renewed opposition to Taylorism—the machine shops were, after all, the principal locus of applications of Taylorism—and the government ownership of the arsenal provided an opening. The Watertown strike was settled by an agreement for a public investigation, and in fact several actions followed: a Congressional inquiry, mobilization of AFL opposition to Taylorism, a serious academic evaluation of Taylorism in practice, and a legislative ban on the introduction of stopwatch and premium-pay methods into military enterprises.[31] Most importantly, the strike alerted all organized labor to oppose Taylorism.

The growing labor opposition to scientific management, especially after the highly publicized troubles at Watertown, ended the possibilities for a scientific management solution to the firm's crisis of control. It would be implemented in some cases—one optimistic contemporary estimate sug-gested that about 1 percent of all industrial workers labored under the system—and in certain firms it would be dominant. But labor, especially the highly organized machinists, had learned to be on the lookout for the appearance of the "time-and-motion man" on the factory floor. Their opposition disproved the claim that "science" could eliminate the worker's ability to soldier or, more accurately, that Taylor's system could build worker-boss harmony and could decisively turn the shop-floor battle in management's favor.[32]

Yet the scientific management movement was one of those failed (or only partially succesful) experiments from which much was learned. First, the chaff needed to be discarded: daily instruction cards, the silliness of extreme time and motion studies, functional foremanship, the differential-rate piecework plan all had to be abandoned or heavily modified. One important element that did endure was the aggressive attempt to gain management control over the special knowledge of production—what Harry Braverman has brilliantly described as the "separation of conception from execution."[33] Another element that survived was the notion that each worker's job should be carefully defined, including standards of "adequate" performance. The basic impulse to define jobs in terms of output rather than simply obedience to the foreman's orders would be picked up later by the structural control systems. Yet another lesson was the need to subject management itself to management control, specifically by breaking the power of foremen to act as absolute rulers of the shops. Functional foremanship would never catch on, but the transfer of hiring, disciplining, wage-setting, work directing, and other functions to personnel departments and planning or industrial design offices would take hold.

Undoubtedly the greatest lesson that capitalists learned from the efficiency engineers was that rational methods and large resources could be devoted to the management process and be made to pay handsome dividends. With their investments in welfare capitalism, employers sensed that they had obtained little return on their money. Scientific management had not really paid off either, but the

---

[29]Milton Nadworny (1955), p. 28. Daniel Nelson and Stuart Campbell (1972), pp. 12–13.

[30]Watertown account based on Hugh Aitken (1960).

[31]Hugh Aitken (1960), Chapter 4 and Milton Nadworny (1955), pp. 79–84.

[32]C.B. Thompson (1915). See the discussion by Bryan Palmer (1975).

[33]Harry Braverman (1974), Chapter 4.

prospects seemed much more promising. The difference was no doubt due to the fact that scientific management directly addressed the issue of power relations in the workplace, whereas welfarism seemed peripheral. If the Taylorites had not found quite the right mechanism, they were at least looking in the right place.

BIBLIOGRAPHY

AITKEN, HUGH. *Taylorism at Watertown Arsenal.* Cambridge, Mass.: Harvard University Press, 1960.

BRAVERMAN, HARRY. *Labor and Monopoly Capital.* New York: Monthly Review Press, 1974.

BRODY, DAVID. "The Rise and Decline of Welfare Capitalism." In *Change and Continuity in Twentieth-Century America: The 1920s,* edited by John Braeman et al. Columbus: Ohio State University Press, 1968.

DRUCKER, PETER. *The Practice of Management.* New York: Harper and Row, 1954.

EDWARDS, RICHARD C. "Stages in Corporate Stability and the Risks of Corporate Failure." *Journal of Economic History,* June, 1975. [1975a].

HOXIE, ROBERT F. *Scientific Management and Labor.* New York: D. Appleton and Company, 1915.

NADWORNY, MILTON. *Scientific Management and the Unions, 1900–1932.* Cambridge, Mass.: Harvard University Press, 1955.

NELSON, DANIEL, and CAMPBELL, STUART. "Taylorism Versus Welfare Work in American Industry: H.L. Gantt and the Bancrofts." *Business History Review,* Spring, 1972.

PALMER, BRYAN. "Class Conception and Conflict: The Threat for Efficiency, Managerial Views of Labor, and the Working Class Rebellion, 1903–1922." *Review of Radical Political Economics,* 1975.

TAYLOR, FREDERICK W. "The Principles of Scientific Management" in *Scientific Management.* New York: Harper and Row, 1947. [First published in 1911.]

———. "Testimony Before the Special House Committee," in *Scientific Management.* New York: Harper and Row, 1947. [First published in 1912.]

THOMPSON, C.B. "Scientific Management in Practice." *Quarterly Journal of Economics,* February 1915.

URWICK, LYNDALL, and Brech, E. F. L. *The Making of Scientific Management.* 3 vols. London: Management Publications Trust, 1945, 1946, 1948.

QUESTIONS FOR DISCUSSION

1. To what extent is management a science? Explain.
2. Was Taylor correct in his assessment that money is what the worker wants most?
3. In what kinds of social systems is Taylorism most likely to work? Why?
4. Is Taylorism exploitive of workers? Explain.
5. To what extent is Taylorism valid in an increasingly service economy?
6. Can Taylorism be effectively applied in the public sector? Explain.

SUGGESTED READINGS

COPLEY, FRANK BARKLEY, *Frederick W. Taylor: Father of Scientific Management.* New York: A. M. Kelley, 1969. 2 vols.

DEWAR, DONALD L., "Frederick W. Taylor—Was He All That Bad?," *Quality Circle Digest,* 3 (Feb. 1983), 60–69.

DRURY, HORACE BOOKWALTER, *Scientific Management: A History and Criticism.* New York: AMS Press, 1968.

GULICK, LUTHER, AND LYNDALL URWICK (eds.), *Papers on the Science of Administration.* New York: Institute for Public Administration, 1937.

HABER, SAMUEL, *Efficiency and Uplift: Scientific Management in the Progressive Era, 1890–1920.* Chicago, IL: Univ. of Chicago Press, 1964.

KAKAR, SUDHIR, *Frederick W. Taylor: A Study in Personality and Innovation.* Cambridge, MA: MIT Press, 1970.

KLAW, SPENCER, "Frederick Winslow Taylor: The Messiah of Time and Motion," *American Heritage,* 30 (Aug./Sep. 1979), 26–39.

MERKLE, JUDITH A., *Management and Ideology: The Legacy of the International Scientific Management Movement.* Berkeley: Univ. of California Press, 1980.

NELSON, DANIEL, *Frederick W. Taylor and the Rise of Scientific Management.* Madison: Univ. of Wisconsin Press, 1980.

TAYLOR, FREDERICK WINSLOW, *The Principles of Scientific Management.* New York: Norton, 1967.

14   YES   CAN JAPANESE MANAGEMENT TECHNIQUES BE APPLIED IN THE UNITED STATES?

Japanese Management Philosophy: Can It Be Exported?
Toyohiro Kono

INTRODUCTION

Many papers and books on Japanese style of management are appearing, as Japanese goods are penetrating into the world markets. Many of them state the traits on personnel management or environmental characteristics.

This paper tries to analyse the overall characteristics of Japanese management, with emphasis on strategic level of management practices. There are three characteristics of Japanese management style. (a) Japanese enterprises have traits as innovative organizations. (b) They have features as soft organizations. (c) They have characteristics as community organizations.

(A) INNOVATIVE ORGANIZATION

Organizations adapt themselves to change of environment by a number of models. Organizations may be classified as stagnant, reactive and innovative organizations. Ansoff classified organizations as stable, reactive, anticipatory and initiative.[1] Innovative organization may correspond to the latter two. Innovative organization is growth-oriented and introduces new products at an early stage, and changes strategy and structure frequently. In order to do this, goals are clearly stated and top managements are strong and aggressive.

Stagnant organization is not interested in growth. It is interested in safety, does not change its products, does not undergo any change of strategy and structure. Goals are not clearly shown, and top management is either very autocratic or very weak

(power is scattered).[1-6] (For definition see Ansoff et al., 1976; Rowe and Boise, 1973; H. Mintzberg, 1973; Glueck, 1976; Steiner and Miner, 1977; H. Nystrom, 1978.)

Japanese enterprises have many characteristics common to innovative organizations.

(1) Goals

Missions and Goals Are Clearly Stated. They may be called the philosophy of management. Many Japanese corporations have a clearly stated philosophy.

Table 1 is an example of Matsushita Electric Co. [Editor's note: omitted here.]

Missions and goals have a hierarchy. Missions are the statement of the role the company wants to play in the larger environment. 'To supply the consumer with electric home appliances at a cheap price like water' is a statement of a desired role of the company.

Goals are the highest value of the company, like growth and profit. They have direction (or item), level and timing such as long-term goals and short-term goals.

When missions and goals are clearly stated, they tend to motivate the employee, to increase the sense of identification with the organization. It then becomes easier to understand the meaning of their work, to understand the relationship between the jobs they perform and the society. If they are not

---

From Toyohiro Kono, "Japanese Management Philosophy: Can It Be Exported?" Reprinted with permission from *Long Range Planning*, 15 (June 1982), pp. 90–102. Copyright 1982, Pergamon Press, Ltd.

---

[1]Ansoff, Declerk and Hayes eds., *From Strategic Planning to Strategic Management* (1976).

[2]Rowe and Boise, *Organizational and Managerial Innovation* (1973).

[3]H. Mintzberg, Strategy-making in three modes, *California Management Review*, Winter (1973).

[4]Glueck, *Business Policy, Strategy Formulation and Managerial Action* (1976).

[5]Steiner and Miner, *Management Policy and Strategy* (1977).

[6]H. Nyström, *Creativity and Innovation* (1978).

clearly stated, employees may think that 'the company is company and we are we', and that the values of both are different. They may demand easier jobs with higher pay.

When long-range goals and short-range goals are clearly stated, they have the effect of making it easier to introduce innovation into the company, because the workers can understand the new direction of the company. They can orient themselves to the company's new direction. Without clearly stated goals, it is hard for the organization to change direction or the initiative of the employees and with their co-operation.

There are a number of publications in Japan on compiled business creeds, and there is enough evidence to show that many Japanese corporations have stated business philosophies. Many U.S. corporations have stated philosophies, but in the U.K., not so many corporations have company philosophies. It is impossible to find a business creed displayed on a plant site in the U.K. In my interviews with many British executives, they mentioned two reasons for this. One is that the creeds of companies are very similar from company to company, so it may not be very meaningful. Most of them simply state the responsibilities to the society, to the consumer, to the supplier and to the employees.

Another reason is that the values of the employees in the U.K. are more individualistic than the Japanese. Employees have less sense of involvement with the organization so it does not work if the philosophy is publicly stated. (Some successful British companies do have stated philosophy e.g. ICI, Marks & Spencer.)

Growth Oriented Goals and Long-range Goals. Japanese corporations have long-range views and growth is an important item of goals. Approximately 80 per cent of large Japanese corporations have long-range planning.[7,8] This is evidence of long-sightedness of Japanese corporations.

Table 2 shows what are the important items of goals in long-range planning, and we find that sales and growth are the most stressed. (In this survey U.K. responding companies have long-range planning, so they are much more growth oriented than the other U.K. companies.)

Why is it that Japanese companies are more long-range growth oriented? There are two reasons. One comes from the expectation of life-time employment. To keep the employee for a life-time, the company has to grow. To provide the employees with wage increases and frequent opportunities of promotion, the company has to grow. Another reason is that the pressure from the shareholder is not so strong in Japan and annual profit or quarterly profit is not important. The ratio of paid-in capital (including stock dividend) accounts for less than 10 per cent of total capital (including current debt).

Japanese corporations borrow most of their money from banks and the banks support the long-term growth of the company, because by so doing the banks can cultivate the market to lend the money. Most of the savings of a family goes to bank deposit accounts and the savings ratio is high. It is approximately 20 per cent, whereas in the U.K. it is about 10 per cent.

Welfare of the Employees Is Also Important as One of the Goals. In a depression, Japanese companies will decrease the dividend first to protect employment, but U.S. or U.K. companies will lay-off (or make redundant) the employee first in order to maintain the dividend. This shows the different way of thinking. In long-range planning goals, compensation, value added, labour productivity are stressed (Table 2 does not show the full range of the survey of long-range goals.) Labour productivity is the precedent of good treatment. (The personnel policies of Japanese corporations will be explained later.)

(2) Top Management and Board of Directors

Top Management. The separation of management from ownership is well advanced. As the size of the company grows, and as the successor of the founder has to pay large amounts of inheritance tax so the further separation proceeds. But this is not a unique characteristic of Japanese corporations. What is different in Japan is that there is a management committee at the top level. According to a recent survey, 86 per cent of large corporations have management committees.[7] A group decision-

---

[7]Kansai Productivity Centre, *Survey on Business Organization* (1976).

[8]Ministry of International Trade and Industry, *New Indices for Managerial Capability* (1978).

TABLE 2   Goals Stated in Long-range Planning (by mail questionnaire survey)

	U.K. 74 companies %	Japan 327 companies %
In what specific terms are the goals and policies of your long-range plans stated? (Please tick as many as necessary)		
Basic goals		
(1) Sales	51	88*
(2) Rate of growth (sales or profit)	59	64
(3) Profit		
(a) Amount of profit	53	87*
(b) Profit ratio to total capital (or total assets)	59	42*
(c) Profit ratio to equity capital	18	27
(d) Profit ratio to sales	37	61*
(e) Standard deviation of profit (or limit of profit in the worst case)	0	16*
(f) Earning per share	37	18*
(4) Market share	50	41
(5) Capital structure	41	32
(6) Dividend	30	43
(7) Share price	8	2
(8) Employee compensation	8	39*
(9) Quality level of products	32	13*
(10) Basic policy of growth	49	50
(11) Basic policy of stability	14	34*
(12) Basic policy on profit	47	51
(13) Basic policy on social responsibility	16	19
(14) Other, please describe below	7	—
(15) NA	1	—

Note: Mail questionnaire survey in Japan was conducted by Kono in 1979 and 327 companies were analysed. In the U.K., the survey was conducted jointly by Prof. Stopford of London Business School and by Kono in March 1981 and 74 private companies were analysed here.

*Indicates the level of significance is 10%.

making body at the top began to appear in the 1950s. The average number of members of these bodies is approximately 10. They meet once a week, making decisions as a group. The members are usually the chairman, president (managing director) and four to six executive directors. Each member has broad responsibility for corporate decisions covering several departments, receiving reports from these departments and giving advice to them. They are not identical to department heads. They are in charge of general management and strategic decisions.

In the United States, there is a growing tendency to have a group at the top, but the number of members is smaller than in the Japanese case. In the U.K., management committees are not frequently used, but rather the individual managing director or chairman makes the final decisions. If there is a group at the top, the number of members is usually three to five, and it is often an informal meeting.

Group decisions at the top tend to be innovative. There is some misconception that group decisions tend to be mediocre and slow, but a recent survey found otherwise. Group decisions can be innovative. The reasons are three.

Firstly, by group meetings, information is provided by more participants and uncertainty decreases. Where there is uncertainty, people do not like to make decisions. Secondly, there is more diffusion of responsibility. Thirdly, positive opinions tend to dominate negative opinions in group meetings. The high diffusion of management committees may be one of the causes of greater innovation in Japanese corporations.

Creativity is different from innovation. Innovation means the early adoption of a new idea, whether it comes from outside or not, and creativity means the new creation of the idea. I am not, however, saying that group decisions at all levels of Japanese corporations are always favourable to creativity in organizations. This has to be studied further.

Members of the Top Management. Most of the members of Japanese corporations are university graduates and approximately 45 per cent of them are engineering or natural science graduates. (Kono survey on 102 large manufacturing corporations, unpublished.) This percentage is higher in corporations where the products are more technology oriented (for example, 26 technology related companies have 50.6 per cent natural science graduates).

Where there are more university graduates, the decision at the top tends to be more analytical. Where there are more natural science graduates the decision tends to be more aggressive and innovative, because they have a better understanding of new technological development, and they like to do new things. In the U.K., less than 40 per cent of top management are university graduates and a much smaller percentage are science graduates. (About university graduates, see Channon, 1973.)[9] If accountants or financially oriented management are in power, the decision may be more conservative. (The above analysis is based on the directors of Japanese corporations, i.e. the members of the board of directors. In Japan, there are very few outside directors, so the analysis of directors can be the analysis of top management.)

Board of Directors. The board of directors in Japanese corporations plays a small role. It makes decisions on only legally required matters. If the board consists of many outside directors, as is the case with U.K. and U.S. corporations, and if they play a more important role in final decisions, then the strategy must be more conservative, because

outside directors are not interested in risky decisions. They tend to put more emphasis on short-term profit.

(3) Strategic Decisions

Sensitivity to Opportunities. Innovative organizations are sensitive to change of environment, the scope of research is wider, outside oriented and future oriented. The research is flexible and it does not follow a fixed pattern. The subjects of research need not be very creative, but imitative, and research can lead to innovation, if it is done aggressively at an early stage.

Japanese managements are sensitive to new technology and to new ideas, but they do not necessarily create the original idea. They are quick to introduce foreign ideas and to implement them by conducting development research. For example, Sony produced the small portable transistor radio (1955), television using transistor (1959), video tape recorder (1963), Trinitron colour television tube (one gun three beams) (1968) for the first time in the world, but the original key technology came from the U.S. There is no doubt that Sony is an innovative and successful company. It is introducing a number of new products every year and one division is introducing 100 new products (including improvement) every year.

Scope of research and aggressiveness can be partly measured by R & D activity. Matsushita Electric spends 4 per cent on sales for research (£120m) and it has 10 laboratories with 4000 staff. It has 31,000 patents. Toyota spends 3 per cent on sales for research (£180m), it has two centralized technical centres and one laboratory with 2500 staff.

Taking Japanese industry as a whole, R & D expenditures over sale are 1.48 per cent (electrical appliances, 3.61 per cent), and R & D staff (excluding assistants) over total number of employees account for 3.01 per cent (manufacturing, in case of electrical appliances 5.85 per cent). (White Paper on Science, 1978, by Ministry of Prime Minister.)

Aggressiveness of research can be measured by the performance. Percentage of new products on sale is one of the measurements. Japanese companies are eager to introduce new products. The extent of new products introduced by Matsushita and Toyota is very high and we can confirm this by having a look at the products sold.

---

[9]D. F. Channon, *The Strategy and Structure of British Enterprise* (1973).

Sensitivity to new opportunity is not restricted to technology and Japanese managers are very sensitive to new theories of management.

Theories of organization, methods of planning, methods of production control and methods of quality control were eagerly studied, and experiences were exchanged between companies. At the present, the number of publications on management is quite large, and the study of management is extensive.

Most of the characteristics of Japanese management are not unique, but their implementation of theory goes further than other countries. Japanese businesses grow fast. Many new systems had to be constructed, so it was possible to introduce many new methods and to implement them.

This means that many characteristics of Japanese management do not originate in the uniqueness of their culture, but rather in the positive introduction of new theory and rational decision on continuous improvement.

Interactive Approach.   There is a misconception that innovative organizations should have decentralized decision making structures. How can we expect that risky innovative decisions can be done by a bottom-upwards approach.

There is also a misconception that the decision making in Japanese corporations is bottom-upwards. This is not the case with strategic decisions. Top management takes aggressive action in strategic decisions. Strategic decisions involve a large risk, so it is the area where top management should make decisions.

According to my observation, diversified companies in the U.K. and in the U.S., tend to make strategic decisions at lower levels. For example, in GEC there are only 100 personnel in the head office, and most of the strategic decisions are done by the group or at division level.

Generally speaking, when strategic decisions are done at lower levels, they tend to be conservative and incremental to avoid risk, and it is almost impossible that they should decide to discontinue their own operations. Growth-share matrix models try to correct this tendency and aim at centralization of strategic decisions.

Japanese corporations, have very strong head office staff, and decisions are centralized. Matsushita Electric is a diversified company with 40 product divisions, but still there are thousands of people in the head office and strategic decisions are much more centralized than in similar companies in the U.K. and in the U.S.

With the help of strong staff in the head office, top management interchange information and ideas with the staff, and thus decisions are made by an interactive process, and generally speaking, this process is rather of a top-down process.

In the case of Matsushita Electric, key strategic decisions such as product line policy, foreign investment for multi-national management, drop-out of unprofitable products, change of organization structure are decided by top management with the strong leadership of the founder.

The interactive approach in strategic decisions of Japanese corporations is shown partly by a survey of the planning process of long-range planning. In the case of Japanese corporations, corporate planning departments play an important role in preparing, and management committees in reviewing, the final decision.

Top-down and interactive processes result in an aggressive and analytical process of decisions.

High Diffusion of Long-range Planning. As was stated already, formal long-range planning has a very high diffusion among large Japanese corporations. There are a number of surveys, and these surveys show that more than 80 per cent of large Japanese corporations have formal long-range planning.[7,8] This high diffusion comes from several reasons: (a) top management is future-oriented, (b) in a high growth economy, it is necessary to forecast the long-term future, (c) long-range national economic plans have been published many times since 1956, which stimulated corporate planning and laid out the bases for long-range planning.

(4) Strategies

Competition Orientation.   Competition orientation means two things. Firstly, with a new product, there are many followers. Companies are willing to enter the area if it is a hopeful product, and new entry is done at an early stage of the life cycle. This results in many manufacturers in the same business. This is an 'I will do if others do' attitude, which is different from 'I will not do if others do' attitude. Secondly, it means the will to increase the share of the market at the expense of others, and to try to drive the competitor out of the market by competition, not by acquisition. This results in a frequent change of share of the market.

Competition between the Japanese corporations is very severe. When I interviewed the corporate planner of Toyota, I asked him the most important reasons for the success of the company, the planner answered immediately that 'we had to survive the domestic competition even when there was a barrier to importing cars.' In every new area of hopeful products, there are many new entries and it is quite usual that 10 companies should produce similar products. For example, even now in the passenger car business where approximately 10 million cars per year are produced, there are six companies; Toyota, Nissan, Toyo, Honda, Mitsubishi and Daihatsu. The two largest have a 70 per cent share, but they are losing that share of the market. In colour television, where 9 million sets are produced, there are seven companies, Matsushita, Hitachi, Sony, Sanyo, Mitsubishi, Sharp and JVC. Even in the computer business, there are six companies.

They are competing with each other in the home market and in the foreign market. Some are losing and others are gaining. There are few mergers and acquisitions of companies, so losing out is fatal to the company.

The number of failures including bankruptcies is 16,000 cases in Japan (1978).

Employees of Japanese companies are willing to identify themselves with the company, cohesiveness is very high, and, as a result, competitive attitudes towards other companies which produce similar products is strong. Under the life-time employment system, the companies have to grow and this tends to intensify the competition.[10]

Competition was an important reason for rationalization of operation, for new capital investment, for introduction of new products.

Vertical Grouping.   There is a long-term co-operative relation between the final products manufacturer and parts manufacturers. It is well known in the U.K. that the relations between Marks and Spencer Ltd. and the suppliers to that company are co-operative on a long-term basis. This kind of long-term relationship is very popular in Japan.

Toyota organizes 'Kyoho-kai' which has 172 companies. These parts manufacturers supply parts

only to Toyota. In return, they receive supports, e.g. training on quality control and production control, and general management. They receive support on financing. The buying manufacturers will inspect the method of quality control, but will not inspect the parts. Parts manufacturers of the Toyota group will seldom sell their parts to Nissan or other car manufacturers.

By having such a long-term co-operative relationship, the parts manufacturers can plan the production on a mass production basis and improve the quality with lower prices.

These parts manufacturers are independent as a legal entity, are not controlled either by stock ownership or by directors, excepting some key companies, but they enter long-term contract relationships with the manufacturers.

Japanese manufacturers produce parts internally to a lesser extent. GEC used to produce the cabinets for televisions, but Japanese TV manufacturers do not. BL Cars Ltd. produce transmission and steel wheels, but Japanese car manufacturers do not—instead they buy from outside. In this sense, the extent of vertical grouping is more widespread. Sales channels are encouraged to be exclusive. At least, in the case of consumer durable goods the manufacturers try to build an exclusive sales channel. Matsushita has 120 exclusive wholesalers, and 25,000 'national shops' whose sales account for 80 per cent of total sales and 25,000 'national stores' whose Matsushita sales account for 50 per cent. Matsushita provides a number of helps including special discounts to these shops and stores. Exclusive distribution policy is now under challenge from big stores which exhibit many brands, so it may change in the future.

Grouping is the result of the group orientation of Japanese people. Japanese tend to, and try to have stable relationships. Competition is severe, and to meet the competition it is advantageous to form a coalition with the organizations in the form of a complementary relationship.

More Use of Internal Growth, Less Use of Acquisition.   Japanese companies seldom acquire other companies for diversification, they would rather use internal development, or joint venture by contract. This is easily evidenced by looking at the history of large corporations, or by looking at the statistics.

---

[10]C. Nakane, *Human Relations in Vertical Society* (1966).

The growth of Toyota and Matsushita Electric was done by internal development with few acquisitions. If this strategy is compared with the strategy of U.S. companies and U.K. companies, there is a sharp contrast. When we read Moody's manual, we find that the history of the company is the history of acquisitions.

Growth by acquisition tends to have several problems. Diversification without synergy may be undergone by easy entry using acquisition with the results of failure.

Weak companies which should be driven out of the market might be kept alive by acquisition and the result is a wasting of resources.

Less use of acquisition, and more use of internal development tends to pay more careful attention to the effects of synergy, and results in the concentration of the company strength. It also results in severe competition and in the application of "the fittest will survive" principle.

There was a technology gap between Japan and the U.S. and European countries. It was more profitable to buy the patents than to acquire other companies in the home market.

More important reasons are sociological ones. Even in a low technology industry, acquisitions were not used. They were considered to be shameful behaviour. The Japanese are group oriented and members of the company have a deep identification with their company, and they are hard to integrate with the members of other companies. Wages and promotions are determined by length of service to a great extent, so wages of the same profession are not the same. The labour unions are organized on a company-wide basis, so that unions tend to be against acquisition. The companies guarantee lifetime employment and it is not easy to decrease the number of employees after acquisition. These are important reasons for less use of acquisition.

(B) SOFT ORGANIZATION (OR ORGANISMIC ORGANIZATION)

Burns and Stalker classified the organizations into organismic and mechanistic.[11] Japanese corporations have many characteristics as an organismic (or soft) organization.

---

[11]Burns and Stalker, *The Management of Innovations* (1961).

(1) Jobs Are Ambiguous

Japanese organizations are comparable to the natural stone walls which are seen at the many Japanese castles. The shapes of stones are different from one to another, but they are combined so as to complement each other. Western organizations are comparable to brick walls, which are composed of standardized square bricks.

In Japanese organizations, jobs are ambiguous and they have several characteristics. (a) Jobs are roughly defined, not well defined, and employees are required to do any related jobs, (b) job contents change all the time, (c) employees are expected to present ideas to improve the jobs, (d) rules are less and ignored sometimes.

The opposite model, or bureaucratic models, are as follows. (a) Jobs are clearly defined by contract, (b) change of job is a serious matter, especially when the wage changes and when the membership of the union has to change, (c) it is not necessary to do work other than specified jobs, (d) there are many rules.

It is true that jobs are less defined and less divided in the U.K. than in the U.S., but at the plant site, employees on different jobs wear different colour uniforms. They usually belong to different unions. Operators cannot touch the machines.

The Japanese managers in the U.K. and in the U.S. complain that people there perform only the specified jobs, without willingness to do any related jobs.

In Japanese organizations, sometimes job names are not clear, and wages are paid by status, by performance and by length of service. In this situation employees will perform other duties if required.

There is no problem of job demarcation and there is only one company-wide union.

In the office, people work in a large room. They work as a team. Even the head of department is located in the corner of the large room. This system is quite different from the U.K. or U.S. office layout where each staff member has an individual room and perhaps has a secretary.

Job flexibility is closely connected with job classification. Table 3 is the job classification and grading system of Matsushita Electric. [Editor's note: omitted here.]

In this system, operational jobs on the plant site and administrative jobs are more graded by job content, but in other areas, people are graded by their own capability without any relation to the job they perform. Under this system, jobs need not be well defined.

The reasons for this ambiguity spring from several sources. (a) Wages are related to the job to a lesser extent; they are also related to capability and length of service, (b) a union is organized on company basis, (c) the sense of involvement of the employee is very high.

The effects of this system are to make it easy to change jobs and easy to introduce new technology. This system tends to increase the productivity of labour by mutual help.

(2) Group Decision and Participation

Group decision making and participation are popular. Meetings within the section and meetings of those who have responsibilities throughout the sections are held frequently. This decision style is different from the system where the responsibility of each person is clear and each person does his job in his room with the help of a secretary.

This decision style has many similarities with the decision making style of system IV by R. Likert.[12]

On the plant site, participation is limited, but group meetings are frequently held and each employee is encouraged to present the idea. In the office, people work in a large room, and group decisions are more popular.

A suggestion system is another means of participation, and in many cases each employee might present more than 10 suggestions a year. Matsushita Electric has to deal with 460,000 suggestions a year. In the U.K., 10 suggestions a month in a whole plant is about the average. Japanese workers are willing to present their ideas.

The reason for group decision or participative decision making may be as follows. People have equal capability and should be allowed to participate, and people are willing to participate because of a high sense of involvement.

The effects of these Japanese style group de-

cisions can be stated as follows. (a) Decisions tend to be slow but implementation is quick because everybody concerned knows the issue well. (b) Decisions are better and errors are less because a lot of information and ideas are collected. (c) Morale is high because of participation.

(3) Better Communication, Horizontally and Vertically

Communication from individual to individual tends to be better. This is rather hard to prove, but many Japanese managers of subsidiary companies in foreign countries comment that foreigners do not communicate well with each other.

In the U.K. and the U.S. written memos are frequently used, but in Japan oral communication is more often used. In the relations between individuals, Japanese will communicate better with colleagues and seniors will teach their subordinates well. 'NEMAWASHI' (log rolling) is required before the group decisions. Under the length of service system, people are not competitive with each other, so it is easier to have a good communication system. Under the same system, there is less fear of being out-promoted by a subordinate.

On the plant site, everybody wears the same uniform from plant manager to operator so it is easy for the managers to walk through the plant and to talk with everybody on the site.

In the U.K. office workers never wear uniform, they are provided with a separate lunch room from that of blue collar workers, and in this setting communication tends to be poor.

The above features are similar to the concept of organismic organization by Burns and Stalker.[11] But there are some differences. In the Japanese style, strategic decisions are taken by top-down or interactive approach, because strategic information is held by top level. Authority is not distributed equally in this respect.

Knowledge of the organization itself is emphasized rather than knowledge of specific professional skills. It is rare to find a professional occupation where knowledge is transferable from company to company. Unlike the original concept of organismic organization, people are not loyal to the occupation, but rather to the organization.

---

[12]R. Likert, *The Human Organization* (1968).

(C) COMMUNITY ORGANIZATION (*GEMEINSCHAFT*)

Tönnies founded the concept of *Gemeinschaft* (community organization) and *Gesselschaft* (association).[13] *Gemeinschaft* is like a family or a church where members are combined by mutual love. Getting together itself is a source of joy. People love each other, share the good luck and bad luck as well and help each other, trust each other and understand each other.

Gesselschaft is like a pure profit making economic organization. If there is no reward, people will not work. There is no spiritual unity. People are combined by contract, but they are apart, and in a state of tension. They work by division of labour, within the strict limits of the job, and they become one of the atoms of the organization.

Japanese organization is somewhat similar to *Gemeinschaft*, because the company respects the welfare of employees and gives more equal treatment on a length of service system, and in turn the employees devote themselves to the organization willingly.

(1) Life-time Employment

Once a person enters the organization, he will devote himself for his life-time, and will stay until 55 or 60 years old. He will not move around from organization to organization. The organization will take care of the employee for his life-time, and will not lightly discontinue the employment. Because of life-time employment, recruiting is usually done from among new graduates from high schools and universities. It is seldom done by advertisement. For the employee, leaving or discharge is a serious damage to his career. There are several misconceptions on life-time employment. It is not a contract. It is a way of thinking on both sides—by the employer and by the employee.

Women employees do not stay for their life-time. They leave the company when they get married. Married women will devote themselves to the family. This is another sort of organization orientation. In the case of small sized companies, mobility is higher than larger companies. The life-time employment system originates from the traditional way of thought by Japanese people that devotion to an organization is a value. But this system was reinforced after the war, because it has merits on both sides.

Closely related with this system is the length of service system which is analysed later. In the life-time employment system, a strict merit system disturbs the order, so length of service with loose merit rating is more appropriate. On the other hand, under the length of service system, it is disadvantageous to change the organization.

The merits of stable employment are many. It is possible to spend a lot of money and time on employee training. This benefits both the organization and employee. There is little fear of losing employees who are well trained and have accumulated knowledge of the operation. The organization can this way obtain a good accumulation of knowledge. It is possible to introduce technological innovation, because employment is assured and there is less resistance to change.

When innovation necessitates a change of job employees are transferred within the company from one job to another, but they are not made redundant. To provide the employee with the job, the company has to introduce innovation in order to grow and has to survive the competition. The company is more concerned with the long-term growth. The company has to establish a long-range personnel plan to increase the productivity of labour. It can not decrease the number of employees temporarily; it has to increase productivity on a planned basis, and this will reduce conflict. Where the company can reduce employees easily, rationalization will not have been planned seriously.

The life-time employment system does not mean that the number of employees cannot be reduced. There are a number of methods to cope with the decreased demand for man-hours. Overtime is decreased first. Suspension of new recruits, early retirement with an increased rate of retirement allowance (flexible retirement system), temporary 'going back to country home' with pay, are frequently used. Voluntary retirement is solicited from aged people. The last resort is to decrease the number in employment. In this case older people will be selected first and younger people will be kept.

---

[13]R. Dore, *British Factory–Japanese Factory* (1973).

(2) Frequent Promotion and Frequent Increase of Wage by Length of Service and by Merit

In many cases there are two ladders of promotion, one is the hierarchy of job gradings, another one is the hierarchy of status. In the case of Matsushita Electric, there is only one grading for operational jobs, but for other fields of jobs there are two ladders (Table 3). [Editor's note: omitted here.]

Even for operational jobs, when the skill of one person improves, then he is promoted to a higher grade while he is doing the same job. This kind of flexibility changes job grading to status grading. For clerical and technical jobs, each person is evaluated on the basis of job content and capabilities, and ranked on a grade. An employee can be promoted even when he is performing the same job.

For higher levels, there are three ladders, the administrative job grade, the qualification status grade and professional status grade. Everyone is ranked in a qualification status grade, as is explained in Table 3. [Editor's note: omitted here.]

The general practice of many corporations is that promotion on the status grading is done by taking into consideration the performance and the capability and the length of service. At the lower level an open test is requested in addition to subjective judgment by the superior.

Subjective judgment is used to a great extent to decide promotion on both ladders. The trade unions do not like subjective judgment but management believes that as there is maybe a risk on subjectivity of merit rating, it is better to increase the opportunity of promotion and wage increase.

The wage is related to the job and status. A person may be promoted on status grading while he is doing the same job. If there is no vacancy of higher jobs, his status grading may be higher than his job grading. Wages are related to status if the status is higher than the job rating. There is a difference in speed of promotion, but the length of service plays an important role, and therefore there is not a great difference between the employees. The wage is related to status or the job grade, so that promotion on status is accompanied by financial rewards.

Wages in the same job grade or status grade have a wide rate range. Progression on the rate range is done by merit rating and by length of service. Every year the wages are increased to some extent, and, depending upon the performance there is only a small amount of difference among the employees.

Wage scales are drawn up differently according to the grade of jobs and status. The higher the grade, the higher the standard line of wage by length of service (or age), so promotion results in higher wages.

What are the reasons for this unique system? This system was largely developed after the war. Job grading comes from the import of job evaluation and job classification systems. But outright application of imported systems resulted in failure and they had to be modified to meet the special culture of Japanese organizations.

The status system is a unique system, and is largely based on mutual respect. Promotion by length of service is related with the life-time employment where promotion is necessary because people do not move from one organization to another.

The wage increase system by length of service was useful to adjust the wage to the cost of living when wages were very low immediately after the war. Before the war, skilled workers were more mobile, wages were largely determined by job content and wage differentials between blue collar workers and clerical or administrative staff were much larger.

There are many merits of this system. There are frequent opportunities for promotion. Everybody can be promoted eventually to some grade, usually up to fourth or fifth grade from the bottom and this gives people the hope of advancement.

There is a slight difference of speed of promotion among employees and this gives a strong incentive for productivity and creativity. The same effects can be found in wage increases by length of service, with a slight difference of amount of increase for merit.

Some problems have arisen recently with this system. As the average age of employees increases, and as the retirement age is extended from 55 to 60 years old, the wage cost increases under the length of service system. The result has been to decrease the amount of wage increase by length of service, and put more emphasis on merit rating.

(3) Training

Training within the company is very much emphasized, and it pays under the life-time employment system. Matsushita Electric has seven training centres.

The training system consists of training for new recruits, training for each functional skill, and training for promotion to higher hierarchical level. A Japanese company will spend a lot of money and time on off-the-job-training.

On-the-job-training tends to be better when people are not competitive with each other, because communication is then better. Under life-time employment, and under the length of service system, communication is easier and better.

Good training is necessary where job content is ambiguous and where employees are requested to do any related jobs. It is also necessary when there are more opportunities of promotion. All of them can be sources of satisfaction to employees.

(4) More Attention to Each Employee

Employees are respected as a partner of the organization. They are not considered as one of the elements of resources for production. Life-time employment is the result of this thought. In a depression, employees are kept on at the expense of dividend and profit. In addition to life-time employment, there are a number of systems which try to do good care for people.

(a) Good Personal Records and Self-statement System.   Personal records are mainly comprised of personal career and merit rating record. Records are kept even for the blue collar workers and there is no distinction between blue and white collar at all. These records supply information for reviews for promotion and wage increases.

Self-statement is a statement of jobs, annual goals, self appraisal, extent of use of ability, other jobs where ability may be used to a fuller extent. This is sometimes accompanied by an observation sheet from a supervisor, which states job content, qualification, training given, capability to present job, need for promotion or transfer, training needed, characteristics of personality, etc.

(b) Morning Meeting.   A meeting is held every morning, usually in each section of the plant site. Information is given, and sometimes an employee is asked to give a speech on his or her thoughts and ideas.

Morning meetings are also popular in primary schools and middle schools so this is an easily ac-

cepted habit for new employees in organizations. Unions are not against this kind of meeting.

(c) Group Activity.   Group activity is encouraged on most of the plant sites. The subjects of the activity are selected by the group. They may be quality control, cost reduction, production method, improvement of machines and materials. A group is formed usually within the formal organization, and thus a group activity is to organize an informal group within the formed group. The group leader is selected by the group members. Group meetings are usually held after working hours and overtime is paid for this activity.

Group activity is a kind of job participation. It not only improves the quality of products, but also enhances the sense of identification with the company.

Japanese corporations imported the techniques of quality control and it was accepted enthusiastically. It was implemented as a technical system, but at the same time it was taken up as a subject of group campaign throughout the company, and as a subject of small group activity. Eventually quality control diffused throughout the company, not only as a technique but also as a way of thinking. Here is one of the secrets of the better quality of Japanese products.

(d) Suggestion System.   Suggestion system is again nothing new. But it is implemented well as a means of participation. In the case of Toyota and Matsushita Electric, each employee presents ten to fifteen ideas a year on the average, so the total number is about 450,000 and 900,000 a year. In the case of a U.K. company, ten suggestions a month for a total plant is usually the case.

(e) Welfare System.   Housing provided by the company and resort houses are very popular. In the case of Toyota, the company provides houses for 4200 families and dormitories for 17,200 bachelors. There are seven resort houses. It has one hospital and a number of recreational grounds.

Loan for home ownership, stock ownership with partial aid from the company, company deposit with high rate of interest,—these financial benefits are provided by many companies. (Large bonuses are paid during summer and at the end of the year, which account for more than 5 months of pay. This is not a benefit, it is merely a method of payment.)

* * *

The above are the features of personnel management of Japanese corporations. As a community organization, the company respects the employee. It keeps good record of employees, it encourages participation by group decision, by group meetings, by suggestion systems. It provides the employee with a number of welfare programmes. Welfare is one of the goals of the organization. However, the company is not a benevolent organization nor a charity organization. It has to encourage devotion and to enhance productivity and creativity. Incentive systems are used to a greater extent than in organizations in the U.S. or in the U.K.

(D) SOME ENVIRONMENTAL CHARACTERISTICS

This is not the place to dwell on the characteristics of political systems and social systems at large, but selected important features will be explained here.

(1) Political Stability

Since the end of the war there has been a continuous dominance of the conservative party (Liberal Democrat). The Socialist Party only achieved a majority once (1949). This has meant that a long-term economic policy has been worked out. There are many small groups amongst Liberal Democrats. They compete with and criticize each other, and these small groups helped the conservative party to be viable.

(2) Good Co-operation between Social Subsystems

There is good co-operation between political parties and government bureaucrats, government and business, business and labour unions, business and banks, business and universities. There is competition between the organizations which produce similar products, but there is co-operation between complementary organizations.

(3) Large Number of University Graduates

There are 400 universities excluding 2-year colleges, and two million university students. Approx-

imately 500,000 university graduates are supplied every year to various organizations. It is not rare that in high technology related companies university graduates total more than 20 per cent of employees.

(4) Organization Orientedness

People will select one formal organization, and devote themselves to the organization. Devotion to an organization is a moral value with Japanese people. Individualism which respects the independence of individuals, freedom of individuals and leisure for a private life are not the highest values for the Japanese. Organization orientation springs from the traditional culture of the Japanese people.

(E) UNIVERSALITY OR TRANSFERABILITY OF JAPANESE STYLE OF MANAGEMENT

It is a misconception that Japanese management is unique, that it is based on a unique cultural background, and that it is neither universally appropriate nor transferable. This is not true and most of the characteristics of Japanese management style were formulated after the war by rational thinking (e.g. status system) and many of them were transplanted from the U.S. or European theories and business practices (e.g. management committee, quality control). Some visitors to Japanese businesses have said 'there was no new fish, but the method of cooking is better.'

Of course a management system must fit environmental systems such as political, educational, social and economical systems, and also internal management systems must fit each other, so there are some limitations on transferability of any management system from one country to another. Contingency theory emphasizes this.

In order to discover what kind of Japanese management styles are universal, and what can be transferred to foreign countries, there are two methods. One is to observe the practices of Japanese subsidiaries in foreign countries. Another method is to look at the practices of well managed companies and try to find the similarities. Here the latter approach is used.

ICI is undoubtedly a well-managed company, and there are many similarities of management style to Japanese companies. Corporate philosophy is clearly stated, missions and responsibilities are openly declared.

At the top level, there is a management committee which meets once a week and discusses strategic issues. Five out of twelve directors are technology or science graduates. It has a long-range plan which integrates the strategic projects. It does aggressive research (spending £164m, 3.6 per cent, on sales in 1978), aggressive capital investment (£701m, 16 per cent, on sales in 1978). Even in the paint division, there is a good research laboratory, and facilities are on a large scale. Jobs are hard structured, but job enlargement and job rotation are tried among similar jobs after training.

It has only two centralized negotiation units—joint negotiation committee for weekly paid workers and for monthly paid staffs. Wage contracts are thus centralized.

There are works committees on a corporate level, division level, works level and plant level. On the plant level, the committee (managers and shop stewards) meets once a month, and discusses every problem other than wages. Business and investment committees are another form of joint consultation and deal with strategic problems.

ICI respects people. It encourages managers and supervisors to spend 20 per cent of their time on personnel management. There is no time recorder in paint division, for example. It has reduced the number of employees continuously, not by sudden redundancy, but by a long-range plan, and natural turn-over. It has a profit sharing system. Job

TABLE 4   Transferable and Hard-to-transfer Practices

(I) Japanese management practices universally effective to a great extent, or "transferable"
   (A) (1) Clear long-range goal, more emphasis on long-term profit and growth
          2-1* Management committee
          2-2 Promotion of engineers to higher ranking
          2-3 Large and strong head office
          3-1* Aggressive capital investment for modernization
          3-2 Positive expenditure for research and development
          3-3 Careful assessment for company acquisition
          3-4* Emphasis on quality control
   (B)
          1-1* Centralized negotiation unit
          1-2* Job enlargement, job rotation
          1-3* Participation on many levels
          2-1* Large rooms
          2-2* Group activities and suggestion system
          2-3* Morning meetings
   (C)
          1* Respect for people
          2* More frequent promotion and wage increase by many grades and rate ranges
          3* Detailed personal records

(II) Japanese management practices hard to transfer

   Generally speaking, the following practices are hard to transfer
   (a) Management practices which have good fit with deep core of cultural value, for example, organization orientation
   (b) Management practices which are strongly conditioned by other environmental features, for example, educational system
   (A) (1) Too much expectation from employees to identify with corporate philosophy
      (2) Sacrifice on short-range profit
   (B) (1) Job ambiguity beyond certain extent
      (2) Too much expectation on group activity
   (C) (1) Life-time employment (but respect for people is universal principle)
      (2) Promotion by length of service and wage increase by length of service
      (3)Some kind of fringe benefits, such as housing, large bonus

*Practices which are actually implemented by many Japanese subsidiaries in the U.K., such as Matsushita, Sony and YKK.

grades are many. There are seven grades below supervisor, thus increasing the opportunity for promotion. There is no rate scale for blue collar workers, but there is some extra pay. For white collar workers there are rate scales, and good personal records are held. Job grading and wage scales are standardized all through the company without regard of the union membership.

These features are not necessarily the same as Japanese systems, but there are many similarities and we can see that Japanese systems are not peculiar to Japan.

Transfer of management practice is a kind of organizational change. It is a change of an old balance of sub-systems to a new balance of sub-systems. This change is conditioned by social environment and rigidity of old internal sub-systems.

Generally speaking, management practices which are related to a deep core of cultural value such as individualism or group orientation, and are strongly based on environmental characteristics such as educational systems, are hard to be transferred.

Table 4 lists the transferable practices and hard-to-transfer practices according to the observation of a number of Japanese subsidiaries in U.K., the U.S., Malaysia, Philippines and other countries.

CONCLUSION

There are three characteristics of Japanese style of management.

It is an innovative organization. The goals of the organization are clearly stated, and growth and employee welfare are considered as important. Top management is a team, they are imitative but are sensitive to new opportunities. They are supported by the staff of large headquarter office.

It is a soft organization. Jobs are ambiguous, and employees are willing to do any related jobs. Most of the decisions are done by participation, so a group decision is the usual type.

It is a community organization. Employees are considered as a partner in an organization. They stay in the organization for their life-time. The organization provides more opportunity for promotion and wage increase with small differentials, which operate as incentives.

Some of these features are rooted in the uniqueness of Japanese culture, but many of them were transferred from other countries and modified; many of them were shaped by logical judgement and so many of them are universally effective and transferable.

14   NO   CAN JAPANESE MANAGEMENT TECHNIQUES BE APPLIED IN THE UNITED STATES?

Adopting Japanese Management: Some Cultural Stumbling Blocks
Linda S. Dillon

William G. Ouchi, whose research into Japanese management practice has been largely responsible for the current interest in Japan's highly productive management methods, is fond of telling the story of three men sentenced to die in front of a firing squad. The executioner asked the men—a Frenchman, a

Reprinted by permission of the publisher from Linda A. Dillon, "Adopting Japanese Management: Some Cultural Stumbling Blocks," *Personnel*, 60 (July/Aug. 1984), pp. 73–77. © 1983 American Management Association, New York. All rights reserved.

Japanese, and an American—if they had any last requests. "Oui," replied the Frenchman, "I would like to sing *La Marseillaise* once more before I die." "Granted," said the executioner. "I would like to give my discourse on quality circles one last time," said the Japanese. "Granted," said the executioner, who then turned to the American. "Please," said the American, "Shoot me before the Japanese has a chance to talk about quality circles again."

Ouchi's story illustrates the extent to which American business has bought into the Japanese model—in theory, if not in practice. Ouchi's work describes the American organizations labeled "Type A," which are characterized by short-term employment, rapid evaluation and promotion, specialized career paths, explicit control mechanisms, individual decision making and responsibility, and segmented concern. He compares these with "Type J" (Japanese) organizations, which practice life-time employment, slow evaluation and promotion, nonspecialized career paths, implicit control mechanisms, collective decision making and responsibility, and a holistic concern.

"Theory Z" organizations are those identified by Ouchi as having been able to make the cultural crossover—that is, American firms that have foregone the mistrust of employees and autocratic management style so typical in Type A organizations in favor of the Type J approach, which views employees as the company's greatest resource and assumes that, given the opportunity, employees want to and will do good work. Many writers have examined why Theory Z has worked well for Motorola, Westinghouse, Hewlett-Packard, and the other highly touted Theory Z models. But few have asked why Type J organizations function so well in Japan. An understanding of this cultural perspective should help American managers trying to introduce a Japanese approach into an American organization.

LIFETIME EMPLOYMENT AND THE NONSPECIALIZED CAREER PATH

The willingness of Japanese managers to think of their employees as the company's greatest asset is not so much an example of humanistic concern as an example of their ability to deal with the unpleasant truth. Japan is a resource-poor nation whose land and raw materials are in extremely short supply. Over the past century, Japan's military efforts to alleviate that problem have ended disastrously, and the memory lingers. If the 30 percent of Japan's major corporations who offer lifetime employment do value their employees, it is because they know that they have to compete to get quality and that lifetime employment precludes the availability of a trained labor force from which to choose in filling current needs. This, of course, leads quite naturally to the practice of job rotation. Individuals may not

be so apt to balk at being asked to fill a job they are unqualified for if that requirement is part of the company's basic approach to personnel planning.

But how can you offer lifetime employment when workforce needs vary with the supply-and-demand cycle? The answer in Japan is to use the participation of women in the labor force to buffer the lifetime employment of men. Women are hired as temporary or part-time workers and discarded when demand decreases. This system works well in Japan because 94 percent of the population over 30 years old is married. In this way the majority of women receive financial security in one form or another. But even if we disregard the illegality of institutionalizing a similar approach in the United States, it is easy to imagine the economic and social chaos of using women as a disposable workforce in a country where just 13 percent of the population lives in conjugal units.

SLOW EVALUATION AND PROMOTION

The Japanese practice of slow evaluation and promotion takes on special meaning when seen in terms of another infamous Japanese practice, the examination system. Examinations, which begin in junior high school, are used to determine both high school and college placement. Since the most prestigious firms hire from the most prestigious schools, children realize that their futures may be irreversibly decided at a very early age.

This practice has caused the Japanese to adopt a Japanese counterpart to a uniquely American concept: the "show biz mother." The Japanese alternative, "Kyoeku Mama" or "education mother," spends her day juggling the food budget to pay for after-school classes and hounding her children to do their homework. In feudal times, the Samurai who lost his retainer was called a "ronin" to indicate his predicament as a soldier without a master. Today, "ronin schools" provide extracurricular help for students who score low on examinations, and suicide is still an acceptable way to atone for this failure. The excruciating pace that children are forced to keep eventually pays off: when they achieve lifetime employment with a good firm. The slower pace which follows entrance into the workforce is the logical reward for the years of struggle it requires.

COLLECTIVE DECISION MAKING AND RESPONSIBILITY

Some of Japan's highly productive methods result from efforts to compensate for some very difficult features of her culture. Japan's love of consensus decision making and the use of quality control circles are reasonable reactions to the difficulties of the Japanese language. The Portuguese missionaries who first attempted to translate Japanese termed it "The Devil's Language" when they began to settle in Japan during the 17th Century. Japanese is normally written with a mixture of two syllabaries (Kana) and Chinese characters (Kanzi). There are verb forms representing levels of formality and politeness for any situation you might encounter in addressing the Emperor or your pet cat and all points on the spectrum in between. There are two sets of ordinal numbers that use suffixes to reveal whether you are counting hotels or cows. To be able to read a Japanese newspaper requires knowledge of 2,000 Kanzi, each symbol having several meanings and pronunciations.

The difference between male and female speech is so pronounced that Japanese schools which train seeing-dye dogs for the blind use English commands and teach the blind people English, instead of training a dog in Japanese and thus limiting it to use with just one sex. In the face of this incredibly difficult system of written communication, it is hardly surprising that Japan has come to rely on verbal communication in the form of quality circles and an office seating arrangement that features all employees in one work unit sharing a common office, with desks arranged so that everyone is forced to be aware of what everyone else is doing.

WHOLISTIC CONCERN AND IMPLICIT CONTROL MECHANISMS

An organization that maintains a holistic approach to company decision making forces employees at all levels to deal with each other as human beings and creates a condition in which open communication, trust, and commitment can flourish. Theory J management seeks more than a vote; it seeks agreement. A group member may be asked to accept responsibility for a decision he does not prefer, but which has been arrived at through a collective process.

To be able to put personal preference aside and commit oneself wholeheartedly to company goals is the essence of a holistic approach. "Labor, not the art of management, is the key to Japan's ascendancy," writes B. Bruce-Briggs in his critique of Theory Z," . . . labor does what is expected of it. It is expected to work hard, work right, and not block productive improvements. American labor is told what to do but does not do it reliably; that is the difference."

A holistic approach to corporate decision making and business activities is made easy in Japan by the homogeneity of the Japanese culture and the implicit philosophy that employees share. Japan has one of the lowest interracial marriage rates of any nation, and even today there is social discrimination against Koreans, Chinese, and the burakumin, the descendents of butchers and leather workers who were historically outcast because of the Buddhist prejudice against the taking of animal life. The Japanese today are the most thoroughly unified and culturally homogeneous large block of people in the entire world, with the possible exception of the North Chinese. To say that the Japanese people are all Japanese has no equivalent concept in American culture.

The Christian religions that have dominated American life over the last 200 years have created a "guilt culture" in the United States wherein judgment before the eyes of God is the primary conditioning force. Japan's culture has been characterized as a shame culture rather than a guilt culture. The Japanese fear shame from the judgment of family or society over all else and have developed elaborate systems of duty (giri) and obligation (on) which represent their shared cultural values. These value systems apply equally to business concerns and family matters, and operate efficiently to provide a unified labor force that can easily be motivated toward a common goal. Many of the judgment calls that managers and workers make are made on the basis of a company philosophy that is implicit rather than explicit, communicated by a common cultural perspective that all share. Of course, slow promotion and the common practice of yearly bonus systems that reward all employees on the basis of company profitability combine to ensure that the only way for individuals to profit personally is for the total company to prosper—another factor that rewards a holistic approach.

CONCLUSION

Examination of concepts unique to Japanese management reveals just how closely they are tied to the Japanese culture. Equally apparent is the interrelatedness of each factor with the other. It is not surprising that so few American firms have been able to successfully adapt the Theory Z approach. The real success of the Japanese approach lies in what they were able to learn from the United States in the early post-war years: the value of controlling cost, working hard, saving money, and giving the customer value for his dollar. It was their ability to adapt those concepts to a Japanese culture that led to their productivity gains and subsequent worldwide envy. But it would be a mistake to assume that these techniques can be borrowed and used productively as easily as Japan has "borrowed" American technology in the past. It will take the most creative efforts of America's most skilled managers to adapt the Japanese approach to the American culture.

QUESTIONS FOR DISCUSSION

1. To what extent can Japanese successes in economic development be attributed to Japanese culture?
2. Are any of the cultural features which are conducive to Japanese economic development to be found in the American public sector? Explain.
3. What features of American management practices did the Japanese follow?
4. What effect has the women's rights movement had on economic efficiency and productivity in the United States?
5. To what extent are factors other than management responsible for Japanese economic success?

SUGGESTED READINGS

BOYCE, MICHAEL T., "Can Quality Circles Be Applied in the Public Sector?," *Journal of Collective Negotiations*, 14, No. 1 (1985), 67–75.

BLAIR, JOHN D., STANLEY L. COHEN, AND JEROME V. HURWITZ, "Quality Circles: Practical Considerations for Public Managers," *Public Productivity Review*, 6 (March/June 1982), 9–18.

BRUCE-BRIGGS, B., "The Dangerous Folly Called Theory Z," *Fortune* (May 17, 1982), 41, 44, 48, and 53.

CONTINO, RONALD, AND ROBERT M. LORUSSO, "The Theory Z Turnaround of a Public Agency," *Public Administration Review*, 42 (Jan./Feb. 1982), 66–72.

ELLENBERGER, JAMES N., "Japanese Management: Myth or Magic?," *AFL-CIO American Federationist*, 89 (Apr./June 1982), 3–12.

MCABEE, MICHAEL, "Can Japanese 'Magic' Work Here?," *Industry Week* (Aug. 8, 1983), 46–48.

NAVE, JAMES L., "Z: From Theory to Practice," *Management World*, 12 (May 1983), 10–12.

OUCHI, WILLIAM G., *Theory Z: How American Business Can Meet the Japanese Challenge.* Reading, MA: Addison-Wesley, 1981.

ROLL, JOYCE L., AND DAVID L. ROLL, "The Potential for Application of Quality Circles in the American Public Sector," *Public Productivity Review*, 7 (June 1983), 122–42.

THOMPSON, PHILIP C., *Quality Circles: How to Make Them Work in America.* New York: AMACOM, 1982.

CHAPTER 5
Implementation and Public Policy

Students of public administration are concerned with both the implementation of laws and the wisdom of enacting particular laws. The implementation of laws governs such matters as whether laws will be centrally administered, whether local citizen participation will play a role in the allocation of funds, and whether the private sector should administer or provide public services. This chapter begins with a discussion about one problem that occurs in the relationship between the public and private sector in providing public services—namely the problem of whether government or the private sector delivers services more effectively.

Public policy is at the heart of the democratic process. To some extent, democracy may be defined as a means by which individuals and groups compete about what laws and policies the political community should impose. In the United States, the controversy over public policy issues is vigorous—whether in domestic matters, such as the level of spending in the welfare sector, or in foreign policy matters, such as the wisdom of providing military aid to the Contras who are trying to topple the Sandinista government in Nicaragua.

Much attention in the past few decades has centered on government regulation. As indicated in chapter 1, the demands of different groups for government regulation has been one of the reasons for the growth of government.

As an abstract concept, regulation has not been a liberal or conservative theme. Many liberals, for example, favor government regulation of industry but oppose government regulation restricting individual freedom. Many conservatives favor government regulation of pornography but oppose government regulation restricting certain business practices. This chapter deals with two areas of public policy involving regulation—airlines and broadcasting.

CONTRACTING OUT

One choice that government has to make is whether to perform a particular function itself or to let private enterprise do the job. Some jobs are generally regarded as clearly lying within the necessary functions of government. Armed forces engaged in combat operations is a case in point. The mercenary soldier who sells his services to a foreign army or guerrilla force is popularly regarded as odd if not at times traitorous. But many government functions can easily be performed by either government or the private sector—or by both.

Even in the military sector, airlift is furnished by both the Military Airlift Command and private airlines under government contract. Sanitation services can be performed by either the government or private sanitation companies—or by both.

In the past few decades "contracting out" —in which private companies perform governmental tasks—has become increasingly used at the national, state, and local levels. The Reagan administration particularly, with its championing of private industry, has called for greater government use of the private sector and has recommended that privatization—the use of the private rather than the public sector—be expanded in the management of national parks, in the sale of public power, and in many other areas of government activity. The Grace Commission endorsed privatization, arguing that much money could be saved if private enterprise rather than government could do the jobs previously designated to government.

In cities, privatization has been adopted even in such areas as firefighting and jail management. Cities have turned to private companies to provide services in other areas, such as urban transportation and health care. The major beneficiaries of privatization are clearly the companies and their employees who are the successful contractors of government services. The losers are clearly the government employees who lose their jobs as a result of privatization.

From the point of view of public administration, it is essential to know whether contracting out is an effective means of performing government services. Stephen Moore, a policy analyst with the conservative Heritage Foundation, argues that it is. He points out that the federal government has not implemented contracting out as extensively as the Reagan administration had hoped to do. He makes the following arguments for contracting out as a major initiative in the federal government: (1) It would produce vast savings. (2) It would mean that existing services could be maintained at the same level as exists today. (3) Private contractors tend to be more efficient than their public-sector counterparts. (4) The quality of services provided to the public would be better. In explaining why contracting out has not been adopted as much as he thinks it should, Moore provides supporting evidence for his arguments.

The American Federation of State, County and Municipal Employees (AFSCME) makes the case against contracting out. It argues: (1) Contracting out often produces higher costs. (2) It often results in poorer services for citizens because private contractors supply inexperienced workers, ignore contract requirements, provide inadequate supervision, and often engage in corrupt practices with government. (3) Contracting out results in less accountability by the government to the citizens.

As you read this debate, consider the criteria necessary to compare the efficiency of government to the efficiency of the private sector. Consider, too, whether values of a political system which are reflected in personnel matters in the public sector will be undermined by contracting out.

AIRLINE DEREGULATION

Airline deregulation, unlike many proposed other forms of deregulation, has had the support of both liberals and conservatives. Liberal Senator Edward Kennedy favored it, but so, too, did President Gerald Ford. Jimmy Carter supported deregulation and signed into law the Airline Deregulation Act of 1978.

Prior to deregulation, the Civil Aeronautics Board (CAB) determined not only the routes that individuals carriers could serve but the fare structure, as well. In such a system new carriers were frequently prevented from entering the market since it was believed that they would engage in "cut-throat" competition.

Airline deregulation has revolutionized the character of the airline industry in ways that are described in detail in the debate below. Generally, however, new carriers, such as People's Express and Presidential, entered the market, and price competition has marked the airfare structure. Some of the older carriers have done well under the new conditions; others, however, have done poorly. Some of the older carriers have gone out of business. Others have sold off some of their assets or have been taken over by more successful carriers.

In 1986, for example, the financially troubled Eastern Airlines was sold to Texas Air.

Airline deregulation has affected other aspects of the industry. For example, airline employees have been forced to accept "give-backs" to airlines in which benefits secured by their unions through collective bargaining were voluntarily abandoned in order to allow airline companies which employ them to stay in business. A number of airlines hired nonunion workers, moreover. The CAB itself was terminated as a government agency in 1985, giving hope to some observers that government agencies are not immortal.

Has airline deregulation done more harm than good to the airline industry and the public it serves? Two airline executives argue the point. Wesley G. Kaldahl, Senior Vice President for Airline Planning of American Airlines, takes the Affirmative position. He makes the following points: (1) Financially, the industry is presently in serious trouble. (2) Deregulation has produced excessive competition, resulting in greater cost disparity among individual airlines, overcapacity in certain markets, unsound pricing practices and fare wars, reduction in service to less glamorous markets, and a waste of jet fuel. (3) Deregulation has meant lower fares in a few markets but the same or higher fares in smaller communities. (4) The airline industry now offers fewer nonstop and direct flights and more flights requiring connections than was the case before deregulation. (5) In all, deregulation has been harmful to the public, stockholders, carriers, airline employees, most cities, aircraft manufacturers, and lenders and creditors. In spite of the considerable evidence he offers against deregulation, Kaldahl asserts that airline re-regulation would not be feasible today.

Herbert D. Kelleher, President and Chief Executive Officer of Southwest Airlines, takes the Negative side of the debate issue. He argues that the benefits of airline deregulation are: (1) lower fares, (2) increased service, (3) diversity of service and price alternatives, (4) reduced industry concentration, (5) more efficient allocation of resources, and (6) a more healthy, efficient, and innovative airline industry.

As you read this debate, consider whether the authors disagree about the facts of deregulation or the consequences of the facts. Consider, too, the applicability of the lessons of airline deregulation to other sectors of the economy.

BROADCAST DEREGULATION

For most of American history the print media—newspapers and magazines—provided the news to the American people. Newspapers were free of most government regulation and were protected by First Amendment rights guaranteeing freedom of the press. The print media have varied in objectivity and partisanship. In the twentieth century, the electronic media—primarily radio and television—have become new media forms conveying news to the public. More Americans today get their news from television than from newspapers.

The electronic media have been subjected since 1912 to regulatory laws. The primary agency for regulating the electronic media is the Federal Communications Commission (FCC), which was created by Congress in 1934. The FCC allocates broadcast channels and frequencies and regulates the sale of stations and the renewal of licenses. Congress has passed laws, and the FCC has imposed rules governing the electronic media. The granting of equal time for political candidates competing in elections and for "fairness" in requiring differing viewpoints to be heard are mandatory for the electronic media in a way that is not the case for the print media.

Should electronic broadcasting be deregulated? Such a question was debated when a Senate committee considered a bill (S. 1917), which would have deregulated the electronic broadcasting industry. The debate below is drawn from testimony before that committee. NBC newsman Bill Monroe argues the Affirmative position. He contends: (1) The First Amendment right of freedom of the press requires the electronic media to be free of government regulation. (2) The frequency allocation problem for radio and television stations can be resolved without government intrusion into editorial decisions or program content. (3) Electronic media today—unlike the past—are the principal media forms carrying news to the American people and so should have the same freedom as the print media. (4) Regulation has not improved the electronic media, as its proponents claim, but, rather, it has held it back.

Elaine Donnelly, Special Projects Director of the Eagle Forum—a conservative private group—takes the Negative side. She argues: (1) First Amendment rights of freedom of speech are strengthened by government regulation of broadcasting. (2) Broadcasting media—partic-

ularly television—enjoys a unique role in influencing opinion and so must be constrained by rules requiring fairness. (3) Existing regulatory rules are not cumbersome.

As you read this debate, consider the issue of free speech and whether government regulation of the broadcast media strengthens or weakens that freedom. Compare the characteristics of the electronic media to determine if those characteristics differ so markedly from the print media as to warrant greater regulation.

ISSUES

15 YES   IS CONTRACTING OUT AN EFFECTIVE MEANS OF PROVIDING GOVERNMENT SERVICES?

How to Privatize Federal Services by "Contracting Out"
Stephen Moore

INTRODUCTION

Privatization has come of age. The Reagan Administration's FY 1987 budget argues that considerable budget savings can be achieved without cutting services but by transferring government functions to the private sector—in short, by privatization. A major privatization device is "contracting out," an inelegant term to describe what happens when the government hires private firms to provide government services under contract. A number of highly specialized goods and services for some time have been provided by private contractors. Notable ex-

From Stephen Moore, "How to Privatize Federal Services by Contracting Out," *The Backgrounder* (Washington, DC: Heritage Foundation, 1986), No. 494. Reprinted with permission.

Note: Nothing written here is to be construed as necessarily reflecting the views of The Heritage Foundation or as an attempt to aid or hinder the passage of any bill before Congress.

amples include delivery of sophisticated communications satellites and military weapons procurement. But the greatest potential for budget savings would come from the federal government turning to private firms to supply such routine services as data processing, janitorial services, and maintenance work. These are generally known as "commercial services" because they are activities that are routinely provided in the private sector by commercial firms.

The Reagan Administration has been committed to contracting out commercial services since 1981, but its efforts have been undermined repeatedly. Federal agencies have been ignoring White House directives, while Congress has erected more than a dozen legislative impediments to contracting out federal services. The result: rather than reducing the size of the federal work force engaged in commercial activities, 120,000 additional workers have been added to the federal payrolls since January 1981. And despite the 1983 recommendation of the Grace Commission that 500,000 government positions be contracted to more efficient private firms, the Administration in 1985 reviewed just 2,381 civilian agency positions as candidates for privatization. At the current rate, it would take 100 years to conduct cost estimates for every federal commercial activity.[1]

If he truly intends to reduce federal spending, Ronald Reagan must make contracting out a top administrative priority. And he must seek institutional changes in the contracting out procedure. Studies have documented that 20 to 35 percent savings from contracting out are typical. Because contracting out does not reduce service levels, it provides a painless way to slash the deficit.

In recent months, the Administration has been sending mixed signals on contracting. For instance, the Administration's *Management Report*, accompanying the FY 1987 Budget, makes very useful recommendations for facilitating contracting out—most notably, allowing targeted commercial functions to be automatically contracted to private firms without requiring time-consuming cost comparisons with in-house provision.[2] Yet the Administration seems to be giving these initiatives secondary priority. Greater emphasis seems to be placed on the noble wish, invoked by heads of government from Washington to Moscow, that government productivity be improved. Rather than concerning itself with making government computer operators more efficient, for example, the White House should be asking why the government hires computer operators at all when private firms could provide them at low competitive prices.

To accelerate contracting out, the Administration should change the procedure for awarding contracts so that the bias against private firms is removed. In addition, Congress should overhaul drastically the impediments that it has erected to contracting out. By working together to improve the process, significant reductions in spending could be achieved without reducing services to the American people.

HOW CONTRACTING REDUCES FEDERAL SPENDING

When the federal government contracts out an activity which is commercial in nature, it retains its funding responsibility, but relies on private sector competition to assure that the good or service is delivered at the lowest possible cost and at high quality. The federal government currently employs nearly one million workers who perform 11,000 separate commercial activities. This workforce includes electricians, dentists, janitors, plumbers, caterers, laboratory technicians, and even veterinarians.[3]

Since 1981 at least a dozen studies have investigated the potential savings from contracting with private vendors for such services. Such contracting out now is routine in thousands of cities and is being carried out on a limited basis on the federal level. The findings of eight representative studies are shown in Table 1.

Private contractors tend to be more efficient than their public sector counterparts—not because federal employees are less able, but because they face different incentives. Since private firms operate under competitive conditions, they have a powerful incentive to seek innovative approaches to reduce the cost of providing their service. If they do not keep cost down and quality up, they soon will lose contracts to their rivals. No such incentive exists in the public sector. The lack of competition removes the pressure to be more productive. In fact, there are perverse incentives, for if a public sector agency becomes more efficient at providing a service, then that agency is likely to see its budget cut—to reflect the savings—for the next year.

Injecting competition into the procurement process even generates greater efficiency within the bureaucracy. Example: an analysis of cost comparisons in the Department of Defense reveals that the cost of services provided by federal employees fell by 17 percent when they were forced to compete with private firms. This alone has saved the Department over $100 million since 1982.[4]

---

[1]W. Jackson Coleman, "Implementation of O.M.B. Circular A-76," Hearings, Subcommittee on Human Resources, House Committee on Post Office and Civil Service, October 30, 1985.

[2]For more complete details, see: "Status Report on Federal Procurement," in Office of Management and Budget, *Management of the United States Government*, Fiscal Year 1987, pp. 92–103.

---

[3]Office of Management and Budget, "Circular No. A-76 (revised)," August 4, 1983.

[4]Office of Management and Budget, "Enhancing Governmental Productivity Through Competition: A Program Report on OMB Circular No. A-76," 1984, p. 7.

TABLE 1   Cost Savings Estimates from Contracting Out Studies Conducted Since 1981

Source of Study	Type of Service	Percentage Savings From Contracting Out
Ecodata, under contract with HUD[7]	Municipal janitorial services	73
	Municipal refuse collection	42
	Municipal overlay construction	96
American Public Works Association[8]	Highway and street maintenance	16
Department of Defense[9]	Department services contracted between 1980 and 1982	22*
Department of Defense[10]	Revised 1985 estimate, all DOD contracted services	29*
U.S. Air Force[11]	Review of 132 contracted functions	33
Institute of Transportation Studies, University of California, Irvine[12]	Municipal contracting of urban mass transit	25–50
U.S. General Accounting Office[13]	Federal cleaning costs	50
Office of Management and Budget[14]	Agencywide review of 60,000 positions contracted	24

*Includes savings from activities which remained in-house due to the agency reducing its initial cost estimate.

[7]Barbara J. Stevens, ed., *Comparative Study of Municipal Service Delivery* (New York: Ecodata, 1984).

[8]John L. Whetman, "Contracting and Street Maintenance," Paper prepared for the American Public Works Association, 1983.

[9]U.S. Department of Defense, *Report to Congress on the Commercial Activities Program*, March 12, 1984, p. 5.

[10]Lawrence Korb, Assistant Secretary, Department of Defense, Testimony before the House Armed Services Committee, April 1985.

[11]*Air Force Times*, June 17, 1985.

[12]Roger F. Teal, Institute of Transportation Studies, University of California, Irvine, "Transit Service Contracting: Experience and Issues," Paper presented at the Annual Meeting of the Transportation Research Board, Washington, D.C., January 1985.

[13]General Accounting Office, "GSA's Cleaning Costs Are Needlessly Higher Than in the Private Sector," 1981.

[14]Office of Management and Budget, *Management of the United States Government*, Fiscal Year 1987.

If contracting out were expanded on the federal level, the Congressional Budget Office envisions a $1.2 billion reduction in government costs.[5] The Office of Management and Budget's latest projection puts the figure at $3 billion.[6]

[5]Congressional Budget Office, "Contracting Out for Federal Support Services: The Potential Savings and Budgetary Impacts," 1982.

[6]Office of Management and Budget, "Enhancing Governmental Productivity Through Competition," 1984, p. 10.

Improved Service Quality

The most outspoken opponent of contracting out predictably has been the American Federation of State, County and Municipal Employees. The union charges that while contractors may indeed provide services at lower cost, they "frequently cut corners by hiring inexperienced, transient personnel at low wages, by ignoring contract requirements, or by providing inadequate supervision.[15] This complaint is refuted by performance evaluations of contracted activities which reveal that, if anything, service quality is enhanced by hiring private firms.

A 1984 study of contracted municipal services by Ecodata, Inc., found no diminution in service quality. In fact, it concluded that "for many of the services, the individual cities with the lowest costs of service delivery also achieved among the highest levels of quality."[16] Further corroboration of service quality is found in the California Tax Foundation 1981 survey of 81 local governments. By a margin of two to one, cities indicated that service had improved from contracting over those that complained of poorer service.[17]

These findings were to be expected. Private contractors typically are forced to meet rigid performance specifications, and the quality of services they provide is closely scrutinized. With public delivery, by contrast, such accountability is low or nonexistent.

More Efficient Use of Resources

A 1983 Joint Economic Committee of Congress (JEC) study of federal procurement finds that offering federal contracts to the private sector greatly stimulates business expansion.[18] Equipment and other capital purchased by a private firm to fulfill the terms of a federal contract are likely to be later adopted for other commercial ventures. By contrast, the gov-

ernment, because of its limited flexibility, often has capital sitting idle upon project completion. Technological spin-offs to other commercial markets from government-funded research and development were particularly important, the study notes.

Contracting out also permits the federal government to marshall the specialized talents of private companies on a temporary basis, rather than keeping such expertise permanently within the government. Agencies acknowledge that this option offers the government greater flexibility in responding to changing priorities.

WHY FEDERAL CONTRACTING REMAINS THE EXCEPTION AND NOT THE RULE

The first presidential directive on federal contracting was issued by Dwight Eisenhower in 1955. It specified that "the federal government will not start or carry on any commercial activity to provide a service or product for its own use if such product or service can be procured from private enterprise." The intent of this directive has been thwarted repeatedly for three decades. The reasons:

The Cost Comparison Process Prevents Contracting Out

The original Eisenhower policy statement was stripped of much of its force in 1966, when it was replaced by Office of Management and Budget Circular A-76, which forms the basis of current policy. This new directive requires the federal agencies only to conduct detailed cost comparisons between "in-house government suppliers" and private vendors, and to choose the less expensive alternative. Despite the apparent reasonableness of this approach, the rules which govern the cost comparisons are heavily skewed against private contractors. Examples:[19]

- Unless the private contractor's bid beats the in-house estimate by at least ten percent, to cover government "transition costs," the function automatically re-

[15]Gerald W. Maentee, "The Case Against Privatization," *The Privatization Review*, Fall 1985, p. 7.

[16]Stevens, *op. cit.*, p. iv.

[17]California Tax Foundation, "Contracting Out Local Government Services in California," May 1981, p. 9.

[18]Robert Premus, David Karns, and Anthony Robinson, "Socioeconomic Regulations and the Federal Procurement Market," Joint Economic Committee, December 1984.

[19]A comprehensive analysis of the cost comparison process and its flaws is examined in William D. Russell, Testimony before the Subcommittee on Human Resources, House Post Office and Civil Service Committee, October 20, 1985.

mains in house despite the potential savings from contracting out.

- The private bidder must submit a "firm contract" proposal with a fixed price, whereas the agency is only required to submit a cost estimate. This places the private bidder at a significant disadvantage; if he underestimates his costs he will have to swallow the loss. The agency, on the other hand, is not penalized by submitting low cost estimates. If its estimates prove to have been too low, it pays no penalty nor does it lose the contract. It simply draws additional agency funds.

- The commercial firm's bid must include an allowance for indirect costs, such as corporate salaries and other administrative expenses; the agency's need not. The U.S. Chamber of Commerce estimates that this alone constitutes a 20 to 30 percent handicap to the private bidder.

- Costs are added to the bid submitted by private providers to pay for government monitoring of contract performance; no cost for checking quality is added to the agency cost estimate.

- Very low bids may be rejected as being "outside the competitive range." This discourages breakthrough innovation and means that in many cases the selected proposal from private bidders is not always the lowest bid. It also leads to more decisions in favor of the agency provider.

This biased cost comparison process has placed private bidders at an estimated 35 percent cost handicap.[20] According to the Congressional Budget Office, eliminating the 10 percent rule alone would increase contracts awarded to commercial sources by 14 percent.[21]

The Campaign in Congress to Prevent Contracting Out

The unfair cost comparison process tilts decisions against private vendors. An even greater problem is that restrictions imposed by Congress ensure that only a small share of federal commercial activities are even subject to competitive bidding.

In recent years, Congress has passed over 20 separate prohibitions on contracting out. Congress usually justifies the impediments to contracting of Pentagon commercial activities, for example, by claiming that contracting out would jeopardize "national security" interests. But it is certainly in the interest of U.S. national security for the Pentagon to get maximum value from its defense dollars. Every dollar saved by contracting out routine Department of Defense commercial activities is an additional dollar to protect national security in other areas. And it is important to stress that if congressional restrictions from contracting such activities as firefighting and security guard functions on military bases were lifted, the Secretary of Defense would still have the authority to prevent contracting where legitimate security considerations arise.

In fact, mounting evidence suggests that Congress merely uses the "national security" motivation as a guise to conceal more parochial concerns. Congressman Bill Nichols (D-AL), who has played a lead role in restricting contracting out by the Department of Defense, acknowledges that one of his goals has been "to protect [military civilian] jobs."[22]

Congressionally imposed restrictions on civilian agencies are equally insidious. The General Services Administration, for instance, is prohibited from contracting out guard, elevator operator, messenger, and custodian services. These exemptions cost federal taxpayers $32 million each year.[23]

The Veterans Administration (VA) is expressly prohibited from contracting its medical care activities, whatever the savings, unless in-house facilities can not fully handle the patient load. The Grace Commission found that when VA nursing home care was contracted out, the average cost per day was more than cut in half: $45 per day versus the $109 per day the VA charges. Quality of care concerns which motivate the VA restriction are dubious as well: the Air Force often contracts out for similar hospital care without degrading service quality. The VA restriction costs the federal taxpayers at least $100 million annually according to the Grace Commission.[24]

The cost impact of these congressional obstacles to contracting is considerable. Thanks to the restrictions, only an estimated 30 percent of the government's $20 to $30 billion tab for commercial

[20]Ibid., p. 4.

[21]Congressional Budget Office, p. 22.

[22]As quoted in "Contracting Out: Win Some, Lose Some, Some Rained Out," Government Executive, 1985, p. 41.

[23]OMB, Management of the United States Government,

[24]William R. Kennedy, Jr. and Robert W. Lee. A Taxpayer Survey of the Grace Commission Report (Ottawa, Illinois: Green Hill Publishers, 1984), p. 2.

services is even eligible for the savings that contracting out offers.

Opposition to Contracting Out Within the Agencies

The Administration must share the blame for the unsatisfactory progress on fully implementing the A-76 directives. Congressional restrictions do not explain why less than 2,000 cost reviews were conducted in civilian agencies in 1984, and only 2,300 in 1985. The Executive Branch employs over 20,000 "program analysts" who should be undertaking comparisions, yet the number actually conducted is very small. The problem evidently begins with the heads of such Administration agencies as the National Oceanic and Atmospheric Administration, NASA, and the General Services Administration. Charges the General Accounting Office, "The commitment of agency heads to the reform effort has not been demonstrated and agency officials interviewed by GAO believe they do not have to follow the [Circular A-76] policy guidance."[25]

Even when the cost comparisons are reluctantly performed by an agency, the bureaucracy can skew the process so unfairly against the private bidder or delay the proceedings for so long, that few contracts ever get out the door.

Typical of such footdragging is at the General Services Administration. The GSA spends $250 million more to clean offices with its own custodians than it would cost to contract out this service. According to the GAO this waste of taxpayer money occurs "despite GSA's knowledge that it costs more to clean with its in-house custodial staff. . . . Instead of actively pursuing the spirit of A-76, GSA is only slowly converting to contract cleaning."[26] If the agency proceeds at its current pace, it could take fifteen years for janitorial services to be privatized. The message is clear: without a forcing mechanism attached to the A-76 program, agencies

will not even try to obtain the saving achievable through contracting out.

FIVE STEPS BY WHICH THE WHITE HOUSE WOULD IMPROVE AND EXPAND CONTRACTING OUT

1. *Issue an Executive Order to reconfirm the Reagan commitment to contracting out.*

   The Office of Management and Budget's contracting out initiatives are doomed to failure without Ronald Reagan's explicit and wholehearted support. Through an executive order, he should require federal agencies to classify all of their functions as either "inherently governmental" or "nongovernmental," with the second category eligible for contracting out. Once these designations have been made they should be reviewed for consistency by OMB, and made subject to appeal by private contractors. This general classification would eliminate time-consuming disputes and inconsistency. The President should also direct all agencies to conduct cost studies for a fixed number of civil service jobs each year that are subject to contracting.

2. *Eliminate the cost comparison process when private sector delivery is clearly less expensive.*

   Certain inherently commercial activities, such as janitorial services, automatically should be contracted out to private firms. This would free up agency personnel to conduct reviews on more complicated cases. In early 1986, the Office of Management and Budget recommended this reform. The proposal would permit agencies to bypass the cost comparison process for certain activities.

3. *Hold agency heads and lower level appointees accountable for any failure to execute A-76.*

   A chain of responsibility in each agency should be established to assure that cost comparisons are made and conducted in a fair and speedy manner. Progress reports from all program administrators should be required and carefully reviewed. Political appointees who fail to make progress in executing A-76 should be removed and replaced with those who will. Political appointees should also be required to publish information on the positive results of A-76, to counter public employee union lobbying.

4. *Replace method specifications with performance specifications on most federal contracts.*

   Bids by private contractors have to cover the cost of rigid, and in many cases unnecessary, agency specifications. Contract solicitations routinely exceed 100 pages. A 1983 Joint Economic Committee investigation found that for 67 percent of businesses that had voluntarily reduced their participation in federal

---

[25]General Accounting Office, "Progress of Federal Procurement Reform Under Executive Order 12352," 1983, p. ii.

[26]General Accounting Office, "GSA's Cleaning Costs Are Needlessly Higher Than in the Private Sector," 1981, p. ii.

procurement, "complexity of contract requirements" was a major factor in this decision.[27] If requirements were simplified and related more to contract performance and progress rather than to the method the contractor employs to fulfill the terms of the contract, competition would be enhanced, costs would be reduced, and contracts would be awarded faster.

5. *Contract out the contracting out process itself.*

As long as the authority to determine whether or not an activity will be contracted out rests on the shoulders of the agency itself, contracting out will remain the exception rather than the rule.

The contracting out decision must be removed from the hands of the agency bureaucrats. A number of municipalities already use independent auditors. Example: Phoenix created a separate auditing department that not only evaluates outside bids, but verifies the accuracy of the in-house estimate. It computes the proper allocation of overhead and whatever indirect costs could be eliminated by contracting out. The auditor awards the contract and monitors its performance, whether it is being delivered by private firms or by public workers.[28]

The federal government should experiment with such an approach. An auditing office, for instance, could be added to OMB or GAO. Failure by a cabinet department to provide information quickly to the auditors could result in functions being contracted out by default. Reporting to such an independent auditing department would mean that performance standards would apply equally to contractors and the agencies, since in-house performance would be monitored.

There is no reason why this independent agency need be a government department. In fact, the federal government should consider contracting out the contracting out process. The President could nominate a panel of private auditing firms, subject to Senate confirmation, to undertake the cost comparisons. The private auditors would be responsible for making cost estimates, awarding contracts, and monitoring performance problems. Perhaps the auditors could receive payment based upon savings to the government and satisfactory performance of the contracts they awarded and managed.

---

[27]Joint Economic Committee, p. 39.

[28]Innovating approaches to contracting out employed in Phoenix and other cities are described in Robert W. Poole, Jr., "Departments vs. Contractors," *Fiscal Watchdog*, February 1984.

FOUR STEPS FOR CONGRESS TO PROMOTE CONTRACTING OUT

1. *Remove legislative restrictions on contracting out.*

With few exceptions, congressional restrictions on contracting out have ill served the public. Where national security questions arise, the appropriateness of utilizing contracts should be determined by the Secretary of Defense. Where quality of care objections have prompted restrictions, as with veterans' health care, independent auditors, free of constituency pressure, should ensure that contractors live up to quality commitments.

2. *Modify competitive bidding regulations to eliminate biases against contracting out.*

The competitive bidding process imposes a 35 percent handicap on the contractor. The rules tend to keep contracts inside the government when taxpayer savings would be realized by contracting out. Legislation is needed to remove unreasonable restrictions. Representatives Robert Smith (R-OR) and Charles Stenholm (D-TX) have introduced the Contract Savings Act, which tackles the problem of congressional red tape.

3. *Review the Service Contract Act and the Davis-Bacon Act.*

The objective of government procurement should be to assure that taxpayers' money is being spent wisely. In 1972 the Commission on Federal Procurement warned that "the cumulative effect of *regulations* already imposed on the procurement process and the addition of those contemplated could overburden it to the point of breakdown."[29] Nearly 15 years later, federal procurement is more burdened than ever, with only the most skillful and experienced contractors able to wiggle through stacks of paperwork requirements and red tape. On the federal level alone, 4,000 provisions of federal law, covering 64,000 pages, affect procurement and contracting.

Congress should reevaluate those existing contract regulations that are concerned with social policy, while placing a moratorium on new ones. This reassessment should look first at the labor requirements affecting A-76. The Davis-Bacon Act requires that workers on federally contracted construction projects receive the prevailing wage in the area where the work is performed. The Service Contract Act is the counterpart of the Davis-Bacon Act, applying to service contract workers. Surveys of contractors have found that Davis-Bacon is considered the single most burdensome regulation affecting federal contracts. The Service Contract Act is only slightly less inhib-

---

[29]United States Commission on Government Procurement, Vol. 1, 1972, p. 114.

iting. These two regulations cost the taxpayer $1.3 billion.

4. *Reform the small business and minority business set-aside rules.*

These set-aside programs restrict eligibility on specified government contracts by mandating that they be awarded to small and minority-owned businesses. Aside from the questionable effectiveness of this method of promoting the growth of targeted businesses, there is strong evidence that the biggest winner from set-asides is the bureaucracy. The reason is that if no small or minority business is able to match the agency in-house bid, which is frequently the case, the bidding is not then opened up to large contractors. Rather, the activity remains in-house. If Congress genuinely wants to assist small businesses through federal contracts, it should do so by reducing regulations rather than eliminating competition.

CONCLUSION

The goal of government procurement, set down by the 1972 Commission on Federal Procurement, is to obtain "products and services of the needed quantity at the lowest reasonable price available." But thanks to congressionally imposed restrictions

on contracting out, and the "civil disobedience" characterizing bureaucratic responses to contracting initiatives, the taxpayer has been denied the full benefits of contracting out under Ronald Reagan. In 1986 there are more federal workers performing commercial activities than ever before, and the competitive procurement process is more regulated and restricted than it has ever been.

Most of the privatization initiatives proposed by Reagan's FY 1987 budget must travel the treacherous route of winning congressional approval. By contrast, a more aggressive contracting out campaign can be undertaken immediately by the Administration, independent of Congress.

The Gramm-Rudman-Hollings timetable for federal deficit reduction means that Congress and the White House must seize every opportunity to cut unnecessary spending. Since contracting out cuts spending while preserving the level of services to beneficiaries—and in many cases improves the quality of service delivery—there is every reason why lawmakers should step up the pace of contracting out. Failure to do so will indicate that Washington is still not serious about cutting the deficit with the minimum of service disruption.

---

15   NO   IS CONTRACTING OUT AN EFFECTIVE MEANS OF PROVIDING GOVERNMENT SERVICES?

Look Before You Leap: How Contracting Out Can Be Dangerous to Your Budget—and the Integrity of Government
American Federation of State, County and Municipal Employees

This book is about the contracting out of public services—the use of private companies to perform the work of state and local governments. That may seem like pretty dry stuff, but contracting out now costs billions of dollars a year in tax money and

From American Federation of State, County and Municipal Employees, "Look Before You Leap: How Contracting Out Can be Dangerous to Your Budget—and the Integrity of Government," *Passing the Buck: The Contracting Out of Public Services* (Washington, DC: AFSCME, 1983), pp. 7–18. Reprinted with permission.

directly affects the quality of life and sometimes the substance of life itself for every person in this country.

Before exploring contracting, let's take a quick look at what a public service is. A public service is anything government does to meet its constitutional and legislative responsibilities to serve the common good. Ensuring that your kitchen tap water is clean, disposing of your waste materials, educating children, protecting the quality of the air, guarding convicted lawbreakers, and much more: All these tasks are necessary if we are to have a civilized society.

Generations ago we could do some of these things for ourselves or with the help of friends and neighbors, but that is no longer possible. We cannot personally repair the street or patch a broken sewer line or inspect the hamburger meat at a fast-food restaurant. Instead, we look to our local or state or federal governments to do these tasks for us. We share the costs of them by paying taxes, and we call the performance of these tasks public service.

The range of these services has grown over the years. Some critics claim that there are now too many. It is worth remembering, however, that in the overwhelming majority of cases we the people asked government to provide a service—to do something we thought necessary to serve the common good—because no other institution could or would do the job.

Giving contracts to private, profit-making companies to perform these public services has been tried before and found wanting. Yet, the push to contract out public services continues. State and local governments can avoid repeating the mistakes of the past by becoming aware of the many issues involved in contracting out as presented in this book. This chapter provides a background, examining the arguments of contracting advocates, and presenting the major problems with the practice. . . .

THE PENDULUM OF HISTORY

Historically, American government has provided most public services directly, but there has always been some degree of contracting out, particularly at the federal level. In the early years of this century, cities and towns around the country turned to private companies to run local streetcar systems, to collect garbage, to provide fire protection and to perform other basic public services, often because their communities lacked the needed public resources. But there were problems: contractors frequently overcharged municipalities; under-the-table payoffs by contractors were common; contractor-provided services were often poor. It was also the era of big city political bosses—for example, Tammany Hall in New York and later James Curley in Boston—and municipal contracts became a favored way of lining pockets and rewarding political cronies.

"Because of gross abuses," Ralph W. Widner, staff vice president of the Urban Land Institute, has noted, "the reform movement of the 1920s tried to professionalize the delivery of quality public services by making them part of the municipal government." Prodded by reformers, many municipalities decreased their dependence on contractors and delivered more services using the public work force. Now, in recent years state and local governments have been turning again to private contractors. In 1982, Widner noted, contractors were on the ascendancy in state and local governments. "The pendulum is swinging back the other way," he said. "It will continue to swing until there is another round of abuses and scandals and then [will] swing back the other way."

THE BUSINESS OF PUBLIC SERVICE

Contracting out has become big business; in 1980 alone state and local governments paid an estimated $66 billion to private firms to provide public services. The growth has not only been in such traditional areas of contracting as waste collection or consulting and architectural services but also in building maintenance, food services, health care, transportation, social welfare, security services and even police and fire protection. Big corporations such as ARA Services, Inc. (food services and health care), Waste Management, Inc. (waste collection and disposal) and the Marriott Corporation (food services) have moved vigorously into the public sector in recent years—and have profited handsomely. (Similar trends toward greater private-sector involvement in the delivery of public services have occurred in Canada, Great Britain, and West Germany.)

The federal government, especially, has seen a dramatic rise in contracting since World War II. By 1982, federal expenditures on contracting totaled almost one-fourth of the entire federal budget. The federal contracting system has been typified by enormous cost overruns for major weapons systems, by overpriced and useless consultants' studies, and by a lack of real competition in the awarding of most contracts. In addition, and perhaps more dangerous, corporations and think tanks under government contract have frequently shaped basic public policy in such areas as defense, energy and space exploration. Although there is ample evidence of abuses in federal contracting, state and local governments continue to follow the federal government's lead.

Contracting out is a high-stakes game. On one side of the issue are the contractors, their trade associations, local chambers of commerce, many state and local public officials, as well as many powerful federal figures. These powerful advocates of "privatization" claim that contracting out is a way for financially burdened state and local governments to trim budgets, to hold the line on taxes, and to improve the delivery of services. In seeking to involve the private sector more heavily in the delivery of basic public services at all levels of government, this group echoes a basic philosophy of the Reagan Administration: that we have too much government, that government provides too many services and that the private sector can provide whatever public services are needed more efficiently and more cheaply than public workers.

On the other side of the issue are public employees, public interest organizations, and many state and local government officials and community organizations who have experienced contracting out failures in their own jurisdictions. To these groups, it is clear that contracting out, rather than providing a panacea for state and local fiscal and service delivery problems (as its advocates claim), often increases governments' woes.

THE EXTENT OF CONTRACTING

Supporters and opponents agree that contracting out has been increasing in recent years, but accurate figures are hard to come by regarding the number of state and local jurisdictions that use contractors, the types of services they perform, and the total dollars involved. Still, several studies roughly indicate the extent of the practice and the trends.

In 1973, the Advisory Commission on Intergovernmental Relations sampled 2,375 local governments nationwide and identified 66 types of contracted services. Most frequent were refuse collection (14 percent of the jurisdictions sampled), street lighting (13 percent) and electricity supply and engineering services (11 percent each).

A 1979 survey of public works contracting in 620 cities by Dr. Eileen Berenyi, senior research associate at the Columbia University Graduate School of Business, found that 57 percent of the localities contracted for street paving, 30 percent contracted for solid waste collection, 19 percent for street lighting and 11 percent for vehicle maintenance.

A study published in 1979 by Patricia S. Florestano of the University of Maryland's Institute for Urban Studies and Stephen B. Gordon, coordinator of education and professional development at the National Institute of Governmental Purchasing in Washington, D.C., examined contracting for public services in counties and municipalities with populations of more than 500,000 in the United States and Canada.

Twenty-eight local government purchasing officials responded to the Florestano/Gordon survey. They reported contracting for 168 services; refuse collection and equipment maintenance led the list with 18 jurisdictions using private firms for these tasks. Half also contracted for building repair and maintenance and vehicle maintenance, while one-third contracted for ambulance service and food service for public employees. The study also found that many contracts were made without competitive bidding.

Another Florestano/Gordon study, published in 1980, reported on 89 localities with populations under 50,000. In these smaller communities, the study found that the most frequently contracted services were street construction, professional services (architects, attorneys, and so on), building repairs, and solid waste collection, with the biggest dollar-volume contracts being in the areas of professional services, solid waste collection, and street construction. The authors said that the results indicated that local governments' use of private contracts would expand rapidly in the future.

A more recent survey by the Southeast Michigan Council of Governments in 1982 disclosed that 127 of 195 local governmental units in the state—or 65 percent—contracted for some public services. Garbage collection was most common, with more than 100 localities using private firms.

The extent of contracting by state and local governments varies from state to state and community to community. The extremes run from localities which contract no services to a city such as Phoenix, Arizona, which had 450 outside contracts in effect in the early 1980s.

SQUEEZE PLAY ON GOVERNMENT

Although private firms regularly seek government contracts even in good economic times, a combination of factors in the 1970s and early 1980s has accelerated private marketing activity. The recession, coupled with increased foreign competition in many markets, has caused many private firms to look increasingly to the public sector for new sources of revenue. At the same time, state and local governments are becoming increasingly cost-conscious. They have been hurt by inflation and their revenues have been cut by recession.

In addition, property tax-cutting initiatives, such as Proposition 13 in California and Proposition 2½ in Massachusetts, further reduced available revenues. By 1981, this combination of inflation, recession and taxing limitations had placed state and local governments in the difficult position of having to raise taxes or reduce services, or finding other ways to reduce the costs of government.

The Reagan Administration has made the fiscal prospects for states and localities even bleaker. President Reagan has accelerated cutbacks in federal aid to states and particularly to localities, and he has proposed a massive transfer of federal responsibilities to the state and local governments. If the total program should become a reality, the private, nonprofit Urban Institute observed, "by 1991 federal aid to state and local governments would be almost as low a share of these governments' budgets as in 1933." Because of this, the Administration's approach has generated intense opposition from state and local public officials.

The fiscal situation has been particularly precarious for the cities. As the United States Conference of Mayors reported in late 1981: "Recently enacted federal budget cuts are imposing immense burdens on city budgets, resulting in massive layoffs, service reductions, tax increases and postponement of needed capital improvements." President Reagan's cuts in federal aid to cities in fiscal year 1982 were particularly hard on certain services; these included public schools, employment and training programs, parks and recreation programs, housing, police, fire and sanitation services, street and bridge maintenance, public transit, community and economic development programs, and water purification programs. Localities were also

forced to cut back or defer plans to acquire garbage trucks, buses and other city-owned equipment and to reduce maintenance of existing vehicles and equipment.

In addition to the economic pressures on localities and states to contract out, there have been political pressures as well. Within months after taking office, the Reagan Administration was actively lobbying local public officials to contract out more of their services. The U.S. Department of Housing and Urban Development began a series of "privatization" conferences and seminars limited to contractors and public officials and also scheduled a number of regional pro-contracting out conferences. The underlying theme was that local governments could no longer depend on federal assistance to fund public services and thus local officials had to "respond to changing fiscal realities." The conference agendas heavily emphasized the need to find "alternatives for public service delivery," using such devices as "contracting out, user fees, voucher systems, subsidies, franchising, volunteers and self-help programs." Assistant HUD Secretary E.S. Savas, a main Administration spokesman for contracting out, made it clear that federal help to the cities would concentrate on spreading the gospel of "privatization" rather than on federal dollars.

Another contracting advocate, Edward Wesemann, the former city manager of Mount Lebanon, Pennsylvania, said that he believed that "the Scottsdale case notwithstanding," public safety services —fire and police—should not be contracted out. Wesemann's reference was to Scottsdale, Arizona, where firefighting services are performed under private contract. The Scottsdale example is often cited by contracting out boosters as a major example of private-sector efficiency in providing public services and as an example that public safety services need not be handled by public employees. Wesemann, however, said that his own analysis of cost per fire and cost per capita indicated that fire protection in Scottsdale was more costly than for similar-sized cities where fire services are not contracted out.

With economic conditions deteriorating in recent years, and with city and state officials anxiously searching for ways to cut government operating costs, contracting out has sounded especially appealing. Private businesses, faced with depressed markets and often intense foreign competition, have viewed contracts in the public sector as a way to alleviate their own fiscal woes. Thus, on the surface contracting would appear to be a perfect match, offering state and local governments a way out of their managerial and financial problems while giving private firms a new market in the public sector.

Unfortunately, the partnership is too often unequal. Private-sector firms, indeed, often make substantial profits, but while state and local governments sometimes realize short-term benefits through lowered personnel costs, they are stuck with long-term disadvantages; they retain the responsibility for management, the quality of the services is often diminished, and costs after an initial drop begin to escalate.

THE ARGUMENTS FOR . . .

Advocates often say that contracting out costs less and provides better performance of a particular public service. As the Urban Institute, which leans toward the use of contracting out, has put it: "Competition and the profit motive are presumed to act in the same way in government purchase-of-service agreements as they do in private contracting."

Contracting advocates also contend that the system produces better management in state and local programs by bringing sophisticated cost-cutting and efficiency programs to public services. Contract managers can single-mindedly devote their time to improving a particular service without having to be caught up in the day-to-day administrative issues that drain so much of the time of public-sector managers. Conversely, its supporters say, contracting frees public administrators from managing day-to-day operations of a particular service, and gives them more time to plan future programs while requiring them to exercise only a monitoring role over the contractor.

Another often-cited advantage of contracting out is that it can provide specialized skills that are unavailable within government and for which it would cost too much to recruit new personnel and then put them on the permanent public payroll. In addition, contracting advocates claim, the use of private firms often permits "rapid initiation of new projects without large initial outlays for facilities, equipment, and training of personnel" by those private suppliers that have already made such an investment.

Advocates also contend that contracting out part of a service and keeping the other part in-house provide a yardstick to compare the costs and efficiency of the contractors' operations with public employees' performance of the same tasks.

Finally, advocates maintain that private-sector managers, motivated by the goals of self-advancement and monetary gain, have a stronger incentive than public managers to perform well. The other side of this, of course, is that the private-sector manager's first loyalty is to his or her firm, and not to the public, and steps taken to improve personal status and the company's profits may not consider the public good. This profit motivation argument is certainly an insult to all public managers, many of whom consider service to others as a major professional motivation.

Proponents of these views feel that when any service can be performed by the private sector—such as trash collection, snow removal, or street paving—it is unfair competition to allow the public sector to do such work exclusively. Public employees, so this argument goes, have a "monopoly" on such services and are not required to compete to survive, as their counterparts must do in the private sector. According to this philosophy, because workers and managers do not share in a profit or compete, they have little incentive to deliver low-cost, effective service; conversely, the private sector, with a profit motive and competition, must perform as efficiently and as cheaply as possible.

THE ARGUMENTS AGAINST . . .

Whatever the philosophic merit of these arguments, experience with contracting out at the state and local levels has demonstrated severe weaknesses in the practice of using private firms to deliver public services.

For example, rather than saving money for state and local governments, contracting out often results in higher costs—especially when all the true costs of contracting are actually considered. Private companies exist to make a profit; the necessity of a profit drives up the costs, if not immediately, then eventually. In addition, there are government's "hidden" costs such as contract preparation, the administration and monitoring of the contractor's performance, and the use of public facilities and materials. (These hidden costs are discussed in Chapter 2.)

Another key argument against contracting out is that it too often results in poorer services for citizens. Contractors are also looking for ways to reduce their costs, and frequently this has meant they "cut corners" by hiring inexperienced, transient personnel at low wages, by ignoring contract requirements, or by providing inadequate supervision.

The age-old problem of corruption in contracting out has not improved over time. As documented in an earlier AFSCME book, *Government for $ale*, and discussed further in Chapter 5, contracting is all too often associated with bribery, kickbacks, and collusive bidding. Also, contracts have frequently become a tool of political patronage to reward supporters of successful candidates—just as in the days of the spoils system, when public jobs were doled out to winning candidates' backers.

Contractors also go in and out of business; sometimes they may be unable to complete a contract, leaving a jurisdiction high and dry. When a city finds it necessary to remove a contractor for poor performance, it is often forced to make expensive interim arrangements.

Cities and states frequently find that a contract, originally awarded at an attractive rate, becomes more and more expensive. This common practice among contractors, called "buying in" or "lowballing," is notoriously evident in major defense contracts, at the federal level. In order to obtain the contract and thus get a foot in the door, a firm offers a very low price to perform a particular service. As contract performance continues, however, the city or state finds itself dependent on the particular contractor to such an extent that it cannot change contractors or take back service. This often occurs in long-term contracts for services, such as trash collection, which require expensive equipment that must be well maintained. After contracting out such a service, a municipality often sells its equipment, leaving it no realistic alternative but to use a contractor. The contractor who gets a contract with a "lowball" bid can thus obtain substantial price increases on subsequent contracts because the government is left with no options.

Another major problem with contracting out is in the drafting of appropriate job specifications. State and local governments often discover to their chagrin that is extremely difficult to write a contract which ensures that government gets what it wants for the agreed-upon price. Or, they learn that work tasks performed as a matter of course by public employees turn out not to be covered under the agreement with a contractor. Public managers directing a public work force have a large degree of flexibility to respond to unforeseen circumstances; on the other hand, a contractor has the clear right to refuse to do anything—even the smallest task— that isn't in the contract. Even experienced contract writers find it extremely difficult to design a document for complex services that covers all unforeseen circumstances and emergencies. When a contract's performance specifications are too narrow or contain loopholes, the inevitable result is a decrease in the quality of services for the public.

True competition for contracts is more often the exception than the rule in many state and local governmental jurisdictions. Contracts for trash collection, social services, and architectural, engineering and consulting services are often awarded under no-bid or negotiated-bid conditions. Where bidding ostensibly occurs, there is often collusion, as the ongoing paving and electrical contracting scandals demonstrate. . . . In addition, contracts often are "wired" by contracting officials, written so that only one favored or politically connected firm can possibly meet the specifications.

Contracting out results in less accountability by the government to the citizens. When citizens complain about a contracted service, government can often do little more than complain in turn to the contractor or enter into costly contract renegotiations or termination proceedings. At a time when many citizens feel that government is too removed from the people it serves, contracting out pushes the level of accountability and responsiveness one more giant step away. In addition, a dual system of government is created—one with workers who are subject to strict personnel regulations and pay and benefit schedules, all of them public—and another with workers who are subject only to the rules set by their private employers.

Dr. Rosaline Levenson, associate professor of political science at the California State University–Chico and a specialist on public personnel, put it this way: ". . . The private contractor and consultant affect policies and decisions of the agency with which they have a contract, yet the lines of control and accountability are unclear. . . . Private contracting could open the door to circumvention of personnel ceilings and standards, as well as to political patronage if contracts are awarded to supporters of the administration in power."

Contracting is frequently used to mask the inadequacies of public officials who can't manage their own departments properly. Any state or local governmental agency with skilled managers should be able to effect the same kinds of economies and efficiencies that good private managers achieve— and without the added problems that contracting out brings.

With competent public management, there would be no need even to consider contracting out in many of the instances in which it is now used. Paul D. Staudohar, professor of business and economics at California State University—Hayward, has written: "There is no innate reason why private employees should perform better than their public-sector counterparts. . . . Waste and inefficiency are found in all levels of service—private and public."

A LOOK AT THOSE "BENEFITS"

Even some organizations which generally favor contracting out have found numerous pitfalls in the policy of relying on the private sector for public services. As the Urban Institute noted in its 1978 report on contracting out: "The long-term benefits to local governments from many of the contracting arrangements examined were uncertain. Comprehensive, in-depth analysis of contracting, when undertaken, shows that contracting results in markedly lower costs in some cases but, in other instances, similar or even higher costs."

Particularly illuminating was a June 1981 study published by another pro-contracting out organization, the California Tax Foundation, whose board of trustees is dominated by executives of major corporations, utilities, and a bank. The Foundation, the research and education arm of the California Taxpayers Association, said the purpose of the study was "to illustrate how tax dollars can be saved through contracting out" as well as "to describe procedures, pitfalls, advantages and disadvantages of local officials desiring to begin or expand cost-effective contracting out."

Especially interesting were the comments of unnamed municipal officials. Although some were glowing in their praise of contracted services, others who had had direct experience with the practice were not enthusiastic. "The cost saving to be realized by contracting out is often grossly exaggerated," said one. "The benefits tend to be in what is *avoided* (the government 'red tape' and personnel problems) rather than what is actually saved."

Another official commented that among the "several drawbacks" of contracting out "is an attempt on the part of private contractors to view government contracts as 'easy money.' There is a significant segment of the private sector which operates under the assumption that minimum standards and high costs are normal operating practices for government." Another local official, who said his community had "drifted away from private contracts," contended that "we have found that in most cases the cost savings have been eaten up by increased administrative costs." Still another complained that his community's experiments with industrial refuse collection and grounds maintenance contracts "were unsatisfactory experiences not only in cost but in public relations. The contractors' employees lacked the sensitivity to individual citizens' problems. Consequently, city staff monitoring time was increased."

Even some of the strong advocates of contracting out raised warning flags. For example, one official who stated that "contracting services is the way of the future" went on to warn that "performance monitoring is difficult unless the city employs staff persons with skills that are being contracted for either in the private sector or from other governmental agencies. Often, contracting with the private sector is less expensive . . . but without technical skills or staff to monitor the contracts, one must trust the contractor to perform satisfactorily." The official noted that "when a city is burned once or twice by private contractors," it often goes back in-house for the service. "Our city hasn't had the problem to any great degree, but we have been cautious because of warnings from others."

The California Tax Foundation sent questionnaires to 310 municipalities, counties, school districts and special districts and received responses from 87. The study stated that most of the responding governmental units "reported they had experienced increased costs with contracting." However, the study also noted that many of these local governmental entities "do not have cost accounting systems which permit relevant comparison of total costs (direct and indirect) on a 'before' and 'after' basis." Therefore, the study continued, "it often cannot be accurately determined whether any cost increase occurring after contracting was greater, less, or the same as that which would have been the case had the service continued to be performed in-house."

In effect, this major study by a pro-contracting group found that many governmental units either have not saved money by contracting out or they don't really know whether they did or not.

In addition, the Foundation reported that some 49 percent of the cities and 42 percent of the counties surveyed had "difficulty monitoring contracts." Also, 28 percent of the cities and 42 percent of the counties felt that contracting out was disadvantageous because of the "unreliability of contractors."

Such statistics should carry a sharp warning to jurisdictions seriously contemplating contracting for basic services.

Too often, however, public officials ignore these warnings as well as the larger philosophical question of the proper role of government. Instead, relying on scanty evidence or isolated examples, they tout contracting out as *the* answer to mounting costs and inefficiencies in the delivery of public services—when the solution more often than not is to improve public management.

This book, with its numerous documented examples, has a simple message for state and local government officials: Thoroughly explore the alternatives to contracting out as part of your decision-making, before contracting out. You may be able to avoid the costly and disruptive mistakes made by others.

QUESTIONS FOR DISCUSSION

1. What criteria should be used in determining whether a public service should be operated by a public agency or a private firm?
2. Why do governments turn to the private sector to perform tasks traditionally provided by government agencies?
3. Is contracting out more likely to be effective at the local rather than the national level? Explain.
4. Is contracting out likely to lead to corruption of government officials? Explain.
5. Is the private sector more efficient than government? Why?

SUGGESTED READINGS

BUTLER, STUART M. (ed.), *The Privatization Option: A Strategy to Shrink the Size of Government.* Washington, DC: Heritage Foundation, 1985.

CALLISON, CHARLES H., "The Fallacies of Privatization," *Environment*, 25 (Oct. 1983), 7, 17–20, and 37.

HEIN, C. J., "Contracting Municipal Services: Does It Really Cost Less?," *National Civic Review*, 72 (June 1983), 321–26.

HOLMES, PETER A., "Taking Public Services Private," *Nation's Business* (Aug. 1985), 18–24.

LIBECAP, GARY D., "Problems of Privatizing," *Journal of Contemporary Studies*, 7 (Winter 1984), 29–33.

MCENTEE, GERALD W., "City Services: Can Free Enterprise Outperform the Public Sector?," *Business and Society Review*, No. 55 (Fall 1985), 43–47.

President's Private Sector Survey on Cost Control: Report on Privatization. Washington, DC: Government Printing Office, 1983.

RUNGE, CARLISLE FORD, "The Fallacy of 'Privatization'," *Journal of Contemporary Studies*, 7 (Winter 1984), 3–17.

SAVAS, E. S., *Privatizing the Public Sector.* Chatham, NJ: Chatham House, 1982.

U. S. CONGRESS., *Privatization of the Federal Government*, Hearings before the Subcommittee on Monetary and Fiscal Policy of the Joint Economic Committee, 98th Cong., 1st Sess., 1983, Parts 1 and 2.

16 YES
HAS AIRLINE DEREGULATION DONE MORE HARM THAN GOOD TO THE AIRLINE INDUSTRY AND THE PUBLIC IT SERVES?

Let the Process of Deregulation Continue*
Wesley G. Kaldahl

Under deregulation, events in the airline industry have moved so rapidly that we have tended to lose track of major milestones—and the places events occupy in time. It therefore comes as somewhat of a surprise to note that deregulation is now six years old. After all, wasn't it only yesterday that airline representatives were camped outside CAB headquarters, waiting to apply for dormant route authority?

Whether it was yesterday or not, one thing is clear: the Deregulation Act of 1978[1] ushered in for the nation's airlines a revolution as profound and far-reaching as the revolution upon which our nation was founded. After Congress and the President acted in 1978, the airline business was changed forever. The question on this sixth anniversary, however, is whether all of the upheaval and dramatic change that have characterized the industry's adjustment to deregulation have been good or bad, both for the industry and for the public it serves?

In my view the jury is still out on that question. But the record should also show that there is mounting evidence to support the view that deregulation has done more harm than good. I may make this statement with a touch of irony because American Airlines on the whole has adjusted well to the new environment. I also strongly believe that the industry is now down the road of change much too far to turn back. Nevertheless, one cannot deny the excruciating difficulties that have beset the industry—and most especially the large, established carriers like American—in this tough new age.

During the initial phases of debate on deregulation, American was among the staunchest op-

From Wesley G. Kaldahl, "Let the Process of Deregulation Continue," *Journal of Air Law and Commerce*, 50, No. 2 (1985), pp. 285–97. Reprinted with permission.
*This article is taken from a speech prepared by Mr. Kaldahl in early 1984.
[1]Airline Deregulation Act of 1978, Pub. L. No. 95–504, 92 Stat. 1705 (1978) (amending Federal Aviation Act of 1958, 49 U.S.C. § § 1301–1552 (1982)).

ponents of deregulation. At that time, the question was rather clear-cut: Should the existing regulatory system be *retained* or should it be *discarded* in favor of a new, deregulated order? In that context, American argued for keeping the regulatory system. Without question, there were elements of self-interest, but the overriding concern was for the air transport system itself (of which American was a key component). The regulatory system, although not without flaws, had served the industry and the public extremely well for forty years. American maintained that any requirement to stimulate price and route competition could be accomplished within that structure. American pointed out that deregulation, with its uncertainty and instability, could not avoid producing a detrimental effect on the airline system, including airports and airport operators.

Over time, however, the fundamental question before the nation changed. No longer was it a choice between regulation and deregulation, but only a question of what form deregulation should take. American then came out forcefully for total and immediate deregulation as the preferable alternative to the piecemeal proposals that would leave the industry half free and half restrained. Ultimately, in what could only be termed a supreme philosophical contradiction, the piecemeal approach prevailed, and the industry found itself partially deregulated.

How the industry has fared since that fateful day in October of 1978 best illustrates the onerous effects of the deregulatory scheme finally enacted. Financially, of course, the industry is presently in serious trouble. Supporters of deregulation, however, quickly point to the industry's outstanding profit performance in 1978. Indeed, 1978 was an exceptional year for the airlines. As a group, the majors alone reported operating earnings of almost $1.2 billion, and some carriers, including American, set individual profit records.

In no way, however, can these results be attributed to the positive effects of deregulation. The Airline Deregulation Act was not passed until late

October of 1978. Several months elapsed before the new regulatory order began to have a competitive impact, and consequently to have an effect on the airlines' financial results. In truth, 1979 was the industry's first full year of deregulation. By the end of that year, the industry was awash in the red ink that has since been flowing freely among most of the airlines.

The numbers speak for themselves. Between 1979 and 1982, the major airlines had combined operating losses of over $1.2 billion. Losses have continued for some carriers, even in a supposed recovery. Although some individual carriers have shown improvement, the majors as a whole had net losses of more than $181 million in 1983 with rough financial weather continuing into 1984. Even Delta, one of the industry's traditional profit leaders, suffered financially in the 1983 fiscal year.[2]

Significantly, the industry is losing money and continues to struggle financially in spite of several developments which, on the surface, should be improving airline balance sheets. For example, fuel prices have declined, saving the industry about $100 million a year with each one cent drop in the price per gallon. Various wage and work-rule concessions by labor unions are saving some carriers many millions of dollars each year. Agreements by major lending institutions are assisting certain struggling airlines either by restructuring their debt or by forgiving portions of their debt entirely. Furthermore, some airlines are reducing overall costs by contributing less to employee pension funds.

Each of these developments has produced tens of millions of dollars in savings for the struggling carriers. Nevertheless, these savings have not been enough to prevent the massive losses that have been making business page headlines for more than three years. Something in the airline environment, then, must be standing in the way of renewed profitability. Is the industry suffering from some chronic financial deficiency? Or is the industry simply suffering from the effects of a lingering and pronounced recession? There can be no denying that the recession has hurt; yet to suggest that the recession is our sole economic problem and that deregulation has been entirely beneficial is to deny the history of the last six years. Deregulation has had and continues to have a profound complicating effect on the financial health,

not only of the airline business, but also of aircraft manufacturing and other allied industries. The answer may be stated in two words: excessive competition.

When Congress enacted deregulation, it fully expected that the new law would intensify competition. What Congress did not anticipate, however, is the ruinous degree to which this competition has developed. Amid the oversimplifications that sometimes prevail when a legislative body considers an issue as complex as airline operations, Congress tended to equate increased competition with a set of perceived social benefits, most notably lower air fares and more service. Congress overlooked the less than obvious risks of deregulation.

More airline players, for example, mean less control over the critical economic factors that play such key roles in day-to-day business decisions and "long-range planning." More players mean greater cost disparity among individual airlines, placing some carriers at a serious competitive disadvantage not necessarily of their own making. More players mean excessive capacity in certain key markets, encouraging unsound pricing practices and even sparking some disastrous fare wars. And, conversely, more players mean a serious reduction in service in many less glamorous markets. More players mean a waste of precious jet fuel as more carriers fly more empty seats over more routes. As history has unfolded, these risks have become some of the harsh economic realities of deregulation, creating a business climate not conducive to making money. Such has been the crux of the industry's problems for the past six years.

At the same time, deregulation has not delivered to the public all of the benefits that were suggested would flow almost automatically. The lower fares that were to become a natural consequence of increased competition provide a good illustration. In actuality, fares have fallen in a few markets, though not in the smaller communities. Although competition under deregulation has indeed intensified, that competition has tended to be highly concentrated around a handful of major cities. It is on these routes and in these cities where most of the fare cutting has been initiated. In those markets where competition has not developed or has declined, fares have remained at much higher levels and, in some cases, are higher than they might have been without deregulation.

---

[2]See 1984 MOODY'S TRANSPORTATION MANUAL 1427–28.

Perhaps the most vivid example of concentration in competition is the New York–Los Angeles and New York–San Francisco markets. Under the old system, each route was aggressively and adequately served by three nonstop carriers: American, United and TWA. Within a year after the Deregulation Act became effective, seven nonstop carriers were competing in the New York–Los Angeles market while six were competing on the New York–San Francisco route. Intense price cutting ensued, making those two markets much less rewarding for everyone.

Listing those cities whose air service has increased by at least forty daily departures since 1978 provides another example. The list contains just twenty-two cities or markets. At the top is New York/Newark. Others are such major metropolitan centers as Houston, Dallas/Fort Worth, Denver, Phoenix, Minneapolis/St. Paul, Atlanta and Los Angeles. There are only a few modestly sized cities on the list. Significantly, none are in the category of medium or small markets.[3]

Although destructive competition has raged in the largest cities, more cities have lost service or experienced service reductions than have gained service or seen existing service increased. On the basis of total weekly scheduled departures, for example, 364 markets had declined or remain unchanged between 1978 and March of 1983, while only 289 markets had increased. Similarly, 436 markets had lost total weekly seats since 1978, while only 217 markets had gained. In other words, between March of 1979 and March of 1983, 116 cities have lost *all* air service while only 40 cities have service today that never had it before. Losers have outnumbered gainers by almost three to one!

Moreover, many of those cities adversely affected are important commercial and population centers. The list includes cities such as Chattanooga, Tennessee; Charleston, West Virginia; Columbia, South Carolina; Jackson, Mississippi; and Monroe, Louisiana. The inescapable conclusion is that a few large markets have prospered from deregulation while many smaller markets have suffered.

The effects on air fares are equally confusing. One of the glaring flaws of the pricing structure in the new environment has been its lack of fairness and equity for consumers, a deficiency that has damaged the credibility of the entire industry. The examples are already notorious. In January of 1982, a passenger could fly 2,500 miles from New York to San Francisco for $99, but would pay $268 to fly 1,800 miles from Memphis to San Francisco.[4] This disparity made no sense economically and seemed grossly unfair to the consumer, but it was a reflection of the competitive realities that existed at the time. Unforunately, competition still produces the same results in certain markets. Deregulation implied lower fares for most, but has delivered them only to the chosen few. Most passengers are now paying higher fares or at least more than they might be paying if fares were still regulated.

Meanwhile, the fare system has had a disastrous effect on the industry. The explosion of new fares under deregulation created nothing short of chaos for airline personnel and travel agents. And outrageous discounting, often below costs, almost brought the industry to its knees financially in 1981 and 1982. The mileage-based pricing system introduced by American early in 1983 has improved the situation by eliminating some of the worst fare inequities. In many markets, fares are now being offered on a more sensible and economically realistic basis. The problem has not been solved, however. The competitive dynamics of this industry are such that the potential for renewed chaos and complexity always exists, as the events of 1984 are proving. Hopefully, though, the members of the industry have learned from the bitter financial lessons of the past few years.

Other anomalies abound. The industry, for example, is offering less nonstop and effective single-plane service than under the old system, because of the extensive development of hubs and their emphasis on connecting services. In the days of regulation when route franchises were clearly defined, airlines could afford to operate on a nonstop or single-plane basis between many pairs of cities. Accordingly, the public became accustomed to this level of convenience and came to associate it with good airline service. Business travelers, for whom schedule frequency and convenience are para-

---

[3]CAB Staff Study, Report on Airline Service, Fares, Traffic, Load Factors and Market Shares (Issue No. 26, June 1983).

[4] Official Airline Guide, North American Edition (Jan. 15, 1982).

mount, in particular, grew dependent on this level of service.

Under the extreme competitive and economic pressures of deregulation, however, airlines have had to find new and more efficient ways of scheduling their flights. The result has been less nonstop, or point-to-point, flying and a dramatic shift to the hub-and-spoke system (where flights from one part of the system feed into an intermediate point and exchange passengers and freight with flights going to other parts of the system). This massive realignment of schedules and routes into huge hub-and-spoke operations has developed into one of the most significant themes of the deregulation era and is being practiced by dozens of airlines, large and small, in all parts of the country. Indeed, the practice is so widespread today that even the hubs themselves compete with one another for passengers and freight.

The emergence of hubs has fostered a dramatic change in air travel patterns. Today there are fewer opportunities to fly nonstop to a final destination because there are fewer nonstop flights available. Most passengers also find themselves traveling the entire distance with the same airline, rather than making interline connections to another airline at the intermediate point, because most airlines built their hubs with the aim of keeping passengers within their respective systems.

The numbers once again tell the story. Over the past six years, the percentage of passengers using on-line service (that is, those remaining within a single airline's system) has jumped from 84 percent to 92 percent. At the same time, however, the percentage of passengers using single-plane service to their final destination has dropped significantly in all but a token number of markets. In the Louisville–Los Angeles market, for example, 62.2 percent of all passengers used single-plane service in 1978 but only 3.7 percent did so in 1982.[5] Boston–Nashville is another example. On that route, 78.7 percent were single-plane passengers in 1978 but only 36.4 percent flew single-plane in 1982.[6] The point is further illustrated by a recent study which showed that 24 percent of American Airlines'

on-line passengers required connecting flights in 1982, as compared with 8 percent in 1978.[7] Thus, a system that was to produce better service has instead led the industry to offer fewer nonstop and direct flights and more flights requiring connections.

Yet another anomaly exists in that one-stop or connecting flights are often cheaper than nonstop flights in many large markets like New York–Los Angeles. The desire of airlines to promote their hubs by luring passengers away from airlines with nonstop services in particular markets accounts for this pricing contradiction. A few years ago, for example, a competitor of American established a major hub in Denver and began offering coast-to-coast fares over the Denver hub that seriously undercut the already low fares in effect for transcontinental nonstop flights. To protect its market position, American was forced to match the hub fares over its connecting center at Dallas/Fort Worth, even though the fares were clearly unwise and unrelated to the production costs of connecting service. In effect, the attractive one stop flight required the passengers to be handled one additional time on the ground and to be flown on 727 aircraft that are not as efficient per seat mile as the wide-body aircraft used in the nonstop transcontinental markets. It simply does not make sense to offer lower prices for a product that costs more to produce. Neither does it make sense to use fares to discourage nonstop travel while promoting service that involves greater circuity and elapsed travel time. And it does not make sense to divert traffic to less efficient and less productive aircraft. Logic and reason, however, are often overshadowed in the new age by the demands of competition.

One of the major complaints about the old regulatory system was that passengers in short-haul markets were subsidized through generally higher fares paid by passengers on long-haul routes. One of the curious ironies of deregulation is that subsidization still occurs. Today, the cost of traveling between the New York area and Los Angeles can be as low as $119 each way. But to fly from Memphis to Phoenix (just half the distance) will cost $341.[8] The higher fare paid by the Memphis passenger helps to underwrite the big transcontinental

[5] Civil Aeronautics Board, Origin—Destination Survey of Airline Passenger Traffic Domestic, Table 12, Fourth Quarters of 1978 and 1982.

[6] Id.

[7] Id .

[8] Official Airline Guide, North American Edition (Oct. 15, 1984).

discount. Scores of other hidden examples can be found throughout the system.

Another anomaly of the new age is that while some cities are losing service or are seeing a decline in the frequency of their service, schedules are being built around hub airports. These schedules are entirely out of proportion to the local passenger demand in hub cities. The Los Angeles market illustrates this point. For years, American operated nonstop service between Nashville and Los Angeles. With the emphasis on hubs in the new environment, however, it became prudent to discontinue the Nashville nonstops and instead route those airplanes through the DFW hub. In order to build the DFW hub, American increased its nonstop frequency between DFW and Los Angeles and even added widebody airplanes on the route. The end result, of course, is that Dallas/Ft. Worth residents flying to Los Angeles have six daily nonstop flights to choose from, but Nashville residents, who once could fly nonstop to Los Angeles, now have to change planes at DFW. The proponents of deregulation did not allude to this consequence when selling the concept of deregulation to Congress and the public.

The proponents of deregulation also failed to indicate that new airlines entering the industry in the new environment would receive the kind of preferential treatment that has been accorded such newcomers. The federal government, for example, has given many new airlines loan guarantees, and thus lower costs, to facilitate aircraft acquisitions. From its founding until 1983, about two years ago, People Express enjoyed CAB exemptions from the baggage liability and denied boarding compensation rules that apply to the rest of the industry. The CAB granted the exemption on the theory that People's Express was a new, low-fare airline and therefore should not be expected to bear the same expense burdens as established carriers. People's Express stated that the administrative burden—for an airline with less than 50 aircraft—would be in excess [of] $3 million annually. Imagine the cost to a huge, established airline! Strangely, of course, there was no similar CAB edict to prevent People's Express from using its low fares to steal traffic from the rest of the industry. The inconsistency in the government's logic is astounding.

Looking back over the last five years, it is evident that deregulation certainly has not lived up to its euphoric billing. Additionally, the new air transport system which has emerged under deregulation has done very little for the industry's major constituents. *The public* has not benefitted. There is less nonstop service, most lengthy trips require stops at intermediate hubs, and fares are widely inconsistent and tend to favor the few chosen markets. *Stockholders* have not benefitted. Most carriers have struggled financially in the new age, eroding stockholder equity and preventing the kind of solid, sustained profitability that leads to renewed or increased dividends. *Airline employees* have not benefitted. Layoffs, wage cuts, benefit reductions and other austerity measures have almost become the norm in the industry as airlines fight for survival in an intensely competitive environment. *Most cities* have not benefitted. More cities have lost service than have gained service. Airline schedules have become concentrated around hub airports in a few major cities at the expense of many small markets. *Aircraft manufacturers* have not benefitted. As losses have mounted over the past few years, airlines have been forced to cancel orders, delay aircraft deliveries, and discontinue plans for new orders that, absent deregulation, would have been placed. As a result, the manufacturers themselves are struggling and are finding it hard to compete in world markets where some competitors are backed by foreign governments that assist their manufacturers in luring new orders with various financing incentives. *Lenders and creditors* have not benefitted. Some airlines— Braniff, Continental, Air New England, Altair, Air Florida, Golden West—have gone bankrupt. Other carriers with serious financial troubles have had to seek debt restructuring and other concessions that impede the recovery of massive investments in the industry. Airlines now have a "bad name" in the financial community. Lenders already heavily committed to poor-risk carriers now have little money for the good-risk airlines who need capital for growth and revitalization.

Should these harsh facts suggest that the industry return to some form of regulation? I would respond an emphatic "no." The industry is too complex, too dynamic and too far down the road of deregulation ever to be reregulated in any equitable, sensible way. The deregulators intended to totally dismantle the economic structure of regulation. The deregulators sought to throw the industry completely open so that free market forces alone would determine the prices charged, the markets served, and the manner of doing business. Though the results are open to question, the attempt itself was a complete success, as far as it went.

On every economic front, the industry has been revolutionized. All of the old boundaries and restrictions have vanished. The airlines move today through a new and largely uncharted terrain. The boundaries of a former age, however sensible and beneficial they may look in restrospect, can no longer be erected in any logical way. Any attempt by legislators to undo deregulation and put the old system back together would simply make conditions in the industry worse. Again, this is an extremely complex industry. There was little congressional understanding of these complexities during the deregulation debates of the 1970's, and there is no reason to believe that Congress, as a whole, is any more knowledgeable today. The airlines could just as easily again become the victims of misguided notions and simplistic judgments.

Many in the airline industry have paid a heavy price for change. When deregulation was enacted, the industry found itself with the wrong airplanes, with a cost structure that was too high, with too many point-to-point routes, with too many employees, and with airport facilities that were too large in some markets and too small in others. Adaptation has not been easily achieved, but American is finally adjusting to the new environment. American's hubs are in place, it is whittling away at its

cost structure; employment levels are more realistic, it is acquiring new, more efficient aircraft, and it is bringing airport facilities in line with the needs of a realigned route network.

To complete the task and prosper once again, a higher degree of labor/management cooperation than has been historically practiced in the industry is essential. Under deregulation no high-cost airline can hope for long-term profitability. American's labor and management are working hard to effect the transition from high to low cost without sacrificing the income or the jobs and security of career employees.

Now, just as American's reputation, service skills, marketing and operational abilities, and revamped route structure are beginning to come together, some suggest that perhaps the industry should reverse itself in midstream and undo everything that has been accomplished since 1978. Such a suggestion is not only naive, it is unrealistic. The wiser, sounder course is to complete the adjustment to deregulation that is already well underway. At this advanced stage in the game, it is clearly preferable that the *marketplace*, rather than the government, determine American's future and the future of the industry. While the government continues to hold an important position in matters pertaining to safety, other issues are best left to free enterprise and open competition, just as the proponents of deregulation intended.

16 NO HAS AIRLINE DEREGULATION DONE MORE HARM THAN GOOD TO THE AIRLINE INDUSTRY AND THE PUBLIC IT SERVES?

Deregulation and the Troglodytes—How the Airlines Met Adam Smith
Herbert D. Kelleher

Almost 200 years after his death, Adam Smith's ethereal invisible hand swept across the American airline industry, brushing aside in its wake a regu-

From Herbert D. Kelleher, "Deregulation and the Troglodytes—How the Airlines Met Adam Smith," *Journal of Air Law and Commerce*, 50 No. 2 (1985), pp. 299–318. Reprinted with permission.

latory structure which for forty years had bred the arrogance, slothful inefficiency and unresponsiveness inherent in an industry which has substituted paternal "regulation" by a supposedly omniscient regent for the competitive impetus of a free marketplace. Through a single broad stroke, enacted with the support of a newly-enlightened regulatory agency under the leadership of Chairman Alfred

Kahn, Congress set the airlines free of the regulatory strictures which had constrained the innovation of service alternatives, restricted market entry and discouraged price competition. As might be expected of a troupe of competitive troglodytes emerging from the protective cocoon of a regulated existence, some members of the newly liberated sect suffered, and some prospered, while some fell into a boiling caldron.[1]

Because deregulation of the airline industry provided much of the stimulus for a general reevaluation of the beneficence of economic regulation of other potentially competitive industries (such as communications,[2] trucking,[3] and financial services[4]), it may be of some moment, although perhaps somewhat premature, to evaluate the impact of airline deregulation upon the industry, the communities it serves and, most importantly, upon the consumers the industry exists to serve. Although the view is far from unanimous,[5] the weight of evidence and experience strongly suggests that despite tremendous unforeseen obstacles arising from the unprecedented escalation of fuel costs, a severe economic "recession" which might be more aptly described as a "depression" in the airline industry, unprecedented high interest rates and the disjointing of our national air transportation system caused by the PATCO [Professional Air Traffic Controllers] strike,

deregulation has served our nation well. Indeed, a strong case can be made that it was only the flexibility and creativity made possible by deregulation that saved the airline industry from unmitigated disaster during the period from 1978 to 1983.

In reality, the Airline Deregulation Act of 1978[6] did not instantaneously deregulate the airline industry, but instituted a gradual process of regulatory change, culminating in the abolition of the Civil Aeronautics Board (CAB) in 1985.[7] Perceptive economists had for some time recognized that CAB regulation resulted in greater inefficiency and higher fares than would otherwise have existed.[8] These views gained support from the successful introduction of efficient low-fare air service in the intrastate markets of California by PSA and Air California, and Texas by Southwest Airlines, where state regulatory agencies adopted liberal entry and pricing policies approximating economic "deregulation."[9] In 1975, the CAB appointed a special staff to study proposals for regulatory reform, resulting in a staff recommendation that public utility-type controls be eliminated

---

[1] Cf. The Three Little Pigs (in which the boiling caldron was reserved for one who tried to eat too many little pigs in one day).

[2] See, e.g., United States v. American Tel. & Tel. Co., 552 F.Supp. 131 (D.D.C. 1982), aff'd sub nom. Maryland v. United States, 103 S.Ct. 1240 (1983); Repeal of the "Regional Concentration of Control" Provisions of the Commission's Multiple Ownership Rules, 49 Fed. Reg. 2,478 (1984) (to be codified at 47 C.F.R. pt. 73) (proposed Jan. 20, 1984); Multiple Ownership of AM, FM and Television Broadcast Stations, 48 Fed. Reg. 49,438 (1983) (to be codified at 47 C.F.R. pt. 73) (proposed Oct. 24, 1983), corrected, 48 Fed. Reg. 50,907 (Nov. 4, 1983).

[3] See Motor Carrier Act of 1980, Pub. L. No. 96–296, 94 Stat. 793 (codified at 49 U.S.C. §§ 10101–11917 (1982)).

[4] See Depository Institutions Deregulation and Monetary Control Act of 1980, Pub. L. No. 96–221, 94 Stat. 132 (1980) (codified in scattered sections of 12 U.S.C.); see also Gorinson, Depository Institution Regulatory Reform in the 1980s: The Issue of Geographic Restrictions, 28 ANTITRUST BULL. 227 (1983).

[5] See Kay, All Flights Cancelled, TEXAS BUSINESS, May 1984, at 36: Deregulation Foes in Counterattack, Los Angeles Times, July 3, 1983, pt. VI at 8, col. 1.

[6] Airline Deregulation Act, Pub. L. No. 95–504, 92 Stat. 1705 (1978) (codified as amended at 49 U.S.C. §§ 1301 –1552 (1982)).

[7] An entertaining commentary on the "causes" of the airline Deregulation movement can be found in Callison, Airline Deregulation—Only Partially A Hoax: The Current Status of the Airline Deregulation Movement, 45 J. AIR L. & COM. 961, 962–64 n.4, 965 (1980). Mr. Callison, the Senior Vice President-General Counsel for Delta Air Lines, concludes that:

> Viewed by hindsight, the leaders of the airline deregulation movement were Senators Cannon and Kennedy, Congressman Elliot Levitas, Dr. Alfred Kahn, and the Ford Administration, spurred on, of course, by the various academic economists who pushed the theory in the beginning and throughout. The Carter Administration also played a role, but its major contribution was appointing Alfred Kahn to the CAB.

Id. at 964 n.4.

[8] G. DOUGLAS & J. MILLER, ECONOMIC REGULATION OF DOMESTIC AIR TTRANSPORT: THEORY AND POLICY (1974); Keeler, Airline Regulation and Market Performance, 3 BELL J. ECON. & MGT. SCI. 399 (1972); W. JORDAN, AIRLINE REGULATION IN AMERICA (1970); R. CAVES, AIR TRANSPORT AND ITS REGULATORS: AN INDUSTRY STUDY (1962).

[9] See SIMAT, HELLIESON & EICHER INC., AN ANALYSIS FOR THE INTRASTATE AIR CARRIER REGULATORY FORUM, VOLUME 1 SUMMARY REPORT (1976); Note, Is Regulation Necessary? California Air Transportation and National Regulatory Policy, 74 YALE L.J. 1416 (1965).

within three to five years.[10] The report concluded that the airline industry "is naturally competitive, not monopolistic," and that regulation caused higher-than-necessary costs and prices, weakened the ability of carriers to respond to market demands and narrowed the range of price/quality choices available to the consumer.[11] Thus, the industry was hardly shocked when Senator Kennedy's Subcommittee on Administrative Practice and Procedure recommended that the focus of the nation's aviation policy should shift from promoting the well-being of the aviation industry to making its service economically available to more of the American public.[12] Nor was the industry surprised when President Ford sent to Congress a comprehensive program of reform entitled the Aviation Act of 1975, which was designed to allow greater pricing flexibility and freedom of entry.[13]

The transition to deregulation began in 1977 with the appointment of Dr. Alfred Kahn as Chairman of the CAB. Under the leadership of Dr. Kahn, the CAB commenced its first major low-fare route case, in which it expressly requested parties to explore whether the authority to enter a market should be permissive and whether more than one applicant should be granted authority in each city-pair market.[14] A year later, the CAB went further and proposed to award multiple authority to all qualified applicants by nonhearing show cause proceedings, eliminating the lengthy hearings of the comparative selection process and the restriction of entry to a single carrier.[15] About the same time, the CAB also began approving individual carriers' proposals for discount and promotional fares, such as Texas International's "Peanuts" fare,[16] and American's "Su-

persaver" fare from New York to the West Coast.[17] By the late fall of 1977, the CAB had decided not to intervene through promulgation of discount fare policies and had adopted the view that allowing airlines to implement their own pricing strategies could significantly improve the economic performance of the industry.[18]

The CAB's decision to reduce price restrictions coincided with the most favorable part of the business cycle for the industry, so that substantial fare reductions tapped price-sensitive segments of the public and resulted in a substantial increase in demand for air service. In 1978, traffic grew markedly in response to the wide availability of deep discount fares. Average fares (adjusted for inflation) fell almost nine percent. Load factors increased more than five points, and carrier profits increased markedly.[19]

Thus, by the time President Carter signed the Airline Deregulation Act on October 18, 1978, the theories of the deregulation economists and the experiences of intrastate carriers in Texas and California seemed confirmed by the real-life experiment of limited deregulation of the CAB-regulated carriers. The trunk carriers were experiencing substantial increases in loads, enjoying healthy profits, and aggressively plotting their own post-deregulation courses. Aircraft manufacturers were enjoying bountiful orders for new aircraft. Deregulation appeared to be a panacea to everyone associated with the industry.

In 1979, however, things began to turn sour for much of the industry. Events in the Middle East precipitated a sudden rise in fuel prices. Between the first quarters of 1979 and 1980, the CAB permitted average fares to increase by thirty-one percent, but even this could not keep pace with the rapid increase in costs occasioned largely by the more than doubling of the price of fuel.[20] The economy then began a prolonged recession. Interest rates skyrocketed, wreaking havoc on the balance sheets of highly leveraged carriers who had the misfortune

---

[10]Report of the CAB Special Staff on Regulatory Reform (1975).

[11]Executive Summary of Report of the CAB Special Staff on Regulatory Reform at 1 (1975).

[12]SENATE SUBCOMM. ON ADMINISTRATIVE PRACTICE AND PROCEDURE, 94TH CONG., 1ST SESS., AIRLINE REGULATION OF THE CIVIL AERONAUTICS BOARD (Comm. Print 1975).

[13]S. 2551, 94th Cong., 1st Sess., 121 Cong. Rec. 33,505–509 (1975).

[14]Chicago-Midway Low-Fare Route Proceeding, 78 C.A.B. 454 (1978).

[15]Oakland Service Case, 78 C.A.B. 593 (1978).

[16]Texas International Airlines "Peanuts" Fares Proceeding, 72 C.A.B. 868 (1977).

---

[17]American Airlines "Supersaver" Fares Proceeding, 73 C.A.B. 1066 (1977). The "Peanuts" fare and "Supersaver" fare decisions were made under Chairman John Robson, who preceded Alfred Kahn as CAB Chairman.

[18]E. BAILEY, D. GRAHAM & D. KAPLAN, DEREGULATING THE AIRLINES—AN ECONOMIC ANALYSIS 121 (1983).

[19]Id. at 39–40.

[20]Id. at 42.

to have recently-acquired or floating-rate debt. Carriers such as Braniff, which had aggressively acquired new aircraft and entered new markets in the anticipation of reaping a deregulation bonanza, and Republic, which borrowed heavily to acquire Hughes Airwest, were among the hardest hit.

In 1981, which was marked by the disruption following the PATCO strike, the former trunk airlines,[21] in the aggregate, had an operating [loss] of approximately $480 million. For 1982, the operating losses widened to approximately $650 million, not including losses suffered by Braniff or Texas Air, the holding company parent of Continental.[22] Adding Braniff and Continental increased the 1982 operating losses by over $67 million.[23]

Does this dismal aggregate performance by the largest, and formerly most regulated, members of the airline industry render deregulation a failure? Even assuming all the airlines' woes were attributable to deregulation, which they clearly are not, the answer would still be "no." Deregulation has produced substantial societal benefits in the form of lower fares, increased service, diversity of service and price alternatives, reduced industry concentration, more efficient allocation of resources and, in the long run, a more healthy, efficient and innovative airline industry.

Analysis of the effect of deregulation on airlines fares must begin with a recognition of the fact that between 1976, the last year before relaxation of regulation began, and 1983, the year after the CAB's route, rate and tariff authority ended,[24] airline costs increased by seventy-one percent, yet fares increased by only forty-five percent. Between the year ending September 1978, just before the Deregulation Act was passed, and June 1983, costs increased by fifty-four percent while fares increased thirty-nine percent.[25] Thus, it appears that the cost-plus method

of pricing, which existed under CAB regulation, has been destroyed and that, in the aggregate, consumers are enjoying the benefits of substantially lower fares than would otherwise exist. Under regulation, the CAB adjusted fares with a focus on industry profitability. From 1960 to 1974, the Board set fares to achieve an average 10.5 percent rate of return for the industry based on actual industry operating costs. Beginning in 1974, the Board set fares to yield a twelve percent return based on "optimal" industry load factors and seating density.[26]

The benefit of the substantial aggregate savings resulting from deregulation has not, of course, been spread evenly. The CAB adjustment of fares operated uniformly for all markets, without regard to market density or level of competition. Fare levels were generally related to distance, with long-haul fares set substantially above cost and short-haul fares deliberately set below cost.[27] Consequently, the CAB-regulated carriers frequently allowed their quality of service on the unprofitable short-haul routes to reflect their disdain for these markets.[28]

With carriers now free to set their own pricing policies, prices tend to reflect market forces as well as cost. Although subject to temporary distortions, fares are generally tending to find their natural level, reflecting the price at which service can economically be provided on a market-by-market basis. The competitive market forces now shaping the airlines' fare structures reflect, in a way government regulators never could, the actual cost of providing the most efficient service to a specific market. The presence of actual and potential competition in every market provides strong discipline against pricing practices which would produce super-normal profits.

The impact of actual competition on fares has been dramatic in many markets. For example, when Southwest opened its first interstate route from Houston to New Orleans in early 1979, the one-way standard coach fares in the market were $50 to $52. Southwest entered the market offering un-

[21]American, Braniff, Continental, Delta, Eastern, Northwest, Pan American, TWA, United and Western. Republic and U.S. Air have, since deregulation, been added to the list of "trunks."

[22]Derchin & Tortor, First Boston Research Aviation Bulletin, Mar. 7, 1983.

[23]Civil Aeronautics Board Report to Congress, Implementation of the Provisions of the Airline Deregulation Act of 1978, Appendix D (1984).

[24]49 U.S.C. § 1551(a) (1984).

[25]Civil Aeronautics Board Report to Congress, supra note 23, at 20.

[26]E. BAILEY, D. GRAHAM & D. KAPLAN, supra note 18, at 103.

[27]Id. at 102–44.

[28]See Texas Aeronautics Comm'n v. Braniff Airways, 454 S.W.2d 199, 202–03 (Tex. 1970) (record of cancelled flights and late flights on routes served by CAB certificated carriers in the Dallas, Houston and San Antonio markets).

restricted fares of $30 for every seat on every flight before 7:00 p.m. on weekdays, and $20 on weekends and weekday evenings.[29] Six years later, despite precipitous increases in fuel costs and six years of inflation, Southwest serves that market with hourly flights and unrestricted fares of $55 and $40. Today Southwest offers unrestricted weekend and evening fares for every seat substantially below the prevailing standard coach fares offered by the old CAB-regulated carriers in 1979. And several competitors match Southwest's fares, although most do so on a "restricted" basis.[30]

The benefits of actual competition have, to be sure, taken longer to reach some markets than others. For example, in March 1984, when Southwest commenced service between Dallas and Little Rock, the standard coach fare offered by incumbent carriers was $139 and $149, and the lowest restricted fare was $89.[31] Southwest entered the market offering unrestricted coach fares of $47 for every seat on weekdays before 7:00 p.m., and $32 for every seat on weekends and weekday evenings. The incumbent carriers suddenly discovered that they, too, could economically provide service at those fares, albeit on a restricted basis.[32] Other low-fare carriers, such as People Express and Northeastern, have brought about similar dramatic fare reductions upon entering new markets.

Although fares are markedly higher in markets not served by new, low-fare entrants, even in these markets the threat of competition from potential new-market entrants serves to discipline pricing practices. The freedom of airlines to enter markets at will has caused most airline city-pair markets to become readily contestable. The major economic barrier to entry into specific markets is the acquisition and location of aircraft. Aircraft, however, are readily movable from one market to another, and do not represent the type of "sunk costs" which, once sunk, become a true barrier to entry.[33]

The principle of market contestability means that a carrier which overprices its product risks market entry by a lower-priced competitor. In the three years from 1978 to 1981, 122 of the 200 most heavily traveled markets experienced entry by at least one new carrier.[34] A prudent competitor will seek out markets that are underserved or overpriced, for these markets present the greatest potential for profit. Moreover, experience demonstrates that lower fares and increased competition serve to increase traffic, making underserved and overpriced markets particularly attractive. For example, with the entry of Southwest Airlines' low fares and frequent service in 1971, air traffic between Dallas and Houston increased 127.5% from 1970 to 1974, while ten similar high-density CAB-regulated markets grew an average of only 9.8 percent during the same period.[35] Similar experiences have been encountered repeatedly as Southwest has entered new markets with its low fares and frequent flights. This increase in total traffic, generally resulting in high load factors for Southwest, is frequently accomplished without a significant impact upon the incumbent carriers' traffic in the market. In part, this is attributable to the incumbents' own reduction in fares and is, in part, the result of traffic which is newly generated or attracted from surface transportation in short-haul markets.

The impact of fares upon traffic is demonstrated on a more global scale by the experience of carriers as a whole under deregulation. In 1978, fare rates per revenue passenger mile (RPM) fell by 8.5% while traffic grew by 16.7% The next year fares again fell, this time by only 5.3% while traffic again grew, by a more modest 11.1%. In 1980, however, impelled by higher fuel costs, fares rose by 13.5%. Traffic, consequently, fell by 5.4%. In 1981, fares rose by 2.5% and traffic dropped by 3.7%.[36] In 1982, the carriers' fares fell 3.76%; traffic rose 6.2%.[37] In 1983, fares fell by 0.5%, and traffic climbed by a strong 11.2%.[38] The pattern is unmistakable.

[29]OFFICIAL AIRLINE GUIDE, NORTH AMERICAN EDITION (February 1, 1979) [hereinafter cited as OAG].

[30]OAG FARE ISSUE, supra note 29 (March 1, 1984).

[31]OAG, supra note 29 (Mar. 1, 1984).

[32]OAG, supra note 29 (Apr. 15, 1984).

[33]Bailey & Panzar, The Constestability of Airline Markets During the Transition to Deregulation, 44 LAW & CONTEMP. PROBLEMS 125, 128–29 (1981).

[34]E. BAILEY, D. GRAHAM, & D. KAPLAN, supra note 18, at 90.

[35]Id. at 22.

[36]Id. at 40. These fare figures are adjusted for inflation.

[37]M. Derchin & R. Tortora, supra note 22.

[38]M. DERCHIN & R. TORTORA, AIRLINE INDUSTRY: FOURTH QUARTER AND FULL YEAR 1983 RETROSPECTIVE (Mar. 7, 1984). Derchin and Tortora's fare figures are not adjusted for inflation. The magnitude of the 1983 and 1984 fare decreases is therefore understated.

The impact of potential competition on fares is demonstrated by the fact that ticket prices at slot-constrained airports tend to be higher than those at airports that are not slot-constrained.[39] Similarly, markets with only one CAB-certificated carrier in 1979, when market entry still generally entailed cumbersome CAB proceedings, had statistically higher fares than those with multiple authorized carriers. Markets with only one authorized carrier averaged fares at ninety-seven percent of the standard industry fare level (SIFL), while those markets with more than one authorized carrier, where actual or potential entry was readily possible, averaged ninety percent of the SIFL.[40]

Experience with fare deregulation suggests that markets which continue to endure noncompetitive fares either cannot economically support service at lower fares, or have simply not yet been "found" by an aggressive competitor ready to cut fares to gain market share. If the former is the case, then there should be little room for complaint, since the market is receiving exactly the level of service it is capable of supporting. If the latter is the case, time and natural market forces will resolve the situation in due course. Perceptive airline route managers regularly scan maps, airline boarding figures, and prevailing fare levels in search of market openings. In any event, it is clear that the free market can better tell airlines where to cut fares than the government can (which it seldom did).

Discussion of air service to small communities since deregulation has frequently centered upon two misconceptions: (1) that the rate of loss of air service to small communities has increased with deregulation; and (2) that the loss of service that has occurred is attributable to deregulation. Each of these assumptions is incorrect.

During the ten years from 1968 to 1978, the CAB deleted 127 points from carrier certificates, often concluding that the subsidy cost did not justify continued service. Suspension of service without replacement was permitted at another 64 points.[41] Thus, the Board was deleting points at a rate of over one per month prior to deregulation, and even the points receiving service frequently received inadequate or unsatisfactory service (with flights at inconvenient times to remote locations). The Deregulation Act sought to halt this trend with the establishment of the Essential Air Service (EAS) Program. Under this program, the CAB was charged with assuring through subsidies or carrier "lock-in" procedures that "essential air service" is provided to any community receiving service from only one certificated carrier on October 24, 1978, to any community whose service was thereafter reduced to only one carrier, and to any community whose service was authorized, but had been suspended, on October 28, 1978.[42] The CAB was also responsible for resuscitating service to communities whose service had been deleted from carrier certificates before deregulation.[43] Between 1978 and 1983, the number of departures at EAS points actually increased by 5.2%, although the number of seats in these markets decreased by 13.7%.[44] This increase in departures and decrease in seats is largely attributable to the improved suitability of aircraft size to markets.

Convenient air service, especially in thinly traveled markets, is far more related to frequency of service than to the number of available seats. If the frequency is available, the market will have an opportunity to demand for itself the number of seats necessary to serve the market. Although the size of aircraft serving small communities has generally decreased, the quality of service has probably improved overall. Small communities now receive more flights and greater service to small hubs than before, giving them better access to major commercial centers and connecting flights, rather than the "milk runs" they historically had received.[45]

While the facts suggest that small communities have benefitted from the passage of the Deregulation Act, the continued comparatively high level of

---

[39]Graham, Kaplan & Sibley, *Efficiency and Competition in the Airline Industry*, 14 Bell J. Econ. 118. 124 (1983); Note, *Airline Deregulation and Airport Regulation*, 93 Yale L.J. 319, 328 (1983).

[40]Bailey & Panzar, *supra* note 33, at 137–38.

[41]Civil Aeronautics Board Report to Congress, *supra* note 23, at 47–49.

[42]49 U.S.C. § 1389(2) (1982). Authority over the EAS became housed in the Department of Transportation when the CAB was dismantled on December 31, 1984. 49 U.S.C.A. §1551(b)(1)(a) (West Supp. 1984).

[43]49 U.S.C. § 1389(b) (1982). The Department of Transportation now exercises this authority. 49 U.S.C.A. § 1551(b)(1)(a) (West Supp. 1984).

[44]Civil Aeronautics Board Report to Congress, *supra* note 23, at 49.

[45]E. Bailey, D. Graham, & D. Kaplan, *supra* note 18, at 94–96.

government regulation of small-to-medium markets may actually be injuring efforts of those communities to attract air service by larger carriers. Unlike other unregulated markets, EAS points may not be freely exited by the "last" carrier providing service. A certificated carrier must give the CAB ninety days notice before exiting the market. Even after the ninety-day waiting period expires, the carrier is subject to being "locked-in" and prevented from leaving the market until a replacement carrier is found.[46] This well-meaning attempt to protect communities from the total loss of air service represents a formidable obstacle to a carrier seeking the most efficient allocation of its resources. Although the carrier is entitled ultimately to be reimbursed for any "losses" incurred after the ninety-day notice period,[47] trunk and major regional airlines are not likely to be attracted by the prospect of a government subsidy to cover "losses" whose calculation may be subject to lengthy and contested proceedings. Airlines looking at the commitment of an aircraft costing at least $15 million are more likely to be deterred by the knowledge that they cannot easily remove the aircraft to a market where it can make a profit. Thus, the spirit of entrepreneurial experimentation which might lead prudent businesspersons in a free market to "take a chance" on many smaller communities may well be dampened. The obligation of the "last carrier" to continue service indefinitely has, moreover, undoubtedly hastened the departures of numerous "next to last" carriers seeking to "bail out" before being saddled with an essential service obligation. To the extent that small communities can complain of their inability to attract "major" carriers since deregulation, their frustrations might, in some cases at least, be more appropriately directed at the remnants of regulation rather than deregulation.

Airline routes and service patterns have undergone substantial change since market entry was made discretionary and the rules for market exit were greatly liberalized. On the average, a carrier served about the same number of nonstop routes in 1983 as in 1978, but only about forty percent of its nonstop routes were between the same points.[48] The origins of the regulated domestic route structure can

be traced back to the Hoover Administration, which granted transcontinental mail route authority to the predecessors of American, TWA, and United, and established Eastern as the north-south carrier on the East Coast.[49] Piecemeal route awards by the CAB for the new single-plane or nonstop service hardly contributed to the creation of rational or economic route structures for the regulated carriers. Route applications sometimes took years for decision. In addition, the choice between competing applicants was frequently influenced by a carrier's economic need.[50]

Quite predictably, the carriers, once given the opportunity, set about reorganizing their route structures. The trunk airlines have generally sought to convert to "hub-and-spoke" networks centered at major airports where they can gather and sort passengers. Through the use of hubs,[51] carriers hope to dominate traffic in their respective geographic regions. Such a system has strong economic justification, allocating resources quite efficiently. For example, a connecting complex serving 20 points actually services 400 potential city-pairs with every complete "turn." Many markets, including small and mid-size markets, which could not otherwise support the level of service they receive, are thereby afforded efficient single-carrier through and connecting service to much of the country. Through its connecting complex at the Dallas–Fort Worth International Airport, for example, American provides passengers from Lubbock, Amarillo, Midland–Odessa and virtually every other sizable city in the Southwest efficient single-carrier connecting service to New York, Boston, Detroit and even London—service of a quality that those and comparable cities would likely lack in the absence of a "hub-and-spoke" system.

Deregulation has certainly resulted in the loss of nonstop and single-plane service in some markets, but such service has also been added to others. The proportion of passengers receiving single-plane

[46]49 U.S.C. § 1389(a)(6).

[47]Id. § 1389(a)(7)(B).

[48]Civil Aeronautics Board Report to Congress, supra note 23, at 28–29.

[49]E. BAILEY, D. GRAHAM & D. KAPLAN, supra note 18, at 55.

[50]Id. at 59–61.

[51]Among the trunk carriers, American has established an outstanding hub at Dallas-Fort Worth International Airport; Delta and Eastern, at Atlanta; United at Chicago, Denver and San Francisco; and US Air, at Pittsburgh. Other major hubs include Continental at Houston Intercontinental and Denver, TWA at St. Louis, Frontier at Denver, Northwest at Minneapolis-St. Paul, Ozark at St. Louis, Western at Salt Lake City, and People Express at Newark.

service has actually increased from 73% in 1978 to 74.7% in 1983. The percentage of passengers able to complete their journey on a single carrier has also increased, from 89.1% in 1978 to 96.7% in 1982.[52] Although isolated examples of loss of non-stop and single-plane service can undoubtedly be cited, the statistics suggest that the airlines' reorganization of their route systems has improved rather than diminished the quality of service. While Nashville, for example, may have lost its American nonstop flights to Los Angeles, it gained the benefit of American's efficient connecting complex at DFW, giving it single-carrier service throughout much of the Southwest and West. Furthermore, if the service that was lost were in sufficient demand, another carrier would likely fill the void in due course. Airlines, like nature, abhor a vacuum.

Moreover, the movement to "hub-and-spoke" systems has created the opportunity for new market initiatives by aggressive competitors. Piedmont, for example, has developed "hubs" at such relatively less congested points as Charlotte, Dayton and Baltimore and has actively promoted its "bypass" strategy of allowing passengers to avoid congested major hubs. Southwest, of course, has significant hubs at Dallas Love Field and Houston Hobby Airport, both previously abandoned by the trunk carriers.[53] Southwest has also successfully introduced point-to-point nonstop service in numerous markets, bypassing its hubs in order, for example, to fly San Antonio passengers nonstop to El Paso, Phoenix, Los Angeles and the Rio Grande Valley. Austin passengers likewise have nonstop service to Midland–Odessa, Lubbock, El Paso, the Rio Grande Valley and Phoenix. Other airlines evaluating opportunities for their own markets will undoubtedly take notice of these successful route systems bypassing major hubs. In 1985, however, unlike 1975, public demand for the service, rather than governmental decisions or mere happenstance, will dictate the airlines' decisions to enter new markets.

The product of free price competition and market entry has been an unprecedented array of service

alternatives for the consumer. The rigidity of the regulatory structure allowed passengers few choices of fares or of levels of service. Rivalry among carriers tended to be in the form of nonprice competition —flight frequency, food and beverage services, flight equipment and advertising. The former regulatory scheme encouraged this cost-increasing nonprice competition and necessitated fare increases justified only by the rising costs for which it was responsible.[54]

With the advent of deregulation, the market has experienced new levels of service and fare competition. Newly certificated carriers have adopted widely varying business strategies. The success of People Express has proven that a substantial percentage of airline passengers are not willing, given the choice, to pay for such amenities as meals or baggage checking. People Express charges extra even for such amenities as soft drinks and sells tickets on the airplane while the passengers are in the air. But it offers the lowest fares in the industry, has extremely high load factors, and generally makes money. At the other end of the "new entrant" spectrum, Air One offered nothing but first class service, flew 727 aircraft equipped exclusively with first class seats four abreast, and served complimentary meals on china while charging standard coach and discount fares and went bankrupt. New York Air started as a low-fare carrier, but has successfully converted to a more business-oriented service, charging comparatively higher fares and offering what is perceived as a higher quality of service. Midway has similarly shifted corporate strategy from its initial low-fare concept to its upscale business-class "Metrolink" service, offered at standard coach fares. Muse Air introduced its service as the nonsmoking airline by banning smoking on all flights. Jet America has found its market niche by providing standard services between Southern, through the satellite Long Beach Airport, California and major cities such as Chicago and Dallas–Fort Worth. Southwest has maintained its strategy of offering unrestricted low fares, high frequency and single-class service while expanding its service from Texas to ten additional states since deregulation.

These newly certificated carriers, and others like them, have brought something unique to the

---

[52]Civil Aeronautics Board Report to Congress, *supra* note 23, at 35.

[53]Since it was reopened to commercial service by Southwest in 1972, Hobby Airport has undergone a complete revitalization and is presently served by American, Delta, Republic, Ozark, Muse, and Southwest, as well as several commuter carriers.

[54]Phillips, *Airline Mergers in the New Regulatory Environment*, 129 U. Pa. L. Rev. 856, 856 (1981).

markets they serve. The widespread impact and acceptance of these new services is evidenced by the decline in the proportion of passengers traveling on standard "Y" coach fares from sixty percent in 1977 to twenty-five percent in 1982.[55] Such innovation and variety would have been unlikely under a regulatory scheme which in forty years had never awarded a single major route to a new entrant.[56]

The ability of new carriers to start service and the opportunity for expansion by existing carriers have, contrary to some predictions, reduced the level of concentration in the airline industry. New entrants represent the fastest growing segment of the industry. Between 1976 and 1982, the trunk carriers' share of domestic traffic dropped from eighty-eight percent to seventy-nine percent.[57] This limited deconcentration of the industry has coincided with widespread public acceptance of the fare and service alternatives offered by the new entrants.

The ultimate standard by which deregulation is measured, however, often is the effect of deregulation on the economic health of the airline industry itself. As suggested earlier, it is at least arguable that deregulation came along just in time to save the airline industry, and the nation itself, from a major debacle. Given the inverse relationship between fares and passenger boardings, what would have happened to passenger traffic if fare levels had followed the historical cost-plus approach of regulation and actually exceeded, rather than falling 15 points short of, the fifty-four percent increase in costs between 1978 and 1983? It is not difficult to imagine the incantation of the regulated carriers: "We need even higher fares because of the lower loads caused by our high fares." In the airline industry, the cost of a flight is affected relatively little by the number of passengers. The incremental cost of carrying one additional passenger is slight while the loss of that passenger represents a disproportionate loss of revenue. Put another way, a decrease in the number of passengers results in an increase in the average cost per passenger because total costs are relatively constant regardless of the number of passengers. The rising fare/declining load cycle may feed on itself, potentially sending airlines balance sheets into a death spiral.

Moreover, if not for deregulation, airline costs would probably have increased much more rapidly than they did between 1978 and 1983. Deregulation both enabled and compelled the formerly regulated carriers to seek ways to cut costs. Regulation had done little to promote efficiency or economy, since higher costs could simply be built into every new fare level approved by the CAB. The reorganization of the carriers' route structures allowed the carriers to achieve substantial "economies of scope."[58] By increasing the numbers of related city-pairs through "hubbing," carriers were able to achieve "network" economies in the form of more efficient airport facility usage, improved scheduling and more optimal equipment utilization. For example, by eliminating nonstop flights between Nashville and Los Angeles, a carrier could use a moderate-size 727 aircraft to carry passengers going to Dallas and a dozen other cities to its DFW hub, where the Los-Angeles-bound passengers might join passengers from twenty other mid-size cities aboard a larger and more efficient DC-10 for the trip to Los Angeles. Airport facilities in Nashville and Los Angeles could also be efficiently utilized as bases for additional flights to DFW or other stations of the carrier's choice. Further network economies could then be realized. In addition, this network can better satisfy passenger preference for single-carrier service, which is widely preferred over inter-carrier connections.

Deregulation also forced the airlines to reevaluate the level of utilization of their aircraft and employees. Years of public utility-type regulation produced inefficiencies reflected in the regulated carriers' cost structures. Most of the new entrants, who built their organizations under deregulation, have achieved more efficient, less costly structures. For example, in 1981 Southwest's fully allocated cost per passenger for a 200 mile market was $24

[55] E. Bailey, D. Graham & D. Kaplan, *supra* note 18, at 130.

[56] Civil Aeronautics Board Report to Congress, *supra* note 23, at 7.

[57] E. Bailey, D. Graham & D. Kaplan, *supra* note 18, at 44.

[58] Phillips, *supra* note 54, at 864–65 n.28. "Economies of scope exist if the cost of producing given levels of outputs of two (or more) products in a single enterprise is less than that of producing the same products in separate enterprises." *Id.* Such economies "have found a home in the corporate planning and strategy field . . . under the vague concept of 'synergy.' " *Id.*

as compared to $58 for United.[59] This cost difference was due in large part to the higher productivity of Southwest's employees. Southwest's pilots and flight attendants flew more hours than their counterparts with the regulated carriers. Southwest's pilots flew 73 hours per month in 1981 while United's pilots averaged only 43 hours per month. Southwest operated its aircraft 9.5 hours per day in 1981; United operated its aircraft only 5.2 hours per day.[60] Southwest keeps its planes in the air with its unparalleled ten-minute turnaround at the gates. If its average turnaround time were increased by just ten minutes, Southwest would require five more aircraft, costing over $16 million each, to operate the same number of flights. Finally, Southwest's frequent flights enable it to more fully utilize its airport facilities and employees.

These economies were forged in the heat of the competition which Southwest has experienced since its inception. Lack of price competition reduced the regulated carriers' incentives to control costs and promote efficiency. In a competitive environment, the successful firm will be one which can reduce its costs and provide its product at an attractive price to the consumer. Regulation denied society the benefit of an efficient airline industry.

Although the transition has been difficult for many airlines, the industry has finally been forced to consider the efficient allocation of resources. In 1983, the airline industry realized its first profitable year since 1979, with an aggregate operating profit over $500 million.[61] The effects of the transformation of the industry will continue to be uneven, however. American, which made a record profit of $228 million in 1983, followed by a 1984 profit of $234 million, has brilliantly positioned itself (with its strategic DFW hub, strong balance sheet, revised labor contracts, and planned deliveries of new aircraft) to be a dominant member of the airline industry well into the 21st century. Undoubtedly, some others will fare less well.

In a freely competitive market, the future can never be predicted with certainty. The one certainty of the future is that as long as the temptation to let the government do "just a little" re-regulating can be resisted, a deregulated airline industry will deliver its product efficiently and economically. We can be assured of this, not by any government edict, but only by the competitive forces of the marketplace which dictate that the slothful, the unresponsive, and the arrogant will not survive.

[59]E. BAILEY, D. KAPLAN & D. GRAHAM, *supra* note 18, at 179.
[60]*Id.* at 180–181.

[61]M. DERCHIN & R. TORTORA, *supra* note 38.

QUESTIONS FOR DISCUSSION

1. Who have been the winners and the losers in airline deregulation? Explain.
2. To what extent has airline deregulation lived up to its initial objectives?
3. What effect has deregulation had on labor–management relations?
4. Does the experience with airline deregulation offer any lessons for deregulation in other industries? Explain.
5. Is it possible to re-regulate the airline industry? Explain.

SUGGESTED READINGS

COOPER, ANN, "Free-wheeling Airline Competition Is Apparently Here to Stay," *National Journal*, 16 (June 2, 1984), 1086–90.
DERTHICK, MARTHA, AND PAUL J. QUIRK, *The Politics of Deregulation*. Washington, DC: Brookings Institution, 1985.
HARDAWAY, ROBERT M., "Transportation Deregulation (1976–1984): Turning the Tide," *Transportation Law Journal*, 14, No. 1 (1985), 101–51.
JAMES, GEORGE W., "Airline Deregulation: Has It Worked?," *Business Economics*, 20 (July 1985), 11–14.
LABICH, KENNETH, "Fare Wars: Have the Big Air-

lines Learned to Win?," *Fortune* (Oct. 29, 1984), 24–28.

LEINSTER, COLIN, "How American Mastered Deregulation," *Fortune* (June 11, 1984), 38–40, 43, 45, 47, 49, and 51.

MEYER, JOHN R., AND CLINTON V. OSTER, JR., WITH MARNI CLIPPINGER et al., *Deregulation and the New Airline Entrepreneurs.* Cambridge, MA: MIT Press, 1984.

MORASH, EDWARD A., "Airline Deregulation: Another Look," *Journal of Air Law and Commerce*, 50, No. 2 (1985), 253–82.

U. S. CONGRESS, HOUSE, *Review of Airline Dereg-*

ulation and Sunset of the Civil Aeronautics Board, Hearings before the Subcommittee on Aviation of the Committee on Public Works and Transportation, 98th Cong., 2nd Sess., 1984.

U. S. CONGRESS, SENATE, *Sunset of the Civil Aeronautics Board*, Hearing before the Subcommittee on Aviation of the Committee on Commerce, Science, and Transportation, 98th Cong., 2nd Sess., 1984.

U. S. GENERAL ACCOUNTING OFFICE, *Deregulation: Increased Competition Is Making Airlines More Efficient and Responsive to Consumers.* Washington, DC: G. A. O., 1985.

17 YES SHOULD ELECTRONIC BROADCASTING BE DEREGULATED?

Statement Before Congress
Bill Monroe

The United States began the twentieth century with a free press. It is approaching the end of that century with one third of the press free, two thirds of it regulated by government, and an apparently growing acceptance of the idea that government guidance is superior to freedom of the press in providing a diverse and satisfying news service to the public.

The printed press, which is cited by one third of Americans as their primary source of news, remains free under the stout shield of the First Amendment. But the electronic, or broadcast, press, which is the primary supplier of news to two thirds of our people, is subject to compliance with government imposed rules for the treatment of issues and the coverage of politics. It must answer to a Washington bureaucracy in complex, and often costly government proceedings and court cases over interpretation of those rules. The broadcaster cannot escape awareness that a federal commission, appointed by the President, holds the ultimate power to terminate his license and put him out of business.

We have drifted, first by accident and later by inertia, into this situation where, for the first time in American history, the people are receiving the

bulk of their information from sources not independent of government influence. Obviously, it is a situation which the First Amendment was expressly designed to prevent.

In the early decades of this century broadcasting did not look like an extension of the traditional American press either in technology or in function. It was not something palpable and enduring to be held in the hands and read and, sometimes, to be filed away and re-read. And, whereas the front page of the newspaper featured news almost exclusively, the "prime time" of the new media featured entertainment almost exclusively.

The early radio stations didn't even cover the news. They ripped news off of wire service machines, news that for the most part came from newspapers. Announcers and disc jockeys read it on the air. In 1947 I became the first journalist ever to work for a New Orleans radio station. It was hard to make any connection between this wobbly, upstart new medium and so majestic a concept as freedom of the press.

There was also the necessity of assigning frequency locations to individual radio stations and, later, television stations. With these infant media not looking like the press we were accustomed to, and indeed not looking initially very important in the scheme of things, the government naturally took

From U.S. Cong., Senate, *Freedom of Expression*, Hearings before the Committee on Commerce, Science, and Transportation, 97th Cong. 2nd Sess., 1982, pp. 131–38.

on the role of channel assignment and then moved, somewhat uneasily to be sure, into evaluation of program content as a rationale for decisions between competing applicants.

As a journalistic medium, television was not much more impressive than radio in its early days. Typically, the local television station had a 15-minute early evening newscast followed by a 15-minute network newscast, perhaps John Cameron Swayze with the Camel News Caravan. Then news gradually began expanding into half-hour news periods, even full hour news periods, and late evening news reports. The Today show, daringly, ventured into breakfast time with two full hours of news and information. The expansion into longer news periods and untried time slots, into all-news stations and all-news cable programs, continues to this moment.

During political conventions, election nights, space launchings, television soon discovered it could devote its own front page, the evening hours, to news. On November 23, 1963, the morning after the assassination of President Kennedy, I was at my desk as Washington bureau chief for NBC News when I got a phone call from New York that startled me: word that for the next day or so, until the Kennedy funeral was over, we would provide continuous live news coverage. Not only would entertainment programs be swept off the air but the coverage would not be interrupted by a single commercial. I wasn't sure we could manage that long a stint of continuous coverage. But we did.

Today the names of Murrow, Huntley and Brinkley, Cronkite, Chancellor and others drive home the existence of the electronic media as American press of the first rank. But still there is obstinate resistance to according radio and television clear and complete First Amendment status.

One basis for this resistance, I think, is a persistent elitist tendency among opinion leaders—professional, managerial, intellectual—to dismiss television as vulgar in its dependence on a mass audience and fatally contaminated by its show business ancestry. The centrality of television's press function to the American democracy of today is not self evident to civic, cultural and business leaders who, in fact, for the most part continue themselves to rely on newspapers for most of their own current information.

There is also a generation gap at work on attitudes toward television. It is notable, for example, that on the longstanding issue of equal access for television to coverage of courtrooms, the younger lawyers and judges are much more amenable than the older to admission of cameras, and the opening of courtrooms to electronic coverage, which was going nowhere 20 years ago, is now gaining ground year by year.

But, however explainable these attitudes are, if the present general acceptance of government-regulated media is not challenged, the First Amendment will, inexorably, waste away to nothing. It will be repealed, not by any deliberate process of government, but by a slow undermining process on two levels: technological and philosophical. Indeed, the repeal process has already gone a long way on both levels.

Technological repeal is taking place in that the electronic media, requiring channel allocation, are perceived as not-quite-press. We define these media on the basis of irrelevant technology not on the all-important basis of function. Thus, the flow of two thirds of American news is already contaminated by government policymaking in areas that used to be the clear prerogative of journalists.

People who favor permanent relegation of the electronic media to second-class status under the First Amendment like to argue that there is something in the technology, something in the frequency allocation problem, that compels government interference. It is a totally empty argument. There are many possible ways to accomplish frequency allocation while placing a hard barrier in the way of government intrusion into editorial decisions or program content. All we have to do is start out with a consensus, based on function, that American electronic media are American press, that they can, and must, be free under the First Amendment, and we will find ourselves free to choose the method of accomplishing that deeply conservative purpose, which is nothing less than preservation of a meaningful First Amendment.

As it is, the printed press itself is ominously endangered by the erosion of its constitutional protection—not only because newspapers are moving in the direction of electronic distribution but also because our present toleration of media regulation, as applied to electronic media, challenges head-on the whole philosophy of press freedom inherent in the First Amendment.

Channel allocation is a mere excuse for the

present regulation of broadcasting. The actual philosophy behind it, which is sometimes plainly stated by its proponents and sometimes only implied, is that government guidance *improves* American news media, provides more fairness and balance, for example, than would otherwise be the case. It is a straight-on anti-First Amendment argument. The First Amendment says that the most essential condition for the American press in our system of checks and balances is independence from the government. It does not guarantee a perfect press or a fair press or even a responsible press. It guarantees only an independent press, a press untouchable by government: "The Congress shall make no law . . . abridging the freedom of speech, or of the press." It protects the citizenry by setting up free and diverse sources of information—a competitive flow of ideas, facts and argument.

But the very existence of government rules fastened on two thirds of the American news flow increasingly argues that the First Amendment is out of date. It tells us that modern America not only accords a secondary value to independent journalism but is, in fact, willing deliberately to place journalism under government oversight and set up government standards of fairness and balance in the hope of obtaining more dependable reporting. If we accept this idea which, in fact, we have already put into practice, the idea that government guidance can improve electronic media, then obviously, it can improve printed media as well. Under these circumstances, the philosophical bedrock under the First Amendment is going or gone. And the newspaper monopolies of this country, at some crisis point in the future, will find themselves friendless in their efforts to maintain an independence which, in terms of both American practice and American opinion, no longer has legs to stand on.

At this point, however, it is my hope and belief that we have not drifted so far into the practice and philosophy of press regulation that we can't catch ourselves and undertake the restoration of full freedom to all American media before it is too late. Because we have gotten where we are by drift, without much public awareness or discussion, that process should be reversible by a newly rising awareness of danger now becoming apparent and by a process of national debate, if those who are concerned can get it going. I am encouraged in that regard by the new attention being paid to this subject in recent years by you, Mr. Chairman, and by others of your colleagues, including, Senator William Proxmire and former Senator Eugene McCarthy.

If we follow through on this national debate, I am convinced that political and intellectual leaders and a majority of the American people will gradually turn against the idea of captive media responsible to a government agency. I believe they will come to see the kind of regulation we have not only as wrong in principle and destructive of the First Amendment but as inhibitory and unworkable on the practical level, and destructive of the kind of journalistic vigor essential to the health of our democracy. Regulation has not improved electronic journalism. It has held it back, stultified it, made it wary and defensive in its effort to live by government rules.

For example, the "equal time rule" has come closer to serving the political interests of presidential candidates than the public interest. Until recently, the candidates used it to hide behind if they did not want to debate.

The rule says that broadcasters, unlike newspapers, cannot hold debates among major presidential candidates without inviting all the obscure candidates that may be on the ballot in one state or another. Its practical effect has been to make it impossible for broadcasters to arrange such debates for the benefit of voters.

But in 1960, Senator John F. Kennedy and Vice President Richard M. Nixon, neither an incumbent president at that time, decided they wanted to debate. So they passed discreet signals to their adherents in the Congress, Congress waived the rule for that year, and the networks, because the candidates were willing, could stage three history-making presidential campaign debates.

But in subsequent presidential contests—Johnson–Goldwater (1964), Humphrey–Nixon (1968), Nixon–McGovern (1972), one or both candidates didn't want a debate. The Congress, accordingly, declined to waive the rule and the public was deprived of the kind of campaign debates they had watched in huge numbers in 1960. Here was a regulation purportedly to protect the public interest being manipulated cynically to promote or protect the campaign interests of political candidates.

To round out the story, in more recent elections the Federal Communications Commission has set up a loophole that permits evasion of the "equal time" rule by a transparent strategem. The League of Women voters invites the major candidates to debate. When the candidates have agreed to a time, place and format, the networks discover, under the rules of this subterfuge, that a news event is about to take place and they arrange to "cover" it. As everyone knows, of course, including the candidates, the League, the networks, the Congress, the FCC and the public, the League is setting up a debate expressly for network distribution to the nation because broadcasters, unlike newspapers and wire services, are not allowed to do it themselves. The New York Times can, and does, arrange its own debates without the complicating services of middle men or women. But broadcasters have to go through a hypocritical, cumbersome, three-cornered process to accomplish the same result.

There are many examples of the political manipulation of the regulatory process. One occurred during the Carter–Reagan campaign of 1980. This involved the so-called "reasonable access" provision of the Communications Act. The Carter–Mondale committee applied to the networks to buy political time. Each network declined on the basis that it was too early in the political season to schedule campaign broadcasts. The Carter–Mondale committee appealed to the Federal Communications Commission, which ruled in the committee's favor. The favorable vote was cast by the four Democrats on the commission, with the three Republicans all voting no. In effect, a decision that should have been made by journalists was made by presidential appointees acting as political partisans.

A newsman who once worked in a highly reputable television news organization in a middle-sized city told me of an incident involving a powerful United States senator. In a hot local controversy, involving water control and dam projects, he was under fire as a supporter of large dams, which critics said did more harm than good. The senator insisted vehemently that his critics were mistaken, that he had vigorously worked for small dams. The local station news editor asked a reporter to check on the senator's record. It turned out he had voted consistently for big dam projects and only rarely for small dams. When the station aired the story in a newscast, the senator was indignant. Without challenging the accuracy of a single fact in the story, he made a strong argument to the station manager

that the account had put him in a bad light and was not indicative of his basic attitude.

The station wound up giving the senator ten minutes of free time in which he was able to bolster his position by a combination of selected facts and personal charm. It should be noted that there was no specific compulsion, under law or regulation, for the station to have supplied such a gift of time. But the television editor who related the incident felt that, in the general climate of broadcast regulation and the uneasiness broadcasters feel about their dependence on a Washington bureaucracy, the station management just didn't want to incur the long-range hostility of their own senator, a man of national standing. The station did not offer any other parties in the controversy time to reply to the senator. The station's newsroom wound up feeling embarrassed and somewhat chastened. They had aired a legitimate, factual story. But the station then acted, in response to the senator's anger, as if the story had been unfair or distorted. It had taken an action that had about it an aura of apology.

I have not, of course, identified the newsman acquaintance who related this incident or the station involved. He asked me not to. Although he is no longer working at the station, he did not wish to embarrass his former employer.

This understandable and honorable inhibition underlines the problem of getting at specifics of instances in which government regulation has intimidated broadcasters. Nobody wants to admit to being intimidated. Nobody wants to admit to trimming his sails to stay out of trouble with the bureaucracy. I once asked five radio station executives whether they had ever allowed themselves to be intimidated by government regulation. They all said no. I then asked them whether they had ever paused, in the making of a journalistic decision, to consider whether it might get them in trouble with the government. They all said yes.

There is also a Catch 22 at work in this area that militates effectively against candor. The FCC has said, on at least one occasion, that broadcasters are not supposed to make journalistic decisions with the intention of avoiding difficulties with the commission. If any broadcaster did that, said the FCC, he or she would be regarded unfavorably. Thus, broadcasters are under regulatory rules to which they feel they have no choice but to react defensively, and at the same time they are on notice not to admit it in public. So there is a bureaucratic inhibition, on top of a natural inhibition, against confessions of intimidation. And one result of this is that rank-and-file journalists—correspondents, reporters, editors and producers—often don't know when their own news organizations have made decisions yielding to anxiety about the regulatory process. The executives above them avoid their own embarrassment and possible trouble with the FCC by not telling them.

The fairness doctrine, like the equal time concept, produces, under the fine banner of the public interest, abuses of the public interest. A former communications lawyer, Steven Simmons, wrote a book on the subject a few years ago: "The Fairness Doctrine and the Media," published by the University of California Press. He began his research personally in basic accord with the idea of government overseeing media. But by the time he got through interviewing judges, lawyers, bureaucrats and journalists, and looking through court decisions and regulatory pronouncements, he concluded it was an area of endless bureaucratic-legal confusion and frustration in which nothing was clear and predictable. He described this bureaucratic dogma as an "unfairness doctrine"—unfair to the public because it did not expand coverage of public issues, unfair to broadcasters because it interferes with editorial judgments and inhibits controversial broadcasting, and open to abuse by presidents, political parties and special interests.

In fairness to former and present FCC commissioners, some of whom I know, I should note an observation of Simmons with which I agree. It is that there is nothing venal or sinister about the commissioners as people. Most of them are highly dedicated and entirely favorable to the abstract concept of press freedom. But they are asked to do an impossible job: to reconcile regulation of program content with the abstract principle of press freedom. The result, inevitably, is confusion, frustration, decisions and reversals, tortured language, unpredictability.

The famous Pensions case is a good example. I didn't happen to have any personal involvement in the preparation of the NBC documentary, narrated by Edwin Newman, which focused on abuses in the private pension system. Like any other viewer, I watched it at home on television. I found myself profoundly moved by the agony of several old men

who were interviewed, men who felt bitter and cheated. Some of them wept as they told of the disappearance of pensions they had been led to believe would be there when they turned 65. Expecting dignified retirements, they were suddenly struggling with poverty and dependence. When it was over, I felt angry—and proud of NBC News for producing a powerful and compelling program.

So I was startled when Accuracy in Media subsequently complained to the FCC that although NBC was deliberately targeting several pension plans that were fraudulent, the program should have included balancing material, to make it clear that all pension plans were not fraudulent, that most were all right. The FCC proceeded to declare the program in violation of those U.S. government rules of fairness which would have astonished Thomas Jefferson.

NBC could then have gotten off the hook at that point by afflicting innocent viewers of the Today show with a bewildering five-minute interview on pension plans that work just fine. Instead, to its credit, the network went to court to uphold the principle that it had a right to target abuses without wasting time in defending the general system in which they occurred. Eventually, the courts reversed the FCC. But it had cost NBC $100,000 to make the point.

Simmons made this comment on the case in his book: Unfortunately, the fairness doctrine, held constitutional by the Supreme Court, inevitably leads to unhealthy Commission intervention in broadcast journalism and healthy yet tortured court decision, such as Pensions, to rectify the First Amendment balance.

The fairness doctrine metes out harassment to big and little broadcasters alike. A Spokane television station, hit by what seemed to be an unreasonable fairness complaint, was, like NBC, angry enough to fight it—and eventually got it thrown out. But not until it had spent $20,000 and an estimated 480 supervisory man hours defending itself.

The fairness doctrine inculcates a code of play-it-safe, don't rock-the-boat journalism to stay out of trouble with the FCC. Tackle tough issues and you court trouble with the government. Avoid controversy and there will be no obstacles to license renewal. Fred Freed, a producer of outstanding documentaries for NBC, once said, "If you do something controversial, you know you will spend months defending yourself to the government. That's not conducive to doing something controversial."

If a station presents a documentary on a subject that arouses emotions, it risks stirring up complaints to the FCC from one group or another. If the FCC gets indignant letters challenging the fairness of the program, it will write to the station manager and direct him to defend the program's compatibility with government rules. The station manager then goes through a long, meticulous process of consultation with the program producer, the news director, local attorneys, Washington attorneys. For the next week or ten days he cancels some of the appointments on his schedule to see the process through. Finally, a careful, detailed document is sent to the FCC justifying the program.

In most cases, the FCC writes back indicating its acceptance of the station's position. But what happens the next time that documentary producer seeks to do a program on another controversial issue? Would it, or would it not, be human for the station manager to steer the producer toward a safe subject, one less likely to stir complaints? Would it, or would it not, be human for him to want to avoid, any time soon, another hassle with the FCC?

The tendency of broadcast executives and lawyers to play it safe is certainly not modified by the aura of confusion and unpredictability about the whole process. A case in point involves former Democratic party chairman Larry O'Brien. After President Nixon had made five prime-time speeches, primarily about Vietnam, CBS provided O'Brien half an hour of reply time. In response to that, much to the astonishment of the Democrats, the Republicans asked for time to answer O'Brien. O'Brien, they said, had not stuck to the issue of Vietnam. The FCC bought the Republican argument and ordered CBS to give the GOP time to answer O'Brien's answer to Nixon. It turned out, eventually, to be another case in which a court overturned the commission.

After working as a journalist for a wire service and local newspapers, for a radio station, for a television station and 21 years for NBC News, I continue to be struck by a broad and vital area in which broadcasting remains relatively bland and timid compared with its print brethren—the area of opinion journalism: editorials and commentary.

Pick up any decent American newspaper and you'll find a range of informed, hard-hitting opinion. Some of it comes from the national columnists:

Evans and Novak, Joseph Kraft, Anthony Lewis, William Safire, Tom Wicker, James J. Kilpatrick, Mary McGrory, and others. They add a tremendous flavor of vigor and vitality to editorial and op-ed pages. And alongside their essays there is usually a rich diet of local opinion: columns, editorials and special op-ed pieces.

Where is the counterpart of all this intellectual salt and pepper on local and national television news programs? It almost doesn't exist. In contrast to this daily newspaper diversity, the networks offer occasional generally guarded comments by John Chancellor and Bill Moyers. Chancellor and Moyers, to be sure, are intellectual and journalistic equals of the print columnists but their total output is tiny indeed compared to the varied spectrum of their newspaper brethren. The local station that offers daily personal opinion of any kind is rare. Television editorials tend to inveigh heavily against potholes and shoplifting and for the United Fund.

Pick up any American newspaper and alongside its array of journalistic opinion you'll find an array of popular opinion in the letters column where readers can take the newspaper to task and, if they want to, rage at city hall and the state legislature. Networks and local stations have, here and there, dabbled half-heartedly in audience response programs with occasional phone-in productions and scattered letters-to-managers hours stuck away in odd time spots. But, as a living, breathing, daily institution, television just doesn't have a letter-to-the-editor section. With most newspapers, you can complain about the city editor's news judgment and the political reporter's interpretation of the election campaign, and you can get your complaint printed where it's visible to the same audience they have. With television, for all practical purposes, you're frozen out of answering back before the same audience.

Why is television, which does so remarkable a job in news presentation, so deficient, so sterile, so pallid, so bland in its handling, or non-handling, of opinion? Because in my opinion, it is a government regulated medium, because regulation sets up an atmosphere in which it is prudent not to invite controversy, and the avoidance of opinion of any kind is one way to stay clear of controversy.

Outsiders don't understand, and often don't believe, the existence of this inhibitory cloud. Many insiders don't understand it and some of them deny it. Skeptics will tell you that so few station licenses are taken away it is not rational for station owners to fear the possibility. Maybe it's not rational. But the regulatory apparatus is real, the rules are confusing, the lawyers must be consulted, the proper papers must be carefully drawn up and submitted in triplicate, occasionally a station does lose its license on the vote of a bureaucratic body, and there's no way station executives, who possess every bit as much integrity as newspaper publishers and editors, can relish challenging a process which can, conceivably, strip them of their livelihoods.

People who have worked exclusively in broadcasting, many of them, do not themselves understand the difference between genuine press freedom, with its clear boundaries marked by the First Amendment, and the kind of limbo in which they operate with its boundaries ever shifting according to the changing attitudes of Congress, the courts and the FCC. All they know is that you can make a profit in broadcasting, you can make some satisfying contributions to the public weal, you can cover the news and you can venture a strong, outspoken editorial occasionally—with accent on occasionally —without stirring up too much trouble. In general, they obey the unwritten rule against plain talk and blunt opinion on any kind of regular basis. And they consider themselves functioning in comfortable enough freedom, which, by comparison with the Soviet Union and Argentina, perhaps they are. First Amendment freedom it is not.

When I made the transition from associate editor of a daily newspaper to news director of a television station in the same city, I could feel the atmosphere of a different, inferior, less comfortable order of freedom in broadcasting. I once suggested to my television bosses that the station broadcast an editorial criticizing the Chairman of the FCC. They agreed readily with the basic idea but immediately said that, first, we would have to consult legal counsel. Not once, in some years of writing editorials for a newspaper, had I heard an editor or publisher suggest that, before criticizing a government official, we had better check with a lawyer.

Broadcast news has gradually, one by one, assumed all of the special functions of print news. Beginning with the general and the obvious—news, sports and weather—it has moved into the same specializations as newspapers: business correspondents, experts on the law, science reporters. But,

arriving at the realm of journalistic opinion, it has stopped on the threshold, unwilling to develop the same free, robust clash of opinions traditional to newspapers. So, in an average American city, we have a monopoly newspaper providing news and all sorts of opinion and we have four or five competitive television stations providing news but, with a few wan exceptions, avoiding opinion as if their lives depended on it.

That may be exactly the way station owners and managers feel, though they might not admit to it: that their commercial lives, in fact, depend on minimizing controversy and the embroilment with the FCC which it entails. Broadcasters don't feel free to follow their consciences as journalists because they have to answer to a bureaucratic conscience with its close-packed pages of rules, regulations and precedents. So the electronic media, by contrast with what the First Amendment intended, are stifled and stunted. In a sort of unacknowledged collusion with government, they have already accustomed us to a public policy that allows news on our television screens but not the panoply of opinion that gives such character to newspapers.

I'm not suggesting that, if full First Amendment freedom were suddenly bestowed on broadcasting, a journalistic millenium would be upon us. I am suggesting that broadcasting is now a relatively bland and timid medium by comparison with print. I believe that difference is due to the stultifying effects of government regulation. If that regulation disappeared, television would simply acquire the same relative boldness, the same freedom to bring us a robust mix of opinion, for example, that newspapers now have. Television networks and stations would not, despite the fears of some, go charging off in all directions, espousing wild causes and wallowing in political bias. Like the newspapers, if freed from unhealthy government pressure, they would still respond to the constraining imperatives of mass media—the need to please a wide audience of diverse views, the pressure to maximize audience size, the need to attract advertisers. America is now enjoying some of the finest newspapers the world has ever seen. There is no reason why television, free of government constriction, should settle on any lower journalistic standards than those guiding the print media. And there is one reason to expect even higher standards: the electronic media are disciplined more by competition than are the print media. With First Amendment protection, television would simply become more lively and more interesting, more effective in acquainting the American people not only with current events but with the kaleidoscope of current thinking. And, more important, in the event of some future national crisis, if the government tried to pressure news media to angle the news in its favor, the electronic media would have the same independence as print of withstanding the pressure.

As to how we should go about assuring genuine First Amendment status to broadcasting, I am just not sure. A new constitutional amendment applying to the electronic media would certainly accomplish the purpose. But I am skeptical that we can expect the Congress to take such an initiative. My perception is that too many congressmen and senators feel comfortable with, and perhaps see some advantage in, their ability to manipulate and pressure media that are answerable to government. I may be underestimating, however, their willingness, when confronted with the issue, to act on principle and take the historic action of restoring clearcut American freedom to the new media. If Congress does not act, it is my hope that the Supreme Court will

one day recover from its present myopia toward the electronic media and undo its early decisions consigning them to second-class citizenship. In the meantime, I note that groups who should be interested in this issue are not much concerned about it: newspaper editors, lawyers and judges, intellectuals, broadcasters themselves. Until such groups become interested, we may not see public opinion develop toward the necessary general support for freeing electronic media.

But it is a fact that the steady year-by-year erosion of the First Amendment is becoming increasingly visible. It is a fact that the present proliferation of electronic media has nullified the common argument that their scarcity precluded full freedom for them. And your own interest in the matter, Mr. Chairman, along with that of others, suggests that we are not going to just let press freedom waste away, that we are going to face the issue and make a conscious decision to rebuild the First Amendment by extending it to all media. That is the only way to preserve that signal American guarantee of free and independent sources of news, a press not beholden to government.

17 NO   SHOULD ELECTRONIC BROADCASTING BE DEREGULATED?

Statement Before Congress
Elaine Donnelly

Mr. Chairman and members of the Senate Commerce Committee, I am Elaine Donnelly of Michigan, Special Projects Director of Eagle Forum, a national organization of activist women and men that has been leading the pro-family movement since 1972. I have more than eleven years of experience in practical applications of the Federal Communications Commission's Fairness Rules, and I have participated in numerous F.C.C. Rulemaking Proceedings. I am the author of the handbook "One Side vs. the Other Side—a Primer on Access to the

Media," which has been successfully used by grassroots activists all across the country since 1981.

Arguments for the deregulation of television may sound very persuasive, but only from the perspective of those fortunate few who happen to own or control television stations. It is understandable that broadcasters want even more power and the right to be accountable to no one, but I cannot understand why the interests of the two other parties concerned in this matter have been almost totally ignored in the testimony presented to date before this committee.

Mr. Chairman, I appreciate this opportunity to remind the members of this Committee that broadcasters do not own the First Amendment, even if they think they do.

From U.S. Cong., Senate, *Freedom of Expression Act of 1983*, Hearings before the Committee on Commerce, Science, and Transportation, 98th Cong., 2nd Sess., 1984, pp. 139–42.

Actually, there are three groups with an interest in the concept of free expression: (a) Broadcasters; (b) Individuals and candidates who need access to the airwaves; and (c) Members of the general public who need to be informed as citizens and voters. All three groups are important, but the U.S. Supreme Court ruled in 1969 (Red Lion Broadcasting vs. FCC) that the rights of the third group—the public—are paramount.

Please remember that broadcasters are in a position to greatly diminish the first amendment rights of the other two groups. New technologies that are not universally available do not change the fact that no one can gain access to television unless the time is given or sold to them by station-managers.

As an activist woman who has been involved in the public debate surrounding a number of controversial issues of public importance, I know from personal experience how easy it is for a broadcaster to deny free expression to those whose views do not agree with the "media elite." Let me give you just one concrete example. At the end of over ten years of debate over the proposed Equal Rights Amendment, a survey of the official video record of evening network news programs showed that out of 11 hours of total coverage from March, 1972 to June, 1982, 95 percent of the time was devoted to spokespeople for the pro-ERA side, while opponents appeared only 5 percent of the time.

This shocking record of biased coverage on that issue alone demolishes the self-serving testimony of network correspondents like CBS's Dan Rather who appeared before this Committee last year to complain about the unfairness of the Fairness Rules. Dan Rather, the National Association of Broadcasters, and the other media moguls that you have heard from are not just ordinary citizens. Their power to influence public opinion by setting the agenda of public discussion is far "more equal" than that of the rest of us.

It was bad enough that the opponents of ERA enjoyed only 5 percent of the network coverage over a period of ten years, but it was even more hurtful that in most of the coverage overall of those difficult years, the broadcast media managed to almost totally conceal from the American people the important and undisputed information that passage of ERA would have resulted in the drafting of women for combat duty in a future war. If it were not for the Fairness rules that the women of Eagle Forum

invoked at the local level, as a means to exercise our rights of free speech, it is entirely possible that the ERA would have been ratified without any real public understanding of its true effects. That would have been unfair to women, and to the general public which still has the paramount right to be informed about this and other issues of the day.

Incidentally, this same argument could be made by proponents of ERA, if their side has been the one that was held to only 5 percent of the network news coverage. The Fairness Rules are neutral in their impact—available to liberals and conservatives, pros and cons alike—no matter what the issue might be.

Mr. Chairman, the Supreme Court ruled that censorship of a medium not open to all is no more acceptable than censorship by the government. Nevertheless, statements in favor of concepts such as objectivity in journalism, professional ethics, fairness, and the responsibility of broadcasters to serve the public interest by allowing conflicting viewpoints to be heard are conspicuously absent in your hearing record to date. The Supreme court upheld the minimal Fairness Rules as a means to protect the true "marketplace of ideas," which should not be confused with the lucrative commercial marketplace of broadcasting.

The testimony you have heard about new technologies such as Teletext and Direct Broadcast Satellites is most intriguing, but it does not change the fact that surveys show that over 65 percent of the people still get most of their information from conventional "free" television. This percentage is not likely to change because space-age technologies are expensive, and the demand for them is already leveling off because of that expense. Mr. Chairman, we cannot afford to become a nation of information "haves" and "have-nots."

Joel Chaseman, President of the Post-Newsweek Stations, Inc. suggested in a speech before the Town Hall of California (Los Angeles, January 27, 1981) that "the Federal Communications Commission has become a home for technology hedonists, falling in love with each new development they meet, committed to none, apparently believing that invention is the mother of necessity." Mr. Chaseman declared in that speech that it is the height of bureaucratic arrogance to suggest that the First Amendment rights of the public will be served if only every household is wired for cable TV at the rate of at least $16.50 per month (for starters), or if everyone buys a home computer or an earth station costing several hundred dollars plus an additional monthly charge. The suggestion that ordinary people will have to pay dearly for access to diverse points of view on television is tantamount to suggesting that everyone has the right to vote, but only if they can afford to pay a poll tax for the privilege.

Please remember that the broadcasting networks enjoy a unique monopoly that already distorts the marketplace of ideas in a way that cannot be equalled by the print media. Among local newspapers, even those owned by the big publishing conglomerates, there is no equivalent to the impact and dominance of the network news programs. Local newspapers can set their own agendas of editorial discussion, and choose from a vast spectrum of additional "op-ed" pieces from columnists that reflect the wide diversity of opinion on national issues of the day. . . .

By contrast, the networks offer only one commentator per program, such as Bill Moyers on CBS and John Chancellor on NBC. Affiliate station managers who usually limit their editorials to local issues are no competition for the media giants; nor are the cable stations and community access programs that are midgets in the world of the media elite. It is important to remember, too, that the same giants that have dominated the communication industry to date, such as Time, Inc., Warner-Amex, Westinghouse, and networks such as ABC are now using their considerable economic clout to take over cable TV and other systems, in the same way that many newspapers have been swallowed up by the big conglomerates.

The testimony you have heard about how much easier it supposedly is to buy a television station than it is to buy a newspaper is entirely beside the point. What about the First Amendment rights of those who are not in a position to buy either?

99.9 percent of the candidates and issue advocates in this country can always buy a paid newspaper ad or produce their own publication, but they cannot have access to television unless someone gives or sells the time that is needed. S. 1917 would greatly expand the rights of broadcasters to deny the First Amendment rights of others. The deregulators' suggestions that people who are being censored out of the media should go out and buy a TV or radio station is the modern electronic equivalent of Marie Antoinette's "Let them eat cake."

EQUAL TIME RULES

In addition to abolishing the Fairness Doctrine that relates to the coverage of controversial issues of public importance, S. 1917 would abolish the Equal Time rules that are necessary [to] ensure fair elections and an informed electorate. If S. 1917 is enacted, stations would be free to sell all of their time just before a local, state, or national election to one Party's nominees, at bargain rates, to the exclusion of all the other Party's candidates from the President on down. How would the public be served if broadcasters could use their monopoly of the airwaves to endorse candidates, allow personal, unanswered attacks against opposing candidates, and to censor those opposing candidates right off the air without any responsibility to anyone?

Would any Senator on this Committee be content to buy commercial time for his next campaign on a dozen 5-mile radius low-power stations, instead of the most-watched network affiliate stations in the state? That kind of effective censorship, as authorized and encouraged by passage of S. 1917, would constitute a violation of your First Amendment rights of free expression, and there is no way that that would serve your interest or that of the public.

The Equal Time rules have sometimes been cumbersome, and it has been necessary to adjust and reinterpret their meaning from time to time in order to protect the rights of both the major and minor candidates. However, the total elimination of Equal Time rules would serve only to expand the power of broadcasters, moneyed interests, and those who have favor with the decidedly liberal media elite. (For a scholarly analysis of the liberal leanings of the recognized media elite, see the 1983 Lichter/Rothman study published in Public Opinion.) Our entire system of free and fair elections could be permanently distorted as a result.

THE EXAGGERATED COMPLAINTS OF BROADCASTERS

In my opinion, the various complaints of station managers and broadcasters that have been expressed before this Committee are utterly unconvincing.

Anyone who takes the time to study the Fairness Rules as printed in the Federal Register can see just how minimal they really are. For example, the Fairness Doctrine does not require equal time, and the F.C.C.'s skimpy record of enforcement demonstrates that station managers have little to fear from the bureaucrats in Washington. Actually, anyone who has filed a legitimate complaint with the F.C.C. knows that the Commission is one of the weakest and most ineffective agencies in the government. Contrary to the impression given by some of your previous witnesses, the government does not monitor what goes on the air; the broadcaster—not the government—has the sole right to decide how the general principles of fairness in the public interest are to be met. The only reason that the rules work at all is because they serve as a useful standard and starting point for cooperation between station managers, those who seek access to the media, and the general public that has a right to expect free access to the "marketplace of ideas."

If a station manager feels that it is too much to ask that he allow the public to hear a variety of opinions, then he should exercise his option to sell the station to one of the many applicants who would like to take his place.

Witnesses before your Committee have expressed great alarm at the prospect that electronically-transmitted newspapers are threatened by an all-powerful bureaucracy that could step in and tell them how to run their newspaper. I have not encountered so much paranoia since I read the story of Chicken Little. Even if the Supreme Court upheld this fearsome intrusion into the realm of the print media (and it hasn't), Congress would have all the power in the world to resolve the problem. The sky is not about to fall on the Wall Street Journal or USA Today. There is no reason for panic, or legislation that ignores the interests of the majority while catering to the wildest fears of the powerful minority.

Mr. Chairman, the Fairness rules of today are carefully balanced to protect the rights of broadcasters as well as other parties with an interest in the First Amendment. If these reasonable guidelines to protect the public interest are sacrificed on the altar of the commercial marketplace, the true marketplace of ideas would be narrowed to serve the interests of only those with power, influence, or popularity among the media elite.

QUESTIONS FOR DISCUSSION

1. What is the difference in impact on audiences between the print and electronic media?

2. Does it matter whether the electronic media are fair in offering equal time to oppose candidates in elections? Why?

3. Does it matter whether the print media are fair in providing objective coverage of opposing candidates in elections? Why?

4. Would deregulation of the electronic media benefit liberal or conservative causes? Why?

5. Is television news biased? If so, how?

SUGGESTED READINGS

"Broadcast Deregulation: Pro & Con," *Congressional Digest*, 63 (Apr. 1984), whole issue.

CORN, ROBERT L., "Broadcasters in Bondage," *Reason* (Sept. 1985), 31–34.

DIAMOND, EDWIN, NORMAN SANDLER, AND MILTON MUELLER, *Telecommunications in Crisis: The First Amendment, Technology, and Deregulation*. Washington, DC: Cato Institute, 1983.

FOWLER, MARK, "Unregulations in the Eighties," *Lincoln Review*, 2 (Winter/Spring 1982), 3–9.

KAUFMAN, IRVING R., "Reassessing the Fairness Doctrine," *New York Times Magazine* (June 19, 1983), 16–19.

ROWAN, FORD, *Broadcast Fairness: Doctrine, Practice, Prospects: A Reappraisal of the Fairness Doctrine and Equal Time Rule*. New York: Longman, 1984.

SMITH, R. C., AND NEIL HICKEY, "Should the Government Regulate TV News?," *TV Guide* (Aug. 6, 1983), 38–40.

U. S. CONGRESS, HOUSE, *Broadcast Regulation Reform Proposals*, Hearing before the Subcommittee on Telecommunications, Consumer Protection, and Finance of the Committee on Energy and Commerce, 97th Cong., 2nd Sess., 1982.

U. S. CONGRESS, SENATE, *Freedom of Expression Act of 1983*, Hearings before the Committee on Commerce, Science, and Transportation, 98th Cong., 2nd Sess., 1984.

U. S. FEDERAL COMMUNICATIONS COMMISSION, *The Law of Political Broadcasting and Cablecasting: A Political Primer*. Washington, DC: Federal Communications Commission, 1984.